THE

LAW MAGAZINE;

OR

QUARTERLY REVIEW

OF

JURISPRUDENCE,

FOR AUGUST, 1839; AND NOVEMBER, 1839.

VOL. XXII.

———————

LONDON:

SAUNDERS AND BENNING, LAW BOOKSELLERS,

(SUCCESSORS TO J. BUTTERWORTH AND SON,)

43, FLEET STREET.

——

1839.

59.112

CONTENTS.

  Page

CONTENTS.

THE LAW MAGAZINE.

ART. I.—FOURTH CRIMINAL LAW REPORT.

Fourth Report of Her Majesty's Commissioners on Criminal
Law, dated the 8th Day of March 1839 ; presented to both
Houses of Parliament by command of her Majesty.

IN conformity with the directions issued during the reign of
his late majesty, requiring the Commissioners " to proceed in
forming a Digest of the Criminal Law, as well written as unwritten, into one statute, with such partial alterations as might
be considered by them to be necessary or expedient for more
simply and completely defining crimes and punishments, and
for the more effectual administration of criminal justice," we
have before us the above-named Report. As we propose to
make this the subject of a careful examination, it is satisfactory to be able to state at the outset, that a much more pleasing and profitable task awaits us than was our lot in reviewing
for our twenty-seventh Number the First Report on Criminal
Law. In that we found little which we did not feel compelled to censure, in this we find much to praise ; and as we
ventured to pronounce that deficient both in reasoning and
information, so are we obliged to acknowledge this replete
with both those qualities, and calculated to be useful and instructive to the legislature. The present Report indeed, treating mainly of the same topics as the first, often contains its
best refutation, apart from any strictures of ourselves or others.
On many most material points the two express totally different
opinions, a few of which we shall notice incidentally ; and

further we are gratified to observe, that as the later opinions are those we generally desire to hold by, so are they in some instances identical with those put forward in our former Review.

The present Report however, as might fairly be anticipated from a task of so much difficulty, is not without its faults, and whilst acknowledging the general excellence of its observations and doctrines, we must say that there is not unfrequently a want of logical arrangement and of perspicuous expression likely to detract a good deal from its general utility. This is the more to be complained of, because the Commissioners, as regards the latter fault at least, set out by saying, " We have studiously endeavoured to express the definition of crimes, and the rules connected with them, in the most simple and intelligible language ;" and again, " Elegance of diction must be regarded as a matter of inferior importance in the declaration of abstract propositions and rules ; and we have not hesitated to use plain and even homely language in our articles where a neater construction of the sentences, and more refined expressions, would not have contained so effectually the meaning of the law." The reader will by and by have some opportunities of judging how far this promise has been kept.

This Report consists principally of a dissertation on the nature and classification of crimes ; of a short anticipatory notice of the amendments hereafter to be proposed in punishments ; of an essay and digest relating to the law of " offences against the person," and of the same relating to the law of " criminal violations of the right of property ;" besides an appendix containing the whole of the statute law of crimes now in force, arranged according to the scale of punishment. We propose to give a brief account of the most important subjects discussed in each of these sections, with such observations as occur to us ; and we shall venture, in so doing, sometimes to point out two sorts of imperfection with which it seems to us that the Report is chargeable, first where the Commissioners propose to introduce novelties and alterations in the law without sufficient cause, and, secondly, where they leave unaltered things not essential features of the law, yet easily and properly alterable. In deprecation of any censure on the latter account they say indeed,

" From this statement of the authority under which we now act, it will be obvious that it does not extend to the construction of a new Criminal Code, but is limited to the reduction and consolidation of the existing law of England, as well written as unwritten, concerning crimes; for although we are authorized to make partial alterations, we apprehend that we should not be justified in making such changes in the essential features of the law as would alter its nature and character. We have therefore confined our attention chiefly to a reduction of the existing law by more simply and completely defining crimes and punishments, and have only in a few extreme cases ventured to remove positive and apparent inconsistencies in principle. Where defects have occurred to us in the prosecution of our task which involved more extensive changes, we have noticed them in the Prefatory Remarks to the several classes of crimes, or in the Notes to the Digest, in order that, if it be thought expedient to remove them, the attention of the legislature may be directed to that object. It will be readily understood that the declaration of an existing law, to which our authority is limited, is an undertaking of a very different nature and extent from the composition of a new system. In the formation of a new system the several rules and definitions might be expressed in uniform language, and the several classes of crime might be so arranged as always to bear a just proportion to each other and to ensure the complete harmony of the whole; but in the reduction of the common and statute law of England, we have been compelled, in order to preserve its identity and character, to retain much that a strict regard to principle and propriety of language would have induced us to reject."

This is a far more temperate and self-denying tone than that prevailing through the First Report, the authors of which seemed to consider themselves called upon to create rather than to digest, to emulate Napoleon more than Comyn; but as the Commissioners *are* empowered to introduce " such partial alterations in the Criminal Law as may be considered by them necessary and expedient," we may animadvert on omissions of this sort, if such there be, without unfairness.

The Report commences by pointing out some of the more considerable difficulties which necessarily impede the framing of a good Digest even for Criminal Law. Among these one is indicated which, if we mistake not, has escaped the observation of most advocates for the codification of the law of crimes ; and as it is very ably stated here, we extract it, though somewhat lengthy.

" It is in the first place material to advert generally to the relation which the criminal branch of the law bears to the whole system. Every system of municipal law consists necessarily of two distinct parts, which may be distinguished as substantive and adjective laws. The former comprehends the definition of civil rights and obligations, while it is the office of the latter to prevent the occurrence of certain grave infractions of such rights and obligations. And one mode of prevention, namely, the infliction of punishment on those who offend, in order, by example, to deter others from offending, constitutes the great principle, on which the law respecting crimes and punishments is founded. The legitimate objects therefore of penal legislation are the selection of those violations of right, which are sufficiently dangerous to the good order of society, to justify, and require the infliction òf punishment to repress them, and the adaptation of the degree of punishment to the purpose of repressing such violations.

" This consideration is an important one, as it limits the subjects of penal legislation to violations of such rights and obligations, as are presumed to be already defined in another department of the law. It may, for instance, be proper to punish one who, being under a legal obligation to repair a public bridge, by reason of his tenure of particular lands, has omitted to do so ; but to define, under what circumstances one who holds lands shall be bound to repair a bridge, does not properly fall within the province of penal legislation. It is a question of substantive obligation to be decided by the laws which concern the tenure of land. Were any such obligation to be announced or enacted by means of a penal law, the latter would no longer be merely adjective or accessary to the enforcement of the substantive law, but would form part of that law. The definition of crimes, therefore, does not in any case involve the necessity for defining de novo substantive rights ; yet as the existence of a substantive right or obligation is frequently assumed in the definition of a crime, and as in the course of judicial investigation the incidents and extent of such right or obligation often become material, any imperfection in the law by which they are constituted necessarily introduces a corresponding defect into the criminal definition or the administration of the penal law. For instance, on charges of homicide, or cutting and maiming in resistance to a lawful apprehension, the guilt of the offender may often depend entirely upon a nice and difficult question, belonging to the civil branch of the law, such as the technical regularity of civil process, or the precise duty of a minister of justice in its execution. In like manner, in ascertaining the penal responsibility of the offender in crimes of omission, an inquiry into the nature of the duty or liability, the breach of which forms the substance of the crime, is obviously essential. Thus in cases of homicide, where death has been occasioned by the omission to discharge the legal obligation imposed by some civil relation existing between the deceased and some other person, such as the supply of sufficient food in the case of parent and child, or master and apprentice, or the application of due skill and caution in the case of surgeon and patient, the particulars of the civil rights and liabilities of parties so circumstanced become absolutely essential to the determination of the criminal responsibility of the accused.

" It is clear therefore that a system of criminal law, into the administration of which nice distinctions belonging to any other branch of jurisprudence are sometimes necessarily imported, must partake of all the imperfections to which those distinctions themselves are liable ; and consequently that if the law concerning civil rights and obligations be uncertain and indefinite, the criminal law (however accurately defined in general), must be uncertain and indefinite in its application in every case in which those distinctions become essential. From the absence of sufficient definitions of rights and obligations in our civil law, the examination of such rights and obligations has not unfrequently become the subject of embarrassing discussion in courts of criminal judicature ; but the remedy for this evil must be sought in the improvement of the civil branch of law, and cannot be comprehended within any scheme for digesting and amending the Criminal Law alone."

This remedy, we fear, will long be sought for in vain. The question of the practicability of defining such rights and obligations 'is in fact the question of general codification revived in another shape. We have already repeatedly given utterance to our opinions on this much controverted matter. But fortunately the objections are far weaker to a criminal than to a civil code, whilst the inducements are incomparably greater; and thus those who have been most forward to ridicule or to condemn the theory of general codification, have directed their criticism against civil, or have expressly excepted criminal legislation. Even Rossi, although he prefers the plan of special and individual statutes to that of a general digest of the Criminal Law, declares that in every point of view the question of a penal code is wholly foreign to that of codification in a general sense, and considers the creation of the former in some shape or other as a necessity admitting no alternative;[1] although no one has more clearly perceived the difficulties arising from the variability of relative evil in different countries, and different states of society. We hold with him that a statutory declaration of crimes and their punishments is essential to the good administration of the penal laws in any state, and this without being insensible to the absurdity or danger of even criminal codification by men partially or wholly ignorant of the habits and feelings of the countries for which they legislate; of the fabrications of a Bentham for the Western, or of a Macaulay for the Eastern Indies. It is true that the most able statutory enunciation of the criminal law in a state must be but an imperfect and transitory good. Obscurities and contradictions must in course of time arise from contrary judicial interpretations; the spirit of humanity growing with the growth of civilization will require an alleviation of punishment; the increase or diminution of temptations to particular offences will necessitate an alteration of their relative position in the scale of criminality. There is no finality in legislation even respecting things so immutable as the nature of evil and of man.

[1] Traité de Droit Pénal, l. iv. c. 3.

But let us hear the Commissioners further on the limits, which they have thought it right to prescribe to themselves in the prosecution of their task.

" We are fully aware, as we have already intimated, that the attempt to describe all the minute variations and combinations of facts which compose crimes, with metaphysical exactness, is visionary and absurd ; but we conceive it to be quite possible, by means of correct definitions and subsidiary rules, to give to written laws such an approximation to certainty, as may facilitate the practical administration of justice, and at all events introduce an improvement upon a system so vague and indefinite as the present common law of England respecting crimes and punishments. In order to remove the uncertainty introduced into our law by the various causes to which we have above alluded, we have carefully endeavoured to reconcile the definitions of common law crimes with the modern decisions, by which their nature and qualities have been ascertained ; and by such definitions (including, of course, all supplementary rules) to ensure, as far as possible, the simple and concise expression of every thing essential to the constitution of each offence. Still, whatever pains may be taken to render a digest of the law perfect, much must necessarily be left to judicial interpretation. A digest or code does not undertake to decide, with certainty, every supposeable case ; it establishes directory principles—it defines much that was before indefinite—it supplies imperfections, and removes inconsistencies—it effects upon system, and simultaneously with respect to the whole law, that which a variety of statutes has at different periods attempted to effect, with respect to particular parts of the law. But it can never supersede the necessity for judicial construction, which rightly understood, and applied within certain limits, is not only necessary but beneficial.

" In distributing crimes within their proper limits, and so defining their component parts as to promote the great ends of all penal laws, two opposite evils are to be avoided. If the predicaments of fact which constitute crimes are framed too largely, and if the same penal consequences are applied generally to an extensive class of criminal actions, a wide range of discretion in their application becomes necessary, in order to avoid injustice in particular cases; and thus judicial discretion, the exercise of which, within defined limits, is not only salutary but necessary, is too largely substituted for legal certainty. In this state of things, the uncertainty of the penalty diminishes the fear of offending, and tends to confound the gradations of crime, which ought always to be plainly marked by corresponding gradations of punishment. If, on the other hand, the penal predicaments are too narrow, one of two inconveniences results; it is necessary either to multiply legal distinctions, the certain effect of which is the partial obstruction of justice, or to enlarge the boundaries of offences beyond their prescribed limits, by technical interpretations, and forced constructions. It is, however, a material object in defining crimes, to enlarge the terms of the definition to as ample a range of subject-matter as convenience and a due regard to the above consideration will permit, as by this means the multiplication of special provisions is avoided, and the law is rendered more simple, and therefore more easily applicable. For instance, the crime of theft embraces the removal of every species of property capable of being removed; and this generality, as to the subject-matter, supersedes the necessity of various express provisions for the protection of particular kinds of property from depredation."

In direct opposition to the suggestions of their former Report, the Commissioners intend to continue the present distribution of offences into the three classes, Treason, Felony, and Misdemeanor. " As we propose," so they go on to say, " to retain these general divisions, with certain changes and modifications, it is necessary to explain our views and reasons." But although they proceed to suggest many valuable improvements in the classification of crimes under those several heads, supposing them to be retained, we have searched these pages in vain for any argument or authority in support of the propriety of retaining them. As the Report contains a recommendation, in which we most heartily concur, to abolish for the future the incident peculiar to convictions of treason, the additions, namely, to the simple punishment of death; and to abolish, or at least to modify, the incident peculiar to convictions for felony, the forfeiture, namely, of the offender's property; and as modern humanity has assimilated the course of procedure in all criminal trials, as far as the facilities for defence are concerned, we cannot perceive the utility of retaining a difference in name, which will be no longer indicative of any material difference in fact. At present the Commissioners admit that the distinction between felonies and misdemeanors is quite arbitrary, and affords no just line of division between a higher and a lower degree of criminality, and, although they propose to mitigate this evil by a better classification, it must still sometimes occur, from the peculiar facts of particular cases, that of two offences the more heinous will bear the lighter appellation, and escape accordingly, not only with the less share of punishment, but also, considering how mankind are led by names, with the less share of reprobation; a mischief serious in the eyes of those who consider it of the first importance, as we do, to make pure morality, penal legislation, and public feeling harmonize as entirely as the imperfection of human institutions will admit. Unless then, some positive arguments can be found for the maintenance of these unmeaning titles, on this account alone we see sufficient reason for abolishing them altogether.

Supposing the position established, that it is desirable on the whole, to maintain or introduce some arbitrary classification or other for crimes under distinct and several titles, we quite admit that the Commissioners will do well to retain the antique nomenclature. Neither the writings of criminal jurists, nor the systems in use by other countries, supply any arrangement more simple or more rational. The distinction between felony and misdemeanor is wise and innocuous, compared with that between *crime* and *délit* according to the *Code Pénal* of France, between *Verbrechen* and *Vergehen* according to the *Strafgesetzbuch* of Bavaria; in both of which the name of an offence depends upon the quantity of punishment assigned to it, and that quantity of punishment, upon matters often unconnected with the degree of guilt in the offender. Thus, by the Bavarian Code, theft is called *Verbrechen* or *Vergehen*, as the booty happens to be worth more or less than twenty-five florins.[1] " Such a division of offences," observes Rossi of the French Code, indignantly and well, " is

[1] Art. 215.

saying to the public—Trouble not yourselves about the intrinsic nature of human actions.   Look at the powers that
be—if they cut a man's head off, conclude that man is a
great villain.   There is such a contempt for the species in
this, such a pretension to despotism in all things, even in
morality, that without risking over much, one might judge of
the spirit of the whole code by the first article."[1]

As an improvement on the law of Treason, the Commissioners recommend the limitation of that crime to cases of
direct attack on the person or authority of the Sovereign, as
head of the state.   They propose to remove from the present
list of Treasons, all offences which do not come within this
category, and to insert them under the titles of Felony or
Misdemeanor, with appropriate punishments.   Those who
know the length to which the doctrine of constructive Treason
had of old been carried ; how it fastened indifferently on the
importers of bad coin, and the demolishers of meeting-houses,
will admit this to be a most desirable change.

We pass on to a subject of paramount importance, on which
the Commissioners have barely indicated their general views.

" We propose to reduce all punishments in respect of indictable offences to those specified in the following or some
other similar scale, by which the classes shall be greatly
reduced in number, so as not, at the furthest, to exceed twenty.

" 1. Death on conviction of treason, or conviction of
    felony.

" 2. Transportation for life, or some less term of years,
    or imprisonment not exceeding five years.

" 3. Transportation for fifteen years, or some less term,
    or imprisonment for any term not exceeding four
    years.

" 4. Transportation for the term of ten years, or imprisonment for any term not exceeding three years.

" 5. Imprisonment for any term not exceeding five years.

" 6. Imprisonment for any term not exceeding four years.

" 7. Imprisonment for any term not exceeding three
    years.

" 8. Imprisonment for any term not exceeding two years.

" 9. Imprisonment for any term not exceeding one year.

[1] Traité de Droit Pénal, i. 54.

" 10. Fine at discretion, either simply, or in addition to some other punishment.

" 11. Fine not exceeding five hundred pounds, either simply, or in addition to some other punishment.

" 12. Fine not exceeding two hundred pounds, either simply, or in addition to some other punishment.

" 13. Fine not exceeding one hundred pounds, either simply, or in addition to some other punishment.

" 14. Fine not exceeding fifty pounds, either simply, or in addition to some other punishment.

" 15. Fine not exceeding twenty pounds, either simply, or in addition to some other punishment."

" In suggesting this scale, in which the maximum of punishment only is mentioned in each class, we are desirous that it should be regarded merely as a specimen of the form into which we think it will be desirable to reduce the various penalties assigned to crime. When the definitions of crimes are completed, it will be necessary to consider the classes of punishments with the most scrupulous care, in order to ensure the consistency of the whole system; but this must, for obvious reasons, be one of the last operations to be performed.

The introduction of fourteen degrees of punishment short of death, is strangely at variance with the Second Report of the Commissioners, which recommended three degrees only. Of those, too, they proposed to fix by law the minimum as well as maximum, but we do not clearly collect whether this is also intended with the present augmented number. If it is, the discretion of a judge will be small indeed under the new system, to say nothing of the bad principle involved in the introduction of minima at all; but we confidently hope that it is not.

Another deviation from the previous Report, the reduction of the proposed maximum of imprisonment from a term of ten to five years, has our entire approval. It is true that many of the foreign codes recognize the expediency of incarceration even life-long, but apart from the consideration, that with most other countries no punishment of transportation is practicable,[1] the value set in England on personal liberty is so

[1] Professor Haus, the celebrated commentator on the Belgian code, commences a solemn dissertation on the merits of transportation as a punishment, with the

much greater, that we are convinced even a ten years' imprisonment would be regarded by the public at large, as not less cruel or terrible than death itself.

The Commissioners doubtless intend, although they are silent on the point, to retain the two aggravations of imprisonment, hard labour and solitary confinement. The utility of the former is beyond all question,—of the latter, when employed with discretion, scarcely so questionable as to be worth dispute. But it may be doubted, whether the duration of it has been sufficiently abridged by the late statutes, whether too much discretion is not still left in the hands of an over severe judge. It may be remembered, that, previously to the Victoria acts, the Court possessed an authority, unlimited as to time, to direct solitary confinement for some offences, whilst for others, and those often very serious,—such as offences under the 9 Geo. IV. c. 31, the Court had no authority of the kind. But by the Statutes passed in the first year of her present majesty's reign, in cases of forgery, robbery, and offences against the person, burglary, stealing in dwelling-houses and from the person, piracy, destroying buildings and ships, and of certain offences before punishable with death or transportation for life, the application of solitary confinement was restricted to one month at any one time, or three months in any one year; and by the more general provision of c. 90, s. 5, the same restriction was extended to all such offences as were before liable to this punishment for an unlimited period. This still left some felonies, and misdemeanors generally, exempt altogether. We should have no objection to see the power of appending solitary confinement to every sentence of imprisonment, entrusted to the Courts, but we think the power they at present exercise in some instances too great. Thus, it is no unfrequent practice of a learned judge, of acknowledged ability in the discharge of his criminal functions, to alternate three months of solitary confinement in imprisonments of only six months' duration. This seems contrary to the spirit, at least, of the clause

remark, that as to Belgium, " la question est tranchée, nous n'avons pas de colonies."—Obs. sur le Projet de Code Pénal Belge, vol. 1, p. 89. This reminds one of the mayor's twelve reasons for not firing a salute. " In the first place, we have no cannon."

in the Victoria Acts, allowing only three months in any one year, and the proportion there indicated of one in four for the whole period of imprisonment, is perhaps one which to exceed would be dangerous rigour. So terrible an infliction is this punishment considered by foreign writers, that Professor Hans whilst approving it, recommends that it shall be introduced into the sentence of great criminals, in the proportion of one month for the first year, and fifteen days for the following years,[1] during their term of confinement.

We hope to see the imposition of Hard Labour also legalised as an aggravation of all sentences of imprisonment at the discretion of the Court. At present justice is frequently baffled through the impotence of our tribunals in this respect. We may instance the case of common assaults, however brutal and violent, where the offender, if, as mostly happens, a person of low rank and dissolute habits, thinks it a positive boon to be consigned to a comfortable abode, where he finds food and lodging at least as good as he has been used to, without any of the toil of earning them.

The Report, as before stated, recommends the abolition of all additions to the simple punishment of death. Consistently with this advice, we are at a loss to understand what is meant by the proposal to change the offence of slaying a chancellor or judge from treason to felony, as aggravated murder. Aggravated murder surely implies a punishment greater than that of ordinary murder; if not, it is an expression totally devoid of meaning, or at least of effect. The French code in cases of aggravated murder still retains the horrid punishment of mutilation;[2] the Bavarian superadds to the usual solemnities of execution, half an hour's previous exposure in the pillory.[3] Few will be found in these days to defend the enactment of the former code, but it is not perhaps so clear whether that of the latter is to be condemned. At any rate, if the expression of aggravated murder deserves to be imported into our criminal law, it ought to be sanctioned by some exemplary addition to the penalty of death, not involving further bodily suffering to the criminal.

[1] Obs. sur le Projet de Code Pénal Belge, vol. i. p. 159.
[2] Art. 299.   [3] Arts. 5, 6.

On the subject of transportation, the Commissioners briefly observe:

"It will be seen that we have placed transportation among the secondary punishments in the above scale. In so doing, we merely deal with it as a punishment provided by the existing law, without intending to express any opinion as to its general efficacy as a punishment, or as to the propriety of its continuance. This subject is at present under the consideration of the legislature, and the recommendation contained in the recent Report of a Committee of the House of Commons, may possibly lead to some extensive modifications of the practice. On this ground alone it would be impolitic to recommend a final scheme of punishments, founded upon the present state of the law, as the abolition of transportation would necessarily occasion a total change in the whole system of secondary punishments."

On the subject of this punishment, we have little to add to the text. The many interesting topics involved in the consideration of it have been fully discussed in former numbers. But as far as we can perceive, the difficulties attending this question remain unremoved and irremoveable; the evils of the present system are admitted universally; but the ingenuity of those who most condemn it, fails to suggest any adequate or effectual substitute. One objection, however, to this punishment, that it is not correctional, must, we fear, lose weight as we progress towards a right understanding of human nature and penal economy. With a doubtful reservation for the case of juvenile offenders, it is our sad conclusion that the reformation of the criminal is too generally hopeless to justify its being adopted as a material element in the problem of the best possible arrangement of punishments. It is remarkable, that, whilst in England and America the benevolent theory of correctional methods is still entertained by many of those whose opinions are most entitled to respect, it seems generally abandoned by the jurists of the Continent, where the subject of punishments in general has been more thoroughly studied and analysed. Even Rossi, with all his sanguine benevolence, on this point seems almost to despair.[1]

---

[4] Traité de Droit Pénal, l. iii. c. 3.

On the important subject of Accessories, the Commissioners observe : — " Another remarkable characteristic of felony, which we have noticed in our First Report, is the distinction between accessories before the fact and principals,—a distinction not recognised in treason (although, as before stated, every treason is considered to include a felony,) nor in misdemeanors. The penal liability of an accessory after the fact, in harbouring or comforting a known offender, is also peculiar to crimes of the degree of felony. We have already remarked generally upon the present state of the law with regard to this distinction, and a more particular account of the reasons by which we have been governed in our proposed alterations, will be found in the parts of our Digest which relate to Accessories. We think it expedient, however, at once to intimate our opinion that the limitation of the criminal responsibility of an accessory after the fact, to offences of the degree of felony, does not rest upon any reasonable foundation. If a person, who is not a party to the commission of an offence, afterwards aids the criminal, in acquiring the fruits of his crime, or in withdrawing himself from punishment, he is guilty of an obstruction of public justice, and should be punished for that offence, whatever may have been the nature of the crime of the original offender. In the most complete of the modern codes of Germany such an offence is carefully defined as a substantive crime, and the punishment is distributed into several degrees, according to the quality of the principal crime and other circumstances; and it seems to us that this offence ought not to be limited as it is in our law by the technical distinction between felonies and misdemeanors."

No part of the present Digest, however, is found to relate to Accessories. We are, therefore, at a loss to conjecture what will be the alterations proposed hereafter by the Commissioners. But it is greatly to be hoped that they do not intend to confine their ameliorations of the law in this respect to accessories after the fact. The extreme severity of the English system, with regard to accessories before the fact, calls, we submit, for some amendment. When Blackstone wrote his celebrated work, he laid it down as a general proposition that accessories before the fact were punishable, as principals, at common law.   Notwithstanding his general inclination to see as few defects as might be in the system he so fondly comments on, he was sensible of the mischief involved in this maxim, inasmuch as it gives a direct motive to accessories to become principals.   " Perhaps," he says, " if a distinction were constantly to be made between the punishment of principals and accessories, even *before* the fact, the latter to be treated with a little less severity than the former, it might prevent the perpetration of many crimes, by increasing the difficulty of finding a person to execute the deed itself; as his danger would be greater than that of his accomplices by reason of the difference of his punishment."[1]   In spite of the obvious good sense of this remark, most of the penal statutes passed in the two last reigns confirmed the common law by clauses declaring the accomplice punishable as the principal. A distinction between the two, however, was introduced into the important act relating to offences against the person, 9 Geo. IV. c. 34, the thirty-first section of which makes accessories before the fact liable to transportation for not more than fourteen years, or imprisonment for not more than three years, in all cases under the act, short of murder.   But of the acts prepared by the Commissioners in 1837, the 1 Vict. c. 85, s. 7, revives the severer punishment, and declares accessories before the fact to *all* offences against the person punishable as principals are, whilst the clauses concerning accessories in the remaining acts continue the indiscriminate harshness of the old law.   This augurs ill, it must be owned, for the intentions of the Commissioners in this respect.

It is curious that a rule contrary to reason and justice, and unsanctioned either by the Roman or the Canon law, should have been adopted by the legislators of so many nations in modern Europe.   The Austrian and French codes both contain it; and the latter goes even further in condemning accessories after the fact to the same punishment as principals, in some cases, even where the sentence is death.[2]   The Bavarian code, on the contrary, whilst it exempts all accessories from the same amount of punishment as principals, divides, perhaps with an excess of refinement, accessories be-

[1] Com. vol. iv. p. 39.   [2] Arts. 62, 63.

fore the fact—" Gehülfe," and accessories after the fact—
" Begünstiger," into three classes each, and pronounces each
liable to a different amount of punishment, according to the
degree of participation.[1] It seems not improbable that the
excessive severity of English legislation on this subject has
resulted from the limited interpretation put upon the phrase,
" principals in the second degree," by holding it to include
only those actually present at the perpetration of the offence,
to the exclusion of the absent contrivers of it. If the word
" principals" could once be defined to mean, in law, as it
already does in common sense, all who have been the authors
either of the resolution or the execution of a crime,[c] the propriety of some mitigation in the existing punishments of mere
accomplices, would, we think, become manifest to all.
Meanwhile we would not be understood as undervaluing the
recommendation of the Commissioners, that the restriction of
Accessoryship after the fact to cases of felony should be
removed

We next proceed to that portion of the Report which treats
specifically of Offences against the person. The introductory
dissertation on the law of homicide thus begins:

" The order we propose to observe in treating of the law of
homicide is, first, to take a brief survey of the characteristic
incidents which belong to the subject, and by which it may be
conveniently defined and limited ; secondly, to consider the
mode in which the class of offences comprehended under the
general denomination of homicide is regulated by the existing
law ; and thirdly, to submit our general conclusions.

" To every culpable homicide two circumstances are essential ; first, the fact of killing ; secondly, an evil disposition
of mind on the part of the offender.

" In respect of the mere fact of killing, it is necessary, in
order to bring the offence within the jurisdiction of any criminal tribunal, that death should have been occasioned by
some external act, or some criminal omission ; for although
in foro conscientiæ one who designedly kills another through
the medium of mental excitement, as by working on the imagination, be just as guilty as one who effects his purpose by

---

[1] Arts. 73 to 87.   [a] Rossi, Traité de Droit, l. ii. c. 35.

actual violence, the two cases are not equally the subject of legal animadversion. The law cannot satisfactorily judge of or punish intention, except it be manifested by some act of physical violence, or some criminal omission.

" The essential distinctions between culpable homicide, and such as is justifiable or excusable, as also between the different degrees of culpable homicide, necessarily depend upon the following considerations :

First, the mind and intention of the party doing the act which occasioned death.

Secondly, the particular occasion of the act, and circumstances attending it.

Thirdly, collateral grounds of legal policy.

" I. So far as the intention of the author of the death is concerned, the case admits of the following distinctions :

" 1st. He may directly intend to kill the deceased or some other person. Or, without intending to kill, he may intend to do bodily harm to the deceased or some other person. And the harm so intended may be great bodily harm or mere slight harm. And such bodily harm, whether greater or less, may either be the immediate or the collateral object of the offender.

" 2dly. Being regardless of the safety of human life, he may wilfully do an act attended with manifest peril to human life.

" 3dly. He may be guilty of negligence or want of due caution, either in doing an act not under the circumstances attended with manifest peril to life ; or in doing an act which in fact was attended with such peril, but without wilfully and consciously incurring that risk."

However good its substance, there is a perplexing deficiency of logical arrangement in this analysis. We have first an order of three things not at all co-ordinate: the characteristic incidents of homicide, the existing law thereon, and the general conclusions of the Commissioners. Then we have the division of incidents, into the fact, and the disposition of mind. A limitary definition of the fact follows, and we then look for a definition of the disposition, instead of which we have a division of something else into three parts, the first of which itself involves a definition of this disposition. There is no fault to find with the positions laid down, but the manner in which they succeed each other, and the language in which they are expressed, make a clear perception of them very difficult. The Report proceeds to enlarge on the above-mentioned distinctions, but without doing more than defending the present state of the law respecting them. Then follow these interesting remarks upon the legal doctrine of implied malice:

" The crime of murder, the highest class of culpable homicide known to our law, and the law of most countries, is, in the laws of England, characterised by its having been committed with premeditation, or what the English law terms malice prepense, or malice aforethought. But as this class comprehends not only those instances where the offender acts from a motive of ill will against another, and an express intention to destroy or injure him, but also other cases where there is no express malice, but where it is necessary, on grounds of policy, to punish homicide with the highest degree of severity; the term ' malice aforethought' is often applied to a state of circumstances where malice does not exist, in the ordinary sense of the term, but is only malice in a legal sense by construction of law.

" If A. shooting at B., with intent to kill him, were to miss B., and kill C., without intending to kill him, he would be guilty of killing C. of implied malice. Or, if A. were to throw a great stone from a house into a street, in which he knew that numbers of persons were continually passing, and to kill B., a mere stranger, he would be guilty of implied malice in killing B.

" If the various facts and circumstances which constitute implied malice were sufficiently defined, there would be no particular inconvenience in the use of the term as a descriptive ingredient in the crime of murder. But implied malice, according to the law of England, is loosely defined, or is rather not defined at all. It is stated by an eminent authority on the subject (Mr. Justice Forster), to be a pure question or conclusion of law, from all the circumstances of the case; and it is made to depend on a very abstruse and technical doctrine, by which a criminal intention, wholly unconnected with any personal injury, in connexion with a

c 2

purely accidental killing, is, in some instances, made to constitute the distinction between the higher and lower species of culpable homicide, and in others, to bring an accidental killing within the scope of manslaughter.

"Mr. Justice Foster says, ' When the law maketh use of the term malice aforethought, as descriptive of the crime of murder, it is not to be understood in that narrow restrained sense to which the modern use of the term ' malice' is apt to lead one, a principle of malevolence to particulars ; for the law, by the term ' malice,' in this instance meaneth, that the fact hath been attended with such circumstances as are the ordinary symptoms of a wicked, depraved, and malignant spirit.' Again he says, ' the *malus animus,* which is to be collected from all circumstances, and of which, as I before said, the court, and not the jury, is to judge, is what bringeth the offender within the denomination of wilful malicious murder.' Again : ' And I believe most, if not all the cases which in our books are ranged under the head of *implied malice,* will, if carefully adverted to, be found to turn upon this single point, that the fact hath been attended with such circumstances as carry in them the plain indications of a heart regardless of social duty, and fatally bent upon mischief.'

"It is scarcely necessary to observe, that the conclusion of Mr. Justice Foster supplies no certain boundary for distinguishing the crime of murder ; all that is concluded is, that to constitute murder the fact must have been attended with such circumstances as, in the opinion of the court, not of the jury, are ' the ordinary symptoms of a wicked, depraved, malignant spirit ;' of ' a heart regardless of social duty, and fatally bent upon mischief.' It is a description of that which is rather a matter of fact than of law, for whether, in any particular instance an offender, in doing what was perilous to human life, acted in wanton and wicked disregard of the probable consequences of this act, is to be decided by the consideration of a variety of circumstances, which are properly matters of fact, upon which a jury may be able to draw the conclusion ; but where the court would not, by the aid of any mere technical rules, be able to deduce any legal results from the facts.

"When an attempt to explain implied malice, by so high

an authority as Mr. Justice Foster, on a review of all the cases, ends in a description so vague and indistinct as is contained in the above terms, it may, without hesitation, be inferred, that the common law afforded no certain test of that malice which was essential to the crime of murder: had the law furnished any more specific definitions on the subject they would not have escaped the search of so diligent an inquirer.

" We proceed to offer some observations and illustrations, with a view to show that in the ordinary case, where death is occasioned by the doing an act attended with manifest peril to life, the conclusion is properly one, not of law, but of fact, and that it is for the jury to decide whether the offender wilfully exposed life to manifest peril. Upon their affirming or negativing this proposition, the question, whether he be guilty or not of murder, ought, we think, to depend.

" The *mens mala*—the heart regardless of social duty, are figurative expressions used to denote the criminal apathy or indifference with which an act is wilfully done, which puts human life in peril. Whether such a peril be wilfully occasioned is a question, not of law, but of fact, depending on a consideration of the nature of the act done, the circumstances under which it was done, the probability that the act, under those circumstances, would be fatal to life, and the consciousness, on the part of the offender, that such peril would ensue.

" It is the *wilful exposure* of life to peril that constitutes the crime. If one, knowing cakes to contain deadly poison, was to scatter them in a public street, and death were the consequence, the act would be murder, for the offender knew that which he did was likely to occasion loss of life; but if one did the same act, without knowing or suspecting that the cakes contained poison, he would be innocent in law, as well as in morals, for though the act be in truth equally dangerous, whether knowledge exist or not, in the one case great peril of life is wilfully occasioned, and in the other not. And so in all cases it is essential to the criminality of the act, both in law and morals, not only that the act should, in its own nature, under the circumstances, be attended with peril to life, but that the offender should be aware of such peril. Where the offender does an act attended with manifest danger to life, wilfully, that is, with knowledge of the consequences, he may properly be said to have the *mens mala*, or heart bent on mischief.　In such cases, therefore, it is plain that implied malice, or malice in law, according to Mr. Justice Foster's notion, means nothing more than the state or disposition of the offender's mind, when he wilfully does an act likely to kill, or wilfully intends to put life in peril ; but this is a conclusion to be drawn from the facts, viz. the probability that death will result from the act under the particular circumstances of the case, and the intention of the offender to occasion the peril, regardless of the consequences.　No facts or symptoms evidencing brutality or malignity of mind, could possibly be material to the inquiry, except so far as they tended to show the wilful intention to occasion the risk, and when that was proved the offence would be complete."

We are not sure that we agree with these remarks.　The condemned expressions of Mr. Justice Foster, are, perhaps, not so clear and happy as the usual excellence of his writings might lead us to expect, but we doubt if they are substantially erroneous.　Further, we doubt if there is much practical difference between his doctrine and that of the Report after all.　When he says that the Court is to judge of the malus animus to be collected from all the circumstances, we understand him to mean, that the judge is bound to tell the jury, that, supposing they find the circumstances to have been such and such, they ought to go on to find a verdict of murder, because given a certain state of circumstances,—call these circumstances implying malice, denoting wilful exposure of life to peril, or what you will,—the law has said the name of this offence is murder.　But the circumstances, in the largest sense of the word, are entirely for them, not for him.　Let us take the case put by the Report : It is a question of fact for the jury only, whether the prisoner knew that the cakes were poisonous ; whether he was the person who scattered them ; whether the place in which he scattered them was notoriously frequented by other persons ; whether the deceased came by his death in consequence of eating them: but supposing these facts all proved in the affirmative, is not the judge justified in directing the jury, that if they so believe, they must find the prisoner guilty of murder; for that every killing of malice aforethought is murder, and malice aforethought is, malice either express, or implied, and that when a person lays poison, knowing it to be such, in a place where other persons are likely to swallow it, the law implies malice against the public, and therefore against the individual member of it who suffers. Certainly, if indictments, instead of the phrase " of malice aforethought," contained that of " thereby wilfully intending to expose life to peril," the judge might tell the jury instead, that, in such a case as this, the law implied, not malice aforethought, but a wilful intention to expose life to peril. But the inference is a fair legal inference on either supposition, not at all depending on the facts of the particular case, but upon this general principle of morals, that when one, knowingly, endangers the life of another by his act, he must be concluded to do it with a wilful intention, or *malo animo,* or with express or implied malice.

As far as the practical application by judges of the doctrine goes, we should say, that according to experience, the whole usurpation, if usurpation it be, of the province of the jury is, the taking from them the right to draw a metaphysical conclusion as to the state of the offender's mind at the time the offence was committed. The judge does not tell the jury, that from the particular circumstances of the case before them the law implies malice, but he tells them, that wherever one individual voluntarily causes the death of another, if no express malice be shewn, the law implies malice in the causer's mind, although, whether it certainly existed there, no human ingenuity can discover. It is a legal presumption, disproveable by evidence, but not requiring, and indeed impossible, to be proved. The cases so often put, of a man casting a large stone from a house top, or firing a loaded pistol in a crowded street, are exactly similar—it is a natural and therefore a legal presumption, that men doing such acts intentionally do them maliciously, and why then are the jury to undertake the impracticable task of analysing human motives in any particular case? It is for the protection of society that the law presumes malice in every homicide till the contrary be proved, and when this presumption is negatived by positive evidence, the verdict is practically the decision of the jury on the point of law, however much the judge may refine on the doctrine of implied malice in his summing up.

Such is the view which our experience of the charges of judges would lead us to take respecting this questionable point. But it must be admitted, that Mr. Justice Foster's expressions are over-strong, and that the Commissioners, according to their interpretation of them, have a right to argue the matter as they have done. We are only surprised at their representing it as one of practical importance in our days, if it was ever practically important. The case put by the Commissioners in support of this their representation is surely inapplicable. " On words of provocation, a man threw a broomstick, at a distance, at a woman and killed her, and the judges not being unanimous, a pardon was advised." Here a party, who undoubtedly committed culpable homicide, escapes altogether, on the sole ground that the question was a question of law, not of fact, which nevertheless the judges, as a question of law, were unable to resolve. We do not see how any inquiry as to *implied* malice could possibly have arisen here. If the offence was murder, it was so with " *express* malice," the man's enmity to the woman, and intent to do her *some* bodily harm, being clear. " If," says Blackstone, " upon a sudden provocation one beats another in a cruel and unusual manner, so that he dies, though he did not intend his death, yet he is guilty of murder *by express malice.*" [1] And the Commissioners inform us in their Digest, that " the killing of another is of express malice, where death results from a deliberate intention to kill or do great bodily harm. [2] Now, in the case before us, as the provocation was one of words alone, the extenuation of heat of blood could not be admissible; the act therefore would be regarded as deliberate, and, as the Commissioners and Sir Edward H. East [3] agree in saying, the real doubt would depend on " the probability of a fatal result under the circumstances; for, if that probability was considerable, the prisoner wilfully placed life in peril." If he did so, he killed her with express malice, and the offence was murder. If he did not so, the offence being only manslaughter, malice could not be in question.

[1] 4 Bl. Com. 199.   [2] Art. 14.   [3] East, P. C. 235, 6.

In pursuance of the same line of objection, that questions of fact have been perverted into questions of law to the disadvantage of criminal justice, the Report goes on to say:

" The question, whether for want of due caution, a party were to be considered guilty of manslaughter, or the death was merely accidental, has also been regarded as a question of law under circumstances which seem to make it more properly a question of fact. An instance of this kind, reported by Kelyng, is cited by Mr. Justice Foster, with just disapprobation, as being a hard case, and of very extensive influence. A man found a pistol in the street, which he had reason to believe was not loaded, *having tried it with a rammer*; he carried it home and shewed it to his wife, and she standing before him, he pulled up the cock, and touched the trigger. The pistol went off and killed the woman. *This was ruled manslaughter.* This was decided then as a matter of law, but in such a case the law seems plainly to depend on a question of fact, viz. whether that reasonable degree of caution was used which is usual and ordinary in like cases.

" The law may well pronounce as to the consequences where death results from the want of due caution, but whether, in the particular instance, there was a want of due caution, is a mere question of fact, to be decided on a consideration of the circumstances of each particular case.

" In a case very similar to the above, the same learned judge states, that he left it to the jury to say whether the prisoner had reasonable grounds for believing that the gun was not loaded, and upon that direction the prisoner was acquitted."

We are disposed readily to acquiesce in the conclusion, that want of due caution is a question for the jury alone. But there is little analogy between this and implied malice. In deciding the point of caution, the juror has merely to consider, whether his own judgment would lead him to act in the same way if placed in similar circumstances; in deciding the point of malice, he has to calculate the workings of another's mind. We cannot, however, sympathise in the " just disapprobation" of the learned judge. Supposing that the point had been left to the jury, whether the man had or had not reasonable grounds for thinking the pistol unloaded, could the verdict have been other than it was, when the jury must have concluded from the evidence one of two things; either that the statement of " trying" was not true, or that the man tried so negligently, as actually to mistake a loaded pistol for one unloaded, whereas the most ordinary degree of care enables any one to ascertain such a fact correctly? Would it not be absurd to say that a man who tries a loaded pistol with a ramrod, and thereupon believes it to be unloaded, has " reasonable grounds" for believing it unloaded? On reference to the " case very similar," it turns out very different. A. went to church, leaving his gun unloaded in a friend's house, and in his absence B. secretly and unlawfully took it from its place, used it, and replaced it loaded. A. returning from church, had reasonable grounds for believing it unloaded, and could not therefore be guilty of manslaughter, because going off accidentally it killed his wife.[1]

Of homicide committed in pursuit of an unlawful purpose, the Report observes:

" It may be very questionable, whether in point of principle an effect wholly unexpected and unconnected with the intention and act of the party, except by accident, can properly be made the foundation of criminal responsibility, for as the object of punishment is the prevention of crime, it ought properly to be annexed to such acts as are in themselves culpable, by reason of their mischievous tendency, and the intention with which they are done, and not to such as are simply accidental and unintentional. By the law of England, this doctrine is in many instances reversed, and the criminal intention incident to the act intended, but not perpetrated, or not in question, is supposed to be transferred to the act which was the mere accidental consequence. Thus, a party doing the same act in the same manner, but who by mere accident, and not through want of caution, kills another, may be according to his intention in doing that act, though such intention be wholly unconnected with the accidental result, guilty either of murder, when his intention was to commit a felony, or of manslaughter, where his intention was to commit a bare misdemeanor, or. trespass, or an act *malum*

---

[1] Discourse on Homicide, p. 265.

in se, or purely innocent, where the act, although unlawful, was merely malum prohibitum.

" Mr. Justice Foster says, ' In order to bring the case within the description of homicide by misadventure, the act on which death ensueth must be lawful; for if the act be unlawful, I mean if it be malum in se, the case will amount to felony, either murder or manslaughter, as circumstances may vary the nature of it. If it be done in prosecution of a felonious intention, it will be murder; but if the intent went no farther than to commit a bare trespass, manslaughter; though I confess Lord Coke seemeth to think otherwise.' The instances cited by Mr. Justice Foster, in illustration of this doctrine, are not inapt to shew the want of principle exhibited by such a rule. ' A. shooteth at the poultry of B., and by accident killeth a man; if his intention was to steal the poultry, which must be collected from circumstances, it will be murder by reason of that felonious intent; but if it was done wantonly and without that intent, it will be barely manslaughter.' ' But,' he adds, ' that if an unqualified person shoots at game, and the same accident happens, it is excusable; for,' he says, ' the statutes prohibiting the destruction of game under certain penalties, will not, in a question of this kind, enhance the accident beyond its intrinsic moment.' This may be a very satisfactory reason in the latter case, but it is equally, if not more strongly, applicable in the former. There seems to be no good reason why a trespass relating to a man's fowl should be enhanced beyond its intrinsic moment, which is in law a liability on the part of the trespasser to pay the value to be recovered in a civil action; whilst the shooting at game without a qualification is not *merely a civil injury,* but an offence punishable by a penalty to the amount of much more than the value of a fowl. If the distinction is to depend on the intrinsic illegality of the wrong done, it ought to be applied in favour of the mere trespasser."

In the reasoning of this passage we concur, but the criticism on Mr. Justice Foster is unjust. The critic assumes the civil injury of trespass to have been committed by the unqualified person in the pursuit of game. The judge clearly contemplates the case of an unqualified person killing game without committing any trespass. The Report afterwards proceeds:

" For the above reasons we have thought it expedient to obviate this defect in the digest, by modifying the existing law. Whilst we think that a mere accidental killing in the endeavour to do an illegal or criminal act, wholly unconnected with any danger or mischief to the person, cannot on any just principle be brought within the scope of the law of murder, it appears to us that the same objections do not apply with the same force to the case where death is occasioned in the endeavour to commit a crime with violence to the person or habitation of another, and consequently is attended with some degree of risk to the person, although it may not be so great as to constitute murder without resorting to the consideration of the offender's intention. For here the result is not a matter of pure accident, wholly unconnected with the criminal intent; and consequently the enhanced punishment is justified by one of the main principles of penal laws, namely, the prevention of crimes of violence attended with danger to the person. For these reasons, we do not think it necessary to do more than restrain the present generality of the law in this respect, by confining the rule to cases where death results from the endeavour to commit some crime with force against the person or habitation."

Without disputing for a moment the propriety of holding homicide accidentally resulting from the commission of any offence involving violence to the person murder, it may be asked why the felon who accidentally kills whilst breaking into another's house, is more to be punished than he who does so whilst stealing another's horse? There is no more risk of *accidental* killing in the one case than the other, although there may be of *intentional* killing, as the parties are more likely to come to a personal encounter, and there is more temptation to kill, if they do so, with the burglar than the horse stealer. Professor Haus, in his criticism upon the severity of the French code in this respect, (it punishes all homicide committed in the pursuit of other *crime*, though not *délit*, with death,) suggests, we think, the correct principle. He would have the other crime only taken into account in so

far as it affords evidence of premeditation in the homicide.[1]
The Bavarian code[2] goes farther, and establishes as a general
rule, that a criminal committing a greater offence than he
intended, is only guilty to the extent of his design.

The Commissioners conclude the essay on homicide, by
recommending the abolition of Deodands, a reform which it
is to be hoped they will succeed in effecting.

The following analysis and summary will serve to explain
the arrangement of the Digest of the law of homicide. The
Digest itself we could wish to give entire, but its length will
not admit of this.

" Criminal homicide is,
>   I. Murder;
>   II. Manslaughter; or
>   III. Self-murder.

" Homicide not criminal is justifiable, excusable, or by
misadventure.

>   I. Murder is of three kinds:

1. Voluntary homicide not justifiable, excusable, or extenuated by circumstances.
2. Homicide in committing, or attempting to commit,
   specified crimes.
3. Homicide committed in unlawfully resisting officers
   or others acting in execution of the law.

" Homicide is justifiable or excusable:

> For the execution or advancement of the law;
> For defence of person or property;
> For self-preservation.

" Homicide is extenuated where it is not deliberate, but is
committed—

> Under the influence of provocation arising from a *suffi-
> cient* cause;
> Or, is attributable to the influence of fear, or effect of
> surprise.

>   II. Manslaughter is either,

1. Voluntary but extenuated homicide;
2. Involuntary homicide, not merely by misadventure.
   > Involuntary homicide not by misadventure includes—
1. Homicide resulting from any act or omission (done or

[1] Projet de Revision, vol. ii. p. 202.   [2] Art. 42.

omitted) with intent to occasion bodily harm to any other person.

2. Homicide resulting from any wrong occasioned to the person of another.

3. Homicide in committing, or attempting to commit, offences attended with risk to the person.

4. Homicide resulting from any act or unlawful omission (done or omitted) without due caution.

III. Self-murder."

We must again take leave to complain of a want of arrangement, which induces a want of clearness, and superfluity of words. Why might not the analysis stand thus, using the very words of the Report, except in one instance, yet much shorter, and with the advantage of the propositions following in regular connexion.

Homicide is either criminal or not criminal.

A. Homicide not criminal is justifiable, excusable, or by misadventure.

Homicide is justifiable or excusable:

For the execution or advancement of the law;

For the defence of person or property;

For self-preservation.

Homicide by misadventure is involuntary homicide without any unlawful act or unlawful omission on the part of the person killing.[1]

B. Criminal homicide is,

I. Murder;

II. Self-murder;

III. Manslaughter.

I. Murder is of three kinds,

1. Homicide in committing, or attempting to commit, specified crimes.

2. Homicide committed in unlawfully resisting officers or others acting in execution of the law.

3. Voluntary homicide not extenuated by circumstances.

Homicide is extenuated when it is not deliberate, but is committed—

Under the influence of provocation arising from a sufficient cause;

---

[1] This is a definition according to the present state of the law. The Commissioners' definition (Art. 69) is according to the proposed change of the law.

Or, is attributable to the influence of fear, or effect of surprise.

II. Self-murder.

III. All other homicide is manslaughter.

The following are the articles of the Digest of Murder.

" Art. 10. Whosoever shall of malice aforethought kill any other person shall be guilty of murder, and shall suffer death.

" Art. 11. The killing is of malice aforethought whensoever it is voluntary, and is not justified, excused, or extenuated, as hereinbefore mentioned.

" Art. 12. The killing of another is voluntary whensover death results from any act or unlawful omission (done or omitted) with intent to kill or do great bodily harm to any other person, or whensoever any one wilfully endangers the life of another by any act or unlawful omission likely to kill, and which does kill any other person.

" Art. 13. In all other cases the killing of any other person is involuntary.

" Art. 14. The killing of another is of express malice when death results from a deliberate intention to kill, or do great bodily harm to the person killed.

" Art. 15. Any other killing hereby declared to be murder, is of implied malice.

" Art. 16. It is murder where means used with intent to kill one person through mistake or accident occasion the death of another person, and whether the offender be present or absent, when such means occasion injury.

" Art. 17. It is murder whether the offender wilfully putting life in peril intend mischief to the deceased or any other person in particular, or wilfully do an act, or be guilty of an unlawful omission likely to occasion death, without intending the mischief to light on any person in particular.

" Art. 18. Whosoever shall persuade another person to kill himself, and shall be present aiding and abetting such killing, shall be deemed guilty of murder.

" Art. 19. Bearing false witness on a capital charge, with intent to destroy the life of any person, by reason whereof such person suffers death by the sentence of the law, shall not be deemed to be murder."

In a note to the last article, as one ground for settling in the negative the hitherto disputed question of law involved in it, the Report, adopting the opinion of Mr. Justice Blackstone,[1] observes that " there are strong grounds of policy against admitting this offence to be murder, founded on the danger of deterring witnesses from giving evidence in capital cases, if it must be at peril of their own lives." Notwithstanding the authority quoted, we must humbly contend that this mischief is wholly imaginary. No witness of truth would be deterred from giving evidence by the contingent risk of a false charge of murder, any more than of a false charge of perjury. In fact, unless human nature be wholly different from what we believe it, the witness of truth would never feel the slightest apprehension of either. There is only one other argument, the extreme difficulty of proof in charges of murder of this kind ; and this, if it be deserving of attention, must, be it observed, refute the first, for the harder the proof of the charge, the less the fear and danger of the charge being falsely made with success. We may therefore be allowed to doubt whether it is desirable to except from the designation and the punishment of greatest enormity so enormous an offence.

We proceed to quote the articles on " Extenuated Homicide."

" Art. 40. The guilt of the offender is extenuated where the act, being done under the influence of passion from sudden provocation, or of fear, or of alarm, which for the time suspends or weakens the ordinary powers of judgment and self control, is attributable to transport of passion or defect of judgment so occasioned, and not to a deliberate intention to kill or do great bodily harm.

" Art. 41. When passion is excited by any act done, or attempted, or threatened to be done of an injurious or insulting character to the person of the party killing, or of any other person, or by any other grave cause of provocation of the like character offered to the party killing, or any other person, such cause shall be deemed to be sufficient to extenuate the guilt of killing, provided that in fact the killing be attributable to heat of blood so occasioned, and not to deliberate intention to kill or do great bodily harm, regard being especially had to the kind and degree of violence used as compared with the cause of provocation.

[1] Com. vol. iv. p. 196.

" Art. 42. It is otherwise, where in respect of a slight cause of provocation, a return is made so excessive and disproportionate to the cause of provocation, that the killing cannot be attributed to mere heat of blood, arising from the provocation given.

" Art. 43. The rule contained in the last preceding article, applies whensoever upon provocation given by mere words, or gestures of reproach, contempt or derision, the party provoked uses a deadly weapon, or otherwise makes a return wholly disproportionate to the affront offered."

" We have experienced great difficulty in framing these rules respecting provocation. It is not every trivial cause of provocation which ought to be considered as an extenuation of the crime, even although a violent and irascible person was, in fact, excited by that cause to a pitch of passion, which had it arisen from a just cause, might by reason of the temporary suspension of the judgment have properly extenuated the offence. To allow this in respect of very trivial causes of affront, would, if it did not encourage sudden outbreaks of ungovernable passion, at least weaken a salutary check and withhold a signal mark of disapprobation stamped by the authority of the law. In this respect the Bavarian, and several other German codes, by admitting generally as an extenuation of homicide, the existence of passion, however caused, have introduced a dangerous latitude into the law on this subject. On the other hand, as a necessary allowance for human infirmity, and the actual subjugation of the judgment to uncontrolable passion are the grounds of extenuation, it is manifest that to punish a man as a murderer by virtue of any peremptory rule limiting the cause of provocation, may be in effect to inflict punishment not so much in respect of the particular act of deliberate malice, as of a want of habitual control over a mind naturally impetuous, and ready to break forth on slight occasions. We have framed the above article as nearly as we could in conformity with the authorities, which, whilst they in many instances recognise very slight causes of extenuation, do not extend an express negative beyond the limits of our rule. It seems to us, however, to be very questionable whether this rule, large as it may seem, is strictly in accordance with principle, for words or gestures may often be more irritating and provoking than a personal injury of a trivial nature. It is extremely difficult, if not impossible, to define all the causes of provocation which ought to extenuate homicide, and we do not see any mode by which the object of the law can be satisfactorily accomplished, unless it be by making the existence of reasonable provocation within certain limits, a matter of fact, to be decided by a jury. In France, the difficulty has been in a great degree evaded by the law introduced in 1832, enabling juries to find 'attenuating circumstances,' and though we think a general law of this kind is liable to serious objection, the occasional introduction of a similar principle, where precise definition is impracticable, might perhaps be desirable."

" Art. 44. If an interval occur between the provocation given and the act done, it is a question of fact, whether the passion excited by such provocation had subsided or still continued, and if it continued, whether the act was attributable to transport of passion or defect of judgment so occasioned, and not to a deliberate intention to kill, or do great bodily harm.

" Art. 45. The plea of provocation is available, although the offender by accident kill not the party who offered the provocation, but some other person.

" Art. 46. The plea of provocation is not available where the offender either seeks the provocation as a pretext for killing or doing great bodily harm, or endeavours to kill or do great bodily harm before provocation given.

" Art. 47. Homicide is neither justified nor extenuated by reason of any consent given by the party killed.

" Art. 48. Where upon any sudden quarrel, parties fight in heat of blood, and one be killed, the offence, if attributable to heat of blood, is extenuated.

" Art. 49. In such cases, it is immaterial which of the parties was guilty of the first affront or assault.

" Art. 50. If two parties deliberately agree to fight with deadly weapons, and one be killed, the offence of the other is not extenuated.

" Art. 51. If one seeks a quarrel, or takes advantage of a quarrel, with another person, with intent to kill or do great bodily harm, and a contest ensues, in which he kills such other person, the offence of the person so killing is not extenuated, although such provocation has intervened as might otherwise have extenuated the offence.

" Art. 52. If one upon a sudden quarrel with another person, and before any provocation given sufficient to extenuate the offence, endeavours to kill or do great bodily harm to such other person, and afterwards, upon a combat ensuing, kills him, the offence of the person so killing is not extenuated."

We cannot concur in the opinion, somewhat doubtfully expressed in the note to the forty-third article, suggesting the expediency of adopting into England the French practice of permitting the jury to alter the sentences of criminals, by finding, with their verdict of guilty, what are technically called " attenuating circumstances." In a former article, written about six months after this innovation on the *Code Pénal* by the law of the 18th of April, 1832, we mentioned, whilst asserting our own disapproval of the scheme, that we had understood from high authority, that it had hitherto worked well in France. But the experience of seven years has led to the contrary conclusion. The result inevitable, as we believe, of entrusting to unskilled and inexperienced persons, so delicate an arbitrament as that of the degree of punishment due to a particular offender, has been to moderate the severity of the laws, not so much in instances where the facts of the case made some mitigation of punishment desirable, but where the majority of the jury happened to be of unusually lenient disposition, or what is far more pernicious, where the proof of the charges was incomplete, and they could not consequently agree on a summary verdict of " guilty" or " not guilty." As an instance of the last sort, we may point to the trial of La Roncière, the wonder and the shame of the French jury system. It is beyond the province of this article to enter into details of that case. Besides, to most of our readers it is already well known ;[1] to those who are unacquainted with it, we can only recommend the perusal of a story unparalleled in the annals of criminal tribunals for its perplexing difficulty and absorbing interest. It is enough to state here, that if La Roncière, who was charged with an attempt at rape, and a' wounding of the person in the attempt, was guilty, the circumstances attending the offence rendered it one of wholly unexampled atrocity. But it was doubtful, most doubtful as we think, whether he was guilty at all,

---

[1] See an account of it, Law Mag. No. 32

whether the charge was not a mere fabrication; and the jury, in the conflict of opposite opinions, found a way out of their embarrassment by finding him " guilty with attenuating circumstances;" a verdict that to the feelings of all who knew the evidence, involved a most revolting perjury. Yet this so-called improvement of the code, was introduced mainly. on the plea, that owing to the severity of the law, juries had hitherto been in the habit, to the great scandal of the public conscience, of acquitting parties clearly guilty, to save them from immoderate punishments; a practice which went by the name of jury " *omnipotence*," in France, as the similar practice in England, provoked by a similar cause, used to be called " pious perjury." As if the scandal to conscience, the outrage to all morality, were not as great in finding the man whose crime was wholly without facts of excuse or mitigation, " guilty with attenuating circumstances," as " not guilty"—as if a jury capable of committing the latter perjury, would not just as readily commit the former—as if too the remedy were not manifest to the dullest comprehension, that, if over-severe in general opinion, the law itself should be improved, not the evasion of it by falsehood facilitated. Nevertheless, such or similar were the chief arguments for the innovation urged to the French Deputies in 1832.

" The system of attenuating circumstances," said M. Dumon, the reporter of the Committee to the Chamber, " helps to evade some serious difficulties that occur in criminal legislation ; it will obviate in practice the strongest objections to the punishment of death, to the theory respecting subsequent offences, accomplices, and attempts at crime. What does it matter in reality, that the punishment of death is equally a punishment for all, and one which consequently cannot with justice be applied to crimes often unequal, if the admission of attenuating circumstances allow of discarding the punishment of death in the more favorable cases ? What does it matter that the subsequent offence does not always proceed from progressive immorality, and consequently does not always deserve an aggravated punishment? What does it matter that the offence of the accomplice, so various in its forms and its degree of guilt, cannot always with justice be assimilated to that of the principal, if the admission of attenuating circumstances re-establish the distinctions which by the general assimilation of the accomplice to the author of the crime have been neglected? What, in fine, does it matter that the law makes the attempt and the act itself equal in all cases, although according to public opinion the gravity of the offence is partly to be measured by the result it has produced, if the admission of attenuating circumstances allows the judge, (*query jury*) to give credit to the accused for his good fortune in failing to effect his crime? Consider this well! All these questions, so arduous, so much controverted, in the examination of which it would be so difficult to formulise distinctions, and to mark degrees, are solvable with as much facility as justice, by the system of attenuating circumstances, confided to the rectitude of a jury."

It may be thought waste of time and space to quote such arguments. We can only say, that we do so because we can find no better in the numerous and lengthy dissertations of foreign jurists, on the doctrine of attenuating circumstances. Professor Haus, of Ghent, the able commentator on the Belgian code, has in particular devoted many pages of his work to the argument. But he adds little to the reasons already stated, except when he contends that, apart from mere considerations of practical utility, the true principles of jurisprudence lead to the conclusion of entrusting this function to the jury. He maintains, that as they are admittedly the proper persons to find the fact, so the fact they ought to find is not simply the naked fact of guilt or innocence, but the fact with all its circumstances before and after; and that admitting the application of punishment to be the province of the state, and therefore of the judge its representative, still this application should be according to *all* the circumstances the jury find, and therefore should take into account attenuating circumstances, if these are found; and that the punishment being shifted only one degree in severity thereby, the judge may still exercise his discretion also, by choosing between the maximum and minimum of that degree. The fallacy of his argument consists, we think, in this, that ad-

---

[1] Obs. sur le Projet de Revision, vol. i. p. 50, et seq.

mitting all the propositions of Haus to be correct, he does no more than make out a case for the expediency of a jury sometimes finding a special verdict, as we call it. His reasoning is good to the extent that they may fitly state such and such circumstances to have attended the commission of the crime. But his conclusion goes unwarrantably further. They are not only to be permitted to find that these special facts existed, but that these facts in their opinion attenuated the crime. This is the capital mistake, as counter, we believe, to just views of human nature as of criminal law.

The question, whether a certain fact does or does not exist, is a question which any juryman of average intelligence can decide as well as any judge. To such an inquiry, the learned and the unlearned, the experienced and the unexperienced, the wise and the simple, come with equal qualifications for arriving at the truth, or rather we may even say, that the humble and comparatively uneducated man has a juster appreciation of the veracity of witnesses, a keener perception, and more unerring judgment about facts, the subjects about which his mind has been habitually exercised, to the exclusion of higher speculations, than the man of imagination and reflection. But when the inquiry proceeds to the moral quality of those facts, their weight in the metaphysical balance of good and evil, the disposition of heart they indicate, the degree of their relation to the point at issue ; the superiority of the more elevated and more cultivated intellect asserts itself, the simpler and less practised becomes puzzled and obscured ; the judge's opinion is incomparably more valuable than the jury's. It is true, inquiries of this sort must sometimes be partly left to juries in particular branches of circumstantial evidence, but experience teaches how uncertain then the correctness of their conclusions becomes, when they do not, as is generally the case, follow blindly in some course of ratiocination, suggested by advocate or judge. It may, therefore, be quite right to say, that the jury ought to find a precedent fact, but this does not prove that they also ought to draw a conclusion from it. In a case of homicide—for example, that put by the Report—the jury might find properly enough that a certain act of provocation took place so many minutes or moments previous to the fact of killing, but it does not therefore follow, that they ought to find whether the former fact was any extenuation, or in what degree an extenuation, of the latter. It is curious that Haus himself, in another place, seems to express juster notions of the province of a jury, for with regard to the offence of *Recidive*, relapse, subsequent offence, as we term it, he would have, (as it does not always import greater criminality than a first offence,) a larger discretion than usual as to the punishment left to the judge.[1] It is, at any rate, to be remembered, that the argument in favour of the system of attenuating circumstances drawn from foreign codes, being founded on the excess of severity which must otherwise sometimes occur when the judge's discretion is limited as to the minimum as well as maximum of punishment, does not apply to England, where, generally speaking, the judge's power is unrestricted as to the mitigation of his sentence, a salutary power which we trust there is no intention of abolishing. On the whole, then, we cannot agree with the opinion of the Report, that this anomalous function might, in some cases, be usefully imposed upon an English jury.

It is hardly necessary to remark, as the distinction is palpable, that the doctrine of attenuating circumstances is wholly unconnected with the power, given in some cases to juries by our law, of finding the party charged guilty of a minor offence. In practice this may be open to the same objection, namely, that a jury will sometimes, when the evidence is clear, indulge their merciful inclinations at the expense of truth, and find the housebreaker, or murderer in intent, guilty of larceny, or assault only, in order to ensure him a less punishment; but the principle upon which they are allowed to do so, is not that of suffering them to consider whether there are circumstances of extenuation, but merely that of securing justice, sometimes only of saving time, by enabling them to append a conviction for an offence which the evidence does meet to an acquittal for the offence charged which the evidence does not meet, without the necessity of preferring a fresh indictment. Whether the practice is not a bad one, and the abuse indicated a sufficient ground for putting an end to it, is another question. It would not have been worth while to point

---

[1] V. i. p. 83.

out so clear a distinction, had we not seen the clause in the 1 Vict. c. 85, allowing convictions of common assault to take place under all indictments for offences against the person, instanced as an introduction of the system of attenuating circumstances into the law of England; a mistake partly caused, we suspect, by the confused way in which the Second Criminal Law Report recommended the extension of the jury power to convict for a minor offence, when a greater was charged in the indictment.[1]

The following are two principal sections of the Digest relating to offences against the person, other than homicide.

" Art. 74. Whosoever shall administer to or cause to be taken by any person, any poison or other destructive thing, or shall stab, cut or wound any person, or shall by any means whatsoever, cause to any person any bodily injury dangerous to life (*a*). with intent, in any of the cases aforesaid, to commit murder, shall suffer death.

" (*a*) We think it here proper to observe, that in the draft of the statute 7 Will. 4 and 1 Vict. c. 85, as originally prepared by the Commissioners, the punishment of death was to be inflicted in respect of the crimes of administering poison; attempting to drown, suffocate or strangle; stabbing, cutting, or wounding; or doing actual bodily harm, by any means manifesting a design to kill, with the intent, in any of those cases, to commit murder. According to this scheme, the capital crime consisted in any attempt to murder, effected by any of the means above enumerated, the *corpus delicti* was complete so soon as any of the specified acts of violence was committed with the intent to murder, and did not depend upon the extent of injury effected by them, or the accidental fact of resulting danger to the life of the individual against whom they were employed.—*See Correspondence between the Secretary of State for the Home Department and the Commissioners*, pp. 11 and 20. The clause, as it now stands in the statute, makes the capital offences as follows :—Administering poison, stabbing, cutting or wounding, or causing any bodily injury dangerous to life, with intent in any of such cases to commit murder. It appears to us to be objectionable to make the issue of a capital charge depend upon the opinion formed by a jury, respecting so doubtful a question

[1] See Law Mag. No. 34.

as danger to life : besides which, in the above article, which merely contains the words of the recent statute, the application of the principle of danger to life, is partial and inconsistent, inasmuch as it is confined to that member of the clause which contains the general words, ' whosoever shall, by any means whatsoever, cause any bodily injury dangerous to life,' and does not extend to the administration of poison, or cutting, stabbing, or wounding. The practical inconsistency arising from this is, that the offence of a person who, with a murderous intent, strikes another with a bludgeon and fractures his arm, (provided the fracture does not endanger his life), is not within the clause, whereas a person who inflicts the most insignificant cut or wound upon the arm, with the intent to commit murder, is guilty of a capital crime, within the terms of the law."

" Art. 75. Whosoever shall attempt to administer to any person any poison or other destructive thing, or shall shoot at any person, or shall, by drawing a trigger, or in any other manner attempt to discharge any kind of loaded arms at any person, or shall attempt to drown, suffocate, or strangle any person, with intent, in any of the cases aforesaid, to commit the crime of murder, shall, although no bodily injury shall be effected, incur the penalties of the ——— class."

It is much to be desired, that the Commissioners would propose a restoration of the original clause mentioned in the note to Art. 74. Their objections to the present state of the law are wholly unanswerable ; and no deference to the opinion of the legislature should prevent their urging the amendment. But such are not the only objections which may be taken to the late statute respecting offences of this kind. The friends of humanity complain, that the administering of poison, without any bodily injury following, and the infliction of the most insignificant cut, or wound, if the intent to kill be inferred, are to be followed by the extreme punishment of death. The advocates of equal justice remark, that the administering and the attempt to administer poison are noted as different offences in the scale of punishments, although, supposing no injury to the person follow, they are often precisely the same offence. This error proceeds, as we believe, from a neglect by English legislators hitherto of the important distinction between an offence not effected, but which the offender has done all in his power to effect, and a mere attempt at the same offence ; between "*crime manqué*" and "*simple tentative,*" a distinction much insisted on by all foreign jurists, as indispensable to the framing of a good penal code. An example will best show the meaning of the position it is our object to establish.

1. A., with intent to kill, administers poison to B., which, though it fails of its whole effect, does him serious bodily harm.

2. A., with intent to kill, administers poison to B., which by some accident does B. no harm.

3. A., with intent to kill, attempts to administer poison to B., as by mixing it with a potion which he places in B.'s hand, and as B. is raising it to his lips, A. leaves him, and flies to a distance. By accident B. drops the glass, and does not swallow the poison.

By the present law of England the two first cases are capital, but not the third, which was heretofore also capital by 9 Geo. 4, c. 31, s. 11; but now, by 1 Vict. c. 85, s. 3, is punishable with transportation for life.

It seems to us that, admitting it to be expedient to punish any of these offences with death, it is only the first, which should be so punishable. True, in the second and third cases the criminal intent is as fully developed, and the act, as far as the agent is concerned, is as perfect as in the first case; or, to use the accurate language of foreign jurists, the crime is complete, "subjectively" considered, in all three; true, also, the intended result not being effected in either, the crime in all is incomplete as regards the destined victim, or incomplete "objectively." But then the difference of personal injury being sustained or not, should be allowed, in accordance with the universal feeling of society, to make some difference in the punishment. At any rate thus much is clear, that the third case is exactly the same offence as the second, for it has all its characteristics. It is as much subjectively complete as the second, for by flying to a distance at the instant, A. puts it wholly out of his power to prevent the consequences of his attempt. It is not more incomplete objectively, for in both cases no consequences to the object follow. To condemn, then, the second offence to a heavier punishment than the third, under all possible combinations of circumstances, is to commit a practical injustice. The framer of such a law has been misled by a verbal inaccuracy in the expressions " administer" and " attempt to administer." In the cases put, if either is to be called an attempt, one is as much an attempt as the other; each is an attempt to kill by poison, wholly failing of effect. But neither is in strictness an attempt only, but a crime complete as regards the agent, incomplete as regards the patient,—a *crime manqué.* Just so the imaginary distinction in guilt at present drawn by English law, between with intent to kill, shooting at a person but missing him, and administering poison to a person but doing him no harm, is open to a similar objection. The former is not capital, the latter is, though as much a crime incomplete objectively, a *crime manqué,* as the former.

" Art. 80. Whoever, with intent to procure the miscarriage of any woman, shall unlawfully administer to her, or cause to be taken by her any poison or other noxious thing, or shall unlawfully use any instrument or other means whatsoever with the like intent, shall incur the penalties of the —— class."

We remarked in a former article on the curious omission of the words " pregnant or with child," from the 1 Vict. c. 85, s. 6, suggested by Lord Lyndhurst ; whence it follows, that a person may be found guilty of an offence impossible to be committed, when the woman is not with child at all. It seems that the Commissioners are willing to retain this anomaly in legislation. We do not see why an attempt to murder a dead man should not be made punishable on the same principles. The Bavarian Code, Art. 173, takes a distinction as to the magnitude of this offence of procuring abortion, accordingly as the mother is or is not a consenting party to it ; and Professor Haus strongly reprobates the Belgian Code for not introducing the same distinction. We hold, however, with the principle implied in the 47th Article of the Digest, that consent in crimes against the person cannot extenuate.

Of the many other important articles concerning "Offences against the Person," we regret that our limits do not permit us to take notice, but compel our proceeding at once to the other portion of the Digest relating to " Criminal Violations of the Right of Property."

The following prefatory remarks are highly valuable.

" Offences against personal and moveable property are distinguishable in the first instance into two classes :

" 1. Such as consist in the fraudulent appropriation by the offender to his own use of the property of another.

" 2. Such as consist in the malicious destruction of, or injury to, the property of another.

" Each of these two classes comprises offences which must be prohibited by the criminal law, but these need not, and ought not, to be punished in equal degree, or to the same extent. Here consequently arises a necessity for legal distinction; for laws against fraudulent appropriations are capable of a more general application than those which regard malicious injuries to property. Thus, although the fraudulent taking of another man's goods must usually constitute the same offence in specie, whatsoever kind of chattel be taken, policy may require a very different rule in respect of malicious destruction of, or damage to, property. Whilst the stealing of many kinds of property is necessarily punishable as a crime, the malicious destruction of the same property is an injury in respect of which a civil remedy to the proprietor may be deemed sufficient without treating the act as a crime.

" Offences of the former class, that is, those which consist in fraudulent appropriations, are also distinguishable for legal purposes into two classes :— First, those where a mere wrong-doer fraudulently takes and appropriates, or takes with intent to appropriate, that which belongs to another, and by so doing commits a wrong in the first instance ; secondly, those where one having possession of property without wrong, by consent of the owner, or other lawful means, fraudulently converts such property. In the first case, the original taking or obtaining possession of the property is wrongful, and may properly be made penal ; in the latter, it is not the taking, but the fraudulent appropriation of the property, which is criminal. This distinction is important, as serving to establish a boundary between the two offences of theft and embezzlement ; to the former an original *wrongful taking* is essential, whilst the latter is committed by a *wrongful appropriation*, consequent upon a possession originally lawful.

" In the one case as well as the other, the prevention of

fraudulent appropriation is the object of the law, but it is useful to distinguish them, because the offence of embezzlement is
for the most part limited by the necessity of proving some
actual fraudulent appropriation, but the offence of theft is
capable of a much more extensive application.   *   *   *

" A wrongful taking into possession may either be without
the consent of the proprietor, as where a chattel is taken clandestinely, or by force, or with his consent induced by fraud, or
extorted by intimidation.   *   *   *

" The obtaining and taking are equally wrongful, whether
the property be taken secretly, without the knowledge or
consent of the owner, or with his knowledge, by force or
fraud ; and therefore the taking or obtaining possession by
any of those means may equally be regarded as a sufficient
overt act to constitute the offence of theft. When, however,
possession is obtained by fraud, there is a material distinction
between the consent to part merely with the temporary possession of property, and the consent to part with the entire
interest. The distinction is important on grounds of extrinsic
policy, rather than by reason of any intrinsic considerations in
respect of the act itself, or its consequences. There is little
reason, so far as either the immorality or the mischief of the
act is concerned, for distinguishing between the case of an
owner defrauded of his money under a false pretence, and an
engagement for repayment in a month, or that of a horse obtained under the pretence of hiring it, and returning it at the
end of the month. The fraudulent intent may be the same,
and the loss the same, and for many, even legal purposes, the
contract may be equally void by reason of fraud. In point
however of legal policy, there exists a wide difference between
the case where the owner parts with the *temporary possession*
of a chattel to be returned in specie, and of one who parts with
his entire interest in the specific money or chattel.

" To constitute any obtaining of money or goods a theft
where the owner meant, even although he were induced by
fraudulent means, to part with his entire interest, would be
inconvenient and dangerous. Every loan of money or sale of
goods, where the borrower or buyer made default in payment
or repayment, might be made the subject of a prosecution by
the disappointed creditor, and the guilt of the accused would

be made to depend on the mere secret intention of his mind, without such aid from circumstances as his conduct respecting property, in which he had but a temporary interest, would usually afford."

" This objection applies only to a law which would generally constitute a taking of property penal whenever the owner was, with a fraudulent intention on the part of a wrong-doer, induced to part with his entire interest in such property; it does not apply where the fraudulent means can be specifically defined, and are such as of *themselves constitute overt acts of fraud,* sufficiently demonstrative of intention to constitute, in conjunction with such intention, a substantive offence in conformity with the general principle to which we have above alluded.   For as the want of an overt act plainly manifesting the intention to defraud constitutes the principle of exception, it ought not to operate where the very means indicate such intention.

" The obtaining of money or goods by *false pretences* is, conformably with these principles, a mode so clearly indicative of fraud, as properly to constitute an offence, notwithstanding the intention of the owner to transfer his right of property; and the same principles govern the class of cases usually denominated cheats, where false and deceptive cards, dice and other such instruments are used to defraud a person of his property.   Consistently with these principles, it may be questionable whether the offence of obtaining moveable property under false pretences ought not rather to constitute a branch of the law of theft, than a substantive and distinct offence."

" By the existing law, however, the two offences are regarded as distinct, and although they agree in one material and characteristic circumstance, viz. that the original taking is *by wrong,* yet they differ in one other essential circumstance, that a taking by consent of the owner to part with his entire interest, however fraudulently obtained, cannot amount to theft, although it may constitute an offence of a different kind.   We think it, therefore, more convenient that the offence of obtaining property by false pretences, and the kindred offences of defrauding by means of false weights and measures, and other such practices effected by defined fraudulent devices, should constitute separate classes of offences."

These remarks will more particularly strike those who are already acquainted with the First Report of the Commissioners, which also contained an elaborate dissertation on the fraudulent appropriation of property, not so much because they are in most respects an improvement upon that report, as because they in many respects inculcate a directly opposite course of legislation. For example, the First Report was for confounding all the species of fraudulent appropriation under the single title of theft ; whereas the Fourth ably contends for the propriety of classifying the same species as several distinct offences. The following is an attempt at a synopsis of what in the Report extends beyond the limits of quotation.

Crimes against property are either of malicious injury, or of fraudulent appropriation.

Fraudulent appropriation is either with possession lawfully obtained, which is Embezzlement, or with possession unlawfully obtained.

Possession unlawfully obtained is either, by force, which is Theft, and if violence or threat of violence to the person be used, Robbery ; or by Fraud.

Possession unlawfully obtained by fraud is either, when the possession only is parted with by the owner, which is Theft ; or when the property also is parted with, which are False Pretences, and Cheats.

In the treatise on the Offence of Theft in particular, the Report takes exceptions to the present state of the law which regards possession by the owner of the article stolen essential to the commission of the crime ; whereas its true essence consists only in the fraudulent appropriation of, or the fraudulent attempt to appropriate, that which belongs to some other person. It is from this inaccurate view of this offence, as they observe, that the perplexing fiction of *constructive* possession has grown up, which was invented to bring as many cases as possible of fraudulent appropriation, when there was clearly no actual possession by the owner, within the purview of the law of larceny. But " the doctrine of constructive possession is objectionable as well because it is indistinct and uncertain as a rule, as also because it affords after all but an inadequate remedy for the inconvenience felt." We find a difficulty in reconciling this statement of the matter with the remarks that follow, or those remarks indeed with one another.

" The position that *actual possession of property by the owner is necessary* in order to make the taking of it by another theft, is best illustrated by example. If property be delivered to a carrier to be carried, the constructive as well as the actual possession of the proprietor ceases, and the carrier is not guilty of theft although he fraudulently sell the property; but if he do any wrong inconsistent with the contract, as by breaking open the box or package containing the property, he puts an end to the contract, and then, although he continues to be in the actual possession of the property, yet in construction of law the possession re-vests in the proprietor; being so re-vested the carrier is deemed to be as guilty of theft in taking any part of such property as if he had independently of any contract fraudulently taken it from the possession of that proprietor. But though this be the law in case of an ordinary carrier, yet if the owner of a horse deliver him to another upon a bargain made that the latter shall take the horse to some distant place and there leave him, the possession is deemed constructively to remain in the owner, and the agent would be guilty of theft in taking and selling the horse contrary to the contract.

" It is difficult to discover any certain principle which would reconcile such decisions, or prescribe any certain rules for determining, amongst the almost infinite variety of circumstances under which the possession of property is parted with, whether the constructive possession is to be still considered as continuing. The doctrine of re-vesting possession seems to be of too complicated and indefinite a nature to serve as a practical test of criminality; what particular wrongful acts shall operate to re-vest the constructive possession, and under what circumstances the bailment or contract shall be considered as determined by effluxion of time, performance, or otherwise, are questions frequently of a doubtful nature as matters of civil right; and the rules on which they depend are as little calculated to define the boundaries of criminal liability.

" In another and most important point, the law, even extended by the doctrine of re-vesting possession, is greatly defective. Its application depends altogether upon the fortuit-

ous existence of circumstances which are by no means essential to the justice of the case, or the effectuating of any general
principle.   For although it be certain that the carrier or other
agent has, contrary to his duty and the trust reposed in him,
been guilty of a fraudulent appropriation, yet can he not be
convicted unless it can be proved that previous to that offence
he committed a wrong by which the possession was constructively re-vested.   The obvious remedies are to make possession by the owner in all cases immaterial to the offence of
theft, and to embrace at once, by a direct substantive law, offenders who having lawful possession of property are guilty
of fraudulent embezzlements.   Should this suggestion be
sanctioned by the legislature, it is hoped that all the anomalies
and difficulties which have arisen from strained and ineffectual
attempts to bring embezzlements within the limits of the law
of theft, by resorting to the fiction of a constructive re-vesting of possession, will be swept away, and that embezzlements
will be adequately punished as frauds committed upon owners
by offenders having the actual possession."

Whose position is it, we would ask, that *actual* possession
of property by the owner is necessary to make the taking of it
theft?   It is not the position of the existing law, for that re-
cognises constructive possession.   It is not the position of the
Commissioners, who object to possession by the owner being
required at all.   Nor is it the position of the examples given,
which are instances of constructive possession.   Again, if by
a substantive law the offence called embezzlement is made to
comprehend all cases where a fraudulent appropriation by one
having the lawful possession, but not the property, takes place,
is not such a law in itself a complete remedy for all the evils
now experienced in this respect?   It certainly would be so for
all the evils stated in the text at least, as arising from the
existing doctrine of constructive possession.   And although
there are other cases where constructive possession is held to
arise by legal implication, which no generalization of the
offence of Embezzlement could embrace or affect, these are
not such as are likely to give rise to difficulty or failure of
justice.   Such are, for example, where A. has a temporary
use or bare charge of B.'s property, or where A. finds B.'s
property in some spot where he has lost or unguardedly left

E

it, in which cases the possession is held still to remain constructively in B.[1] But cases of this kind are neither perplexing nor numerous, and we cannot think that they furnish any sufficient foundation for the favorite theory of this Report, that the possession of the owner ought to be held an immaterial circumstance in all questions of fraudulent appropriation. If it be an immaterial circumstance, what then can be the use of constituting a separate crime of embezzlement, which only differs from theft as far as the incident of possession is concerned? To this dilemma must the Reporters come at last; if the possession of the owner is an useless requirement of the law, the carefully elaborated distinction between theft and embezzlement is useless, as was maintained in the first Report; if theft and embezzlement would be well employed, which we believe, to designate two modes of fraudulent appropriation, then there exists no need to reject possession by the owner as a constituent element of the former offence; whereas there is much reason for retaining it, as it aids that most important object of criminal procedure, certainty with respect to the offence charged. We shall see too, presently, that the digest is at variance with the commentary in this matter.

As it is not very long, and contains many illustrations of the views taken by the Commissioners as to the principles of the law of theft, we extract the whole of the digest relating to it.

Art. 1. "Whosoever shall, without such consent as is hereinafter specified, wrongfully take and remove any thing, being the property of any other person, and, unless when it shall be otherwise provided, of some value, with intent to despoil the owner, and fraudulently appropriate the same, shall be guilty of theft, and incur the penalties of the —— class."

This article is a more careful and laborious definition of the offence of Theft, the word the Commissioners wish to substitute for Larceny, than any we have met with in looking into the codes of other European countries. Compare it with two of the most famous.

French Code, art. 379: "Whoever has fraudulently abstracted a thing which does not belong to him is guilty of theft."

---

[1] See *post*, p. 53.

Bavarian Code, art. 209 : " Whoever knowingly of his own accord takes possession of moveables not his, without consent of the person entitled thereto, but without violence to any one, with intent unlawfully to hold the same as his property, is a thief."

We abstain from comment on the comparative merits of these three definitions. But it must be observed, that as the laws of France and Bavaria do not recognise the principle of English law, which holds the attempt at fraudulent appropriation, provided an asportavit has taken place, the same substantive offence as the effecting it, the framers of the articles last quoted were exempted from the difficulty of devising expressions to embrace both offences, which the Commissioners have endeavoured to do by the words " take and remove," in substitution for the hitherto accredited expression, " take and carry away." That they regard this as a great improvement is evident from the many passages in the Report dilating on it, and condemning the old version of asportavit as so different in its popular from its legal sense. Perhaps we undervalue the alteration, but it seems to us that the word " remove" conveys the intended meaning hardly better than " carry away." To remove is to move *re*, back, or away; and its only superiority consists in this, that " move" is a word conveying a more general idea of change of place, however caused, than " carry." The Commissioners however maintain that they have succeeded in expressing thus that idea of taking to any distance, however small, which has been held to consummate the crime of theft. And yet they hardly seem to feel entire confidence in the marvellous quality of their substituted phrase, when we find such articles as the fourteenth, fifteenth[1] and sixteenth devoted to defining the definition. Be this as it may, there is in this first article an ambiguity which has escaped the framers' notice. The words " and fraudulently appropriate," according to grammatical construction, are as fitly to be attached to the member of the sentence " take and remove anything," as to that " with intent to despoil the owner." From the former it would result that a completed appropriation is necessary to the offence of theft, from the latter that an intended appropriation is all the

[1] See *post*, p. 53.

law requires. Of course the last sense is that designed ; but the ambiguity might have been avoided by a word of two letters, " and fraudulently *to* appropriate" being unequivocal.

" Art. 2. A taking upon consent given by the owner, or any other person authorised to consent, such consent being given without intent to transfer the right of property in the thing taken, is not theft unless such consent be yielded to violence or threat of violence to the person of the party consenting or of some other person.

" Art. 3. The rule contained in the last preceding article applies, although consent be obtained by a false pretence or other fraud, whensoever the owner or other person authorised to consent intends and consents to part with the right of property, whether he intends and consents to transfer such right to the wrongdoer or to any other person.

" Art. 4. It is not theft where the owner consents to part with the temporary possession of the thing taken, provided such taking be not with intent to despoil the owner, and fraudulently appropriate the thing taken.

" Art. 5. It is theft where the offender fraudulently procures or avails himself of such consent with intent to despoil the owner, and fraudulently appropriate the thing taken.

" Art. 6. Where possession is fraudulently obtained under pretence of hiring or other agreement for the temporary possession of moveables, it is not material that the agreement should be for any definite time ; nor is an actual appropriation by the offender of the thing taken essential.

" Art. 7. It is theft, although the owner knowing that a theft is meditated suffers it to be accomplished, provided he do not procure or induce it to be committed.

" Art. 8. No taking or fraudulent appropriation by one who has lawful possession of any property, such possession being distinct from that of the owner, amounts to theft.

" Art. 9. The rule contained in the last preceding article comprehends all cases of possession by carriers intrusted with goods to be carried, millers with corn to be ground, artificers or workmen with materials to be wrought, hirers of goods, pawnbrokers, and all others, who by virtue of any express or implied consent, or by authority of law, or by any finding or other casualty or means whatsoever, have a lawful possession of any property distinct from that of the owner.

" Art. 10. A taking and fraudulent appropriation by one who has the bare charge or use of any property, but has no lawful possession distinct from that of the owner, amounts to theft."

Here we have the doctrine of constructive possession fully recognised in the two articles preceding, which we must reconcile as we can with the prefatory remarks before considered. And so in the following.

" Art. 11. The rule contained in the last preceding article applies whensoever servants or others have the lawful custody or charge of their master's property to be exercised upon his premises, or elsewhere under his superintendence or control, or guests or inmates have the temporary use of plate or other property, or artificers or workmen have the charge of materials to be wrought in the house or on the land of the employer, and generally whensoever any owner employing, permitting, or authorising another to deal with his property in his house, or on his land, or elsewhere, for any purpose subject to his own continuing possession and control, does not intrust him with any possession of the property distinct from his own.

" Art. 12. The rule contained in article 10 applies whensoever one has the temporary possession of any property subject to the continuing possession of the owner or his agent, with a view to a sale or transfer, or other special purpose.

" Art. 13. The law of theft comprehends every species of wrongful taking and removal, without regard to the means by which the offender effects his purpose, whether he take and remove the thing clandestinely or otherwise without consent, or subject to the above exceptions with consent, or under pretence or colour of legal process or other lawful authority, or by means of any other device, or under any other pretence whatsoever, practised with intent to despoil the owner, and fraudulently appropriate the thing taken.

" Art. 14. Any act of taking, by which the offender has such possession of the thing taken that he is enabled to remove it at his will to any distance, however small, so that no portion of the thing removed occupy the space it did before, is a taking and removing sufficient to constitute theft.

" Art. 15. The rule contained in the last preceding article

comprehends every kind of removal, by lifting, carrying, or otherwise; or by driving, leading, or otherwise, where an animal is the subject of theft; provided that such removal be effected by the offender in furtherance of his intention to despoil the owner, and fraudulently appropriate the thing removed.

"Art. 16. It is not essential to the offence that the thing taken be completely removed from any place of deposit in which it may have been taken, or completely freed from all impediment to further removal.

"Art. 17. The law of theft shall be deemed to extend to all moveable property; and also to property severed from the realty, although it be severed at the time, and for the purpose of taking and removing the same.

"Art. 18. It shall be limited, unless otherwise provided, to property which is either of value to the amount, at the least of the lowest denomination of the current coin of the realm, or of value to the owner to that amount, although it would be of no value to any other person; but it shall extend to property, the taking or severance of which diminishes to the owner the value of any other property to that amount.

"Art. 19. Theft may be committed by the taking and removing of the property of another, though the actual owner be unknown.

"Art. 20. The rule contained in the last preceding article shall be deemed to comprehend the wrongful taking of waifs, estrays, treasure-trove, and wreck, previously to the vesting thereof respectively in the crown, or the lord of the franchise.

"Art. 21. Where the taking is upon the finding or other casualty, the quality of the act depends upon the intention of the party at the time; and it is not theft, unless he took with intent to despoil the owner, and fraudulently appropriate the thing taken, although such owner be unknown.

"Art. 22. Theft cannot be committed by one who is either the sole, or a joint, or a part owner of the thing taken.

"Art. 23. Nor by a wife in taking the property of her husband.

"Art. 24. Provided that no delivery from the wife of the property of her husband, or consent by her to any taking or removing of such property, shall in any wise justify or excuse the taking or removing of such property by one intending to despoil the husband, and fraudulently to appropriate the thing removed.

" Art. 25. The law and all rules concerning theft shall be equally applicable, whether the thing taken be the property of a sole owner, or of several owners, or of a body corporate, and also whether any such owner have or have not a right to the present possession of the thing taken, and also whether any such owner be or be not in possession of the thing taken.

" Art. 26. The taking and removing are with intent to despoil the owner, and fraudulently appropriate the thing taken, whensoever these acts are done with intent to deprive the owner of the thing taken, and to have or deal with it as the property of the offender or some other person, in fraud of the owner, without regard to the offender's motive for committing spoliation, or the particular use to which he intends to apply, or does apply the thing taken.

" Art. 27. It is not theft, unless the intent to despoil and fraudulently appropriate exist at the time of taking and removing.

" Art. 28. It is not theft whensoever the acts of taking and removing, although wrongful, are done under a mistake of right or authority, or through inadvertence or by accident.

" Art. 29. It is not theft where the intent is to deprive the owner of the temporary possession only, and not of his absolute property in the thing taken.

" Art. 30. Neither the right of property, nor of possession, is in anywise altered by the theft.

" Art. 31. No restitution to the owner of a thing taken by theft shall absolve the offender.

" Art. 32. Whosoever shall commit the crime of theft, in respect of any property, shall be deemed to steal the same."

The length to which this article has already extended precludes our doing much more than name the titles of the remaining members of the Digest. These are—Robbery, Aggravated Thefts, Extortion by Threats, Obtaining Property by False Pretences, Cheats, Embezzlements, Malicious Injuries to Property, and a very strange ungainly member which comes halting in at last, styled " Special Provisions for the Protection of Particular Property," under which head we find various offences collected, some of which are Thefts, some Aggravated Thefts, some Offences against the Person, for what purpose relegated to this awkward squad of crimes we have not been able to discover in the absence of all explanation by the Report.

The Commissioners propose to reduce the offence of "Robbery" in future to a taking by or by threat of personal violence, and on the other hand to extend the limits of the offence of "Extortion by Threats." In the Digest of Robbery we find the following articles together.

" Art. 41. Actual fear is not material, provided the act of stealing be accompanied by such threats or menaces as are calculated to create an *expectation* that force will be used in case of resistance.

" Art. 42. Where no actual violence is used, and the threats or menaces used either do not create any *apprehension* of violence, or such apprehension has ceased to exist at the time when the property is taken, the offender is not guilty of robbery."

Thus, although actual fear in the person plundered is not material to the crime, apprehension is : a very nice distinction if apprehension is to be understood in its popular sense. It must therefore, we suppose, be understood in its primitive and unusual sense of expectation. Why not then, instead of creating the needless obscurity, have continued the latter word in the forty-second article, as it is used in the forty-first.

"Aggravated theft" includes sacrilege, stealing from the person, or in dwelling-houses. The fifty-second Article is curious.

" Whosoever shall commit any of the offences contained in the last preceding Article," (stealing, namely in certain buildings,) " such offence being attended with any two of the following aggravations, viz.

1. Breaking into such dwelling-house, shop, warehouse, or counting-house ;
2. Putting any one being therein in bodily fear by any menace or threat ;
3. Property being stolen to the value of 5*l.* or more;

shall incur the penalties of the   class."

This is the only instance we find in the Report which introduces into English law that peculiar feature of foreign codes, of surrounding a substantive offence with aggravatory satellites to be taken by ones, twos, and threes, according to the phases of their principal. It is, we must humbly contend, a bungling and indolent mode of legislation, invented to save a few words at the expense of perspicuity and neatness, and wholly counter to the important principle of making the offence and its consequences manifest to common understandings. The notion here seems borrowed from the Bavarian Code, Art. 224, a code of which we must observe, that with all its singular excellencies, the subjects of the country where it is in force have in general but little chance of comprehending its meaning, so subtle and involved are its provisions.

In treating of False Pretences, the Commissioners thus limit the extent of the cases they consider properly within the bounds of this offence.

" In order to avoid the inconvenience of too great generality, it is essential that such pretence shall consist in some false and fraudulent representation, as to the existence or non-existence of some specific fact by the credit given to which, either wholly or in part, the property is obtained. Were the offence to be extended to an obtaining by means of any representation or promise fraudulent merely because it was not meant to be fulfilled, the offence would be without any sufficient limit. This distinction is sufficiently plain for practical purposes. If a man purchasing goods promise to call and pay for them the next day, this is a mere prospective engagement, but no misrepresentation as to any specific fact; but if he be entrusted with goods, on giving his promissory note in payment, falsely representing that the banker to whom such note is directed has 1,000*l.* of the maker's in his possession, the specific false pretence may be justly and conveniently dealt with as a crime."

" The offence in principle extends to all property so obtained, whether it be moveable or not at the time of the pretence made. And also to pretences made by signs or actions, which if made by words would come within the principle."

And equally well of Cheats they observe,

" The question is, how this offence can be conveniently

limited and defined in respect of the means used. It may be
stated negatively that the offence cannot, consistently with
the above suggestions, be extended to any fraud committed
solely by the aid of any mere false assertion, be it oral or
written. To make a fraud criminal in respect of a mere false
or deceitful representation, whether oral or written, beyond
the class already observed upon, of obtaining by false pretences, would be inconvenient on account of its generality,
and not sufficiently warranted upon any principle of necessity. On the other hand, all cases, where the fraud is effected
by means of any instrument or thing falsely constructed and
used for the purpose of deceiving, may be made penal in
furtherance of the great object of this branch of the law, the
protection of property, without incurring the danger of inconvenience from laxity of definition, the use of such an instrument or thing supplying a definite limit to the offence, and
affording a practicable test of guilt. Within this description
would fall every case where a false and deceptive instrument
was used to defraud ; the rule would include false weights
and measures, and any other instrument for ascertaining the
weight and magnitude or quality of any commodity ; all
false seals or tokens, all forged writings, every thing in short
false in its construction, and adapted to and used for the purpose of fraud."

The following are the articles which define the offence of
Embezzlement.

" Art. 79. The crime of embezzlement is characterized by
an actual fraudulent appropriation.

" Art. 80. Whosoever being for any special purpose entrusted under any contract express or implied, or other lawful
authority, with the possession, or with power to take or deliver the possession of any moveable property or fixture, being
of the property of any other person, shall wrongfully and fraudulently embezzle the same or any part, or any proceed thereof, shall incur the penalties of the —— class.

" Art. 81. The term ' embezzle' shall be deemed to comprehend every kind of fraudulent appropriation, provided the
offender by some act manifest his intention to make such
fraudulent appropriation."

In a note to the eightieth article the Commissioners observe,—" It may perhaps be proper to introduce a still more general clause, including the embezzlement of property not specifically entrusted to the offender." Surely the arguments employed in the several introductions to the different portions of the Digest, of which we have extracted what is most material, place this beyond a conjecture. The definition of the Bavarian Code for this offence is brief and good. Embezzlement, " Unterschlagung des anvertrauten," is described thus: " Whosoever holds a thing for another in possession or safe custody, and unlawfully appropriates the same, is guilty of embezzlement."[1]

In the Digest relating to " Malicious Injuries to Property," we regret to see retained, by the hundred and third article, without any condemnatory remark, the provision of the 7 & 8 Geo. IV. c. 30, s. 8, by which the *beginning* to demolish certain buildings is made the same offence as the actual demolition or destruction of them, and therefore punishable like that with death. However, the alarm excited by the agrarian war of 1830-1 may have justified for a time this merciless enactment in the eyes of society, there no longer exists any sufficient reason for retaining it. It will be remembered, that at the trials under the Special Commission of that period the offence was held to be proven, wherever it appeared that any the slightest demolitory act had taken place, though the agent was straightway interrupted without any material injury being done, unless the interruption originated in his own choice, and not in extraneous circumstances. And such, doubtless, is the true interpretation of this law. But it is a law, we venture to think, as inconsistent with the true principles of legislation as of humanity. Grievous as the offence of beginning to demolish a house may be, yet if the offender be interrupted, (although up to the time of the interruption he manifests not the slightest intention of desisting voluntarily,) it is not a complete offence. As regards the criminal intention even, he might, if left to himself, have desisted voluntarily; it is impossible to predicate that he would not have done so. The offence then is not complete even as regards intention,—not subjectively complete in other words; it is

[1] Art. 329.

not *crime manqué,* a crime imperfect only in the execution but merely an attempt to commit a crime. The guilt of the individual is therefore less than if he had effected the demolition, and so far he deserves a less punishment. On the other hand, the injury done, the only ground besides for aggravating the punishment is less, probably very much less than in the case of complete demolition; perhaps there is no injury at all. On both grounds, therefore, the punishment of death seems too severe for this offence. And it should not remain as a blot upon our now generally humane statute book, that a mob, who declaring they will pull down a house, take off one tile, and are then frightened away by a posse of constables, are all guilty of a capital felony.

A great many opinions, both critical and suggestive, have been thrown out in the course of this article, without apology or restraint. Let it not therefore be supposed, that we entertain any exalted notion of our right or capacity to dictate on a subject of such extent and difficulty. But we should not do our duty as reviewers, if we suffered our respect for the personal merits of the Commissioners, or our sense of the importance and utility of their labours, to interfere with the honest expression of doubt, where doubt is entertained, of the correctness of some of their views. Some observations have been made with a pretty confident reliance on their justice, others with no decided opinion one way or the other, some with no other view than that of drawing the attention of the reader to a topic of decided interest; but none without a full sense of the manifold qualifications required for dealing with a subject so vast and profound as the consolidation of the Criminal Law of England. We take our leave of this Report by heartily recommending it to the careful perusal of all those who take delight in such inquiries, and with the confident belief that it will be introductory to many valuable improvements in the legislation of this country.

S.

ART. II.—EQUITY JURISPRUDENCE IN ENGLAND AND AMERICA.

Commentaries on Equity Jurisprudence, as administered in England and America. By Joseph Story, LL.D. Dane Professor of Law in Harvard University.

THE treatise we now propose to examine, is written by the author of the work upon pleading, which we reviewed in our last number. It will perhaps occur to our readers, that this treatise should have been offered to their notice in the first instance, and that the principles of equitable jurisprudence should have been submitted to their consideration before they inquired into the forms of pleading, in which it assumes a practical shape. We certainly should recommend a student of equity to make himself acquainted with these Commentaries, before he passes to works of detail and practice. We fear that such is not the course commonly adopted. The student generally begins with the actual work of a pleader's office. He is brought in medias res. He commences a bill or answer, and hopes that in the course of their completion he may make acquaintance with the principles upon which they are framed. The consequence is, that lawyers are more frequently found to be correct in practice, and well versed in the rules of pleading, than acquainted with principles or capable of taking general views of the rights which are enforced. One cause of this difference is, that the principal object of a young lawyer is to acquire that peculiar species of knowledge which leads to early fame, and to an immediate increase of fortune. Another reason, we believe, to be the want of a comprehensive treatise upon equitable jurisprudence. The treatise on equity, attributed to Mr. Barlow, is a very meagre work in comparison with the extent of his subject, and although the notes of Mr. Fonblanque, which have been added to it, are executed with consummate ability, still from their very nature they are wanting in the arrangement and course of reasoning, without which a student is rarely induced to follow a long train of study. Blackstone's Commentaries contain a very short explanation of some of the leading equitable doctrines. He has pursued the discussion, so far as he has carried it, with his usual acuteness of thought and elegance of style; but he has advanced so very small a distance, that no foreign jurist, rising from the perusal of his work, would entertain the slightest notion of the extensive application of equitable doctrines to all kinds of property in England.

The work before us supplies the defect. " My main object," says the author in his preface, " has been to trace out and define the various sources and limits of equity jurisdiction, as far as they may be ascertained by a careful examination of the authorities, and a close analysis of each distinct ground of that jurisdiction, as it has been practically expounded and applied in different ages. Another object has been, to incorporate into the text some of the leading doctrines which guide and govern Courts of Equity in the exercise of their jurisdiction; and especially in those cases where the doctrines are peculiar to those Courts, or are applied in a manner unknown to the Courts of common law. In many cases I have endeavoured to show the reasons upon which their doctrines are founded, and to illustrate them by principles drawn from foreign jurisprudence, as well as from the Roman civil law." He afterwards explains in the following words the mode in which he treats his subject. " The work is divided into three great heads. First, the concurrent jurisdiction of Courts of Equity; secondly, the exclusive jurisdiction; and thirdly, the auxiliary or assistant jurisdiction. The concurrent jurisdiction is again subdivided into two branches; the one, where the subject-matter constitutes the principal (though rarely the sole) ground of the jurisdiction; the other, where the peculiar remedies administered in equity constitute the principal (though not always the sole) ground of jurisdiction."

Looking to the vast range of subjects included in this inquiry, we naturally fix our attention upon our author's preliminary investigation into " the true nature and character of equity jurisprudence." This is the title of the first chapter. There is perhaps no other subject connected with our Courts of justice, which so often comes under discussion, and yet gives rise to such frequent mistakes. The error pervades not merely laymen, but also a large number of those who practise in Courts of Common Law. It is supposed, that any wrong for which common law provides no remedy, may be relieved in equity. " In the most general sense," says our author, " we are accustomed to call that equity, which, in human transactions, is founded in natural justice, in honesty and right, and which properly arises ex æquo[1] et bono." In the same way equity has sometimes been supposed to depend upon the boni viri arbitrium. No person at all acquainted with our Courts of Equity, we might indeed say no person who has paid attention to the administration of justice in any country, can suppose that equity, such as prevails in English Courts, can fall within such a description. It would include those claims which are called by Doctor Paley, rights of imperfect obligation. For instance, the right of the best candidate for public appointments to be preferred to his inferiors ; that of unfortunate persons to be relieved by the rich; that of a benefactor to enjoy the gratitude of him who is benefited. The reason why claims of this description are not enforced by courts of justice is, not that the violation of them is less injurious to the state than breaches of statute law, but that the enforcement of them must necessarily be of an arbitrary character, and must be accompanied with inquisitorial examination. As Doctor Paley observes, " A man[2] who by a partial, prejudiced, or corrupt vote disappoints a worthy candidate of a station in life, upon which his hopes, possibly a livelihood depended, and who thereby grievously discourages merit and emulation in others, commits, I am persuaded, a much greater crime than if he filched a book out of a library, or picked a pocket of a handkerchief, though in the one case he violates only an imperfect right, in the other a perfect one."

Our author notices another opinion of the nature of equity, which we believe owes its origin to Aristotle. The sense here alluded to, is that in which it is used in contradistinction to strict law, or " strictum et summum jus." [3] The principal passage of Aristotle upon this subject may be translated in the following words :—" Justice[4] then and equity are of the same character, both of them are excellent, but equity is the

---

[1] Page 1.
[2] Paley, Moral Philosophy, 1, 91, 94.
[3] Page 4.
[4] Aristot. Ethic. lib. 5.

better of the two. The difficulty is, that equity is a species of justice, not however according to law, but as a correction of that justice which is established by law. For the law is laid down generally; but there are some subjects on which general rules cannot be laid down with success." This definition of equity is less extensive than the preceding definition, confining it to those subjects to which law is applicable. The jurisdiction of the Roman Prætor seems to have worn the same character. " Jus prætorium est quod prætores introduxerunt adjuvandi, vel supplendi, vel corrigendi juris civilis gratiâ, propter utilitatem publicam, quod et honorarium dicitur ad honorem prætorem sic nominatum." We need hardly observe that the equity defined in this term, is quite distinct from the equity as administered in this country, as there are numerous rights enforced in our Courts of Equity on which the statute and common law are altogether silent. When we remember the arbitrary notions, which during the earlier periods of our history prevailed in all departments of state, we cannot be surprised that Courts of Equity should have assumed the exercise of a very wide discretion, and that in the dicta of the Chancellors of those days language should be found in favour of the largest interpretation of the province of equity. For instance, that Lord Bacon should say, " Chancery is ordained to supply the law, and not to subvert the law," or that in the treatise on equity it should be observed, " every matter therefore that happens inconsistent with the design of the legislator, or is contrary to natural justice, may find relief here. For no man can be obliged to any thing contrary to the law of nature; and, indeed, no man in his senses can be presumed willing to oblige another to it."[1] In truth, equity was in ancient times " most gigantic in its sway." Selden's rebuke was correct in fact. " For law we have a measure, and know what we have to trust to.— Equity is according to the conscience of him that is chancellor; and as that is larger or narrower, so is equity. 'Tis all one as if they should make the standard for the measure the chancellor's foot. What an uncertain measure would this be? One chancellor has a long foot, another a small

---

[1] Page 13.

foot, a third an indifferent foot. It is the same thing with the chancellor's conscience." But as in the progress of constitutional doctrines, restrictions have been fixed upon political power, a change similar in character has taken place in the administration of justice. We have learnt that the judgment of an individual can never be relied upon; that although that judgment be the boni viri arbitrium, still it cannot compensate for the advantages of certainty, and that a few decisions, founded upon more exalted principles, would less conduce to public happiness, than laws of an inferior character, enforced with uniformity and strictness. Justice Story quotes abundant instances in which equity so completely follows the law, that it ventures to offer no correction in matters admitted to be mischievous. But it is not merely by statute or common law, that the judgment of the equity judge is fettered. He is equally bound by the judgments of his predecessors. Previous decisions receive the force of a compact code, and enable the suitor by reference to cases already determined, to ascertain the decision which his own case will receive.[1]

Justice Story, after explaining what English and American equity is not, proceeds to explain what it is, by giving a general view of its operations, and then defining it in the following terms :—" Perhaps the most general, if not the most precise, definition of a Court of Equity, in the English or American sense, is, that it has jurisdiction in cases of rights recognised and protected by the municipal jurisprudence, where a plain, adequate, and complete remedy cannot be had in the Courts of Common Law.[2]" The rights must be such as are recognised by municipal jurisprudence, that is, they cannot be rights founded merely on moral considerations, on those of charity or gratitude, or personal merits. On the other hand, they must be such rights as are not completely protected at common law. If partially protected, they will receive relief in equity, so far as legal aid is defective. If not protected at all, the protection which they will find in equity will be complete.

[1] " The principles are as fixed and certain as the principles on which the Courts of Common Law proceed." Per Lord Redesdale, Bond v. Hopkins, 1 Sch. & Lef. 429. [2] P. 32.

It is not, however, by the study of a definition that the knowledge of this extensive subject is to be acquired. Where law ends and equity begins, is a question which does not rest upon definite principle. The insertion of three words in a conveyance defeats the statute of uses, and converts the most important rights over an estate from legal into equitable rights. Almost all the principles which law could have applied to the property in its descent, transfer, or liability to incumbrance, are equally applicable to it in the Court of Equity. It is this coincidence which gives rise to the question alluded to by our author at the end of this chapter. "Many[1] persons, and especially foreigners, have often expressed surprise that distinct Courts should in England and America be established for the administration of equity, instead of the whole administration of municipal justice being confided to one and the same class of courts, without any discrimination between law and equity." In the first instance the distinction arose from a combination of different circumstances, the limited character of our laws, and the desire to evade either forfeitures or the absolute authority of the churchmen, who happened to be Chancellors. To enter into the question whether the distinction ought to be maintained, would of course far exceed our limits. We may, however, observe, as the point on which the question turns, that there are many functions performed by Courts of Equity which differ from those performed by Courts of Law in the machinery which is required for them, the manner in which the subject of suit is to be treated, and the results to be obtained. We may mention, as an example, the specific performance of an agreement, which is to be modified. A Court of Law would inquire what loss a party had sustained through its non-performance; and would make the inquiry by means of a jury. But no jury could fairly consider the claim of a party to have it modified; and the two questions are so distinct from one another, that no advantage would be gained by the union of the two inquiries in proceedings before the same tribunal. Let us take, as another instance, an executory trust to purchase property for a particular purpose:—No jury could ever inquire whether the property proposed to be purchased corresponded with the terms of the trust, whether the title of it could safely be accepted, whether the conveyance was properly drawn and executed. An officer of the character of a master is wanted for the determination of these questions; or, in other words, there is need of that species of machinery which is found in a Court of Equity. We do not mean to say that many improvements may not be introduced into our present system; but it must be borne in mind that, although the same subjects are common to suits and actions, still they give rise to questions totally distinct in character, which require for their determination tribunals differently formed, and conducted upon different principles. There is no excellence in mechanical arts without division of labour: if we may trust our experience in England, the same principle is applicable to jurisprudence.

To return to the subject of the first chapter. The doctrines there laid down suggest an inquiry of the following nature, with a view to ascertain whether any given claim falls within the province of equity. In the first place is it a claim protected by municipal jurisprudence? If so, is it adequately protected at common law? Should such be the case, there will, generally speaking, be no concurrent jurisdiction in equity; though this must be matter of careful observation. But if the protection at common law is incomplete, or there is no protection at all, relief may be obtained from Courts of Equity, in the former case to supply the defects of legal proceedings, in the latter to protect and enforce the entire claim.

Having thus discussed the nature of equity jurisprudence, Mr. Justice Story gives a short account of its origin and history, tracing it from the earliest periods of arbitrary doctrine, to the maturity of the present system. He adds a short account of the different forms in which it has been introduced into the United States.[1]

[1] The following curious passage, from Camden's Britannia, is introduced in a note, p. 41, vol. i. " The Chancery drew that name from a chancellor, which name, under the ancient Roman emperors, was not of so great esteem and dignity, as we learn out of Vopiscus. But now-a-days, a name it is of the highest honor, and chancellors are advanced to the highest pitch of civil dignity; whose name Cassiodorus fetcheth from cross-grates or lattices, because they examined matters within places (secretum) severed apart, enclosed with partitions of cross bars,

The next part of the subject, of which our author treats, seems to us to be an admirable introduction to the great body of his work. He brings before his readers " some few maxims and rules of a general nature, which are of constant, and tacit, and sometimes of express reference in most of the discussions arising in equity." Such maxims as, " equity follows the law ;" " where there is equal equity, the law shall prevail ;" " he who seeks equity, shall do equity;" " equality is equity, or, as it is sometimes expressed, equity delighteth in equality ;" " equity looks upon that as done, which ought to be done." Each of these maxims he explains as to its nature, and the mode of its application. He places them, where the maxims occur in Euclid, at the commencement of the treatise, to be used according to the same example, in connecting together the series of arguments which arise in the legal problems. Thus he completes the substratum of his work. Having explained what equity is, how and when its doctrines arose and became recognized, and having brought forward many of the maxims which it is accustomed to employ, he has prepared his readers with all that preliminary information which is required for an accurate study of the province of equity jurisprudence.

Our author next proceeds to ascertain the true boundaries of the jurisdiction at present exercised by Courts of Equity, and commences with that portion of the concurrent jurisdiction, in which the subject-matter constitutes the principal

---

which the Latins call cancelli.—Regard (saith he to a chancellor) what name you bear. It cannot be hidden which you do within lattices. For you keep your gates lightsome, your bars open, and your doors transparent as windows. Whereby it is very evident that he sat within grates, where he was to be seen on every side ; and thereof it may be thought he took his name. But minding, it was his part, being as it were, the prince's mouth, eye and ear, to strike and slash out with cross lines, lattice like, those letters, commissions, warrants and decrees passed against law and right, or prejudicial to the commonwealth, which, not improperly, they called to cancel. Some think the name of chancellor came from this cancelling. And in a glossary of a later time, this we read—a chancellor is he, whose office it is to look into and peruse the writings of the emperor, to cancel what is written amiss, and to sign that which is well." However, antiquaries differ much upon the origin of the word chancellor. Some derive it, a cancellis, or latticed doors, and hold, that it was a denomination of those ushers who had the care of the cancelli or latticed doors, leading to the presence chamber of the emperors and other great men.

ground of equitable interference. Accident is the first head of which he treats. Accident, by unforeseen events, misfortunes, acts or omissions, which are not the result of negligence or misconduct in the party : accident, by loss of important instruments, by payments to creditors and legatees which the true state of the assets will not warrant, or by defective execution of powers. The jurisdiction upon this head is laid down in very comprehensive terms. " It may now be stated generally, that where an inequitable loss or injury will otherwise fall upon a party from circumstances beyond his own control, or from his own acts done in entire good faith, and in the performance of a supposed duty, without negligence, a Court of Equity will incline to give him relief."

Under the head of Mistake, an interesting discussion is introduced respecting the common maxim " Ignorantia legis neminem excusat." The doctrine is not in a very satisfactory state ; and perhaps will scarcely admit of definite limits, for excessive ignorance borders on imbecility, and while a Court of Equity gives relief from a contract made under the influence of imbecility, it will leave a person who has acted in ignorance of law to the consequences of his own act. Lord King[1] is reported to have said, in one case, that " this maxim was in regard to the public, that ignorance cannot be pleaded in excuse of crimes, but that it does not hold in civil cases." But in truth, there is the same difficulty in criminal as in civil proceedings. No idiot or madman is punished for crime. Each tribunal must ascertain whether the party in question has the excuse of imbecility. In civil proceedings, the cases generally brought forward as exceptions to the general rule, appear to include points for consideration which are quite independent of mere ignorance of law. In one case there is misplaced confidence, in another surprise, often imposition, or undue influence. We do not mean to say that there is no case which is really an exception, but we think that most of the apparent exceptions, if they are rigidly scrutinized,[2] will be found to depend upon peculiarities of their own, independent of mere ignorance of law. This is the view of the law taken by our author after a notice of all the principal decisions. " Without undertaking to assert that there are none of

---

[1] P. 129.   [2] See cases quoted in chapter on " Mistake."

these cases which are inconsistent with the rule, it may be affirmed, that the real exceptions to it are few, and generally stand upon some very urgent pressure of circumstances. The rule prevails in England in all cases of compromises of doubtful, and perhaps in all cases of doubted rights; and especially in all cases of family arrangements. It is relaxed in cases where there is a total ignorance of title, founded in the mistake of a plain and settled principle of law, and in cases of imposition, misrepresentation, undue influence, misplaced confidence and surprise." He goes on to say that the law in America is in a more satisfactory state. "In America the general rule has been recognized as founded in sound wisdom and policy, and fit to be upheld with a steady confidence. And hitherto the exceptions to it (if any) will be found, not to rest upon the mere foundation of a naked mistake of law, however plain and settled the principle may be, nor upon mere ignorance of title, founded upon such mistake."[1]

The next head to which our author passes, in his inquiry into cases of concurrent jurisdiction, is Fraud. After quoting several definitions of fraud, he seems to prefer the definition given by Labeo, which is in the following words, "Dolum malum esse omnem calliditatem, fallaciem, machinationem ad circumveniendum, fallendum, decipiendum alterem adhibitem." He then explains some of the numerous characteristics of circumstances, which are treated as frauds in Courts of Equity. For instance, the misrepresentation must be of something material; it must be made with the intent to mislead another; it must be of some circumstance which is not equally open to the examination of both parties, and it must have been the misrepresentation itself, which actually produced the mischief to the complaining party. The recent case of Small v. Attwood was decided in the House of Lords upon this last principle. Without inserting here the particulars of a case so universally known, we may at once mention the point upon which it turned. There seemed to be no doubt that the representations made to the company on the part of Mr. Attwood were incorrect. The works in question were more expensive and less productive than the account which he gave of them led the company to expect. But then came

---

[1] P. 154.

the question, whether the company could reasonably have been supposed to have acted upon that account. It was proved that, before the contract was actually agreed upon, the company were put in possession of the works; that they had the opportunity of satisfying themselves as to their real value; that the whole was left under their superintendence, and that they did not *close* the bargain, until ample time for the experiment had been allowed. It was reasonable to suppose that they had turned such an opportunity to advantage, and that they had been misled, if misled at all, not through the vendor's misrepresentations, but through their own negligence in making the experiment. On the other hand it was no less reasonable to suppose, that no misrepresentation was intentionally made on the part of the vendor, who gave to his purchaser the best possible means of discovering the truth. These considerations appear to have received too little attention in the Court below, but in the House of Lords they prevailed with the majority of the legal Peers.[1]

Having commented at some length on the suggestio falsi, our author next proceeds to the suppressio veri. He there traces the principle of fraud in dealing with idiots, lunatics, and persons in a state of intoxication, persons " under duress, or the influence of extreme terror, or threats, or apprehensions short of duress."[2] " And circumstances," he says, " of extreme necessity and distress of the party, although not accompanied by any direct restraint or duress, may, in like manner, so entirely overcome his free agency, as to justify the Court in setting aside a contract made by him on account of oppression, or fraudulent advantage or imposition." We cannot help thinking, that, in some of these heads, our author has been in some measure misled by his wish to generalize. They are cases rather of force than of fraud. *Calliditas* and *machinatio*, the terms employed in the definition of Labeo, are inapplicable to cases of this description. To bring the distinction clearly into view, let us refer to the criminal law.

---

[1] The opinion of the profession is much divided as to this case, and the above is after all only a peculiar mode of looking at it. By the way, how came the Earl of Devon to be reckoned a law-lord? A question which we submit with the fullest conviction of his legal acquirements and capacity.—*Edit.*

[2] P. 243.

A man, who is threatened with instant death, if he does not give up his watch, is not subjected to any fraud, but to theft accompanied with violence. In such a case, were an indictment laid for fraud, it would undoubtedly fail. But if a person is induced to give money by the representation of fictitious claims on the part of a petitioner, the offence committed against him consists in fraud and not in violence. We cannot see the advantage of confounding two classes of cases which differ essentially from one another, and we even believe that fictions of this nature render the study of the law less acceptable than it would otherwise be, and the law itself an object of suspicion.

An error of the same nature appears to have been committed in the chapter on constructive frauds. Under this head are classed contracts in restraint of marriage, and bargains in restraint of trade. Such contracts and bargains may be at variance with public policy, but they do not appear to contain the ingredients of fraud. It would be quite sufficient, without having recourse to a supposition of fraud, to lay down as a rule, that Courts of Equity will not enforce any contract which is at variance with public policy, just as it refuses to enforce an usurious contract, or an agreement, of which the consideration is future illicit intercourse, or the commission of a crime, the violation of a law, or the omission of a duty. Such contracts are contrary to public policy, and contain in them abundant reason, why they should not be recognised in a Court of justice ; but, in calling them frauds, while they contain nothing of a fraudulent character, jurists indulge their love of comprehensive classification, at the expense of the ordinary meaning of language.

The objection attaches as much to the definition of constructive fraud, which our author has given, as it does to some of the instances which he brings forward in illustration. " By constructive frauds, are meant such contracts or acts, as, though not originating in any actual evil design, or contrivance, to perpetuate a positive fraud or injury upon other persons, are yet, by their tendency to deceive or mislead other persons, or to violate private or public confidence, or to impair or injure the public interests, deemed equally reprehensible with positive fraud, and therefore are prohibited by law, as within the same reason and mischief, as contracts and acts done malo animo." We can quite understand why all such acts should be subject to the restraints of courts of justice; the difficulty is to explain why they are all to be classed as frauds. That they have a tendency " to impair or injure the public interests," is no sufficient reason for terming them fraudulent. Mr. Justice Story himself seems to distrust the propriety of such a classification ; for he adds ; " though at first view, the doctrines on this subject may seem to be of an artificial, if not of an arbitrary, character ; yet, upon closer observation, they will be found to be founded in an anxious desire of the law to apply the principle of preventive justice, so as to shut out the inducements to perpetrate a wrong rather than to rely on mere remedial justice after the wrong has been committed." The apology here offered for the incorrectness of the definition does not seem to be of much weight. It implies that a Court of Equity cannot interfere upon these subjects, unless it attributes to them a fraudulent character.

The chapter on constructive frauds, contains a long catalogue of circumstances which are of that character; in all of which, excepting such as we have mentioned, there is clear fraud either in the acts themselves, or else in their necessary consequences. The mischief of a marriage brocage bond is, that it induces the exercise of undue influence in the promotion of marriages, and exposes the fortunes and happiness of innocent persons to the temptations of flattery and pretended friendship. The tendency of a bargain for a public office,[1] is to introduce unfit persons into places of great public trust, and to defraud the public of the services of the most efficient candidates for office. A long list of constructive frauds arise out of the peculiar relation subsisting between different persons; and the frauds are termed constructive, as distinguishable from actual frauds, because the obligation, which is supposed to be violated, is one which the party has undertaken rather in presumption of law, than in reality. For instance, a trustee to sell property is presumed to undertake that he will obtain the highest possible price for the property entrusted to him. A solicitor is presumed to devote all his abilities to the service of his client, and if he exercises over

[1] P. 292.

him any influence improperly, or takes advantage of the confidence placed in him, he commits a breach of the obligation,
which attaches to his position.　On the same ground, Courts
of Equity watch with scrupulous jealousy all transactions
between parent and child, guardian and ward, trustees and
cestui que trust, principal and agent.　The relation of principal and surety is a very remarkable illustration of similar
doctrines.　" The contract of suretyship imports entire good
faith and confidence between the parties in regard to the
whole transaction.　Any concealment of material facts, or
any express or implied misrepresentation of such facts, or any
undue advantage, information or surprise taken of the suretyship by the creditor, will undoubtedly furnish a sufficient
ground to invalidate the contract.　So the creditor is in all
subsequent transactions with the debtor bound to equal good
faith to the surety."

A large class of cases falling under this head, depends on
the determination of the Court to prevent men from making
unconscionable bargains, and to check fraud not merely as
between the actual parties to the contract, but also in relation
to strangers.　Bargains with heirs, expectants, reversioners,
and remainder-men are set aside.　They savour in a greater
or less degree of usury, and are effected by a cunning imposition upon needy and unwary men, who attach too small a
value to that which will not be in possession for some time
to come, and think that the future enjoyment is not to be
weighed against immediate relief.　It may be very justly
doubted, whether the interference of Courts of Equity has
not been extended too far upon matters of this description.
If men who have reached years of discretion, and who are in
reality acquainted with all the circumstances in which they
stand, choose to make a large prospective sacrifice with a
view to present relief, it is very questionable in policy, whether Courts of justice ought to set aside the contract.　We
suspect that the imputation of fraud to these transactions,
often gives protection to spendthrifts, who contract the more
carelessly, because they think that the hardness of the bargain will become their protection.　The cause of public
morality will probably be uninjured if such persons are left to
their fate; and the property which they recover by aid of the

Court will be used by them with as little advantage to the community, as it would have been used, but for the Court's interference, by those to whom they sold it. Usury laws have driven dealings with money into a class inferior in morals, and ready to take dishonest advantages; they have made the position of a spendthrift rather worse than better, and without any advantage by way of compensation, have interrupted the free circulation of money. We suspect that the interference of Courts of Equity, to which we have just alluded, often produces results of a similar character. Indigent men fall into worse hands, are drawn into harder contracts, and after all this increase of suffering can obtain no corresponding redress, except through the vexation and protracted inquiries of a suit in equity. We attribute little weight to the principle, not unfrequently advanced, of fraud[1] upon the ancestor. It is not till after his death that the inheritance sustains any injury, or is subject to any transfer; the evil is wholly unknown to him, and the Court, if it aims at his protection, seems rather to indulge sentimental feeling than to pursue any substantial benefit. We must, however, admit that we are calling in question a system of law, which, as our author observes, has prevailed under the Macedonian decree, under the Roman and many other codes of law, and has been successively enforced by our ablest chancellors.

Next come those cases in which the fraud is upon strangers, and not upon any one who is an actual party to the contract. Our author's remarks shew that these cases have been the subject of the civil law, and also, from a very early period, of the common law of this country. " The common law has adopted similar principles, which have been more fully carried into effect by the statutes of 50 Edw. 3, c. 6, and 3 Hen. 7, c. 4, against fraudulent gifts of goods and chattels, and by the statute of 13 Elizabeth, c. 5, against fraudulent conveyances of lands to defeat or delay creditors, and the statute of 27 Elizabeth, c. 4, against fraudulent or voluntary conveyances of lands to defeat subsequent purchasers, which have always received a favourite and liberal construction in suppression of fraud." Voluntary conveyances, under the circumstances for which these statutes provide, are treated as

---

[1] P. 329.

fraudulent, because there is always a fair presumption of fraud, though perhaps no fraud in reality. The common doctrine of Courts of Equity is, that if property is conveyed to one person, while another pays the consideration, the conveyance is made for the benefit of the latter: equity looks to the quarter from which the consideration moves. If then no consideration is acknowledged, the same principle induces a belief that the conveying party is not acting for the benefit of any other person, but is seeking some advantage for himself. So far there is ground for suspicion. When it afterwards comes to light that he has creditors, or that he makes a fresh conveyance to a third party, an intention to commit fraud, in whichever of these positions he happens to stand, is connected in the eye of the Court with the original conveyance. It is not then without good reason that these statutes are introduced in this place, as intended to give relief against constructive fraud.

The same principle of fraud introduces our author to a discussion upon notice implied or express, the registry acts, the effect of lis pendens, and the tacking of mortgages. But we cannot dwell any longer upon this portion of the treatise, except to offer to our readers the general concluding remarks, in which Mr. Justice Story brings strongly into view some of the principal advantages of proceedings in equity:

" The flexibility," he says, " of Courts of Equity, too, in adapting their decrees to the actual relief required by the parties, in which their proceedings formed so marked a contrast to the proceedings at the common law, is illustrated in a striking manner in cases of accident, mistake and fraud. If a decree were in all cases required to be given in a prescribed form, the remedial justice would necessarily be very imperfect, and often wholly beside the real merits of the case. Accident, mistake and fraud are of infinite variety in form, character and circumstances; and are incapable of being adjusted by any single and uniform rule. Of each of them one might say, mille trahit varios adverso sole colores. The beautiful character or pervading excellence, if one may so say, of equity jurisprudence is, that it varies its adjustments and proportions so as to meet the very form and pressure of each particular case, in all its complex habitudes. Thus, (to present a summary of what has already been stated) if conveyances or other instruments are fraudulently or improperly obtained, they are decreed to be given up and cancelled. If they are money securities, on which the money has been paid, the money is decreed to be paid back. If they are deeds, or other muniments of title, detained from the rightful party, they are decreed to be delivered up. If they are deeds suppressed or spoliated, the party is decreed the same rights as if they were in his possession and power. If there has been any undue concealment or misrepresentation, or specific promise collusively broken, the injured party is placed in the same situation, and the other party is compelled to do the same acts, as if all had been transacted with the utmost good faith. If the party says nothing, but by his expressive silence misleads another to his injury, he is compellable to make good the loss; and his own title, if the case requires it, is made subservient to that of the confiding purchaser. If the party, by fraud or misrepresentation, induces another to do an act injurious to a third person, he is made responsible for it. If, by fraud or misrepresentation, he prevents acts from being done, equity treats the case as to him as if it were done; and makes him a trustee for the other. If a will is revoked by a fraudulent deed, the revocation is treated as a nullity. If a devisee obtains a devise by fraud, he is treated as a trustee of the injured parties. In all these and many other cases which might be mentioned, Courts of Equity undo what has been done, if wrong, and do what has been left undone, if right." [1]

We have enlarged so much upon these three great heads of concurrent equitable jurisdiction, that we are obliged to pass rapidly over the subjects which follow. They are—account in all its various shapes, matters of apportionment, contribution and average, liens, rents and profits, tithes and moduses, and waste, matters of administration, legacies, and marshalling of assets, confusion of boundaries, matters of dower, marshalling of securities, matters of partition, and matters of partnership. The course of discussion adopted upon all these subjects is to inquire in the first instance what are the general rules of statute and common law, and how far relief can be obtained independently of the Courts of Equity; afterwards to ascertain the principles upon which those Courts proceed, and to trace the application of them in the several forms which those cases assume. There is, however, one passage in the chapter upon "account," to which, as it closely affects a question constantly occurring in practice, and seems to settle it in very

[1] P. 421.

distinct terms, we wish to direct particular attention. The question is, whether there are any, and if any, what are the true boundaries of equity jurisdiction in matters of account cognizable at law? Some expressions in the reports would make the jurisdiction extremely wide, including every matter of contract and account.[1] Some are so vague as to leave the whole to a criterion scarcely more distinct than convenience; for instance, "such an account as cannot be taken justly and fairly in a Court of Law."[2] Other judges have said that the accounts must be complicated accounts,[3] or mutual accounts.[4] Mr. Justice Story, after alluding to all the principal authorities, gives his version of the law in these terms:—

"On the whole, it may be laid down as a general doctrine, that in matters of account growing out of privity of contract, Courts of Equity have a general jurisdiction, where there are mutual accounts, (and à fortiori where these accounts are complicated,) and also where the accounts are on one side, but a discovery is sought, and is material to the relief. And on the other hand, where the accounts are all on one side, and no discovery is sought or required; and also, where there is a single matter on the side of the plaintiff seeking relief, and mere set-off on the other side, and no discovery is sought or required; in all these cases Courts of Equity will decline taking jurisdiction of the cause."

We are not aware that in any other treatise there is contained any definition of matters for equitable account, which explains so satisfactorily as this passage the proper limits of the jurisdiction.

The next branch of concurrent jurisdiction is that in which the peculiar remedies afforded by Courts of Equity constitute the principal, though not the sole ground of the jurisdiction. In law, for instance, the lips of the parties themselves are closed. Transactions which have taken place between the principals in the absence of witnesses, and unaccompanied with writings, are absolutely veiled from investigation A Court of Equity elicits the information by the bill of discovery. Again, a person possessed of a deed, fraudulent in its character, may fail at law in case he puts it into suit; still he keeps it in his

[1] Vol. i. 438; Billon v. Hyde, 1 Atk. 127, 8.
[2] Ibid. 440; Frietes v. Santos, 1 Y. & Jerv. 574.
[3] Ibid. 439; O'Connell v. Spaight, 1 Sch. & Lef. 309.
[4] Ibid. 439.

possession. Those whom it affects, are aware that he has it as a weapon of offence to be employed at a fitting opportunity, perhaps too with success, in case he is favoured by the deaths of witnesses, or by other contingencies. Relief in such a case is given by a Court of Equity, upon the principle, as it is technically called, quia timet, by the rescission, cancellation,[1] or delivery up of the dangerous document.

On the other hand, the person who seeks the assistance of the Court may wish not to get rid of an agreement, but to have it carried into execution. At law he can have no redress except that of a certain amount of damages, such as the jury may consider a fit compensation for the loss of the benefit of the contract. No agreement is necessary to show that in many instances such relief cannot be satisfactory, as there are many circumstances, most important to the contracting party, which cannot enter into the consideration of the jury. Here then equity steps in, and acts upon the well-known principle of placing parties in the state in which they would have stood, if the object of the contract had been honestly fulfilled. This is the decree for specific performance, which Mr. Justice Story treats under three separate classes of agreements, those which respect personal property, those which respect personal acts, and those which respect real property.

In discussing the execution of these agreements, a question is introduced, on which we wish to offer some observations, as it appears to us not to have been very successfully determined. " Before Lord Somers' time, the practice used to be in bills for a specific performance to send the party to law ; and if he recovered any thing by way of damages, the Court of Chancery entertained the suit, otherwise the bill was dismissed. And hence the opinion was not uncommon, that unless damages were recoverable, no suit could be maintained in equity for a specific performance." [2] In contending against this principle, our author quotes the observation of Lord Macclesfield in the case of Camel v. Buckle. " Neither is it a true rule—that where an action cannot be brought at law on an agreement for damages, there a suit will not lie in equity for a specific performance." On examination of the cases, and

---

[1] Page 5.　　　　[2] Vol. ii. p. 44.

of the remarks of Mr. Justice Story, we cannot help thinking that upon this subject equity follows the law much more closely, than the language generally used would lead one to suppose.   The contract which Lord Macclesfield enforced in the case above quoted, was perfectly good in itself at the time of its creation ; it became suspended at law, because at law the wife and husband are of necessity one and the same person; but not in equity, because the same technical rule is not in force.   Another case frequently quoted is, Winged v. Lefebury,[1] in which a tenant in fee made a lease and covenanted for himself and his heirs to renew.   He sold the reversion.   The lessee died.   In this position of the parties, there could be no action at law for the representatives of the lessee ; but a decree for specific performance of the agreement to renew was made in equity.   Sir Edward Sugden,[2] in his work upon Vendors and Purchasers, quotes several other cases. But upon all of them there arises this remark, that the agreement was not, in itself, bad at law.   That there was a difficulty in enforcing it, on account of the peculiar circumstances which had arisen, but that in itself it was a good agreement. In considering the uniformity or discrepancy supposed to prevail between law and equity upon this subject, we must pay attention to the position of parties, to the forms of pleading, and to the general machinery of the respective Courts.   Just as upon the subject of evidence,[3] we endeavoured, in a recent article, to show that if these peculiarities are fairly weighed, there is no difference between the rules of the two Courts. " Equity," says Sir Edward Sugden,[4] " cannot contradict or overturn the grounds or principles of law."   We suggest the consideration above mentioned, as one which removes all difficulty upon the question.   Equity would contradict law, if it declared that to be an agreement, which law declared to be a nullity ; it does not do so by merely carrying into effect that which law does not deny to be an agreement, but is prevented from enforcing by its peculiar forms, and by the want of proper machinery.

The same consideration supports the harmony between law and equity, upon many other subjects mentioned in this

[1] 2 Eq. Ca. Ab. 32.   [2] V. and P. p. 213.
[3] Law Mag. vol. xviii. p. 136.   [4] V. and P. 214.

chapter. A contract, not in writing, is no ground for damages at law ; but why ? because at law there can be no discovery. In equity, the defendant confesses the agreement in his answer, and the court acts upon the confession, which is held to be a sufficient compliance with the statute. It is enacted in the statute, not that the verbal agreement is a nullity, but only that it is not to be the subject of an action. Nor is it inconsistent with this distinction, that, if the answer sets up the statute, no decree can be obtained upon the confession of the agreement. " Quisque renuntiare potest juri pro se introducto." By confessing the agreement and omitting to set up the statute as a defence, the defendant is assumed to waive the benefit which the statute supplies. Similar observations arise upon the doctrine of part-performance. If a person were allowed to enter upon property and enjoy it, and afterwards to give it up, because the agreement under which he entered was not in writing, he would be disappointing the expectations which the vendor had justly formed from his conduct. Or if the vendor, having allowed him to enter and to spend upon it considerable sums of money, could then expel him by process of ejectment, very serious injustice would be done. Courts of Equity enforce the agreement in each case ; still without violating the statute, for they found jurisdiction, not upon the verbal contract, but upon the acts done, the partial enjoyment, or the outlay in improvements. The principles established upon all these questions are most carefully developed in the work before us, and the advantages, derived from equitable interference, are put into powerful contrast with the meagre relief attainable in a Court of Law.

In the chapter on Interpleader our author remarks with great ability upon a leading principle which in other treatises has not been sufficiently explained. " In cases [1] of tenants seeking such relief, (i. e. relief by interpleader,) it must appear that the persons claiming the same rent, claim in privity of contract or of tenure." Again, " let us suppose that two persons should claim the same property under independent titles, not derived from the same common source ; the question would then arise, whether a third person, bonâ fide and

---

[1] Vol. ii. p. 118.

lawfully in possession of the property as the agent, consignee, or bailee of one of the parties, could maintain a bill of interpleader against the different claimants standing in privity with one only of them.   It would seem that he could not; and that the analogies of the law and the doctrines of Courts of Equity equally inhibit it.   " The question which is here examined arises in this way.   A person lets land to a tenant, and commits property to the custody of an agent, and, when he comes to ask rent for the one, or the restoration of the other, is met by a bill of interpleader.   Then it is for the tenant or agent to show that the relation which subsisted at the time of the lease or bailment, has been changed by some subsequent act. A tenant cannot dispute his landlord's title.   A servant must conform to his master's orders.   These relations, and the duties belonging to them, continue unchanged until some act is done by landlord or master."

We have no space for a lengthened notice of the chapters upon bills of quia timet, bills of peace, or injunction.   But under the latter head there is one passage applying with so much force to one of the crying sins of the day, that we must call to it the especial attention of our readers.   It respects the publication of private letters, and the claim of the receiver to use them as he pleases :—

" A question has been made, and a doubt suggested, how far the like protection ought to be given to restrain the publication of mere private letters on business or on family concerns, or on matters of personal friendship, and not strictly falling within the line of literary compositions.[1]   In a moral view the publication of such letters, unless in cases where necessary to the proper vindication of the right or conduct of the party against unjust claims, or injurious imputations, is perhaps one of the most odious breaches of private confidence, of social duty, and of honourable feelings, which can well be imagined.   It strikes at the root of all that free and mutual interchange of advice, opinions, and sentiments, between relatives and friends, and correspondents, which is so essential to the well being of society, and to the spirit of a liberal courtesy and refinement.   It may involve whole families in great distress, from the public display of facts and circumstances, which were reposed in the bosoms of others, under the deepest and most

---

[1] Perceval v. Phipps, 2 V. & B. 24, 27, 28.

affecting confidence, that they should for ever remain inviolable secrets. It may do more, and compel every one in self-defence to write, even to his dearest friends, with the cold and formal severity with which he would write to his veriest opponents, or most implacable enemies. Cicero has with great beauty and force spoken of the grossness of such offences against common decency. ' Quis enim unquam, qui paulum modo bonorum consuetudinem nôsset, literas ad se ab amico missas offensione aliquâ interpositâ in medium protulit palàmque recitavit? Quid est aliud tollere e vitâ vitæ societatem, quàm tollere amicorum colloquia absentium? Quàm multa joca solent esse in epistolis, quæ, prolata si sint, inepta videantur! Quàm multa seria, neque tamen ullo modo divulgenda.' It would be a sad reproach to English and American jurisprudence, if Courts of Equity could not interfere in such cases." [1]

We have already occupied so much space, that we can do no more than mention the heads of the several subjects discussed under the latter divisions of the works. Under the head of the exclusive jurisdiction, we find trusts express and implied, trust terms, mortgages, rights of assignees, wills, testaments and legacies, election and satisfaction, charities, relief from penalties and forfeitures on the non-performance of conditions and covenants; the proceedings in respect of the peculiar relations and personal character of parties, as infants, idiots, lunatics, and married women; and proceedings upon certain writs, as the writ ne exeat regno and supplicavit. The last head is the auxiliary or assistant jurisdiction; which, our author says, is exclusive in its own nature, but, being applied in aid of the remedial justice of other courts, may well admit of a distinct consideration[2]—as bills of discovery, and bills to preserve or perpetuate evidence.

We strongly recommend the entire work to the perusal of our readers. In the work upon equity pleading we found excellent arrangement, a clear statement of cases, and a satisfactory explanation of all received doctrines. In this work, far higher qualities have been displayed. Maxims are laid down and traced in their operation. The history of the jurisdiction is stated, the principles are developed upon which it is maintained, and the entire equitable

[1] Vol. ii. p. 221.   [2] Vol. ii. 629.

system assumes a philosophical character, with which it has never been invested by any preceding author. The student finds an easy introduction to all the principal characteristics of equitable doctrines, and, while he learns to view them with interest, is invited to further and more accurate investigation. " Let not, however, the ingenuous youth imagine that he also may here close his own preparatory studies of equity jurisprudence, or content himself for the ordinary purposes of practice with the general survey, which has thus been presented to his view." It would be impossible, within the compass of such a treatise as this, to supply so elaborate a discussion upon the subject, as not to leave ground for this observation. But our author has unfolded the map, and has pointed out the first landmarks and the main roads. The student must take his own course in following the several byepaths and intricate windings into which men are driven by the business and vicissitudes of life. " The minute details, the subtile contrivances, and the various arrangements, which are adapted to the general exigencies and conveniences of a polished society, remain to invite the curiosity of the student, and to stimulate his love of refined justice."[1]

. *C.*

ART. III.—NOTICE TO QUIT.

THERE are few branches of the law which embrace a greater variety of topics or involve a greater complication of legal principles, than that concerning the relation of landlord and tenant. At the same time there is scarcely one of which a practitioner is required to have a more accurate knowledge, or in which a more ready application of that knowledge is called for. It is proposed, at present, with a view chiefly to the convenience of our country readers, to treat generally of those points which more immediately relate to the determination of a tenancy by a notice to quit.

A notice to quit is necessary wherever there is a holding as tenant for any indefinite term. This proposition involves two

[1] V. ii. p. 747.

points : first, that there be a holding as tenant, and this presupposes a contract of letting between the parties; secondly, that such tenancy be for a period consisting of a succession of years, months, or weeks, according to the nature of the holding, to go on until one of the parties shall think fit to determine it.

In the absence of direct proof of a contract, the payment of rent *eo nomine* is the general criterion of a holding as tenant. A person let into possession under an agreement to purchase does not become tenant· in this sense without payment of rent, however long he may continue, and if the agreement ultimately goes off, he. may be turned out without a half-year's notice, though not without a previous demand of possession, —(Right v. Beard, 13 East, 210); and where a person, having agreed with a lessee to· take an assignment of his lease and pay for it by instalments, besides paying him the rent reserved thereby, and that upon default of any instalment the agreement should be forfeited, took possession and paid the rent, but failed to pay the instalments, it was held, that as the payment of rent was referable to the proposed assignment, he might be ejected without a notice to quit.—(Doe v. Lander, 1 Stark. 308.) But had the party been in possession as a yearly tenant, before the agreement was made, as the forfeiture remitted him to his original situation, a notice would then have been necessary.—(See John v. Jenkins, 1 C. & M. 230.)

A person who claims by title paramount, need not, for the same reason, give a notice to quit. Hence, if tenant for life let the lands, he in remainder may eject without notice, unless, by acceptance of rent or attornment, a new tenancy has been created.—(Doe v. Watts, 7 T. R. 83.) As the title of a tenant by elegit relates back to the judgment, he may in like manner avoid any demise subsequent thereto.—(Doe v. Hilder, 2 B. & A. 782.)

A mortgagee need not give a notice to quit to a tenant let in by the mortgagor subsequently to the date of the mortgage ; but if the demise were made before the mortgage, the tenancy continues, and the mortgagee, by virtue of the statute 4 Ann. c. 16, s. 9, becomes by the conveyance ipso facto landlord, and after default made, he may either put an end to the tenancy by notice, or, upon giving notice to the tenant to pay him the rent, entitle himself not only to the accruing rents, but also to those which were in arrear at the time of the notice.—(Birch v. Wright, 1 T. R. 378.)　　But until notice the mortgagor continues landlord.　　The statute expressly protects a tenant as to all payments actually made before notice.

· The situation of a tenant let in by the mortgagor after the mortgage, is essentially different.　　As against the mortgagee he is not even tenant at will, but a trespasser, and may be turned out without any notice.—(See Birch v. Wright, 1 T. R. 382 ; Thunder v. Belcher, 3 East, 449 ; Doe v. Maisey, 8 B. & C. 767 ; Doe v. Giles, 5 Bing. 421.)　　It has often been said, that a mortgagee has the option of treating the mortgagor, and all persons claiming under him, either as tenant or trespasser.　　But this position is not correct.　　The relation of landlord and tenant can only be created by the assent of both parties, for it is founded on contract.　　Hence the mortgagee cannot, by giving notice to the tenant, entitle himself either to the accruing or the back rents. If the tenant refuse to pay, all the mortgagee can do is to eject him.—(See Partington v. Woodcock, 6 Ad. & Ell. 690.)　　Yet, if he chooses to pay, he may justify such payment as one of necessity, to save an eviction, upon the same principle that he may set off a payment of ground-rent, or rent-charge.—(Johnson v. Jones, 17 L. J. 124, Q. B.)　　Whether such payment constitutes the tenant a tenant to the mortgagee, depends of course upon its quality. If the notice require him to pay his accruing rents to the mortgagee, one payment of rent *quasi* rent is sufficient, and he cannot afterwards justify paying the mortgagor ; but if it merely require payment of a given arrear, in discharge of interest due, payment of that amount does not alter the tenancy.

But the dealing with the tenant even in that way, operates as an admission that his possession is at that period lawful, and to a certain extent precludes the mortgagee from treating him as a trespasser.　　In Doe v. Hales, 7 Bing. 322. the tenant was applied to in April, by an attorney, acting on behalf both of the mortgagor and mortgagee, for rent, " to pay the interest."　　He had before received rent from the tenant for the mortgagor, and out of it he had paid the interest, and accounted for the residue to the mortgagor. He told the tenant, that unless the rent were paid he should distrain. He afterwards did distrain on behalf of the mortgagor, and by his authority, but had never been authorized to do so by the mortgagee. The latter subsequently brought this action against the tenant, laying the demise in the December preceding. It was contended, that not having received rent from the tenant, or done any act to make himself landlord, the mortgagee was entitled to recover, but the Court held, that whether he had become the landlord or not, as he had by his agent admitted the tenant to be in rightful possession in April, and had availed himself of that possession, he could not afterwards say that he was a trespasser in the preceding December; " but," observed Alderson B., " had the demise been laid subsequently to April, the question might have been very material." The Court of Queen's Bench, on another occasion, pointed out the fact that the mortgagee had applied to the tenant and got his interest out of the rent, as forming the distinction between this and the case then before it, and held, that the receipt of interest from the mortgagor, without any application to the tenant, did not prevent the mortgagee from laying his demise on a day prior to that for which the interest had been paid.—(Doe v. Cadwallader, 2 B. & Ad. 473.)

It will probably become necessary before long, to consider what is the effect of a recognition of the tenant's possession, with regard to the future rights of the mortgagee. Whatever it may be, the lying by and suffering the mortgagor to deal with the property in such a manner as to lead a tenant to believe that he is the owner, and induce him to take a lease, and perhaps to expend money on the premises, ought, it should seem, upon every principle of justice, to be deemed as much a recognition as the receipt of interest from him. The opinion of Lord Denman, C. J. on the point is thus expressed in a recent case. Speaking of the doctrine that a mortgagee may always treat the mortgagor and those who claim under him as trespassers, he says, " For my part, I wish to guard myself upon that, it being very doubtful, whether the mortgagee may not bind himself by his own conduct so as to be prevented from treating his mortgagor's lessee as a trespasser. What conduct might amount to a recognition, seems to me rather matter of evidence than law, but I confess Doe v. Hales appears to me to be well decided, although doubted by my brother Littledale in Doe v. Cadwallader. I am by no means prepared to admit that a jury might not be warranted in inferring a recognition of the tenant's right to hold, from the mere circumstance of the mortgagee knowingly permitting the mortgagor to continue the apparent owner of the premises as before the mortgage, and to lease them out exactly as if the property continued unaltered."—(Evans v. Elliott, 17 L. J. Q. B. 51 ; S. C., 1 P. & D. 256; and see per Lord Mansfield in Keech v. Hall, Doug. 22.)

The case before the Court was an action of replevin, in which the mortgagee attempted to justify distraining on a tenant let in by the mortgagor subsequently to the mortgage, nothing having been done to create that relation. Notice had been given by the mortgagee requiring the tenant to pay the rent to him, notwithstanding which he had paid it to the agent of the mortgagor. The judgment was against the mortgagee. Now, if under such circumstances, the mortgagee could not have maintained an ejectment, when, it may be asked, could he get into possession ? Having no means of getting at the rents, must he suffer the tenant to hold out till the expiration of a long lease ? Without presuming to anticipate what the opinion of the Court may be in such a case, it does appear to us, that the only effect of a recognition should be to give the tenant an option of becoming tenant to the mortgagee, and that if he persists in paying his rent to the mortgagor, after notice, an act which clearly amounts to a disclaimer, the mortgagee should not be barred from at once asserting his right of possession. The question seems to have been virtually decided, though in another shape. It appears to be settled, that a tenant having complied with the notice to pay his future rents to the mortgagee, may plead the facts as an eviction, and thus show that his lessor's title has expired.— (See per Parke, J. in Pope v. Biggs, 9 B. & C. 250 ; Partington v. Woodcock, 6 Ad. & Ell. 690.) We have indulged in this little digression, as the point is one of great importance both to mortgagees and tenants.

No notice is requisite, where the duration of the tenancy is marked by the terms of the contract, If a house is taken for a year, month, or week certain, the tenant's interest ceases at the expiration of that period. So if a person enters under an agreement for a lease, not amounting to a demise, and pays rent, and no lease is executed, he holds on the same terms as if it had, and may be ejected at the period when the lease would have expired without notice, though not before. So if lands be let by parol for a term exceeding three years, and the tenant enter and pay rent, though the lease is void as a lease, there arises a tenancy from year to year until the expiration of the stipulated term, and then the tenancy *ipso facto* ends.—(Doe v. Stratton, 4 Bing. 446 ; Doe v. Smith, 6 East, 530.) In like manner, if a house belonging to one of several partners be occupied by another of the firm " during the continuance of the partnership," the latter may be turned out upon a dissolution, without a notice to quit.—(Doe v. Miles, 1 Stark. 181.) It has been ruled, that a hiring of lodgings by the week, does not involve a stipulation for a week's notice to quit, but that if either party insists upon notice, proof of usage must be given.—(Per Parke, B. in Huffell v. Armistead, 7 C. & P. 56.)

A holding over after the expiration of a lease, with intent to continue tenant, gives the landlord the option of treating the party either as tenant or trespasser, and if he assents thereto, a new contract arises, and then a notice to quit becomes necessary. The question here is *quo animo* the party continued in possession, and this is a question of fact. Payment of rent, *eo nomine,* is conclusive, but it is always a question for the jury whether the payment was made as rent or merely as a compensation for the trespass. If the latter, no notice is of course requisite, because there is no tenancy. Where an executor, at the expiration of a lease made to his testator, tendered the keys to the lessor, but the latter refused to receive them, because an under tenant of the executor refused to quit, and a few months afterwards, having obtained possession, the executor again tendered the keys and a proportionate part of the rent for the time he held over, it was holden there was no evidence of a new contract, and that the lessor was not entitled to recover more than such proportion.—(Ibbs v. Richardson, 17 L. J. Q. B. 126.) So where the lessees of a coal-mine, having power to determine the lease by notice at a given period, had done so, but held over for two months after its expiration, and during that time worked the coals as before, it was holden a question for the jury whether they continued to work the mine with intent to waive the notice, and the jury having found the negative, the court refused a rule for a new trial.—(Jones v. Shears, 4 Ad. & Ell. 832.) On the other hand, if the lessor distrains for subsequent rent, he thereby admits the tenancy; and a notice to quit in the usual form would have the same effect, because it admits a holding as tenant. So the acceptance of rent by a remainder man under a lease by tenant for life or in tail, void as against the former, though it cannot set up the lease, yet constitutes a tenancy from year to year, which can only be determined by notice to quit.—(Doe v. Watts, 7 T. R. 83.) But if a notice to quit has previously been given, no evidence of a tenancy arises from the receipt of rent.—(Sykes v. ——, cited 1 T. R. 161.)

But the rent here spoken of, the payment of which is evidence of a new tenancy, means that which is paid as a composition for the land. Where upon a lease determinable on lives, a rent of thirteen shillings and fourpence was reserved, which rent the steward of the lessor continued to receive for some years after the lives had dropped, in apparent ignorance of that event, it was holden that no contract as of a tenancy from year to year could be presumed from such payments. —(Mildmay v. Shirley, cited 10 Ea. 164.)

A disclaimer by the tenant entitles the landlord to eject him without notice. According to a modern authority, any act or expression by the person in possession, whether it asserts a right in himself inconsistent with the relation of tenant, or not, if it goes to repudiate the title of the owner, and is such as, if acquiesced in, would be evidence against him, amounts to a disclaimer. Premises had been devised to a *feme sôle* for life, who afterwards married. The husband let them to the defendant as tenant from year to year. The wife died, and there being no devise over, the lessor of the plaintiff claimed them as heir at law to the devisor. His solicitor wrote to the tenant, inclosing a copy of the claimant's pedigree, and offering to give any further information that may be required, to which the latter replied, that he had not hitherto considered the claimant as his landlord, nor could he pay him any rent without the risk of being thereafter called upon to pay it again to the person who might fancy and perhaps prove that he had a better title; that he should be at all times ready to pay the arrears to any person who should be proved entitled, but, without wishing to dispute the connection in blood of the claimant, he must decline taking on himself to decide on that claim without more satisfactory proof in a legal manner. The claimant upon this brought an ejectment, and the court, upon a point reserved, were unanimously of opinion that the letter of the defendant was a disclaimer. "A notice to quit," observed Best, C. J. "is only necessary where a tenancy is admitted on both sides, and if a defendant denies the tenancy there can be no necessity for a notice to end that which he says has no existence."—(Doe v. Frowd, 4 Bing. 537.) There appears to be no difference in principle between this case and that of Doe v. Pasquali, Peake, 195. There the will of the lessor had been contested in the ecclesiastical court; the devisee under it claimed the rent. The tenant, doubting the validity of the will, refused to pay, but expressed his readiness to do so to any person who was entitled to receive it, and actually paid a part to a person who had collected for the lessor in his life time. Lord Kenyon considered that this was not such a disavowal as entitled the devisee to proceed without giving a notice to quit. His lordship's opinion seems to have been influenced by the consideration of hardship on the tenant, who was ready to pay the devisee, provided he had a reasonable assurance that he could do so with safety. But the hardship would have been the same, had the devisee distrained; the tenant must then at his peril have determined on the validity of the will.—(See Doe v. Grubb, 10 B. & C. 316; Doe v. Pitman, 2 N. & M. 672.) The mere payment of rent to another person is not of itself sufficient evidence of a disclaimer. It must be shown to have been made against the will of the landlord.—(Doe v. Parkes, Gow, 180.)

An eviction from part of the demised premises gives the same option to the tenant which a disclaimer gives to the landlord, whether it be made by the lessor himself or his assigns, or by a person having paramount title. For as by the contract of letting, the lessee stipulates for the enjoyment of the whole, if any part be taken from him he is at liberty to treat that contract as rescinded. If he chooses to remain, the law makes a distinction between an eviction by the lessor, and an eviction by a stranger. In the former case the whole rent reserved is suspended (Bull. N. P. 165, 177); in the latter, it must be apportioned (Ewer v. Moyle, Cro. Eliz. 771; Stevenson v. Lambard, 2 Ea. 575); but [in both, the contract being broken, the tenant may quit the whole if he pleases.

Hence if one of several lessors, joint tenants, give a notice to quit for himself alone, the tenant may treat it as a notice to quit the whole, for as the person giving it may recover his share, the tenant would otherwise be compellable to hold a part only.

So if the premises become, through the fault or neglect of the landlord, unfit for the purposes for which they were let, this is equivalent to an eviction and justifies the tenant in quitting without notice. Thus it was holden, that the putting in a number of workmen to repair the party wall, which occasioned so much inconvenience that the lodgers quitted the house, and the tenant was obliged to take lodgings for his family elsewhere, was an answer to an action for the rent, though the tenant left in the middle of the quarter.—(Edwards v. Hetherington, 7 D. & R. 117.) In another case the tenant had entered under an agreement in writing, by which he undertook to *keep* the premises in tenantable repair. After some time they became unwholesome, by reason of the defective state of the drains, which the landlord refused to repair, and it appeared they could not be put in order at a less expense than 60*l*. or 70*l*. Bayley, J. ruled that as the premises were not fit for comfortable occupation, and could not be rendered so without an extravagant and unreasonable outlay for a tenant to make, he was justified in quitting without notice. (Collins v. Barrow, 1 M. & R. 112.) It must be observed that to entitle the tenant so to put an end to the holding, the complaint must be one which goes to the very root of the contract. Where the inconvenience or expense is but trifling, the remedy in the one case is by action; in the other the tenant must make the repairs himself, if the landlord will not, and set off the amount against the rent. A lodger has no right to quit without notice, from an apprehension, however well founded, that his goods will be distrained for the land-lord's rent.—(Ricketts v. Tullich, 6 C. & P. 66.)

The last circumstance we shall notice, as dispensing with a notice to quit, is that of a surrender. By the statute of frauds, 29 Chas. 2, c. 3, s. 3, it is enacted, "that no leases, estates or interests, either of freeholds or terms of years, or any uncertain interest, not being copyhold or customary inte-rest, of, to, or out of any messuages, manors, lands, tenements, or hereditaments, shall be surrendered, unless it be by deed or note in writing, signed by the party so surrendering, or his agent, thereunto lawfully authorized by writing, or by act and operation of law." Little need be said of the qualities of a surrender in fact. It may be laid down in brief, that any in-strument or memorandum in writing, expressing an immediate purpose of giving up the estate on the part of the tenant, if accepted by the landlord, will be good as a surrender. Where by indenture a mortgage term of five hundred years was cre-ated, which had become forfeited by non-payment at the sti-pulated time, a memorandum, incorporated in the receipt by the mortgagee indorsed on the deed, in these words, " And I do hereby release and discharge the within premises of the said mortgage money," was holden a valid surrender. (Farmer v. Rogers, 2 Wils. 26.) But a notice to quit at a future time, given by the tenant, cannot operate as a surrender. If it be regular, it puts an end to the term; if not, but the parties act upon it, there is a surrender by operation of law; but if either refuses to act upon it, the term continues, for a surrender must operate in *presenti*.—(Doe v. Milward, 3 M. & W. 328.)

A surrender by operation of law is an accord executed, and may be effected in three ways. 1st. By taking a new lease of the demised premises, or of some part thereof; 2dly, By agreeing to a lease of such premises granted to a third party; and 3dly, by the giving up and acceptance of the premises to and by the lessor or landlord.

1st. The taking of a new lease of any part of the demised pre-mises, or of any interest therein, inconsistent with the existing lease, operates as a surrender *in toto* of the latter. Hence, if the landlord of a tenant from year to year, enter into an agree-ment with him for a lease, which operates as a present demise, the effect is to sink the accruing half year's rent.—(See Doe v. Benjamin, 1 P. & D. 440.)   It is immaterial for what term, or what quantum of interest the second conveys, or when it is to commence, provided it be during the existence of the former.—(Roll. Ab. tit. Surrender.)   A lease for fifty years will in this way be surrendered by a demise from year to year; a lease by indenture, by a demise by parol; a lease to the party alone, by a demise to him and another; and a lease in possession, by one to commence *in futuro*.   So if a husband possessed of a term in right of his wife, take a new lease of the same lands to himself, the former will be surrendered.— (Roll. Ab. Surr.)   The effect is the same if lessee accepts a grant of a rent-charge out of the same lands commensurate or inferior in duration to his term (Roll. Ab. Surr.); or a right of common or an easement, the enjoyment of which necessarily presupposes an extinction of his former right.— (Gyburn v. Searl, Cro. Jac. 776.)   But the lessee of a manor may accept a grant of steward or bailiff of the same manor; and the lessee of a park, the office of park-keeper, because these franchises are collateral and do not confer an interest in the estate.—(Ib.)   A tenant by elegit will in the same way lose that estate by taking a lease of the same lands.—(Roll. Ab. *supra*.)

The principle upon which this doctrine is founded, seems to require that the second lease should be granted by the same party who granted the first, or by some one claiming through or under him, but it need not be made to, if it be for the benefit of, the same parties, for if a lease be granted to A. in trust for C., and then another to B. in trust for C., the first is surrendered.—(Wilson v. Sewell, 4 Burr. 1975.)   It is settled that the second must be a good and valid lease, in order to have this effect, and therefore where the reversion came by devise to a tenant for life, with power to grant leases, and the lessee took from him a new lease, executed not according to the power, it was holden that as the latter purported to originate from the power, and not from the party's life interest, and was not conformable thereto, it did not work a surrender of the first.—(Roe v. Archbishop of York, 6 Ea. 86; Davison v. Stanley, 4 Burr. 2210.)   Where, however, the second is merely voidable, it seems that as the lessee takes some interest, though defeasible, it operates as a surrender.—(Roll. Ab. *supra*.)

2. Instances of the second kind frequently occur in respect of parol demises from year to year. If the tenant underlet, or assign his interest to another, and the landlord accept the latter as his tenant, as by receiving the rent as landlord, the first is discharged; his tenancy and interest in the lands *ipso facto* ceases.—(Sparrow v. Hawkes, 3 Esp. 505; Stone v. Whiting, 2 Stark. 235; Phipps v. Sculthorpe, 1 B. & A. 50; Thomas v. Cook, 2 B. & A. 119.)

The principle of this doctrine is well known, and brought into daily practice in the case of an assignment of a lease. If the lessor accept rent from the assignee, the action of debt cannot be afterwards sustained against the lessee. The privity of estate being gone, he is no longer chargeable as tenant of the lands, and were there no express covenant he would not be liable at all, for the covenant implied from the words " yielding and paying" is co-extensive only with the occupation and enjoyment. The difference between this and the case of a parol tenancy is therefore obvious. In the first place, there is in the latter no contract to outrun the privity of estate. When that is gone, all is gone. And in the next place, a contract under seal cannot be discharged before breach, but by a contract of equal solemnity. So that if the lessor were expressly to agree by parol, upon receiving rent from the assignee to discharge the lessee, the agreement would be of no effect. But if the demise were not under seal, such an agreement, coupled with the acceptance of the assignee as tenant, would amount to a surrender by operation of law, and the original lessee would be discharged notwithstanding he had undertaken to pay rent during the whole term.

Hence, whether the tenancy were created by a written agreement or by parol only, the acceptance of a new tenant under circumstances amounting to evidence of an agreement to discharge the original lessee, will constitute a surrender by act and operation of law. This is strikingly illustrated by the case of Reeve v. Bird, 1 C. M. & R. 31. The plaintiff sued in assumpsit for the breach of an agreement to repair.

The agreement, which was in writing, amounted to a demise for seven years from Midsummer 1826, of a messuage, three cottages, a stable, yard and garden, and the defendant agreed to pay rent during the term and to keep the premises in repair. The stable and yard were occupied by the defendant; the dwelling-house by one Prince, and the cottages by three different tenants. The defendant paid rent for the whole till January, 1832, when becoming embarrassed, he agreed to assign the premises to one Bullock. At this time he paid to the plaintiff the rent up to Christmas, and a further sum intended to cover the period during which he continued tenant before the assignment to Bullock. Prince remained in possession of the dwelling-house, and paid his subsequent rent to the plaintiff's agent, from whom he took a receipt as for the rent of premises held of the plaintiff. Bullock also paid the rent of the stable and yard to the plaintiff. During the year 1832, the tenants of two of the cottages left, and the plaintiff's agent let them to other parties and received the rents. In the month of August in that year, the whole of the premises were advertised by the plaintiff to be let or sold. There was no evidence of the premises being out of repair previous to January, 1832. Under these circumstances the Court held there was clear evidence of a surrender of the term by act and operation of law in January, 1832, and consequently, that the defendant was not liable.

So if a lessee consents to give up his lease, and that the lessor shall grant a new lease to a third party, and that is done, the effect is the same as if he took a new lease to himself; the first is surrendered.—(See Walker v. Richardson, 2 M. & W. 882.) And where two tenants holding adjoining lands, under different landlords, agreed to exchange, and took possession of each other's accordingly, and the agent to both landlords upon being informed thereof assented to the arrangement, in was holden that the original tenancies were surrendered, and each became the tenant of the other's landlord, though no rent had been actually paid by him, (Bees v. Williams, 2 C. M. & R. 581.[1] See further on this point Woodcock v. Nuth, 8 Bing. 170; Graham v. Whichelo, 1 C. & M. 188;

[1] The pleadings in this case do not appear correct.

Matthews v. Sawell, 8 Taunt. 270; Rex v. Banbury, 1 Ad. & Ell. 136.)

3. Another familiar instance of a surrender by operation of law is, where the tenant and landlord agree to put an end to the tenancy in the middle of the term, and possession is accordingly given up and accepted. This species of surrender differs from the last only in circumstance; the principle of both is, that the tenant gives up and the landlord resumes possession. Hence, the agreement must be actually executed, and, therefore, though the tenant or landlord accept an irregular notice to quit, irregular from its expiring at a wrong period, or from its being given too short a time, yet if at the expiration of such period either the one refuses to quit or the other to accept possession, the agreement is void. In the case of Doe v. Johnstone, (M'Clel. & Y. 141,) the tenant gave a three months' notice to quit instead of half a year, which however was accepted by the landlord, and the premises were put up to be let by auction. The tenant attended the sale and bid, but the premises were knocked down to a higher bidder. The tenant then refused to quit, upon which the landlord brought an ejectment, and contended first, that the offer to quit, and acceptance thereof, followed by the reletting of the premises, amounted to a surrender by operation of law, and secondly, that as there was a mutual agreement to waive a half year's notice, and adopt one for a shorter period, the latter was a *reasonable* notice, which was all the law required. But it was holden that the facts did not amount to a surrender, and that an agreement to take a shorter notice than the law requires, not being part of the original contract, cannot make that notice good. The landlord subsequently distrained for double rent, and failed on the same ground. (Johnstone v. Huddlestone, 4 B. & C. 922.) It will be observed that the one ingredient wanting to constitute a surrender of the second class, was the *consent* of the tenant to the second letting. The bidding was adverse to him, and this circumstance nullified all that had taken place before. (See Doe v. Milward, 3 M. & W. 328; Brown v. Burtenshaw, 7 D. & R. 603.) In another case the landlord and tenant having quarrelled, went before a magistrate, and upon

his recommendation came to a mutual resolution to put an
end to the tenancy, the landlord agreeing to receive a proportion of rent for so much of the second quarter as had
then elapsed. The defendant accordingly quitted the premises, but the landlord refused to accept either the rent or
the key, and it was holden there was no surrender. (Thomson
v. Wilson, 2 Stark. 379.) But if he had accepted possession
the cases of Whitehead v. Clifford, 5 Taunt. 518, and Grim-
man v. Legge, 8 B. & C. 324, show that the tenancy would
have been legally determined. (See Mollet v. Brayne, 2
Camp. 104.)

Still it is not necessary that the quitting and taking possession should be concurrent acts. It is sufficient to bar his
claim for any further rent, if the landlord enter before the
next payment falls due. In Walls v. Atcheson, 3 Bing. 462,
the defendant quitted at the end of the first quarter some
apartments which he had hired by the year from Michaelmas. In January the landlord let them to another person,
and continued to let them until July, when being unable to
procure another tenant, he sued the defendant for the balance
of the year's rent. The court held, that having precluded
the defendant from occupying the apartments by letting them
to another person, he must be taken to have rescinded the
agreement; that if he had meant, as it was alleged, to let
them on behalf of the defendant, he should have given notice
thereof. (Hall v. Burgess, 5 B. & C. 332, S. P.) A mere
attempt to let by putting a bill in the window is not enough.
(Redpath v. Roberts, 3 Esp. 225.) Where the landlord,
about a fortnight after the tenant had quitted, caused a fire
to be lighted in the kitchen, and used it for the purpose of
roasting a hare, Abbot, C. J. ruled that as it was proper a
fire should be lighted, the making such a use of it was not
such a taking of possession as deprived the landlord of his
rent. (Griffith v. Hodges, 1 C. & P. 419.)

From the case of Gore v. Wright, (17 L. J. Q. B. May,
1838,) it would appear doubtful whether cases of this kind
can properly be pleaded as a surrender. There, in answer to
an action of debt for rent on a demise, the tenant pleaded an
agreement between him and the plaintiff, that he should quit
at a given period and should thenceforth be discharged from

the payment of rent; that he did accordingly quit, and that the landlord accepted and had ever since retained possession, and concluded that thereby the term was *surrendered*. Issue being taken on the quitting by the defendant and the acceptance of possession by the landlord, and found for the defendant, the plaintiff moved for judgment *non obs. veredicto,* on the ground that the plea amounted to a surrender, and as it was not alleged that there was any note in writing, the surrender was not valid. After taking time to consider, Lord Denman, C. J. gave judgment for the plaintiff. " The motion was made," said he, " on the ground that the plea showed no valid surrender of the term. We do not, however, consider it to be a plea of a surrender, but only as showing an excuse for the party's not paying the rent claimed in the declaration, and we take it to be a valid plea for that purpose." Perhaps the judgment proceeded on the form of the plea. It is not easy to see why the facts should not be pleaded as a surrender. The only difference which strikes the mind upon a consideration of the cases between a surrender in *pais,* and a surrender by act and operation of law is, that the former is executory, and the latter executed ; in the one, the delivery of possession is symbolical; the surrender is complete though the tenant remain in possession, and hence it is required to be in writing; in the other, there must be an actual delivering up. The gist of the one is the *agreement,* of the other the execution of it.

It is now settled that a tenant from year to year has an interest which goes to his executors, and that they stand precisely in the same situation as the deceased as to giving and receiving notice to quit. (Doe v. Porter, 3 T. R. 13.) And in case of bankruptcy the interest is one which the assignees may claim, and which if they do not the bankrupt may deliver up pursuant to the 6 Geo. 4, c. 16, s. 75. (Slack v. Sharp, 3 N. & P. 390.)

It was determined by the House of Lords in Hewitt v. Adams, 1782, that a composition for tithes conveyed an interest analogous to a tenancy of land, and that the like notice was required to determine it. This doctrine has been established by many subsequent decisions. Hence if a lessee of tithes enter into a composition, and afterwards assign over or grant an underlease ; neither the assignee nor sub-lessee, nor the tenant of the land can demand or pay in kind without a regular half's year's notice. (Wyburd v. Tuck, 1 B. & P. 458.) But at the expiration of the lease the composition *ipso facto* ceases, unless by some act or admission a new contract has been created between the tenant of the lands and the tithe owner. (Cox v. Brain, 3 Taun. 95.) A composition however is a personal contract between the parties, which ceases with the interest in respect of which it was made. Thus, if a tenant enter into a composition for a term of years, and quits the same before the term has expired, the incoming tenant cannot avail himself thereof without a new agreement express or implied. (Paynton v. Kirkby, 2 Ch. 405.) In like manner the death of an incumbent puts an end to a composition made by him. But as a composition made by the owner of tithes binds his lessee, it would seem that a composition made with the owner of the land would bind his tenant. (See Eagle on Tithes, 2d vol. 25.) And though a composition ceases with the occupancy of the land, yet if the tenancy of the latter expire in the middle of the year of composition the tenant must pay for the whole year, unless there be an agreement to the contrary. (Hulme v. Pardoe, M'Clel. 393.)

The notice to quit may be given either by the party himself or by an agent duly authorized. In point of form it must appear to be the notice of the principal, and therefore when given by an agent, it must express that he gives it as " agent."

If the party with whom the contract was made as landlord be alive and his interest continue, he is the party to give the notice, though he have not the legal estate, and his representative, or the person claiming under him, has the same right. Where the agreement was made by one of three partners in his own name, a notice by him alone was holden good, though the receipts for rent had been given in the names of all the partners. (Doe v. Baker, 8 Taun. 241.) But in the absence of evidence of letting, the person to whom the rents are paid is *prima facie* landlord. If the lessor has parted with his interest, of course the purchaser is the proper party to give the notice.

Where the property is owned by several joint tenants, any one of them may, as before observed, put an end to the tenancy by a notice to quit; and it seems to be immaterial whether such notice purport to be given on behalf of all or of himself only. It is clear he may recover his own share whether the other joint tenants will concur or not. (See Doe v. Chaplin, 3 Taun. 120; Doe v. Read, 12 Ea. 97.) And as a tenant is not bound to continue tenant of part only of what he took under an entire demise, he is at liberty to treat a notice from one, in his own name only, as a determination of the tenancy in the whole. So far both principle and authority concur. But the other branch of the proposition, viz. that the other joint tenants may also avail themselves of such a notice and compel the tenant to quit the whole, rests upon the authority of the dicta found in the case of Doe v. Summersett, 1 B. & Ad. 135. Aslin and Finch were executors and joint devisees under the will of Ricketts. The defendant had held over after the expiration of a lease from Ricketts, and paid rent for some years to Aslin. Finch gave a notice to quit, signed by himself " on behalf of the trustees of the late John Ricketts." The plaintiff had a verdict, which the defendant moved to set aside on the ground that the notice having been signed by one only of two joint tenants was insufficient. The plaintiff contended, 1st, that the bringing the action upon the joint demise of the trustees was an adoption of the notice, which made it of the same validity as if it had been signed by both; and 2dly, that without such adoption a notice by one of two joint tenants put an end to the tenancy as to both. The court held that the latter position was right. " Where joint tenants join in a lease," said Lord Tenterden, C. J. in delivering the judgment of the court " each demises his own share, and each may put an end to that demise as far as it operates upon his own share, whether his companions will join with him in putting an end to the whole lease or not, so that upon the notice to quit in this case, no doubt a third[1] might have been recovered, had there been a separate demise. But although upon a joint lease by joint tenants each demises his own share, this is not the only operation of such a lease. Joint tenants are seised not only of their respective shares *per my*, but also of the entirety *per tout*. The rent reserved will

---

[1] A moiety must have been meant.

enure jointly to all the lessors, and if any of them die, the
lessee shall hold the whole as tenant to the survivors.   Upon
a joint demise by joint tenants upon a tenancy from year to
year, the true character of the tenancy is this, not that the
tenant holds of each the share of each so long as he and
each shall please, but that he holds the whole of all so long
as he and all shall please, and as soon as any one of the joint
tenants gives a notice to quit, he effectually puts an end to that
tenancy ; the tenant has a right, upon such a notice, to give
up the whole, and unless he comes to a new arrangement
with the other joint tenants as to their shares, he is compellable so to do.   The hardship upon the tenant, if he were not
entitled to treat a notice from one as putting an end to the
tenancy as to the whole, is obvious, for however willing a man
may be to be sole tenant of an estate, it is not very likely
he should be willing to hold undivided shares of it, and if
upon such a notice the tenant is entitled to treat it as putting
and end to the tenancy as to the whole, the other joint tenants
*must have the same right.   It cannot be optional on one side,
and on one side only.*"   The soundness of this conclusion is
very questionable.   If one joint lessor were to require the
tenant expressly to quit his share only, the latter would clearly
have a right to give up the whole.   This is a right founded
on strict justice and deducible from the very nature of the
contract, as stated in the foregoing judgment.   But to hold
that such right is reciprocal is to lose sight of the principle
upon which it rests.   For by this reasoning, if a person, claiming by title paramount, or even the lessor himself, were to
evict the tenant from part of the lands demised, he would instantly acquire a right to eject him from the whole, because
in these cases the tenant may, if he pleases, give up the
whole.

The case it will be observed did not require a proposition
so extensive.   The notice professed to come from both, though
it was signed only by one ; the tenant therefore had sufficient
information by it, and the question whether the one who
signed had the authority of the other to do so, though a
question of fact to be found by the jury, was one which, in
the absence of evidence to the contrary, the circumstances
would seem to warrant a direction to find in the affirmative,

just as from evidence of a demand and refusal a jury would be directed to find a conversion.

The case of Right v. Cushell, 5 Ea. 491, is distinguishable in this respect, that the stipulation in the lease by which either party was to be at liberty to determine it at the end of the first seven years, expressed " that if the landlord or tenant or *their respective heirs, executors, &c.* should give six months' notice in writing under *his or their respective hand or hands,* &c. the term should cease. There it was holden that a notice signed by two or three executors, who were jointly seised, on behalf of themselves and the third was insufficient.

Whether a notice given by a third person " as agent" to the lessor, but who is in fact unauthorized at the time to give it, can be made good by a subsequent recognition, is a point upon which the cases, at first sight, present some difficulty.

The validity of a written notice to quit, when given by a third person, must depend, we conceive, on the affirmative of the two following questions, which are perfectly distinct in their nature, and triable in a different way. First, does it appear on the face of it to be given by the authority of the landlord? And, secondly, was it so given in point of fact? The one is to be decided by the court, the other by the jury. The object of a notice is to inform the tenant that the landlord wills the tenancy to be determined. It would be of no avail for this purpose, that he authorised another to give a notice for him, if that other failed to do so, or, what is the same thing, if he gave it in such a form that the tenant could not collect from it that it had the landlord's sanction. And, on the other hand, if it had not, it could not be a valid notice, whatever its form might be. If it discloses information, which, assuming it to be true, would make the instrument valid, it is *primâ facie* good ; the truth of the information is a fact which the tenant must ascertain at his peril. Hence we conclude that there is an essential difference between a notice from A. requiring the tenant to quit the premises of B., and one of the same tenor, but signed by A., as the agent of B. The one does not give such information as the tenant can act upon. For aught that appears the landlord is a stranger to it. But the other does; and if the tenant has any doubt of the authority, he should make inquiry. If he does not, there is nothing unreasonable in supposing that he looked upon it as correct. And then proof that the landlord subsequently adopted such notice is evidence, from which a jury might and should be directed to infer a prior authority. This is all that is meant by the maxim "omnis ratihabitio retrohabitur et mandato æquiparatur." Its applicability to a notice to quit was expressly asserted in the case of Goodtitle v. Woodward, 3 B. & A. 689. The action was brought on the demise of several trustees. The notice to quit was signed by one Charles King, and it purported to be given by him as agent for all the lessors. When served the tenant made no objection to it. Before the trial King died, and to show his authority, a written authority was produced bearing the signatures of all the trustees, but it appeared that at the time the notice was served the paper had been signed by a part only, and that the rest had signed it subsequently. Best, J. at the trial was of opinion that the notice was sufficient, but upon the authority of a case cited he nonsuited the plaintiff, giving him liberty to move. Upon the argument the distinction just noticed was taken. It was contended that the instrument being in form good was such as the tenant might have acted upon with certainty at the time it was given, and that the reasoning in Right v. Cuthell did not therefore apply. That the tenant could only look at the notice, and the authority to give it need not be shown him. The Court of Queen's Bench acceded to this reasoning, and held that the subsequent adoption by the other parties gave validity to the notice. The case of Doe d. Walters, 10 B. & C. 626, which occurred some years afterwards, was this: the lessor had quitted England, leaving the defendant tenant from year to year, and had committed the management of his affairs to Grylls, a banker and attorney, to whom the tenant paid his rent. The notice to quit was given by Grylls, as agent to the lessor. No evidence was given to show that the lessor ever knew of the notice or of the action. At the trial a verdict passed for the plaintiff, which the defendant moved to set aside, on the ground that a receiver of rents had no authority to give a notice to quit. This being the only point in question, the case is of no value, except for the dicta of the judges in the course of argument; and that was addressed not so much to the question of a general authority, to be inferred from the character of the agency, as to that of a recognition of the notice, by bringing the action, which, under the circumstances, afforded no evidence whatever of a recognition, for the lessor was as ignorant of the one as of the other. " The notice," observed Parke, J. " ought to be such as the tenant could act upon with security at the time it was given. What assurance had the tenant that the landlord would accept possession at the end of the half year ?" Littledale, J. said, " the agent ought at the time when he gave the notice to have had authority to determine the estate of the tenant, for the notice is valid only by reason of its being the notice of the landlord. If the landlord therefore gave authority to the agent after the six months mentioned in the notice began to run, the tenant would not have six months' notice." To this it was answered, that wherever an act is done by an agent, it is done in some measure at the peril of the party towards whom it is done. If he doubts the authority he should make inquiry. That the same principle applied to sales or purchases made by an agent, to demands in trover, distresses in replevin, and entries on lands. The case was ultimately sent back to the jury to determine whether Grylls had, or had not, authority to give the notice. And Littledale, J. repeated the opinion, " That the ratification of the act on the day after the notice was given, or after the half year began to run, would not be sufficient, because in that case the tenant would not have six months' notice ; the notice being valid only from the time when it becomes the notice of the landlord. Parke J. expressed himself dissatisfied with the reasons given for the decision in Goodtitle v. Woodward. " But assuming," said he, " that a subsequent recognition of the authority of an agent can in any case be sufficient, it ought at all events, in this case, to have been before the day of the demise laid in the declaration, for the plaintiff must show a right to the possession on that day. If Grylls had no authority to give the notice at the time when it began to operate as a notice, it seems to me that it was insufficient, and that the lessor of the plaintiff would not be entitled to recover." The decision was right beyond dispute, for the fact of authority had not been left to the jury. Neither can it be doubted that the positions laid down by the learned judges are sound law, and that if it be found as a fact that the agent had no authority at the time the notice began to run, or even perhaps at the time he gave it, it cannot be good. But the mistake appears to us to be in confounding the two questions above noticed ; in taking that which is only evidence of a fact for the fact itself. The court cannot pronounce a subsequent adoption to be equivalent to a prior authority, any more than it can pronounce a demand and refusal to be a conversion. It is to give effect to rules of policy and convenience that the jury are directed in both cases, in the absence of any contrary evidence, to presume the one from the other.

The conclusion, however, to which the court justly came, fully sustains the distinction here contended for. The question to be submitted to the jury was, whether the agent *de facto* had authority to give the notice. To be a legitimate deduction from the reasoning above quoted, this further question should have been put, whether the defendant *knew* the fact or not? But this was treated as immaterial, for the only possible reason, because the notice informed him of it. Had it not expressed that Grylls gave it as agent to the landlord, it would have been invalid, whether authorised or not, and there would have been nothing to go to the jury. In Doe v. Robinson, 3 B. N. C. 678, the Court of Common Pleas appears to have taken the same view as the Court of Queen's Bench, in Goodtitle v. Woodward, by observing, upon sending the case back, that the question of authority might be specifically put to the jury, the notice purporting to come from an agent, " there should have been evidence of an authority to give the notice, *or of a subsequent recognition.*"

The doctrine, if correct, appears to be applicable to a notice given by one tenant in common, if not to the case of joint tenants.

A person appointed to receive rents has no authority to determine a tenancy, but where a receiver appointed by the Court of Chancery had power by the terms of his commission to let the lands, it was holden that he had an implied authority to determine such lettings.—(Doe v. Read, 12 East, 67.) The agent must give the notice himself, he cannot delegate his authority to another.—(Doe v. Robinson, sup.)

In cases of a tenancy from year to year, either party may give notice to quit. It is repugnant to the nature of such an estate that it should not be determinable at the pleasure of either. In Doe v. Browne, 8 East, 165, the defendant held under a written agreement, by which, in consideration of 40*l.*, the lessor agreed to let and defendant agreed to take the premises at 40*l.* per annum, payable quarterly. And it was further agreed that plaintiff should not raise the rent, *nor turn defendant out so long as the rent was duly paid, and the defendant did not sell anything injurious to the plaintiff's business.* It was admitted that the defendant had not broken either of the stipulations, and the only question was, whether the lessor, having given a regular notice to quit, was entitled to recover contrary to his own agreement. Lord Ellenborough asked what estate the defendant was contended to have, for if it might endure at the option of the tenant so long as he lived, then it would be an estate for life, which could not be created without deed ; if not for life, being for no assignable period, it must operate as a tenancy from year to year, in which case it must be open to either party to determine it. " The notion of a tenancy from year to year," said Lawrence, J., " the lessor binding himself not to give notice to quit, which was thrown out by Lord Mansfield, has been long exploded." The plaintiff accordingly had a verdict. But, on the other hand, where a lease is made for a term certain, it may be made determinable at any given period, at the option of one of the parties. Indeed a proviso in a lease that it shall be determinable at the end of seven, fourteen, or twenty-one years, without saying by whom, has been construed to give the option only to the tenant.—(Denn v. Spurrier, 3 B. & P. 399.) If it be meant that both shall have the power to do so, it must be so expressed.

The first point to be observed in framing a notice to quit is as has been shown, that it should purport to come from the demising party, or if more than one, from all of them. The next is, that it should so specify the premises as to inform the opposite party that the *whole* subject of the demise is to be given up. The landlord cannot require the tenant to quit a part, nor can the tenant insist on giving up a part of the premises ; and hence a notice to quit a part only will be bad.

But the courts will, if possible, so construe the reference to the premises as to make it embrace the whole. A lease demised several distinct farms and premises, describing them as " all those parts and parcels of the barton or farm called Town Barton, that is to say," &c. " Also all those several overlands," &c. " And also all those parts and parcels of the barton called Shippen Barton, that is to say," &c., and reserving distinct rents for each. Either party was to be at liberty to put an end to the lease at the expiration of the first fourteen years. The notice ran thus:— " Agreeably to the terms of the covenant between us, I hereby give you notice to deliver up possession of *Town Barton, &c.* on the expiration of the fourteenth year of your term ;" and it was holden that the " &c." might well be taken to include all the premises demised, especially as the notice referred to the lease, and that only gave the lessor power to determine the whole.—(Doe v. Archer, 14 East, 245.) So the tenancy of a messuage and lands, together with certain great and small tithes, which were let together at a gross rent, was holden well determined by a notice requiring the delivery up of " all that messuage, tenement, or dwelling house, farm, lands, *and premises, with the appurtenances,* which you rent of me."—(Doe v. Church, 3 Camp. 71.) The liberality of construction put upon this part of a notice is well illustrated by the following case. The premises consisted of a public house called " the Bricklayer's Arms." The notice was " to quit the premises which you hold of me called the Waterman's Arms." The tenant held no other premises of the plaintiff, nor was there any house in the parish called the Waterman's Arms. Lord Ellenborough, therefore, ruled that the tenant could not have been misled, and that the variance was immaterial.—(Doe v. Cox, 4 Esp. 185.)

Another requisite is, to indicate that the party is to give up possession at the period when the tenancy may be lawfully determined. But before looking at the form of the notice in this respect, it will be convenient to consider, first, At what period the tenancy may be put an end to ; and, secondly, What length of notice is required before it can be legally determined.

A tenancy from year to year can only be put an end to by

notice at the expiration of the year, or rather on the anniversary of the day when the tenancy commenced. In like manner, to determine a holding for a shorter period, as half a year, quarter, month, or week, the notice must expire on the half yearly, quarterly, monthly, or weekly day corresponding with that on which the holding began. This rule arises ex vi termini from the contract itself. As soon as a yearly tenant passes over the anniversary of his tenancy, the contract is renewed for another year, and he must hold to the end of it.

In the absence of an express limitation, the nature of the tenancy is ascertained by reference to the rate at which the rent is calculated, not by the periods at which it is made payable. If a house is let at so much per year, it is a yearly tenancy, though the rent be payable quarterly, monthly, or weekly; but if rated at per quarter, month, or week, that will be evidence of a quarterly, monthly, or weekly holding. This is the only criterion to which the courts resort, where the nature of the tenancy is not expressed. A stipulation for a quarter's notice to quit, unless it appear on the face of the contract that the parties mean the notice to be operative at any quarter, will be taken to mean a quarter ending at the expiration of the year.—(Doe v. Donovan, 1 Taun. 555.) And even where it is so expressed, the notice must expire on one of the regular quarter days, unless the tenancy commenced on some intermediate day, and then it must expire on some day being at the distance of three, six, or nine calendar months from the time of such commencement. In no case will it be construed to mean a notice expiring in the middle of any quarter, reckoning from the commencement, unless so expressed.—(Kemp v. Derrett, 3 Camp. 510.)

A general letting at a yearly rent, as before observed, constitutes a tenancy, not for one year only, but from year to year, which cannot be determined without notice, but notice may be given so as to put an end to it at the end of the first year. But a letting "*for a year and so from year to year,*" is a letting for two years at least.—(Bellasis v. Burbrick, Salk. 413; see Birch v. Wright, 1 T. R. 380.) So where upon an agreement for purchase of the premises, the vendor stipulated that C., who was then in possession, "should continue tenant not for one year only but from year to year;" it was holden that the vendee could not turn out C. at the end of the first year.—(Denn v. Cartwright, 4 East, 29.) The authority of these cases has been recently confirmed. The agreement expressed that " J. C. hath agreed to let, and the said W. G. hath agreed to take for *one year from the date hereof, and so on from year to year,* until the tenancy hereby created shall be determined as after mentioned, a house, &c. at the yearly rent of 10*l.* to be paid quarterly. The rent to commence from the 5th January, 1836, and three months shall be sufficient notice to be given from either of the parties. And it is further agreed that it shall be lawful for the said J. C. or the said W. G. to determine the tenancy by either of us giving unto the other three months' notice of either of their intentions." This was holden to constitute a tenancy for two years at least.—(Doe v. Green, 17 L. J. Q. B. 100.) In the case of Thomson v. Maberley, 2 Camp. 572, the agreement was "for twelve months' *certain,* and six months' notice *afterwards;*" and this was considered to mean " if the tenant should hold on after the year," but that he was at liberty to quit at the end of the first year, upon giving the usual half year's notice.

As to the commencement of a tenancy, this is *primâ facie* on the day when the contract was made, but independently of some express stipulation on the point, which is generally inserted, other circumstances frequently occur to repel this presumption and fix the commencement to some other day. Thus if a party enters as yearly tenant in the middle of a quarter and pays a proportion of the rent up to the ensuing quarter day, this will be evidence that the tenancy commenced on the latter day.—(Doe v. Johnson, 6 Esp. 10; Doe v. Stapleton, 3 C. & P. 275.) Where a lease becomes void by reason of the death of tenant for life, who granted it in the middle of a quarter, and the remainderman accepts rent at the times mentioned in the lease, though such acceptance creates a new tenancy from year to year as between him and the lessee; yet as the payment has reference to the original entry the tenancy will be deemed to have commenced at the anniversary of that period, and not from the time when the new relation arose; consequently the notice to quit must expire at the time when the lease began.—(Doe v. Weller,

7 T. R. 478.) The same rule applies where the tenant of a mortgagor upon notice pays his rent to the mortgagee and thus creates a new tenancy. A lease by parol for more than three years, and therefore void by the statute of frauds, yet regulates the terms of holding, and the tenant can only be turned out at the season when the lease was to have commenced.— (Doe v. Bell, 5 T. R. 471.) If, by consent of the parties, a new tenant be substituted, whereby the interest of the former becomes surrendered by operation of law, and the new tenant enters in the middle of a quarter, but continues to pay rent at the same time as the old tenant, the notice must expire at the time of the year when the original tenancy commenced.— (See Doe v. Johnson, sup.; Doe v. Samuel, 5 Esp, 173.) So if new terms are come to between the landlord and tenant in the middle of the year of holding, such as an increase of rent, unless there appears an intention to create a new tenancy from that time, it will be deemed for this purpose to be a continuation of the original term.—(Doe v. Kendrick, Ad. Eject. 129.)

A difficulty frequently occurs in country lettings, where the premises are entered upon at different times, to ascertain from which of the periods of entry the tenancy is to be considered as commencing. The rule is, to regard the time of entry on that which is the principal subject of demise as the substantial commencement. Thus in Doe v. Snowdon, 2 Black. 1224, the agreement being to hold the arable land from Old Candlemas, the pasture from Old Lady Day, and the meadow from Old May Day, the rent being reserved at Old Michaelmas and Lady Day, the court considered that the substantial holding commenced at Lady Day, and that as to the arable land the agreement operated merely as a licence to the tenant to enter and prepare it for the lent corn, and it was mentioned by the court, as an argument in favor of this construction, that if the landlord was bound to give six months' notice before Candlemas, it would be only giving the tenant an opportunity to injure the land by taking a second crop of hay from the meadows. The same question afterwards arose in Doe v. Spence, 6 East, 120. The defendants had taken possession at Old Lady Day, and by agreement, dated 17th July following, they were to become tenants of the farm described as then in their occupation, " and to enter on the premises as follows, viz. on the tillage land at Candlemas last past, and on the house, and all other the premises at Lady Day following ;" and a stipulation was added, " that whenever they left the farm, they should quit the same according to the times of entry as aforesaid." The defendants also agreed to pay the rent half-yearly, at Michaelmas and Lady Day. The notice was given on the 23d August, to quit " at the end of the year," being more than half a year's notice, if the tenancy commenced at Lady Day, but less than that, if it began at Candlemas. As to the stipulation to quit according to the time of entry, the court considered it was no more than the law would have implied, and determined, on the authority of the preceding case, that the substantial time of entry was Lady Day, with a privilege to the tenant, on the one hand, to enter on the arable land before that period, for the purpose of preparing it, and on the other hand, a stipulation by him, when he quitted the farm, to allow the same privilege to the in-coming tenant. In both these cases, the rent was made payable from one of the days of entry, and this was considered a circumstance of some weight in determining the question. In the following cases that circumstance was wanting. The premises, consisting of messuages or dwelling houses, outhouses, mills, and other manufacturing buildings, meadow and pasture lands, and bleaching grounds, though there was not much of the latter, together with all watercourses, &c., were holden under a written agreement for a lease, dated 1st January, 1792, for thirty-five years, " *to commence*, as to the meadow ground, from the 25th of December then last past, as to the pasture ground (except a certain field called the Bull Hill, for training in), from the 25th March then next, and as to the said field called the Bull Hill, and the housing, mills, outhousing and other buildings, and all the residue of the said premises, from the 1st of May then next, at the yearly rent of 250*l*., payable on the day of Pentecost, and on the feast day of St. Martin ; the first payment to begin and be made on the feast day of Pentecost next." The defendants were bleachers, and the premises were intended solely for manufacturing purposes. The notice was served on the 28th September, requiring the defendants to quit at the expiration of the then current year of their holding. The demise was laid on the 11th June following. It was argued that the occupation of the meadow ground, on the 25th December, was as beneficial for manufacturing purposes, as that of the house on the 1st of May, and that, at all events, this case was distinguished from those above cited, inasmuch as here there was an express stipulation that the term of thirty-five years " should commence" on that day. But the court held that the substantial part of the demise was the houses, buildings, and watercourses, which were to be entered upon on the 1st of May; that every thing else was auxiliary thereto, and that the notice was consequently sufficient.—(Doe v. Watkins, 7 East, 550.) In Doe v. Howard, 11 East, 498, the question assumed a different shape. The demise was of a messuage, with the appurtenances, then in the possession of the defendant, together with several closes of land described as thereunto belonging, containing thirteen acres, for the term of eleven years, to hold the lands from the 2d February, and the house and other premises from the 1st of May then next, at a rent payable at Michaelmas and Lady Day, the first being payable at the Michaelmas ensuing the commencement of the term. The notice was given for the first of May. At the trial, the learned judge was of opinion, that the *land* was the principal subject of demise, and on that ground nonsuited the plaintiff. Upon a motion to set aside the nonsuit, Lord Ellenborough observed, " It must, in all these cases, depend upon the relative value and importance of the house and of the land let together, which is the principal, and which is the accessary." In this case, the learned judge, upon consideration of the whole subject-matter of the demise, thought that the land was the principal, and the house the auxiliary, and it lies upon you who impeach his opinion, to show that the house was the principal. If you disputed the fact assumed by him, you should have desired him to leave it to the jury to say which was in fact the principal." And Le Blanc J. remarked, " when once the inquiry is let in, as to which was the principal and which the accessary, in these cases, a question of fact was necessarily let in, which, if not agreed upon, the jury must decide."

It was once considered that a notice to quit, regular in form and regular also in point of duration, was, if not returned or objected to, *primâ facie* evidence for the lessor, that the tenancy commenced at the period specified in the notice, and that it lay on the tenant, at the trial, to show the contrary. But this, as a general proposition, has been long since exploded, as being contrary to first principles, that a man's own act should be evidence for himself.—(Doe v. Calvert, 2 Camp. 387.)   If indeed the notice be served on the tenant himself, and he reads it and makes no objection as to the time when it requires him to quit, his conduct amounts to an indirect admission that the notice is correct.—(Doe v. Harris, cited 1 T. R. 161 ; Thomas v. Thomas, 2 Camp. 648 ; Doe v. Foster, 13 East, 405.)   Just as a letter or declaration of the party is often introduced, not as *evidence*, but to found a presumption from the conduct and demeanour of the party addressed in relation thereto.   If therefore the tenant either cannot or does not read the notice, when delivered, no such inference can be raised.   Where the tenant, upon receiving the notice, merely said he should go out as soon as he could suit himself with another house, Lord Ellenborough put it to the jury, whether he meant that rather than involve himself in litigation, he would quit as soon as he could, though he could not legally be turned out, or whether he must be understood as admitting that the tenancy would be thereby regularly determined.   The jury found the latter.—(Doe v. Wombwell, 2 Camp. 559.)   In another case, this expression by the tenant on receiving the notice, " I pay rent enough, it is hard to use me thus," was considered by the court merely as the answer of an angry man, but the case was sent back that the question might be decided by a jury.—(Oakapple v. Copons, 4 T. R. 361.) This kind of evidence, it must be remembered, is only presumptive. The tenant may repel its effect, not merely by proof that the tenancy commenced at a different time, but also by any evidence explanatory of the act, or conduct, from which the inference is sought to be raised.   But if an admission be made for a specific purpose, and with the view to induce the landlord to act upon it, the party will be estopped from showing the contrary.   Hence, where the tenant being applied to by the solicitor of a devisee of the estate, who was about to sell it, to know when his tenancy commenced, told him that it commenced at Lady Day, and the purchaser, to whom this answer was communicated, gave him notice to quit at that period, Lord Ellenborough would not permit the tenant to show that his holding commenced at a different period.—(Doe v. Lambley, 2 Esp. 635.)

The terms " Michaelmas, Lady Day," &c. in a lease or other written instrument, are construed with reference to the new style, and evidence is not receivable to show that they were meant to designate old Michaelmas, old Lady Day, &c. —(Doe v. Lea, 11 Ea. 312.) But where the demise is by parol, such evidence is receivable, and it becomes a question for the jury whether the holding was according to the new or the old style.—(Farley v. Wood, cited 11 Ea. 313, but differently reported, 1 Esp. 198.) So where these words are used in a notice to quit, though *primâ facie* they refer to the new style, yet they may be construed by reference to the lease or holding to mean either the new or the old style.—(Ib.; Dean v. Walker, Peake, Ad. Ca. 194 ; Doe v. Vinie, 2 Camp. 256.)

Secondly,—As to the length of notice. It was determined so long ago as the reign of Henry the Eighth, that in order to determine a tenancy from year to year of lands, half-a-year's notice must be given, and the same rule was subsequently applied to houses, (Right v. Darby, 1 T. R. 159,) and to a composition for tithes.—(Hewitt v. Adams, Dom. Proc. 1782.) So if a lease be made determinable at a given period, notice must be given half a year before.—(Goodright v. Richardson, 3 T. R. 462.) " Six months " therefore is not the proper expression for a notice where the holding commenced on a feast or quarter-day, for taken to mean lunar months, as it must in legal construction, it would not amount to the period designated by " half a year," while " six calendar months " would be either too much or too little.—(See Parker v. Constable, 3 Wils. 25 ; Johnstone v. Huddlestone, 4 B. & C. 932.) On the other hand " half a year " from either of such days is always sufficient.—(Rex v. Doe, 6 Bing. 574.) But if the holding commenced on any other day, there must be a six calendar months' notice, and then either that or the phrase " half a year " may be used. By the custom of particular places, a shorter or a longer notice may be good or necessary, but, like all other customs in opposition to the common law, it must be strictly proved.—(Roe v. Charnock, Peake, 4.) In one case evidence was given of a custom in a town for a tenant to give three months' notice, but the court held it insufficient to govern a tenancy at a village eight miles distant, there being no express proof that it extended there.— (Roe v. Dickinson, cited Co. Litt. 270 b, n. 1.) Where the tenancy is by the week, month, or quarter, a week's, month's, or quarter's notice, even if necessary, (Huffell v. Armistead, *ante,*) is at all events sufficient, (Doe v. Hazell, 1 Esp. 94,) unless there be an express agreement to the contrary.—(Roe v. Ruffen, 6 Esp. 4.)

It is not too late to give the notice on the quarter day, since it is to expire *on* and not *before* the anniversary of the day when the tenancy commenced. For example, a notice to quit at Michaelmas may be served on Lady Day.—(Per. Ld. Ellenborough in Doe v. Green, 4 Esp. 198.) The tenant is not bound to quit on the day before. And even on a weekly tenancy, where the holding commenced on a Monday, it was holden that the tenant had not made himself liable to another week's rent by not quitting until the middle of a Monday. "I cannot say," said Parke, B. "that a week has been exceeded by holding for six days, and two fractions of a day."

The notice must indicate the time when the tenancy is to end with reasonable certainty, and that must be the proper time, or the notice will be bad. Hence a notice to quit on the 11th of October, being old Michaelmas Day, was holden bad for new Michaelmas, though it was served more than half a year before the latter day.—(Doe v. Lea, 11 Ea. 312.) It has been ruled however that a notice on the 26th September to deliver up the premises " on *or about* the end of six calendar months from the 29th September next ensuing" was good for Lady Day, as being equivalent to "half a year."—(Howard v. Wemsley, 6 Esp. 53. But see Adams' Eject. 124.)

A notice that "from henceforth" the party will set out his tithes in kind, the tithes becoming payable within six months afterwards, is insufficient to determine a composition, either for that or the subsequent year; for taking it to apply to the present year, it is too short, and there is nothing to show that it means the next year.—(Goode v. Howells, 4 M. & W. 199.) But where the tithes for the current year had all become due, a notice by the landlord that "for the time to come" he should require them to be paid in kind was deemed sufficient, as necessarily referring to the next year's tithes.—(Leech v. Bailey, 6 Price, 506.)

It is therefore enough to show generally an intention to end the tenancy at the proper and legal period, as "at the expiration of the term for which you hold the same."—(Doe. v. Lamb, Ad. Eject. 277.) Or "at the expiration of the year of your tenancy which shall next happen after the expiration of half a year from the service hereof."—(Doe v. Butler, 2 Esp. 590; Doe v. Scott, 6 Bing. 362; Doe v. Smith, 5 Ad. & Ell. 351.) The only disadvantage belonging to this general mode of stating the time, is that the landlord gains no evidence upon the service, upon which to build the presumption we have just noticed.

Following out the principle of construction, which is invariably applied to an instrument of this kind, it has been holden that a notice dated on the 27th September and served on the 28th, requiring the tenant to quit "at Lady Day next, or at the end of your *current* year," the year in fact expiring on the 29th September, was good for the Michaelmas of the following year.—(Doe v. Culliford, 4 D. & R. 249.) So a notice served at Michaelmas 1795, to quit at Lady Day "which will be in the year 1795," was considered good for the ensuing Lady Day.—(Doe v. Kightley, 7 T. R. 63.) The plaintiff in this case perhaps received some aid from evidence of a conversation between the person serving the notice and the tenant, in which the former observed that he was instructed to give a notice for "Lady Day next," but the court remarked that the words "will be" clearly must have given the tenant to understand that the date of the year was a mistake. So a notice on the 22d October 1833 "to quit at the expiration of half a year from the delivery of this notice, or at such other time or times as your *present* year's holding shall expire after the expiration of half a year from the delivery of this notice," the tenancy having commenced in February, was holden sufficient for February 1835, the Court rejecting the word "present" as surplusage.—(Doe v. Smith, 4 Ad. & Ell. 350.) And in Doe v. Wightman, 4 Esp. 5, Lord Kenyon ruled that a notice to quit "on the 25th of March or the 8th of April next" was good for whichever day was the right one.

The notice must be given to the tenant of the party giving it. not to an under tenant, or any other person, notwithstanding he may be in possession, so long as the original relation continues.—(Pheasant v. Benson, 14 Ea. 234.) We have before observed that the acceptance of rent *quasi* rent from the person in possession constitutes the relation of landlord and tenant, and then the notice must be given to him. So where the lessor, having power to put an end to the lease, has accepted rent from the assignee, the notice must be given to him, and not to the lessor. Where A. had been tenant, and upon his quitting B. took possession, but neither had paid any rent, it was holden that B. might be presumed to have come in as assignee of A., and that notice to quit given to him was therefore regular.—(Doe v. Williams, 6 B. & C. 41.) A tenancy from year to year, as before observed, is an interest which passes to the assignees in case of bankruptcy, but until they have by some act or expression signified their acceptance thereof, the bankrupt continues tenant, and consequently the notice must be given to him. If the tenant dies, the notice must be given to his personal representative ; but where the widow of the tenant continued in the house after his death and notice was given to her, it was holden unnecessary for the landlord to prove that she was the representative, but the onus of proof to the contrary lay on her.—(Rees v. Perrott, 4 C. & P. 230.)

On the other hand, if the lessor die, become bankrupt, or part with the property, the notice must be given to his heir, devisee or executor, assignee or vendee, as the case may be. The statute of 4 Anne, c. 16, which abolishes attornments, permits the tenant, until he has had notice of the sale, to consider the vendor still as his landlord, so far that he is not to be prejudiced by payment of rent to him. Perhaps a notice to quit, given to the vendor in ignorance of the sale, would by the equity of this proviso bind the vendee.

No date need be put to the notice, nor need it be addressed to any one. If addressed to the wrong person, though served on the right, its validity would be doubtful.—(Doe v. Woodman, 8 Ea. 23.) But where a notice was directed to a tenant by a wrong Christian name, but he did not return it, Lord Ellenborough ruled he should be bound by it, it being shown there was no other tenant of that name.—(Doe v. Spiller, 6 Esp. 70.) It is not advisable that there should be an attesting witness, because of the difficulties this formality often engenders in respect of proof.—(See Doe v. Durnford, 2 M.& S. 62.)

Service of the notice should be effected, if possible, on the tenant himself, particularly if it be expedient to provide such evidence of the commencement of the tenancy as is afforded by his acquiescence. For this purpose, the person serving it should wait till the tenant reads it, or if he cannot read, to read it to him. Personal service may be effected any where. If this cannot be accomplished, the service may be made on the wife, (Pulteney v. Shelton, 5 Ves. 261, n.) or domestic servant of the tenant, or some other person standing in such a relation as to make it his duty to give it to the tenant, and then a presumption arises that he did his duty. A service in this way should be made on the premises, though, if given to the wife off the premises, and it be shown that she at the time lived with the husband, it would be sufficient.

Still this kind of service is only *prima facie* good; if the tenant show satisfactorily that the notice never came to his hands, or not till a considerable time after it had begun to run, the service would be defective.—(See Jones v. Marsh, 4 T. R. 464; Doe v. Dunbar, M. & M. 10.) Merely leaving the notice at the tenant's house will in no case suffice.—(Doe v. Lucas, 5 Esp. 153.)

If two or more tenants hold the premises jointly, service on one is good for all. In Doe v. Cuck, 5 Esp. 196, the landlord sent for one of the defendants and told him he should want the premises, which he and his brother held, to take into his own occupation, and should expect them to quit at Michaelmas. This was holden a good notice to determine the tenancy as to both.

A notice may be waived either by express agreement, or by some act indicating an intention to continue the tenancy. Thus the payment and acceptance of rent, which accrued due after its expiration, amounts to a waiver, but then it must be found by the jury to have been paid and received *as rent*, for there is nothing to prevent a landlord from receiving as a compensation for the trespass, what he would recover in an action for mesne profits. *Primâ facie*, payment of the stipulated amount, without protest or explanation, will be a waiver, and it lies on the party affirming the contrary to show that it was not made for rent, but for a compensation.—(Goodright v. Cordwent, 6 T. R. 219.) A distress for subsequent rent, acquiesced in, is conclusive. (Zouch v. Mullingate, 1 H. Bl. 311.) Where a banker, to whom the rents had been usually paid, being ignorant of the notice, received from the tenant rent for a period after its expiration, it was holden that such receipt did not bind the landlord.—(Doe v. Calvert, 2 Camp. 387.) Payment of double rent under the statute, though for a twelvemonth, affords no evidence of a renewal of the tenancy.—(Booth v. Macfarlane, 1 B. & Ad. 906.)

A second notice to quit, given after the expiration of the first, recognizes a subsisting tenancy, and amounts therefore to a waiver of the first, (see Doe v. Palmer, 16 Ea. 53,) but this must be understood of a notice to quit at the expiration of another year or period of holding. A notice " to quit the premises which you now hold of me in fourteen days, or I shall require double value," given after the expiration of the first, cannot be so understood, having for its object merely the recovery of double value.—(Doe v. Steel, 2 Camp. 116; see Messenger v. Armstrong, 1 T. R. 53.) Where the landlord, after ejectment, brought upon the first notice, served another in case he should fail in proof of the former, and in that described the premises as then held of him, the Court considered there was no necessity for expressing the purpose thereof in the second, for as an ejectment was actually pending in the first, the tenant could not have supposed that the landlord intended to waive it.—(Doe v. Humphreys, 2 Ea. 237.) So where the landlord, after the notice expired, told the tenant he should not be turned out until the premises were sold, this was holden to be merely an indulgence, and not a waiver of the notice.—(Whiteacre v. Symonds, 10 Ea. 13.)

L.

ART. IV.—LIFE OF LORD ERSKINE.

A COMPLETE life of this master of forensic eloquence has yet to be written. In the volumes of his speeches,—reported with elaborate care, and the collection of those State Trials which darkened the close of the last century, there is raised indeed a tablet to his memory as durable as our language,—the κτῆμά ἐς ἀεί, which the Greek historian congratulated himself, and not in vain, on erecting. But of Erskine's daily skirmishes and triumphs in the courts, of his gay and happy temperament, of his social and companionable excellencies, of his wit and repartee, of those qualities of head and heart, which made the orator forgotten in the man, the traditions are becoming each year more faint as the cotemporaries who loved him pass away, with all their vivid recollections. In this neglect he has shared, it is true, the common fate of eminent lawyers, the best and greatest of whom, Nottingham, and Somers, and Hardwicke, have failed to obtain a faithful cotemporary chronicler. It was also reserved for this Magazine to record the memorabilia of Holt and Camden, nor will the difficulty of the task deter us from attempting to offer a similar tribute to the still higher merits of Erskine. There is no name more dear to the profession which he gladdened, adorned, and exalted; no legal memory which is held in more affectionate esteem by the people. It will be our endeavour to concentrate the rays of light that illumine his character, as the idol of special juries, and glory of Westminster Hall;—to bind together the Sibylline leaves which illustrate his life and conversation;—to amass the materials that may hereafter be moulded and chiselled by more skilful hands into a monument worthy of his genius.

The Honourable Thomas Erskine, third and youngest son of Henry David Erskine, tenth Earl of Buchan, in Scotland, was born in Edinburgh, in January, 1750, or, according to some accounts, in January, 1748. The name is derived from the barony of Erskine, in the shire of Renfrew, and as a local surname proves the high antiquity of his race. The earldom of Buchan can be traced to the time of William the Lion. Its lineage included the John Cumyn, whose wife placed the

crown on the head of Robert Bruce, at his coronation at
Scone;—James Steuart, son of Jane Queen of Scotland and
the Black Knight of Lorn; Sir Thomas Erskine sent ambas-
sador to England by Robert III. and styled in the royal
commission "consanguineus noster;" Alexander Lord Erskine, Governor of Dumbarton Castle in the reign of James
the Fourth; John, thirteenth Lord Erskine and Earl of Mar,
Regent of Scotland in 1571, and John, second Earl of Mar,
Lord High Treasurer of Scotland in 1603. During a space of
four hundred years this noble family filled the highest situa-
tions of public trust that could be held by a subject, but
without increasing the number of their paternal acres or
amassing wealth. In the middle of the eighteenth century,
the representative of a race, which had swayed as regents the
kingdom of Scotland, could not boast of a higher income than
200*l.* a year. These reduced circumstances prevented his
youngest son from being trained for any of the learned professions, then the usual destination of the younger scions of
Scottish nobility. He received, however, the rudiments of a
classical education at the High School of Edinburgh and
University of St. Andrew's, these seminaries affording the
same advantages to boys which the English universities were
originally intended to provide. In 1769 he went to sea as
midshipman in a ship of war commanded by Sir John Lind-
say, nephew to Lord Mansfield, quitting at eleven years of age
those native shores which he never revisited till raised to the
peerage,—as ex Lord Chancellor and invested with the Order
of the Thistle. He made voyages to North America and the
West Indies, and became so warm an admirer of the character
of the British sailor, that in after-life he could not endure the
notion of a change. He would hardly listen to the notion of
making them sober and orderly on shore. "You may scour
an old coin," he wrote, "to make it legible, but if you go on
scouring it will be no coin at all." Young Erskine did not remain in the service long enough to obtain the commission of
lieutenant, though by the friendship of his commander he acted
for some time in that capacity. However much attached to
his shipmates, the chance of promotion appeared so slender to
the unfriended middy, that he quitted his vessel in despair,
after cruising about for five years, and at eighteen entered the

army as an ensign in the Royals or 1st Regiment of Foot. Before accompanying his regiment to Minorca, where it was stationed for three years, he committed an act of improvidence, and was married to a lady of good family, but of a fortune as narrow as his own. On the 29th of March, 1770, he was united to Frances, daughter of Daniel Moore, Esq., M.P. for Marlow, and though subject at first to many privations, he had no reason to repent of his precipitancy. She became the fond parent of a numerous offspring, and lived till within a few years of her husband's attaining the seals, having well deserved his tribute on her monument, that she was the most faithful and most affectionate of women. During his long sojourn at Minorca, the married ensign solaced his leisure hours with reading aloud the old English authors. He was more familiar with Shakespear, we are informed, than almost any man of his age, and Milton he had nearly by heart. The noble speeches in Paradise Lost may be deemed as good a substitute as could be discovered by the future orator for the immortal originals in the Greek models. The works of Dryden and Pope were next read and committed to memory with the avidity of a re-fined and well-formed taste. Nor were the hours of a garrison life, spent out of study, wholly wasted or unprofitable. The ensign, just verging to manhood, acquired among his brother officers that knowledge of the world, that frank and gallant bearing, the self-confidence and self-respect, which are among the best passports to professional eminence. For the military profession, Erskine professed no enthusiasm, though he would talk with some exultation of having handled a musket. The duties of parade and military evolutions, the monotony of the camp and the barrack-room, presented too narrow a sphere for his talents, especially when cabined and confined in the quarters of a petty island. On the return of the regiment in 1772, he mixed much with the literary coteries of the metro-polis, and appears to have attracted the notice of the great lion Dr. Johnson. "On April the 2d, 1772," writes Boswell, "I dined with Dr. Johnson at Sir Alexander Macdonald's, where was a young officer in the regimentals of the Scots Royals, who talked with a vivacity, fluency and precision, so uncommon, that he attracted particular attention. Mr. Erskine (throughout this memoir we shall reject the prefix Mr. as an impertinent addition to such a national name) told us that when he was in the island of Minorca, he not only read prayers, but preached two sermons to the regiment." The editor, Mr. Croker, has added in a note, " Lord Erskine was fond of this anecdote. He told it to the editor the first time that he had the honour of being in his company, and often repeated it with an observation that he had been a sailor and a soldier, was a lawyer and a parson. The latter, he affected to think the greatest of his efforts, and to support that opinion, would quote the prayer for the clergy in the Liturgy, from the expression of which he would (in no commendable spirit of jocularity) infer that the enlightening them was one of the greatest marvels that could be worked." But this was in later days, when Lord Erskine loved to multiply the echoes of fame, and to announce the speedy publication of a work which should strike all readers by its title-page, " Sermons preached on Ship-board and in the Camp, by the Right Honourable Thomas Lord Erskine, late Lord High Chancellor," thus bearing under one hood the character of sailor, soldier, lawyer, peer and divine.

The cause of his second change has been variously ascribed —to the persuasions of his mother, a lady of excellent discernment—to the admiration called forth by the exercise of his talents in conversation and debate—to the " res angusta domi," and the claims of an increasing family—and lastly, to the ennui produced by a desultory course of life, which his occasional pamphlets on the abuses of the army could not furnish sufficient occupation to remove. To his happy determination the whole of these causes with combined force probably contributed ; the success of his brother Henry at the Scottish bar, of which he was for many years the grace and ornament, affording also a felicitous precedent. " At the house of Admiral Walsingham," says Cradock, " I first met with Erskine and Sheridan, and it was there the scheme was laid that the former should exchange the army for the law ; and in consequence our excellent friend, Mr. Hinchcliffe, was applied to, who kindly received him at Trinity Lodge, and obtained for him a nobleman's degree. He was now twenty-six, and to save further loss of time entered his name on the boards of Trinity, Cambridge, as fellow-commoner, and kept terms simultaneously as student at Lincoln's Inn. His sole object in taking a bachelor's degree being to dispense with two out of the five years' noviciate, according to the then regulations of the inns of court, he did not enter the senate house for honours, and confined his attempts at university distinction to the gaining a college prize for a declamation on the Revolution of 1688. To this little triumph Erskine reverted with complacency when defending Paine. ' I was formerly called upon, under the discipline of a college, to maintain these truths, and was rewarded for being thought to have successfully maintained that our present constitution was by no means a remnant of Saxon liberty, nor any other institution of liberty, but the pure consequence of the oppression of the Norman tenures, which, spreading the spirit of freedom from one end of the kingdom to the other, enabled our brave fathers not to reconquer, but for the first time to obtain, those privileges, which are the inalienable inheritance of all mankind.' "

During the intervals of his residence at college, Erskine studied in the chambers of Mr. Justice Buller, then practising as a special pleader, and afterwards with Mr. Wood, a lawyer in the strictest sense of the term, under whom he continued to imbibe black letter for a year after his call to the bar. He had taken lodgings in Kentish Town, and would occasionally call for his wife at the house of a connexion, who kept a glass shop in Fleet Ditch and used to talk of him as "Our Tammy." He was a constant visitor at the villa of Mr. Reynolds, an eminent solicitor, near Bromley, in Kent, whose son, the noted dramatist, in his " Life and Times," has given the following history of their guest. " The young student resided in small lodgings near Hampstead, and openly avowed that he lived on cow beef because he could not afford any of a superior quality, dressed shabbily, expressed the greatest gratitude to Mr. Harris for occasional free admissions, and used boastingly to exclaim to my father, ' Thank fortune ! out of my own family I don't know a lord ! ' But the end of difficulties and privations was at hand. Born with the heroism of a light heart, they had tended rather to sustain than to subdue his exertions." In Trinity term, 1778, according to the most authentic report, in his 31st year, the very best age for adventuring the legal profession, Erskine was called to the bar by the Society of Lincoln's Inn, just before the commencement of the long vacation, and immediately on its close saw a long vista of wealth and fame opening before him. But the story of his success has been too graphically told by himself to admit another narrative. "It was at the King of Clubs," says Adair, "that I heard Erskine detail his early professional life. His tale is an instructive exemplification of those golden opportunities, which occur but rarely in human affairs. Yet, though what is vulgarly called luck had its share in urging along his most rapid and prosperous career, never was chance so well seconded by great talent, by chivalrous zeal, and proud integrity of heart and conduct."

"I had scarcely a shilling in my pocket when I got my first retainer. It was sent me by a Captain Baillie of the navy, who held an office at the Board of Greenwich Hospital, and I was to show cause in the Michaelmas term against a rule that had been obtained in the preceding term, calling on him to show cause why a criminal information for a libel reflecting on Lord Sandwich's conduct as governor of that charity should not be filed against him. I had met, during the long vacation, this Captain Baillie at a friend's table, and after dinner I expressed myself with some warmth, probably with some eloquence, on the corruption of Lord Sandwich as First Lord of the Admiralty, and then adverted to the scandalous practices imputed to him with regard to Greenwich Hospital. Baillie nudged the person who sat next to him, and asked who I was. Being told that I had just been called to the bar, and had been formerly in the navy, Baillie exclaimed with an oath, 'Then I'll have him for my counsel!' I trudged down to Westminster Hall when I got the brief, and being the junior of five, who would be heard before me, never dreamt that the court would hear me at all. The argument came on. Dunning, Bearcroft, Wallace, Bower, Hargrave, were all heard at considerable length, and I was to follow. Hargrave was long-winded, and tired the Court. It was a bad omen; but, as my good fortune would have it, he was afflicted with the stranguary, and was obliged to retire once or twice in the course of his argument. This protracted the cause so long, that, when he had finished, Lord Mansfield said that the remaining counsel should be heard the next morning. This was exactly what I wished. I had the whole night to arrange in my chambers what I had to say the next morning, and I took the court with their faculties awake and freshened, succeeded quite to my own satisfaction (sometimes the surest proof that you have satisfied others), and as I marched along the Hall after the rising of the judges, the attorneys flocked around me with their retainers. I have since flourished, but I have always blessed God for the providential stranguary of poor Hargrave."

Erskine related this anecdote with those raptures of retrospection which are among the richest luxuries of minds that have triumphed over fortune. His pleading for Captain Baillie will be long remembered as a splendid monument of his eloquence, which never rose to loftier heights than in the exposure of oppression and injustice, and in dragging public corruption to shame and infamy. It was a long struggle against the court, and against Lord Mansfield in particular, who once or twice exhorted him to moderate his language, but interposed with his usual mildness and urbanity. He went on without abating one jot of his vehemence, and, though a young man who had never heard the sound of his own voice before in a court of law, he astonished the whole bar and the auditory by his intrepidity and firmness. The case was indeed one well calculated to call forth the youthful energies of the high-spirited advocate, and to "awaken his dormant thunder."

Captain Baillie, then Lieutenant-governor of Greenwich Hospital, having detected various abuses in the administration of that national charity, presented several petitions to the directors and governors, and (failing in his humane object) to the Lords of the Admiralty, with a prayer for inquiry and redress. He printed and circulated a statement of the case among the general governors of the Hospital, animadverting with much severity upon the introduction of landsmen into the Hospital, and insinuating that they had been placed there to serve the electioneering purposes of Lord

Sandwich. Indignant at these charges, the Board of Admiralty suspended the adventurous captain; and certain officers of the establishment, whose conduct had been the subject of his invective, were hardy enough to move the Queen's Bench for a criminal information. This audacity on their part excited a burst of vituperation from the young and enthusiastic orator. "That such wretches should escape chains and a dungeon, is a reproach to humanity and to all order and government, but that they should become prosecutors is a degree of effrontery that would not be believed by any man who did not accustom himself to observe the shameless scenes which the shameless age we live in is every day producing. Far different was the treatment his client met with from the seamen. They surrounded his apartments, and testified their feelings by acclamations which sailors never bestow but on men who deserve them." The rule was discharged, with a general concurrence of opinion that Erskine's happy hardihood had ensured the result. The judge's displeasure at the freshman's boldness was probably modified by his aristocratic birth and connexions. His bearding the first lord of the Admiralty, and persisting to drag him before the court in defiance of Lord Mansfield, might not have been tolerated in a tyro of less pretension; and even had the spirit of the advocate persisted in his license of remark, there would have ensued an appearance of altercation with the Bench most fatal to his interests in the fears of wary attorneys.

His naval education and successful debût soon afforded the opportunity for another triumph,—the defence of Admiral Keppel. This parlour officer, better adapted for campaigns at the west-end of London than for braving the battle and the storm, had been brought to a court martial on the accusation of Sir Hugh Palliser, on grave charges of incapacity and misconduct. The counsel originally retained, Dunning and Lee, were wholly ignorant of those sea phrases, without some knowledge of which the case was in a great degree unintelligible, and Dunning recommended his young friend as eminently qualified for the task. The powers of counsel before a court martial are restricted within narrow bounds. He has neither the privilege of addressing the court, nor of putting any questions to the witnesses. But Erskine did all that could be done, in the full and admirable defence which he wrote out for Admiral Keppel. To prepare himself for the task he personally examined all the captains in the fleet. The speech was highly applauded, and his client, being honourably acquitted as much by the skill of the apology as the merits of his case, evinced his gratitude in the munificent gift of a bank note for 1000*l.* Erskine hastened in high glee to his friend Reynolds to display this epitome of wealth, and exclaimed with natural triumph, "Voila the non-suit of cow beef, my good friends !"

Another case to which he was recommended as well by his early renown as by former professional associations, though curious and highly characteristic of his high-toned independence, is little known. His client, Lieutenant Bourne, had been convicted on two indictments for libel and assault on Sir James Wallace. Numerous affidavits were read, when Lieutenant Bourne was called up for judgment, from which it appeared that he had taken his passage for the West Indies in the ship of which Sir James Wallace was admiral, that he behaved himself fractiously on the voyage, that the tempers of both became exasperated by collision, till at length he had shouldered Sir James on the quarter deck, refusing to give way an inch, that his superior officer might have room to pass. On this fresh provocation the admiral said to the next in command,—" Understand, sir, it is my order that Mr. Bourne does not walk on the same side of the deck with me." The order was rigorously enforced, and on their return to England Lieutenant Bourne sent him a challenge. The admiral refusing to grant a meeting, and alleging some former pusillanimous conduct as an excuse, Mr. Bourne, in a frenzy of passion, inserted a libel on his enemy in the newspapers, and meeting him in the streets at Bath, lifted up his cane and inflicted a severe wound upon the head. In mitigation of punishment for this violent assault, Erskine urged every topic that ingenuity could suggest, and poured forth a vehement strain of lofty declamation :—" I build my principal hope of a mild sentence upon much more that will be secretly felt by the court, than may be decently expressed from the bar; for, although I am convinced that your lordships have all those nice sensations which distinguish men of honour from the vulgar, and that your genuine feelings for the defendant must be rather compassion and approbation than resentment; yet I cannot address myself to your lordships, sitting on that bench and clothed in the robes of magistracy, in the same language by which I think I could ensure your favour to my client in another place. It is, indeed, very unfortunate for the gentleman, whose cause I am defending, that your lordships are bound, as judges of the law, to consider that as a crime in him against the society in which he lived, which yet, if he had not committed, that very society would have expelled him, like a wretch, from its communion; and that you must speak to him the words of reproach and reprobation for doing that, which if he had not done, your lordships would scorn to speak to him at all as private men. Surely, my lords, this is a harsh and a singular situation. . . . I profess to think with my worthy friend, who spoke before me, that the practice of private duelling, and all that behaviour which leads to it, is a high offence against the laws of God; and I agree with that great prince (he mentioned Frederick II. of Prussia), that it is likewise destructive of good government amongst men; a practice certainly unknown to the most refined and heroic people which the revolutions of time and manners have produced in the world, and by which the most amiable man in society may be lost by an inglorious death, depending upon mere chance. But though I feel all this, as I think a Christian and a humane man ought to feel it, yet I am not ashamed to acknowledge that I would rather be pilloried by the court in every square in London, than obey the law of England, which I thus profess so highly to respect, in a case, where that custom, which I have reprobated, warned me that the public voice was in the other scale. My lord, every man who hears me, feels that so would he: for without the respect and good opinion of the world we live in, no matter upon what foundation it is built, life itself is a worse imprisonment than any which the laws can inflict; and the closest dungeon, to which a court of justice can send an offender, is far better with the secret pity, and even approbation of those that send him there, than the range of the universe with the contempt and scorn of its inhabitants." After reading voluminous affidavits to his character, Erskine continued—" a man in possession of such a character as this, justly acquired, will not consent to sacrifice it to the pride of any man; it is a just and sacred pledge; and he to whom God in his providence has given it, deserves every sort of reproach, if he parts with it in a light cause. . . . Unquestionably the captain may desire every officer, whose duty it is to walk the quarter deck, to go to the top of the mast of the ship; but he cannot do that without an adequate cause, and without subjecting himself to the disgrace and punishment of a court martial. I have had the honour to sail with a man who is an honour to that profession; a gentleman, I believe, the most accomplished that this nation or world can produce, and who has the honour to be nearly allied to your lordship. Under him I learned what idea ought to be entertained on this subject, and what respect ought to be paid to officers in all stations; and the result of what I saw there, joined with my own original feelings, is this—that, although I was placed on board his ship to reverence him as my father, by the command of my own; and although at this hour I do reverence him in that character; yet I feel that if he had treated me in that manner, I should not have made Jamaica or Bath the limits of my resentments, but would have sought him through all created space, till he had answer made, and done me justice! . . There are some injuries which even Christianity doth not call upon a man to forgive or to forget; because God, the author of Christianity, has not made our natures capable of forgiving or forgetting them. . . . I must plead for the infirmities of human nature, and beseech your lordships once more to consider what the honour of an officer is; consider that, and say what punishment this gentleman deserves. You have before you a young military man, jealous, as he ought to be, of his fame and honour, treated with the grosest indignity by his superior officer, smothering his honest resentment as long as the superior duties of military service required that painful sacrifice; and after pursuing the man, who had dishonoured him, with a perseverance, certainly, in criminal opposition to the law, but in obedience to what I may, without offence even here, term generous infirmity in his nature, nourished by the long established, though erroneous, customs of the world. . . . I rely with confidence upon the justice, the humanity, and the honour, of the court !''

Mr. Law, who appeared as counsel for Admiral Wallace, treated this novel vein of rhetoric, opened with so much intrepidity by the quondam naval officer, in his usual tone of rough displeasure :—" I think I shall be warranted in desiring your lordships to forget, for a little while, the laws of chivalry and the wild maxims of romance, with which the court has been so liberally entertained to day; and to return with me to the good old laws of England, and the wholesome correction they administer to such high-handed violence as this. . . If this quarter-deck order be such an insult, entailing on the person who suffers it such infamy as will warrant him, in the language of my learned friend, to hunt Sir James Wallace through all created space, I am sure my ideas on the subject are much too narrow to enable me to comprehend the soreness and jealousy which belong to the character of a man of honour.'' The officers of the different militia corps in England having signed a written testimonial to the propriety of Lieutenant Bourne's conduct, Mr. Law added, "I would not for the world's wealth have set my hand to that foul paper ; I would not have condemned an officer in matters of discipline and honour without hearing that officer, and knowing that he had no defence. Let these gentlemen feel as they may, their sentiments of honour and mine are widely different, I am not ashamed of my own.'' Mr. Law concluded with a striking antithesis :—" His countrymen cannot be so ungrateful as to forget Sir James Wallace, the enemies of his country have felt his bravery too deeply to do so.'' The glories of this rhetorical field-day were not yet over. Mr. Justice Willes felt sufficiently elated by the occasion to transgress the reserve so becoming to the bench, and deliver a lecture on the code of honour, which, however salutary to the young, must have astonished the grave old lawyers. " Can such a violent blow be justified ? No ! Your counsel did not pretend to do it till some of them, from a meritorious zeal for your service, lost themselves in the wilds of chivalry, and adopted the romantic notions of knight-errants. And now I am come to that fairy ground in which I mean to examine your conduct as a man of honour. If you thought your shaking your cane over Sir James Wallace at the bath not sufficient, as a man whose conduct was to be sanctified by the rules of honour, you might, when you met him in the streets, have flung your glove in his face, or have given him a touch on the arm, with a declaration that you meant to strike him; instead of which you, in a most barbarous and ungentlemanlike manner, struck him in the cruel way I have before described!" The sentence was severe, but only adequate to the offence : that, for the assault, Lieutenant Bourne be imprisoned two years, and find sureties for seven years ; and for the libel, that he pay a fine to the king of fifty pounds.

The eloquent appeal which Erskine made in defence of Lord George Gordon, his third great triumph in little more than a year,—and what advocate but he was ever selected to defend a prisoner for high treason in the second year from his call to the bar?—has commanded, as it deserves, universal admiration. His emphatic oath, after commenting most indignantly on the witnesses for the crown, " By God ! that man is a ruffian, who shall build on such slender foundations evidence of guilt," was a bold and novel figure, forged on the instant, but which drove conviction into all who heard it. This celebrated trial at the bar of the King's Bench, in February 1781, is too well known to require more than a passing notice. Lord George Gordon, having been elected president of the Protestant Association, proceeded at the head of upwards of forty thousand persons to the House of Commons to present their petition for a repeal of some indulgences lately conceded to the Roman Catholics. In this procession originated the fatal riots, and hence the charge of treason against their enthusiastic and misguided, but not malignant, chief. The following passages from Erskine's powerful peroration are selected to mark his independent character, to point attention to the bold defiance which he scrupled not for a moment to hurl at the law officers of the crown.

" I have all along told you that the crown was aware it

had no case of treason, without connecting the noble prisoner with consequences which it was in some luck to find advocates to state, without proof to support it. I can only speak for myself, that small as my chance is (as times go) of ever arriving at that distinction, I would not accept the high office on the terms of being obliged to produce (as evidence of guilt) against a fellow citizen that which I have been witness to this day . . . It is indeed astonishing to me that men can keep the natural colour in their cheeks, when they ask for blood in such a case, even if the prisoner had made no defence. There was not even a walking-stick to be seen amongst the procession which he led. What then has produced this trial for high treason? What! but the inversion of all justice, by judging from consequences instead of from causes and designs! What! but the artful manner in which the crown has endeavoured to blend the petitioners in a body, and the zeal with which an animated disposition conducted it, with the melancholy crimes that followed; crimes which the shameful indolence of our magistrates, which the total extinction of all police and all government suffered to be committed in broad day, in the delirium of drunkenness, by an unarmed banditti, without a head, without plan or object, and without a refuge from the instant gripe of justice: a banditti, with whom the associated Protestants and their president had no manner of connection, and whose cause they overturned, dishonoured and ruined. How unchristian then is it to attempt, without evidence, to infect your imaginations, who are upon your oaths, dispassionately and disinterestedly, to try the offence of assembling a multitude with a petition to repeal a law, which has happened so often in all our memories before, by blending it with all the future catastrophe, on which every man's mind may be supposed to retain some degree of irritation? O fie! O fie! it is taking advantage of all the infirmities of our nature! Do they wish you, while you are listening to the evidence, to connect it with consequences in spite of reason and truth, to hang the millstone of prejudice round his innocent neck to sink him? If there be such men, may God forgive them for the attempt, and inspire you with fortitude and wisdom to do your duty to your fellow citizens with calm, steady, reflecting minds . . . You will then restore my innocent client to liberty, and me to that peace of mind, which, since the protection of that innocence in any part depended upon me, I have never known."

Such language might well startle all who heard it, for similar licence of remark had rarely, if ever, been adventured in that court before. The remarks with which the solicitor-general commenced his reply prove how trenchant was the blade which his assailant wielded, and what a deep wound it had inflicted. "If I was to believe, or if any man could believe, what has been very frequently, very boldly, very hardily asserted, I might be afraid of sharing in that blame and that censure, which, in a manner perfectly new in English courts of judicature, has been cast upon my learned friend as the author of this prosecution, as well as upon the witnesses who have appeared in the cause, and upon all who have had any thing to do with it; and, if the word of a gentleman, who has boldly, adventurously, and licentiously, inveighed against every man who has had any thing to do in the conduct of this cause, is to be taken against evidence, against reason, against law, I should have indeed a very terrible trial to undergo: I must fear very much for my reputation: I must fear the imputation of persecution, of cruelty, of an attempt to support an unjust and groundless persecution by shameful ignominious evidence, for this is the result of frequent assertions made with a boldness perfectly new to me in my short experience in English judicature, but which however makes no impression upon me. Though a learned gentleman at the bar shall tell me ten times a day to my face that I am a ruffian, I shall not think that I deserve it, because he says it; nor will any such abuse frighten me from doing the duty of an English advocate." Neither the matter nor manner of the crown-orator could subdue Erskine, who refused to retract, qualify, or explain away, one word that he had spoken.

The same fearless temperament and commanding genius, which always seized the exact moment for resistance and clothed the best reasons in the most attractive language, wrought a still higher achievement to the cause of constitutional law in the celebrated trial of the Rev. Dr. Shipley, dean of St. Asaph, for publishing a seditious libel. The work was unimportant in itself, a dull and tedious dialogue, written by

Sir William Jones, then a judge in India, between a farmer and a gentleman on the duty of resistance, and on the evils of the representative system. But the principle which his eloquent advocate maintained and at length succeeded in establishing is of vital efficacy, that the fact of publication should not alone be submitted to a jury, but the intent of publication also,—that the jurors and not the presiding judge should decide on the work published, whether libellous or not. To contend for such a privilege for the twelve honest men in the box was deemed a hopeless attempt of legal knight-errantry. Bearcroft, who led for the prosecution, asserted boldly the doctrine of the time: that libel or no libel was a question of law for the court, and that the adverbs and epithets were not for gentlemen of the jury. "At the hazard of any libel that any set of men may choose to throw at my head," continued the conservative lawyer, "I have no difficulty to say that the man, who maintains this proposition: that every man of twenty-one has a right, by this constitution, to choose his representatives in parliament, is either a fool or a knave. If he believes it himself, he is an idiot, if he does not, he is a dishonest man. This country would be worse than a Polish diet if that scheme were to take effect. These ideas would not be so extravagant, perhaps, if the kingdom of England consisted of no more subjects than a district ten times as large, inhabited by a few Indians half civilized. You would do well, perhaps, to have such a nation sit in a ring and give their opinions." Erskine, after a vehement denial of his friend's law, volunteered his own concurrence in the obnoxious pamphlet. "I desire to be considered the fellow criminal of this defendant, if by your verdict he should be found one, by publishing in avowed speaking my hearty approbation of every sentiment contained in this little book." Mr. Justice Buller, in summing up, denounced with all the weight of authority the legal position contended for by the dauntless advocate: "You have been pressed very much by the counsel, and so have I, to give an opinion upon the question, whether this treatise is or is not a libel. It is my happiness to find the law so well settled, and so fully, that it is impossible for any man, who means well, to doubt about it." In the angry discussion which ensued between the

bench and the bar on the finding of the jury "guilty of publishing only," the judge displayed more warmth than discretion, and the advocate, in defying the threat of committal, rendered his profession excellent service, not more by the courage
of the resistance, than by the happy selection of the time and
the exact propriety of his manner. The temerity of his old
master quailed beneath his rebuke, and the menace died
away unheeded. Erskine's argument on the motion for a
new trial on the ground of misdirection, that Judge Buller
had submitted as the only question to the jury the fact of
publication, has been considered the most perfect union of
reasoning and eloquence ever delivered in Westminster Hall,
and was described by Fox as a speech so luminous and so convincing, that it wanted in opposition to it not a man but a
giant. It was addressed to judges, whose minds he knew to
be so firmly prepossessed against him, as to preclude even the
most distant expectation of success, and met with the most
disheartening of all receptions, an indulgent indifference.
" That revered magistrate, Lord Mansfield, treated me," said
Erskine, " not with contempt indeed, for of that his nature
was incapable, but he put me aside with indulgence, as you
do a child, when it is lisping its prattle out of season. Such
a judicial practice, the judges decided on the precise point,
from the revolution down to the present day, was not to be
shaken by arguments of general theory or popular declamation." But it was shaken into fragments by that very discourse, whose argument, so contumeliously treated, is declared
by a subsequent act of parliament to have been the law. This
was " the last key-stone that made the arch" of Erskine's
early fortune. With a just appreciation of his own powers,
he had, in his fourth year, altogether refused to accept
of junior briefs at Nisi Prius, and was sought for with such
avidity that he soon commanded the distinction of a silk
gown. To prevent his seniors from being thrown out of
professional business on the circuit and at Guildhall, he
was presented by Lord Loughborough, at the instance of
Lord Mansfield, with a patent of precedency in 1783, though
he had not yet attained the statutable period of five years,
the sine quâ non of modern legislation. It was arranged

that he should take precedence of Piggot, considerably his senior in standing, and Piggot lost caste with the bar by acceding to this proposal. Mr. Scott, with a more fitting pride, declined to take rank as junior to Erskine who had been called later than himself, and had his claim to precedence allowed in the final distribution of honors. None who saw and heard Erskine were at a loss to account for this rapidity of success. The magic of his eloquence can only be fully appreciated by those who are acquainted with, what has been well termed, its music and its statuary,—the grace of his person, and the perfectness of his elocution. The following admirable tribute has been paid to their power by a first-rate judge of eloquence, Lord Brougham—more eloquent in the senate, and occasionally almost as eloquent at the forum.

"Nor let it be deemed trivial, or beneath the historian's province, to mark that noble figure, every look of whose countenance is expressive, every motion of whose form graceful, an eye that sparkles, and pierces, and almost assures victory, while it speaks audience ere the tongue. Juries have declared that they felt it impossible to remove their looks from him, when he had riveted, and as it were fascinated them by his first glance ; and it used to be a common remark among men, who observed his motions, that they resembled those of a blood horse, as light, as limber, as much betokening strength and speed, as free from all gross superfluity or incumbrance. Then hear his voice of surpassing sweetness, clear, flexible, strong, exquisitely fitted to strains of serious earnestness, deficient in compass indeed, and much less fitted to express indignation, or even scorn, than pathos, but wholly free from harshness or monotony. All these, however, and even his chaste, dignified, and appropriate action, were very small parts of this wonderful advocate's excellence. He had a thorough knowledge of men, of their passions, and their feelings—he knew every avenue to the heart, and could at will make all its chords vibrate to his touch. His fancy, though never playful in public, where he had his whole faculties under the most severe control, was lively and brilliant; when he gave it vent and scope it was eminently sportive, but while representing his client it was wholly subservient to that, in which his whole soul was wrappped up, and to which each faculty of body and of mind was subdued—the success of the cause. His argumentative powers were of the highest order, clear in his statements, close in his applications, unwearied, and never to be diverted in his deductions, with a quick and sure perception of his point, and undeviating in the pursuit of whatever established it; endued with a nice discernment of the relative importance and weight of different arguments, and the faculty of assigning to each its proper place, so as to bring forward the main body of the reasoning in bold relief, and with its full breadth, and not weaken its effects by distracting and disturbing the attention of the audience among lesser particulars. His understanding was eminently legal, though he had never made himself a great lawyer, yet he could deliver a purely legal argument with the most perfect success, and his familiarity with all the ordinary matters of his profession was abundantly sufficient for the purposes of the forum. His memory was accurate, and retentive in an extraordinary degree, nor did he ever during the trial of a cause forget any matter, how trifling soever, that belonged to it. His presence of mind was perfect in action, that is, before the jury, when a line is to be taken in the instant and a question risked to a witness, or a topic chosen with the tribunal, on which the whole fate of the cause may turn. No man made fewer mistakes, none left so few advantages unimproved; before none was it so dangerous for an adversary to slumber and be off his guard, for he was ever broad awake himself, and was as adventurous as he was skilful, and as apt to take advantage of any the least opening, as he was cautious to leave none in his own battle. But to all these qualities he joined that fire, that spirit, that courage, which gave vigour and direction to the whole, and bore down all resistance. No man, with all his address and prudence, ever adventured upon more bold figures, and they were uniformly successful, for his imagination was vigorous enough to sustain any flight; his taste was correct, and even severe, and his execution felicitous in the highest degree."

" His action," says another eye-witness, " was always appropriate, chaste, easy, natural, in accordance with his slender and finely-proportioned figure and just stature. His features regular, prepossessing, as well as harmonious, bespoke him of no vulgar extraction. The tones of his voice, though sharp, were full, destitute of any tinge of Scottish accent, and adequate to every emergency, almost scientifically modulated to the occasion. His movements were rapid, according to the character of his mind, a peculiarity shown in his hand-writing. From their characteristic autographs, it would appear that Dunning's was a pretty neat hand; Lord Eldon's a beautiful clear hand, indicating a clear head; Erskine's professional, but quick, as if from a quick perception."

With those who met him at Westminster or on circuit, (such was the strength of his constitution, that he never absented himself from the courts for a single day during 28 years) the charm of his oratory was effaced by the playful grace of his manners. His gaiety of temper and unruffled urbanity, which clothed as in a court-dress his wit and repartee, made him a favourite with all classes; popular alike with the grave judge, and the mercurial tyro. The rugged Lord Kenyon was strongly opposed to his politics; the colour and complexion of their minds was wholly different; they came often into collision, and their sentiments upon the judicial questions, which so frequently arose in cases of libel and sedition, in a period of bitter intestine division, were as far asunder as the poles. Yet even in those bad-humoured times that venerable lawyer spoke well of Erskine; and if any one could rightly take offence at his tone and manner, which were occasionally indignant even to vehemence, it was the old judge, from whose eyes the tears would sometimes start, after some little bickering had arisen between them. Mr. Adair relates a conversation he had with the Chief Justice concerning Erskine. "I know not what perversity of feeling came across me, nor do I recollect precisely what I objected to that eminent man, but it was a repetition of some of the ill-tempered animadversions of Westminster Hall, that were then current. 'Young man,' said the Chief Justice, 'what you have mentioned is most probably unfounded, but these things, even if they were true, are only spots in the sun!' As for his egotism, which they are so fond of laying to his charge, they would talk of themselves as much as Mr. Erskine does of himself, if they had the same right to do so. His nonsense would set up half-a-dozen of such men as run him down." In his turn, Erskine was grateful and affectionate to Lord Kenyon, although not a little disposed occasionally to circulate epigrams and indulge in pleasantries upon the eccentricities of that honest magistrate, whose dress in particular— a very old pair of black velvet breeches, that had sat at the Rolls and at Nisi Prius for twelve years—was always considered fair game. His co-mates on the Bench formed not unfrequently the subject of his jest, and these little squibs flew about the barristers' benches, and lighted up with laughter the sombre precincts of the King's Bench.

One or two of them deserve to be repeated. Mr. Justice Ashurst was remarkable for a long, lanky visage, not unlike that which Cervantes has sketched as Don Quixote's. Erskine scribbled this ludicrous couplet on a slip of paper :—

> " Judge Ashurst, with his lanthorn jaws,
>   Throws light upon the English Laws."

The other was a Latin distich, more envenomed than his wont, upon Mr. Justice Grose :—

> " Qualis sit Grotius judex, uno accipe versu,
>   Exclamat, dubitat, stridet, balbutit, et—errat."

Erskine would affect to discover a striking likeness between the yellow lion on the royal arms, and the jaundiced complexion of Mr. Justice Grose, and would descant on the advantage of the long vacation, when, on resuming his seat, the judicial resemblance of colour seemed still more complete. With these, and a thousand passing gibes, the idol of the Court delighted the idle barristers, who were never tired of crowding round him. The lawyer of the people was the most unassuming man living, and in the intervals of professional toil the most amusing; without a particle of pride, yet with every apology for being proud, and, though in hourly conflict, free from asperity. Of the manner in which his witticisms were received during play-hours, and of his overflowing good nature, Dr. Dibden gives, from his own experience, the following testimony :—" Cocked hats and ruffles, with satin small-clothes and silk stockings, at this time, constituted the usual evening dress. Erskine, though a good deal shorter than his brethren, somehow always seemed to take the lead both in pace and in discourse, and shouts of laughter would frequently follow his dicta. Among the surrounding promenaders, he and the one-armed Mingay seemed to be the main objects of attraction. Towards evening it was the fashion for the leading counsel to promenade during the summer in the Temple Gardens, and I usually formed `one in the thronging mall of loungers and spectators. I had analyzed Blackstone, and wished to publish it, under a dedication to Mr. Erskine. Having requested the favour of an interview, he received me graciously at breakfast before nine, attired in the smart dress of the times, a dark green coat, scarlet waistcoat, and silk breeches. He left his coffee, stood the whole time looking at the chart I had had cut in copper, and appeared much gratified. On leaving him, a chariot and four drew up to wheel him to some provincial town on a special retainer. He was then coining money as fast as his chariot wheels rolled along."

" Adequately to estimate what Erskine was at this period," says a brother barrister, " we must forget all that the English Bar has produced after him. They will afford no criterion by which he can be appreciated. They are all of inferior clay, the mere sweepings of the Hall, in comparison. Nor is it easy to form any tolerable idea of him, but by having seen him from day to day, from year to year, in the prime and manhood of his intellect, running with graceful facility through the chaos of briefs before him; it is only by that personal experience that it is possible to form any notion of the admirable versatility with which he glided from one cause to another, the irony, the humour, the good nature with which he laughed down the adverse cause, and the vehemence and spirit with which he sustained his own."

" I never saw him grave," is the testimony of Espinasse, " but with a constant flow of animal spirits, he enlivened those who surrounded him with whimsical conceits and jokes on what was passing. I had a full share of his jeux d'esprit, as my place in court was directly at his back." Erskine observed, how much confidence in speaking was acquired from habit and frequent employment : " I don't find it so," said Lamb, " for though I have a good share of business, I don't find my confidence increased ; rather the contrary." Why," replied Erskine, " it is nothing wonderful that a Lamb should grow sheepish." His squibs in verse were full of wit, though sometimes too broad. A witness was put into the box, who travelled to get orders. This description of persons go indiscriminately by the name of riders and travellers, but most affect the latter. " You are, I understand, a rider ? " " A traveller, sir," was the reply. " Pray," said Erskine, " are you addicted to that failing usually imputed to travellers ? " Another of the fraternity having baffled his cross-examination, he suddenly remarked, " You were born and bred in Manchester, I perceive." The witness admitted that it was so. " I knew it," said Erskine carelessly, " from the absurd tie of your neckcloth." The traveller's weak point was touched, for he fancied that his dress had been perfect; and the counsel gained his object—the man's presence of mind was gone. When induced to make a personal observation on a witness, Erskine divested it of asperity by a tone of jest and good humour. In a cause at Guildhall, brought to recover the value of a quantity of whalebone, a witness was called of impenetrable stupidity. There are two descriptions of whale-bone, of different value, the long and the thick. The defence turned on the quality delivered, that an inferior article had been charged at the price of the best. A witness for the defence baffled every attempt at explanation by his dulness. He confounded thick whalebone with long in such a manner that Erskine was forced to give it up : " Why, man, you don't seem to know the difference between what is thick and what is long. Now, I'll tell you the difference. You are a thick-headed fellow, and you are not a long-headed one ! " In a cause at Guildhall, Mingay spoke of one Bolt, a wharfinger on the Thames, who loved litigation and whose name regu-larly appeared as plaintiff or defendant in the cause-paper of the sittings after term, in very harsh terms, for his dishonest and litigious spirit. " Gentlemen," replied Erskine, " the counsel has taken unwarrantable liberties with my client's good name. He is so remarkably of an opposite character, that he goes by the name of Bolt-upright." This was all invention. In this mirthful spirit Erskine loved to play occasionally with the partialities of Lord Kenyon. When any matter of law was started at a trial, the Chief-Justice pricked up his ears, and prepared his note-book to take down the point with great formality. In an action for assault, which was tried before him at Guildhall, the plaintiff, a man of great size and bodily power, kept a public-house of some notoriety, called " The Cock," at Temple Bar. It was a house much frequented by country attornies. A spruce little member of that profession came into the public room one evening, booted and spurred as if just off a journey. He took his seat in a box, but soon became so noisy and troublesome that the other guests wished to have him turned out, and called on the land-lord to do so. The lawyer demurred, and when pressed, assumed an attitude of defence. The landlord, acting under the authority of a habeas corpus of his own issuing, took pos-session of the person of his puny antagonist, by catching the little man up in his arms, and bearing him in triumph towards the door. The publican's embrace, which resembled the friendly hug of a bear, roused all the indignant energies of the lawyer; and being furnished with no weapons of defence except his spurs, he sprawled, kicked and spurred so violently that the knees and shins of the host of the Cock were covered with blood. For this assault the action was brought, and the defendant pleaded that plaintiff had made the first assault on him, by forcibly taking him in his arms and turning him out of doors. Erskine defended him: he described the combat in the most ludicrous terms, and, with assumed gravity, appealed to the jury if instinct had not pointed out to every animal the best means of its defence; that his client had no weapon of any sort to oppose to the violence of the plaintiff, except his spurs, which he had therefore lawfully used for self-defence. The turn which Erskine's manner of treating it gave to the case, caused much laughter in the court, and he was not dis-posed to stop it. To the law cited on the other side, he said he would oppose a decisive authority from a book of long standing, and entitled to the highest credit. Lord Kenyon, expecting that some text book or reporter was going to be cited, took up his pen, and put himself into the attitude for taking down the point. " From what authority, Mr. Erskine?" said the Chief-Justice. " From Gulliver's Travels, my lord," was the reply. The whimsical contrast in appearance of plaintiff and defendant then on the floor, presented the bur-lesque representation of Gulliver dandling in the arms of his Brobdignag friend. No other barrister would have ventured to trifle so far with the gravity of the Chief; but he knew that his anger was sheathed against himself, and that if he did shake the head reproachfully, it was in good humour at the jest. The licensed joker of the court, the petted school-boy of the robing-room, the gay oracle of consultation,—he would follow his whim further than barristers in general feel inclined to pursue it, and would sport with that privileged class, the attornies. He was aware that they could not dispense with his talents of advocacy, and that whether offended with his witticisms or not, the principal anxiety of each on the morrow would be, who should be first with his retainer. " He attached too little consequence," says Espinasse, " to consultations : he relied solely on himself. As they always took place in the evening, and his return from court had not many hours preceded them, he had very rarely read his brief, but reserved it for perusal at an early hour in the morning. He therefore sought to relieve his mind from the fatigues of the day by unbending it in conversation, or diverting it to something which amused him, but which required little thought. I have often observed the disappointment of his clients, who attended his consultations, expecting to hear their cases canvassed with some degree of solemnity and attention, to find that he had not read a line of his brief, but amused himself with talking upon subjects either trifling or wholly unconnected with them. I recollect accompanying a client to a consultation at his house in Serjeants' Inn. We found on the table thirty or forty phial bottles, in each of which was stuck a cutting of geranium of different kinds. Our client was all anxiety for the appearance of Erskine, and full of impatience for the commencement of the consultation, sure that he should hear the merits of his case and the objections to it accurately gone into, and the law of it canvassed and well considered. When Erskine entered the room, what was his disappointment at hearing the first words which he uttered : Erskine—' Do you know how many kinds of geraniums there are ?' ' Not I, truly,' was my reply. ' There are above 100,' he said. He then proceeded with a detail and description of the different sorts, and indulged in a discussion of their relative beauties and merits. This lecture on geraniums evidently disconcerted our client. He listened with patient anxiety till he had finished, hoping then to hear something about his cause, when he heard him conclude : Erskine— ' Now state the case, as I have had no time to read my brief.' With my statement of it the consultation ended. But our client's disappointment of the evening he found amply compensated by Erskine's exertions on the following morning, when he heard every point of his case put with accuracy and enforced by eloquence. To his consultations, in fact, no feature of deliberation belonged. If in the course of them any thought struck him, he did not reserve the communication of it for a more fit occasion, but uttered it as it occurred, though it broke in on the subject under discussion, and was wholly foreign to and unconnected with it. At a consultation, in which I was junior, Christie, the auctioneer, attended to give some information. In the middle of it Erskine exclaimed, ' Christie, I want a house in the neighbourhood of Ramsgate, have you got such a one to dispose of?' ' What kind of a house do you want,' inquired the auctioneer. Erskine described it. ' I have,' said Christie, ' the very thing that will suit you, and what is more, I'll put you into it as Adam was put into Paradise, in a state of perfection.' These playful humours the fortunate lawyer would sometimes carry to an excess, bordering on burlesque. He had a large and favourite dog, called Toss, which he had taught to sit upon a chair with his paws placed before him on the table. In that posture he would put an open book before it, with one paw placed on each side, and one of his bands tied round his neck. This ludicrous exhibition was presented to his clients, who came to attend his consultations. No one would have ventured on such a childish experiment, but one who felt that the indulgence of a trifling whim did not detract from the dignity of his professional character, and with the perfect assurance of a superior mind, that his clients could find no equal to him at the bar, or in fact do without him.

The auctioneering flourishes of this Christie once afforded Erskine a favourable opportunity for winning a verdict by dint of laughter from the jury. He was conducting a case for the plaintiff, in an action to recover the deposit money for an estate, which his client had credulously purchased on Christie's representation of its beauties. In one of those florid descriptions which abounded in all his advertisements, the house was stated as commanding an extensive and beautiful lawn, with a distant prospect of the Needles, and as having amongst its numerous conveniences an excellent billiard-room.

" To show you, gentlemen," said Erskine, " how egregiously my client has been deceived by the defendant's rhetoric, I will tell you what this exquisite and enchanting place actually turned out to be, when my client, who had paid the deposit on the faith of Mr. Christie's advertisement, went down in the fond anticipations of his heart to this earthly paradise. When he got there, nothing was found to correspond to what he had too unwarily expected. There was a house to be sure, and that is all—for it was nodding to its fall, and ' the very rats ' instinctively had quitted it. It stood, it is true, in a commanding situation, for it commanded all the wind and rains of heaven. As for lawn, he could find nothing that deserved the name, unless it was a small yard, in which, with some contrivance, a washerwoman might hang half a dozen shirts. There was, however, a dirty lane that ran close to it ; and perhaps Mr. Christie may contend that it was an error of the press, and therefore, for ' lawn,' we must read ' lane.' But where is the billiard-room? exclaimed the plaintiff, in the agony of disappointment. At last he was conducted to a room in the attic, the ceiling of which was so low that a man could not stand upright in it, and therefore must, per force, put himself into the posture of a billiard player. Seeing this, Mr. Christie, by the magic of his eloquence, converted the place into a ' billiard room.' But the fine view of the Needles, gentlemen ; where was it ? No such thing was to be seen, and my poor client might as well have looked for a needle in a bottle of hay ! "

[*To be continued.*]

ART. V.—PIRACY OF MARKS OR SIGNS OF MERCHANTS AND TRADERS.

It is well known that commercial men have long been in the habit of affixing to their different goods and merchandise certain arbitrary marks or signs, by which they may be distinguished from similar articles belonging to other persons in the same trade. These marks usually consist of fanciful words or devices, sometimes with and often without the name or initials of the owner. The convenience of the plan seems obvious, and cannot be more clearly evinced than by the fact that its general use has led to the establishment, in almost every branch of business, of a sort of conventional or technical language, whereby not merely the species, but the quantity, and degrees of quality, of the goods are ascertained and referred to through the medium of such symbolical distinctions. Some of these vocabularies and characters are so peculiar as to be utterly unintelligible beyond the sphere of their immediate application, and not unfrequently beget a ludicrous association of ideas in uninitiated minds. In very many instances the knowledge and use of them are not confined to the members of the trade, but extend to the great body of the consumers and customers. In all cases the reliance placed upon them is most implicit, and, from the foreign and wholesale commerce of the greatest mercantile houses down to the more humble retail dealer, any violation of good faith in the employment of them cannot but be attended with most prejudicial consequences. Whenever such a violation occurs, it may be very properly regarded in the two-fold light of an invasion of a private right, and a fraud upon the public. It is proposed to consider, how far the right to the exclusive enjoyment of these marks or signs has become judicially recognised, and what are the remedies which exist for its infringement, either at law or in equity. In the first place, we shall take a brief review of the cases at law.

The earliest which we find is in Popham's Reports, page 144, where Mr. Justice Doddridge mentions a case in the 22nd of Elizabeth as follows : " An action was brought upon the case in Common Pleas by a clothier, that whereas he had gained great reputation by the making of his cloth, by reason whereof he had great utterance to his great benefit and profit ; and that he used to set his mark to his cloth, whereby it should be known to be his cloth ; and another clothier perceiving it, used the same mark to his ill made cloth, on purpose to deceive him ; and it was resolved that an action did well lie."

In the case of Sykes v. Sykes, 3 B. & C. 541, the plaintiff had been in the habit of affixing the mark, " Sykes's Patent," to shot belts and powder flasks manufactured by himself, and his articles were well known by that distinction. The plaintiff had then in fact no subsisting patent. The defendant, also named Sykes, made use of the same mark on similar articles manufactured by him, and the plaintiff brought his action, alleging that the defendant sold his articles as and for those of plaintiff, and that defendant's goods were of inferior quality. The jury found a verdict for the plaintiff, and the court refused a new trial. Lord Tenterden said, " It is established most clearly that the defendants marked the goods manufactured by them with the words " Sykes's Patent," in order to denote that they were of the genuine manufacture of the plaintiff, and although they did not themselves sell them as goods of plaintiff's manufacture, yet they sold them to retail dealers, for the express purpose of being resold as goods of the plaintiff's manufacture. I think that is substantially the same thing, and that we ought not to disturb the verdict." The next and last case, at law, upon the subject is Blofield v. Payne, 4 B. & Adol. 410. The declaration stated that the plaintiff was the inventor and manufacturer of a metallic hone for sharpening razors, &c., which hone he was accustomed to wrap up in certain envelopes, containing directions for the use of it, &c., and that the said envelopes were intended, and served to distinguish the plaintiff's hones from those of all other persons ; that the defendants wrongfully, and without his consent, caused a quantity of metallic hones to be made and wrapped in envelopes resembling those of the plaintiff, and containing the same words, thereby denoting that they were of his manufacture, which hones the defendants sold, so wrapped up as aforesaid, as and for the plaintiff's, whereby the plaintiff was prevented from disposing of a great number of his hones, and they were depreciated in value and injured in reputation, those sold by the defendants being greatly inferior. The defendant pleaded the general issue. At the trial, the questions left to the jury were, first, whether the plaintiff was the inventor or manufacturer, and secondly, whether the defendant's hones were of inferior quality, but Lord Denman stated to them that, even if the defendant's hones were not inferior, the plaintiff was entitled to some damages, inasmuch as his right had been invaded by the fraudulent act of the defendants. The jury found for the plaintiff one farthing damages, but stated that they thought the defendant's hones were not inferior to his. A motion for a nonsuit, on the ground of there having been no special damage, was refused : Mr. Justice Littledale said, " The act of the defendants was a fraud against the plaintiff, and if it occasioned him no specific damage, it was still to a certain extent an injury to his right." Mr. Justice Patteson said, " It is clear the verdict ought to stand ; the defendants used the plaintiff's envelope and pretended it was their own ; they had no right to do that, and the plaintiff was entitled to recover some damages in consequence." From these authorities it may be considered as clearly established, that the exclusive enjoyment of a particular sign, mark or label, is the subject of a legal right, and that an action at law may be brought for an invasion of the right, even though no special damage have been sustained thereby.

It generally happens, however, that the injury caused by the piracy of a mark or sign is too complicated and ramified to be easily computed, and it may be wholly irreparable. It is not limited to the immediate pecuniary loss of profits, by the supply of the market *pro hac vice* with the spurious commodity, but it detracts from the goodwill, and often, being resorted to for palming off an inferior article, assails the trading reputation of the rightful owner. Whatever redress can be obtained in a court of law, by way of damages for past *tort*, may be a very inadequate remedy. It is, therefore, in the next place, proposed to inquire what assistance can be afforded by a court of equity. The inadequacy of the legal remedy, under the circumstances just mentioned, appears to bring the case directly under the ordinary equitable jurisdiction by injunction; and we proceed to ascertain whether the authorities bear out this view.

Until the late case of Motley *v.* Downman (post, p. 154), the only reported case directly bearing upon the equitable point was of ancient date, and rather tended to discountenance than support the granting of injunctions to secure the exclusive use of marks or signs : we allude to Blanchard *v.* Hill, 2 Atk. 485, in which a motion was made on behalf of the plaintiff, for an injunction to restrain the defendant from making use of the *Great Mogul* as a stamp on his cards, to the prejudice of the plaintiff, upon the suggestion that the plaintiff had the sole right to this stamp, having appropriated it to himself conformably to the charter granted to the Card Makers' Company by King Charles the First. Lord Hardwicke refused the injunction, mainly on the ground of the invalidity of the charter ; but in the course of his judgment he delivered sundry general dicta upon the subject of marks. " The motion is to restrain the defendant from making cards with the same mark which the plaintiff has appropriated to himself, and in this respect there is no foundation for this court to grant an injunction. Every particular trader has some particular mark or stamp, but I do not know any instance of granting an injunction here to restrain one trader from using the same mark with another ; and I think it would be of mischievous consequence to do it." Alluding to the beforementioned case at law, cited in Popham's Reports, Lord Hardwicke proceeds, " It was not the single act of making use of the mark that was sufficient to maintain the action, but doing it with a fraudulent design to put off bad cloths by this means, or to draw away customers from the other clothier ; and there is no difference between a tradesman putting up the same sign and making use of the same mark with another of the same trade." He then states that if the injunction is to be obtained, it must be on the charter of the crown, and after showing the illegality of the charter, his lordship added, " An objection has been made, that the defendant, in using this mark, prejudices the plaintiff, by taking away his customers; but there is no more weight in this than there would be in one innkeeper setting up the same sign with another."

It is probable that nearly a century ago, when the above case arose, marks or signs did not occupy so prominent and influential a place in mercantile transactions as they do now, because, allowing that a balance of mischievous consequences or hardships is a proper mode of deciding upon such a question, it seems palpable, that the preponderance of evil results must now be greatly on the side of permitting the piracy to be practised with impunity.

The case of Canham v. Jones, 2 V. & B. 218, is sometimes cited as carrying out Lord Hardwicke's opinion; there a bill was filed for an injunction, to restrain the defendant from selling a medicine under the title or sign of " *Velno's* Vegetable Syrup," alleging that the plaintiff was solely entitled to the recipe for preparing the medicine, and that the defendant sold a spurious article under the same name. The defendant put in a general demurrer for want of equity, which was allowed by Sir Thomas Plomer, on the ground that the plaintiff had claimed an exclusive right to the medicine, which he could not maintain, and that the defendant did not in fact represent that he sold the plaintiff's medicine, but merely one of as good a quality, which he was perfectly at liberty to do. It seems scarcely necessary to point out, that the wrong there complained of was not the piracy of the plaintiff's mark, but of the recipe for the medicine; and fraudulent representation being out of the question, this decision is in reality no authority against the equitable interference under consideration. The next case, of which any printed note is extant, is Day v. Day, Eden on Injunctions, 314, where an injunction was granted to restrain a manufacturer of blacking from using labels in imitation of those employed by the plaintiff.

Many injunctions of this description have been granted by the present Vice Chancellor, but none of the cases have appeared in the reports of that Court, although several are well known to counsel, and are often referred to. Among the principal are : 1. a case relating to watches exported to Turkey, having inscribed thereon, as a mark or sign of the plaintiff, a word in foreign characters, signifying " warranted," which was pirated by the defendant ; 2. a case of Ransome v. Benthall, (1st December, 1833,) where the defendant had used on plough-shares the mark " H. H.," which belonged to the plaintiff; an injunction was granted, after opposition, the Vice Chancellor observing, that he had examined the specimens and private marks, and it was evident the defendant had used the plaintiff's marks for the purpose of fraud, and he would therefore grant the injunction to the fullest extent, for the protection of the plaintiff and the public : 3. Hutton v. Forster (24th December, 1833), in which an injunction was granted (also after opposition), to restrain the defendant from using on the wrappers of woollen goods, exported to the Gold Coast of Africa, certain fanciful devices of the plaintiff's, painted in bright and glowing colors, which had been found most effective in attracting the custom of the natives.

In addition to these traditionary authorities there have very recently appeared, in the Equity Reports, three other cases, which, considering the great importance of the subject, and the previously unsatisfactory state of the authentic records of the law thereon, cannot but be of essential service to the profession and the public. The first of these cases is Knott v. Morgan, 2 Keen's Reports, 213. Certain of the proprietors of the London Conveyance Company filed a bill for an injunction against the defendant, stating that their omnibuses were of a novel and superior construction, and that the defendant, with the view of fraudulently depriving the plaintiffs of custom, began to run an omnibus on the same line of road as the plaintiffs, on which was painted " *Conveyance Company,*" and " *London Conveyance Company,*" so as to resemble the same words on the omnibuses of the plaintiffs ; and that certain symbols on the defendant's omnibus were also imitations of the plaintiffs. It appeared that the defendant had made some colorable variation in his inscriptions, and an injunction was granted to restrain the use on the defendant's omnibus of the above words, or any other names, words or devices, in such manner as to form or be a colorable imitation of the names &c. on the omnibuses of the plaintiffs.

The Master of the Rolls observed, " The only question is, whether the defendant fraudulently imitated the title or insignia used by the plaintiffs for the purpose of injuring them in their trade. It is not to be said that the plaintiffs have any exclusive right to *the words,* but they have a right to call upon this Court to restrain the defendant from fraudulently using precisely the same words and devices which they have taken for the purpose of distinguishing their property."

The next case is Motley v. Downman, 3 M. & Cr. 1. The facts were shortly thus.—The mark " *M. C.*" had long been used to distinguish tin manufactured at particular works in Carmarthen. The plaintiff had been a *lessee of those works,* and had used the mark *there.* He subsequently removed to other tin-works, about forty miles distant, and continued to use the mark " M. C." at the latter works during several years, while the Carmarthen works were unoccupied. Afterwards, the defendant took the Carmarthen works, and commenced using the mark on tin manufactured there. The Vice-Chancellor granted an injunction to restrain the defendant from using the mark, but on appeal the Lord Chancellor reversed his Honor's decision, on the ground that the mark, having been once attached to the Carmarthen manufactory, the real question was, whether the plaintiff had acquired a right to prevent the tenants of those works from enjoying it. His Lordship said, if the case had stood upon the use of the mark by the plaintiff, and there had been nothing but the fact of another company, forty miles off, assuming the same mark, the injunction would have been granted, even though the defendants had made an addition to the mark, which was not sufficient to prevent deception. This case was not one of mere piracy, because there the defendant relied on an earlier title, which the plaintiff must supersede before he could establish an exclusive right in himself, and the Lord Chancellor clearly recognized the general right of the lawful owner of a mark to restrain the piracy of it. It is worthy of observation, that in the last case is to be found an element not contained in any of the preceding authorities; viz. that a mark may be attached to a particular manufactory, so as to be enjoyed as appendant or appurtenant thereto, and that non-user for a considerable length of time, during which the manufactory was unoccupied, will not necessarily destroy the right.

Whatever doubts may have formerly prevailed, it may with confidence be said, that the foregoing investigation unequivocally shows that courts of equity will now interfere by injunction to prevent the piracy of marks or signs used in trade. This remedy is no less speedy than it is sufficient:—

a bill is filed, praying for an injunction, and usually asking, at the same time, for an account of the profits made by the piratical use of the mark ; the injunction is granted on motion, either *ex parte* or after notice to the defendant, according to circumstances. If the plaintiff files his bill immediately or without any unnecessary delay after he discovers the piracy, he may obtain his injunction at once ; and it is curious to remark, that the court which has acquired the reputation of being proverbially cumbrous and tardy in its machinery and movements, is on these occasions made one of the most prompt and summary tribunals in the country; a few hours only being necessary for procuring its aid in matters involving interests and property of the greatest importance and value.

The spirit of rivalry now so extensively pervading every branch of trade, and the unfair means often resorted to by the unscrupulous and overreaching, has lately brought this subject into such general discussion as fully to justify these observations, which, it is hoped, have placed the law in a perspicuous light, although they are insufficient completely to exhaust the topic.

ART. VI.—TOWN *v.* COUNTRY—PROVINCIAL COMPLAINTS OF AGENCY.

Observations on the Unprofitable State of Country Equity and Common Law Practice, &c., with Suggestions for Relieving it from Town Agency, &c. &c. London. 1837.

WE are sorry to see that the diminution of law business is producing an effect which almost follows on the deterioration of a trade : the partners are beginning to quarrel amongst themselves. A short time since we had attorneys calling on their fellows to conspire for the purpose of cutting down the fees of the bar ; and here we have a practitioner of long standing and evident respectability summoning his provincial brethren to join with him in sweeping town-agents from the face of the earth, from a firm conviction that, locust-like, they devour the fruit and leaves, and leave little besides the bare dry branches for their principals.

Lord John Russell says somewhere, that a proverb is one man's wit and many men's wisdom. It may be doubted whether the very old and familiar proverb—" A house divided against itself cannot stand,"—comes within the denomination of wit, but we are quite sure that it would be many men's wisdom, if adopted and acted upon by the legal profession ; and Menenius' fable of the belly and the members might also be studied with profit by several of us. The author of this publication, however, has convinced himself that an immediate strike on the part of a peculiar section is advisable, and as he expresses opinions which are much more largely disseminated than could be wished, we think it right to devote a few pages to an examination of them. He begins as follows :

" It is a matter beyond dispute, that the professional receipts of country attorneys very inadequately correspond with the expenses incurred in their education and admission, the responsibility attending their practice, their superior intelligence and activity, or the extensive influence they possess through the latter qualifications. With incomes inferior to those made by the middle class of tradesmen, they are expected, nevertheless, to take a more elevated rank in society, and to live in a style requiring a larger expenditure. A practice yielding 300*l*. per annum is not enjoyed by one-half of the members of the profession ; a business producing the double of that income is not very frequently met with ; whilst the profits of few offices exceed 1000*l*. a-year. I speak, of course, of the sums made by individuals,—a return of two, three, or four thousand a-year from one connexion being generally, if not always, divided amongst many partners.

* * * * * *

" A superficial observer may contend, that the small amount of professional incomes is solely attributable to the existence of too great a number of practitioners ; and that the pursuit of the law, as a means of livelihood is not exempt from the operation of competition, which regulates alike the profits of trades and professions. I have often heard this assertion made by country attorneys, and have lamented the tendency of the opinion to prevent improvement in their condition. The suggestion not unfrequently made for augmenting the stamp-duty on articles of clerkship, or for throwing additional difficulties in the way of admission, has no other support than this notion ; and I conscientiously believe, that the lately-revived examination of clerks is not unfavourably regarded by a considerable portion of the profession, from a conviction that it will in time materially check the further increase of practitioners.

" Without calling in question the tendency of competition to reduce the profits of attorneys engaged in practice in the country, I simply contend that the present narrowness of their incomes is not alone owing to the influence of that principle, but, for the greater part, to the operation of other and more powerful causes. These causes I have for some time made the object of diligent investigation ; and although at first, I confess, they appeared too formidable to be assailed with success, upon a closer examination I found them, in many instances, susceptible of partial or complete abatement. Every portion of country practice has been for years, more or less, in a depressed condition ; but without doubt the most unprofitable branches, for a long time past, have been those of Equity and Common Law. These two legitimate and important sources of profit to the country practitioner under a well-regulated system of judicial administration, are at present nearly choked with artificial and unnecessary obstructions, and, consequently, are of comparatively insignificant value to the profession. If restored to a healthy state, I have little hesitation in maintaining that they would be equal, if not superior, in point of profit, to every other kind of business transacted by the country attorney. I intend to devote the following pages to a consideration of the means of rescuing these two branches of practice from their present mischievous restrictions : at a future season I may direct my observations towards the improvements of the other kinds of professional business pursued in the country."

The first step in the discussion is to establish the facts, and this is done satisfactorily enough : first, by laying before us the average profits of his own business ; secondly, by references to returns, shewing that the majority of country practitioners are worse off than himself. His own accounts shew that his common law business produced 165*l.* profit in 1835 and 173*l.* in 1836 ; from which he deducts 75*l.*, the salary of a clerk employed exclusively in that branch of practice ; but he admits that he lost 76*l.* in 1835 and 88*l.* in 1836 by bad debts ; i. e. by costs which the parties were unable to pay, or which he was loth to demand under the circumstances. The general rate of profit he estimates by multiplying the number of writs issued, trials had, executions sued out, &c. &c. in

1834 (as stated in the Appendix to the First Common Law Report,) by the average amount of taxed costs allowed for each, and dividing the product amongst the attorneys of that year : computing the metropolitan business at a third of the whole, and deducting three-fifths of the gross amount set down to the account of country business for agency. Thus, out of 1,592,284*l.*, the gross amount of taxed costs in 1834, only 424,610*l.* remains for 7075 country practitioners,—about 60*l.* each. Even this small sum is subject to deductions on account of clerks, office expences, interest on capital, &c. ; but on the other hand he forgets that, far from strictly abiding by the taxation, attorneys in most cases very properly demand and frequently receive the difference from their own clients. Still the main conclusion is undeniable, that country practitioners derive small incomes from the common law ; and having made up his mind as to the existence of the evil, the author sat down and indited the following epistle to his agent :

    " My dear Sirs,   " Nov. 2d. 1836.

    " Upon a careful examination of your bills of costs for agency during the last year, I find that you have paid away out of pocket, on account of matters connected with my common law business, 140*l.*, and that your profit from that source was 182*l.*

    " Allow me to state, that on account of the same business, I have (with the remittance mentioned in the accompanying letter) paid away 445*l.*, and have cleared 173*l.* And that from this latter sum is to be deducted the salary of a common law clerk, whose time is entirely devoted to that branch of my practice, and to whom I pay 75*l.* per annum.

    " From the profit of each of us, also, may be deducted, if it be thought necessary to arrive at our respective clear gains, the interest of the money laid out, or capital employed, as well as the ordinary expenses for stationery, &c. From your profit, also, is to be deducted a portion of a clerk's salary ; but only a portion, since you do not keep a clerk for each client's business.

    " But all these deductions will still leave you much greater gainers than myself, from my year's common law practice. This is not peculiar to the past year : it has been so (I think, without exception) ever since I began practice ; and instead, therefore, of being the result of accident, it must be considered as the natural consequences of the existing method of conducting agency.

" The professional connexion between your house and myself has continued twenty-two years, during which period, notwithstanding an almost daily correspondence upon matters of business, I believe neither of us can remember the slightest difference ever having occurred between us. In addition to this, I may also allude to the strong feelings of friendship and attachment which unite ourselves and our families. I mention these matters merely by way of preface to what I am about to propose, in order that you may be satisfied that I treat you with sincerity and candour, and that you may treat me so in return.

" My proposition is, that a more equal division of the profit arising from my common law connexion should be made between us, by dividing such profit rateably, according to the capital we respectively employ, and the time, labour, and attention we respectively contribute to that branch of my business.

" I am aware of very many powerful objections to this arrangement, to be urged on your part; whilst the overwhelming reason on my side, for making the proposal, is, that unless accepted, I do not think I shall cultivate that part of my connexion any longer.

" I am sure you will give me credit for not having written this letter, containing what you may deem an extraordinary proposition, without having pondered long and deeply on the subject.

" I am, dear sirs,

" Yours most faithfully,

" ———— ————."

With characteristic promptitude, we are informed, came the answer :

" ———— ————.

" Dear Sir,   " 5th November, 1836.

" We have duly considered the contents of your letter of the 2nd instant, and we intend to reply to it in the same spirit of frankness with which we are certain it was written. We beg to say, at once, that we decline your proposal.

" In the first place, if we accepted it, it would have the effect of creating a partnership between us,—by making us joint participators in the gains and losses attending a particular business : this, without any other reason, is sufficient to induce us to negative your proposition.

" We are quite sure that you do not entertain any vulgar notion that agency business is attended with any extraordinary degree of profit. We don't know whether it has happened to you, but to many of our clients it has, more than once, to have received letters from professional gentlemen in town, offering to transact agency business for something less than what is generally considered to be the established charges. This fact alone speaks volumes upon the subject of the amount of our gains. There cannot be a doubt for a moment, in the mind of any thinking man, that competition has not only brought down our charges to the lowest remunerating figure, but has also so subdivided old connexions, and distributed agency business, as to reduce the incomes of the members of the profession engaged in carrying it on, to the lowest point consistent with their making a decently respectable appearance in the world.

" We readily acknowledge that your business is a very valuable one to us as agents, not only from the gentlemanly and agreeable manner in which it has always been conducted on your part, but also from the large profit we obtain from it, when compared with the outlay or trouble it puts us to in the course of the year. *But you will allow us to remind you, that agencies are taken one with another; and that where one pays well, like yours, there are three or four that do not.* If we are not in error, we, some time ago, in confidential conversation with you, alluded to the fact of our having no less than four agency accounts (one of them of considerable amount), the balances of which had gone on increasing for so long a period, that, in three of them, we had just opened communications with the parties, intending to take a half of the amounts due; and *that* even at a future time, rather than be kept any longer in a state of uncertainty about them. In the agencies, also, of large convey-ancing connexions in the country, with two or three of which we are favoured, where a great deal of Chancery business takes place, the extravagant sums out of pocket, in fees to counsel and to offices, with the oppressive yearly bills of our clerk in court, diminish the profits to a degree that would not remunerate us, *un-less the deficiency were supplied from the more profitable businesses like yours.*

" Although a great many agency houses, and not those alone with small connexions, have of late undertaken business on terms less favourable to themselves than what, for nearly a century, we believe, have been understood to be established between principals and agents, we are quite averse to such a system. Although we have several agencies, we have not one tainted with any such ar-rangement. Whenever we have begun business with a country client, it has been without a word passing as to the charges; im-pliedly we were to make the regular charges in all matters of busi-ness. If now we were to consent to your proposal, we do not see

how, as men of honour, we could continue our connexion with our
other clients, without informing them of it; nor, having informed
them of it, do we see how we could refuse their desire to enter
into a similar arrangement with us, as the one we had made with
you. This would completely cut up our business.

" As we refuse your particular proposal, so we should also be
disinclined to make any arrangement by which our charges should
be lessened in your favour, although not to the amount you have
required. A trifling reduction of charges amongst all our clients
(and we cannot insist upon it too strongly, that one of them must
not secretly fare better than another,) would materially cripple our
incomes. That, however, we might possibly bear, and it does not
constitute, therefore, the ground of our objection. Our aversion
to any reduction of the kind is, that immediately you cease to remunerate the professional man, according to his deserts, his exertions become paralyzed, and his activity or attention is no longer
to be depended upon. With his interest go his feelings of professional honour. Of this we are firmly convinced. Within the last
fifteen years, agency business has not been conducted in town in the
same way as it was before the galling competition arose, which is
now pulling us all to pieces. We are well persuaded that as these
new and private arrangements creep into the profession, it will
proportionably decline in integrity, capacity, and respectability.

" The melancholy view you present of your common law business grieves us. We hoped that you had done better with your
excellent connexions. *But your case is by no means singular; the
complaints from the country being loud and frequent.* We need not
add that this correspondence must not interrupt the feelings of
friendship that have existed between us so long. We frankly own
to you that we are under heavy obligations to you; to which, however, we trust we have a set-off in the unceasing attention we have
ever paid your business.

" We are yours, truly obliged and very sincerely,
" For myself and my partner,
—— ——.""

There is one clear fallacy in this letter. An agent has no
more right to make his good agencies insure him against the
bad, than a tailor has to charge a customer who pays regularly with a portion of the loss incurred by his own loose
system of giving credit. The remedy in either case is the same
—due caution in the choice of connexions or customers. But
in other respects, the answer seems to have proved so far

convincing that the individual attempt to lower the agent's charges was given up, and the system which renders agency a necessary evil is thenceforward the grand object of attack—

"In arguing that the agents' share of profit is more than it nominally appears, I do not desire to be understood as contending that such share is greater than it ought to be. Quite on the other hand ; I am of opinion that it cannot well be less, so long as the present system, which requires the intervention of agency, remains intact. Men of honour, integrity, and information, and many such, I am happy to know, are to be found amongst that class of the profession in town, must be adequately remunerated for their attention, and the exercise of their skill. Nothing that I can say can add to the cogency of the reasoning upon this point, contained in Messrs. —— and ——'s letter upon the subject. I am quite satisfied that, without the introduction of ignorant, unskilful, or unscrupulous men into the portion of the profession in question, or fraud or negligence into its practice, the present moderate profits of agents cannot be diminished, so long as the actual judicial system lasts.

"If the agents' share of profit cannot be reduced, so as effectually to relieve the country practitioner without producing the mischiefs alluded to, it must not be attempted. This, however, does not prevent the question of relief to the country attorney being raised in another shape ; and we must turn our attention to the possibility, or practicability, of introducing such a change into the administration of judicial affairs, as to render the intervention of agency unnecessary for carrying on common law or equity suits. The London agent is called into existence from the law and equity business of the country at large being transacted, during some of its most important stages, whilst rigid personal and daily attention is required, at a common centre,—the metropolis,—where, of course, country practitioners cannot by possibility be present. So long, therefore, as business is centralized in this manner, the services of agents are required, and of necessity they must absorb a considerable part of the gains. The only mode of putting an end to the employment of agents, and of the draught they necessarily make upon provincial profits, is for the country business to be withdrawn from this common centre, and transacted in the neighbourhood of the country attorney, so that he can give his own personal and constant attention to it in all its stages, instead of retaining an agent, and sacrificing to him a moiety of his profits for that purpose. In other words, the provincial profession wants Local Courts,"

But the annihilation of agency is not the only benefit to be anticipated from the plan. Bad debts are to be avoided, no money out of pocket or preliminary outlay of any sort is to be required, and business is to increase in a ratio which will soon place provincial attorneys on a level with landlords and farmers during the war.

A complete exposure of the visionary nature of such expectations would involve a variety of topics which have been already nearly exhausted in this work, and which there is no pressing occasion to repeat. We will, therefore, simply indicate a few of the unfounded assumptions on which this gentleman, and those who think with him, proceed.

1. He assumes that when the London agents are exterminated, the seven thousand country attorneys will grow richer in the exact ratio of the spoil, as an Indian warrior believes that the strength of a dead enemy is transferred to him with the scalp. But a trifling acquaintance with political economy might suggest, that, if the practice were transferred from the town to the country, the practitioners would accompany it, and the seven thousand be soon augmented to ten. The transplanted practitioner might lie under some disadvantage at starting, but he would not die without a struggle, and if other means failed, it is just possible that a system of underselling might be pursued. At all events, there can be no doubt that the number of country attorneys would increase.

2. He assumes that country attorneys could do what is now done by London agents, with equal cheapness and expedition, in other words, that the principle of division of labour, confessedly beneficial in most other walks of life, is inapplicable to law. The example of the bankers' clearing-house affords an apt and familiar illustration of this fallacy. If a London banker were obliged to send a clerk on a distinct errand with every bill or cheque brought to the banking-house, not only would much valuable time be lost, but he would be obliged to have a great many more clerks on his establishment, and would of course require to be remunerated in some shape or other by his customers. By the simple expedient of a clearing-house, one clerk does in an hour what might otherwise occupy twenty for a day. Now London may

M 2

be regarded, in some sense, as the great legal clearing-house; and the slightest attention to the nature of legal proceedings and the mode of conducting actions, will shew that the community is very greatly benefited by the circumstance.

Both before and after an action is brought to trial, the parties or their attorneys have necessarily frequent occasion to communicate; they have not merely the ordinary pleadings to exchange and the ordinary notices to give, but various incidental matters, commonly termed interlocutory, are constantly occurring, in respect of which meetings and communications must take place. Many of these meetings, too, must take place in the presence of the judge. A party, for instance, makes a false step, and wishes for an opportunity of retrieving it, or requires an enlargement of the time within which it is in strictness incumbent on him to plead or go to trial; in either of these cases due notice would be given to the adversary, and the point would be decided in the presence of both parties by the judge. The number of such interlocutory applications is very large under all systems, but it is generally found to be largest where the fewest steps are specifically marked out,—for the simple reason, that, where precise rules are wanting, the parties have no alternative but to apply for the equitable interposition of the judge. Under any local system, the grievance of these interlocutory applications would be intolerable; for every process, pleading, summons, and notice, to be served or delivered, a distinct journey must be taken by the attorney or his clerk; and in every case of application to a judge, the party applying, (or both parties, if the application be opposed,) must repair to that part of the country in which the judge may be sitting at the time, and wait till he is at leisure to attend to them. All this is avoided by our present system of agency: the moment a country attorney is retained to prosecute a suit, he authorises his agent in town to do all that may be necessary in the course of it; the attorney employed to defend it does the same; and all future communications as to the formal steps preceding and following the actual trial, are almost exclusively confined to the London agents of the two. The London agents have various modes of lightening labour, besides those which the having offices in each other's immediate vicinity supplies : and the good understanding prevailing amongst them is perhaps as beneficial to the suitors as to themselves. For instance, we believe it to be a rule with respectable agency firms, never to take advantage of an omission of mere form, where no real interests are affected by it; and we know that it is by no means uncommon for equitable arrangements of the matter in difference to be proposed and completed by them. But the most prominent advantage of the system is the ease and cheapness of interlocutory applications. The judge is close at hand in a fixed place; under the new arrangements one is always in town, and that one is a member of the metropolitan court, thus insuring a certain degree of uniformity, which is little less important in decisions upon points of practice than in decisions upon contested questions of right. By the abolition of agency, therefore, the expense of law proceedings would be materially increased.

3. He assumes that the parties generally reside in the same district, and is unconsciously legislating for those good old times when a man made his will before setting out from York to London, and the saving clause of *God willing* was attached to an advertisement that the Dispatch coach would make the journey in three weeks. But coaches and rail-roads have effected mighty changes; dealings are no longer confined to neighbours, even amongst agriculturists, generally regarded as the most stationary part of the community, the larger part of whose business is now transacted at the great central markets and fairs : and with regard to the manufacturing and commercial classes, their credits are extended to the remotest quarters of the kingdom by means of correspondents and travellers. A Birmingham or Liverpool tradesman, therefore, would gain nothing, and a London tradesman would lose incalculably by the change.

4. He assumes that under a local system the legal charges would be sufficiently high to make the bringing of actions the occupation of a gentleman ; which strikes us to be the most preposterous assumption of the whole. In his scale of prices, for example, he proposes 2*l.* 2*s.* for the service of the summons ; he may think himself happy if the odd two shillings are allowed. In arguing against any limitation of jurisdiction, he remarks : " If parliament decree a limitation, and

confine the jurisdiction to cases of insignificant **value**, the profession must prepare to submit to Sir Robert Peel's **scale** of remuneration—*ten shillings per cent.*—in two-thirds of the business of the country." Our own opinion is, that if any sort of unlimited local jurisdiction be carried, the profession must prepare to submit to a scale of remuneration, which will be no remuneration at all to any one above the condition of a bum-bailiff; and therefore let them look to it in time.

"The country attorneys (he continues) are better represented in the House of Commons than any body of men in the country; for it is to them that nearly every member owes his seat. In the House of Peers their interest is scarcely less, for obvious reasons. This should be borne in mind. But let them, also, be active out of doors; let them combine; let them follow the course that always leads to success, in struggles with the legislature; let them have their district meetings; let them have their central association of deputies, from all parts of the kingdom, to deliberate upon the common good. Let them animate their organs in Parliament; and, from one end of the kingdom to the other, let them arrange the means of spreading intelligence and information connected with the cause they maintain."—p. 106.

We think they had better remain quiet instead of helping to make sport for the Philistines. They would probably find little difficulty in persuading the public that agency is an unjustifiable extortion; that there is no need of uniformity in the administration of justice; and that the various alleged advantages of a metropolitan system are fanciful. But we doubt whether it would be equally easy to inculcate a belief that the other branches of the profession should be liberally maintained.

H.

DIGEST OF CASES.

COMMON LAW.

[Comprising 7 Adolphus & Ellis, Part 4; 1 Perry & Davison, Parts 2 & 3; 5 Bingham's New Cases, Parts 2 & 3; 6 Scott, Parts 3 & 4; 4 Meeson & Welsby, Part 4; 7 Dowling's Practice Cases, Part 2; and a selection from 8 Car. & Payne, Part 4 :—omittting all cases included in former Digests.]

ACCOUNT.

A plea of plene computavit, in an action of account, against a tenant in common and bailiff, is not satisfied by proof that the defendant rendered an account of the produce of sales of goods belonging to himself and the plaintiff, together with an account of the charges attending the sales; he ought also to render an account of the loss, if any, arising from the sales; or an account showing an agreed balance between him and the plaintiff. (Fitz. N. B. 117, D. note (d)) —*Baxter* v. *Hosier*, 5 Bing. N. C. 288.

AFFIDAVIT.

(*Sworn before the attorney of the party.*) The statement of a party that A. B. is her attorney, is sufficient to support an objection to an affidavit, founded on the rule of H. T. 2 Will. 4, c. 6, on the ground that it was sworn before A. B., although it is not positively sworn on the other side that he was the attorney employed.—*Haddock* v. *Williams*, 7 D. P. C. 327.

AMENDMENT.

An agreement between the defendant and two others of the one part, and the plaintiff of the other, but executed only by the plaintiff and defendant, was described in the declaration as an agreement between the plaintiff and defendant: Held, that this was a variance amendable under the 3 & 4 Will. 4, c. 42, s. 23.—*Boys* v. *Ancell*, 5 Bing. N. C. 390.

APPRENTICE.

The justices at sessions have no power, under the stat. 5 Eliz. c. 4, s. 35, on making an order for the discharge of an apprentice from his apprenticehood, to direct the return of any part of the premium already paid to the master, or the non-payment of any part of it remaining unpaid.

Semble, per Alderson, B., that the statute does not apply to cases where a premium is given with the apprentice, but only to compulsory bindings without premium. (1 Stra. 69.)—*East* v. *Pell*, 4 M. & W. 665.

ARBITRATION.

1. (*Authority of arbitrator over costs.*)　An action at law, and a suit in equity by the defendants in that action, for an injunction, were referred to an arbitrator, the costs of the action and suit *to abide the event of the award.* The arbitrator found, as to some of the issues in the action, for the defendants; and as to so much of the suit as regarded those issues, against the defendants, on the ground that they had a defence at law; as to the other issues he found for the plaintiffs, with 5*l.* damages, but as to so much of the suit as regarded them, he awarded that the plaintiffs should not proceed to recover the damages nor costs: Held, that the arbitrator had not exercised such a discretion over the costs as the reference meant to exclude, but had merely exercised a power over them necessarily resulting from the reference, and without which he could not have properly adjudicated on the suit in equity.— *Reeves* v. *M'Gregor,* 1 P. & D. 372.

2. (*Award, finality and certainty of.*)　Where parties, by mutual bonds, submitted all matters in difference to arbitration; and the award, after reciting the submission, awarded (not stating it to be of and concerning the premises) that a certain sum *was due and owing* from the one party to the other: Held, that the award must be intended to be made on all the matters referred.

It also appeared by affidavit that the claims of one of the parties consisted of items for money due, and also for prospective damage, in consequence of a contract between the parties being put an end to·by the other party; but as it also appeared that both of these claims were investigated by the arbitrator, it was held that the general finding, that a balance was due to one of the parties, was sufficient.

Where, on a reference, one of the parties admits the claim of the other, but seeks to reduce it by a set-off, it is sufficient for the award to state that a certain sum is owing to the one side or the other, without further noticing the set-off.— *In re Brown and Croydon Canal Company,* 1 P. & D. 391.

3. (*Election of umpire by lot.*)　Where an umpire in an arbitration is chosen by lot, the assent of the parties to the umpire chosen does not make the election good, unless they know the manner in which he was chosen, and all the circumstances relating to his election. (3 B. & Ad. 248; 5 B. & Ad. 488; 4 Ad. & E. 945.)—*In re Greenwood,* 1 P. & D. 461.

4. (*Setting aside award on extrinsic facts.*)　An arbitrator, with the view of enabling one of the litigant parties to make an application to the Court, after the publication of his award, stated matters which showed that he had put a mistaken construction on the rule of reference, and had misdecided accordingly. The Court received affidavits of these facts, and set aside the award, although on the face of it there was no objection.—*Jones* v. *Corry,* 5 Bing. N. C. 186; 7 D. P. C. 299.

5. (*Costs.*)　The plaintiff declared, in a special count, for the breach of a contract to accept timber, and in a general count, for goods sold and delivered. The cause was referred to an arbitrator, who awarded that the defendant was liable to pay, and ordered him to pay to the plaintiff 75*l.*; he found also that certain of the timbers shipped by the plaintiff were the property of the plaintiff, and at his disposal: Held, that this sufficiently appeared to be a finding on both counts, and that the Master was therefore right in taxing the costs on all the issues in favour of the plaintiff.—*Rennie* v. *Mills,* 5 Bing. N. C. 249; 7 D. P. C. 295.

6. (*Authority of arbitrator.*) To an action commenced on the 27th of June, the defendant pleaded, by way of set-off, a claim against the plaintiff, which was not payable until the 1st August, although the consideration had been received by the plaintiff before her action was commenced. Under a judge's order, dated July 27th, by consent of both parties, " all matters in difference between the parties, including the claim of the defendant in her set-off in the said action," were referred to arbitration : Held, that the claim made in the set-off was properly entertained by the arbitrator as a matter in difference, although not payable until after the date of the action and the judge's order.—*Petch* v. *Fountain*, 5 Bing. N. C. 442.

7. Where, on a reference of a cause to arbitration, the costs to abide the event, the arbitrator finds in favour of the defendant upon a plea which covers the whole cause of action, it is no objection to the award that on other issues the arbitrator has found for the plaintiff without damages.—*Savage* v. *Ashwin*, 4 M. & W. 530.

8. (*Validity of award made by arbitrators without umpire—Attachment.*) By agreement of reference, a cause was referred to two arbitrators, with power to appoint an umpire, the costs of the cause to abide the event ; and the said parties thereby bound themselves to stand to, obey, and keep the award " of the said two arbitrators and their umpire, so as the award of the said arbitrators and their umpire was made before a certain day." An award was made by the two arbitrators only, and they found two issues for the plaintiff and one for the defendant, and directed that " the costs of the said cause, and of the several issues found therein, shall be paid to the plaintiff, or to the party entitled thereto :" Held, on motion for an attachment, that the validity of the award, being made by the two arbitrators only, was too doubtful to grant an attachment upon it ; and secondly, that it was void as to the adjudication of the costs of the cause.—*Hetherington* v. *Robinson*, 4 M. & W. 608.

And see Costs, 13.

ARREST.

1. (*Discharge from, for irregularity.*) The defendant was arrested at the suit of M. by S., who had a warrant against him from the late sheriff, but none from the present. There was at that time another writ against the defendant in the sheriff's office, at the suit of R. ; the warrant on which, from the present sheriff, was in the hands of N. N. delivered this warrant to S., and the undersheriff altered it, by inserting the name of S., and detained the defendant at the suit of the plaintiff, P. : Held, that the defendant was entitled to be discharged from custody at the suit of the plaintiff. (9 Bing. 566.)—*Pearson* v. *Yewens*, 5 Bing. N. C. 489.

2. (*Discharge from, for irregularity.*) Where a defendant was arrested under an attachment out of the Court of Chancery for non-payment of costs, and a capias utlagatum out of this court, at the suit of the same party who was the plaintiff in the equity suit, was on the same day lodged with the sheriff ; and the arrest under the attachment was afterwards set aside by the Court of Chancery for irregularity : Held, that the defendant was entitled to be discharged as to the capias utlagatum also.— *Hall* v. *Hawkins*, 4 M. & W. 590 ; 7 D. P. C. 200.

3. (*Discharge from, on ground of privilege.*) A party privileged from arrest redeundo was arrested on a writ of capias ad respondendum, and applied for and obtained a judge's order for his discharge in that action, on the ground of his pri-

vilege. At the time of his arrest other writs of ca. sa. against him were in the hands of the sheriff: Held, that the sheriff was justified in detaining him on those writs, notwithstanding notice of the judge's order.—*Watson v. Carroll*, 4 M. & W. 592; 7 D. P. C. 217.

ASSIGNMENT. See LEASE, 2.

ASSUMPSIT.

1. (*Assumpsit or Covenant.*) The defendant, lessee of certain premises, *granted* and assigned them by indenture to the plaintiff; who being distrained upon for rent in arrear to the superior landlord before the assignment, brought assumpsit to recover the money paid under the distress, relying on an express promise by the defendant to repay it: Held, that as covenant would lie on the word *grant*, assumpsit could not be maintained on any implied contract to indemnify the plaintiff, not founded on a new consideration. (Hutton, 34; Cowp. 128; 2 Str. 1027; 2 T. R. 100; 3 B. & Cr. 789.)—*Baker v. Harris*, 1 P. & D. 360.

2. (*Consideration.*) Where a deed of separation between the plaintiff and his wife had been drawn up, but not executed by him: Held, on error, (by Patteson, J., Alderson, B., and Littledale, J.—Lord Denman, C. J., and Lord Abinger, C. B. dissenting), that the petitioner's executing such deed was a legal consideration for a promise by the defendant to pay certain debts and expenses, for which the plaintiff was solely liable.—*Jones v. Waite*, 5 Bing. N. C. 341.

ATTORNEY.

1. (*Re-admission.*) An attorney re-admitted in Queen's Bench, is thereby entitled, under 1 & 2 Vict. c. 45, to practise in the other Courts.—*Exparte Thompson*, 5 Bing. N. C. 380; see also *Exparte Martin*, 7 D. P. C. 334.

2. (*Costs of taxation of bill.*) On an application to compel an attorney to pay the costs of taxation, the Court will not entertain a question as to the mode in which the allocatur has been obtained. Nor will they allow items to be added to the bill which has been taxed.

However small the sum is beyond one-sixth which is taken off on taxation, the attorney is equally liable.—*Swinburn v. Hewitt*, 7 D. P. C. 314.

3. (*Same.*) An attorney is not compellable to pay the costs of taxation, on the ground of more than one-sixth having been taken off his bill, unless there have been either an undertaking by the party to pay the bill, or money brought into Court, with an agreement by the party that it shall be appropriated to that purpose; since otherwise it is not within the stat. 2 Geo. 2, c. 23, s. 23.—*Rogers v. Peterson*, 4 M. & W. 588.

And see VENUE, 3.

BANKRUPTCY.

1. (*When specific appropriation of money is revoked by.*) O. & Co. carried on business as a commission house at Liverpool, and were connected with several houses abroad, in which they were partners, but the foreign partners were not partners in the Liverpool house. H. & J. were in the habit of consigning goods to O. & Co., to be sent abroad to their foreign houses for sale, and the proceeds were remitted to O. & Co. on account of H. & J. H. & J. being indebted to R. & Co., wrote to O. & Co. a letter, authorising them to pay the net proceeds of their shipments, after payment of their own balance, to R. & Co., on which O. & Co.

wrote to R. & Co. stating that they would pay the money accordingly on receiving their guarantee, which R. & Co. thereupon gave. Before the proceeds were
received by O. & Co. H. & J. became bankrupts, and their assignees gave O.
& Co. notice not to pay anything on account of the bankrupts : Held, that the
goods being afterwards received and sold by O. & Co., the proceeds were not recoverable by the assignees ; for that the letter of H. & J. contained a specific
appropriation, or an equitable assignment to R. & Co., which was not revocable
by the bankrupts or their assignees. (5 Ad. & E. 107 ; 10 B. & Cr. 44 ; 3 B.
& Cr. 842 ; 8 B. & C. 448.)—*Hutchinson* v. *Heyworth,* 1 P. & D. 266.

2. (*What passes to the assignees.*) The retiring pension of a military officer in the
East India Company's service, does not pass to his assignees on his bankruptcy ;
for if no bankruptcy had intervened, he could not himself have sued the Company for arrears of his pension.—*Gibson* v. *East India Company,* 5 Bing. N. C.
261.

3. (*Right of assignees to enforce contract of bankrupt.*) In an action by the plaintiffs as assignees of O., a bankrupt, against the defendant, for the non-performance of a contract to deliver railway shares, the issue raised was, whether O.,
and the plaintiffs as his assignees, had been always ready and willing to perform
it : Held, that the bankruptcy and insolvency of O., and the insufficiency of his
assets, were circumstances from which the jury might properly infer that he and
his assignees had not been ready and willing.

The contract was to be performed on the 1st July, 1835 ; and another issue
was, whether the plaintiffs had abandoned it : Held, that they were bound to
make their election within a reasonable time, and that not having taken any decisive step until January, 1838, the jury might fairly infer that they had abandoned the contract.—*Lawrence* v. *Knowles,* 5 Bing. N. C. 399.

4. (*Set off against assignees.*) To a count for money had and received to the use of
assignees of a bankrupt, the defendant pleaded that although the money mentioned remained and was in the possession of the defendant after the bankruptcy,
yet that it was in fact received before the issuing of the fiat, and from thence remained in the defendant's possession ; that before and at the time of the issuing of
the fiat, the bankrupt was indebted to the defendant in a larger sum ; and that at
the time he so gave credit to the bankrupt, he had no notice of any act of bankruptcy : Held, that this was not a good ground for a set-off (which the plea
concluded with), and that it was therefore bad. (6 M. & Sel. 295 ; 2 Bing. N.
C. 138.)—*Wood* v. *Smith,* 4 M. & W. 522 ; 7 D. P. C. 214.

And see PLEADING, 4 ; WITNESS, 7.

BILLS AND NOTES.

1. (*Re-issuableness of.*—*Stamp.*) Where a note, payable on demand, has been indorsed for the accommodation of the maker, in order to be deposited with his creditor, to secure the debt due, if the maker pays the debt, and the bill is thereupon re-delivered to him, it is no longer negotiable, and therefore under the
stamp act, 55 Geo. 3, c. 184, s. 19, cannot be re-issued.—*Bertram* v. *Caddy,* 1
P. & D. 207.

2. (*Pleadings.*) In trover for a bill of exchange, the defendant pleaded, that the
plaintiff indorsed the bill in blank ; that R. became the holder ; and that the
defendant, believing that R. had authority to dispose of the bill, took it of him
as a pledge to secure the payment of a debt : Replication, that at the time of

taking the bill from R. the defendant knew he had not authority to pledge it: Held sufficient.—*Hilton* v. *Swan*, 5 Bing. N. C. 413.

And see EVIDENCE, 5; PLEADING, 16; STAMP, 2; USURY.

BURGLARY.

If a person commit a felony in a house, and break out of it in the night-time, this is burglary, although he were lawfully in the house as a lodger.—*Reg.* v. *Wheeldon*, 8 C. & P. 747.

BYE-LAW.

Where the master, wardens, and assistants of a corporation, were authorised by their charter to make bye-laws, with penalties to the use of the corporation, a bye-law imposing a fine on any one of the livery refusing to take upon himself a certain office, and reserving the penalty to the master and wardens only *for the time being*, for the use of the corporation, is valid. But where debt for the penalty was brought by parties who were the master and wardens at the time when the fine was incurred, but who had ceased to be so at the time of action brought: Held, on demurrer, that a plea that the plaintiffs were not master, &c., was an answer to the action, for non constat, but that they were strangers to the corporation at time of action brought.

Semble, also, that the corporation at large could not have maintained the action on this bye-law, nor the master and wardens at the time of action brought, for the right of action did not pass to them by succession.—*Graves* v. *Colby*, 1 P. & D. 235.

And see MUNICIPAL CORPORATION ACT.

CERTIORARI.

A prosecutor is not bound, by 5 Geo. 2, c. 19, s. 2, to enter into recognizances, in order to obtain a certiorari to remove an order of sessions for quashing a conviction. The statutable regulations for suing out a certiorari apply to defendants only. (6 N. & M. 28.)—*Exparte Spencer*, 1 P. & D. 358.

COGNOVIT.

(*Entering up judgment on.*) By a cognovit, it was declared that judgment should not be entered up until default made in payment of an instalment of the debt, with costs to be taxed by the master, as between attorney and client: Held, that on default in payment of an instalment, the plaintiff was entitled to sign judgment, although he had not taxed costs. (3 M. & W. 54.)—*Barrett* v. *Partington*, 5 Bing. N. C. 487.

COMMON. See POOR-RATE, 3.

COSTS.

1. (*Setting off.*) Where a lessor in ejectment obtained a verdict in 1834, and taxed his costs, and sued out a writ of possession, which in 1837 was set aside for irregularity, with costs: Held, that as he had not revived the judgment by *sci. fa.*, he could not set off his costs on the judgment against the defendant's costs on setting aside the writ of possession. (Tidd, Pr. 1103.)

Semble, the defendant's costs on setting aside the writ, though after final judgment, are interlocutory costs within the rule of H. T. 2 Will. 4, c. 93.—*Doe d. Stevens* v. *Lord*, 1 P. & D. 388.

2. (*On plea puis darrein continuance.*) The defendant cannot, after pleading bankruptcy puis darrein continuance, force the plaintiff to reply, and the latter may

discontinue without payment of costs. (1 M. & P. 138 ; 4 B. & Cr. 117 ; 2 Smith, 659 ; 5 B. & Ad. 925 ; 2 M. & W. 617.)—*Woller* v. *Smith*, 1 P. & D. 374.

3. (*Of attachment.*) An attachment for non-performance of an award was ordered to remain suspended, to await the result of an inquiry before the master, but was to be discharged on payment of the costs of the attachment, if the defendant performed certain conditions within a certain time. The defendant having failed in doing so, the attachment issued, and the defendant then complied with the conditions : Held, that the costs of the inquiry were to be considered as part of the costs of the attachment.—*Tyler* v. *Campbell*, 5 Bing. N. C. 193.

4. (*Taxation on higher scale—Certificate for.*) Where a cause was referred by order of nisi prius, with power to the arbitrator to certify whether the cause was a proper one to be tried before a judge of assize, and he certified that it was, but the judge died before the arbitrator's certificate was made known to him : Held, that the Court had no power to make the order for full costs. (3 D. & P. C. 339.)—*Astley* v. *Joy*, 1 P. & D. 460.

5. (*Certificate under 43 Eliz. c. 6, revocation of.*) Quære, whether a judge has authority to revoke a certificate granted by him to deprive the plaintiff of his costs ; but at all events he cannot revoke it after the lapse of a reasonable time ; and it was held that he could not do so after fourteen months.—*Whalley* v. *Williamson*, 5 Bing. N. C. 200 ; 7 D. P. C. 253.

6. (*Discretion of master over.*) In an action for 1000*l.*, on an I. O. U., the master having disallowed the costs of a second counsel's brief, and of the attendance at the trial in London of the attorney who had conducted the cause in the country, the Court, on an affidavit showing that the circumstances of the case justified the employment of two counsel, and the attendance of the attorney, directed a review of the taxation.—*Madison* v. *Bacon*, 5 Bing. N. C. 246.

7. (*Set-off.*) The plaintiff signed judgment and taxed his costs on the 16th July, 1838. At that time certain costs were due to the defendant on a rule of the plaintiff's which had been discharged. The defendant, to avoid execution, paid the debt and costs in the action, at the same time insisting that he was entitled to set off the costs of the rule, but not making any formal demand of them. The Court afterwards, on motion, directed that the plaintiff should pay those costs.—*Abernethy* v. *Paton*, 5 Bing. N. C. 276.

8. (*Of interlocutory rules.*) The sheriff, having paid into Court a sum paid to him by a defendant upon his arrest on a bill of exchange, the plaintiff obtained and made absolute a rule to take it out of Court ; but did not enter an appearance for the defendant. A rule of the defendant's for allowing the money so paid into Court to be deemed equivalent to bail, was discharged. In neither of these rules was there any mention of costs. A year afterwards the defendant obtained a rule for the plaintiff to deliver up the bill of exchange on payment of costs : Held, that the plaintiff was entitled to the costs of this latter rule, but not of the two former.—*Hannah* v. *Willis*, 5 Bing. N. C. 385.

9. (*In trespass.*) Trespass for an assault. Pleas, not guilty and son assault demesne. The defendant having a verdict on the latter plea, and the plaintiff on the former, the defendant is not entitled to the costs of the issue on the former.—*Mullins* v. *Scott*, 5 Bing. N. C. 423.

10. (*Security for.*) In trespass against magistrates for turning the plaintiff out of a cottage, at the instance of parish officers, who claimed the premises as part of

the poor house, the Court refused to call upon the plaintiff to give security for costs, on the ground that the action had been instigated and encouraged by a third person, who had petitioned the House of Lords on the subject, and had expressed his determination to see the plaintiff re-instated.—*Hearsey* v. *Pechell,* 5 Bing. N. C. 466.

11. (*Of Magistrates.*) Where a magistrate obtains a verdict in an action against him for an act done in his judicial capacity, he must obtain the certificate of the judge who tried the cause, as a condition precedent to his demand of double costs, under the 7 Jac. 1, c. 5. (2 Vent. 45; Dougl. 307; 7 T. R. 448.)—*Penny* v. *Slade,* 5 Bing. N. C. 469.

12. (*In error.*) The costs of settling a bill of exceptions are costs in the Court of Error.—*Doe* d. *Harvey* v. *Francis,* 7 D. P. C. 193.

13. (*Of first trial.*) Where a cause is referred at nisi prius, and the award being set aside, a second trial is had, the party succeeding on the second trial is not entitled to the costs of the first. (1 Price, 310; 5 Burr. 2693; 1 C. & J. 354.) —*Wood* v. *Duncan,* 7 D. P. C. 344.

14. (*Double costs, how to be calculated.*) In an action against a public company for injury to the plaintiff's watercourse, the declaration contained several special counts, charging various wrongful acts. The defendants pleaded not guilty to the whole declaration, and also several special pleas. A verdict was found for the defendants on the general issue, and for the plaintiff on the other pleas. The act incorporating the company contained a clause giving them treble costs in the event of a verdict for them in an action for anything done in pursuance of the act: Held, that they were only entitled to treble costs on the issues raised on those counts which were within the protection of the statutes.

The proper mode of taxing treble costs for a defendant is, first, to calculate the defendant's costs, then treble them, and from that amount deduct the plaintiff's costs.—*Wilson* v. *River Dun Company,* 7 D. P. C. 369.

15. (*In trespass.*) To trespass quare clausum fregit, and carrying away divers large quantities of straw, the defendant pleaded, first, not guilty; secondly, that the straw was not the property of the plaintiff; thirdly, a justification to the whole cause of action: to which last plea the plaintiff demurred, but judgment was given on the demurrer for the defendant. At the trial the jury found a verdict for the plaintiff on the first issue, with 1s. damages, and for the defendant on the second, and the judge did not certify under the 22 & 23 Car. 2, c. 139: Held, that the plaintiff was entitled to no more costs than damages.—*Patrick* v. *Colerick,* 4 M. & W. 527; 7 D. P. C. 201.

16. (*Of pauper.*) When a plaintiff, suing in formâ pauperis, succeeds upon one of several issues, the defendant is not entitled to any set off in respect of the costs of other issues found for him.

Semble, that the admission of a party to sue in formâ pauperis, after the commencement of the suit, is improper, such admission being in contravention of the statute 23 Hen. 8, c. 15, s. 2.—*Foss* v. *Racine,* 4 M. & W. 610; 7 D. P. C. 203.

And see ARBITRATION, 5; COURTS OF REQUESTS; ELECTION PETITION; PRACTICE, 11.

COURTS OF REQUESTS.

The plaintiff sued in the Court of C. P. a defendant residing within the jurisdiction of the Blackheath Court of Requests, for 2*l.* 15*s.*, but recovered only

1*l.* 2*s.* 6*d.* : Held, that the defendant was entitled to his costs, under the Black-heath Court of Requests Act, 6 & 7 Will. 4, c. 120, for that the sum recovered was to be deemed the sum *sought to be* recovered, within the meaning of the 1 & 2 Vict. c. 89, s. 2.—*Cross* v. *Collins,* 5 Bing. N. C. 194.

COVENANT.

(*For quiet enjoyment, by what words implied.—How restrained.*) The word *demise,* in a lease, implies a covenant for title, and a covenant for quiet enjoyment ; but both branches of such implied covenant are restrained by an express covenant for quiet enjoyment. (4 Rep. 80, b ; 4 Taunt. 329.)—*Line* v. *Stephenson,* (in error,) 5 Bing. N. C. 183.

And see ASSUMPSIT, 1.

CUSTOM.

A custom for *all* victuallers to erect booths on a common, being parcel of the waste of a manor (selected by the lord for holding fairs yearly, every fortnight), and to place posts and tables there a reasonable time before the Monday next after the Feast of Pentecost, and to continue them so erected until the Feast of All Souls, each paying therefore to the lord a compensation of 2*d.,* is good.—*Smith* v. *Tyson,* 1 P. & D. 307.

DEBT. See MUNICIPAL CORPORATION ACT.

DESCENT.

(*Precedency of heir exparte paternd.*) The heir on the part of the great grandfather has a prior claim to the heir on the part of the maternal grandfather.—*Davies* v. *Lowndes,* 5 Bing. N. C. 161.

DEVISE.

1. (*Operation of word " estate."*) A testator, seised of an estate pur autre vie to himself and his heirs, by his will, after bequeathing several legacies to his children (omitting his eldest son), devised as follows :—" Also, I give and devise unto my wife all my money, securities for money, goods, chattels, and *estate,* and effects, of what nature or kind soever, and wheresoever the same may be at my death." Held, that the word *estate* conveyed all the testator's interest in his real property, although the lease creating the estate pur autre vie contained a provision against assignment without the license in writing of the lessor, and therefore the effect of a devise of it might be to work a forfeiture. (2 T. R. 659, n. ; 1 Cox. 362 ; 14 East, 370 ; 5 Madd. 38.)—*Doe d. Evans* v. *Evans,* 1 P. & D. 472.

2. (*Vesting of remainder.*) Devise to A. H. for life, remainder to R. H. for life, and to his sons in tail ; and for default of issue, to A. D. H. for life, remainder to his sons in tail ; and for default of issue, to " such person bearing the name of H. as shall be the male relation nearest in blood to the said R. H., and his heirs for ever :" Held, that the ultimate remainder vested in interest on the death of the testator.—*Stert* v. *Platel,* 5 Bing. N. C. 434.

3. (*Construction of inconsistent devises.*) A testator devised his two houses and gardens to his wife during her widowhood ; and after the determination of that estate, to the use of all and every of his child or children by his said wife, equally to be divided between them, share and share alike, and the lawful issue of their or her or his bodies or body ; and for default of such issue, to the use of his nephew in fee. By a subsequent clause, he devised and bequeathed to his daughter F. the sum of 300*l.,* to be paid when she attained twenty-one, and the house wherein

she then lived [one of those before devised], after her mother's decease or marriage, and to his daughter R. the sum of 300*l.*, to be paid when she attained twenty-one, and the house in the occupation of D. [the other of those before devised], after her mother's decease or marriage ; and in case of either of his daughters dying without lawful issue before the said sum or sums were paid, then the share or shares of her or them so dying to be divided amongst the survivors or survivor of them.

The testator had no other property but the two houses, and no children except the two daughters, who both survived him and his wife. F. married, had a child which died, and died, leaving her husband and also her sister F. surviving her : Held, that on the construction of the whole will, an estate for life was given (subject to the devise to the widow) to each daughter in severalty in one house, with remainder in both to the testator's children as tenants in common in tail ; and therefore that R. was entitled, on F.'s death, to recover a moiety of the house devised to F.

Semble, that F.'s husband was entitled to the other moiety thereof as tenant by the curtesy, F.'s estate for life therein having merged in her estate tail.—*Doe* d. *Amlot* v. *Davies*, 4 M. & W. 599.

EASEMENT.

A parol license from A. to B. to enjoy an easement over A.'s land, is countermandable at any time whilst it remains executory ; and if A. conveys the land to another, the license is determined at once, without notice to B. of the transfer, and B. is liable in trespass if he afterwards enters upon the land.—*Wallis* v. *Harrison*, 4 M. & W. 538.

EAST INDIA COMPANY. See BANKRUPTCY, 2.

EJECTMENT.

1. (*Adverse possession—Competency of witness.*) The owner of a cottage divided into two parts, in 1808 put in two servants, H. and W., to occupy it, who occupied each part severally till his death in 1814, without paying any rent. They continued to occupy undisturbed after his death, until 1821, when H. died, having by his will devised his moiety to W. H., some time before his death, took in L. to live with him as a servant, and after H.'s death L. continued in possession : Held, on ejectment brought by W., that by proving L. to have come in under H., he had shown a primâ facie title.

The defendant in the above ejectment, who defended under the landlord's rule, proposed to call L. as a witness, on the ground that he was not the tenant in possession, but a mere servant : Held, that H. was incompetent, the defendant having by the rule admitted him to be tenant in possession. (5 Taunt. 183 ; 6 Bing. 394.)—*Doe* d. *Willis* v. *Birchmore*, 1 P. & D. 448.

2. (*Service.*) In ejectment against the Southampton Railway Company, service pursuant to the 4 & 5 Will. 4, c. lxxxviii. s. 204, held sufficient.—*Doe* d. *Martyns* v. *Roe*, 6 Scott, 610.

3. (*Same.*) Service on the sexton, who held the keys of a dissenting chapel, held sufficient.—*Doe* d. *Scott* v. *Roe*, 6 Scott, 732 ; *Doe* d. *Dickens* v. *Roe*, ib. 754.

4. (*Staying proceedings till payment of costs of ejectment.*) Where an unsuccessful defendant in ejectment brings an action against the lessor of the plaintiff for seizing goods on the land in question, and is nonsuited, but obtains a rule for a new trial, the Court will not stay proceedings on that rule until payment of the costs of the ejectment.—*Carnaby* v. *Welby*, 7 D. P. C. 315.

5. (*Service.*) Where it did not sufficiently appear that there are no tenants in possession of premises held under a lease, and although service had been effected on a servant at the house of the lessee, not part of the premises in dispute, and a copy stuck on the premises in dispute, the Court will not grant judgment against the casual ejector.—*Doe* d. *Burrows* v. *Roe*, 7 D. P. C. 326.

ELECTION PETITION.

(*Costs.*) The certificate of the speaker of the House of Commons, under the 9 Geo. 4, c. 22, is a primâ facie case for the party who appears on the face of it to be entitled to costs, and the onus is on the defendant to show that the plaintiff is not so entitled ; and the certificate is conclusive as to the amount of costs mentioned in it.

- The action on the certificate may be brought against any one of several persons named in it as liable. (2 Tyr. 616.)—*Fector* v. *Beacon*, 5 Bing. N. C. 302; 7 D. P. C. 265.

EMBEZZLEMENT.

A., one of several proprietors of a coach, horsed it from Hereford to Worcester, and employed B. to drive it when he did not himself drive it ; B. having all the gratuities whichever drove. It was B.'s duty, each day when he drove, to tell the bookkeeper at Malvern how much money he had taken ; the bookkeeper thereupon entering that sum in a book and on the way-bill, together with what he had himself taken, and then paying over the latter to B., who was to give both sums to A. B. gave true accounts to the bookkeeper, who made true entries ; but B. accounted for smaller sums to A., saying those were all. All the proprietors were interested in the money, but A. was the party to receive it, and was accountable to his co-proprietors : Held, that this was embezzlement, and that B. was rightly described in the indictment as the servant of A., and the money was properly laid as the money of A.—*Reg.* v. *White*, 8 C. & P. 742.

ESCAPE.

To an action of escape against the marshal, a plea that the prisoner escaped without the defendant's knowledge to places unknown to the defendant, and voluntarily, and without the knowledge of the defendant, returned into his custody, is insufficient : the plea ought to aver that the defendant had no knowledge where the prisoner was at any time during his absence. (2 T. R. 126 ; 1 Bos. & P. 413.)—*Davis* v. *Chapman*, 5 Bing. N. C. 453.

EVIDENCE.

1. (*Seal of Court.*) The seal of the Insolvent Debtors' Court proves itself.—*Doe* d. *Duncan* v. *Edwards*, 1 P. & D. 408.

2. (*Receipt given by one partner.*) In an action by a partnership firm for a debt, evidence is admissible to show that a receipt given for the debt by one of the plaintiffs was fraudulently given without the knowledge of the others. (1 Campb. 392.)—*Farrar* v. *Hutchinson*, 1 P. & D. 437.

3. (*Pedigree.*) A pedigree purporting to have been compiled from monumental inscriptions, family records, and history, is not admissible in evidence.—*Davies* v. *Lowndes*, 5 Bing. N. C. 161.

4. (*Best evidence—Admission by debtor in action against surety.*) Where the defendant, as surety for N., had received and promised to pay an account which he was informed had been agreed to by N. ; and on the trial of an action brought against him by the plaintiff, the employer of N., the defendant, refused to produce such

account: Held, that without calling N., the plaintiff might prove by the witness who produced a duplicate, that that was the account which N. had gone over, and that he had said it was correct.—*Ward* v. *Suffield*, 5 Bing. N. C. 381.

5. (*To vary written instrument.*) A bill of exchange was expressed in figures to be drawn for 245*l.*; in words for two hundred pounds, value received; with a stamp applicable to the higher amount : Held, that evidence to show that the words " and forty-five" had been omitted by mistake, was not admissible. (Marius, 32 ; Beawes, 441 ; 2 East, Pl. Cr. 951.)—*Saunderson* v. *Piper*, 5 Bing. N. C. 425.

EVIDENCE IN CRIMINAL CASES.

1. In a case of felony, in order to prove that a prisoner did *not* state a particular fact before the magistrate, his examination must be put in and read.—*Reg.* v. *Taylor*, 8 C. & P. 726.

2. (*Confession.*) It is the opinion of the judges that any confession is receivable, unless there has been some inducement or threat held out by some person in authority. If a person not in any office or authority hold out to an accused party an inducement to confess, this will not exclude a confession made to that person : but if a person in authority over the prisoner was present at the time of such confession, and expressed no dissent, it is not receivable.—*Reg.* v. *Taylor*, 8 C. & P. 733.

FINE.

1. Where L., a devisee of S., taking if no heir to S. should be found, and on condition that he changed his name to S., took possession of the property, claiming it as his own, twelve years after the testator's death, and adopted the name of S., and levied a fine with proclamations in the name of S. : Held, that such fine was a bar to a writ of right brought by an alleged heir of S., and need not be specially pleaded.—*Davies* v. *Lowndes*, 5 Bing. N. C. 161.

2. (*Amendment of Welsh fine.*) The Court amended a fine levied at the Cardigan great sessions of 1830, by indorsing the proclamations, it appearing to have been the practice in that Court to proclaim all fines, and that two proclamations (the first and last) were actually made of the fine in question, though not indorsed. (4 Bing. N. C. 633.)—*Evans* v. *Davies*, 5 Bing. N. C. 229 ; 7 D. P. C. 259.

FIXTURES.

(*Trover for.*) The first count of a declaration in trover stated that T., before his insolvency, was possessed of certain goods, chattels, and *fixtures*, to wit, &c. (enumerating, amongst many chattels, cupboards, grates, &c.,) and that he casually lost the same out of his possession, and the same came to the possession of two of the defendants by finding, and that *the said* defendants converted, &c. The second count was on a conversion by *the said defendants* of goods, chattels, and *fixtures*, after the insolvency : Held, first, that the words " said defendants" must be taken after verdict to mean all the defendants. Secondly, that the term *fixtures* did not necessarily mean things actually annexed to the freehold; and that as it might have a sense which would support the declaration, the Court was bound, after verdict, so to construe it. (2 C. M. & R. 78.)—*Sheen* v. *Rickie*, 7 D. P. C. 337.

FOREIGN JUDGMENT.

To a declaration in trover, the defendant pleaded that he, the defendant, being within the jurisdiction of the Admiralty Court of Sierra Leone, the plaintiff recovered a judgment against him in that Court for the same cause of action : Held bad. (2 H. Bl. 411 ; 11 East, 124.)—*Smith* v. *Nicolls*, 5 Bing. N. C. 208 ; 7 D. P. C. 283.

FORGERY. See SESSIONS.

FREIGHT.
The freighter of goods on which freight was to be paid on delivery at the port of destination, is bound to pay the whole freight originally contracted for, where transshipment has been found necessary, and the goods have been delivered at the port of destination, although the master of the ship consigned the goods under fresh bills of lading in the second vessel to his own agent, and the freight was at a much lower rate than that originally contracted for. *Semble*, also, that if the freight in the second vessel exceeded that contracted for by the original bill of lading, the freighter would be liable for the additional freight also. (Abb. Shipp. 240.)—*Shipton* v. *Thornton*, 1 P. & D. 216.
And see INSURANCE.

GAMEKEEPER.
(*Notice of action to.*) A gamekeeper acting under a deputation granted and registered before the stat. 1 & 2 W. 4, c. 32, is not entitled to notice of action under the 47th section of that act. (4 Bing. N. C. 41.)—*Lidster* v. *Borrow*, 1 P. & D. 447.

GRAND JUNCTION RAILWAY COMPANY.
(*Liability of, as carriers.—Notice of action to.*) The declaration stated, that the defendants were the *owners and proprietors of* a certain railway, and of certain engines and carriages for the conveyance of passengers, cattle, goods, &c. : that the plaintiff caused to be delivered to the defendants certain horses, *to be safely and securely carried and conveyed* by the said railway from Liverpool to Birmingham, and there to be delivered to the plaintiff. Breach, that the defendants took so little care about carrying and conveying the horses, that the carriages containing them were thrown off the railway and down an embankment, and one of the horses was killed, and the others injured.

The company was incorporated by act of parliament, for the purpose of making a railway, and the act contained a clause enabling them to carry on the railway passengers, cattle, goods, &c. on their own account, if they should think fit. There was also a clause requiring fourteen days' notice of action for anything *done or omitted to be done* in pursuance of the act.

It appeared that the horses in question were delivered to the defendants to be carried on the railway from L. to B. : that while the train was proceeding at its usual rate, it was thrown off the rails in consequence of coming in contact with a horse which had strayed from an adjoining field, and lain down on the railway : the fence which separated the field from the railroad had been removed by some labourers of the company.

Held, 1st, that the defendants having elected to become carriers, the carriage of the horses was an act done by them in pursuance of their duty as common carriers, and therefore no notice of action to them was necessary.—*Palmer* v. *Grand Junction Railway Company*, 7 D. P. C. 232.

GRAVESEND PIER ACT.
By the Gravesend Pier Act (3 & 4 Will. 4, c. 101, s. 18), the corporation are empowered to appoint clerks, treasurers, collectors, and such other officers or

assistants as they may think necessary for the purposes of the act. By sect. 19, it is provided that it shall not be lawful for the corporation to appoint the person who may be appointed the clerk in the execution of the act, the treasurer for the purposes of the act; and a penalty is imposed on any person, being the clerk, or his partner or clerk, who shall in any manner officiate for the treasurer: Held, that, by the latter section, the corporation were prohibited from appointing the clerk to such officer as assistant treasurer: but where the corporation had so appointed the clerk, and he had discharged some of the duties of the treasurer, held, that it was a question for the jury, whether he did so bonâ fide and in the belief that he was legally appointed by them as an independent officer, or colourably and in evasion of the act; and that, in the former case, he would not be liable to the penalty for officiating for the treasurer, but in the latter he would.—*Hawkings v. Newman*, 4 M. & W. 613.

GUARANTEE.

Assumpsit on a written guarantee given to the plaintiffs for goods to be supplied by them to one G., to the extent of 400*l*. The guarantee provided, that the plaintiffs were to have full liberty to extend the period of credit to G., and to hold over or renew bills, notes, or other securities given by him, "and to grant to G. and the persons liable upon such bills, notes, or securities, any indulgence, *and to compound with him or them respectively, as the plaintiffs might think fit, without the same discharging or in any manner affecting the liability of the defendant by virtue of the guarantee."* The declaration then averred the supply of goods exceeding the guarantee, of which sum 168*l*. was unpaid by G. of which the defendant had notice, and was requested to pay that sum, but had not done so.

Plea, that after the debt was incurred by G., and before action brought, the plaintiffs became parties to a composition deed between G. and his creditors, whereby he assigned all his stock in trade, &c. for the benefit of his creditors; and that, in consideration thereof, the plaintiffs and the other creditors, parties thereto, granted a general release to G. of all debts and demands against him. The plea then averred, that the promise in the declaration was only made by the defendant as surety, and that the plaintiffs, by the deed, released G. without the privity of the defendant, and without notice.

Held, on demurrer, that under the express terms of the guarantee, the security war not discharged by the release of the principal debtor.—*Cowper v. Smith*, 4 M. & W. 519.

HABEAS CORPUS.

An application for a writ of habeas corpus must be supported by the affidavit of the prisoner himself, unless it appear from the circumstances that it cannot be obtained. (13 East, 195.)—*In re Canadian Prisoners*, 7 D. P. C. 208.

HOLIDAYS. See PRACTICE, 10.

HUSBAND AND WIFE.

1. (*Conveyance by married woman.*) The Court of Common Pleas authorised a feme covert, under the 3 & 4 Will. 4, ss. 79, 91, to convey her copyhold property without the concurrence of her husband, he having resided abroad for many years with another woman.—*Exparte Shirley*, 5 Bing. N. C. 226; 7 D. P. C. 258.

2. (*Acknowledgment by married woman abroad.*) An affidavit of acknowledgment by

a feme covert, taken before a notary public in Illinois, held sufficient.—*Ex parte Mann*, 5 Bing. N. C. 226.

And see ORDER OF REMOVAL, 1.

INDICTMENT.

1. (*Conclusion contra formam statuti—Subsequent felony.*) In order to warrant a sentence of transportation for life on an indictment for larceny after a previous conviction, the indictment need not conclude contra formam statuti.—*Reg.* v. *Blea*, 8 C. & P. 735.

2. (*Description of prosecutor by name of dignity.*) In an indictment for larceny of goods the property of a peer who is a baron, he is sufficiently described as A. Lord B.—*Reg.* v. *Pitts*, 8 C. & P. 771 ; *Reg.* v. *Elliot*, ib. 772, n.

3. (*Misjoinder of counts.*) To an indictment for stabbing (containing the usual counts) was added a count for a common assault, which was not discovered till the trial had considerably advanced. The case proceeded, and the jury found the prisoner guilty of an assault, and the verdict was entered on the count for stabbing with intent to do grievous bodily harm. The judges held the conviction good.—*Reg.* v. *Jones*, 8 C. & P. 776.

And See MURDER. PERJURY.

INCLOSURE ACT. See WAY.

INFANT.

(*Liability of.*) Where an infant, living in a style of some pretension, purchased of the plaintiff, in the course of four months, silks to the amount of 35*l.*, some of which were delivered in the presence of her mother, and some sent to a fashionable hotel, where she and her mother resided : Held, that the defendant might be liable for the amount, although the plaintiff had omitted to make any inquiries of the mother whether the articles were or were not necessary for the defendant. —*Dalton* v. *Gib*, 5 Bing. N. C. 198. For an inquiry into the circumstances of the infant is not a *condition precedent* to the right to recover against him, but only has the effect, that the tradesman trusts him at the peril of proving by other means that the articles were necessary.—*Brayshaw* v. *Eaton*, ib. 231.

INSOLVENT.

The first three sections of the 1 & 2 Vict. c. 110, do not apply to insolvent debtors adjudged to be discharged at some future period ; but by sect. 85, their case is excepted altogether out of the operation of the act ; and therefore such prisoners may be detained by capias or detainer, without a judge's order or writ of summons.—*Turnor* v. *Darnell*, 7 D. P. C. 346.

INSURANCE.

(*On freight—Description of interest—Inception of risk.*) The plaintiff, owner of a ship, effected a policy *on freight*, at and from the Coromandel coast to Bourbon. The ship put into a port on the Coromandel coast for repairs : the plaintiff purchased a cargo, and had it ready to be sent on board, about seven miles from the port. The ship was lost by an accident in going out of dock.

Held, that the plaintiff's interest in the profit of conveying the cargo was properly described as *freight* (1 B. & Adol. 45) ; that, the cargo being ready when the ship was about to leave the dock, the risk had attached (13 East, 331 ; 1 B. & Adol. 45) ; and that the loss was a loss within the terms of the policy, which covered perils of the seas, and all other perils, losses, and misfortunes.—*Devaux* v. *J'Anson*, 5 Bing. N. C. 519.

INTERPLEADER ACT.

(*Costs.*) Where a party has succeeded on an issue directed under the Interpleader Act, to try the right to certain property, he is entitled, as against the unsuccessful party, to the costs of applying to the Court in order to obtain the property in question from the stakeholder, an application having been made to the latter, and he having properly awaited the decision of the Court before he gave it up.— *Barnes* v. *The Bank of England,* 7 D. P. C. 319.

JOINT STOCK COMPANY.

By an act of parliament constituting a joint stock company, it was directed that the company should apply the first moneys received under the act, in discharge of the expenses incurred in obtaining the act : Held, that a member of the company might sue the company in debt for his time and trouble and money expended in obtaining the act. (4 B. & C. 962.)—*Carden* v. *The General Cemetery Company,* 5 Bing. N. C. 253 ; 7 D. P. C. 275.

JURY.

On a motion for a new trial, the Court would not receive an affidavit by the attorney of an admission made to him by one of the jurymen, that the verdict was decided by lot.—*Straker* v. *Graham,* 7 D. P. C. 233.

JUSTICES.

(*Actions against.*) In the borough of P., seven borough magistrates, including the mayor, assembled to appoint overseers. The mayor took out of his pocket two blank forms, with three seals already attached to them, filled them up with the names of two persons of his own political party, handed them to the two magistrates sitting next to himself, and on their being signed, immediately despatched them by a constable to be served. As soon as the constable had left the room, the four other magistrates, who had not observed the mayor's proceedings, desired him to nominate two other overseers, and on his refusing to do so, appointed them without his concurrence. In an action of trespass brought against the mayor for a distress made under his warrant for nonpayment of a rate made by the overseers first appointed, the jury found the appointment not to be *fraudulent.* The Court refused a new trial, which was moved for on the ground that, whether fraudulent or not, it was *void,* as being a judicial act done by the minority of the justices assembled, without an opportunity of deliberation afforded to the entire body.—*Penney* v. *Slade,* 5 Bing. N. C. 319.

And see Costs, 11.

LANDLORD AND TENANT.

1. (*Estoppel on tenant by payment of rent.*) Parochial trustees, under the authority of a local act of 17 Geo. 3, had built a workhouse on lands belonging to charity trustees in the same parish ; in 1821 disputes arose between the two sets of trustees, as to whether any rent was therefore payable, and the question was brought before the Master of the Rolls by an amicable suit in 1821, who decreed that a certain rent should be paid by the parochial trustees, which was accordingly paid until 1833 : Held, that use and occupation might be maintained for the rent in arrear after 1833, as the decision of the Master of the Rolls was binding on the parties, and that the payment of rent under the circumstances was an estoppel on the parochial trustees.—*Allason* v. *Stark,* 1 P. & D. 183.

2. A lease for one year, " and so on from year to year until the tenancy hereby created shall be determined as hereinafter mentioned," with a provision that it should be lawful for either party to determine the tenancy by three months' notice, creates a tenancy for two years certain, and cannot be determined by a three months' notice to quit at the end of the first year. (2 Campb. 573 ; 3 Campb. 510 ; 1 T. R. 378.)—*Doe* d. *Chadborn* v. *Green*, 1 P. & D. 454.

3. (*Pleadings.*) In an action of trespass, the defendant pleaded lib. ten., and leave and license. The plaintiff denied the license, and to the other plea replied a demise from year to year, commencing on the 16th November, 1836, the defendant by his rejoinder denied the demise. There was evidence that the 16th of November was the first day of each year of the tenancy, but from the evidence it seemed that the tenancy must have commenced before 1836. The ground of defence was, that at the time of the letting the plaintiff had agreed to give up the possession whenever the defendant required to have the land : Held, 1, that the allegation of the tenancy was, inasmuch as a tenancy from year to year is considered as recommencing every year ; 2, that the defendant could not avail himself of the above defence on these pleadings, but the stipulation for giving up possession should have been made the subject of a rejoinder.—*Tomkins* v. *Lawrance*, 8 C. & P. 729.

And see PLEADING, 8.

LAND TAX.

Where a party has been returned in the schedule of the collector of land tax for a particular parish, under the 48 Geo. 3, c. 141, as in default for a sum assessed upon him for land tax in that parish, and the schedule having been duly certified to this Court, a writ of levari facias has issued, under which such sum has been levied on his goods, and paid into the receipt of the Exchequer, the Court cannot afterwards set aside the writ, on the ground that the party has been assessed in the wrong parish.—*In re Glatton Land Tax*, 4 M. & W. 570.

LEASE.

1. (*Lease or agreement.*) A., being in possession as a yearly tenant, entered into the following memorandum of agreement with B. his landlord, in the middle of a current half year :—" B. agrees to let the farm of C. to A. for the term of fourteen years, determinable at the end of seven years, at the option of either party, on giving twelve months' notice, at the yearly rent of 20*l.* a year, payable half yearly, without any deduction whatever. A lease to be drawn up on the usual terms ; and the said A. agrees to take it on the said terms." Held, that this instrument amounted to a lease, although the effect of it might be to cause a surrender of the previous term, and to merge the rent accruing due for the current half year. (15 East, 244 ; 5 T. R. 165 ; Com. Dig. Estates, G. 8 ; 8 Bing. 178 ; 3 Tyrw. 170.)—*Doe* d. *Phillip* v. *Benjamin*, 1 P. & D. 440.

2. (*Assignment or agreement to assign.*) An agreement to assign on payment of 200*l.* by instalments, the assignee to save the assignor harmless from liability to the lessor, and the assignor to re-enter on nonpayment of any of the instalments : Held, to be an agreement for an assignment only, and not an actual assignment. —*Hartshorne* v. *Watson*, 5 Bing. N. C. 477.

LIBEL.

(*What matter is libellous—Innuendo.*) The following publication was held to be no libel :—" Notice. Any person giving information where any property may be found belonging to G., a prisoner in the King's Bench prison, but residing within the rules thereof, at &c., shall receive 5l. per cent. on the goods recovered, for their trouble, by applying to &c.: Held also, that the following innuendo, "thereby meaning that the plaintiff had been and was guilty of concealing his property with a fraudulent and unlawful intention," was an enlargement of the sense of the alleged libel.—*Gompertz* v. *Levy*, 1 P. & D. 214.

LIMITATIONS, STATUTE OF.

(*Merchant's accounts—Payment.*) Accounts not in writing are not accounts excepted by the statute of limitations.

Where a debtor owes his creditor some debts from a period longer than six years, and others from a period within six years, and pays a sum without appropriating it to any particular debt, such payment is not a payment on account, so as to take out of the statute of limitations the debts due longer than six years. (1 C. M. & R. 252 ; 2 C. M. & R. 45, 723.) But the creditor may at any time apply such payment to the debts due longer than six years. (1 Mer. 572 ; 2 B. & Ald. 39; 2 B. & Cr. 65 ; 2 Vern. 606 ; 5 Taunt. 596.)—*Mills* v. *Fowkes*, 5 Bing. N. C. 455.

LIQUIDATED DAMAGES. See PENALTY.

MALICIOUS PROSECUTION.

In a declaration for a malicious prosecution before a magistrate, it is not necessary to state that there was an information ; it is sufficient that the defendant procured a warrant to be issued : but if the declaration state that the defendant made information upon oath, and that upon that information the magistrate granted the warrant, the information must be proved in the regular way, and a recital of it in the warrant is not sufficient.—*Gregory* v. *Derby*, 8 C. & P. 749.

MANDAMUS. See MIDDLESEX COUNTY RATE.

MANOR.

(*Custom to demise copyholds—Mandamus to lord.*) By the custom of a manor, the tenants had a right to demise for any period not longer than three years without a license, and for every license to demise for a longer period, the lord was entitled to 4d. for every year of the term granted. Several licenses were shewn, the earliest in 1729, under which various terms of years, but not exceeding forty-seven, had been granted. Under these circumstances, the Court discharged a rule for a mandamus to the lord to grant a license to demise for two several terms of forty and twenty-one years.

The Court discharged a rule for a mandamus to the lord of a manor to compel him to grant a license for a tenant to dig brick earth, for the purpose of making bricks, there being no evidence of any custom to grant such licenses, except that they had frequently been granted since 1729, on payment of 21l. for each acre.—*Reg.* v. *Hale*, 1 P. & D. 293.

MASTER AND SERVANT.

1. If a person hired on a yearly service as clerk, to conduct an establishment for his master, set up a claim to be a partner, although in a respectful manner and *bonâ fide*, it is sufficient cause for the master to dismiss him without notice.—*Amor* v. *Fearon*, 1 P. & D. 398.

2. B., by a memorandum of agreement signed by himself only, agreed to work for

the plaintiff, a manufacturer of powder flasks, and for no other person whatsoever, from the 17th August, 1833, during twelve months, and so on from twelve months' end to twelve months, and until he should give the plaintiff twelve months' notice in writing to quit : Held, that as this agreement contained nothing binding on the plaintiff, it was *nudum pactum*; and that, although B. served under the agreement until April, 1836, when he left the service and worked for the defendant, who was shown the agreement in question, and warned that B. was the plaintiff's hired servant ; in an action against the defendant for harbouring the plaintiff's servant, it was competent to the defendant to shew that the contract of hiring was altogether void. (2 H. Bl. 511 ; 4 Taunt. 876.)—*Sykes v. Dixon*, 1 P. & D. 463.

3. To an action for wrongfully discharging the plaintiff from the defendant's service before the expiration of his year of service, it is no answer that the plaintiff *obstinately refused* to work.—*Jacquot v. Bourra*, 7 D. P. C. 348.

MIDDLESEX COUNTY RATE.

On an appeal against a rate under the Middlesex County Act, 3 Geo. 4, c. cvii., the justices confirmed the rate, subject to the opinion of the Court of Queen's Bench on a case. The certiorari directed the justices to send up an order of sessions " with all things touching the same :" the Court of Queen's Bench quashed the order of sessions. The sessions, after such order, were applied to to quash the rate, but refused to do so, on the ground that the *rate* had not been removed into the Court of Queen's Bench, and there was no longer any appeal against it. The Court of Queen's Bench refused a mandamus to compel them to enter continuances, and quash the rate : first, because, by so doing, the parties who had been engaged in the collection of the rate might be exposed to an action ; secondly, because the Court could not compel the sessions to decide in a particular way.

A subsequent rate having been made by the sessions pending the argument on the case, open to the same objection, but against which no appeal was made : Held, that the rate, being good on the face of it, could not be quashed on certiorari.—*Reg.* v. *Justices of Middlesex*, 1 P. & D. 402.

MONEY HAD AND RECEIVED. See Principal and Agent.

MORTGAGOR AND MORTGAGEE.

1. Where a lease is granted by a mortgagor after the date of the mortgage, notice by the mortgagee to the tenant to pay the rent does not constitute a tenancy between the mortgagee and the tenant, so as to enable the mortgagee to distrain for rent arrear after the notice : and where, after notice, the mortgagee distrained for half a year's rent, due Lady day, 1833, and rent was paid by the tenant subsequently to the distress : Held, that this did not constitute a tenancy by relation back, so as to entitle the mortgagee to distrain for the rent due previously. (5 Nev. & M. 672 ; 9 B. & C. 245 ; 1 Dougl. 21 ; 2 Bing. N. C. 538 ; 4 Ad. & E. 299.)—*Evans v. Elliott*, 1 P. & D. 256.

2. (*Construction of mortgage deed.*) Premises in which the business of a wine and spirit merchant was carried on, were assigned, together with the license, to the plaintiff by way of mortgage. The occupier forfeited the license, and the plaintiff's mortgage was paid off; afterwards the assignee of the mortgagor obtained a new licence, which he sold to a new occupier of the premises : Held, that the plaintiff could not sue him for the amount obtained on the sale of such license. —*Manifold v. Morris*, 5 Bing. N. C. 420.

MUNICIPAL CORPORATIONS ACT.

(*Reserved rights of freemen, remedy for.*) Declaration in debt against the corporation of S. stated, that in the year 1762 an act of parliament passed for dividing and inclosing two pieces of open land in the borough, over which the corporation had immemorially exercised the sole right of pasturage, and enacted that they should be divided between and allotted to the lord of the manor and the corporation in certain shares, and that the corporation should have power, from time to time, to make leases of the allotments so vested in them, for such terms, and with such covenants and agreements, as the burgesses in common hall assembled should think proper. The declaration then sets forth a " rule, order, and ordinance " of the burgesses in common hall assembled, made on the 1st of April, 1762 ; whereby, after reciting that they were of opinion that the most beneficial mode for the corporation of inclosing the lands would be to grant leases of them for long terms to such burgesses as were willing to take the same, under covenants to inclose them, it was ordered, that no lease should be made to one burgess in the same lease of more than fifty or less than five acres ; and " it being their desire and opinion that every burgess residing within the borough should receive a benefit from the said inclosure," it was further ordered, that certain annual sums out of the rents arising from the inclosure should be paid and distributed yearly, by the common attornies of the borough for the time being, on every 2nd of November, among the twelve senior burgesses residing within the borough ; and that no burgess who should take a lease should be entitled to receive any of such money. The declaration then stated the granting of the leases ; that the plaintiff, after the passing of the Municipal Corporation Act, 5 & 6 Will. 4, c. 76, viz. for a year ending 2nd of November, 1836, was one of the twelve senior burgesses : that defendants had received from the rents of the land sufficient to satisfy the sums so ordered to be paid ; and that the office of common attorney was abolished by that statute.

Plea, that on the 2nd of November, 1836, the defendants necessarily, and as they were legally required and bound to do, paid and applied all the rents of the said lands, together with and amongst other rents and sums of money, in payment of certain lawful debts then due and owing to divers persons from the defendants, in their corporate capacity, out of the property of the borough, and by law then payable in priority and preference to the payments to the twelve senior burgesses, or any of them.

Replication, that on the 2nd of November, 1836, a surplus annual income from the said rents, and from other property of the borough, belonging to the defendants in their corporate capacity, remained to the defendants, wherewith to pay the annual sums before mentioned, after payment of the interest of all lawful debts chargeable on the land so allotted as aforesaid, together with the salaries of municipal officers, and all other lawful expenses which, on the 5th of June, 1835, were chargeable on the same.

Held, 1st, that the declaration was good ; for,

(1.) That the ordinance of 1762 was a valid bye-law ;

(2.) That an action of debt was maintainable on it at common law, by the parties to whom pecuniary benefits were granted by it ; (6 Mod. 26.)

(3.) That under the 5 & 6 Will. 4, c. 76, s. 2, such action was maintainable against the corporation at large.

Held, also, that the plea was bad on general demurrer, as not showing that there existed no surplus rents for the purpose of making the payments to the burgesses, after payment of the interest of debts chargeable on the particular lands,

Semble, that the plea was bad also, as not showing with sufficient distinctness that the debts, in respect of which the rents had been applied, existed at the time of the passing of the statute 5 & 6 Will. 4, c. 76.—*Hopkins* v. *Mayor of Swansea*, 4 M. & W. 621.

MURDER.

1. (*Of illegitimate child—Proof of name.*) An illegitimate child, six weeks old, was baptized on a Sunday, and from that day to the following Tuesday was called by the name of its baptism, and its mother's surname : Held sufficient evidence to warrant the jury in finding that the deceased was properly described by those names in an indictment for murder. (1 Mood. C. C. 402, 457.)—*Reg.* v. *Evans*, 8 C. & P. 765.

2. (*Of legitimate child—Description of child.*) An indictment against a married woman for the murder of her legitimate child, described it as " a certain infant male child of tender age, to wit, of the age of six weeks, and not baptized :" Held insufficient, as it neither stated the name of the child, nor stated it to be to the jurors unknown.—*Reg.* v. *Biss*, 8 C. & P. 773.

NOTICE OF ACTION. See GAMEKEEPER; GRAND JUNCTION RAILWAY COMPANY.

ORDER OF FILIATION.

1. (*Notice of application for, how to be signed.*) The notice of application for an order of maintenance on the putative father of a bastard child under 4 & 5 Will. 4, c. 76, ss. 72, 73, must be signed by a majority of the parish officers, including the churchwardens.—*Reg.* v. *Justices of Cambridgeshire*, 1 P. & D. 249.

2. (*Same.*) Notice of an intended application for an order in bastardy may be signed by the churchwardens and overseers of a parish, although it forms part of a union, and returns a member to the board of guardians, under the 4 & 5 Will. 4, c. 76.—*Reg.* v. *James*, 1 P. & D. 422.

3. An order of filiation, made upon the oath of the mother, and upon evidence in corroboration thereof, without stating to be in some material particular, is bad.—*Reg.* v. *Read*, 1 P. & D. 413.

4. Where a justice is called upon to enforce an order of filiation, under 49 Geo. 3, c. 68, s. 3, on proof of the weekly sum ordered to be paid being due to the parish, and of the reputed father's refusal to pay, he has no jurisdiction to inquire how the weekly sum is expended ; and therefore, where a justice refused to commit the father to the house of correction, on the ground that the weekly sum expended by the parish officers was not wholly employed in the maintenance of the bastard child, the Court of Queen's Bench issued a mandamus to the justice to compel him to make the committal.—*Reg.* v. *Codd*, 1 P. & D. 456.

ORDER OF REMOVAL.

1. By an order of removal, dated 4th of September, the wife of a prisoner, confined in gaol for debt for one hundred days, expiring on the 21st of November, was removed from the parish where she had resided with her husband, and in which the gaol was situated, to her husband's settlement parish. During the imprisonment, she had liberty to visit her husband : Held, that the order of removal was bad, as a separation of man and wife. (5 East, 113 ; 4 B. & Ald. 498.)—*Reg.* v. *Inhabitants of Stogumber*, 1 P. & D. 409.

2. (*Removal of legitimate children—Statement of grounds of appeal.*) Legitimate

children above seven years of age, but under sixteen, of a woman who has married again, if chargeable to the parish where they reside with their mother and father-in-law, may be removed to their late father's settlement notwithstanding the 4 & 5 Will. 4, c. 76, s. 57. (6 Ad. & E. 301 ; 7 Ad. & E. 819 ; 1 M. & W. 129.)]

No objection which is not stated in the grounds of appeal can be taken, either at the sessions or in the Court of Queen's Bench, to an order of removal, even though such objection appear on the face of the case sent up from the sessions. (6 Ad. & E. 273.)—*Reg.* v. *Inhabitants of Stafford,* 1 P. & D. 415 ; *Reg.* v. *Inhabitants of Costock,* ib. 417.

OVERSEERS.

(*Vesting of lands in.*) A devise of lands, as to one moiety for the relief of poor and needy people, of good life and conversation, of a certain parish, and as to the other moiety for putting out poor boys apprentices, does not constitute the lands parish property, so as to vest them in the churchwardens and overseers of the parish, under the 59 Geo. 3, c. 12, s. 17.

Semble, that statute does not operate to take parish property vested in *trustees* out of the trustees, and vest it in the churchwardens and overseers. (10 B. & Cr. 885.)—*Allason* v. *Stark,* 1 P. & D. 183.

And see WITNESS, 4.

PATENT.

A patent was taken out in respect of new machinery for preparing flax, and improved machinery for spinning flax. The improvement in spinning consisted in spinning at a shorter reach than had before been practised : but the contraction of the reach was rendered practicable by the maceration of the flax in the new machinery for preparing it ; for spinning machines, varying in the distance of the reach, had been in use before : Held, that the patent was void, although the machinery for preparing the flax was new and useful. (2 H. Bl. 463 ; 4 B. & Ald. 541.)—*Kay* v. *Marshall,* 5 Bing. N. C. 492.

PEDIGREE. See EVIDENCE, 3.

PENALTY.

(*Penalty or liquidated damages.*) The defendant agreed to grant a lease with the usual covenants, and the plaintiff agreed to execute a counterpart, and to pay the expenses : and for the true performance of the agreement, each of the parties bound himself " in the penalty of 500*l.*, to be recovered against the defaulter, as liquidated damages :" Held, that the 500*l.* must be considered as a penalty, and not as liquidated damages. (2 Bos. & P. 346 ; 3 Bos. & P. 630 : 1 Bing. 302 ; 6 B. & Cr. 216 ; 6 Bing. 141 ; 7 Bing. 735.)—*Boys* v. *Ancell,* 5 Bing. N. C. 390.

PERJURY.

(*Indictment.*) An indictment for perjury, committed before a magistrate, stated that the defendant went before the magistrate and was sworn, and that being so sworn, he did falsely, &c. " say, depose, swear, charge, and give the said justice to be informed" that he saw the prosecutor commit a crime : Held, that this allegation sufficiently shewed that the oath was taken in a judicial proceeding.

An assignment of perjury, that the prosecutor did not, at the time and place sworn to, " or at any other time and place," commit a certain crime with an ass, (as sworn to), " or with any other animal whatsoever," is sufficiently proved by the evidence of two witnesses falsifying the deposition of the defendant.—*Reg.* v. *Gardiner,* 8 C. & P. 737.

PLEADING.

1. (*Plea of payment—Operation of particulars.*) Debt for 180*l.*, the amount of two years' rent. Plea as to 135*l.*, parcel, &c., payment to a superior landlord, to avoid a distress. Replication, admitting the payment, but stating that that sum had been deducted at the time from the rent due to the plaintiff, and that 135*l.* was due to the plaintiff over and above the sum so deducted. Rejoinder, that the said sum of 135*l.* was not deducted, *absque hoc* that 135*l.* was still due to the plaintiff. The plaintiff, in his particulars of demand, gave credit for payment of the first year's rent, minus 16*l.* 2*s.* 6*d.*, and he proved that 106*l.* 16*s.* 2*d.* was due to him, after allowing for all payments : Held (before the rule of T. T. 1838), that the particulars were not to be taken as embodied in the declaration; that the plea of payment of 135*l.* did not apply to the mere balance of 106*l.* remaining after deduction of the sum for which credit was given in the particulars, and that the plaintiff was entitled to a verdict for such balance.—*Ferguson* v. *Mahon,* 1 P. & D. 194.

2. (*Plea of payment.*) Declaration in assumpsit for 883*l.*, stating that although 664*l.*, parcel, &c. had been paid, the remainder had not. Plea, payment of all sums in the declaration mentioned. Replication and new assignment, as to 175*l.*, parcel of the monies in the declaration mentioned, that the action was brought, not for the causes of action in respect of which the defendant paid that sum, but for other causes of action ; and denial of payment of the residue. Pleas, 1, payment generally ; 2, that the causes of action newly assigned were other and different ; and issue thereon : Held, that the plea to the declaration was not to be taken as pleaded to the balance only, and that the replication did not admit payment of 175*l.* as part of the balance, so as to entitle the defendant to a verdict on proof of payment of such a sum as, together with the 175*l.* admitted in the replication, was equal to such balance. (4 M. & W. 4.)—*Alston* v. *Mills,* 1 P. & D. 197.

3. (*In action for malicious prosecution.*) Declaration that the defendant had arrested the plaintiff, and that the plaintiff had been detained in custody until he was discharged by reason of the defendant's not having declared against him : that the defendant might have procured judgment in that suit, if he had thought fit ; but that he afterwards, without any reasonable or probable cause, *maliciously* arrested the plaintiff a second time for the same cause of action, without leave of any judge of the Court. Plea, of the pendency of the former suit : Held, on demurrer to the plea (Lord Denman, C. J., *dubitante*), that the declaration was good, as it must be taken that the second arrest was made maliciously, without the contemplation of any benefit to himself.

Quære, whether the declaration would have been good on special demurrer.— *Heywood* v. *Collinge,* 1 P. & D. 202.

4. (*In debt on bond—Profert—What passes to assignees of bankrupt.*) To debt on bond the defendant pleaded that a fiat in bankruptcy had issued against the plaintiff, under which certain persons had been appointed his assignees ; and that by reason of the premises they had become entitled to sue upon the bond. Replication, that by an indenture, reciting the plaintiff to be indebted to certain persons, upon a cognovit, in more than the amount of the bond, the plaintiff had assigned the bond to them as a further security, with a proviso for redemption ;

and that the balance of the debt remaining unpaid was larger than the amount of the bond; and that the action was brought for their benefit: Held, on special demurrer, 1, that the plaintiff was not bound to make profert of the indenture: 2, that the replication was right in setting out facts to shew in what way the bond was prevented from vesting in the assignees of the bankrupt, and that it was not bad for argumentativeness, in not traversing that the bond did vest in them: 3, that although the bond was stated to have been given only as a further security, and there was a proviso for redemption of it on payment of the debt, the bankrupt had no possibility of interest to pass to his assignees, as the balance of the unpaid debt exceeded the amount of the bond, and it did not appear that any other valuable security had been given.— *Dangerfield* v. *Thomas*, 1 P. & D. 287.

5. (*Plea of second judgment, after fieri facias on first.*) To a count for a false return to a *fieri facias*, on a judgment of the King's Bench against B., the defendant pleaded, that, after the suing out of the said writ, and after the return, the plaintiff sued B. in the King's Bench upon these judgments, and recovered judgment thereon, which still remained in force: by means of which premises, the said judgment in the said count first mentioned became merged and satisfied, the *fieri facias* abandoned, and the defendant discharged: Held, on special demurrer, that the plea was no answer to the action.—*Pitcher* v. *King*, 1 P. & D. 297.

6. (*Special traverse.*) To a declaration in trover by the assignee of a bankrupt, alleging a joint conversion by three defendants, two of them pleaded that, after the bankruptcy, and more than two months before the issuing of the fiat, under which the plaintiff had been appointed assignee, and before the committing of the grievance, &c., the plaintiff, as assignee (to wit, by reason of the relation of his title as such assignee to the time of the bankruptcy), was the owner of and entitled to the goods in the declaration mentioned, as of his property as such assignee: and the bankrupt was then (subject only to such title of the plaintiff as aforesaid) possessed of and entitled to the said goods; and thereupon, after the bankruptcy, and more than two months before the fiat, one of the defendants *bond fide* bought at a fair price from him the said goods; that the two defendants had no notice of the act of bankruptcy; whereupon the defendant, who had so purchased the goods, became possessed of them as of his own property; and that while he was so possessed, and at the said time when, &c, in the declaration mentioned, he in his own right, and the other defendant by his command, converted the said goods, which is the grievance in the declaration mentioned: *without this*, that at the time of the said conversion, the goods were the property of the plaintiff as assignee, or of right belonged to him as assignee: concluding to the country: Held, on special demurrer, that the inducement in the plea was matter of confession and avoidance, and that the subsequent traverse, therefore, made the plea bad. (1 Saund. 207, e, n. (5)).—*Pearson* v. *Rogers*, 1 N. & P. 302.

7. (*Immaterial traverse.*) Debt for 6*l.* for goods sold and delivered. Pleas, 1, as to all but 1*l.* 13*s.* *nunquam indebitatus*: 2, as to 1*l.* 13*s.*, parcel, &c., the Westminster Court of Requests' Act; with an averment " that the defendant was not indebted to the plaintiff to a greater amount than the said sum of 1*l.* 13*s.*:" Held, on special demurrer, that the plea was bad, on the ground that a traverse of that allegation would have raised an immaterial issue.—*Burroughs* v. *Hodgson*, 1 P. & D. 328.

8. (*Form of plea in action for fraudulent removal of goods to avoid distress.*) Trespass for breaking and entering plaintiff's house and taking her goods, on 2nd March, 1837. Plea, as to the breaking and entering, &c. and taking the said goods, that S. was the defendant's tenant of a house at a certain rent, payable, &c.; that on the 25th December, 1836, rent was in arrear, and from thence until the time when, &c.; that the said goods, being then the property and in the possession of S., were, on the 25th February, 1837, fraudulently removed by him from the said demised house, and were then, with the privity and consent of the plaintiff, placed by S. in the plaintiff's house. The plea then justified the entry and seizure (under the 11 Geo. 2, c. 19, s. 1), and concluded with a verification : Held, on special demurrer, 1, that the plea should have been confined to a justification of the breaking and entering ; and that the plaintiff's property in the goods ought to have been denied by a separate plea : 2, that if the plea were to be taken as a denial that the goods were the plaintiff's, it was bad, as being argumentative ; or if it were taken to admit them to be the plaintiff's, the case was not brought within the statute ; and so in either view the plea was bad : 3, that the plaintiff's possession of the goods was *not* admitted, either in the introductory words of the plea, or in the averment that they then, being the property and in the possession of S., were placed in the plaintiff's house with her privity and consent.—*Fletcher* v. *Marillier*, 1 P. & D. 354.

9. (*Plea of judgment recovered.*) On the day for completing the purchase of a house, on which 300*l*. deposit had been paid, the purchaser threw up the contract, on the ground that the vendor was not ready to complete ; and sued him in special assumpsit for 300*l*. money had and received. The jury found a verdict for the defendant, on the ground that he was ready to complete the contract. After the writ in that action was sued out against the vendor, he disposed of the house to another person ; and the former purchaser sued him again for the 300*l*. had and received, to which action he pleaded the judgment recovered in the former : Held, that as the former action failed on the sole ground that it was prematurely brought, the judgment so pleaded was no bar.—*Palmer* v. *Temple*, 1 P. & D. 379.

10. (*Several pleas.*) In an action for false imprisonment, the Court allowed the following pleas to stand together : 1. That the plaintiff had forged the acceptance of a bill of exchange ; 2. That he had issued a forged acceptance, knowing it to be forged ; 3. That the defendant had reasonable cause to believe that the plaintiff had forged the acceptance ; and 4. That the plaintiff had obtained money on the bill by false pretences.—*Currie* v. *Almond*, 5 Bing. N. C. 224 ; *S. C.* nom. *Curry* v. *Arnott*, 7 D. P. C. 249.

11. (*Judgment for want of plea.*) In debt for 150*l*., the defendant pleaded *to the whole action* payment to the plaintiff of 50*l*. The plaintiff signed judgment by nil dicit for 100*l*. : Held irregular. (1 Salk. 179 ; 1 Bing. N. C. 353 ; 2 M. & W. 72.)—*Wood* v. *Farr*, 5 Bing. N. C. 247 ; 7 D. P. C. 263.

12. (*Actionem non.*) Held, that a plea pleaded to part only of the plaintiff's demand ought to commence with the actionem non, whether pleaded in bar of part of the demand, or only against the *further* maintenance of the action in respect of that part.—*Upward* v. *Knight*, 5 Bing. N. C. 338. [Sed quære ; see *Putney* v. *Swann*, 2 M. & W. 72.]

13. Quære, whether *de injuriâ* is a good replication in an action of debt.—*Hebden* v. *Ruel*, 6 Scott, 442.

14. (*What is an issuable plea.*)   The bankruptcy of a sole plaintiff before action is an issuable plea.   (4 Bing. N. C. 144, 714.)—*Willis* v. *Hallett*, 5 Bing. N. C. 465.

15. (*Same.*)   In an action for wrongfully refusing to permit the plaintiff to appraise goods distrained, the defendant, being under terms to plead issuably, pleaded that plaintiff was tenant to defendant, and that the goods were taken as a distress for rent ι Held, an issuable plea.—*Sealey* v. *Harris*, 7 D. P. C. 195.

16. (*Frivolous demurrer.*)   To an action on a promissory note, the defendant pleaded that, after the making of the note, the plaintiff drew a bill on the defendant, which the defendant accepted and the plaintiff received iu satisfaction of the note.   Replication, that the plaintiff did not draw, defendant did not accept, and plaintiff did not receive the bill in satisfaction.   The Court refused to set aside a demurrer to this replication, on an affidavit that the plea was totally false.—*Edwards* v. *Greenwood*, 5 Bing. N. C. 476.

17. (*Plea in defence of possession of dwelling-house, how proved.*)   A plea, to trespass for assault and battery, that the defendant was in possession of a dwelling-house, and that the plaintiff disturbed him in possession, wherefore he turned him out, is not sustained by proof that the defendant was a lodger, occupying one room in a house, the landlord keeping the key of the outer door   (2 Bing. N. C. 617.)—*Monks* v. *Dykes*, 4 M. & W. 567.

18. (*Profert of deed, how excused.*)   Where the profert of a deed is requisite, it is not sufficient to allege as an excuse, that the deed *has been delivered* to the opposite party.—*Wallis* v. *Harrison*, 4 M. & W. 538.

19. (*Replication to special plea of set-off.*)   Declaration in assumpsit by the assignee of W., an insolvent debtor, surviving partner of A., for money received by the defendant to the use of W. and A.; on an account stated with W. and A., with a breach in nonpayment to W. and A., or to W. since A.'s death.   Plea, as to 451*l.*, parcel, &c., that after making the promises as to that sum, and in the lifetime of A., W. and A. were indebted to the defendant in 490*l.* for money lent, &c.; and afterwards, to wit, on &c., an account was stated between W. and A. and the defendant concerning such moneys, and the defendant then set off and allowed to W. and A. thereout the said sum of 451*l.*, parcel, &c., and exonerated and discharged W. and A. therefrom, in full satisfaction and discharge of the promises in the declaration mentioned, and of all damages sustained in respect thereof, which set-off and allowance W. and A. accepted and received from the defendant in full satisfaction and discharge as aforesaid.   Replication, that W. and A. were not indebted to the defendant in manner and form, &c.: Held, on special demurrer, that the replication was good, and that it was not necessary also to traverse in terms the accounting alleged in the plea.—*Learmouth* v. *Grandine*, 4 M. & W. 658.

20. (*Effect of denial of tenancy.*)   Declaration in case stated that the defendants were tenants to the plaintiff of a farm, and by reason thereof it was their duty, as such tenants, to manage and cultivate the farm in a good and husbandlike manner, according to the custom of the country; and assigned breaches in overcropping, &c.   Pleas, 1st, not guilty; 2ndly, that the defendants were not, nor was either of them, tenants to the plaintiff of the said messuage, &c., in manner and form as in the declaration alleged: Held, that this latter plea only put in issue the fact of the tenancy, and not the holding subject to a duty to cultivate according to the custom of the country; and that the defendant could not therefore object, on this record, that a lease, under which the land had been originally taken, was not produced by the plaintiff, in order to show that it did not exclude the custom.—*Hallifax* v. *Chambers,* 4 M. & W. 662 ; 7 D. P. C. 342.

21. (*Plea of payment into Court, effect of.*) A plea of payment into Court, under the indebitatus counts, only amounts to an admission of a liability on some one or more contracts, to the extent of the sum paid in. But a similar plea to a special count is an admission of *the* contract declared on, and of the breach. (4 B. & Adol. 673 ; 5 C. & P. 486 ; 5 Bing. 28 : 8 C. & P. 508.)—*Hingham* v. *Robins,* 7 D. P. C. 352.

22. (*Account stated.*) In an action by husband and wife, the declaration was on an account stated, on the 1st October, 1838, after the marriage, between the husband, on behalf of himself and the wife, and the defendant, concerning monies lent by the wife *dum sola* to the defendant, and on a promise to pay the sum found due on such accounting, *on the 1st October then next ensuing :* Held, that the declaration was bad, 1st, on the ground that the promise alleged, viz. to pay at a future time, was different from and inconsistent with that implied by law from the accounting, viz. to pay on request ; and 2ndly, because it did not appear that the debt was due at the time of the account stated.—*Hopkins* v. *Logan,* 7 D. P. C. 360.

And see BANKRUPTCY, 4 ; FIXTURES ; MUNICIPAL CORPORATIONS ACT ; LANDLORD AND TENANT, 3.

POACHING.

Where three persons went out together night poaching, one being armed, and two of them stood in a road and set nets in the hedge of a field of A., and sent their dog into the field to drive hares into the nets ; and the third afterwards, leaving them in the road, went to poach by himself in another field of A. : Held, that this would not support an indictment against the three for night poaching on land of A., under the stat. 9 Geo. 4, c. 69, s. 9. (6 C. & P. 398.)—*Reg.* v. *Nickless,* 8 C. & P. 757.

An indictment for night poaching, which charges that A. and B., together with another person, entered certain land, " the said A. and B. then and there being armed," is not supported by proof that the third person was armed, and that A. and B. were not so. Under the 9 Geo. 4, c. 69, a constructive arming is not sufficient.—*Reg.* v. *Davis,* 8 C. & P. 759.

POOR LAWS' AMENDMENT ACT. See ORDER OF FILIATION, 1, 2, 3 ; ORDER OF REMOVAL, 2.

POOR RATE.

1. (*Assessment of buildings and machinery.*) In a rate laid on buildings to which machinery is attached for the purpose of manufacture, the real property ought to be assessed according to its actual value as combined with the machinery, without considering whether the machinery be real or personal property, and liable or not to distress or execution, or whether it would go to the heir or executor, or, at the expiration of a lease, to the landlord or tenant. (6 Ad. & E. 634.)—*Reg.* v. *Guest,* 7 Ad. & E. 951.

2. (*On corporation property.*) Corporation property of a borough within the Municipal Corporation Act, 5 & 6 Will. 4, c. 76, the rents and profits of which are received by the treasurer of the borough, under sect. 92 of that act, is not rateable to the poor. (7 B. & C. 61, 70, n. ; 2 Myl. & Cr. 613.)—*Reg.* v. *Mayor of Liverpool,* 1 P. & D. 334.

3. (*Rateability of common.*) Where freemen of a municipal corporation enjoyed the right of depasturing an uninclosed moor, and of digging turves, clay, &c., cutting whins and furzes, getting limestones and slates from the quarries, and sowing grass seeds on the moor, according to regulations framed by the corporation; and the corporation had inclosed a part of the common 100 years back, which they still retained in severalty : but it appeared that the rights of the freemen originated in grants of right of common and turbary, there being no evidence to show that any larger rights had ever been granted to them ; and also that a rent of 2*s. per annum*, which had been reserved on the grant of the right of turbary, was still paid to the lord of the manor : Held, that the freemen possessed only a right of common, although with large and unusual enjoyments, and that therefore it was an incorporeal tenement, not rateable to the poor.—*Reg.* v. *Chamberlains, &c. of Alnwick*, 1 P. & D. 343.

PRACTICE.

1. (*Judgment as in case of nonsuit.*) In a country cause, issue was joined on the 12th June, but no notice of trial given for the next assizes : Held, too soon to move for judgment as in case of a nonsuit in the ensuing Hilary term. (6 D. P. C. 367, 505, 772.)—*Williams* v. *Davis*, 5 Bing. N. C. 227; 7 D. P. C. 246.

2. (*Same.*) Where issue was joined in Easter term, and notice of trial given for the second sitting in Trinity term : Held, that the defendant could not move for judgment as in case of a nonsuit until Michaelmas term. (1 C. & M. 494; 2 C. & M. 213; 1 C. M. & R. 819; 2 H. Bl. 558.)—*Phillipps* v. *Yearsley*, 6 Scott, 602.

3. (*Same.*) Obtaining a rule for a special jury, after a peremptory undertaking, the cause being a proper one to be tried by a special jury, is not such a default as is contemplated by the stat. 14 G. 2, c. 17.—*Twysden* v. *Stuls*, 6 Scott, 434.

4. (*View.*) In an action on a contract for building a chapel, the Court refused to grant the plaintiff a rule for a view.—*Newham* v. *Taite*, 6 Scott, 574.

5. Where a party came to the Court to cure a trifling irregularity, such as ought to be disposed of at chambers, he was not allowed costs, but they were made costs in the cause.—*Robarts* v. *Lemon*, 6 Scott, 576.

6. (*Judgment for want of a plea, time for.*) A judgment signed on the morning after the time for pleading expired, while the parties were attending a judge on a summons for time to plead, returnable before the judgment was actually signed, was held irregular. (2 D. P. C. 447.)—*Abernethy* v. *Paton*, 6 Scott, 586.

7. (*Misnomer.*) Where, in the writ and declaration, in an action not upon a written instrument, the defendant is described by the initials of his name, the only remedy is by summons to amend, under 3 & 4 Will. 4, c. 42, s. 11 ; and the Court will not set aside the proceedings for irregularity.—*Rust* v. *Kennedy*, 4 M. & W. 586; 7 D. P. C. 199.

8. (*Judgment as in case of nonsuit.*) Where the defendant has become insolvent since action brought, a rule for judgment as in case of a nonsuit will be discharged with costs, unless a stet processus be accepted. (5 D. P. C. 91.)—*Holland* v. *Henderson*, 4 M. & W. 587.

9. (*Same.*) Where the plaintiff gave notice of trial, and both parties attended on the day mentioned in the notice, but, before the cause was called on, the plaintiff proposed, and the defendant's attorney agreed to, a reference, and the record was withdrawn : Held, that the defendant could not afterwards have judgment as in

case of a nonsuit, although, by the default of the plaintiff, the reference was delayed, and the agreement of reference was never executed.—*Hansby* v. *Evans*, 4 M. & W. 565 ; 7 D. P. C. 198.

10. (*Observance of holidays.*) The 3 & 4 Will. 4, c. 42, s. 43, which enacts that Christmas-day and the three following days shall be kept as holidays, has qualified the 8th rule of H. T. 2 Will. 4 ; therefore, where a declaration was filed on the 24th December, with a notice to plead in four days, judgment signed for want of a plea on the 29th was set aside for irregularity.—*Wheeler* v. *Green*, 7 D. P. C. 194.

11. (*Costs of the day—Stay of proceedings.*) A defendant is not entitled, on motion for costs of the day, to a stay of proceedings until such costs are paid.—*Gibbs* v. *Goles*, 7 D. P. C. 325.

12. (*Right to begin.*) To a declaration on an agreement for not repairing premises in a reasonable time, the defendant pleaded that he did repair within a reasonable time : Held, that on these pleadings the plaintiff should begin ; for if no evidence were offered on either side, the defendant would succeed.—*Belcher* v. *M'Intosh*, 8 C. & P. 720.

13. (*Same.*) In replevin, if the defendant avow for rent arrear, and the plaintiff reply riens in arrear, the plaintiff must begin.—*Cooper* v. *Egginton*, 8 C. & P. 748.

14. (*Same.*) In an issue under the Interpleader Act, the plaintiffs averred that certain goods were not the property of the plaintiffs, or either of them. Plea, that the goods were the property of the plaintiffs, or one of them : Held, that the defendant had the right to begin.—*Hudson* v. *Brown*, 8 C. & P. 774.

PRACTICE, IN CRIMINAL CASES.

1. (*Election between several counts of indictment.*) The application for a prosecutor to elect is an application to the discretion of the judge, founded on the supposition that the case extends to more than one charge, and may therefore be likely to embarrass the prisoner in his defence. Therefore, where an indictment for arson contained five counts, each charging a firing of a house of a different owner, but it was opened that they were all in a row, and one fire burnt them all, the judge refused to put the prosecutor to elect.—*Reg.* v. *Freeman*, 8 C. & P. 727.

2. (*Giving copy of depositions.*) Where a principal felon is admitted as a witness for the crown against a receiver, the latter will be allowed to see the depositions returned against the former.—*Reg.* v. *Walford*, 8 C. & P. 767.

PRINCIPAL AND AGENT.

(*Liability of agent to principal.*) The plaintiff, in Calcutta, wrote to his agent in England to transmit him a sum of money through the defendant's house, to be placed to his credit there. The agent shewed his instructions to the defendant, and paid them the money, which they placed in their books to the credit of their correspondents in Calcutta, and sent them a letter of advice to account for it to the plaintiff. Before this letter reached Calcutta, their correspondents failed ; but the defendants had, between the date of the letter and the failure, accepted bills drawn by their correspondents before the receipt of the letter, to an amount exceeding the money paid in on account of the plaintiff : Held, that the money could not be recovered from the defendants, for that they had done all that they were instructed or were bound to do, and the situation in which they stood towards their correspondents had been thereby altered.—*M'Carthy* v. *Colvin*, 1 P. & D 429,

PRINCIPAL AND SURETY. See Evidence, 4 ; Guarantee.

PRISONER.

(*Discharge under 48 Geo. 3, c. 123.*)   *Semble*, that the imprisonment which is to entitle a defendant to his discharge under the 48 Geo. 3, c. 123, must be immediately preceding the application.—*Stubbing* v. *M'Grath*, 7 D. P. C. 328.

PROCESS.

1. (*Writ of summons—Description of defendant.*)   A defendant was described in a writ of summons as "of Newcastle upon Tyne, in the county of Northumberland:" Held sufficient; certain townships in the county of Northumberland being by the 2 & 3 Will. 4, c. 64, included within the boundary of the borough of Newcastle upon Tyne, as well as the *town* and *county* of Newcastle upon Tyne.— *Rippon* v. *Dawson*, 5 Bing. N. C. 206 ; 7 D. P. C. 247.

2. (*Same—Teste of alias writ.*)   Where a defendant's place of abode could not be discovered at the time of issuing a writ of summons, he may be described as of his last known place of abode.— (See also Bettyes *v.* Thompson, 7 D. P. C. 322.)

   By leave of the Court or a judge, a writ of alias or pluries summons, or a distringas thereon, may be issued and bear teste after the previous writ of summons has expired.   (2 Scott, 506; 3 Bing. N. C. 478.)

   An alias pluries to compel appearance, taken out after a distringas had been obtained for the purpose of proceeding to outlawry, was held available, notwithstanding such distringas, the distringas never having been acted on or delivered to the sheriff.—*Norman* v. *Winter*, 5 Bing. N. C. 279 ; 7 D. P. C. 304.

3. (*Writ of summons—Description of action—Indorsement.*)   A writ of summons stated the action to be "action on the case promises :" Held insufficient, and the Court set it aside for irregularity.   In the indorsement on the writ of an *attorney's* residence, the *county* need not be stated, unless otherwise it would be calculated to mislead.—*Youlton* v. *Hall*, 4 M. & W. 582.

RAPE.

A boy under 14 years of age cannot in point of law be guilty of an assault with intent to commit a rape : and if he be under that age, no evidence is admissible to show that in point of fact he could commit the offence of rape.—*Reg.* v. *Philips*, 8 C. & P. 736.

SESSIONS.

(*Jurisdiction of, in criminal cases.*)   An indictment for forgery found at the Quarter Sessions is a nullity, and if it be transmitted to the assizes, the judge will direct it to be quashed, and a new indictment prepared.—*Reg.* v. *Rigby*, 8 C. & P. 770.

SET-OFF.

When a verdict is found against a defendant on a plea of set-off, he is estopped from suing the plaintiff for the demand specified in the set-off. (3 East, 346.)— *Eastmure* v. *Laws*, 5 Bing. N. C. 444.

SETTLEMENT.

1. (*Exceptive hiring.*)   In a case sent by the sessions to the Court of Queen's Bench, it was stated that the pauper, when hiring himself for a year, told the master he should want a holiday to go to his feast, and the master agreed that he should have one for that purpose ; the time, and the duration of the absence, were not specified.   When the feast was at hand, the pauper, on a Sunday, told his master he wanted to go, and the master said he might go till Tuesday night,

which he did. The sessions thought a settlement was gained, as there was no distinct period named for the holiday. But the Court held it an exceptive hiring, and the order of sessions was quashed.—*Reg. v. Inhabitants of Threkingham*, 7 Ad. & E. 866.

2. (*By renting.*) Under the 6 Geo. 4, c. 57, no settlement is gained by the hiring and occupation of a tenement as joint-tenant, although the portion of the rent paid by the pauper amount to or exceed 10*l.* (1 Ad. & El. 232; 5 Ad. & E. 261.)—*Reg. v. Inhabitants of Caverswall*, 1 P. & D. 426.

SHERIFF.

1. (*Liability of, for false return by officer of county court.*) Case against a sheriff, stating that the plaintiff, at the county court of the defendant, as sheriff, recovered judgment against B.; that the plaintiff thereupon sued out a fieri facias of the defendant, directed by the defendant to his bailiffs, commanding them to levy, &c.; that although there were divers goods &c., yet the defendant, intending, &c. did not nor would levy, and that the defendant's bailiff, by the direction of the defendant, falsely returned, &c.: Held, that this declaration disclosed no cause of action against the sheriff. (2 B. & Ald. 473; 2 C. M. & R. 298; M. & Malk. 52.)—*Pitcher v. King*, 1 P. & D. 297.

2. (*Attachment against.*) Where the sheriff takes a bailbond with one surety only the Court will not set aside an attachment obtained against him, on an application at his instance. (2 Bing. 227; 2 D. P. C. 140.)—*Reg. v. Sheriff of Middlesex, in Lane v. Griffiths*, 7 D. P. C. 313.

SLANDER.

(*New trial in, where damage under* 40*s.*) The jury having given a verdict for 20*s.* in an action of slander, the Court refused to grant a new trial at the instance of the plaintiff.—*Rendall v. Hayward*, 5 Bing. N. C. 424.

STAMP,

1. (*On agreement—Several stamps.*) A cargo of goods, part of which belonged to T. alone, and part to T. & W. as partners, being in the hands of the consignee, T. on application for both parcels, signed an undertaking to pay freight for them, in the name of T. & W., but commencing with the words, " I hereby engage to pay," &c., and the goods were thereupon delivered to him. In an action against T. for the freight on his own parcel: Held, that the agreement was admissible with a single stamp impressed; because although the agreement related to the goods of the partnership as well as his own, he could not bind his partner as to the latter, but had made himself personally liable for the whole, and therefore the agreement was entire. (13 East, 241; 8 B. & Cr. 565; 1 B. & Cr. 407.)—*Shipton v. Thornton*, 1 P. & D. 216.

2. The following letter, sent to the holders of the fund out of which payment was to be made, was held not to require a bill stamp :—" We now authorize you to pay to Messrs. R. & Co. (having revoked the former order in their favour), after you have paid yourselves the balance we owe you from the net proceeds of our shipments to your foreign establishments to the present date, one-half of the remainder of the proceeds of the said shipments, provided the same shall not exceed the sum of 5000*l.* H. & I." (2 B. & Cr. 318; 6 M. & Sel. 144; 1 B. & Ald. 36; 1 Brod. & B. 78.)—*Hutchinson v. Heyworth*, 1 P. & D. 266.

And see BILLS AND NOTES, 1.

STOPPAGE IN TRANSITU.

M. purchased lead of the plaintiff at Newcastle, without specifying any place of delivery. After a time, M. desired that it should be forwarded to him in London, and the plaintiff gave M.'s agent at Newcastle an order on his servant for its delivery. The agent indorsed the order to a keelman, who received the lead and put it on board a vessel for London. The vessel arrived in London on the 21st June, and the defendants, as wharfingers, undertook the delivery of the lead. On that day M. failed; on the 23rd and 24th M. demanded the lead from the captain of the vessel, who refused to deliver it, although the freight was tendered, alleging that the defendants had stopped it on account of the failure of M. On the 28th a letter arrived from the plaintiffs, ordering the stoppage of the lead, which was then on board a lighter of the defendants: Held, that the transitus was not at an end, and that the plaintiff was in time to stop the lead. (3 T. R. 466; 7 T. R. 440; 3 East, 381; 1 M. & W. 20; 2 Bing. N. C. 81.)—*Jackson v. Nichol*, 5 Bing. N. C. 508.

TENDER.

A tender is not vitiated by the person making it saying at the time, that "it is all the defendant considers to be due."—*Robinson v. Ferreday*, 8 C. & P. 752.

TRESPASS. See COSTS, 5, 15; PLEADING, 17.

TROVER. See VENDOR AND PURCHASER.

USE AND OCCUPATION.

The defendants occupied, as tenants from year to year, a second floor, which, during their occupation, was consumed by accidental fire: Held, that they were nevertheless liable for use and occupation for the period which elapsed between the fire and the regular determination of their tenancy. (4 Taunt. 45; Ambl. 619; 1 C. M. & R. 172; 3 Ad. & Ell. 659.)—*Ixon v. Gorton*, 5 Bing. N. C. 501.

USURY.

A loan of money at more than 5*l*. per cent. interest, on the security of the deposit of a lease, of a warrant of attorney, and of a promissory note, is not protected by the 3 & 4 Will. 4, c. 98, s. 7. (1 Deac. 459; 2 Ad. & E. 326.)—*Berrington v. Collis*, 5 Bing. N. C. 332.

VENDOR AND PURCHASER.

1. (*Forfeiture of deposit.*) By an agreement for the purchase of a house, 300*l*. was paid by the purchaser, " by way of deposit, and in part of the purchase-money." The purchase was to be completed on a certain day, and it was agreed that if either party should refuse to perform the agreement, he should pay the other 1000*l*. as liquidated damages: Held, that on this agreement it was not intended that the 300*l*. should be forfeited on failure of the purchaser to complete the contract.—*Palmer v. Temple*, 1 P. & D. 379.

2. (*Lien of unpaid vendor of goods.*) The defendants sold the plaintiffs wheat, for which the plaintiffs were to pay by a draft on a London banker, to be remitted on receipt of the invoice and bill of lading. The defendants delivered the wheat to a carrier by water, and sent the bill of lading to the plaintiffs, but retook the wheat and sold it, because the plaintiffs failed to send a draft on a London banker according to their contract: Held, that the plaintiffs could not sue the defendants in trover for the wheat. (4 B. & C. 941.)—*Wilmshurst v. Bowker*, 5 Bing. N. C. 541.

VENUE.

1. The fact that there are only a small number of special jurors in the county, is of itself no ground for changing the venue.—*Doe* d. *Lloyd* v. *Williams* 5, Bing. N. C. 205.

2. In an action for non-execution of a contract relating to works on the Bedford Level, the Court refused to remove the venue from Cambridgeshire, on an affidavit that a large proportion of the property in that county is liable to the rates imposed by the Bedford Level Corporation.—*Thornton* v. *Jennings*, 5 Bing. N. C. 485.

3. (*Privilege of attorney as to.*) An attorney plaintiff has no privilege to retain the venue in London.—*Bradshaw* v. *Burton*, 7 D. P. C. 329.

WAY.

(*Extinguishment of, under Inclosure Act.*) By an inclosure act, it was enacted that all ways over a common field, called the West Field, should be extinguished as soon as M. should have made a carriage way across it : provided that nothing in the act contained should deprive A. of the right of ingress and egress to and from a certain watercourse there, for the purpose of opening certain hatches erected thereon, and cleansing the watercourse : Held, that A.'s right of way to the hatches along the side of the watercourse was not extinguished by M.'s having made a more circuitous track to the hatches, at a little distance from the side of the watercourse.

The occupier of a meadow irrigated by means of the hatches was held to be a competent witness in an action by the reversioner for the obstruction of the above way. (1 Bing. 257.)—*Adeane* v. *Mortlock*, 5 Bing. N. C. 236.

WITNESS.

1. (*Competency.*) In assumpsit on a bill of exchange, by indorsee against acceptor, issue being joined on a plea of payment, a prior indorsee is a competent witness for the defendant, although he acknowledge on the voir dire that he received money from the defendant to pay the plaintiff the bill.—*Reay* v. *Packwood*, 7 Ad. & E. 917.

2. (*Same.*) A witness for the plaintiff stated on the voir dire that "he had as agent employed the original attorney for the plaintiff; that the attorney was dead; that he was not released ; that no demand had been made upon him ; and that he did not state that the attorney was to look to the plaintiff, and not to himself:" and nothing further appeared to show that the witness had an interest in the suit, or had made himself liable to the new attorney : Held, that the witness was competent. (3 B. & Ald. 47 ; 1 B. &. Cr. 160.)—*Shipton* v. *Thornton*, 1 P. & D. 216.

3. (*Same.*) In case against a broker for negligently delivering goods without payment, the plaintiffs called their servant, whose duty it was to deliver under the orders of the defendant, and who had delivered without such orders : Held, that he was an interested witness, and therefore not competent to prove that the defendant was informed of such delivery in time to stop the goods and prevent loss to the plaintiffs, and that he neglected to do so. (1 Campb. 251 ; Peake, 117; 8 Taunt. 454.)—*Boorman* v. *Browne*, 1 P. & D. 364.

4. (*Competency of overseers.*) Overseers of the poor of a parish are not competent witnesses on an appeal against an order of removal, notwithstanding the

54 Geo. 3, c. 170. (7 T. R. 664; 1 Moo. & M. 402; 3 East, 7.)—*Reg.* v. *Recorder of Bath*, 1 P. & D. 469.

5. (*Competency.*) In an action against an assignee of a term for rent, a witness was called for the plaintiff, who had himself occupied the premises during a part of the time for which the defendant was called upon to pay : Held, that he was *primâ facie* an interested witness; but that the objection to his competency should be taken on the *voir dire*; and that, on showing that he was under-tenant and not assignee, he was a competent witness for the plaintiff.—*Hartshorne* v. *Watson*, 5 Bing. N. C. 477.

6. (*Same.*) In an action for a tailor's bill for clothes supplied to the defendant's servant, the servant is a competent witness for the plaintiff, his name being indorsed on the record.—*Robinson* v. *Ferreday*, 8 C. & P. 752.

7. (*Same.*) A creditor of a bankrupt's estate, who has sold his debt, is a competent witness in support of the fiat.—*Pulling* v. *Meredith*, 8 C. & P. 763.

And see EJECTMENT, 1 ; WAY.

WRIT OF ERROR.

(*From inferior Court—Return to writ of false judgment.*) A return to a writ of false judgment, that the plaintiff in error has not given security for prosecuting his suit, is bad ; the 19 Geo. 3, c. 70, ss. 5 & 6, do not apply to such a case. —*Crookes* v. *Longden*, 5 Bing. N. C. 410.

WRIT OF RIGHT. See FINE.

WRIT OF TRIAL.

(*What actions triable under.*) The first count of the declaration was for wrongfully discharging the plaintiff from the defendant's service; the second count for wages, the sum laid in each being 100*l.*; the sum indorsed on the writ of summons was 12*l.* 19*s.*; the particulars stated the action to be brought for 5*l.* 19*s.*, arrears of wages, and *also such damages* as the jury might give by reason of the defendant having discharged the plaintiff without due notice. The plaintiff obtained a verdict for 15*l.* 19*s.* : Held, that the sheriff had no jurisdiction to try this cause under the 3 & 4 Will. 4, c. 42, s. 17. (2 M. & W. 53 ; 5 D. P. C. 736 ; 6 D. P. C. 668.)—*Jacquet* v. *Bower*, 7 D. P. C. 331.

EQUITY.

[Containing 3 Mylne & Craig, Part 3 ; 2 Keen, Part 3 ; 8 Simons, Part 4 ; and 3 Younge & Collyer, Part 2.]

ABATEMENT.

(*Dismissal of bill.*) Where a sole plaintiff became bankrupt, it was ordered, on motion by defendant, that the bill should be dismissed without costs, unless the assignees filed a supplemental bill within six weeks.—*Holt* v. *Hardcastle*, Y. & C. 236.

ADMINISTRATION.

1. (*Parties.*) In a suit by landlord to compel an equitable mortgagee to accept an assignment of a lease from the representative of a deceased lessee ; *semble*, that letters of administration limited to attend, supply, substantiate and confirm the proceedings in the suit, or in any other suits, concerning the premises, were not sufficient to constitute a representative for the purpose of making the required assignment.—*Moores* v. *Choat*, Sim. 508.

2. (*Relation of.*) An objection was taken to a bill by a husband for a legacy due to his late wife, that administration had not been taken out till after bill filed ; the objection was overruled, partly because the administration had relation to the time of the death ; *Humphreys* v. *Humphreys*, 3 P. W. 394 ; partly because, before taking out administration, the husband had an equitable interest.—*Moses* v. *Levy*, Y. & C. 359.

ADMINISTRATION OF ASSETS.

1. (*Concurrent suits.*) After a bill filed by a residuary legatee against executors, but before decree in such suit, a creditor filed his bill upon a bond, upon which no interest had been paid, and of which there had been no acknowledgment made for upwards of twenty years, but the executors by their answer admitted the debt ; afterwards the plaintiff in the first suit obtained the usual decree, and the defendants, the executors, obtained an order to stay proceedings in the second suit. The Lord Chancellor, on appeal, discharged such order, made the common decree in the second suit, and directed the report to be made in both causes.—*Budgen* v. *Sage*, *Rawdon* v. *Sage*, M. & C. 683.

2. (*Interest on bond debts.*) Where, in a creditors' suit, bond creditors had been allowed their principal and interest up to the penalties in the bonds, and had received an apportionment upon such sums, and further funds became available : Held, that they ought to be allowed out of such new funds further interest upon so much as remained due, after such payment as above, of the principal sums severally mentioned in the conditions of each bond, provided that such interest, together with what remained due under the previous allow-

ance, should not exceed the penalty in each bond.—*Walters* v. *Meredith*, Y. & C. 264.

3. (*Mortgage—Exoneration.*) A testator seised of an estate subject to a mortgage for a debt which the Court held to be his own, devised that estate, together with another estate, to certain persons in fee, " *the whole* subject to the payment of the mortgage debt :" Held, that the personal estate was not discharged.

Some stress was also laid upon this, that there was a declaration that his personal estate should be subject to payment of his debts, except such debts as were specified, and this was not specified ; and there was also another devise of mortgage property, with an *express* exemption of the personalty from payment of the debt.—*Bickham* v. *Cruttwell*, M. & C. 763.

4. (*Pleading.*) Judgment creditors, filing their bill on behalf of themselves and other specialty creditors, do not thereby waive their priority over creditors by bond.—*Berrington* v. *Evans*, Y. & C. 384.

5. (*Proof by creditor having a lien.*) Where a vendor had obtained a decree for specific performance, with a declaration that if the purchase-money was not paid by a day to be fixed by the master, the estate should be sold for payment of the debt, and in case of a deficiency, that the purchaser should be charged therewith ; and after day fixed, but before the arrival of such day, the purchaser died insolvent, and a creditors' suit was instituted for administration of his estate : Held, that, according to the terms of the above declaration, the vendor could not prove as a creditor in that suit, for the purchase-money, till the estate had been sold, and the proceeds applied ; but the question was reserved, whether he might then prove for the whole, or for the unpaid balance. Distinction between this case and that of Mason v. Bogg, 1 Russ. & Myl. 185. —*Rome* v. *Young*, Y. & C. 199.

ADOPTION.

(*Maintenance.*) A testator who had voluntarily entered into a bond with a parish, to pay a weekly maintenance for a natural child as his son, and had continued such payments up to his death, was considered to have so far placed himself *in loco parentis* to such child as that interest was payable from his (testator's) death, upon a legacy given by him to such child to be paid at twenty-one.—*Rogers* v. *Soutten*, Keen, 598, Coop. 96.

AGREEMENT.

(*Consideration—Privity.*) Where, in consideration of a bill deposited by A. with B., the latter had promised to provide for payment of another bill accepted by A., and held by C. ; it was, upon a bill of discovery in aid of an action by C. against B., considered a fair question for argument at law, how far C. was entitled to sue upon the agreement, and some observations were made by the Court upon the question itself.—*Thomas* v. *Tyler*, Y. & C. 255.

ANNUITY.

(*Inrolment—Value of lands charged.*) The 10th section of the 53 Geo. 3, c. 131, provides that no inrolment shall be required of an annuity charged upon lands of equal or greater annual value than the annuity, and whereof the grantor is seised in fee simple or fee tail in possession, or whereof he is enabled to charge the fee simple in possession. Land of the annual value of 100l. was devised in trust for the testator's daughter, a married woman, for life, remainder to all her children by her then present or future husband, as tenants in common in fee, subject to a proviso that if the daughter should die without having issue of her body, the land should go over. The daughter, having at the time six children, joins with three of them in granting an annuity of 48*l.* charged on the devised estate : Held, that such annuity was within the above exception, because the present value of the interest charged was 50*l.*, and because the gift over was only to take effect in the event of the daughter's death without having had children.—*Walford* v. *Marchant,* M. & C. 550 ; see *S. C.* 2 B. & Adol. 315.

APPEAL.

(*Against separate orders—Practice.*) Where there had been an original bill to which defendant pleaded, and a supplemental bill to which he demurred, and both plea and demurrer had been allowed, a petition of appeal against both orders was held irregular, but the appellant was allowed to elect at the hearing as to which order he would confine his appeal, upon undertaking to amend the petition accordingly.—*Boys* v. *Morgan,* M. & C. 661.

BILL OF DISCOVERY.

1. (*Against witnesses.*) It is improper to join as defendants in a bill of discovery parties who may be examined as witnesses at law, the only exception to the rule being that of a bill against the devisee and witnesses of a will.—*Jones* v. *Maund,* Y. & C. 347.

(*Doubtful question.*) It is sufficient to support a bill of discovery, that there should be a reasonable doubt as to the question to be tried at law ; and where there is such doubt, the Court will not decide upon it.—*Thomas* v. *Tyler,* Y. & C. 255.

BANKRUPT. See ABATEMENT ; RESTRAINT UPON ALIENATION.

BILL OF EXCHANGE.

(*Delivery up of.*) Where a party sues in equity for the delivery up of a bill to which, it appears, he has a good defence at law, it is not sufficient for him to show that such defence at law, as it depends upon testimony, is liable to fail through the death of witnesses, he must also show that the defendant in equity came into possession of the bill in a wrongful manner, or that he is not equitably entitled to recover upon the same. Where the grounds of the legal defence are apparent on the face of the instrument, equity will in no case interfere to have it delivered up.—*Jones* v. *Lane,* Y. & C. 280.

And see AGREEMENT.

BOND DEBT. See ADMINISTRATION OF ASSETS, 2.

CHARGE.

(*Covenant.*) A covenant to pay debts by a certain day, and in default thereof to sell so much of covenantor's estates as should be necessary for that purpose : Held, in an administration suit, and as against judgment and bond creditors, not to create a lien, or entitle the covenantees to rank as judgment creditors ; and it was the opinion of the Court that the covenant was a mere personal undertaking. The word " heirs" was not used.—*Berrington* v. *Evans,* Y. & C. 384.

CHARGE OF DEBTS.

1. (*Power to mortgage.*) A devise in trust, subject to payment of debts, gives the trustee a power to mortgage for the purpose of paying debts ; and where the trustee says the money is wanted for such purpose, the lender is not bound to inquire further.—*Ball* v. *Harris,* Sim. 485.

2. (*Substituted estates.*) Where there was a devise upon various trusts, but subject to a charge for payment of debts, with a power to sell, and to buy other lands to be held upon the trusts of the will, and the trustee sold part of the de

vised lands, and bought others : Held, that the purchased lands were subject to the charge of debts, and might be mortgaged by the trustee.—*S. C.*

CHARITY.

1. (*Divided parish.*) Where there was one endowment under a will of a free-school to be kept in *the village* of Hampton, and there was, by a subsequent will, a devise in trust to pay the rents to the schoolmaster of the free-school of Hampton, or some other person who would teach six poor children of the *parish* of Hampton, and the parish of Hampton consisted of two parts, called *Hampton-wick* and *Hampton-town*: Held, that no part of the first endowment could be applied in maintaining a school at *Hampton-wick ;* but that, if it should appear beneficial, part of the second gift might be applied in maintaining a schoolmaster there, in connection with the principal school.—*Attorney-General v. Jackson*, Keen, 541.

2. (*Free-school.*) A direction (in a will of the year 1556) to found a *free-school* is not satisfied by the foundation of a *free grammar school ;* but in a *free-school* instruction may be given in all elementary branches of learning, exclusive of the learned languages.—*S. C.*

3. (*Jews.*) A bequest to enable persons professing the Jewish religion to observe its rites, was held lawful.—*Straus v. Goldsmid*, Sim. 614.

4. (*Parish—59 Geo. 3, c. 12.*) This statute, which vests certain estates in the churchwardens and overseers of parishes, does not apply to copyholds, or other lands held upon special trust.—*Re Paddington Charities*, Sim. 629.

And see MORTMAIN.

CONSTRUCTION.

1. (*Deed of revocation and re-settlement.*) A father, by deed, settled certain lease-holds upon his son absolutely, and also a rent-charge and stock in the funds upon him for life, with remainder to his children. He afterwards, by deed, revoked all the benefits given to his son by the first deed, and declared that all estates, shares, right, interest and benefit given to his son by such deed, should be and remain to trustees, their heirs, executors and administrators, upon trust, during the joint lives of his son and his son's wife, to pay the rents, interest, *dividends*, profits and annual income thereof to his son's wife for her separate use, and after his son's death then to her, during life or widowhood, with remainder to the children : Held, chiefly upon the strength of the term " dividends," that the stock and rent-charge (as well as the leaseholds) passed to the wife for her life, and not during the life of the son only.—*Angell v. Dawson*, Y. & C. 308.

2. (*11 Geo. 4 and 1 Will. 4, c. 47.*) Where the Court is empowered by act of parliament to decree a sale, it has power also to decree a mortgage, and the infant devisees of deceased debtors were ordered, in such a case, to join in mortgage. —*Holme v. Williams*, Sim. 557.

3. (*11 Geo. 4 and 1 Will. 4, c. 60.*) This act does not apply to lands out of the queen's dominions ; nor is a party having the legal interest in a debt (which he has been decreed to assign) a trustee of such debt within the act.—*Price v. Dewhurst*, Sim. 616 ; see S. C. ante, 279.

4. (*Parcels—General words—Right of dower.*) Where a husband, who had married the widow of testator, assigned, by deed, all and singular the legacies, debts, monies, estate and effects whatsoever and wheresoever, and of what nature or kind of or to which be the assignor, in right of his wife or otherwise,

was possessed, as well under the will and codicil of the first husband, as in any other manner however: Held, that the assignor's interest (if any) in his wife's right to dower, did not pass by the assignment.—*Brown* v. *Meredith*, Keen, 527.

See CHARGE; WILL, (*passim*.)

COPYRIGHT.

1. (*Fair quotation.*) Extracts from another work may be piratical, though but a small proportion of the book quoted from, if they contain the most valuable portion of it.—*Bramwell* v. *Halcomb*, M. & C. 737.

2. (*Law reports.*) *Quære:* Whether it is an infringement of copyright to print at full length detached cases contained in the Law Reports, though with the addition of laborious notes, and with the view of illustrating particular points of law.—*Saunders* v. *Smith*, M. & C. 711.

And see INJUNCTION.

COSTS.

1. (*Collateral suits.*) A cestui que trust instituted a suit against the representatives of a deceased trustee, to have a breach of trust made good; shortly afterwards, a creditor's suit was instituted against the estate of the same trustee, in which the plaintiff in the first suit came in and proved his claim as a debt. He afterwards brought the first suit to a hearing, for the purpose of obtaining possession of a fund in which some of the trust money was invested. Having obtained a decree, he presented a petition in both suits, praying, among other things, to have his costs in the first suit paid to him, in the second, out of the general assets of trustee: Held, that he was so entitled, on the authority of Illingworth v. Nelson, reported in note. (Affirmed by Lord Chancellor.)—*Costerton* v. *Costerton*, *Clarke* v. *Wenn*, Keen, 774.

2. (*Whether borne by real and personal estate.*) Where a suit had been instituted respecting the disposal of accumulations (void by Thelluson's act), which arose from a mixed fund of realty and personalty, and which by the decree were given proportionably to the heir and next of kin; the Court directed the costs of the suit to be paid *pro rata* by the heir and personal representative; but the decree was reversed as to this point.—*Eyre* v. *Marsden*, Keen, 564.

See EQUITABLE MORTGAGE, 1; EXECUTOR.

DELIVERY UP OF DOCUMENTS. See BILL OF EXCHANGE.

DEMURRER.

(*Amended bill.*) A defendant having fully answered the original bill, afterwards demurred to the whole of the amended bill, though the bill as amended did not materially vary the case made by the original bill, and contained many of the statements in it which the defendant had previously answered: Held, in the first place, that the Court might look at the record for the purpose of comparing the two bills with each other and with the answer; and in the second place, it being admitted that the result of the comparison would be as above stated, that the demurrer was overruled by the answer.—*Ellice* v. *Goodson*, M. & C. 653.

DEPOSIT OF LEASE.

1. (*Liability of depositary.*) The equitable mortgagee of a lease, whether by deposit or agreement, is not compellable to take an assignment at the suit of the landlord; Flight v. Bentley, 7 Sim. 149; which is hereby distinctly overruled, having been decided upon a mistaken view of the case of Lucas v. Comerford.—*Moores* v. *Choat*, Sim. 508.

2. (*Same point.*) Corrected report of the case of *Lucas* v. *Comerford*, 8 Sim. 499. (This case is originally reported in 1 Ves. jun. 235, and 3 Bro. C. C. 166.)

DISCLAIMER.

(*Where sufficient.*) Where parties were made defendants to a bill on the ground that they had set up an unfounded claim to a fund, and had by such claim prevented the trustees of the fund from transferring it to plaintiff, and the bill contained several allegations as to the particulars of the opposition made by the defendants to the due performance of the trust; the latter put in what was intituled an answer and disclaimer, whereby they disclaimed all right, and denied that they had ever made any claim: Held (on appeal), on exceptions taken to this as an answer, that it was insufficient; but it was observed by the Lord Chancellor, that the more regular course would have been to move that the answer and disclaimer be taken off the file. De Beauvoir v. Rhodes, not reported as to this point, stated in judgment.—*Graham* v. *Coape,* M. & C. 638.

DISMISSAL OF BILL.— See Abatement.

DOMICILE.

1. (*Evidence of.*) An inquiry having been directed as to the domicile of a testator who died at Amsterdam in 1696; it appeared that testator, who was a Jew, belonged to the Jewish Synagogue of London as well as to that of Amsterdam, and that in the year of his death he had, as appeared from the will, an establishment in London, but that he had previously to his death greatly diminished his contributions to the Jew Synagogue of that place, and the amount of legacies in his will was stated in Dutch money, and the provisions of his will were in some respects repugnaht to the law of England, but agreeable to the law and custom of Holland: Held, that he was a domiciled Dutchman at the time of his death.—*Bernal* v. *Bernal,* M. & C. 559, (note).

2. (*Foreign will.*) The Court will administer the trusts of a foreign will, as to personal property situate in this country, although such trusts may be inconsistent with the English law.— *Bernal* v. *Bernal,* M. & C. 559, Coop. 51.

DOWER.

(*Before assignment.*) *Semble,* that before assignment of dower, a widow has not such an estate in the lands of her deceased husband, as that a second husband would have in her right any assignable interest therein.—*Brown* v. *Meredith,* Keen, 527.

EQUITABLE MORTGAGE.

1. (*Costs of proceedings at law.*) An equitable mortgagee is entitled to charge upon the estate the costs of such proceedings only as he may reasonably have engaged in, in ascertaining or defending his rights; and where an equitable mortgagee had joined in defending an action of trover for the key of a house: Held, that as he had clearly no right in law to the possession, he was not entitled to charge the costs incurred in the action.—*Dryden* v. *Frost,* M. & C. 670.

2. (*Reference, where debt admitted.*) A decree for sale upon an equitable mortgage is not within the stat. 7 G. 2, c. 20, and in such a case the Court will exercise its general jurisdiction as to costs.—*Aberdeen* v. *Chitty,* Y. & C. 379.
And see Deposit of Lease.

EVIDENCE.

1. (*Answer of co-defendant.*) Where a defendant had been dismissed after an-

swer, the plaintiff was not allowed, in a proceeding by affidavit before the Master, to use his answer as an affidavit against the remaining defendant. *Hoare* v. *Johnstone, Hoare* v. *Campbell,* Keen, 553.

And see PRODUCTION OF DOCUMENTS.

2. (*Interested witness.*) An executor, before probate, is a good witness, in equity as well as at law, to increase the testator's estate. The authority of Croft v. Tyke, 3 P. Wms. 180, doubted. In the principal case, the executor, though he had not formally renounced probate, had declined to prove.—*Hall* v. *Laver*, Y. & C. 191.

EXCEPTIONS.

(*Allowed after amendment.*) Where a defendant answers part of a bill, and demurs to the rest, and such demurrer is overruled, and the plaintiff then amends, such amendment is not a waiver of his right to except to the answer, in respect of such part of the bill as was covered by the demurrer.

In this case the amendment was only by adding parties ; and *semble,* that such an amendment is in no case a waiver of the right to except. Miller v. Wheatley, 1 Sim. 296.—*Taylor* v. *Bailey*, M. & C. 677.

EXCHANGE.

1. (*Title under defective exchange.*) A. being entitled under a settlement to lands for life, remainder to trustees for 1000 years to raise jointure and portions, remainder to himself in fee; and there being a power of sale and exchange given by the settlement to the trustees with A.'s consent, conveys, by way of exchange, some of the settled lands to B., without any reference to the power, and without the concurrence of the trustees. B.'s heir afterwards contracts to sell such lands, and after objection being taken by the purchaser before the Master, in a suit for specific performance against such purchaser, procures certain deeds to be executed by A. and the surviving trustee and himself, which, if executed at the time of the exchange, would have given it validity. Held, that the Court would not compel the purchaser to take the title, but no decision was given as to whether the exchange was validated. An objection was also taken to the deeds, on the ground of the inaccuracies and clerical errors which they contained.—*Cowgill* v. *Lord Ormantoun,* Y. & C. 369.

EXECUTOR.

1. (*Liability of one for the other.*) Two executors, being in joint possession of a residue, divided it, in order that each might pay, out of the portion left in his hands, the residuary legatees that resided in his own part of the country : Held, that one executor was liable for default in payment by the other, a distinction being taken between this case and those where money is paid over by one executor to answer a particular debt or specific legacy. Bacon v. Bacon, 5 Ves. 331. In the principal case some neglect in other respects was imputable to the executor sought to be charged.—*Moses* v. *Levy*, Y. & C. 359.

2. (*Limitation to, how construed.*) A limitation in a settlement, " to the executors, administrators, or assigns of the settlor, to and for his and their use and benefit :" Held, upon a consideration of the objects and context of the settlement, not to confer a beneficial interest upon the executors.—*Hames* v. *Hames*, Keen, 646.

3. (*Suit by.*) An executor having (for the purpose of appealing) revived a suit, after the bill of his testator had been dismissed with costs, was held liable to pay such costs whether he had assets or no.—*Horlock* v. *Priestley*, Sim. 621.

4. (*Waste—Denial of assets.*) Where an executor by his answer denies assets, but states circumstances, from which it appears that, but for misappropriation of the estate, he would have assets, a decree for payment was made against him without an account.—*Rogers v. Soutten*, Keen, 598.

And see EVIDENCE; PARTNERSHIP, 2; PRACTICE, 17; RECEIVER 2; WILL, 9.

FORFEITURE. See JURISDICTION; RESTRAINT UPON ALIENATION; WILL, 2.

FRAME OF SUIT.

(*Legal right in plaintiffs.*) Where a man having, by voluntary deed, assigned to a trustee certain choses in action, and other personal chattels, in trust for himself for life, and after his death for other parties, afterwards by will disposed of the property so assigned, and the trustee and cestui que trusts under the settlement filed their bill against the executors and legatees, praying that after payment of testator's debts, the residue might be paid to the trustee: Such bill was dismissed with costs, on the ground that if such trustee had a legal interest under the assignment, as appeared by the bill, he might enforce it at law; and this decision was affirmed by the Chancellor, who observed, that the suit might have been so framed, by making the trustee a defendant, and by alleging difficulties in the way of the execution of the trusts, as to enable the Court to give relief. He therefore dismissed the bill without prejudice to the institution of any other suit.—*Ward v. Audland*, Sim. 571; Coop. 146.

FRAUD. See JOINT-STOCK COMPANY; PARTIES, 6; POLICY OF ASSURANCE.

HUSBAND AND WIFE.

1. (*Insolvent.*) The wife of an insolvent debtor having filed her bill against the trustees of a sum to which she was absolutely entitled, and such money having been paid into Court: Ordered that the interest should be paid to her for life, and at her death the principal divided among her children, no settlement being directed on account of the smallness of the sum.—*Brett v. Greenwell*, Y. & C. 230.

2. (*Wife's legacy.*) It may be assumed from circumstances, that a husband has authorised payment to his wife, as his agent, of a legacy given to her, though no express assent is proved.—*Moses v. Levy*, Y. & C. 359.

And see ADMINISTRATION, 2; PARTIES, 3; PRACTICE, 15.

INCAPACITY.

(*Partition.*) Where one of three tenants in common was admitted to be incapable, through weakness of intellect, of making a conveyance, a commission of partition was nevertheless granted at the suit of the other two tenants, so that the lands might be held in severalty.—*Hollingworth v. Sidebottom*, Sim. 620.

INFANT HEIR.

(1 *Will. 4, c. 47.*) Held that this statute, which authorises the Court to direct a *sale* of the estate of infant heir for the debts of the ancestor, does not authorise a mortgage.—*Smethurst v. Longworth*, Keen, 603.

And see CONSTRUCTION, 1, 2.

INJUNCTION.

1. (*Acquiescence.*) A party having obtained ex parte an injunction to restrain a railway company from prosecuting their works over his property, on the ground that they were bound by an agreement entered into with a company which had been merged in theirs, to purchase at a certain price another part of his property; the injunction was dissolved upon argument, by the Vice-Chancellor,

and his order confirmed by the Lord Chancellor with costs, on the ground that, assuming the agreement to be binding on the existing company, the plaintiff had lost all right to an injunction, because from the 14th of February, 1837 (when it was proved he was aware of his equity under the contract, if any,) to the 6th of August, 1838, he had taken no steps to enforce it, though he knew it was disputed by the company, and in the meanwhile the company had been at the expense of marking out the line.

It was also observed by the Court, that the equity under the contract was doubtful.—*Greenhalgh* v. *The Manchester and Birmingham Railway*, M. & C. 784. (See, *infra*, Railway, 2.)

2. (*Affidavits, where admissible.*) In a motion for an order to extend the common injunction to stay trial, affidavits were admitted on the part of the plaintiff to explain his apparent delay in not before applying for an injunction, and on the part of the defendant, to show, by a reference to the pleadings at law, that the discovery sought by the bill could be of use in a defence to the action, no objection being taken on either side.—*Thorpe* v. *Hughes*, M. & C. 742.

3. (*At suit of plaintiff at law.*) An injunction was granted at suit of plaintiff at law, to restrain defendant from taking cause to trial by proviso before answer to plaintiff's bill of discovery in equity.—*Thomas* v. *Tyler*, Y. & C. 255.

4. (*Costs.*) Where, after the common injunction, the plaintiffs at law proceeded to trial, and obtained nominal damages, and then made an unsuccessful application to the court at law to increase such damages, the plaintiffs in equity obtained a perpetual injunction, with costs of the suit in equity only.—*Calvert* v. *London Dock Company*, Keen, 638.

5. (*Joint-stock company.*) A shareholder in a joint-stock company, established under the 6 Geo. 4, c. 42, having had an action brought against him by the secretary of the company for payment of his instalments, filed his bill against such secretary, and against other persons who were directors of the company, and by whose fraudulent statement he had, as he alleged, been induced to become a shareholder in the company. To this bill the secretary duly appeared, but the other defendants being in contempt for non-appearance, the common injunction was obtained against *them*. The plaintiff then moved to extend this injunction, to stay trial of the action brought by the last-named defendants in the name of *the secretary*, and such motion having been granted by the Vice-Chancellor, the order was held by the Lord Chancellor to be irregular, because, as there had been no common injunction against the secretary, the sole plaintiff at law, there was no ground for an order to *extend* the injunction against him, and that this therefore, though not in form, was a special injunction against a party not in default, which was contrary to the case of Lord Portarlington v. Graham, Sim. 416.

The Lord Chancellor also observed, that to grant such an injunction as this would defeat the objects of the act empowering joint-stock companies to sue by their public officers, though he admitted such cases might require some departure from the rule above laid down.

In this case, too, it appeared, by reference to the pleadings at law, set forth by affidavit of defendant in equity, that the discovery sought by the bill would not assist the defence to the action.—*Thorpe* v. *Hughes*, M. & C. 742.

6. (*Waiver—Copyright.*) Where the Court was of opinion that the plaintiffs had so acted as to induce the defendants to believe that they would not object to the publication sought to be restrained, the Court refused the injunction, without

giving an opinion as to whether there had been an infringement of copyright or not. (Rundell v. Murray, Jacob, 311.)—*Saunders v. Smith,* M. & C. 711.

And see PRACTICE, 5, 6, 22.

INSOLVENT. See HUSBAND AND WIFE, 1.

INSTITUTION OF SUIT.

(*Authority from plaintiff—Costs.*) Where a suit had been instituted without the authority of one of the plaintiffs, and such plaintiff had rights at variance with the other co-plaintiffs: His name was, at his own instance, after replication filed, ordered to be struck out, and his costs of the suit and the application were ordered to be paid by the solicitor who filed the bill.—*Tabbernor v. Tabbernor,* Keen, 679.

- INTEREST.

(*Judgment debt.*) In 1795 judgment was entered up on a warrant of attorney for the penalty of a bond given to secure an annuity. In 1796 a fund charged with payment of the same annuity was paid into Court, in a suit by grantee of annuity ; but the Court, being of opinion that the reversionary interest only of the grantor was effectually charged, retained the fund, paying the interest to the tenant for life. In 1810 the tenant for life died, the grantor of the annuity being then also dead intestate, and the annuity, which was for the lives of both the latter parties, then expired. In 1834 administration was taken out on behalf of the Crown, to the grantor, no next of kin having appeared in the meantime. The representatives of the grantee of the annuity thereupon filed their bill for payment of the arrears of the annuity with interest thereon : Held by analogy to the legal right of a judgment creditor, both before 3 & 4 Will. 4, c. 42, and under that act, that as against the personal estate of the debtor, and in the absence of creditors, the arrears of the annuity with interest thereon from the year 1810, which considerably exceeded the penalty of the bond, should be paid out of the fund which had remained in Court accumulating.—*Hyde v. Price, Hart v. Cradock,* Sim. 578 ; Coop. 193.

And see ADMINISTRATION OF ASSETS, 2.

JOINT STOCK COMPANY.

(*Illegality—Fraud.*) A joint-stock company, of which the association deed, provided that the shareholders might increase indefinitely the number of shares, and, consequently, the capital of the company, and that the shares might be assigned by deed or will at the discretion of the holders, was held to be illegal because it intrenched upon the prerogative of the crown, and because the clause as to the transfer of shares was manifestly intended to delude the public with the false notion that the shareholders could effectually assign their shares at their own discretion, and so as to get rid of all liabilities for the debts of the company ; and on these grounds a demurrer to a bill by one of the shareholders for a dissolution of the company, and an account of its assets, was allowed, with costs.—*Blundell v. Winsor,* Sim. 601.

See INJUNCTION, 5.

JURISDICTION.

(*Remedies against the crown.*) Where a man who had deposited, as a security for money borrowed, the title-deeds of a leasehold estate, was afterwards convicted of a felony : Held, that the Court could not decree a sale against the Crown as holden of the legal estate, but could only declare that the equitable mortgagee was entitled to hold possession of the property till his lien was satisfied or till the Crown should redeem.—*Hodge* v. *Attorney General*, Y. & C. 342.

LAPSE OF TIME. See TRUST.

LEGACY DUTY.

1. (*Legacy for life, with remainder over.*) A testator directed a sum sufficient to produce 200*l.* a year, clear of legacy-duty, to be invested in the funds, of which he gave the income to A. for life, and the capital in remainder to other parties. And he also directed his trustees to pay the legacy duty upon other legacies given to A., and also on the yearly sum given to or in trust for her. A., as well as the other parties in remainder, being strangers in blood to the testator, and liable to the same rate of duty, it was necessary on investing the sum to pay the whole duty: Held, after A.'s death, that the representatives of testator could not, against the legatees in remainder, retain out of the sum invested such proportion of the money paid for the duty as was paid in respect of the interest in remainder.—*Calvert* v. *Sebbon*, Keen, 672.

MISTAKE.

(*Practice.*) A fresh commission to examine was granted to the defendants upon payment of costs of suing out such new commission, where it appeared that the defendants had omitted to examine witnesses under the first commission, under a false impression that the questions in dispute would be disposed of by the tithe commissioners under the act.—*Wetherell* v. *Weighill*, Y. & C. 320.

And see SOLICITOR and CLIENT, 2.

MORTGAGE.

(*Priority—Notice to first mortgagee.*) The principle of the cases, Dearle v. Hall and Loveridge v. Cooper, 1 Russ. p. 1 and 30, does not apply to real estate; and accordingly where a third mortgagee, without notice of the second mortgage, gave notice of his incumbrance to the first mortgagee, and caused a notice to the same effect to be indorsed upon the settlement in possession of the first mortgagee, under which the mortgagor claimed title: Held, that the third mortgagee did not thereby gain priority over the second. It appeared that the second mortgagee had no notice of the first mortgage.—*Jones* v. *Jones*, Sim. 633.

And see PARTIES, 2.

MORTMAIN ACT.

(*Purchase of land for a charity.*) The Court refused, in consideration of the policy and intention of the Mortmain Act, to sanction that part of a scheme for the management of a charity which proposed, that part of the charity funds should be laid out in the purchase of lands for the purpose of enlarging the charity.— *Attorney General* v. *Wilson*, Keen, 680.

NOTICE. See MORTGAGE; TRUSTEE, 5; VENDOR AND PURCHASER.

PARISH. See CHARITY.

PARTIES.

1. (*Aliquot share of ascertained fund.*) A bill having been filed by parties entitled under a will to one-fourth of a fund, (which since the testator's death had been ascertained and appropriated), against the trustee alone; a demurrer for want of parties was put in, which was reluctantly overruled by the Court on the authority of Smith v. Snow, 3 Mad. 10.—*Hutchinson* v. *Townsend*, Keen, 675.

2. (*Foreclosure suit.*)—Where, after issue joined in a foreclosure suit, the mortgagor had become bankrupt, the plaintiff was allowed to amend his bill by making the assignees parties, still retaining the bankrupt as a defendant.—*Hanson v. Preston*, Y. & C. 229.

3. (*Husband and wife—Misjoinder.*) In a suit to obtain the benefit of a bequest to the separate use of the wife, it is improper to join the husband and wife as co-plaintiffs, but the wife should sue by her next friend, the husband being a defendant.—*Owden v. Campbell*, Sim. 551.

4. (*Injunction suit.*) Where a bill is filed to restrain an ejectment the tenant must be made a party, unless the landlord has been admitted to defend the action at law.—*Poole v. Marsh*, Sim. 528.

5. (*Joint stock company.*) The trustees of an assurance company, not being share-holders, who had as such trustees solely subscribed a policy, brought a bill to set aside such policy as sole plaintiffs, not expressing themselves to sue on behalf of the shareholders, but making parties as defendants the directors of the company ; who, as they alleged by their bill, were the only shareholders whose names they were acquainted with : Held, on demurrer, that there was no want of parties, and that the suit was properly framed.—*Fenn v. Craig*, Y. & C. 216.

N. B. The leading authorities on the subject are summed up in a note to this case.

6. (*Surviving partner of testator.*) The case of Bowsher v. Watkins, 1 R. & M. 207, does not establish the general proposition, that a bill may be filed against the executor and surviving partner of testator without charging and proving fraud and collusion.—*Davies v. Davies*, Keen, 534.

And see Administration, 1 ; Partnership, 2, 3.

PARTITION.　See Incapacity.

PARTNERSHIP.

1. (*Conversion of land into personalty.*) A. being seised in fee of warehouses and land used solely for the purposes of his trade, upon taking his son into partner-ship for twenty-four years, which he does gratuitously, conveys to him in fee, for natural love and affection, certain shares of the houses and land commen-surate with the son's shares in the business ; and, by the articles of partner-ship, it is stipulated that the shares in the land given to the son, as also those reserved by the father, should be taken as part of the joint stock in the part-nership business, and in the event of either party dying before the expiration of the twenty-four years without disposing of his shares, the same were to be sold, a right of pre-emption being reserved to the survivor. Afterwards other shares of the land were conveyed to the son, and at the same time similar shares in the business made over to him, upon the footing of the original arti-cles. Both parties outlive the twenty-four years, and continue after that to carry on business, but without renewing the articles, when A. dies : Held, that as between his real and personal representatives his shares in the land were not converted into personalty. (Bell v. Phyn, 7 Ves. 543.)—*Cookson v. Cook-son*, Sim. 529.

2. (*Retainer of deceased partner's share.*) Where the surviving partners, who were also the executors and trustees of the deceased partner's will, after taking the account of what was due to his estate on account of his share, had merely debited the firm with the balance, which was from time to time diminished by pay-

ments thereout under the will, after a lapse of thirty years, during which several changes had taken place in the firm : Held, that the parties interested under the will of the deceased partner were entitled to an account of the profits made by the successive firms, in respect of so much of the deceased partner's estate as was from time to time retained in the business.— *Wedderburn* v. *Wedderburn*, Keen, 722.

3. (*Suit against successive firms.*) An action having been brought by A. upon a covenant entered into with her in conjunction with two others, who were then her partners in a firm, from which A. afterwards retired, a bill was filed, by the defendant at law stating that A., upon her retirement, had assigned all her interest in the partnership business and debts to B., who thereby became and still was a member of the firm, and stating that by various transactions with B. and the continuing firm, to some of which A. was a party, and by various payments to the new firm, the debt had been extinguished ; and the bill prayed for an injunction to restrain the action, and for an account against the firm in its different states, and also to set aside a sale made for payment of the debt. To this bill a general demurrer was put in, which was allowed, partly on the ground that if it could be proved that A. had authorised the new firm to receive the debt, that would be a defence at law, and unless she had done so, the plaintiff had no equity ; partly because the plaintiff had no right to mix up the successive partners with his account against A., though there might be ground for a discovery of the transactions between A. and B. ; partly because the bill as against the successive partners was for discovery beforehand of what they might say as witnesses at law.—*Jones* v. *Maund*, Y. & C. 347.

PAUPER.

(*Service of order.*) An order to sue *in formá pauperis* is ineffectual till served, and till such service the liability to *dives* costs remains.—*Ballard* v. *Catling*, Keen, 606.

And see PRACTICE, 9.

PAYMENT INTO COURT. See PRACTICE, 18.

PERPETUITY.

(*Term precedent to estate-tail.*) Where a term is in its limitation prior to an estate tail created by the same instrument, and part of the trusts of the term are to take effect upon failure of the estate tail, such trusts cannot be barred by a recovery, and are therefore void, as tending to a perpetuity. An alternative construction put by the Court upon the will was, that the trusts were to take effect upon a general failure of issue, not the issue in tail, in which case they would have been equally void.—*Case* v. *Drosier*, Keen, 764.

And see WILL, 8, 11, 13.

PLEA.

1. (*Effect of allowing.*) The mere allowance of a plea, either in the Court of Chancery or in the Exchequer, does not in any case so far put an end to the suit, as that such suit may not itself be alleged in support of a plea of *lis pendens* ; and such last-mentioned plea was allowed under the circumstances above stated, with costs of the suit, under the 31st order.—*Tarleton* v. *Barnes*, Keen, 632.

2. (*Setting down for argument.*) The setting down a plea for argument (as of a *lis pendens*) does not preclude the plaintiff from taking an objection to such plea

founded on the alleged inconsistency of the statements it contains, with the legal conclusions on which its validity depends.—*S. C.*

PLEADING.

1. (*Demurrer to discovery.*) A bill being filed by a purchaser to set aside a contract for purchase of a secret in trade, which bill inquired into the nature of the alleged secret, of which it denied the existence, the defendant demurred to that part of the discovery sought which related to the nature of the secret: Held, that he ought to have taken the objection by plea, this not being one of those cases in which a demurrer to the discovery alone is allowed.—*Carter* v. *Goetze,* Keen, 581.

2. (*Doubtful statement.*) Where, in a bill filed by a vicar and his lessee, it was stated that the vicar had demised the tithes to the lessee, and an objection for misjoinder was taken at the hearing, which, it was admitted, would have been valid if the demise had been by deed, as the legal as well as equitable interest would then have been divested out of the vicar; the Court assumed in favour of the bill that the demise was by parol.—*Foot* v. *Bessant,* Y. & C. 320.

3. (*Plea to discovery.*) Where a defendant is desirous of pleading a settled account as a defence to the whole bill, which bill charges that such settled account, if any, was fraudulent and collusive, the proper mode is to plead to the *whole relief*, and to all the *discovery*, except that which is made by the answer; and a plea to the *whole bill*, except such parts as relate to the charges of fraud and collusion, is informal; but the plea being right in substance, the defendant in such base was allowed to amend.—*Davies* v. *Davies,* Keen, 534.

4. (*Settled account—Vouchers.*) Where a defendant to a bill, by residuary legatees, pleaded a settled account with their executor, which settled account was noticed in the bill as a pretence, and charged to be false, but the bill contained no charge that plaintiffs could not obtain an inspection of such account, or of the vouchers to which it referred, or that they had applied for them in the proper quarter: Held, that the defendant was not bound to set forth such account, or to aver that he had delivered up the vouchers to the executor.—*S. C.*

5. (*Statute of Limitations.*) Advantage may be taken of the statute upon general demurrer. (Hoare v. Peck, 6 Sim. 51.)—*Fyson* v. *Pole,* Y. & C. 266.

And see Administration of Assets, 3; Demurrer; Disclaimer; Executor; Frame of Suit; Parties, 5; Trustees, 6.

POLICY OF ASSURANCE.

(*Fraud.*) A bill will lie to have a policy of assurance upon life delivered up to be cancelled on the ground of fraud; and the more proper time to institute such a suit is during the lifetime of the party whose life is insured.—*Fenn* v. *Craig,* Y. & C. 216.

PORTIONS.

(*Younger son becoming eldest.*) By a settlement containing the usual limitations to the father for life, remainder to the first and other sons in tail, a provision was made for portions for younger children, to be vested interests in them at twenty-one, but payable only after the father's death; and it was provided that if any of the younger sons should become an eldest, his portion should accrue to the other children. There were two sons and a daughter. The eldest son, on becoming of age, joined his father in suffering a recovery, whereby, in the events that happened, the son acquired a remainder in fee, subject only to his father's life estate. The eldest son died, having devised his remainder in fee to his brother for life, with remainder to his brother's sons in tail. The brother had not then acquired a vested interest in his portion:—Held, that it accrued to the daughter.—*Peacocke* v. *Pares*, Keen, 689.

POWER.

1. (*Construction—Extent of.*) A bequest to trustees, in trust for A. for life, and after her decease in trust for such persons and for such purposes as she should appoint, and in default of appointment in trust for her children, but if she should have no children, then in trust for the testator's other daughters:— Held, to confer upon A. a general power of appointment.—*Mackinley* v. *Sison*, Sim. 561.

2. (*Excess—Partial failure.*) A power to appoint among children, subject to such regulations and directions with regard to the settling the shares in trust for their separate use, and with, under, and subject to such powers, provisos, and other restrictions and limitations over (such limitations over being for the benefit of some or one of them), does not authorise an appointment to grandchildren.

But where under such a power A. appointed shares to certain of her children for life, with remainder to their children, and in case any of her children died in her life-time, she gave the share to his or her issue; and in case there should be no issue, to her surviving children:—Held, that the alternative appointment to the survivors, in the event of any dying without issue in A.'s lifetime was valid.—*Hewitt* v. *Lord Dacre*, Keen, 622.

3. (*Execution—Indication of subject.*) Where a power was to be executed by deed or by will, signed and *published* by donee in the presence of and attested by two credible witnesses, a will expressed to be signed and sealed only, omitting the word *published*, and attested by three witnesses, was held to be a good execution.

And where the property subject to the power was stock in the 3*l. per cents.*, and the donee, who had no other stock, gave legacies to be paid out of the monies invested in her name in the 4*l. per cents.* :—Held, that this was an appointment of the 3*l. per cents.*—*Mackinley* v. *Sison*, Sim. 561.

4. (*Husband and wife.*) A power of appointing personalty to a woman (who was unmarried when the power was created,) held to be well executed by an appointment to the husband, as he thereby took no greater interest than he would if the appointment had been simply to the wife.—*Hewitt* v. *Lord Dacre* Keen, 622.

5. (*Trust raised from power—Conversion.*) The words, " I do empower my wife to sell all my estates whatsoever, and the money arising from such sale, together with my personal estate, she my said wife shall and may devise and proportion among my children, as she shall think proper, or as she shall direct by will,—Held, to confer a life estate on the widow, with remainder in default of appointment to the children in equal shares.

Held, also, to be a conversion of the real estate (which was in fact not sold by the widow) as between the real and personal representatives of a deceased child.—*Grieveson* v. *Kirsopp*, Keen, 653.

6. (*Void condition.*) A direction to retain out of share of appointee a sum due to appointor, though void, does not vitiate the appointment.—*Hewitt* v. *Lord Dacre*, Keen, 622.

And see WILL, 3.

PRACTICE.

1. (*Absent defendant.*) Defendant not appearing at the hearing, plaintiff took such decree as he could abide by, having afterwards found out that there was a defect in the affidavit of service of subpœna to bear judgment, he asked the Court to reinstate the cause, which was refused, as the proper course was to set down the cause at the bottom of the list.—*Evans* v. *Evans*, Keen, 604.

2. (*Contempt.*) A defendant, in contempt for want of an appearance, was not allowed to move to discharge order of sequestration, and set aside writ of sequestration on the ground of irregularity in service of the subpœna, without first entering with the registrar a conditional appearance, to be void if the application succeeded, to be good if it failed.—*Davidson* v. *Marchioness of Hastings*, Keen, 509.

3. *Dismissal — Bankrupt.*) Where the plaintiff in an injunction suit became bankrupt, pending the suit, and the defendants served the assignees alone with notice of motion to dismiss the bill, unless they filed a supplemental bill within a certain time:—Held, that the plaintiff ought to have been served also, and an order obtained under the above notice was discharged.—*Vestris* v. *Hooper*, Sim. 570.

4. (*Dismissal—Costs.*) A plaintiff, who at the time of filing his bill had notice of defendant's insolvency, which terminated in bankruptcy, was not allowed to dismiss his bill without costs, though the answer admitted the receipt and non-application of trust-monies.—*Suckling* v. *Maddocks*, Y. & C. 232. (In the Exchequer.)

5. (*Injunction—Exception.*) A plaintiff having, after declaration served at law, obtained the common injunction, gave notice of motion to extend the injunction to stay trial. The day before that motion was to have been made, defendant filed his answer, to which the plaintiff, having excepted, obtained as of course an order to refer the answer instanter:—Held, that such order was regular, the case coming within the principle of Candler v. Partington, Mad. & Geld. 102. —*Brooks* v. *Huigh*, Sim. 558.

6. (*Injunction—Special motion to dissolve.*)—An injunction having been obtained against a cestui que trust and his trustee, to restrain an action brought in the name of the latter; a special motion to dissolve it (the usual order nisi not having been previously obtained) was held to be regular.—*Sharpley* v. *Perring*, Sim. 600.

7. (*Mode of application to the Court.*) Held, that an application to discharge order for taxation of costs, by a person who had obtained that order, and also to have the re-admission of his solicitor declared void, ought to have been by petition and not by motion.—*Exp. Chambers*, *re Wilton*, Keen, 497.

8. (*Notice of motion.*) Where leave of the Court to make a motion has been obtained, the notice of motion should state that it is to be made by such leave.— *Hill* v. *Rimell*, Sim. 632.

9. (*Pauper.*) It is not necessary that a notice of motion of a pauper should be signed by his six clerk.—*Perry* v. *Walker*, Keen, 663.

10. (*Production of documents.*) The proper mode of objecting to the master's certificate of default in the production of documents, is to wait till the other party has obtained the usual four-day order, and then move to discharge such order, and to take the certificate off the file.—*Kemp* v. *Wade*, Keen, 686. (Vide *Toulmin* v. *Copeland*, Y. & C. 382, as to practice in Exchequer.)

11. (*Re-examination of witness.*) A witness who has been examined by one side before the hearing, may, after decree, be examined before the master for the other side, without leave of the Court.—*Metford v. Peters*, Sim. 630.

12. (*Selection of Court—New orders.*) A bill having been filed before the New Orders of 1837, after the issuing of such orders defendant filed a demurrer, and set it down at the Rolls, whereby he confined the subsequent proceedings to that Court: Held, that the demurrer was properly set down.—*Cane v. Martin*, Keen, 607.

13. (*Service of process.*) Service of a *subpœna* to appear and answer, directed to a defendant who was a Scotch peeress, and claimed by an uncontradicted affidavit to be a domiciled Scotchwoman, and which was left at her usual dwelling-house in London, and delivered to her servant there: Held, to be good service, and service of an order nisi for a sequestration, (founded on such service of subpœna,) upon the defendant personally, she being then in Scotland, was also held good.— *Davidson v. Marchioness of Hastings*, Keen, 509.

14. (*Undertaking to speed—Construction of order.*) Where by the terms of an order plaintiff undertook to set down the cause for hearing, and serve subpœnas to hear judgment in Easter term: Held, that he was bound to serve the subpœna soon enough to allow *the return* thereto to be made in Easter term; and the subpœna not having been served till the last day of Easter term, the bill was dismissed.—*Burgess v. Thompson*, Keen, 763.

(*In the Exchequer.*)

15. (*Answer of married woman.*) A separate attachment having issued against a married woman, for not having put in a joint answer with her husband, which was the construction put upon the order by the Court, a motion by the wife for leave to answer separately, and to set aside the attachment, no special circumstances being adduced in support of such motion, was refused.—*Hardy v. Sharpe*, Y. & C. 377.

16. (*Costs.*) Where an order had been made allowing to a residuary legatee, who was the plaintiff, his costs as between solicitor and client, the Court refused to vary the order, on the ground of its having been obtained without the consent of the other residuary legatees.—*Blenkinsop v. Foster*, Y. & C. 205.

17. (*Executor's lien.*) Payment by an executor, under an order, of money into Court, does not deprive him of his lien on it for costs.—*S. C.*

18. (*Pendency of appeal.*) Semble, that under special circumstances the Court will, pending an appeal, order money found due by decree from defendant to plaintiff, to be paid into Court; but in the present case it was ordered to be paid to the plaintiff, upon his giving security to refund.—*Thorpe v. Mattingley*, Y. & C. 255; see *S. C.* Y. & C. 421.

19. (*Production of documents—Master's certificate.*) An appeal from the master to the Court, upon a decision by the former as to the production of documents, is properly made by way of exception to the master's certificate; and where the master had refused to order production of books, but did not make a certificate, he was directed to make a certificate in such form as to admit of an exception being taken to it.—*Toulmin v. Copeland*, Y. & C. 382. (Vide *Kemp v. Wade*, 2 Keen, 686, as to Practice in Chancery.)

20. (*Re-examination of witness.*) A witness who has been examined in the cause, cannot be re-examined before the master without an order made upon motion,

with notice; Swinford v. Horne, 5 Madd. 579, being overruled; and the notice of such motion must state the names of the witnesses proposed to be re-examined. *Jones v. Thomas,* Y. & C. 227.

21. (*Same.*) Where a witness had been examined before the decree, to prove the amount of a balance that had been due to him from plaintiff, and the decree directed an inquiry as to the items constituting such balance; an order was made for the re-examination of such witness, not as to direct payments forming the balance, but as to collateral facts tending to prove the fact of such payments.— *Barker v. Greenwood,* Y. & C. 393. See *S. C.,* 2 Y. & C. 414.

22. (*Special injunction.*) The Court will not dissolve, upon answer put in, a special injunction made till answer, or further order, until the defendant has had time to inspect the documents admitted by answer to be in defendant's possession.— *Walker v. Corke,* Y. & C. 276.

And see ABATEMENT; ADMINISTRATION OF ASSETS; APPEAL; DISCLAIMER; EXCEPTIONS; INJUNCTION, 2, 5; MISTAKE; PAUPER; PRODUCTION OF DOCUMENTS; RECEIVER; REHEARING; SECURITY FOR COSTS; SHORT CAUSE; SOLICITOR AND CLIENT, 1.

PREROGATIVE. See JURISDICTION.

PRINCIPAL AND SURETY.

(*Work by contract.*) By a contract for the performance of certain works, it was stipulated that three-fourths of the work, as finished, should be paid for every two months, the remaining fourth to be paid for upon completion of the whole. For the purpose it was said of assisting the contractor, more than three-fourths of the work done were paid for, without the consent of the sureties for due performance of the contract, (such extra payments exceeding the amount of the penalty in the bond given by the sureties): Held, that the sureties were thereby discharged of their responsibility for the due performance of the contract.— *Calvert v. The London Dock Company,* Keen, 638.

See SURETY.

PRODUCTION OF DOCUMENTS.

1. (*Admitted possession, with claim of privilege.*) Where a defendant by his answer admitted possession of documents, but stated that several of them were privileged, as written since the institution of the suit: He was, on a motion for production of documents, allowed to withhold such as he stated by affidavit to have been written after the said time.— *Parsons v. Robertson,* Keen, 605.

2. (*Answer of co-defendant.*) The answer of a co-defendant cannot be referred to to prove that documents are in the possession or power of another defendant, though such co-defendant was the solicitor of the other, and admitted that he had the documents in his own possession, as the solicitor of the other.— *Kemp v. Wade,* Keen, 686.

3. (*Suspected answer—Practice.*) Although there is strong ground for suspecting the truth of a defendant's answer, yet on a motion for production of documents, founded on that answer, the Court will not disregard the statements which it contains; but where such statements are inconsistent with each other, the plaintiff may adopt that which is most to his advantage; and where the plaintiff was enabled to show that some parts of a document were inconsistent with the description given of it in the answer, an order was made for its production, discharging a previous order which had been made by the Vice-Chancellor for a reference to

the master as to what parts of the document related to the plaintiff's case.—*Bowes v. Fernie*, M. & C. 632.

4. (*Want of privity.*) A. gave B. a power of attorney to get in and manage a residuary estate, to which he was entitled under a will. B. employed C., a solicitor, for the purpose ; and A. afterwards filed a bill for an account against B. and C. : Held, that he was not entitled as against C. to the production of documents relating to the testator's estate and affairs, admitted by C. to be in his possession. Affirmed by Lord Chancellor.—*Adams v. Fisher*, Keen, 754 ; M. & C. 526.

RAILWAY.

1. (*Payment of dividends—Costs.*) Upon the construction of a Railway Act, it was held, that the costs authorised by the act to be given in relation to certain dividends, were the costs of obtaining the order for payment, and not the costs of the payment itself.— *Exp. Adthorpe, re Hull and Selby Railway Act*, Y. & C. 396.

2. (*Substitution of line—Adoption of contracts.*) The B. and C. Railway Company, who were then applying for an act, agree with the plaintiff to give him for fourteen acres and a half of land, required for their proposed line, 20,000*l.*, to be paid by instalments. Afterwards it is agreed, during the proceedings before the committee, between the B. and C. company, and a rival company, called the C. and B., who had proposed another line, that it should be referred to two members of the committee, to choose between the two lines, and that the selected company should take the engagements with the landholders entered into by the others, and this agreement was signed by the agent of the plaintiff. The C. and B. company was slected, and obtained their act, and for their proposed line sixteen acres of the plaintiff's land, in another part of the estate, would be required. After the time at which the first instalment of the 20,000*l.* would have been due, the plaintiff filed his bill against the C. and B. company, alleging the above facts, and also that, relying upon the agreement (for adoption by one company of the contracts of the other), he had not opposed the passing of the act, and praying that the contract of adoption might be declared binding on the defendants, and that they might be decreed to perform the same. To this a demurrer was put in, which was overruled by the Vice-Chancellor, and also by the Lord Chancellor, on appeal, in the latter instance without hearing counsel for the respondents.—*Stanley v. Chester and Birkenhead Railway Company*, M. & C. 773.

See INJUNCTION, 1.

RECEIVER.

1 (*Appointed before answer.*) A motion for receiver by equitable mortgagee was granted before answer, the Court thinking, from the circumstances, that it was a case of danger to the plaintiff, unless the Court interfered.—*Aberdeen v. Chitty*, Y. & C. 379.

2. (*Neglect of executor and trustee.*) It was held sufficient ground for the appointment of a receiver of real and personal estate, that the executor, who was also devisee in trust, should have omitted to raise a sum, which, upon the construction put by the Court upon the will, it was his duty to have raised, as soon as conveniently might be after the testator's death, and that he should have left a considerable portion of the estate outstanding on bad security.—*Richards v. Perkins*, Y. & C. 299.

RE-DELIVERY OF DOCUMENTS.

(*Felony.*) Where upon motion by defendant for re-delivery of documents, after inspection, it was alleged by plaintiff, that he was advised to take criminal proceedings against defendant, in respect of such documents ; they were retained in Court, to see whether he would do so.—*Walker v. Corke*, Y. & C. 277.

REFERENCE TO MASTER.

1. (*Construction of order.*) A master having reported a certain sum due from certain parties, these parties took two exceptions to the report; the 1st, that the master ought not to have found as he did find ; the 2nd, that he ought either to have found that nothing was due, or that a sum, not exceeding a certain amount, was due. Both these exceptions were allowed ; and it was ordered that the master do review his report : Held, that under such order the master was restricted to an inquiry as to whether nothing, or a sum not exceeding the amount mentioned in the second exception, was due.—*Twyford v. Trail*, M. & C. 645.

2. (*Evidence.*) Where it is referred back to the master to review his report, he is at liberty to receive further evidence.—*Twyford v. Trail*, M. & C. 645.

REHEARING.

(*After proper time.*) Where a decree not final in its nature, and still retained in Court for further directions, is in the opinion of the Court clearly erroneous, a petition for re-hearing will be granted, though the ordinary time for presenting it may have elapsed ; and if there be error apparent on the face of such decree, the acquiescence in it for some time of the parties complaining of it, is not sufficient ground for refusing their petition.—*Ackland v. Braddick*, Y. & C. 237.

RESTRAINT UPON ALIENATION.

(*Bankruptcy.*) Where there was a bequest with a gift over, in case legatee should mortgage, change, sell, or expose to sale, or assign or incumber, and the legatee became bankrupt : Held, that the gift over did not thereby take effect.— *Whitfield v. Prickett*, Keen, 608.

RULE IN SHELLEY'S CASE.—See Wills, 18.

SECRET IN TRADE.

(*Contract for sale of.*) Where a man had contracted to sell a secret in trade, and the contracting purchaser filed a bill to be relieved from the contract, denying that there was any secret, and inquiring by his bill what the nature of the alleged secret was : Semble, that the defendant was bound to disclose it, but his demurrer to the discovery was overruled, partly on a point of pleading.—*Carter v. Goetze*, Keen, 581.

Rep. from Vendor and Purchaser.

SECURITY FOR COSTS.

If a plaintiff, who has no fixed residence, gives in his bill a true statement of his then place of abode, his subsequent changes of place, unless he goes abroad, do not entitle the defendant to have security for costs.—*Fraser v. Palmer*, Y. & C. 279.

SETTLED ACCOUNT. See Trust.

SHORT CAUSE.

1. (*Dissent of defendant's counsel.*) A cause will not be set down to be heard as a short cause, where the defendant's counsel states, that in his judgment the cause is not proper to be so heard, and no discussion will be allowed on the question.

—*Reeves* v. *Gill*, Keen, 671. N.B. The practice differs in the Vice-Chancellor's Court, *Ker* v. *Cusac*, 7 Sim. 520.

2. (*When to be set down.*) An application to set down a cause as a short cause cannot be made till after the *subpœna* to hear judgment is returnable.—*Reeves* v. *Gill*, Keen, 671.

SOLICITOR.

1. (*Certificate.*) The omission to take out a certificate does not in any case, notwithstanding the words "*null and void*," in 37 G. 3, c. 90, s. 31, absolutely avoid the admission of a solicitor so as to make admission *de novo* necessary ; but where a solicitor who, within a year after his original admission, has taken out a certificate, afterwards omits to do so for more than a year, he cannot practise without a re-admission, which, *it seems*, he is entitled to obtain without payment of penalty or arrears of duty, if he was not practising during the time he was without a certificate. But if a solicitor has never taken out a certificate, and never practised, *semble*, that he may at any time after his original admission take out his certificate, and begin to practise without re-admission, as the disqualifying clause in the statute refers only to the case of culpable omission, i. e. by a solicitor who is either practising, or has qualified himself to practise, by taking out a certificate.—*Exp. Chambers re Wilton*, Keen, 497.

2. (*Lien of for costs.*) The lien of a solicitor for costs cannot be allowed to interfere with the equities between the parties. Accordingly, where a plaintiff had been declared entitled to have an estate surrendered up to him, upon payment of such balance as might remain, after deducting from a debt due from the plaintiff, the costs of the suit, which were awarded to him : Held, that the solicitor of the defendant, who had in his custody the deeds of such estate, and had a lien thereon for costs as against his client, could not enforce such lien to any extent as against the plaintiff, but that he had a lien on the balance due from plaintiff to defendant.—*Bawtree* v. *Watson*, Keen, 713.

And see INSTITUTION OF SUIT.

SOLICITOR AND CLIENT.

1. (*Lien for costs—Attachment.*) A solicitor does not prejudice his lien for costs, by attaching his client for payment of the same.—*Bawtree* v. *Watson*, Keen, 713.

2. (*Negligence and mistake.*) Where a solicitor had been guilty of great remissness in the conduct of a suit, and had ultimately, through ignorance of the practice of the Court, allowed publication to pass without witnesses being examined on his client's behalf; on the motion of the latter, publication was enlarged, the solicitor paying the costs of the application.—*White* v. *Hillacre*, Y. & C. 278.

3. (*Privileged communication.*) In a bill filed by insurance company A. against company B., and against their solicitor, to set aside a policy of insurance upon a life effected by the latter company with the former; it was stated that B. had first made a proposal to another company to insure the same life, and that in consequence of such proposal the actuary of such last-mentioned company had called upon the agent of company B., and showed to him an unfavourable medical report which had been made on the life, on account of which the insurance was refused by the last-mentioned company. At this interview the then solicitor of company B. was present, which he admitted in his answer, but refused to state what passed, alleging that he was present as the professional and confidential adviser of company B. : Held, that this answer was not sufficient to bring the

case within the benefit of the rule as to privileged communications. Bramwell v. Lucas, 2 B. & C. 745; and Greenough v. Gaskell, 1 M. & K. 98, commented on.—*Desborough v. Rawlins*, M. & C. 507.

4. (*Recovery of costs.*) A solicitor, it seems, cannot file a bill for payment of his costs; but where, upon a solicitor bringing his action at law for costs, the client filed a bill for an account, and to stay proceedings at law, and an agreement was then come to between the parties to refer the costs to the Master of the Court of Law, and a dispute subsequently arose upon such agreement, as to whether certain costs were included therein, and the solicitor thereupon filed his bill for an account of such last-mentioned costs: A demurrer to such bill was overruled.— *Fyson v. Pole*, Y. & C. 266.

SPECIFIC PERFORMANCE.

1. (*Sale of ship.*) The Court will decree specific performance of a contract for the sale of a ship.—*Lynn v. Chaters*, Keen, 521.

2. (*Suit for purchase-money.*) An agreement was entered into for sale of a ship to A. and B., one third only of the purchase-money to be paid at the time; but if default was made in payment of the residue at the specified time, the ship to be resold, and the deficiency be made good by the purchasers. The ship was delivered, and a bill of sale executed, expressing that the purchase-money had been paid, one-third by A., and two-thirds by B., whereas, in fact, one-third only had been paid by A., which was the proportion of his interest in the ship, and bills for the remaining two-thirds accepted also by A. These bills being dishonoured, a suit for specific performance was instituted against B., and he was decreed to pay the balance, or that the ship should be resold, and he make good the deficiency.—*S. C.*

STATUTE OF LIMITATIONS. See INTEREST; PLEADING, 5; WILL. 16.

SURETY.

(*Release of co-surety.*) Where, for considerations that appeared sufficient to the Court, A. executed a deed for the purpose of indemnifying B., one of two co-sureties, against any payments he might have to make in respect of the sum for which he was jointly liable; and B. afterwards, without the concurrence of A., released his co-surety: Held, that as A. was thereby deprived of the benefit of contribution from the co-surety, the indemnity given to B. was restricted to one moiety of the payments which he might have to make as surety.—*Hodgson v. Hodgson*, Keen, 704.

THELLUSON'S ACT.

(*Construction of second section.*) Where the persons, eight in number, described in the will, not by name, but as grandchildren of testator, for whose benefit an unlawful accumulation was directed, were, with the exception of two, the children of three children of the testator, to whom annuities were given out of the fund, of which the surplus was to be accumulated: Held, that the case did not come within the exception of the second section, as to the children of persons taking an interest.—*Eyre v. Marsden*, Keen, 564, (affirmed by Lord Chancellor.)

2. (*Disposal of unlawful accumulation.*) The funds unlawfully accumulated or directed to be accumulated, go as in the case of intestacy, (to the heir or next of kin, according to the source from which they proceed,) to the exclusion of residuary legatees.—*S. C.* (affirmed by Lord Chancellor.)

3. (*Operation of, on will.*) The Thelluson Act does not operate to alter any disposition of the will, except only the direction to accumulate.—*S. C.*

TITHE COMMUTATION ACT.

(*Determination of suit.*) Under the 45th section of the Tithe Commutation Act, which gives the commissioners a discretionary power to determine any suits pending as to the right to any tithes, and to reserve the question for their own decision, specific notice of their intention to do so must be given, and the appointing a time and place for fixing a rent-charge is not sufficient ground for staying proceedings in the suit.—*Wetherell* v. *Weighill,* Y. & C. 243.

TRUST.

(*Lapse of time—Settled account.*) Where the relation of trustee and cestui que trust still subsists, lapse of time is no bar to any right of the latter against the former. Accordingly, an account of the share of a deceased partner taken by his surviving partners, who were also executors and trustees of his will, was reopened thirty-eight years after it had been taken, and thirty years after it had been submitted to the eldest son of such deceased partner (who was one of the plaintiffs), upon his coming of age; who, by deed then executed, expressed himself satisfied with the disclosure thus far made, and the accounts thus far given. Another son, who was also a plaintiff, had signed an absolute release, but the Court was of opinion that he, as well as his brother, was entitled to have the account opened, as the account with the eldest son had been adopted as the basis of the account with the other, and in neither instances had the defendants, the trustees, at the time of such accounts being taken, communicated to the sons the nature of their dealings with the estate of the father, which they had, in fact, retained and used in the partnership.—*Wedderburn* v. *Wedderburn,* Keen, 722.

TRUSTEES.

1. (*Acceptance of trust.*) A sum of money was bequeathed to trustees upon certain trusts; and by the same will a messuage was devised to the same trustees, upon certain trusts, until the testator's grandson attained twenty-one, and then to convey the property to him. The trustees never received the legacy, and never acted in the trusts of the will, except by conveying the messuage to the grandson upon his attaining twenty-one. And in the deed of conveyance it was recited, "that it became unnecessary for the persons named trustees to act in the trust declared by the said will, and in fact they never intermeddled therein:" Held, upon a bill by those interested in the legacy, to make the surviving trustee liable for his neglect in not getting payment of the same, that the execution of the conveyance amounted to an acceptance of the trust.—*Nicloson* v. *Wordsworth,* 2 Swan. 365; *Urch* v. *Walker,* M. & C. 702.

2. (*Appointment of by Court.*) In a suit to appoint new trustees, the Court refused to insert in the will a clause authorising such new trustees to appoint others in their stead.— *Brown* v. *Brown,* Y. & C. 395.

3. (*Compellable to bring actions.*) Where by the terms of a marriage settlement it was declared that a trustee should stand possessed of a debt, upon trust, in the first instance, to *call in or compel payment* of such debt, unless the cestui que trusts consented to its remaining outstanding, and the trustee is requested by the cestui que trusts to call in the debt, he is not entitled to an indemnity from them, previous to his bringing an action, if necessary, for the same; and a trustee under such circumstances was made to pay the costs of a suit, made necessary by his neglecting to bring the action.—*Kirby* v. *Mash,* Y. & C. 295.

4. (*Discretion of.*) Where, upon the conversion of the Navy 5l. per Cents. into New 4l. per Cents., a trustee had refused to accept of the new stock, by means of which, as it was alleged, the trust property had sustained a loss, an

inquiry was directed as to whether the trustee had properly exercised his discretion by dissenting.—*Angell v. Dawson*, Y. & C. 308.

5. (*Liability of, after notice.*) Where a party having a claim, which he afterwards established by suit, against the separate estate of a married woman, had given notice to her trustee to retain so much out of the proceeds of the separate estate as would answer his claim ; and the trustee had nevertheless paid over the whole to the married woman, who disputed the validity of the claim : Held, that he was personally liable for the amount which he was required by the notice to retain.—*Hodgson v. Hodgson,* Keen, 704.

6. (*Primâ facie breach of trust—Pleading.*) Where by the terms of a settlement 7000*l.* stock was vested in trustees upon certain trusts, and it was alleged in a bill to carry such trusts into execution, that 300*l.*, part thereof, had been sold out and misapplied ; and the trustee stated that the 300*l.* was included by mistake in the settlement, and that he had sold it out, and paid it over to the person really entitled to it : Held, that the plaintiffs were entitled to an inquiry into the facts, though they had not prayed for it by their bill.—*Angell v. Dawson*, Y. & C. 308.

VENDOR AND PURCHASER.

1. (*Notice.*) If the same person is either agent for both vendor and purchaser, or himself vendor, and also agent for the purchaser, whatever notice he has will affect the purchaser ; and if the deeds are in possession of a third party, the purchaser is affected with notice of title of such party.—*Dryden v. Frost*, M. & C. 670.

2. (*Possession by purchaser.*) Where a purchaser had entered into possession, as it appeared, without prejudice to an inquiry into the title, but had afterwards continued twenty years in possession, during which time he had taken many frivolous and vexatious objections : Held, that he had forfeited all right to a reference as to title, and he was decreed, with costs, to perform the agreement, and pay four per cent. on the purchase-money from the time of taking possession.—*Hall v. Laver*, Y. & C. 191.

And see EXCHANGE, SECRET IN TRADE, SPECIFIC PERFORMANCE.

VENDOR'S LIEN.

Semble, that the vendor's lien for unpaid purchase-money may be assigned by delivery of title-deeds.—*Dryden v. Frost*, M. & C. 670.

WILL.

1. (*Construction—Accruer.*) A testator gave a mixed fund in trust for his grandchildren living at the time of his decease, equally to be divided among them on the death of the survivor of three persons named in his will, and if any of his grandchildren died without leaving issue before the period of distribution, testator gave their shares equally among his surviving grandchildren, to be paid at the same time and in the same manner as mentioned touching the original shares : Held, that the gift over to the survivor applied to the accruing as well as the original shares.—*Eyre v. Marsden*, Keen, 564.

2. (*Construction—Coming into possession—Presumed knowledge.*) A testatrix gave certain benefits to A. and others of her children, with a proviso, that when any of them came into *possession* of the family property, the benefits given to him or her should go over to the others. By a previous will of testatrix's husband, the family property had been devised to B., an elder brother of A., for life, remainder to A. for life ; with a proviso that if B., on becoming entitled to certain other estates, should not sell them for the purpose of paying off certain charges on the family estates, his interest in the latter should cease as if he were dead. B. did become entitled to such other estates, and advertised them for sale ; but did not

sell them in consequence of an arrangement entered into with A., whereby the latter, in consideration of B. having allowed the forfeiture to take effect, demised to him the family estates during their joint lives at a certain rent : Held, that this was such a possession by A. of the family estates as deprived him of the benefits given by the first-mentioned will.

It was contended on his behalf, that as the arrangement had taken place previous to such will, as the testatrix must be supposed to have known, and as by the terms of her will she pointed to some future coming into possession, she must have intended some other possession than that under the arrangement ; but the argument was overruled, on the ground that it supposed the testatrix to have been privy to an arrangement for evading the first will, of which she was executrix and trustee.—*Wynne* v. *Wynne*, Keen, 778.

3. (*Construction—Continuance of power.*) Where a power of sale was given to trustees, to be exercised during the continuance of the trusts of the will, and owing to the omission of the trustees to convey the estates to the cestui que trusts at the time appointed by the will, such trusts were still subsisting : Held, that the power expired at the time at which the trusts of the will would have ceased if the directions in the will had been complied with.—*Wood* v. *White*, Keen, 664.

4. (*Construction—Cumulative legacy.*) A legacy of annuity given by codicil, which was held to be cumulative, was given expressly for life, but it was held to be subject to a direction in the will, to invest the whole funds out of which such annuity, as well as the annuity given by will, were raisable, in the purchase of lands for the benefit of the annuitant at the expiration of five years.—*Mackinnon* v. *Peach*, Keen, 555.

5. (*Construction—Death under twenty-one.*) Words conferring an absolute interest were followed by a limitation over, in the event of any of the legatees dying without issue in the lifetime of the testator or afterwards, and then by a declaration that none of the legatees should be entitled to any bequest until twenty-one : Held, that the limitation over did not take effect except in case of death (without issue) under twenty-one.—*Monteith* v. *Nicholson*, Keen, 719.

6. (*Construction—Description of subject.*) Testator devised and bequeathed freehold, copyhold, and leasehold property to trustees, their heirs &c., but in declaring the trusts all mention of the copyholds was omitted : Held, that no trust was created in them. (See Stubbs v. Sargon, 2 Keen, 255 ; 3 M. & C. 507.)—*Jackson* v. *Noble*, Keen, 597.

7. (*Construction—Executory devise and bequest.*) Testator gave real and personal estate to trustees in trust for his daughter A. absolutely, provided that if she should marry and have no children, the lands and money should go to his son B., or if he was dead in the lifetime of A. to his children. B. died in the lifetime of A. without children : Held, that as the executory limitation was to have taken effect only for the benefit of B. and his children, A.'s interest on his death became indefeasible.—*Jackson* v. *Noble*, Keen, 597.

8. (*Construction—General intention—Attempted perpetuity.*) A testator bequeathed personalty to trustees to pay the interest to Sir G. A., Bart., for life, and, after his decease, to his eldest son for the time being ; but if he should die, leaving no son, then in trust for the person on whom the baronetcy, which was limited in tail male, should devolve, so that each baronet should take the interest for life, and after the extinction of the baronetcy to fall into the residue of the estate. At

the death of the testator, Sir G. A. had two brothers, on whom the baronetcy successively devolved : Held, on a suit between the representatives of the second brother and the third brother, and to which the representatives of Sir G. A. were not parties, that in consideration of the general intention of the testator to keep the property with the title, the second brother took a quasi estate tail, and therefore an absolute interest in it.—*Mackworth v. Hinxman*, Keen, 658.

9. (*Construction—Gift to a class.*) Testator gave a mixed residue to four persons by name, to be equally divided between them, and to their heirs for ever, which four persons he also appointed to be his executors, and he also in the next sentence appointed two other persons to be executors. It was admitted (on the strength of other expressions) that the gift was conditional upon the legatees accepting the office of executors, and one of them having refused to do so : Held, that his share went to the next of kin, for that this was not a gift to the executors as a class. (Knight v. Gould, 2 Myl. & Keen, 295 ; Hunt v. Berkley, 1 Eq. Ab. 243, expressly overruled.)—*Barber v. Barber*, M. & C. 688.

10. (*Construction—Joint tenancy by implication.*) A testator gave a residue upon trust to pay the produce thereof between his grandchildren A. and B., during their respective lives, in equal shares, and after the death of A. and B. to transfer the capital unto and amongst the children of A. and B. in equal shares, and if there should be no children living at their decease, then upon trust for his personal representatives A. died, leaving children, in the lifetime of B.: Held, that B. was entitled to the whole for life, and that the capital was to be divided *per capita* among the children of A. and B. who might be living at B.'s death.— *Pearce v. Edmeads*, Y. & C. 246.

11. (*Construction—Male descendants.*) A testator, after enumerating certain objects of his bounty, male and female, to be provided for out of a certain fund if they should be in want, added, " and in like manner the male children of the above-named men." In another part of his will he spoke of the persons to be provided for as " descendants of near kindred." In a subsequent part he declared that a preference should be given to the male children of A. This was the will of a Dutchman, but it was construed as an English one, the Dutch law not appearing to be different ; and it was held that the male descendants of A., descended exclusively through males, were solely entitled to the provision.—*Bernal v. Bernal*, M. & C. 559 ; Coop. 55.

12. (*Construction—Same point.*) The words " eldest male lineal descendant" held to designate such male descendants only as were descended exclusively through males ; and *semble*, also, those of the eldest *branch* in preference to those of any younger branch, without reference to the relative age of the different individuals.—*Oddie v. Woodford*, rep. *ex relat.* M. & C. 1821.

13. (*Construction—Period of survivorship—Remoteness*). A testator gave a residue upon trust to invest and pay the annual produce to his several children during their respective lives, and from and after the decease of his said children, upon trust to divide the same produce equally among all his surviving grandchildren who should then be living, until the youngest should attain twenty-one years ; and upon the youngest attaining that age, to convert the residue into money, and divide the same among all such of his said grandchildren, and the children or child of any such grandchild as might then be dead, such children or child to take only the parent's share : Held, that the children of a grandchild, who died before the death of all the testator's children, were not entitled. The

objection of remoteness, which was also strongly insisted on against the claim of such children, was not decided on.—*Smith* v. *Farr,* Y. & C. 328.

14. (*Construction—Quantity of interest.*) An indefinite bequest of the interest and proceeds of personalty to three children, immediately preceded by a like indefinite bequest of 10*l.* per annum to another child, and followed by expressions describing the three as annuitants, and by a direction, reserving in a certain event the annuity of 10*l.* to the other child for *his life :* Held, to confer a life interest only on the three.—*Wynne* v. *Wynne,* Keen, 778.

15. (*Same.*) A testator gave to his brother 300*l.* per annum during his life, and to each of two nephews 150*l.* during their lives, and in case either of the nephews died, the other to inherit the whole 300*l.* ; and if the brother died without issue, the two nephews to inherit from the brother : and he then stated, that the reason why he left only the interest to his brother and two nephews was, that if they died without issue, the money might go to his three cousins. He then desired that his legatees should be paid within twelve months, and added, " it is to be understood I leave it to them and their heirs :" Held, that the brother took only a life interest in the annuity.

The interest of the surviving nephew had become united with that of the testator's residuary legatee, and the claim of the cousins had been rejected in the suit of Lepine v. Ferard, 2 R. & M. 378.—*Ferard* v. *Griffin,* Keen, 615.

16. (*Same.*) By a will in exercise of a power, a fund was appointed in terms which were indefinite, and sufficient to confer an absolute interest ; but this was followed by a clause restricting the bequest to a life interest, with a void gift over to parties who could not take for remoteness : Held, that the absolute gift was not restricted by such attempted gift over.—*Kampf* v. *Jones,* Keen, 756.

17. (*Construction—Remoteness.*) Testator gave a fund among the children of his daughter who should be living at the time the eldest should attain the age of twenty-four years, with a clause of substitution of the issue of such of the children as might then be dead. At the time of testator's death the daughter had three children, the eldest of whom was thirteen, and the youngest nine years old : Held, that as by the terms of the will an after-born child might become the eldest, upon whose attaining twenty-four the bequest was to take effect, it was void for remoteness.—*Dodd* v. *Wake,* Sim. 616.

18. (*Construction—Revival of debts.*) A testator bequeathed a fund in trust, to be equally divided between certain specified creditors, whose debts were barred by the statute : Held, first, that under this bequest they were entitled as creditors and not as legatees, and that therefore no lapse had taken place as to such of them as had died in the lifetime of the testator ; secondly, that their debts were only revived as against the particular fund, and not as against the general assets ; thirdly, that so much of the fund as had been set apart to answer the claims of such of the specified creditors as had not proved, and eventually did not prove, should be divided among those who had proved.—*Williamson* v. *Naylor,* Y. & C. 208.

19. (*Construction—Residue, general or particular.*) In a will which contained other passages indicative of an intention to place the whole of testator's property at the disposal of the legatee, E. M., and upon the strength of which passages administration had been granted to such legatee ; the following passage occurred at the end :—" I guess there will be found sufficient at my bankers to defray and discharge my debts, which I hereby desire E. M. to do, and to keep the

residue for her own use and pleasure :" Held, partly upon the whole context of the will, partly upon the construction of the above passage, and particularly because the direction to pay debts could not be supposed to have been confined to the fund at the bankers, that the general residue passed. (See Dowson v. Gaskoin, 2 Keen, 14, and cases there referred to.)—*Boys v. Morgan,* M. & C. 661.

20. (*Construction—Rule in Shelley's case.*) Testator bequeathed two leasehold houses to his sisters A. and B. during their natural lives, they keeping them in good repair, and at their deaths to be disposed of as follows :—One house to descend to his sister A.'s eldest son or daughter, and the next heir, male or female, until the expiration of the lease, and the other house in like manner to B.'s eldest son or daughter, &c.: Held, that A. and B. took an absolute interest in the leaseholds, and the Court thought, that had it been a devise of freehold, the words would have conferred a fee.—*Exp. Harrison, re Commercial Railway Act,* Y. & C. 275.

21. (*Construction—Specific legacy.*) A bequest, under a power, of certain specified sums of stock, and of all other monies and stocks subject to the power, followed by a bequest in the same sentence, and upon the same trusts, of all the residue of testatrix's personal estate : Held, to be a specific legacy.—*Kampf v. Jones,* Keen, 756.

22. (*Construction—Substitution.*) Where there was a gift of chattels to two daughters, to be divided between them equally, but if either should die without lawful issue, her share to go to her sister, and one daughter died, without issue, in the testator's lifetime : Held, that the gift over to the survivor took effect.—*Mackinnon v. Peach,* Keen, 555.

23. (*Construction—Same point.*) Testator gave all his copyhold and leasehold estates to his widow for life, and at her death the whole to be sold and divided into five parts, and one of such parts to be paid to each of the testator's four sons that should be living at her decease ; and in case of either of their deaths, the share of the one so dying to his issue, or, if without issue, to the survivors : Held, that the child of a son who died in the lifetime of the testator was entitled to her father's share. (Rust v. Baker, 8 Sim. 446.)—*Lejeune v. Lejeune,* Keen, 701.

24. (*Construction—Surplus maintenance.*) Where there was a bequest to an infant of certain shares of a residue, in terms clearly sufficient to carry a vested interest, with a direction that the interest of such shares should be applied to the maintenance and education of the infant till he attained twenty-one, and there was a gift over of " the property bequeathed" in the event of the infant dying under twenty-one, and the infant did die under that age : Held, that such part of the interest on his share as had not been applied to his maintenance and education belonged to his personal representative.—*Burber v. Barber,* 3 M. & C. 688. (See Macdonald v. Bryce, 2 Keen, 517, *infra.*)

25. (*Same.*) Testator, after giving the residue to R. S. *upon* his coming of age, with a gift over in the event of his dying under age, directed his trustees to apply the annual produce of such residue to the maintenance, education, and *benefit* of R. S., as they should judge most advantageous for him. R. S. died under age : Held, that the unapplied part of the annual produce of the residue sunk into the residue for the benefit of those entitled upon R. S.'s death.—*Macdonald v. Bryce,* Keen, 517. See S. C., *suprà,* p. 276. (See Barber v. Barber, 3 M. & C. 688, *suprà.*)

26. (*Construction—Time of payment—Investment.*) A testatrix gave to her executors such a sum as at her decease would purchase 2500*l.* stock, which she directed her executors to purchase, and to pay the dividends to A. for life. She then gave several legacies, and directed all the above-mentioned legacies to be paid within three months after her decease : Held, that the 2500*l.* was to be purchased immediately on her decease, and a considerable delay having occurred in getting in the assets, during which time the price of stocks had risen, that the whole 2500*l.* was nevertheless to be purchased, and a sum equal to the dividends thereon from the time of testatrix's death paid to A.—*Owden* v. *Campbell*, Sim. 551.

27. (*Interest under contract.*) A party having contracted to purchase the fee simple of an estate from a person who was at that time only tenant for life of the same, devised such estate in fee ; afterwards, the vendor having acquired the fee, conveyed the same to a trustee for the testator : Held, that nothing passed by the will.—*Duckle* v. *Baines*, Sim. 525.

28. (*Lapsed share charged with debts.*) Where a testator having devised his freehold and copyhold estates to his children, as tenants in common in fee, and absolutely bequeathed his leaseholds to the same children, afterwards directed that his freehold and copyhold should be the primary fund, and the leaseholds the secondary fund for payment of his debts, and one of the sons died in the lifetime of the testator : Held, that the charge attached to his share, and that it lapsed as to the freeholds to the heir, and as to the leaseholds to the next of kin, subject to payment of debts in either case in manner directed by the will.—*Fisher* v. *Fisher*, Keen, 610.

29. (*Probate—Copy.*) The Court will look only to the probate copy of a will, though strong grounds for suspecting that another copy tendered in evidence is the correct one.—*Bernal* v. *Bernal*, M. & C. 559, note.

And see LEGACY DUTY ; PERPETUITY ; POWER, 5.

APPEAL ON REPORTED CASE.

The judgment of the Master of the Rolls in *Stubbs* v. *Sargon*, 2 Keen, 255, L. M., No. 42, was affirmed in all the points objected to.—M. & C. 507.

BANKRUPTCY.

[Containing Cases in 3 Deacon, Part 2, omitting Cases noticed in former Digests.]

AFFIDAVIT. See Practice, 1, 6, 8.

ANNUITY.

(*Retainer of part of purchase money.*) Where the bankrupt, having received 400*l.*, being the whole consideration for the grant by him of an annuity, half an hour afterwards, and at a different place, paid 100*l.*, part of such sum, to an attorney, whom he had employed in the transaction, and to whom it was not denied that he was indebted to that amount, and who was not shown to have been employed in the business as the agent of the grantee: Held, that this was not a retainer or return of part of the purchase money within the provisions of the Annuity Act, 53 Geo. 3, c. 141, s. 6.—*Exp. Bogue, re Basun, 314.*

ANNULLING.

1. (*Equitable grounds.*) During the pendency of a suit instituted in equity by a creditor against a debtor, for the purpose of realising certain securities, and for an account of what was due, in which suit the liability to pay the greater part of the sum claimed was disputed by the debtor; the creditor proceeded to take out a fiat upon an affidavit of debt, charging the whole amount claimed, without allowing any thing for the securities, and procured himself to be elected provisional assignee, and a meeting was held for the choice of assignees, but no creditors appeared: on petition of the bankrupt, supported by affidavit that he was solvent, and had no other creditor, the Court, in the exercise of its equitable jurisdiction, annulled the fiat. Diss. Erskine, C. J.—*Exp. and re Hall, 405.*

2. (*Evidence—Onus probandi.*) Where there appears sufficient on the face of the proceedings to support the fiat, and the bankrupt has been furnished with copies of the depositions, *semble,* that on a petition by bankrupt to annul, some evidence in disproof of the depositions must be adduced on his behalf, before he can call upon the other party to support the fiat.—*Exp. and re Ford, 494.*

3. (*Infancy.*) *Semble,* that where one of several bankrupts under a joint fiat is an infant, the fiat may be annulled as to him, and yet stand good as to the other.—*Exp. and re Watson, 277.*

APPEAL.

(*Refusal of special case.*) Where, after one of the judges of the Court of Review had refused to certify for a special case, on the ground that the question was one of fact, a petition of appeal was presented to the Lord Chancellor; the latter, after conferring with the judge of the Court of Review, dismissed the petition with costs, but with liberty to apply to the Court below for a rehearing.—*Exp. Woodward, re Turner, 293.*

ASSIGNEE. See Costs.

BANKRUPT.

(*Destitution—Indulgence.*) A bankrupt, who had been committed by the commissioners for not answering to their satisfaction, and who had been lying twelve months in gaol, was, in consideration of his long imprisonment and his destitute condition, ordered, upon his own petition, to be re-examined at the costs of the estate.—*Exp. and re Crossley*, 492.

And see EXPUNGING PROOF; JURISDICTION.

BENEFIT SOCIETY.

(*Bankrupt treasurer.*) Where the bankrupt, on her appointment as treasurer of a benefit society, had agreed to pay interest on 120*l.*, part of the funds delivered over to her as treasurer: Held, that such sum was not converted into a debt, but remained in her hands as trust money.—*Exp. Ray, re Woodliffe*, 537.

CERTIFICATE.

(*Petition to stay.*) A petition to stay the certificate was presented by a partner of the bankrupt, stating that a large amount would be found due to him on account, and alleging, as objections to the certificate, that it had been signed by certain creditors whose debts ought to have been expunged, and that a certain other debt due to the petitioner had been improperly expunged ; but not stating the whole probable amount that would be due to the petitioner, nor alleging that if these errors were corrected, there would not be sufficient in numbers and value of the creditors to support the certificate : Held, by reason of these omissions, and also because the assignees were not made parties, and because it was not alleged that the bankrupt was a party to the improper proceedings, with which the assignees were charged, and because another person, who was a co-partner with the bankrupt and the petitioner, was not made a party, and because it was not stated that all the partnership debts were satisfied ; that the petitioner had not stated a case for staying the certificate. Diss. Sir J. Cross.—*Exp. May, re Malachy*, 382.

CLERK.

(*Six months' wages.*) A clerk who voluntarily leaves his master because he finds him becoming insolvent twelve months before the bankruptcy, is not entitled to six months' salary under 6 Geo. 4, c. 16, s. 49.—*Exp. Gee, re Sawer*, 341.

COSTS.

1. (*New choice of assignee.*) Where an assignee, who had been chosen without his authority, declined to act, the costs of the new choice of assignees were ordered to be paid out of the estate.—*Exp. Pearson, re Stephenson*, 324.

2. (*Notice of prior fiat.*) A party who, as it was shown on the petition, had notice that a country fiat had been actually opened, though such fact was not known at the Bankrupt Office, two days after the time had elapsed for opening such fiat, struck a docket in London, upon which he afterwards applied for a *fiat*, which was refused at the office, when the opening of the country *fiat* was then known ; he then presented a petition for a *fiat*, but it was dismissed with costs.—*Re Wood*, 514.

And see BANKRUPT.

CO-TRUSTEES.

(*Whether to be viewed as partners.*) Held, that the rules preventing proof by joint creditor against the separate estate of one partner while there is another partner solvent, applied to the case of co-trustees.—*Exp. Bauerman, re Lomax,* 476.

EQUITABLE MORTGAGEE.

1. (*Leave to bid.*) An equitable mortgagee, on asking leave to bid, will not be excused from paying the deposit money if he should become the purchaser.—*Exp. Wilson re Maltby,* 545.

2. (*Merger.*) Where an equitable mortgagee, after notice of an act of bankruptcy, took a conveyance of the legal estate : Held, that his equitable mortgage was not thereby merged, but remained good, notwithstanding the invalidity of such conveyance.—*Exp. Harvey, re Emery,* 547.

ESTOPPEL.

(*Admission of payment.*) Where the bankrupt, by deed granting an annuity to the petitioners, acknowleged a certain sum to have been received by him as the consideration for the annuity ; and in a subsequent memorandum of an account between him and the petitioner had admitted the same sum to be due, and had continued for ten years to pay the annuity without objection, an affidavit tendered by him in opposition to proof by the petitioner, stating that a considerable portion of the consideration-money had not been paid him, was considered no ground for rejecting the proof, though the examination of the petitioner himself was in some respects unsatisfactory.—*Exp. Fairman, re Lloyd,* 467.

And see PROOF, 1.

EVIDENCE.

(*Previous contradictory deposition.*) A previous deposition by a witness, at variance with his present affidavit, is a ground only for a *vivâ voce* examination of such witness upon the points upon which he has contradicted himself, and can be received in evidence only for that purpose, and as affecting his general credit.

Quære, whether secondary evidence (by affidavit of by-stander) of such previous deposition is admissible. — *Exp. Chambers,* 1 Dea. 197 ; *Exp. and re Newall,* 333

And see PRACTICE, 10.

EXPUNGING PROOF.

1. (*Petition by bankrupt.*) In a petition by bankrupt to expunge a proof, it should be alleged that there is a probability either of a surplus or of his being entitled to an allowance.—*Exp. and re Pitchforth,* 487.

2. (*Time of objection.*) It is no sufficient reason for expunging a proof that there was a valid objection to it at the time such proof was made, as, for instance, that there was a solvent partner ; if previous to the application to expunge the objection has ceased to exist, as by such partner becoming insolvent.—*Exp. Bauerman, re Lomax,* 476.

JOINT STOCK BANK.

(*Liability to bankrupt laws.*) A shareholder in a Joint Stock Banking Company, established under 7 Geo. 4, c. 46, as amended by 1 & 2 Vict. c. 96, is a trader within the bankrupt laws (unless where he has purchased shares for the purpose of bringing himself within their operation), and by the special provision of those statutes a *fiat* may be sued out against him for a debt due to the concern, upon an affidavit of the secretary or public officer of the company, though according to the general law of partnership one partner cannot be made a bankrupt by another for a debt due to the firm.—*Exp. and re Hall,* 405.

JURISDICTION.

1. (*Concurrent proceedings.*)   The pendency of a petition before the Lord Chancellor to annul a *fiat*, did not prevent the Court of Review from making an order establishing that *fiat* as against another, subject to the decision of the Lord Chancellor on the petition before him.—*Exp. Higgs, re Evans*, 474.

2. (*Discharge of bankrupt from custody.*)   *Quære*, whether the Court of Review has jurisdiction on petition to discharge from custody a bankrupt who has been committed by a Commissioner for not giving a satisfactory answer, or whether the proper mode of redress for the bankrupt is not by writ of " *habeas corpus.*" Such an order was, however, made upon petition.   (*Dubitante*, Sir G. Rose,) —*Exp. and re James*, 515 (and see cases in note).

3. (*Fund in Court.*)   Where, under a former order, money had been paid into Court to the credit of the estate of a creditor deceased : Held, that the Court had no jurisdiction to divide such fund among his creditors ; but an order was made for transfer of the fund to the Accountant General of the Court of Chancery, as soon as the proper bill shall have been filed in that Court for administering the estate.—*Exp. Williams, re Knight*, 378.

NOTICE.

(*Striking docket.*)   The striking a docket is not conclusive evidence against the party doing it, that he had knowledge of an act of bankruptcy ; but in the case of any claim made by him which would be defeated by such knowledge, it throws upon him the *onus* of proving that he had not such knowledge.—*Exp. Swinburne, re Field*, 396.

And see ORDER AND DISPOSITION ; TRUST DEED.

ORDER AND DISPOSITION.

(*Sealed packet — Reputed ownership.*)   The bankrupt handed over to his sister, the petitioner, as a security for money advanced, the certificates of certain shares in a mining company, together with an agreement binding him to complete the transfer when required.   The petitioner inclosed them in a packet, which she *sealed up* and delivered to the bankrupt, in whose house she resided, to be kept in his iron safe : Held, that as the bankrupt could not have got at the shares without breaking the seal, which would, it seems, have been a felony (see 2 Dea. Crim. Dig. 752), they were not in his order or disposition.

It was held also, in the same case, it being proved that the bankrupt, long before his bankruptcy, had given notice to one of the directors of the deposit, and that this director had, on the morning of the day on which the act of bankruptcy was committed, communicated the fact to the board, that the shares (which were in a foreign mining company, see Exp. Pollard, 2 Dea. 496) were not in the reputed ownership.—*Exp. Richardson, re Richardson*, 496.

PARTNERS.

1. (*Debt, joint or separate.*)   A. being indebted to C. on three bills of exchange, B. guarantees the payment of them, one of them being then due, which in consideration of such guarantee is renewed, and afterwards A. and B. enter into partnership ; when the renewed bill falls due, A. and B. remit to C. a portion of the amount and solicit his indulgence for the remainder ; and on a subsequent occasion A. and B. wrote again to C. for indulgence, saying that they were taking means to satisfy all liabilities, and C. among others.   To these letters C. returned no answer, but forbore in each case to take hostile proceedings : Held, on the subsequent bankruptcy of A. and B., that there was not such an adoption

by C. of the firm for his creditors, as to entitle him to prove against the joint estate.—*Exp. Hitchcock, re Worth,* 507.

2. (*Deceased solvent partner.*) The rule which prevents a joint creditor proving against the separate estate of one partner, while there is another solvent partner, does not apply to the case where a partner has died leaving an estate solvent.—*Exp. Baurman, re Lomax,* 476.

And see CO-TRUSTEES ; JOINT STOCK BANK ; PROOF, 2.

PETITIONING CREDITOR.

(*Solicitor.*) A solicitor may take out a fiat as petitioning creditor for his bill of costs *before* it is taxed ; but if upon taxation it is reduced below 100*l.*, the fiat will be annulled.—*Exp. and re Ford,* 494.

And see TRUST DEED.

PLEADING. See CERTIFICATE ; EXPUNGING PROOF, 1.

PRACTICE.

1. (*Affidavit—Filing and title.*) An affidavit in proof of an act of bankruptcy, which was sworn at Manchester before a Master Extraordinary in Chancery, and which was not entitled in any Court, held to be sufficient ; and held also that the same was properly filed in the Registrar's Office of the Court of Bankruptcy:—*Exp. and re Hall,* 405.

2. (*Certificate.*) The certificate of the commissioners under the composition contract clause need not state that no creditor to the amount of 50*l.* resided out of England.—*Exp. and re Butterworth,* 395.

3. (*Competing commissions.*) Where of the five commissioners to whom a *renewed* commission had been directed in 1816, two were since dead, and two were removed to a considerable distance, and a new fiat had been issued ; the Court thought that the *renewed* commission of 1816 ought to be superseded ; but as a petition to supersede the new fiat was pending before the Chancellor, the order of *supersedeas* was made conditional upon the Chancellor rejecting such petition.

The Court observed that there was a difference between superseding an original and a renewed commission.—*Exp. Higgs, re Evans,* 474.

4. (*Direction of fiat.*) The Court refused to alter the direction of the fiat from country to London, merely because a majority of the creditors resided in London. (See Exp. Gregg, 3 Dea. 381.)— *Exp. Rawlinson, re Jones,* 535.

5. (*Incorporation of fiats.*) For the greater advantage of the estates, the Court ordered two prior separate fiats, under which assignees had been chosen and a dividend declared, to be incorporated with a subsequent joint fiat.—*Exp. Lister, re Haddon,* 516.

6. (*Irregular notice, 1 & 2 Vict. c. 110, s. 8.*) Where an affidavit, under the above act, had been filed against the trader, but the notice which ought to have been given after, had been given before the filing of such affidavit, and the creditor, upon discovering such irregularity, had withdrawn the notice ; the Court refused, on petition of the trader, to take such notice off the file, as the creditor was entitled, if he chose, to give a fresh notice.—*Exp. Gibson,* 531.

7. (*Power of attorney.*) One power of attorney from several creditors held to be sufficient authority to the attorney to sign a consent for all to annul the fiat.— *Anon.* 377.

8. (*Revival of order.*) A petition to revive a former order will be granted as of course, unless some hardship arises from the revival.— *Exp. Evans, re Ellis,* 381.

9. (*Standing over.*) The fact of a petition being allowed to stand over at the application of a party, does not, in the absence of a special direction in the order, prevent that party from filing fresh affidavits.—*Exp. Worthington, re Sutton,* 332.

10. (*Same.*) Where a petition stood over for want of an affidavit of service, the Court would not allow it to retain its place, an objection being made by the counsel in the next petition.—*Exp. and re Crossley,* 404.

11. (*Vivâ voce examination.*) The usual course is not to apply before-hand for an order to examine *vivâ voce* on a petition, but if on the hearing the Court see occasion they will direct it.—*Exp. Tate, re Odlin,* 516.

And see JURISDICTION, 1 ; SPECIAL CASE.

PRODUCTION OF DOCUMENTS.

(*Return of, after inspection.*) The party who produces a document to the commissioners, either by compulsion of legal process, or through a threat of being committed, is entitled to have it returned to him after inspection, without reference to his title to retain the same, which the Court will not inquire into.—*Exp. Gilbard, re Malachy,* 488.

PROOF.

1. (*Election—Estoppel.*) Where a creditor who was entitled to elect whether he would prove against the joint estate or the separate estate of two partners, had proved against the separate estate of one, and had received a dividend upon his proofs : Held, that upon refunding such dividend he might retire his proof and prove against the joint estate.—*Exp. Law, re Bailey,* 541.

2. (*Merger of securities.*) The bankrupts, who were bankers, gave a joint and several promissory note to their bankers to secure advances up to 2000*l.* When the advances had amounted to 1957*l.*, one of the bankrupts executed a mortgage to the bankers to secure that sum and all future advances up to 3000*l.* ; and by the same deed all the bankrupts covenanted to pay the 1937*l.* At the time of the bankruptcy the firm was indebted to the bankers 4365*l.* The bankers sold the mortgaged property for upwards of 3000*l.*, and then applied to prove against the estate of one of the partners upon the promissory note, for the balance still due : Held, that they might do so on the authority of Exp. Ladbroke, 2 G. & J. 81. Diss. Sir J. Cross, who thought the lesser security merged in the greater.—*Exp. Bate, re Bishton,* 358.

3. (*Reduction by payment.*) After proof of a debt, but before declaration of a dividend, the creditors received a large portion of the debt from a surety : Held, that his proof ought not to be reduced.—*Exp. Coplestone, re Snell,* 546.

REPUTED OWNERSHIP. See ORDER AND DISPOSITION.

SPECIAL CASE.

The Court adverted to the inconvenience that had arisen from disregarding the terms of the General Order of 22d May, 1833, as to the mode of obtaining the judge's approval of a special case. —*Exp. Woodward, re Turner,* 294.

And see APPEAL.

STAT. 1 & 2 VICT. c. 110. See PRACTICE, 6.

TRADING.

(*Farmer.*) A farmer who was in the habit of buying at a time half as many more sheep as were required to stock his farm, for the purpose, as he alleged, of selecting those he liked best, and selling the remainder ; upon its being shown that the selection was usually left to the buyer, and that in some instances, the whole lot had been sold without shearing or pasturing : Held to be a trader.—*Exp. and re Newall*, 333.

TRUST. See BENEFIT SOCIETY.

TRUST DEED.

1. (*Notice of act of bankruptcy.*) An assignee under a trust deed, who had previously struck a docket against the bankrupt, which (as it stated in his petition) he afterwards abandoned upon the trust deed being executed (and not by reason of any mistake as to the commission of an act of bankruptcy), was held, as against the assignee under a subsequent *fiat*, to have no lien on the property assigned to him for costs incurred and payments made in execution of the trusts of the deed of assignment.—*Exp. Swinburne, re Field*, 396.

2. (*Partners.*) The circumstance of one of several partners having been named as one of the trustees in a deed of composition, which he did not execute : Held not to disqualify the firm as petitioning creditor.—*Re Wood*, 514.

UNCLAIMED DIVIDENDS.

(*Executrix of assignee.*) The Court, on the petition of executrix of surviving assignee, ordered that she should pay certain unclaimed dividends into Court, but declined ordering a release.—*Exp. Raikes, re Tuke*, 494.

HOUSE OF LORDS.

[Containing cases in 4 Clark & Finnelly, Part 3, omitting Cases noticed in former Digests.

ACCOUNT.

1. (*Annual rests—Interest on balance of rent and debt.*)—Where it was agreed between a debtor and his creditor that the latter should accept a certain rent in payment of his debt and the interest thereon, (which interest was not to commence till a certain period,) until debt and interest were satisfied, and that half-yearly rests should be taken, and the rent was in fact not paid for several years: Held, that the creditor was not, upon the construction of the agreement, even supposing it to be legal, entitled to interest upon the unpaid rents—*Page* v. *Broom*, 436.—(See Page v. Linwood, 399, and *infra*.)

2. (*Compound interest.*)—In the course of accounts taken upon the footing of an agreement allowing interest, a balance was struck of the sum acknowledged to be due, including an *item* for compound interest: Held, that this was not sufficient evidence of a settled dealing between the parties to found a charge for compound interest in the subsequent parts of the account.—*S. C.*

EVIDENCE.

(*Entry on journals.*)—Held, that an entry in the journals of the Committee of Privileges was, upon trial of a claim to vote at the election of Representative Peers for Ireland, good evidence of the limitations in a patent of peerage.—*In the matter of Lord Dufferin and Claneboye*, 568.—(See Committee of Privileges.)

MORTGAGEE.

(*Annual rests—Possession as lessee.*)—Where the mortgagor and mortgagee of a house entered into an agreement with a builder to make certain alterations in the house, in consideration of a lease to be granted to him, and it was also part of the agreement, that he should grant an underlease to the mortgagee, at a certain rent and in consideration of a certain sum to be paid to him as the price of such lease, (the effect of such agreement being to postpone the right of the mortgagee to her mortgage money, to the right of the builder to his rent), and upon the completion of the works, the mortgagee entered into possession, but no lease was executed in pursuance of the agreement, either to the builder or the mortgagee, and the mortgagee never paid the 1000*l.*, or the annual rent agreed to be paid by her: Held, that in affirmation of decree of Lord Chancellor Brougham, that upon account taken between her and the representatives of the builder, who had subsequently purchased the equity of redemption from the mortgagor, the mortgagee was in possession as tenant, and not as mortgagee, and the accounts ought not to be taken as against her with annual rests. The suit related to a very complicated state of facts.   See Page v. Broom, 4 Russ. 6, reported upon the hearing before Sir J. Leach, whose decree, except in the above point and also in the point mentioned *supra* in Page v. Broom, tit. Account, was confirmed. —*Page* v. *Linwood*, 399.

PRACTICE.

(*Dismissing appeal on motion.*)—Where an appellant, after receiving indulgence from the House, upon terms, fails to comply with such terms or to appear on the day appointed for the hearing, his appeal was dismissed with costs upon motion on behalf of the respondent, without requiring him to present a petition.—*Mahon* v. *Irwin*, 559.

TIME OF APPEAL.

1. (*Intentional absence.*)—The indulgence, as to time of appealing which is allowed on account of absence, by the Orders of 24th of March, 1726, (No. 118,) as amended in 1829, was refused to a party who went abroad after the decree for the purpose, as the House thought, of avoiding its execution.—(Brooke v. Champernowne, 4 C. & F. 247 ; L. M. No. 44.)—*De Burgh* v. *Clarke*, 562.

2. (*Time saved by subsequent orders.*)—Where proceedings subsequent to the decree had been taken within the time allowed for appealing : Held, that an appeal might be brought against the subsequent orders and the original decree.—*S. C.*

LIST OF CASES.

EQUITY.

BANKRUPTCY.

HOUSE OF LORDS.

ABSTRACT OF THE PUBLIC GENERAL STATUTES.

(2 Victoria.)

CAP. 1.—An Act to amend an Act of the First and Second Year of Her present Majesty for the more effectual Relief of the Destitute Poor of Ireland.
[15th March, 1839.]

CAP. 2.—An Act to apply the Sum of Two Millions to the Service of the Year One thousand eight hundred and thirty-nine. [15th March, 1839.]

CAP. 3.—An Act to authorize the immediate Distribution of a Portion of the Fund applicable to the Relief of Persons entitled to certain Arrears of Tithe Compositions under an Act of the last Session of Parliament to abolish Compositions for Tithes in Ireland, and to substitute Rent-charges in lieu thereof, and for other purposes. [27th March, 1839.]

CAP. 4.—An Act to alter the Powers of Jointuring contained in several Acts for Purchasing and Providing a Residence and Estates for the Duke of Wellington, and to settle certain Articles to go as Heirlooms with the said Estates.
[27th March, 1839.]

CAP. 5.—An Act for Punishing Mutiny and Desertion, and for the better Payment of the Army and their Quarters. [19th April, 1839.]

CAP. 6.—An Act to apply the Sum of Eight Millions out of the Consolidated Fund to the Service of the Year One thousand eight hundred and thirty-nine.
[19th April, 1839.]

CAP. 7.—An Act for the Regulation of her Majesty's Royal Marine Forces while on Shore. [19th April, 1839.]

CAP. 8.—An Act for raising the Sum of Thirteen Millions by Exchequer Bills, for the Service of the Year One thousand eight hundred and thirty-nine.
[14th May, 1839.]

CAP. 9.—An Act for repealing part of an Act of the last Session of Parliament, intituled, An Act for Suspending until the First day of August, One thousand eight hundred and thirty-nine, and to the End of the then Session of Parliament, the Appointment to certain Dignities and Offices in Cathedral and Collegiate Churches, and to Sinecure Rectories. [14th May, 1839.]

CAP. 10.—An Act for enabling the Trustees of the British Museum to Purchase certain Houses and Grounds for the enlargement of the Museum, and making a suitable Access thereto. [4th June, 1839.]

CAP. 11.—An Act for the better protection of Purchasers against Judgments, Crown Debts, Lis Pendens, and Fiats in Bankruptcy. [4th June, 1839.]

S. 1. No judgments hereafter to be docketed under the provisions of the 4 & 5 W. & M. c. 20, but all dockets to be finally closed immediately after the passing of this Act, without prejudice to judgments already docketed and entered, except as hereinafter mentioned.

S. 2. No judgment already docketed and entered to affect lands as to purchasers, mortgagees, or creditors, unless and until the memorandum prescribed by the 1 Vict. c. 110, be left with the Senior Master of the Court of Common Pleas.

S. 3. The date when left to be entered in a book.

S. 4. Judgments, decrees, rules and orders registered since the 1 Vict. c. 110, or hereafter to be registered, after five years from the date of the entry, shall be void against lands, as to purchasers, &c. unless a like memorandum is again left with the master, within five years before the execution of the instrument transferring the estate to such purchaser or mortgagee for valuable consideration, or before the right of the creditors accrued; and so on toties quoties.

S. 5. As against purchasers and mortgagees without notice, none of such judgments, &c. shall bind the land further than a judgment of one of the superior courts would heretofore have done.

S. 6. Nothing in the recited Act, or in this Act, to revive judgments already extinguished or barred, or to affect or prejudice any judgment as between the parties thereto, or their representatives, or those deriving as volunteers under them.

S. 7. No lis pendens to bind a purchaser or mortgagee without express notice, until a memorandum of the suit (as herein prescribed) be left with the Master of the Common Pleas: and the provisions of s. 4 to extend to every case of lis pendens registered under this Act.

S. 8. No judgment, statute, or recognizance obtained or entered into on account of the crown, or inquisition whereby any debt shall be proved due to the crown, or obligation or specialty made to the crown, according to the 33 Hen. 8, c. 39, or acceptance of office by officers where lands shall thereby become liable for arrearages under the 13 Eliz. c. 4, to affect lands as to purchasers or mortgagees, unless registered in C. P. in the manner herein directed.

S. 9. Quietus to debtors or accountants to the crown to be registered in like manner.

S. 10. Empowers the Commissioners of the Treasury, on such terms as they may think proper, to certify that lands of any crown debtor shall be held by a purchaser or mortgagee discharged from all further claims of the crown: or in the case of leases for fines, that the lessees may hold so discharged, without prejudice to the crown's rights against the reversion, and therefore the lands shall be held so discharged respectively.

S. 11. Such certificate, or the discharge of the lands under this Act, not to affect the right of the crown to levy on other lands liable to the debt.

S. 12. Conveyances bonâ fide made and executed by a bankrupt before the date of the fiat, shall be valid notwithstanding a prior act of bankruptcy, provided the party to whom the conveyance was made had not at the time notice of any prior act of bankruptcy.

S. 13. No purchase from a bankrupt bonâ fide and for valuable consideration, where the purchaser had notice of an act of bankruptcy, shall be impeached unless the commission shall have been sued out within twelve calendar months after such act of bankruptcy.

S. 14. Act not to extend to Ireland.

Cap. 12.——An Act to amend an Act of the Thirty-ninth Year of King George the Third, for the more effectual Suppression of Societies established for Seditious and Treasonable Purposes, and for preventing Treasonable and Seditious Practices, and to put an End to certain proceedings now pending under the said Act. [4th June, 1839.]

S. 1. Repeals the 39 Geo. 3, c. 79, s. 27.

S. 2. Penalty of £5 on printers for not printing their name and residence on every paper and book, and on persons publishing or dispersing the same.

S. 3. As to books and papers printed at the University presses.

S. 4. No actions for penalties to be commenced, except in the name of the attorney or solicitor general in England, or the queen's advocate in Scotland.

S. 5. Provisions for staying proceedings now pending for penalties under the 39 Geo. 3, c. 79.

S. 6. The 39 Geo. 3, c. 79, and all acts amending it, to be construed as one act together with this act.

S. 7. Act may be amended or repealed this session.

CAP. 13.—An Act for extending the Copyright of Designs for Calico Printing to Designs for Printing other Woven Fabrics. [4th June, 1839.]

CAP. 14.—An Act for removing Doubts as to the Appointment of a Dean of Exeter, or of any other Cathedral Church. [4th June, 1839.]

CAP. 15.—An Act to provide for the more effectual Execution of the Office of a Justice of the Peace within and adjoining to the District called the Staffordshire Potteries, and for purposes connected therewith. [4th June, 1839.]

CAP. 16.—An Act for improving the Practice and Proceedings of the Court of Pleas of the County Palatine af Durham and Sadberge. [14th June, 1839.]

[This Act introduces into the Court of Common Pleas of Durham alterations in its process and practice analogous to those of the 2 W. 4, c. 39, and the 1 Vict. c. 110.]

CAP. 17.—An Act to secure to Proprietors of Designs for Articles of Manufacture the Copyright of such Designs for a limited Time. [14th June, 1839.]

CAP. 18.—An Act to enable Archbishops and Bishops to raise Money on Mortgage of their Sees, for the purpose of building and otherwise providing fit Houses for their Residence. [1st July, 1839.]

CAP. 19.—An Act to amend an Act of the Sixth and Seventh Years of his late Majesty King William the Fourth, for Consolidating the Laws relating to the Presentment of Public Money by Grand Juries in Ireland, so as to enable the Grand Jury of the County of Waterford to make Presentments on account of the Fever Hospital of the said County, although situate in the County of the City of Waterford. [1st July, 1839.]

CAP. 20.—An Act to authorize the Application of Part of the Land Revenues of the Crown for the Erection of Stables and Stable Offices contiguous to Windsor Castle. [1st July, 1839.]

CAP. 21.—An Act for granting to her Majesty, until the Fifth day of July, One thousand eight hundred and forty, certain Duties on Sugar imported into the United Kingdom, for the Service of the Year One thousand eight hundred and thirty-nine. [4th July, 1839.]

CAP. 22.—An Act to enable Justices of Assize on their Circuits to take Inquisition of all Pleas in the Court of Exchequer of Pleas which shall be brought before them, without a Special Commission for that purpose. [4th July, 1839.]

Justices of assize on their circuits may try causes and take inquisitions of pleas pending in the Court of Exchequer of Pleas, and proceed thereon in like manner as in respect of causes and pleas in Q. B. and C. P. and it shall not be necessary hereafter to issue any commission from the Court of Exchequer for that purpose.

NOTES TO THE LIFE OF LORD ELDON.

We have been favoured by a high legal authority with the following statement of an incident in the Life of Lord Eldon, mentioned in our last number.

"The account of the two gentlemen of the name of Atkinson, and the part which Lord Eldon took with respect to one of them, is partially incorrect.

"There were two gentlemen of that name merchants in the House. Mr. Christopher Atkinson was an eminent corn merchant and factor. In the course of the American war he was employed by the Victualling Office to purchase corn and flour for the navy as a factor, on commission. He was attacked in the newspapers, and it was imputed to him that he had defrauded the Victualling Office by charging higher prices than he paid. He moved for a criminal information against one person who made this charge, and in his affidavit to obtain the information he made oath that he had not in any instance charged more than his commission. Some information was given to the Treasury, upon which a prosecution for perjury was commenced and conducted by the law officers of the crown. The indictment assigned perjury on six instances, in which it was alleged that he had charged higher prices than he had paid. The trial took place in the year 1783, before Lord Mansfield. It was proved that in these several instances he had charged a higher price than he had paid. The defence was, that, although in the particular instances specified he had charged more than he had paid, those prices were merely nominal, for the purpose of obtaining money by way of imprest, and that every six weeks the whole was set right by a balance bill. This defence was not well received by Lord Mansfield, and not sufficiently made out to the satisfaction of the jury, and Mr. Atkinson was convicted. In the next term he did not appear to receive judgment, but went to France. In the course of the next year an error having been discovered in the record, which his counsel thought fatal, he came over, surrendered, and moved an arrest of judgment. On the other hand, the Attorney General moved to amend—the Court did amend. An unsuccessful application was then made for a new trial, and in Michaelmas Term 1784, Mr. Atkinson received judgment of fine and imprisonment and the pillory. The story of his wife standing upon the pillory with him is, I believe, unfounded. About the time the prosecution was commenced the Attorney General had filed a bill in the Exchequer for an account, but the suit had slept. Mr. Atkinson now revived the suit, and called for the account; the account was taken in the Court of Exchequer and occupied considerable time—in the end it was clearly proved that Mr. Atkinson's allegation of the balance bill was true, and that upon the whole he had not charged more than he had paid—in very many instances much less.

"I was present at the argument in the Court of Exchequer, and well remember the feeling manner in which Lord Eldon, then Mr. Scott, who was leading counsel for Mr. Atkinson, commenced his address to the court for his client, who had been "whipped of justice," though now it was proved that he was free from crime.

"Chief Baron Eyre delivered an elaborate judgment in favor of Mr. Atkinson; and his innocence being now established, he received a pardon under the great seal, and for many years afterwards sat in parliament, both in the name of Atkinson and the name of Saville, which after some years he took.

"I knew Mr. Atkinson personally, and remember his being in parliament as late as the year 1808."

EXAMINATION HONOURS FOR ATTORNEYS.

[The following letter is too well written to be thrown away, and we believe we shall best answer the object the writer has in view by printing his own arguments, on which it would not be easy to improve.]

Whitchurch, July 17, 1839.

Sir,

In order to make the law in a degree equal to other professions, and to keep pace with the general progress, the old plan of examination has of late been restored. It was intended to secure a certain amount of talent and character, in a profession which especially calls for the exercise of both. Curiously enough, however, while this object has been partly obtained, another, or rather a more valuable branch of the same object, has been altogether neglected. The examination has been so framed, as to secure a certain, but very small proportion of ability, while all incitements to advance a step beyond have been entirely omitted. All but the very stupid, or the very careless, are sure of a certificate ; but nothing more than a certificate is granted to the industrious or the clever. The consequence is natural. At an age when self-interest has scarcely taken root, and emulation alone is master of the breast, there is no inducement to diligence, because no opportunity for display ; and the moment when, from these motives, every exertion might be made, is suffered to pass by in indolence or dissipation. In other professions the want is remedied by distinctions either present or future. In the church, and to the medical student, early occasions are offered for acquiring recorded fame ; while to the barrister, soldier, and sailor, comes promotion as the reward of merit. The solicitor alone has nothing of an honourable nature to encourage him, and that branch of the profession the most exposed to temptation, and whose members should be most carefully fitted for their calling, is suffered still to continue under the proverb, and treated as unworthy of distinction. This is surely unfair.

I pass by the objection that degrees would be invidious towards those who gained none. I shall not in this age be required to defend the system by which the world is ruled, or to recal the laurel of Wellington because of the murmurings of the coward. To the fool or the knave alone is it an argument, and I believe you will agree with me, that too much weight should not be given to them.

But, in truth, there is no valid objection. If the matter be treated as ridiculous, I reply that the present race of solicitors are, in general, men of education and gentlemanly habits ; and that the medical profession has already public orders of merit in its examinations ; if objected to as needless, I answer that the duties of a solicitor are difficult and delicate ; that emulation is the most powerful motive, and that all mankind possess the feeling.

The only real obstacle is in that aversion to change which, as a sort of instinct, pervades some classes of persons—a sort of *vis inertiæ*, so hard to overcome except by strenuous and repeated exertion.

To me personally the matter is immaterial, as I am established in practice, but I speak for my sons. I educate them as gentlemen, I carefully instruct them in the routine of their profession, I hear other parents boasting of the recorded honours of their children, and I see the benefits which recorded honours bring, but because my son is a solicitor, *I* am deprived of these pleasures, and *he* of the chance of affording them to me.

I trust I may soon see the subject taken up by some one whose name may give authority to his sentiments. To you, Sir, I also earnestly appeal, to consider the matter, and if the result be favourable, to give it your support. This would be of the greatest importance, and if not directly within your usual province, you would be amply rewarded for the trespass. The plan must be adopted ere long, and why delay giving to the rising generation those aids which their successors will undoubtedly enjoy? It is a question about which all are interested,—which seems particularly to deserve the advocacy of the leading law periodical, and, as a humble labourer, I leave it in your hands, begging you to give it your consideration, and to excuse the intrusion of this letter.

I remain, Sir,

Your obedient Servant,

A Country Solicitor.

P.S.—My plan would be to number the candidates as in the *poll* at Cambridge in this manner :—Let the first ten be placed in order of merit in each division of the examination subjects, and then let ten be numbered in a like way on the general balance, so as to ensure general proficiency. This plan is at once simple and without expense, and though it may add in a degree to the trouble of the examiners, I am sure those gentlemen would not refuse to undertake it, if it conduced to the character of their profession.

EVENTS OF THE QUARTER.

NOTWITHSTANDING the solemn assurance volunteered in a speech from the throne, that law reform would receive the earliest and best attention of the government, they have hitherto done next to nothing in this department; and it was left for Lord Lyndhurst to propose a remedy for the most crying of all existing abuses —the ruinous delays of the Courts of Equity, resulting from the extraordinary accumulation of arrears. After waiting till the session was drawing towards its close, to see if the Lord Chancellor or the law officers of the crown had any measure in contemplation, he made a luminous exposition of the present state of these courts, and proved to demonstration that they were hopelessly inadequate to the work, not from any want of energy or capacity in the judges, but from the vast increase of business and the greater degree of deliberation very properly devoted to it. "I believe," said Lord Lyndhurst, "that they (the present equity judges) exercise more time and more energy upon it than any country ought to require of its judges. I am one of those persons who think that a judge should not occupy his mind totally with the administration of justice. There is not any pursuit which does not tend, if a man devotes himself exclusively to it, to narrow the intellect and contract the understanding. A judge ought to look abroad, and to cultivate literature and science, for the lights they so acquire reflect back on the bench, and afford force and vigour to the judgment they pronounce." His proposal was to appoint an additional judge in Chancery, and an additional judge in the Exchequer,—the latter to devote himself exclusively to the equity business of that court, and preside over the judicial committee of the privy council. The Lord Chancellor objected that Lord Lyndhurst's plan did not go far enough, and Lord Langdale seemed to give the preference to a more comprehensive scheme (mentioned in our last number) of his own; but both agreed that the evil was becoming intolerable, and that two new judges might at least lend a helping hand in diminishing it; yet neither would undertake the required bill, which Lord Lyndhurst, mindful of the fate of his former measures, declined; and though Mr. Spence has made a fresh appeal to the public, and Mr. Freshfield has brought the question regarding the Court of Exchequer before the House of Commons, both the Exchequer and the Chancery continue, and seem likely to continue, for some time longer as they were.

The Custody of Infants Bill has passed the House of Commons with little opposition, and was received in the House of Lords in a manner which augurs well for its ultimate success. We allude particularly to the part taken by Lord Denman in the debate on the second reading : " The law (he said) as it now existed was cruel to the wife and debasing to the husband, allowing him with impunity to act the part of the base and corrupt tyrant, while it was ruinous both to the health and morals of the children, who could have no security so complete, when a profligate husband had taken possession of them, as the occasional inspection of the mother,—by her having an opportunity of knowing what was their treatment and the exact situation in which they were placed." Lord Wynford moved the rejection of the bill, but did not press his amendment to a division ; and Lord Brougham did not repeat his statement, that the fifteen judges had held up their thirty hands against the measure.

Lord John Russell's Bill for remodelling the Courts of Quarter Sessions has made no progress, but the Metropolitan Police Court Bill has been favoured by the active patronage of the ministry, because they expect to get from it a good deal of patronage in return. Without quite agreeing in all the objections urged by Mr. Law in his able and spirited speech, we fully go along with him as to the inexpediency of trusting such appointments as those of London magistrates are henceforth to become, entirely to the discretion of the Home Secretary for the time being, who can have little acquaintance with the legal profession, and consequently small means of estimating the qualifications of the candidates ; nor are our fears at all lessened by the recollection of the course pursued by Lord John Russell with reference to the borough magistrates, who have been generally appointed for their politics. The Bill for the Improvement of the County Courts has been referred to a select committee, who have reported in its favour, and made some important alterations. They recommend the judicial appointments to be vested in the Chancellor.

The serjeants are still kept in a harassing state of uncertainty as to their prospects, nor do we exactly understand the present state of the question regarding them. All we know is, that a Bill has been brought in, not to open or to close the Common Pleas, but simply to authorise barristers not of the coif to make or support motions touching the trial of any cause or issue tried elsewhere than in London or Middlesex in which they may have been originally engaged ; from which the plain inference is, that all warrants infringing on the privileges of the serjeants are considered inoperative. London and Middlesex are excepted, to give the serjeants a monopoly of the whole business of the metropolis.

A bill has been introduced, under Dr. Lushington's auspices, for the reform of the Admiralty Court, and the judge is henceforth to receive a fixed salary, instead of a fluctuating income depending on the number of causes he may dispatch.

The Copyhold Enfranchisement Bill has been divested of the compulsory clauses, in consequence of the strong opposition made to them (a), and is now expected to pass. The Bill for Improving the Registration of Electors, and the Bill for Creating a Court of Appeal from the decisions of Revising Barristers, have now no chance of passing ; and though a short declaratory act would have prevented nine-tenths of the uncertainty and apparent inconsistency periodically complained of, even this has been left unattempted by the ministry, in the firm confidence, no doubt, that the blame as usual will fall upon the barristers.

Mr. Serjeant Talfourd has withdrawn his Copyright Bill in consequence of the press of parliamentary business, which rendered perseverance hopeless during the present session. It will be brought forward early in the next, and must pass eventually, notwithstanding the narrow-minded opposition of Mr. Warburton, who exhibits the zeal of a bigot under the guise of a philosopher.

(a) The objections are stongly stated in *A Letter to the Right Honourable Sir E. Knatchbull, relating to the Bill,* &c.

A meeting of the attorneys and solicitors of Ireland was held in Dublin in June last, to oppose a section of the Irish bar, who, it seems, had it in contemplation to apply to parliament for a Bill to authorise the Allowance of Fees to Counsel in Proceedings by Civil Bill in the Sessions Court, where attorneys now enjoy a monopoly. Mr. Ford, the leading speaker, observed : " In Ireland, the barristers never practised at the Quarter Sessions, but they now say, ' Our brethren in England practise at Quarter Sessions, *and receive half-guinea fees*, and why should not we ? ' To this he would answer, that they had never in this country practised in these courts as a body, and why should they go there now ? The barristers in England went to the Quarter Sessions, *because rich England could afford to give them a half-guinea fee.*" We beg leave to assure Mr. Ford, that we have nothing at all analogous to the Civil Bill Court in England, and that an English barrister never receives less than a guinea at our Quarter Sessions, such as they are. Mr. Watt, the second speaker, " concluded by saying that it was a melancholy thing that the Irish barristers were working, not for the 10s. 6d., which the English barrister gets, but only for the fifteen-pence, the half of the 2s. 6d., given by statute to the attorney." It is to be hoped that the barristers of Ireland will get up a meeting to repel this imputation without delay.

Mr. Le Blanc has resigned his situation as one of the masters of the Queen's Bench. He is succeeded by Mr. C. R. Turner, a gentleman much esteemed at the bar, who had neither solicited nor entertained any expectation of the appointment up to the period when Lord Denman's intentions were made known. The choice, and the manner of it, do equal credit to both parties.

We understand that Sir William Horne has accepted the appointment of a Master in Chancery, vacant by the resignation of Mr. Martin.

July 25, 1839.

LIST OF NEW PUBLICATIONS.

The Act for the Amendment of the Poor Laws, (4 & 5 Will. IV. c. 76,) with a Practical Introduction, Notes and Forms. Fifth Edition, with many valuable Additions. By John Frederick Archbold, Esq. Barrister at Law. In 12mo. price 8s. boards.

A Treatise on the Law of Limitations, with an Appendix of Statutes and Forms. By G. B. Mansel, Esq., Barrister at Law. In 12mo. price 6s. boards.

Commentaries on the Law of Nations. By W. Oke Manning, jun. Esq. In 8vo. price 14s. boards.

The Statute Criminal Law of England, as regards indictable Offences : arranged in Classes, according to the Degrees of Punishment, (forming the Appendix to the Fourth Report of the Commissioners on Criminal Law). With Notes. By James John Lonsdale, Esq. of Lincoln's Inn, Barrister at Law. In 8vo. price 14s. boards.

Questions on the Law of Real Property and Conveyancing ; with Answers. By a Member of the Bar. In 12mo. price 4s. boards.

Questions and Answers on the Practice of the Court of Chancery for the Use of Articled Clerks preparing for their Examination for Admission as Solicitors of the Court. By Harding Grant. In 12mo. price 5s. boards.

A Treatise upon the Law and Practice of the Court for Relief of Insolvent Debtors, with an Appendix containing the Acts of Parliament, Rules of Court Forms, and Tables of Costs. By Edward Cooke, Esq. of the Middle Temple, Barrister at Law. Second Edition. In 8vo. price 16s. boards.

A New Law Dictionary, containing Explanations of such Technical Terms and Phrases as occur in the Works of the various Law Writers of Great Britain. To which is added, an Outline of an Action at Law and of a Suit in Equity. Designed expressly for the Use of Students. By Henry James Holthouse, Esq. Price 9s. boards.

A Practical Guide to Executors and Administrators ; designed to enable them to execute the Duties of their Office with safety and convenience ; comprising a Digest of the Law, Stamp Office and other Directions, Forms, Tables of Duties and Annuities, &c. &c. Intended also for the Use of Attornies and Solicitors. By Richard Matthews, of the Middle Temple, Esq. Barrister at Law. Second Edition, corrected to the present Time. In 12mo. price 9s. boards.

The Law of Parliamentary Elections, Part I. from the Issuing of the Writ to the Return of the Members. Including the last Alterations in the Qualifications of Members as fixed by the 1 & 2 Vict. c. 48. By B. Montagu, Esq. Q. C. and W. J. Neale, Esq. Barristers at Law. In 12mo. price 5s. 6d. boards.

The Theory and Practice of Conveyancing. By Solomon Atkinson, Esq. Barrister at Law. Second Edition. Vol. I. in 8vo. price 1l. boards.

London : Printed by C. Roworth & Sons, Bell Yard, Temple Bar.

THE LAW MAGAZINE.

ART. I.—PRIVILEGES OF THE BAR—INFLUENCE OF LEGAL STUDIES.

The Case of the Queen v. Disraeli. With an Argument in Vindication of the Practice of the Bar. By Joseph Stammers, Esq. Barrister at Law. 2d Edit. Lond. 1839.

WE declined noticing this case at the time of its occurrence from an unwillingness to give pain, and it is beside our present purpose to discuss the personal considerations involved in it. But we have long wished for an opportunity of exposing sundry vulgar errors regarding the privileges and practice of the bar, and we can hardly hope to find a better one than the appearance of this pamphlet presents.

Mr. Stammers' argument consists of a concise statement of the precise nature of the principal privilege contended for, with the grounds on which it has been justified by the judges, and the principle on which, in his opinion, it is based. We shall adopt nearly the same method of proceeding so long as our objects are the same, but we have it in contemplation to go a little further than Mr. Stammers, and, after proving that the privileges of the bar are strictly consistent with good sense and good feeling as they stand, to prove that the ordinary practice of the profession,—involving, as it is supposed to do, the indiscriminate defence of right and wrong, and the most complete practical indifference to the guilt or innocence of a client or the truth or falsehood of a case,—does not in reality exercise any bad mental or moral influence upon the mass..

Let us first understand clearly what we are talking about; for we certainly are not about to argue in favour of "the privilege of circulating falsehoods with impunity," nor were we aware, prior to the appearance of Mr. Disraeli's epistle, that the creed of the profession was, that they might say anything provided they were paid for it. Our notion was and is, that if any member of the bar were called upon for an explanation of anything said or done by him in the course of his professional duty,—we mean of course; called upon in the manner sanctioned by custom,—he would neither decline all communication on the subject, nor think it sufficient to reply that he was speaking or acting as counsel in a cause. On the contrary, he would state distinctly that the line of conduct or remark was pursued from a firm conviction of its propriety and tendency to promote the client's interest at the time ; and, as a matter of courtesy, or where the applicant was obviously an innocent sufferer, few, we are quite certain, would hesitate to add an expression of regret or a disclaimer of any personal or individual intention to offend. Would a judicious friend, civil or military, ask more?

In cases calling for legal redress, the same criterion would be applied—were the words relevant to the matter in hand, or were they such as a zealous advocate might fairly be supposed to think relevant? This we take to be the purport of the decision of the Court of Queen's Bench in Hodgson v. Scarlett, where the authorities were thoroughly discussed :

" Lord Ellenborough.—The law privileges many communications, which otherwise might be considered as calumnies, and become the subject of an action. In the case of master and servant, the convenience of mankind requires that what is said in fair communication between man and man, upon the subject of character, should be privileged, if made *bonâ fide*, and without malice. If, however, the party giving the character knows what he says to be untrue, that may deprive him of the protection which the law throws around such communications. So a counsel entrusted with the interests of others, and speaking from their information, for the sake of public convenience, is privileged in commenting fairly and *bonâ fide* on the circumstances of the case, and in making observations on the parties concerned, and their instruments or agents in bringing the cause into Court. Now the plaintiff in this case was not merely the attorney, but was mixed up in the concoction of the antecedent facts, out of which the original cause arose ; he was cognizant of all the circumstances, and knew that the plaintiff had no ground of action in that case, in consequence of having already received more than the amount recoverable by him. It was in commenting on this conduct that the words were used by the defendant. He had a right so to comment, for the plaintiff was mixed up with the circumstances of the case, and was the agent and instrument in the transaction. The defendant then says, he is a fraudulent and wicked attorney. These were words not used at random, or unnecessary, but were a comment upon the plaintiff's conduct as attorney. Perhaps they were too strong. It may have been too much to say that he was guilty of fraud, as between man and man, and of wickedness in *foro divino*. The expression, in the exercise of a candour fit to be adopted, might have been spared. But still a counsel might *bonâ fide* think such an expression justifiable under the circumstances.

" Bayley, J.—The rule seems to me to be correctly laid down in Brook v. Sir Henry Montague, ' that a counsellor hath a privilege to enforce any thing which is informed unto him for his client, and to give it in evidence, it being pertinent to the matter in question, and not to examine whether it be true or false.' No mischief will ensue from allowing the privilege to that extent.

" Abbott, J.—I am of opinion that no action can be maintained, *unless it can be shown that the counsel availed himself of his situation maliciously to utter words wholly unjustifiable.* It would be impossible that justice could be well administered if counsel were to be questioned for the too great strength of their expressions. Here the words were pertinent; and there is no pretence for saying that the defendant maliciously availed himself of his situation to utter them." —1 B. & Ald. 17, 18.

In Flint v. Pike, 4 B. & C. 473, in which the same question came incidentally before the Court, Mr. Justice Holroyd said :

" With a view to the due administration of justice, counsel are privileged in what they say. Unless the administration of justice is to be fettered, they must have free liberty of speech in making their observations, which it must be remembered may be answered by the opposing counsel, and commented on by the judge, and are afterwards taken into consideration by the jury, who have an opportunity of judging how far the matter uttered by the counsel is warranted by the facts proved. Therefore, in the course of the administration of justice, counsel have a special privilege of uttering matter even injurious to an individual, on the ground that such a privilege tends to the better administration of justice. And if a counsel in the course of a cause utter observations injurious to individuals, and not relevant to the matter in issue, it seems to me that he would not, therefore, be responsible to the party injured in a common action of slander; but that it would be necessary to sue him in a special action on the case, in which it must be alleged in the declaration and proved at the trial, that the matter was spoken maliciously and without reasonable and probable cause."

If then a counsel wantonly avails himself of his situation to serve a personal object, and diverges in such a manner that a malicious motive must be inferred, he would be held responsible both in honour and at law, but a very wide discretion must be allowed, or there is obviously an end of advocacy. If parties were willing and able to speak for themselves, they would use very little ceremony towards each other or their witnesses ; charges of fraud and perjury would be freely bandied about, and every body directly or indirectly concerned in the question would come in for a fair share of the spattering. It strikes us that the scandal is at all events not increased by a partial assumption of the same license by their representatives; and it is rather too much to expect of an advocate, that, having necessarily heard only one side of a case, and appearing professedly to make an ex parte statement, he should be as cool as the judge and as indifferent as the bystanders.   In fact, the very nature of forensic contention implies a certain degree of what superficial observers may be apt to designate as intemperance ; it is by the clashing of opposite asseverations, the doubts thrown on character, the uncompromising inquiry into motives, the rough expression of disbelief, that truth is ultimately struck out; and creditors might be cheated, or constituencies corrupted with impunity, if, in proceedings for debt or bribery, no injurious reflections on the honour of the offending party or those connected with him in the transaction were to be allowed.—

" Does this open every view which can bear upon the question ? Does it in the most effectual manner watch the judge, detect perjury, and sift evidence ?—Of what importance is a little disgust at professional tricks, if the solid advantage gained is a nearer approximation to truth.   What an eulogium of a trial to say, ' I am by no means satisfied that the jury were right in finding the prisoner guilty ; but every thing was carried on with the utmost decorum. The verdict was wrong ; but there was the most perfect propriety and order in the proceedings.   The man will be unfairly hanged ; but all was genteel !'   If solemnity is what is principally wanted in a court of justice, we had better study the manners of the old Spanish

Inquisition; but if battles with the judge, and battles among the counsel are the best method, as they certainly are, of getting at the truth, better tolerate this philosophical Billingsgate, than persevere in solemn and polished injustice.[1]"

Were the license of the bar as bad as it is pretended to be, it must be upheld notwithstanding, on the same principle as the press,—because the individual suffering occasioned by the abuse is far more than counterbalanced by the aggregate amount of benefit to the community. Gag the press with a censorship and the bar with an undue measure of responsibility, and you will have done everything that the fellest enemy to free institutions and the pure administration of justice could desire. Our best, our sole reliance as regards each of them must be the progress hourly making in the taste, habits, and feelings of society. Newspaper writers will find out before long that they degrade their own calling, and diminish their own influence, by calling hard names and affecting contempt for one another; and the bar have found out already that undue severity of remark is pretty sure to offend the judge, repel the jury, and deduct materially from their own chances of success. It is undeniable that the great majority of the present leaders of the profession—far more than enough to set the fashion in this respect—are men of polished manners and gentlemanly address, tolerably well versed in the usages and opinions of the world. What reason is there for supposing that they, or such as they, will habitually infringe the known established notions of propriety out of mere wantonness, or scatter imputations at random, when they must know (or they would be very inefficient advocates) that nothing injures a cause more than an attack on character ill supported by the proof. Whenever, therefore, a man like Mr. Thesiger (and we mention him because he has had occasion to use harsh language two or three times in the course of the last year,) gives way to a feeling of indignation, the chances are at least nineteen to twenty that there is something in his instructions, or in his own well grounded conviction of the real merits, to justify it.

But then the understanding is warped by the habit of

---

[1] The Works of the Rev. Sydney Smith, vol. ii. p. 273.

talking on either side for a fee, and a profession can hardly claim credit for good taste or sound moral feeling, who are ready at all times to upset a just claim by a technicality. This objection was thus summarily disposed of by Dr. Johnson :—

" We talked (says Boswell) of the practice of the law. Sir Wm. Forbes said he thought an honest lawyer should never undertake a cause which he was satisfied was not a just one. ' Sir,' said Mr. Johnson, ' a lawyer has no business with the justice or the injustice of the cause which he undertakes, unless his client asks his opinion, and then he is bound to give it honestly. The justice or injustice of the cause is to be decided by the judge. Consider, Sir, what is the purpose of courts of justice? It is that every man may have his cause fairly tried, by men appointed to try causes. A lawyer is not to tell what he knows to be a lie : he is not to produce what he knows to be a false deed ; but he is not to usurp the province of the jury and of the judge, and determine what shall be the effect of evidence,—what shall be the result of legal argument. As it rarely happens that a man is fit to plead his own cause, lawyers are a class of the community who, by study and experience, have acquired the art and power of arranging evidence, and of applying to the points at issue what the law has settled. A lawyer is to do for his client all that his client might fairly do for himself, if he could. If, by a superiority of attention, of knowledge, of skill, and a better method of communication, he has the advantage of his adversary, it is an advantage to which he is entitled. There must always be some advantage on one side or other ; and it is better that advantage should be had by talents than by chance. If lawyers were to undertake no causes till they were sure they were just, a man might be precluded altogether from a trial of his claim, though, were it judicially examined, it might be found a very just claim.' "—*Boswell's Life of Johnson*, Murray's small edition, vol. iii. pp. 16, 17.

It is also obviously a lawyer's duty to take a technical objection if required, or it would be necessary in each individual case to go back to the first principles of legislation.

The law requires the observance of certain forms to give validity to a right. It says, for example, that property shall not pass by will unless attested by two witnesses. A will is attested by only one witness, but the testator's intention was well known. Here is a question of conscience which might occupy the best doctors of the Sorbonne for a month. Some might contend that the devisee was equitably entitled ; others might fairly urge that the nonfulfilment of the statutory condition was decisive even *in foro conscientiæ* against the claim. Is a barrister to decline acting till he has made up his opinion between the two ?

Again, a client admits that he has entered into a contract, but finds it inconvenient to abide by it, and objects that there is no note in writing to satisfy the Statute of Frauds. There may be instances in which such a defence would be justified by the circumstances, but we are supposing one in which no such circumstances appear. If the barrister were to refuse to plead as requested, the statute would be a dead letter, and the bar would thus come in time to usurp one of the most important duties of the legislature.

Choose almost any instance of technicality, and pretty nearly the same considerations will suggest themselves. It follows that so long as a professional man confines himself to giving an honest opinion, and taking or directing the necessary steps, he is no more answerable for the result than any other person officially engaged in the administration of justice—the sheriff who executes an unjust judgment, or the judge who directs the acquittal of a prisoner though morally certain of his guilt. The merits, in fact, are altogether beside the question, and there is consequently none of that mental sophistication which is supposed to exercise so deteriorating an influence on the intellect. The barrister neither deceives himself nor any body else in such an emergency ; he simply says the law requires so and so, and as the party has not complied with its requisitions, he must fail. As Mr. Stammers justly remarks, " he may be called a mere finder of arguments on one side of a given question ;" and it is no affair of his if the client chooses to play Shylock and insist on the very letter of the bond.

A fair mode of testing the present practice in this respect, is to consider what consequences would ensue were it generally understood that a barrister was to be held responsible for the truth of his instructions or the justice of his cause. It is obvious that the establishment of such a rule would compel counsel to take upon themselves much of the work now entrusted to the other branch of the profession, thereby partially, if not wholly, merging the barrister in the attorney, to the manifest deterioration of both.　How the bar would sink, is too obvious to need exposition; and every intelligent solicitor will confess that there is no better check on the less respectable portion of his brethren than the necessity of acting through the bar.　The administration of justice would also suffer from the increased difficulty of finding competent judges.　This is no matter of mere speculation, since the experiment of fusing the profession has been tried both in America and on the Continent, and, to the best of our information, the breed of practitioners produced by the *cross*, will invariably be found filling an inferior rank to that now occupied by English solicitors.

How, too, we should wish to know, are the real merits of a cause, or the propriety of a barrister's conduct in undertaking it, to be tried?　Clearly not by the result, and hardly by the evidence, for up to a given period of the trial he may have had good reasons for believing that the opposing party would break down, or that valid testimony would be produced on his own side?　It strikes us therefore that the upright would often have, as now, little beyond their own characters to fall back upon; whilst the dishonest would find a constant apology for their knavery in the admitted uncertainty of proof.

We make no apology for those, if any such there be, who hire themselves out for the discovery of slips; we merely contend that a counsel employed in the ordinary manner to advise upon a case, is bound to view it in all its bearings, and fully justified (to borrow Dr. Johnson's words) in applying to the points at issue what the law has settled, whether in strict accordance with reason and equity or not; and we deny that either head or heart is likely to suffer from the process, however frequently repeated.　Here again we may appeal to Dr. Johnson:

"Boswell: ' But, Sir, does not affecting a warmth when you have no warmth, and appearing to be clearly of one opinion when you are in reality of another opinion, does not such dissimulation impair one's honesty?　Is there not some danger that a lawyer may put on the same mask in common life, in the intercourse with his friends?' Johnson: ' Why no, Sir.　Every body knows you are paid for affecting warmth for your client; and it is, therefore, properly no dissimulation: the moment you come from the bar you resume your usual behaviour.　Sir, a man will no more carry the artifice of the bar into the common intercourse of society, than a man who is paid for tumbling upon his hands will continue to tumble upon his hands when he should walk on his feet.¹ "—*Boswell's Life of Johnson*, pp. 36, 37.

This illustration is rather far-fetched, and there was no necessity for resorting to it, since life abounds with conclusive instances of analogy. Actors, according to the objector's theory, ought to be finished hypocrites; the diplomatic body (described by Sir Henry Wotton as gentlemen sent abroad to lie for the good of their country) ought to have about the same notion of truth as a blind man of colours; surgeons to be utterly devoid of feeling, and soldiers to be all murderers in their hearts. Nay, we do not well see how any class of the community can escape the corrupting influence of the habit, for most people have prejudices or speculative opinions of some sort which give a one-sided direction to their reasonings; and the majority of Englishmen laudably and patriotically devote their best faculties and a large portion of their time to the discussion of politics; i. e. to the systematic abuse or eulogy of certain prominent characters, and the misstatement or perversion of facts as well as arguments to serve some party object or confirm an opinion suggested by their newspaper. But Dr. Johnson himself affords the strongest illustration of the fallacy, it being undeniable that he combined an inveterate habit of arguing for victory with a scrupulous regard for truth.

The solution of the apparent mystery in all these cases seems to be, that professional men have, as it were, two existences, and acquire a knack of keeping their private sympathies and personal character apart, or that the in-

¹ "See Aug. 15, 1773, where Johnson has supported the same argument."— J. *Boswell, jun.*

" Cicero touches this question more than once, but never with much confidence. 'Atqui etiam hoc præceptum officii diligenter tenendum est, ne quem unquam innocentem judicio capitis arcessas; id, enim, sine scelere fieri nullo pacto potest. Nec tamen, ut hoc fugiendum est, ita habendum est religioni, *nocentem aliquando,* modo ne *nefarium impiumque,* defendere. Vult hoc multitudo, patitur consuetudo, fert etiam humanitas. Judicis est semper in causas *rerum* sequi; patroni, nonnunquam verisimile, etiamsi minus sit verum, defendere.' (De Off. l. 2, c. 14.) We might have expected a less conditional and apologetical defence of his own profession from the great philosophical orator."—*Croker.*

Mr. Croker forgets that the Roman *patron* stood in a very different relation to his clients.

fluence of the adventitious habit or mental process is small in comparison with that exercised by education and society. In the case of the barrister it is so small, that the wonder is how people ever came to fancy that the profession, as a body, could be warped by it. Up to the period of leaving the university his studies are general, so that during the whole of the most ductile season there is nothing to give a bent or bias of any kind. When, at the age of twenty-one or twenty-two, he begins the study of the law, his object is the acquirement of legal *knowledge,* and in applying that knowledge to facts he always does his best to arrive at just, true and logical results. Even when employed as junior counsel in a cause, he has seldom occasion to affect warmth when he has no warmth, or appear to be clearly of one opinion when he is in fact of another opinion; and it is seldom till a man arrives at forty that his occasions of the kind are sufficiently numerous to give plausibility to the supposition, that his morals or intellect are affected by them.

To what, then, does this objection in reality amount?—that, at a period of life long past that at which most men's modes of thought and principles are fixed, some forty or fifty members of a profession composed of thousands, are frequently required to state arguments which they know to be unfounded and support claims which they believe to be inequitable, for the recognized, avowed, legitimate purpose of getting the decision of a court, and with the undoubted consciousness that they are simply discharging a duty without which it could not be well possible for society to exist. The bare analysis is fatal to the fallacy, and mankind show by their conduct that they place no reliance on it, for barristers are not less trusted in private life than other classes of the community.

Still an opinion certainly prevails that the study of the law, if it does not undermine the morals, tends to cramp the intellect, and teaches that over-refined or captious style of reasoning which is commonly stigmatised as special pleading (in utter ignorance of that noble science) by the world. This opinion, we regret to say, is indirectly sanctioned by the authority of Burke, who, in allusion to Mr. Grenville's early education, remarks :—

" He was bred in a profession. He was bred to the law, which is, in my opinion, one of the first and noblest of human sciences ; a science which does more to quicken and invigorate the understanding than all the other kinds of learning put together ; but it is not apt, *except in persons very happily born*, to open and liberalize the mind exactly in the same proportion."[1]

"Except in persons very happily born" any science, branch of knowledge or study exclusively pursued, will have a narrowing tendency, particularly when begun at an early period of life. Law is not ordinarily begun at a very early period, nor is there any positive necessity for making it an exclusive pursuit. On the contrary, much literature and accomplishment may be advantageously combined with it, and the general cultivation exhibited by the present leaders of the bar, with the time the most occupied contrived to set apart for politics, afford a convincing proof that neither leisure nor inclination is wanting. That there is any thing of a contracted or contracting nature in the study itself, is what we must take the liberty to deny. True, the English lawyer appeals full as often to arbitrary rules and positive enactments as to principles, and may be stopped short in the midst of the finest train of reasoning by a precedent ; but the recurrence to principles is quite frequent enough to keep his best faculties in play, and every volume of decided cases contains some in which the highest considerations of policy, the most valuable discoveries of science, or the most interesting speculations in philosophy, are involved.

Whatever might have been the case in Burke's time, (and it must be admitted that too much stress was formerly laid on mere verbal distinctions,) it is now the practice of both bench and bar to take the common sense view of most questions, and in all cases of construction to get at the real meaning of the language. But they keep to the expressions and the context, nor ever suffer extraneous topics of any kind to weigh with them. Now this it is which occasions their mode of reasoning to be stigmatized as quibbling. People in general, having no definite purpose in argument, seldom give themselves the

---

[1] *Speech on American Taxation.* The cause of Burke's dislike to lawyers is explained in the Life of Erskine (*post,* 289), where, also, Erskine's supposed failure in parliament is discussed, (p. 293).

trouble of forming precise notions of any subject till they are compelled; and if you force them to define their own meaning, or confine them strictly to the matter in hand, they are apt to get irritated, and find fault with the logic which convicts them of looseness or inaccuracy.

A country magistrate, for example, contends that certain powers are conferred by an act of parliament; he knows that they were suggested by the framer, and infers that they were intended by the legislature. You show him that the words will not bear such a construction, and he forthwith indulges in a declamation against lawyers, by whom, he declares, the best intentions of parliament are made vain; though the chances are that, if the lawyers had been consulted, the assumed intention would have been fulfilled, and though it is undeniable that, if acts are to be construed by what the framers meant to say instead of what they have said, all would eventually be left dependent on the discretion of the judge.

Any trained reasoner would be exposed to the same style of animadversion as the lawyer, but the misfortune or good fortune of the lawyer is, that he is a member of the only body who are regularly trained as reasoners.

A remark attributed to the late Lord Grenville may be fairly quoted as a set-off to the somewhat invidious one of Burke. He used to say that he always liked meeting a lawyer or two at a dinner party, because he then felt sure of hearing some good topic rationally discussed. This is a fair testimony to that general rectitude of understanding by which the larger part of the profession are characterized.

But it may be asked, why lawyers, whose trade is talking, do not succeed in parliament? to which we answer, that, before endeavouring to explain the reason, we should wish to be satisfied of the fact.

Somers was the parliamentary and political as well as legal oracle of his day; Murray was the only speaker in the house whom the Duke of Newcastle's government could oppose to Pitt (Lord Chatham); Lord Camden's reputation lives chiefly through his speeches in the House of Lords; Thurlow and Wedderburne are strikingly pourtrayed by Gibbon as the two grand supporters of Lord North; Dunning was the right hand of a party which abounded in eloquence; Sir William Grant was more than once selected as the antagonist of Fox ; Percival was Solicitor-General before he became premier ; Romilly, oppressed by a load of professional labour which hurried him to a premature grave, found time to originate more than one scheme of extended amelioration, and support all which partook of his own enlightened spirit of benevolence ; Lord Plunkett was a first-rate debater up to the period of his elevation to the peerage, nor is it possible to suppress the fact that Mr. O'Connell, before aspiring to the dictatorship of Ireland, had attained the highest pitch of reputation as an advocate. In the present House of Lords, Lord Lyndhurst leads one great party, whilst Lord Brougham glitters in the foremost rank of all parties by turns whether they like him for a leader or not ; and in the present House of Commons, Sir William Follett, Mr. Pemberton, Sir Frederick Pollock, Sir Edward Sugden, the Attorney and Solicitor General, Serjeant Wilde, Serjeant Talfourd, Mr. Law, Mr. Kelly, Mr. Creswell, Mr. Erle, &c. &c. will prove amongst them that professional distinctions may be won and kept without any great or lasting sacrifice of knowledge, taste, feeling, imagination, or intellect.

To say that some first-rate advocates like Erskine (who, by the way, would never have been considered a parliamentary failure had he not had so colossal a professional reputation to contend against) fell beneath the expectation of their cotemporaries, is simply saying in other words that it is given to very few to attain the first rank in two departments of excellence. Yet we do not condemn sculpture as a degrading art because Chantrey does not paint as well as Landseer, nor find fault with music because Rossini is not a Moore. Eminence in some one walk, with an average proficiency in the branches of knowledge usually cultivated by those moving in the same rank in life, is as much as can fairly be expected from any but "persons very happily born," and as much as the world will be content to acknowledge until compelled by such a concentration of qualities as may occur once or twice in a century. When a lawyer shines in literature or science, we deny his law ; when his law constitutes the most prominent of his acquirements, we deny his science or his literature.

There is another mode of robbing the profession of its

due. When a man devotes himself so exclusively to it as to leave no time for other reading, and his mind becomes contracted and his language pedantic in consequence, the study is made to bear the blame of a result solely owing to the exclusiveness with which it is pursued ; but when a man, after going through the regular training, leaves it for philosophy or politics and rises to distinction (Bacon, for example, whose " Use of the Law," and other law treatises, show an accurate and extensive acquaintance with his profession ; or Pitt, who went the Western Circuit, and held briefs), not a particle of his celebrity is allowed to be reflected back upon the bar. I short, nothing is to count that is not purely and exclusively professional ; and every thing that is purely and exclusively professional is by the very terms of the question disqualified.

H.

ART. II.—LIFE OF LORD ERSKINE—*continued.*

ERSKINE identified himself too completely with the cause to sacrifice it, or even put it in jeopardy, for the sake of his jest, fool-born indeed when made by counsel at the client's cost. The dervise in the fairy tale, who possessed the faculty of passing his own soul into any body he chose, could scarcely surpass Erskine in the power of impersonating for a time the feelings, wishes and thoughts of others. His entire devotion to the interests committed to him——the absorption of his whole faculties in the progress of the cause——his dogged determination to win, may in part account for the absence of humour generally attributed to his more important forensic efforts. It was only when certain of success that he allowed his humour full range, and gave sport a holiday. The jury had been already won, the cause was secure, before his fancy flashed into merriment.

When taken *special* to Lancaster to defend Mr. Walker on a charge of seditious conspiracy, the case for the prosecution had no sooner broken down, than he ventured to hold up its weakness to ridicule in the following playful fashion :—

" The arms having been locked up, as I told you, in the bed-chamber, I was shown last week in this house of conspiracy, treason, and death, and saw exposed to view this mighty armoury, which was to level the beautiful fabric of our constitution, and to destroy the lives and properties of ten millions of people. It consisted first of six little swivels purchased two years ago at the sale of Livesay, Hargrave, & Co. (of whom we have all heard so much) by Mr. Jackson, a gentleman of Manchester, who is also one of the defendants, and who gave them to Master Walker, a boy of about ten years of age. Swivels, you know, are guns so called because they turn upon a pivot; but these were taken off their props, painted, and put upon blocks, resembling the carriages of heavy cannon, and in that shape may fairly be called children's toys. You frequently see them in the neighbourhood of London, adjoining the houses of sober citizens, who, strangers to Mr. Browne and his improvements, and preferring grandeur to taste, place them upon their ramparts at Mile End or at Islington.

" Having like Mr. Dunn (the witness for the prosecution)—I hope I resemble him in nothing else—having, like him, served his majesty as a soldier (and I am ready to serve again if my country's safety should require it), I took a closer review of all I saw, and observing that the muzzle of one of them was broken off, I was anxious to know how far this famous conspiracy had proceeded and whether they had come into action, when I found that the accident had happened on firing a *feu-de-joie* upon his majesty's happy recovery, and that they had afterwards been fired upon the Prince of Wales' birth-day. These are the only times that, in the hands of these conspirators, these cannon, big with destruction, had opened their little mouths; once to commemorate the indulgent and benign favour of Providence in the recovery of the sovereign, and once as a congratulation to the heir apparent of his crown on the anniversary of his birth.

" I went next under the master-general of this ordinance, Mr. Walker's chambermaid, to visit the rest of this formidable array of death, and found a little musketoon, about so high (describing it). I put my thumb upon it, when out started a little bayonet, like the jack in a box, which we buy for children at a fair. In short, not to weary you, gentlemen, there was just such a parcel of arms of different sorts and sizes, as a man collecting amongst his friends for his defence against the sudden violence of a riotous multitude might be expected to have collected. Here lay three or four guns of rusty dimensions, and here or there a bayonet or broadsword, covered over with dust and rust so as to be almost undistinguishable."

For the result of Hardy's trial Erskine felt too solicitous to hazard more than a scornful jest; and it was only in a moment of exultation towards the close of the proceedings against

Horne Tooke, that a single ray of merriment lit up his severe oratory. " It has not been attempted to prove," he exclaimed, " that our design was to arm : the abortive evidence of arms has been abandoned—even the solitary pike that formerly glared rebellion from the corner of the Court no longer makes its appearance, and the knives have retired to their ancient office of carving !"

When he could find an opportunity to relax from the graver business of banc, he would try hard by pun, and quip, and banter, to win a smile from Lord Kenyon, and, as a reward for the arduous task of unbending the rigid muscles of the Chief Justice, to gain some advantage for the client he was protecting.

A tinman at Plymouth had ‑written with blunt dishonesty to the Chancellor of the Exchequer (Addington) in the following direct terms :—

" Sir,—This day a place in your gift became vacant by the death of A. H., landing surveyor at Plymouth. If you can procure the place for my own use and benefit, I will give you 200*l*., and will also give you my bond in any sum to keep the transaction a secret. Your answer will oblige your obedient humble servant, TH. HAMLIN."

The silly knave had previously borne a good character. He was found guilty on a criminal information, and Erskine sought to obtain for him the contemptuous pity of the Court.

" This poor tinman," he said, " accustomed only to the noise of his own hammer, might think that every thing passed under the hammer, and that it was only necessary to give a person who had the disposal of an office his price for it. As a mark, my lords, of the simplicity of this man, when the information was filed, and the subpœna came down to him with the red seal at the end of it, he vainly believed that the Chancellor of the Exchequer had sent him his appointment to the place."

The laughter of the Court probably saved him from a severer punishment than that to which he was condemned. He was sentenced to pay a fine of 100*l*. and to be imprisoned three months.

In the routine work of Nisi Prius Erskine would often work a vein of pleasantry such as common jurors could appreciate. The two following instances were obligingly communicated to us by Mr. James Smith :—

An action was brought by a gentleman, who, whilst travelling in a stage-coach which started from the Swan with Two Necks, in Lad Lane, was upset and had his arm broken. "Gentlemen of the jury," said Erskine, "the plaintiff in this case is Mr. Beverly, a respectable merchant of Liverpool, and the defendant is Mr. Wilson, proprietor of the Swan with Two Necks in Lad Lane, a sign emblematic, I suppose, of the number of necks people ought to possess who ride in his vehicles."

He once defended Peter Pindar in an action brought against the poet by the late Earl of Lonsdale. West had exhibited in Somerset House a picture of Satan after his fall, and Peter Pindar in a poetical satire alleged that Lord Lonsdale had sat for the likeness. Erskine in behalf of the satirist quoted several passages from Milton to show that Satan was in appearance at least a very majestic person, and concluded his address to the jury as follows :—

" Really, gentlemen, upon the whole, this appears to me to be a libel on the devil." Risu solvuntur tabulæ.

Pleading for a defendant in a case of breach of promise of marriage, where the lady complainant was on the shady side of forty, the cunning counsel drolly submitted to the jury that it would have ruined his client to bring home an old-fashioned piece of furniture, where he had not even a place to hang it up in.

When defending a tallow-chandler, under a similar visitation, nothing could exceed the pathos with which Erskine read the love-letters of the simple swain, in which he had written metaphorically of his love burning clear, of his heart being consumed like the wick of a candle,—of the union of wax and spermaceti ;—or the mock solemnity with which he dwelt on the notable conclusion of a Valentine :—" N. B. I have bad news for your brother; tallow is as high as ever!" The laughter in the jury-box augured ill for the fair plaintiff, whose damages were reduced to a fraction.

There were several among his rivals in the front seats at nisi prius, who could fence at the carte and tierce of raillery with wit as keen, and repartee as clever, as his own. Some of these passages deserve to survive the chance hour of pleasantry that gave them birth.

On a trial relating to the patent for a knee-buckle, Erskine held it up and exclaimed, "How would my ancestors have admired this specimen of dexterity!" The one-armed Mingay concluded his speech in reply with: "Gentlemen, you have heard a good deal to-day of my learned friend's ancestors, and of their probable astonishment at his knee-buckles. But, gentlemen, I can assure you, their astonishment would have been quite as great at his breeches."

In an action against a stable-keeper for not taking a proper care of a horse, "The horse," said Mingay, who led for the plaintiff, "was turned into a stable with nothing to eat but musty hay in the rack. To such feeding the horse demurred."—"He should have gone to the country," retorted Erskine. The jest can only be enjoyed thoroughly by professional readers, being founded on the terms of special pleading; but unprofessional readers may rest assured that it is good as well as technical.

Another of his daily antagonists was Bearcroft, who, for his vein of grave sarcasm, had been chosen Recorder of the Beefsteak Club.

A young gentleman of good family had married a woman of the town. His relatives and acquaintance deserted him. She plunged her husband into debt, and almost ruined him by her extravagance. He mustered courage to defend an action for goods furnished to her at enormous prices. Erskine was counsel for the defendant; and aware of the wife's previous character, was obliged to make it a ground of appeal to the jury. He praised the amiable feelings of the husband, who had sought to restore his wife to the path of virtue, and inveighed against her base ingratitude, to which the plaintiff had lent himself. "For her he gave up his family, and sacrificed all his connexions." When Bearcroft came to reply, he treated Erskine's eulogium of his client's virtue, and the demerits of his wife, as mere burlesque. "My friend reproaches his client's wife with forgetfulness of the debt of gratitude which she owes him, that for her he had given up all his connexions; but the balance of obligation will be found on her side—for, for him, she gave up all mankind."

There was another common jury cause, an action brought by a gentleman against a lady for ten guineas, money borrowed; which, in respect to its emphatic brevity, could not have been decided better before a tribunal at Lacedæmon. Erskine said he should prove the existence of the demand by the defendant's own hand-writing. "Since her love was extinguished, she had adopted the laconic, perhaps the best style of epistolary writing. He should read her letter"——

"Sir, when convenient, you shall have your ten guineas. I despise you. Catherine Keeling."

"That is my evidence," said Erskine, carelessly; "I shall prove the handwriting."——"Is that all?" said Bearcroft. "Yes," said Erskine. "Then I despise *you*," retorted Bearcroft; and Mr. Justice Buller exclaimed, "Call the plaintiff."

Another day, Bearcroft having trespassed too far on the feelings of his sensitive opponent, and bantered him upon a painful passage in his private history, incurred a grave and gentlemanly rebuke. In early life Erskine had fought a bloodless duel with Mr. Dennis O'Brian, in consequence of an altercation in the ball-room at Lewes. He was urging the impropriety of the practice when praying the sentence of the court upon a defendant, for an assault on Dr. Remmett. Bearcroft could not refrain from irony when speaking in mitigation of punishment:

"I feel myself compelled to express a wish that we may all profit by the grave sermon of my learned friend, inculcating the doctrine that no man should take revenge into his own hands, but should apply to the laws of his country. I hope we shall all benefit by this preachment, inasmuch as we know he has always practised this doctrine himself."

Erskine winced at the sarcasm, and replied with more than wonted gravity:

"The defendant has given his counsel instructions to make observations rather more personal, I think, though perfectly good-humored, than is necessary in a case of this sort. Irony is extremely well in private company, but there are too many people around now to hear these sort of allusions. If in any part of my life I have trespassed and offended against the law, to be sure if I had been brought before this court, I should have been punished for it. I am sincere when I say that I think the practice of duelling is a base practice, and I wish it was abolished; but unfortunately men have not sufficient fortitude to refuse a challenge, for bravery does not consist in fighting a duel, but in refusing to fight one."

Mr. Law (afterwards Lord Ellenborough) would sometimes play at these forensic bowls, and not unfrequently give rubbers. In the course of Walker's trial at Lancaster, on the counsel for the prosecution objecting to some questions as inadmissible, Erskine, with that theatrical air and manner which he loved to assume, exclaimed, "Good God ! where am I ?"[1] Mr. Law pithily informed him: " in the Crown Court at Lancaster ;" and when he demanded, in a tone of impassioned vehemence, "How is my client to be exculpated," Mr. Law retorted, " By legal evidence."

On another occasion, when Erskine had been expatiating to the jury on his own love of horticulture, and on the exquisite pleasure a botanist derived from examining different plants, he observed the attorney-general taking notes, and hinted that his friend was probably as great an amateur in botany as himself. " Yes," said Law, " in pot herbs !"

That Erskine's rapid success, which rivalled in celerity, if it did not exceed, that of his most fortunate predecessors, Yorke and Murray, should excite some murmurs of disappointment, and give rise to a few sallies of spleen, was but natural. It is highly to the honour of an ambitious and sensitive profession, that the exhibition of such feelings should have been so rare, and that, when elicited, they should have been at once rebuked into silence. Among the solitary exceptions to the general good humour that pervaded the bar, were Baldwin and Lee. Each of these disappointed rivals tilted with the new champion in no chivalrous spirit, and to the delight of all who witnessed the encounter, had to retire from the field discomfited and disarmed, " *parmâ non bene relictâ.*"

Honest Jack Lee, as he was popularly termed, could not conceal his annoyance when he saw the full stream of business on which he floated turned at once into the channels of the new favourite. Lee was in great professional practice when Erskine came to the bar. They were counsel in opposite sides before a Committee of the House of Commons on a contested election. Erskine, having occasion to observe on

[1] This perhaps suggested Lord Brougham's exclamation during the Queen's trial, " Am I in a court of justice?"

a part of the speech before delivered by Lee, humorously affected to adopt his singular style and action in speaking. Erskine crossed his arms on his breast, and hit off with some degree of humour Lee's tone of voice and manner of concluding his sentences. It was done in the most perfect good humour, but was not so received by Lee. " This gentleman, they tell me, has been a sailor ; they say too, that he has been a soldier ; and he will probably finish his career as a mountebank at Bartholomew fair." Lee gained his laugh at the time, for Erskine had no opportunity of reply ; but with the trials of next term came a heavy retribution.

Erskine usually brought his arguments, says Mr. Espinasse, written at length in a little marble-covered book, from which, even after long experience in his profession, he read and cited his cases. Baldwin, a barrister of considerable standing, distinguished for avarice and jealousy of every rising junior, affected to ridicule Erskine's mode of preparing his arguments, saying on one occasion, with a sneer, that he wished Erskine would lend him his book. " It would do you no harm, Mr. Baldwin," said Lord Mansfield gravely, " to take a leaf out of that book, as you seem to want it."

At the expense of this low practitioner Erskine indulged in one of those *jeux-de-mots* to which he delighted in turning legal phraseology. Baldwin lived in the house which is now Surgeons' Hall, in Lincoln's Inn Fields. Being told that he had sold his house to the corporation of surgeons, " I suppose," said he, " it was recommended to them from Baldwin being so well acquainted with the practice of bringing in the body." Baldwin's business was almost wholly composed of motions of course, this of bringing in the body forming the chief.

In this forbidden ground, the region of puns, wit's lowest story, Erskine would disport himself with more than boyish glee. He fired off a double barrel when encountering his friend Mr. Maylem at Ramsgate. The latter observed that his physician had ordered him not to bathe, " Oh then," said Erskine, " you are ' *Malum prohibitum.*' " " My wife, however," resumed the other, " does bathe." " Oh then," said Erskine, perfectly delighted, " she is ' *Malum in se.*' "

When a military fever overspread the land, he was called with one voice to the command of the Law Association, composed of the Lincoln's Inn and Temple corps. They had greatly miscalculated his fitness for the command. He could not, we are assured, manœuvre the corps through the most simple movements; and in exercising the battalion, which consisted of six companies, he gave his orders from a card prepared for him by his major, Major Reid. If Erskine ever possessed any military ardour, it was at that time nearly extinguished; he did not enter heartily into the duties of his command, and the parade had no longer any charms for him. A friend wishing to banter him on the subject, told him he had just come from the parade of the excise corps, then the worst in London, and that they appeared to him to be superior to his. "So they ought," said Erskine, "why they are all Cæsars (seizers)." In the same facetious spirit he suggested for the motto of his corps, "*Currat lex ;*" and complaining to Bell of his penmanship, declared that his pothooks were nearly as irregular as the Lincoln's Inn volunteers coming to the "present."

An acquaintance having mentioned a relative's illness, Erskine asked the nature of the complaint. Being told, water on the chest, he answered briskly, for the pun interested him more than the invalid, "Then she's not to be pitied; it is lucky in these times to have any thing in one's chest."

But we must beware of pursuing his quiddities further than any but the most inveterate punsters would wish to follow. The worse they were, the more heartily did they seem to be enjoyed by himself, and the more loud and furious grew the laughter of his hearers, few of whom could be sedate enough to resist the infectious witchery of his mirth. For a large portion of the good spirit displayed in his favour by the bar, Erskine was doubtless indebted to his joyous and happy temper, to his hilarity of address and courteous bearing. If any acerbity be detected in the sallies we have imperfectly reported, for writing can only give the wax-work figure, the dead image of pleasantry, that bitterness belongs to his cotemporaries, and not to himself: he appears always acting on the defensive. Twice only during the incessant practice of twenty-seven years, in the midst of that wear and tear of business which exhausts the temper as much as it fatigues the frame, is he proved to have provoked by his petulance any personal altercation; and the circumstances on both occasions display his character in an amiable light.

It was his misfortune, when young in the profession, to have a sharp dispute in court with a poor old barrister in a stuff gown, nicknamed "Frog Morgan!" from his unluckily citing "Croke Jack" (Cro. Jac.) over and over again in his argument, and from a fancied resemblance in tone and visage to a frog. Erskine felt upon reflection that he had gone too far. On the same evening, he called at Morgan's chambers, and apologized for the offence, and on the following day, in full court, he rose and expressed himself to the following effect: "Mr. Morgan, I have already apologized to you in private for what I yesterday intemperately uttered, but, as the offence was public, I think the reparation should be so too. I therefore now beg to repeat my apology."

In the meridian of his fame, when flushed with the excitement of defending Hardy for high treason, he had a sharp altercation with Sir John Mitford, then Solicitor-General, the manner of his falling into which, and the consequent explanations, are highly characteristic.

A question as to the prisoner's declarations being objected to, Erskine proceeded to cite various cases from the State Trials, in which similar questions had been put. The Solicitor-General in reply stated that he thought it would be found that the questions had really been put upon the cross-examination of the witness, and not upon any original examination, and was courteously set right by Erskine: "I hope you will not be offended at me for this interruption, which may amend your last observation. They are all of them taken from the State Trials, and they are all upon original examinations." Sir John Mitford soon after reverted to his first impression:

"Would it be permitted, upon a trial for murder, for instance, to give in evidence, that the prisoner said he would not commit a murder; and yet as far as I have any conception of this, as stated by my learned friend, it was simply that evidence; and therefore I think it must have been upon a cross-examination.

"Mr. Erskine.—I tell you it was not.

"Mr. Solicitor-General.—Then I do not understand it.

"Erskine.—I see you do not.

"Mr. Solicitor-General.—The manner, Sir, in which you have thought proper to conduct yourself towards me, in the course of this trial, has been such as reflects upon my character. I will not submit to any man for knowledge of law ; I am not used to talk of myself, but I will not be taught by you or any other person propriety of conduct, either in a civil or criminal case : I believe I know my duty in both as well as you do, and I trust that I shall discharge it."

To prevent further heat, Chief-Justice Eyre, with his wonted urbanity, interfered—permitting the question to be put, admitting the general rule to be as laid down by the counsel for the crown, but giving his opinion that the political speculative notions which the prisoner entertained touching a reform of parliament might very well be learned from the conversations which he had held at any time or in any place. Erskine, though victor in the argument, asserted his right of explanation :

"I agree with Mr. Solicitor-General that very frequently an improper odium falls upon counsel ; no man can cast his eye upon the State Trials, without seeing that an improper odium has fallen upon counsel conducting causes for the crown, in consequence of that humanity which has ever been the characteristic of the English nation. Thinking so, I did that which perhaps would have been better hereafter : I went out of my way, and, notwithstanding my weak state of health, spoke at some length, and with some anxiety, lest any man should suppose for a moment that I meant to make any such insinuation against any of the gentlemen at the bar : what return I have met with, I leave to others, who have heard it, to judge, without making any observation upon it, because it is not for your lordship to redress it. With regard to Mr. Solicitor-General, thus much I have a right to say, and I am bound for myself to say it, I think that any man who improperly gives offence to another, very much forgets the character that ought to belong to him, and if I had given any just offence to Mr. Solicitor-General, I should have been the first man, without any complaint from him, to have given him satisfaction for it ; but on the contrary, I have a right to complain of him, for when he had asserted (I took it for granted from not having heard what I said), that all the cases I cited were upon cross-examination, I thought it would be unmanly in me, afterwards, to take advantage of that remark in my reply ; therefore to enable the gentleman to make such observation upon the cases I cited, as would belong to them, when he stated that they were upon cross-examinations, out of a proper courtesy, and from that which belonged to the dignity of the bar, I told him that they were on original examinations, and I should have thought that would have satisfied Mr. Solicitor-General, that they were so, for I stated in the course of what I said, that I had personally collected them, and that they were on original examinations. After that, Mr. Solicitor-General goes on, and with great emphasis says, " I shall still think they were on cross-examinations.' I wrote it down, and every gentleman in court heard it, upon which I said, I aver again that they were on original examinations. ' Then,' he said, ' I do not understand them ;' to which I said, ' I see you do not.' Why I would say that to any man that ever existed, here or any where. If a man tells me that what I aver is not so, I would say to that man what I will not say here. So much for that."

In closing his argument, Erskine again made a graceful allusion to his late angry dispute with the counsel for the crown, striving to dispel, as far as in him lay, any lurking uneasiness that might remain :

"It shows us how little dependence is to be had upon words, and how little it is evidence in high treason what men who are warm will say, because we who were thus warm, and who might be imagined to be really disaffected to one another, are persons who live in social life together, on terms of affection and regard ; and therefore I am glad this happens, because persons may see how little we ought to depend upon what may be said by any man when found heated at a tavern."

Whatever may be thought of the petulance which provoked the controversy, all must admire the gentlemanly feeling and thorough courtesy of his full and frank explanation. The ci-devant officer's wit and repartee were in general (to apply Sheridan's illustration) as keen, and at the same time as polished as his sword.

Who would not have predicated that such a cunning master of fence, so quick and ready a disputant in the court, must succeed as completely in the political as in the legal arena ? His friends foretold an ascendancy there, not less rapid than at the bar, that his eloquence and promptitude would fortify or shake the Treasury Bench. Never were expectations more highly wrought, or doomed to receive a more cruel disappointment. " The House of Commons," says Adair, " is a sea

strewed with the mightiest wrecks. It is a course in which
the proudest strength has faltered, and the firmest confidence
grown pale. Erskine's argosy, if we may pursue the metaphor,
though it sunk not there like so many legal freights, lay water-
logged."

The narrative of his entrance and failure is shortly told.
He had adopted with his wonted enthusiasm the liberal politics of his family, and, whilst the elder brother, the Earl of
Buchan, sought to make converts to radical doctrines, he
contented himself with speaking and acting as a zealous whig.
When the coalition ministry perilled the fate of their government on the East India Bill, it was determined to procure
coute qui coute the powerful support of the popular leader of
the bar. A convenient member was easily prevailed upon to
accept the stewardship of the Chiltern Hundreds by one of
those good old arguments which would not have disgraced
the days of Walpole. The bargain is described by Wraxall
as a mere matter of course. The Duke of Richmond arranged
the grant of a pension of 1,000*l.* a-year to Sir William Gordon,
in order that, by vacating his seat for Portsmouth, he might
enable government to introduce Erskine.

The price paid for his entrance shows the extent of public
and ministerial expectation. Nobly born, a thorough gentleman, in the receipt of a large professional income—of commanding presence—heralded by the voice of fame—accustomed to address public assemblies—daily flushed with forensic triumphs—in the prime of manhood—what might he·
not accomplish, endued with all those natural and acquired
advantages, which tell with such effect in the House of Commons? But he felt their weight as oppressive, shrunk from
their clamorous welcome as if "scared at the sound himself
had made," and became the victim of his over-sensitiveness
to applause. Taking his seat on the same night as Mr. Scott,
and rising to speak shortly afterwards, the young member was
disconcerted in his maiden speech by the following dramatic
incident.

Pitt evidently intending to reply, sat with pen and paper in
his hand prepared to catch the arguments of this formidable
adversary. He wrote a word or two. Erskine proceeded, but

with every additional sentence Pitt's attention to the paper relaxed, his look became more careless, and he obviously began to think the orator less and less worthy of his attention. At length, while every eye in the House was fixed upon him, with a contemptuous smile, he dashed the pen through the paper and flung them on the floor. Erskine never recovered from this expression of disdain; his voice faltered, he struggled through the remainder of his speech, and sank into his seat dispirited, and shorn of his fame.

Pitt's pantomimic display of contempt has been deemed by some a clever *ruse de guerre,* a slight-of-hand trick, done designedly to lower the estimation of a formidable antagonist; but we think it more in unison with the supercilious spirit of the man to suppose that the exhibition was unprepared. He had expected a champion worthy to meet him in single combat, was more displeased than pleased at the tyro's feebleness, and took the readiest way of marking his disappointment. It had certainly the effect of silencing the new member, who quailed during the short remainder of the session before a spirit more powerful than his own.

A mind of his elasticity and variety however must have occasionally distinguished itself, but he obviously felt that his place was not in the legislature, and that no man can wisely hope for more than one kind of eminence. Except on some party emergency, he seldom spoke, and never with much expectation of public effect.

Fortunately for him the parliament was abruptly dissolved, and perhaps among the crowd of Fox's Martyrs whom the dissolution dispersed without a chance of immediate re-election, there was not one on whom the blow fell more lightly. He resumed his practice at the bar of the House, where he had won his early laurels, with alacrity; for he there felt secure from interruption and confident of victory.

Being retained by Mr. Carnan, the bookseller, to oppose a bill for continuing the monopoly of the Stationers' Company, he pleaded with a vigour and effect which might be vainly sought for in his parliamentary efforts:

" Mr. Carnan, the petitioner, had turned the current of his fortunes into a channel perfectly open to him in law, and which when blocked

up by usurpation, he had cleared away at a great expense by the decision of one of the highest courts in the kingdom.   Possessed of a
decree, founded too on a certificate from the judges of the common
law, was it either weak or presumptuous in an Englishman to extend
his views that had thus obtained the broadest seal of justice ?   Sir, he
did extend them with the same liberal spirit in which he began, he
published twenty different kinds of almanacks calculated for different
meridians and latitudes, corrected the blunders of the lazy monopolists,
and supported by the encouragement, which laudable industry is sure
to meet with in a free country, he made that branch of trade his first
and leading object ; and I challenge the framer of this bill (even
though he should happen to be at the head of his majesty's government) to produce to the House a single instance of immorality, or of
any mistake or uncertainty, or any one inconvenience arising to the
public, from this general trade, which he had the merit of redeeming
from a disgraceful and illegal monopoly.   On the contrary, much
useful learning has been communicated, a variety of convenient additions introduced, and many egregious errors and superstitions have
been corrected.   Under such circumstances I will not believe it possible, that parliament can deliver up the honest labours of a citizen of
London to be damasked and made waste paper of (as this scandalous
bill expresses it) by any man or body of men in the kingdom.

" And now, Mr. Speaker, I retire from your bar, I wish I could
say with the confidence of having prevailed.   If the wretched Company of Stationers had been my only opponents, my confidence had
been perfect, indeed so perfect, that I should not have wasted ten
minutes of your time on the subject ; but should have left the bill to
dissolve in its own weakness ; but when I reflect that Oxford and
Cambridge are suitors here, I own to you, I am alarmed, and I feel
myself called upon to say something, which I know your indulgence
will forgive.   The House is filled with their most illustrious sons, who
no doubt feel an involuntary zeal for the interest of their parent
universities.   Sir, it is an influence so natural and so honourable
that I trust there is no indecency in my hinting the possibility of its
operation.   Yet I persuade myself that these learned bodies have
effectually defeated their own interests by the sentiments which their
liberal sciences have disseminated amongst you :—their wise and
learned institutions have erected in your minds the august image of
an enlightened statesman, who, trampling down all personal interests
and affections, looks steadily forward to the great ends of public and
private justice, unawed by authority and unbiassed by favour.

" It is from thence my hopes for my client revive.   If the universities have lost an advantage, enjoyed contrary to law, and at the expense of sound policy and liberty, you will rejoice that the courts below have pronounced that wise and liberal judgment against them, and will not set the evil example of reversing it here. But you need not therefore forget that the universities have lost an advantage ; and if it be a loss, that can be felt by bodies so liberally endowed, it may be repaired to them by the bounty of the crown, or by your own. It were much better that the people of England should pay ten thousand a year to each of them, than suffer them to enjoy one farthing at the expense of the ruin of a free citizen, or the monopoly of a free trade."

The hopes thus bravely expressed were not disappointed. He enjoyed the signal triumph of seeing the bill rejected by a majority of forty-five, though ushered in under the auspices of Lord North, then Chancellor of the University of Oxford, and of learning that his brother-in-law, brought down expressly to vote for the second reading, had voted against it, being unable to resist the strong sense of its injustice which the counsel's speech had induced.

Deprived of a seat himself in the spring of 1784, he was selected to oppose two important questions before committees of the whole House: the Westminster Scrutiny, and Mr. Pitt's bill for regulating the affairs of the East India Company. In cross-examining a witness who had attributed misconduct to Fox's agents, Erskine inquired—" Why do you infer they were agents?" The witness replied, that he inferred it, because they appeared as his friends; upon which the counsel exclaimed that, if all Fox's friends were to be considered his agents, every honest man might be so esteemed, who was not a member of that House. Erskine was ordered to withdraw ; and great blame was attributed to the Speaker, who, instead of repressing such disorderly language, allowed it to pass unnoticed. Cornwall admitted that Erskine's conduct was improper, and a resolution of censure was proposed, but Pitt objected to any further notice, saying, with a supercilious sneer, that the learned gentleman's conduct might probably form part of his instructions.

His demeanour when counsel for the East India Company appears to have been characterized by equal boldness,—the term *audacity* would be scarcely misapplied. He eulogized in the warmest terms the rejected measure of his friend, and treated the bill of 1784 as a vile imposture practised on a credulous nation. Indignant murmurs at length compelled the Speaker to interpose his authority—

" If, Mr. Speaker," he continued, ".I have been guilty of any irregularity, it arises solely from a diminution of that respect, which I was accustomed to feel for this assembly, before it was shorn of its dignity, but which no longer animates me since the assumption of the extraordinary powers arrogated and exercised by the present board of control."

He then expatiated on the humility of his present situation standing as a counsel at the bar of that House, of which he had formerly the honour to be a member; and treated of the respect that was still due from a man of his profession addressing an assembly of that elevated and important nature. He said he was well aware that harangues from counsel at their bar were not the species of oratory in which that House took the greatest pleasure, but that it rather submitted to them from the consideration that it was its indispensable duty to receive them by way of physic, as it were, for the benefit of the constitution. He promised to make his dose as palatable as the nature of the patient's case would admit. Occasionally the House expressed their disapprobation of his sarcasms, and the Speaker again interrupted him, when he said the House ought not, at that late hour, to enter upon the discussion of so important a subject. The Speaker told him it did not become a counsel at their bar to hint when they ought to adjourn, and that the House would govern its own proceedings as it thought proper.

A vacancy in the representation of Portsmouth in the following year, reinstated Erskine in the House, but he lost his boldness upon being restored to his place. The friend and second of Fox could not expect forbearance at the hands of his rival, who insulted a foe afraid to meet him in single combat, like some warrior in the Iliad, conscious of superior strength. According to the precedent of that well-fought field, Erskine preferred going out at an earlier period of the evening, and encountering a champion of less prowess. Such was the impression this terrible debater made upon him, that long after Pitt's death he spoke of his eloquence as far exceeding any thing that had ever been exhibited before in any assembly of a civilized country.

By a singular fatality Erskine was doomed to meet with as hard measure from Burke, a comrade in the camp, as from his grand political enemy—the more mortifying to one, whose veneration for that greatest of modern statesmen scarcely fell short of idolatry. Next to the Bible, he had invariably recourse to his writings as the well-spring of eloquence and wisdom, whether he sought to inform, persuade, or subdue his audience; and he never made a speech of moment, without introducing some beautiful text or motto, from those almost inspired pages. No disciple sitting at the feet of Gamaliel, no pupil of the Porch, could look up with more entire submission to his master, even when there escaped from his lips the accents of contumely and scorn.

To a lurking jealousy of the wealth and distinction which Erskine had acquired at the bar, even though Burke might be himself unconscious of the cause, may perhaps be attributed the dislike which he always exhibited towards the popular lawyer. The prejudice formed part indeed of his general antipathy to a profession in which his lot had not been cast, whose unbending technical rules often interfered with his own comprehensive conceptions, whose professors were generally opposed to the principles of the old Whigs, which he most affected, and who thwarted the darling wish of his heart in the impeachment of Warren Hastings.

When Erskine headed the band of lawyers who argued that the impeachment had abated by the dissolution of Parliament,—a doctrine certainly more in accordance with technical reasoning than with the principles of justice or common sense,—the manager of the Commons steeped his words in venom, and searched in his ample armoury for missiles poisoned at the point with obloquy and contempt.

Having cited precedents from a little book according to his wont, Erskine was sneered at for taking the field like David against Goliah, armed with a stone and a sling, but with the difference in his case, that they could do no execution. In answer to his complaint of the length of the trial, Burke borrowed his imagery from that large oriental storehouse in which he had been long expatiating, and asked whether the learned gentleman remembered that, if the trial had continued three years, the oppressions had continued twenty, whether after all there were hour-glasses for measuring the grievances of mankind, or whether they, whose ideas never travelled beyond a Nisi Prius cause, were better calculated to ascertain what ought to be the length of an impeachment, than a rabbit, who breeds six times in a year, was able to judge of the time proper for the gestation of an elephant?

When Erskine had remarked in a deprecating tone, upon another occasion, that lawyers were not at home in that House, Burke retorted in a tone of rude triumph, that they only exercised themselves there in skirmishing with the rights of the Commons, with which in the other House they meant to carry on a war; all they could afford to give members there was a sort of quarter-sessions law, a law *minorum gentium.* " He believed they were not at home there, they were birds of a different feather, and only perched in that House on their flight to another; only resting their tender pinions there for awhile, yet ever fluttering to be gone to the region of coronets; like the Hibernian in the ship, they cared not how soon she foundered, because they were only passengers; their best bower anchor was always cast in the House of Lords."

Erskine replied with mingled truth and grace, that, " if he had meant only to rest in that place in the course of such a pursuit, he should hardly have lighted on that naked bough which supported him, but have sought the luxuriant and inviting foliage which overspread the opposite side of the House, which would have afforded him kind shelter and have accelerated his flight."

The breach was subsequently widened, when the passionate statesman repudiated the term of friend, with which Erskine courteously named him, and asked contemptuously if the learned gentleman knew the meaning of a term he used so glibly; yet such was Erskine's kindly spirit, that these sarcastic insults, the most acute a gentleman of spirit and feeling could receive, left in his heart no rankling resentment. He still spoke of Burke's writings with enthusiasm:

"I shall take care to put Burke's work on the French Revolution into the hands of those whose principles are left to my formation; I shall take care that they have the advantage of doing, in the regular progression of youthful studies, what I have done, even in the short intervals of laborious life; that they shall transcribe with their own hands from all the works of this most extraordinary person, and from the last among the rest, the soundest truths of religion, the justest principles of morals, inculcated and rendered delightful by the most sublime eloquence, the highest reach of philosophy brought down to the level of common minds by the most captivating taste, the most enlightened observations on history, and the most copious collection of useful maxims from the experience of common life, and separate for themselves the good from the bad."

Adverting to his authority on the State Trials, he said:

"I should indeed be ashamed, particularly at this moment, to name him invidiously while he is bending beneath the pressure of a domestic misfortune, which no man out of his own family laments more than I do. No difference of opinion can ever make me forget to acknowledge the sublimity of his genius, the vast reach of his understanding, and his universal acquaintance with the histories and constitution of nations."

Erskine would fain on his death have moved the erection of a national monument in his place in Parliament, but ascertained that the motion was sure to be coldly received, and might even, to the disgrace of England's senators, be rejected. He spoke with equal warmth in old age as in youth of that consummate orator, but, in a conversation with Dr. Clark, at Cambridge, qualified his enthusiasm by the following graphic account of Burke's unfortunate manner in the House. The following is the note taken of it by the learned doctor:

"While we were waiting at Trinity Lodge for the deputation from the senate to conduct the Chancellor, I had a conversation with Lord Erskine upon the qualifications of Burke as an orator; Lord Erskine said that his defect was episode— a public speech, he said, should never be episodical. It is a very great mistake; I hold it to be a rule respecting public speaking, which ought never to be violated, that the speaker should not introduce into his oratory insular brilliant passages, they always tend to call off the minds of his hearers, and to make them wander from what ought to be the main business of his speech. If he wish to introduce brilliant passages, they should run along the line of his subject-matter, and never quit it. Burke's episodes were highly beautiful; I know nothing more beautiful, but they were his defects in speaking. He repeated several specimens from his speeches on the American war. Lord Erskine also told me that Burke's manner was sometimes bad; it was like that of an Irish chairman. Once, he said, I was so tired of hearing him in a debate upon the India Bill, that not liking he should see me leave the House while he was speaking, I crept along under the benches and got out, and went to the Isle of Wight. Afterwards that very speech of his was published, and I found it to be so extremely beautiful, that I actually wore it into pieces by reading it."

Mr. Prior, Burke's biographer, comments in a tone of querulous remark on this conversational criticism, stating that the tone of it belongs to that vague and careless common-place rattle, in which Erskine frequently indulged. " His observation about the Irish chairman is an extravagant exaggeration; and the story of creeping along under the benches (if taken literally), must be a positive untruth, for such a thing was not practicable. The whole conversation bears traces of that loose juvenility of manner to which he was prone."

To the truth of the sketch, however, testimony is borne by contemporary biographers, who prove that the features of this portrait are only slightly exaggerated, and certainly not caricatured. It would be idle to suppose that the narrator meant more by creeping under the benches, than to describe vividly the stealthy manner of his escape.

Of Erskine's own manner in the House, Lord Byron said sarcastically, that, when he heard him there, he wished him at the bar once more. The impression produced by his parliamentary efforts appears to have been favourable on hearers of more good nature, who had no opportunity of contrasting the lawyer with the politician—of making himself his parallel. " Erskine's enemies," says Wraxall, "pronounced his performances tame, and destitute of the animation which characterised his speeches in Westminster Hall. To me, who, having never witnessed his jurisprudential talents, could not make any such comparison, he appeared to exhibit shining powers of declamation."

How completely they failed to captivate those judges of eloquence who had heard him elsewhere, is shown in the diary of Mr. Green, the elegant author of the Diary of a Lover of Literature.

"Left the House at eight, when Erskine was speaking for the bill for restricting Monastic Institutions in this country. The principal speakers — Wyndham, colloquial and ingenious, but desultory and ineffective ; Sir William Scott, solemn, neat, and elegant. After having listened term after term with delight and exultation to this pride of the English bar in his place, I confess I never hear him above stairs but with some emotions of shame for my profession. The constant habit of advocating private suits before a superior tribunal, generates a species of eloquence which, however excellent in itself, appears to cruel disadvantage in a deliberative assembly of statesmen and legislators, debating as equals, seriously and in earnest, the most important interests of the empire. Bearcroft, indeed, whom I once heard on Erskine's libel bill, appeared to suffer little by the change of station : but then, with a vein of the driest and happiest humour I ever met with, there was a solemn gravity in his deportment, and a didactic energy in his manner, which, even at the bar, removed the advocate from sight, and frequently rendered the argument of the counsel more dignified and impressive than the judgment from the bench."

The fact that a man of taste and an admirer should leave the House when Erskine was speaking, proves to demonstration the difference that existed between his fervid eloquence at the bar, and his cold declamation among the assembled Commons. The difference between Philip sober and Philip in his cups was not more striking, and it has been thus accounted for by the highest living authority on matters of rhetoric, Lord Brougham. Admitting the failure in his laudatory notice of Erskine, he explains it in the following manner:

"The ministry of Mr. Pitt did not derive more solid service from the bar in the person of Mr. Dundas, than the opposition party did ornament and popularity in that of Erskine. His parliamentary talents, although they certainly have been underrated, were as clearly not the prominent portion of his character. Nevertheless it must be admitted that had he appeared in any other period than the age of the Foxes, the Pitts, and the Burkes, there is little chance that he would have been eclipsed even as a debater; and the singular eloquence and powerful effect of his famous speech against the Jesuits Bark Bill, in the House of Lords, abundantly proves this position. He never appears to have given his whole mind to the practice of debating; he had a very scanty provision of political information; his time was always occupied with the laborious pursuits of his profession; he came into the House of Commons, where he stood among several equals, and behind some superiors, from a stage where he shone alone, and without a rival; above all he was accustomed to address a select and friendly audience, bound to lend him their patient attention, and to address them by the compulsion of his retainer, not as a volunteer coming forward in his own person—a position from which the transition is violent and extreme, to that of having to gain and to keep a promiscuous and in great part hostile audience, not under any obligation to listen one instant beyond the time during which the speaker can interest, or flatter, or amuse them. Earlier practice, and more devotion to the pursuit, would doubtless have vanquished all these disadvantages, but they sufficed to keep Erskine always in a station far beneath his talent as long as he remained in the House of Commons."

The causes thus clearly given may sufficiently account for Erskine's comparative failure in parliament, but perhaps sufficient stress is not laid upon the main reason, the leading weakness of his mind and temperament, a too keen sensibility to the expressions of adverse feeling, an excessive vanity and inordinate self-esteem. It was necessary that he should be the leading figure, the admired of all beholders, the prominent figure on the platform. Even then he could not brook the slightest appearance of dislike, indifference, or neglect.

He had, says Croly, a morbid sensibility to circumstances of the moment, which sometimes strangely enfeebled his presence of mind; any appearance of slight in his audience, a cough, a rude laugh, or a whisper, has been known to dishearten him visibly. Aware of this infirmity, an attorney, wise in his generation, has been known to plant a man of drowsy appearance and habits beneath the judge, directly opposite the place where Erskine was accustomed to address the jury. Agreeably to his instructions, and nothing loth, the sleepy hind would make a hideous grimace, and give way to the utmost expression of weariness in the midst of the most impassioned sentences. A pause of effect would be broken in upon by a dreadful yawn, and a splendid peroration be interrupted by a titter in the second row, and the cry of silence from the ushers at the too plain indication of a snore. Erskine could not withstand the torture, but sat down abruptly.

Garrow having once fixed his eyes upon him lost in thought, he stooped down to whisper a remonstrance—" Who do you think can get on with that wet blanket of a face of yours before him ?"

Interruption from the jury he could indeed resist, for to them he spoke as a superior, and demanded a patient hearing. " I shall name you, sir, presently," was his instant rebuke to a jury-man, who expressed too openly his dislike of the argument in a state prosecution.

Unjust imputations from the bench he could repel, for he felt that the independence of the bar was embodied in his person : " I shall not sit down ; your Lordship will perform your duty, I shall perform mine," was his answer to an intemperate threat from the judge.

Could he have summoned to his aid the same moral courage in St. Stephen's Chapel, he might have safely braved the premier and his body guard. But fearless in his own forensic field, he had no fund of political courage to resist Cæsar and his legions ; no fund of political knowledge sufficient to contemn the withering sneer of Pitt, and the derisive shouts of his satellites ; and from an excess of wounded self-love he determined to risk himself no more.

It would be unjust to his better nature not to record that his egotism was wholly unmixt with any thing offensive to others, though it might excite a smile at his own expense. Far from seeking to raise himself by their depression, his vanity was of the best natured, most social, and least selfish kind; nay, he always seemed to extol the deeds of others with yet more enthusiasm than he ever displayed in recounting his own. The favourite of fortune, the artificer of his own greatness, he might be pardoned by friendly critics for dilating on his own success, and might well be giddy at the prospect of his rapid elevation.

From a state of privation requiring the strictest economy, he was enabled to return his income to the Commissioners of the Income Tax at 5,500*l.* a year; he could inform Wilberforce in 1796 that he had received sixty-six special retainers of 300 guineas each, and the number was increased to nearly 100 before his elevation to the peerage. He was sought for with such avidity, and enjoyed the plenitude of his fame so fully, that he once told Sir Vicary Gibbs, pointing to a particular cause, " Now would I give 100 guineas if I were in that, for then I should be in every cause in the paper."

With an appetency of applause equal to that of which the celebrated Garrick was accused, he saw the evidences of his triumph daily, and was intoxicated with the incense. The loud laughter, or tears of the audience, the occasional faintings in the boxes, could not more delight the soul of the modern Roscius, open to all the tintillations of vanity, than did the visible emotions of jurymen—their relaxed muscles at the jest —the dark look of indignation at the invective—the plaudits scarcely suppressed in deference to the court—the favourable verdict—gladden the heart of the sensitive orator. Both were alike players, strutting their hour upon the stage, and would alike enact their parts over again, too frequently *encore* their best things at private rehearsals, making their homes a theatre, and their friends an audience.

To enhance the effect of his great performances, when brought down on special retainers, Erskine would sometimes condescend, we are told, to a little theatrical contrivance. He examined the court the night before the trial in order to select the most advantageous place for addressing the jury. On the cause being called, a crowded audience were perhaps kept waiting a few minutes before the celebrated stranger made his appearance, and when at length he gratified their impatient curiosity, a particularly nice wig, and a pair of new yellow gloves, distinguished and embellished his person, beyond the ordinary costume of the barristers of the circuit.

This littleness in so great a man (which he shared with Chatham and Mirabeau) was that species of moral blunder, which in modern ethics is deemed worse than a fault, as it gave frequent occasion of triumph to his enemies and mortification to himself. The effects of his love of the first personal pronoun has been well described by one who must have had a fellow feeling.

" His egotism was remarkable, but there was a bonhommie in it that showed he had a better opinion of mankind than they deserved ; for it implied a belief that his listeners could be interested in what concerned him whom they professed to like. He was deceived in this, as are all who have a favourable opinion of their fellow men in society ; all and each are occupied with self, and can rarely pardon any one who presumes to draw their attention to other subjects for any length of time. Erskine had been a great man, and he knew it ; and in talking so continually of self, imagined that he was but the echo of fame. All his talents, wit, and brilliancy, were insufficient to excuse this weakness in the opinion of his friends : and I have seen bores, acknowledged bores, turn from this clever man with every symptom of ennui when he has been reciting an interesting anecdote, merely because he was the principal actor in it."

One might be excused joining in the cynicism of the preceding observations, when he reads in Lord Byron's journal the following entry, made it would appear at the close of some fatiguing conversation with this dealer in the personal pronoun.

" A goodly company of lords, ladies, and wits. There was Erskine, good, but intolerable, he jested, he talked, he did every thing admirably, but then he would be applauded for the same thing twice over. He would read his own verses, his own paragraphs, and tell his own stories again and again, and then the trial by jury ! ! ! I almost wished it abolished, for I sat next him at dinner. As I had read his published speeches, there was no occasion to repeat them to me."

His style was thus parodied in the Antijacobin, in a pretended report of a meeting of the Friends of Freedom :

" He (Erskine) had not the advantage of being personally acquainted with any gentlemen of the Directory ;—he understood, however, that one of them, (Mr. Merlin,) previous to the last change, had stood in a situation similar to his own.—He was, in fact, nothing less than a leading advocate and barrister, in the midst of a free, powerful, and enlightened people.

" The conduct of the Directory, with regard to the exiled deputies, had been objected to by some persons, on the score of a pretended rigour. For his part, he should only say, that having been, as he had been, both a soldier, and a sailor, if it had been his fortune to have stood in either of these two relations to the Directory—as a man, and as a major-general, he should not have scrupled to direct his artillery against the national representation :—as a naval officer, he would undoubtedly have undertaken for the removal of the exiled deputies ; admitting the exigency, under all its relations, as it appeared to him to exist, and the then circumstances of the times, with all their bearings and dependencies, branching out into an infinity of collateral considerations, and involving in each a variety of objects, political, physical, and moral ; and these again under their distinct and separate heads, ramifying into endless subdivisions, which it was foreign to his purpose to consider."

" Mr. Erskine concluded by recapitulating, in a strain of agonizing and impressive eloquence, the several more prominent heads of his speech :—He had been a soldier and a sailor, and had a son at Winchester school,—he had been called by special retainers during the summer into many different and distant parts of the country—travelling chiefly in post-chaises—He felt himself called upon to declare, that his poor faculties were at the service of his country—of the free and enlightened part of it at least—He stood here as a man—He stood in the eye, indeed in the hand, of God—to whom (in the presence of the company and waiters) he solemnly appealed—He was of noble, perhaps, royal blood—He had a house at Hampstead—was convinced of the necessity of a thorough and radical reform—His pamphlets had gone through thirty editions—skipping alternately the odd and even numbers—He loved the constitution, to which he would cling and grapple—and he was clothed with the infirmities of a man's nature—He would apply to the present French rulers (particularly Barras and Rewbell) the words of the poet :—

' Be to their faults a little blind ;
Be to their virtues very kind,
Let all their ways be unconfin'd,
And clap the padlock on their mind !"—

And for these reasons, thanking the gentlemen who had done him the honour to drink his health, he should propose—' *Merlin, the late Minister of Justice, and Trial by Jury.*' "

In the zenith of his fame there were written under his portrait in the print shops, in large capitals I—I—I, and then in pica mina, *me—me—me*. The editor of the Morning Chronicle, in reporting one of his orations, left many words imperfect, and put an apologetic note to the effect that the printers were out of little i's, and that all the great I's had been exhausted long ago.

How far Erskine's good natured friends joined in these rough jests, and with what keen relish, may be discovered from the following scene in the Hampstead School for Scandal.

Madame D'Arblay, in the memoirs of her father, Dr. Burney, gives a full description of a party at Mrs. Crewe's, at the Hampstead villa :

" Our evening finished more curiously than desirably, by a junction that robbed us of the conversation of Mr. Burke. This was the entrance of Lord Loughborough and of Mr. and Mrs. Erskine, who having villas at Hampstead, and knowing nothing of Mrs. Crewe's party, called in accidentally from a walk. If not accidentally, Mr. Erskine at least would probably have denied himself a visit that brought him into a coterie with Mr. Burke, who openly in the House of Commons, not long since, upon being called by Mr. Erskine his right honourable friend, sternly demanded of him whether he knew what friendship meant ? From this time there was an evident disunion of cordiality in the party. My father, Mr. Elliot, Mr. Richard Burke, and young Burke, entered into some general discourse in a separate group. Lord Loughborough joined Mrs. Burke. The chair of Mrs. Erskine being next to mine, she immediately began talking to me as chattily and currently as if we had known each other all our lives. Mr. Erskine confined his attention exclusively to Mrs. Crewe.

" Mr. Burke, meanwhile, with a concentrated but dignified air walked away from them all, and threw himself on a settee in a distant part of the room. Here he picked up a book which he opened by chance, and to my great astonishment began reading aloud ! but not directing his face, voice, or attention to any of the company. On the contrary, he read with the careless freedom from effort or restraint that he might have done had he been alone ; and merely aloud, because the book being in verse he was willing to add the pleasure of sound to its sense. But what to me made this seem highly comic, as well as intrepidly singular, was that the book was French, and he read it not only with the English accent, but exactly as if the two nations had one pronunciation in common of the alphabet. It was a volume of Boileau, which he had opened at the famed and incomparable *Epitre à son Jardinier.* Yet, while the delivery was so amusing, the tone, the meaning, the force he gave to every word were so winning to my ears that I should have listened to nothing else, if I had not unavoidably been engrossed by Mrs. E., though from her too I was soon called off by a surprise and half alarm from her celebrated husband.

" Mr. Erskine had been enumerating fastidiously to Mrs. Crewe, his avocations, their varieties, and their excess; till, at length, he mentioned, very calmly, having a case to plead soon against Mr. Crewe upon a manor business in Cheshire. Mrs. Crewe hastily interrupted him with an air of some disturbance, to inquire what he meant, and what might ensue to Mr. Crewe? Ob, nothing but losing the lordship of that spot, he coolly answered; though I don't know that it will be given against him, I only know for certain that I shall have 300*l.* (the lady should have written guineas) for it ! Mrs. Crewe looked thoughtful, and Mr. Erskine then finding he enjoyed not her whole attention, raised his voice, as well as his manner, and began to speak of the New Association for Reform, by the Friends of the People; descanting in powerful, though rather ambiguous terms, upon the use they had thought fit in that Association to make of his name; though he had never yet been to the society; and I began to understand that he meant to disavow it: but presently he added, ' I don't know. I am uncertain, whether ever I shall attend. I have so much to do—so little time—such interminable occupation ! However, I don't yet know; I am not decided; for the people must be supported !' ' Pray will you tell me,' said Mrs. Crewe, coolly, ' what you mean by the people? for I never know.' Whether she asked this with real innocence, or affected ignorance, I cannot tell ! but he was evidently surprised by the question, and evaded any answer. Probably he thought he might as well avoid discussing such a point before his friend Mr. Burke; who, he knew well, though lying perdu from delicacy to Mrs. Crewe, would resistlessly be ready upon the smallest provocation to pounce with a hawk's power and force upon his prey, in order to deliver a counter interpretation to whatever he, Erskine, might reply, of who and what were meant by the people. I conjecture this from the suddenness with which Mr. Erskine after this interrogatory, almost abruptly made his bow.

"Lord Loughborough instantly took his vacant seat on the sofa next to Mrs. Crewe, and presently with much grave but strong humour, recited a speech which Erskine had lately made at some public meeting, and which he had opened, to this effect.

"As to me, Gentlemen, I trust I have some title to give my opinions freely. Would you know whence my title is derived? I challenge any man amongst you to inquire? If he ask my birth,—its genealogy may dispute with kings! If my wealth,—it is all for which I have time to hold out my hand! If my talents—No!—of those gentlemen, I leave you to judge for yourselves!

"This renowned orator," continues the celebrated Novelist, "at a convivial meeting at his own house, fastened upon my father with all the volubility of his eloquence, and all the exuberance of his happy good humour in singing his own exploits and praises, without insisting that his hearer should join in chorus; or rather, perhaps, without discovering from his own self absorption, that that ceremony was omitted."

In this clever sarcastic sketch, Miss Burney unconsciously suffers the little secret to escape, that the egotistical lawyer was no great favourite with the authoress of Evelina. But we cannot wonder that literary ladies—the committee of the blue-stocking club—so acute in detecting foibles, and so particular in exacting attention, should visit this particular foible with marked displeasure, and that the self-worshipper should be unpopular in the boudoir. A sister-author accordingly puts on the black cap when passing judgment on his demerits as a volatile but boisterous companion.

"Among the chief talkers at the Bishop of St. Asaph's," writes Hannah Moore, " was Mr. Erskine. To me he is rather brilliant than pleasant. His animation is vehemence; and he contrives to make the conversation to fall too much on himself—a sure way not to be agreeable in mixed conversation. The bar seems to be a fitter theatre for his talents than the drawing-room, where good breeding is still more necessary than wit."

An exception occurs in the person of Miss Seward, with whom he had often exchanged the small coin of compliment :

" The enchanting Mr. Erskine honoured me with frequent attentions in the ball-rooms at Buxton, and with frequent visits at my lodgings, where he often met Mr. Wilberforce. . . . . Did Mr. Erskine tell you of our accidental rencontre on the Chatsworth road? I said to my mind, what an elegant figure is that gentleman approaching us, who, loitering with a book, now reads, and now holds the volume in a dropt hand to contemplate the fine views on his right! There seems mind in every gesture, every step, and how like Mr. Erskine! A few seconds converted resemblance into reality. After mutual exclamations, the graceful being stopt the chaise, opened the door and putting one foot on the step poured all his eloquence upon a retrospect of the hours we had passed together at Buxton; illuminating, as he flatteringly said, one of those seldom intervals of his busy life, in which his mind was left to enjoy undisturbed the luxury of intellectual intercourse."

In a subsequent letter, the literary coquette write : " I have not read aloud less than fifty times this violent story, Spencer's Leonora.[1] Its readers' powers have been represented as Siddonian. Then one party after another petitioned to hear it, till there was scarce a morning in which a party of eight or ten did not flock to my apartments to be poetically frightened. Erskine, Wilberforce, everything that was everything, and everything that was nothing, flocked to Leonora!"

Erskine was always an especial favourite with a character still more open and simple-minded in his vanity, the late Dr.

---

[1] Bürger's Leonora, translated by the Honourable William Spencer.

Parr. Similarity of opinion in politics—an appetite equally ravenous of praise—an equal alacrity to pay as to receive flatteries, and occasional meetings in the same whig coteries, soon ripened their intimacy into lasting friendship.

Delighted with his conversational talents, the doctor exclaimed one day at table—as the highest recompense in his power to bestow—"When you die, I will write your epitaph!" Erskine repaid his compliment with interest, remarking, "It is almost a temptation, my dear doctor, to commit suicide."

A large portion of the correspondence between Parr and Erskine has been preserved, from which we shall draft a few specimens, for several of his letters to the worthy pedagogue present the most lively sketches of character that could be taken, dashed off unwittingly by himself, during the most active part of a busy life, and mark his fervid whiggery in politics, his bonhommie and festivity of temper.

"My dear Sir,

"I have a thousand thanks to send you for your kind and friendly letter. The approbation of such an excellent judge of every accomplishment is a great prize; and I hope to be a candidate for it to better effect in a few months, when Gurney publishes the proceedings, of which you have as yet but an imperfect sketch. Let me also thank Mrs. Parr for her partial judgment, and I hope that in a few months she will be a complete convert to reform of parliament. God knows the news of to-day might work a conversion of itself. All is lost in Flanders; and you may expect to hear in a few days complete and total rout and overthrow. I hope we shall meet soon in London. In the mean time &c.

T. ERSKINE.

"P. S.—Our friend Sheridan has been a constant attendant on the trial, and gave most important evidence for Hardy."

"Aug. 29, 1795.

"I would not have suffered the post to return without my best and warmest thanks for your letter, if I had been in the way to receive it. No wonder you will say when it brought so large a fee for the speech I sent you. It was not for nothing that I left the full monied term of last November at Westminster. No. I am not better than my neighbours. I was only prudently preaching in these days of innovation for coin not subject to be debased in the esteem and approbation of such men as yourself, and I have so far succeeded by the dint of sheer honesty, (for I have little else to boast of,) as to bind so fast in chains both genius and criticism, as to be compared to Demosthenes and Cicero, by one of the very few who are capable of estimating either of them, and who ought to take the lead in England, whether ancient learning and eloquence are to be judged of in the abstract, or compared with the shadows which their descended radiance still gives birth to in our latter days. You say, young Sheridan is with you. My son speaks very highly of him, I am truly glad of it, because I sincerely wish him well. His father, in my mind, is one of the honestest and most manly politicians in England, and I have no doubt will persevere in the good cause of reform of parliament, which is the only thing that can give this unhappy country the smallest chance of safety.

" I am now very busy flying my boy's kite, shooting with the bow and arrow, and talking to an old Scotch gardener ten hours a day, about the same things; which taken altogether are not of the value or importance of a Birmingham halfpenny, and am scarcely up to the exertion of reading in the daily papers. How much happier it would be for England and the world, if the king's ministers were employed in a cause so much more innocent than theirs, and so perfectly suitable to their capacities. Remember me to your worthy and excellent neighbours, the Greatheads. I will forthwith send him the speech. Believe me to be truly, Sir, always your much obliged and very sincere humble servant.

T. E."

The following letters may win a smile from the reader at the follies of the wise, in Erskine's believing young Ireland's forgery, at his forebodings of ruin indulged in common with the Scottish whigs (to the shame of their second sight be it spoken), and at his vivacious vanity as an author. He might well be proud of this offshoot from his teeming brain, the pamphlet on the Causes and Consequences of the War, for it was carried through forty-eight editions by the magic of his name :

" My dear Sir,　　　　　　　　　" London, Dec. 31, 1795.

" I had the pleasure of your kind letter on my return to London from Norfolk. If our proposed association is followed up it may make a mighty revolution in public sentiment; but perhaps it may call for more activity in many quarters than it may receive; great exertions and funds to second them, with discipline, supported by self interest, are fearful odds against voluntary assemblies of men with different views and various opinions. But if it does not succeed, certainly nothing will or can.

"I went to-day to Ireland's from curiosity, and having heard from several quarters that the new Shakspeare was a forgery, and having seen an advertisement from Malone on the subject, all I can say is I am glad I am not the man who has undertaken to prove Mr. Malone's proposition; for I think I never saw such a body of evidence in my life to support the authenticity of any matter which rests upon high authority. I am quite sure a man would be laughed out of an English court of justice who attempted to maintain Malone's opinion, in the teeth of every rule of probability acknowledged for ages as the standard for investigating truth."

"My dear Sir,

"I am highly obliged and flattered by your most friendly letter. I am almost tempted to regret your kind partiality, because it deprives my book of the unbiassed opinion of so complete and perfect a judge of every thing that goes to the composition of literary merit upon all subjects. When I reflect, however, upon your worth and principles, and upon the value of your friendship, I am better contented to have you as a friend than as a critic. I cannot say how much I thank you for remarking the negligence with which it cannot but be filled. I wonder it is not nonsense from beginning to end; for I wrote it amidst constant interruptions, great part of it in open Court, during the trial of causes. I will forthwith send you a copy from the author; and if, in a leisure hour, you will do me the favour to point out errors, &c. I will thank you most sincerely. I always am,

"My dear Sir,

"Your most obliged and faithful servant,

"T. E.

"15,000 copies have been sold in England, besides editions printed at Dublin and Edinburgh, where the sale has been unusual."

"July 4, 98.

"I forwarded your letter, my dear Sir, to our friend Macintosh, and I enclose you one which he sent to me to forward to you. You will be informed no doubt that his lectures are in proper train, and I am persuaded they will contribute greatly to the dignity of the law, and to the advancement of his own reputation. I am glad that you are likely to accommodate the difference that you mentioned to me. I can scarcely figure to myself a situation in which a law-suit is not if possible to be avoided. I have heard with great pain that Lady Oxford has been very ill. She will, I trust, come out again in the spring, with the sun, and like the sun.

"The calamity of Nelson's victory, the greatest that ever befel at least the present ministers of Great Britain, is now beginning to show itself. The few remaining monarchies in the south of Europe are crumbling into dust, and those in the north are in deep consultation whether they choose to follow them. The republic of France, under the nursing care of Pitt, is starting up into new vigour; and such is the stupidity of Englishmen; I call it stupidity, because it has neither the force nor the genius of madness, that they come to him with their gold and silver as a willing tribute for the deliverance of Europe, whose conquest is finishing, and for the restoration of British security, which is utterly annihilated. It is truly astonishing that the high men of this country, who are attached to the monarchy, and interested in the support of their dignities, do not see the precipice, to the edge of which we are hourly advancing. Adieu, my dear Sir."

The last letter in the correspondence proves that the gaiety of the writer was as untiring as his friendship, and that he preserved to the last his pleasing powers of versification:

" My very dear Parr, 　　　　　　" Buchan Hill, Feb. 17, 1822.

"If you wonder why I have not sooner thanked you for your most kind and delightful letter, which I shall keep as an heirloom, it can only be from not having duly considered how difficult it is to find words to acknowledge it. I have read it over and over again, and my children shall read it hereafter. There was an inaccuracy in my little sonnet upon the infant Hampden, which should run thus:

" Thy infant years, dear child, had passed unknown,
　　As wine had flown upon thy natal day;
　　　But that the name of Hampden fires each soul,
　　　To sit with rapture round thy birth-day bowl—
Honest remembrance of his high renown,
　　In the great cause of law and liberty.

" Should Heaven extend thy days to man's estate,
　　Follow his bright example; scorn to yield
　　　To servile judgments; boldly plead the claim
　　　Of British rights, and should the sacred flame
Of eloquence die in corrupt debate,
　　Like Hampden, urge their justice in the field.

" These last lines may one day get this young gentleman hanged unless we can take our just turn in hanging very many who so richly deserve it.

"I have not seen any account of Miss Greathead's marriage, otherwise I should have written to him, as you most properly wished me to do.

　　　　　　" Yours, very affectionately,
　　　　　　　　　　" ERSKINE."

Though not a poet in the highest sense of the term, Mr. Erskine was wont to indite stanzas with more success than usually inspires the gentle tinklings of orators and statesmen. From the date of his residence in college, when he wrote the clever parody to his banker upon Gray's ode, " Ruin seize thee ruthless king," to the octo-syllabic stanzas by which he would fain in old age have whiled away farmers from the cruel sport of shooting rooks, he was never wholly innocent of rhymes.

The following lines were composed by him to the memory of a faithful pony, called " Jack," on whose back he had been accustomed for many years to ride the home circuit :

> " Poor Jack ! thy master's friend when he was poor,
> Whose heart was faithful, and whose step was sure,
> Should prosperous life debauch my erring heart,
> And whispering pride repel the patriot's part ;
> Should my foot falter at ambition's shrine,
> And for mean lucre quit the path divine ;
> Then may I think of thee when I was poor,
> Whose heart was faithful, and whose step was sure."

His epigram on Lady Payne, whether the impromptu of the hour or not, is also turned with considerable neatness. At Sir Ralph Payne's house in Grafton Street, says Wraxall, the leaders of opposition frequently met ; and Erskine having one day dined there, found himself so indisposed as to be obliged to retire after dinner to another apartment. Lady Payne, who was incessant in her attentions to him, inquired when he returned to the company how he found himself. Erskine took out a bit of paper, and wrote on it—

> " 'Tis true I am ill, but I cannot complain,
> For he never knew pleasure who never knew Payne !"

To his *vers de societé*, indeed, a greater permanence is due than to the other gay bubbles of the hour. A favourable specimen has been given in the Memoirs of Mat Lewis.

Among the visitors at Oatlands, we are told, were Lewis, Erskine, and the witty Lady Anne Cullen Smith, who amused themselves in writing one day after dinner what are not inaptly called thread-paper rhymes. It was commenced by the following impromptu from Erskine, on returning Lewis's pencil :

> " Your pencil I send you, with thanks for the loan,
>   Yet writing for fame now and then,
>   My wants I must still be content to bemoan,
>   Unless I could borrow—your pen."

His lordship having indulged in a not very complimentary comparison at the expense of the ladies, was thus answered by Lewis :

> " Lord Erskine at women presuming to rail,
>   Says wives are tin canisters tied to our tail,
>   While fair Lady Anne, as the subject he carries on,
>   Feels hurt at his lordship's degrading comparison.
>   Yet wherefore degrading ? Considered aright,
>   A canister's useful, and polish'd and bright ;
>   And should dirt its original purity hide,
>   That's the fault of the puppy to whom it is tied."

To which Lord Erskine immediately rejoined,

> " When smitten with love from the eyes of the fair,
>   If marriage should not be your lot,
>   A ball from a pistol will end your despair.
>   Its safer than canister shot."

If no higher meed of praise can be awarded to these verses, at least they have the merit of smoothness, nor would it be easy to find a more graceful mode of relief from the fatigues of professional duty or the ennui of old age. Struck off hastily, and in sport, these sparkling trifles may yet be advantageously compared with the idle lyrics of Bolingbroke, or Chatham, or Burke ; from an attentive comparison between whose versification it would appear (and Cicero offers an additional illustration of the theory) that the greater the orator, the worse the poetaster.

Returning with Erskine, as after the interval of a long vacation, to the routine duties of his possession, it may not be uninteresting to follow him into that part of the court which was rarely honoured by his visits, we mean the crown side, and take notes of his practice there as counsel for the prosecution. In that arena, we are free to confess, our admiration of his ability is merged in regret at his want of forbearance, and the homage due to his talents is partly neutralized by a sense of their misapplication. We look in vain for the grave address, temperate demeanor, and measured language, which ought to characterise a counsel for the crown. He rushes into the ring a champion armed at all points and eager to ride down the defenceless, forgetful that the wreath of conquest must be stained with blood, and that the struggle is for human life. Never condescending to enter the criminal court except on a special retainer, he brings with him all the dexdexterity and rhetoric of the nisi prius advocate, and without remorse would make sure of his prisoner were it even by the snares with which he had caught a civil verdict.

Of this perverted power a signal instance is given in the trial of John Motherill for a criminal assault on Miss Wade, the daughter of an officer in the army, then Master of the Ceremonies at Brighton. The trial, though now scarcely known, excited at the time intense interest, from the high respectability of the party injured and the singular circumstances of the case.

The lady was under seventeen years of age, had many personal charms, but was of weak intellect. She had been set down in a friend's carriage at her father's door, about ten o'clock at night on returning from a ball. Unluckily her friends drove off without waiting to see the door opened ; the young lady had returned earlier than was anticipated, and there was no one in the house to receive her. The prisoner, who had been loitering about the door, then came up, took her by the arm, forced her through several streets, making her walk part of the way before him, she being too much fluttered and alarmed to cry out or attempt to escape, till they came to a churchyard, where he effected his purpose. He detained her during the night, compelling her to enter a bathing machine on the shore, and was secured at day-break the next morning attempting to make his escape. The appearance of the poor girl afforded the strongest presumption of his guilt.

This extraordinary case could not but call forth universal sympathy. To aid a father's natural yearning for vengeance,

Erskine was brought down special, and appears to have yielded too much to his anxieties as an advocate and his feelings as a man. The trial came on at East Grinstead, at the Sussex Spring Assizes, 1786, before Mr. Justice Ashurst. The reader when he bears in mind that the prisoner's counsel could not address the jury, and that death was certain to follow conviction, will be startled with us at the glowing language and angry epithets of the speech for the prosecution :

" I beseech you to discharge from your minds every thing you have heard on the subject, and might add too every thing that you have seen, for I am told this wicked and unfortunate wretch has been this morning led about the streets for the benefit of air, and may probably have excited your compassion. I have no objection that you should compassionate him ; a man is more an object of compassion because he is an object of justice ; a man is more an object of pity because his crimes are objects of horror."

After eulogizing her father with much art as an honourable officer, and enhancing their pity for the sufferer as one not of a strong temperament of mind, he goes on to heighten the sympathy of his hearers by the following portrait :

" When she is attentively observed by you, you will probably make this remark, that I confess I made myself upon seeing her, that if you could conceive a painter of the finest genius to be desirous of painting the character of artless simplicity and innocence, he would fix upon the countenance and figure of Miss Wade. What a venial offence (he added parenthetically,) is even murder compared with that with which the prisoner stands charged."

*   *   *   *

" It seems at first view, and has often struck me as a very great hardship, that the prisoner's counsel cannot make those observations which in the commonest civil law action every man's counsel is enabled to make for him, but the law is much wiser than me or any other individual. Custom comes to the protection of the prisoner, and imposes as a duty upon those who prosecute that which perhaps the law does not enforce, viz. that with whatever strength, with whatever clearness, with whatever conclusion the evidence on the part of the prosecution shall appear to day, and whatever art and ingenuity may be employed to defeat the ends of justice, I shall, I can make no reply. If I should see the strength of my evidence as clear as the sun at noontide, and if I should see the weakness of any observations, on the effect of any cross-examination of this young lady, so that I might drag him to justice by the power of your understanding with the aid of the communication I could give it, I shall be silent as the grave."

The advocate then draws a highly coloured sketch of the facts, and proceeds, in a spirit not to be commended, to influence the passions of the jury and insult the prisoner.

" If there is any probability in favour of the prisoner at the bar, in God's name let him have it. But there is no probability in his favour, none that any reasonable mind can for a moment entertain ; for let me ask you this question, whether it be consistent with any thing you ever saw, heard, or read of, that a young lady of hitherto chaste and virtuous life, artless, simple, and innocent in her manners, should all of a sudden go out on a tempestuous night—leave her father's house, not to throw herself into the arms of a lover, who had addressed her and endeavoured to seduce her, but into the arms of a stranger with nothing to recommend him, with nothing upon earth to captivate or seduce the fancy ? It is repugnant to reason to believe it—it is a thing incredible, that the most viciously disposed woman could go into the arms of the squalid wretch before you ! I do not mean to insult him by the expression ; his wickedness renders him an object of compassion. But if he is not to be insulted a virtuous, innocent, miserable, ruined lady is not to pass unredressed ; nor the breach of God's laws and the country's to pass unrevenged. If he dies he suffers less than her, who lives. Oh fie !"

The phrase used by Erskine might have have been echoed back by the squalid wretch at being thus designated.

Fearful that startling improbabilities might be disclosed by his client's imbecility of mind, he concluded with a threat :

" It is a solemn and an unpleasant duty. You are humane I have no doubt, and I am glad you are so. Those who are not humane cannot be just. Justice is all I ask at your hands. If in your consciences you believe that the prisoner at the bar did commit this offence, so shocking to the individual and repugnant to all the principles of justice, you are bound in duty to God and to your country to convict him. If you can go home to night and satisfy yourselves that this young lady either has not been violated in point of fact, or that, having been so, it has been with her own consent ; if you can persuade yourselves of that absurd and improbable proposition, after you shall have heard the evidence, I shall not call your mercy in question; it is a matter which will rest with your own consciences."

The jury withstood this elaborate assault. After a long examination of the unhappy young woman, conducted by Erskine with his accustomed skill, they remained unconvinced that she had resisted to the utmost of her strength. They consulted together for half an hour, and then, after stating their scruples to the court, and being informed that there was no middle course, reluctantly returned a verdict of acquittal.

(To be continued in the next Number.)

ART. III.—FORM OF MORTGAGES.

It is obvious that the present mode in which lands in this country are charged or mortgaged is anomalous and inconvenient. The ancient system of a term of years, with a proviso for cesser of the term on payment of the money, was correct in theory, but it proved insufficient in practice and is now exploded. The usual course is now to convey the fee simple to the lender and at the same time to give him a power of sale in default of payment of the debt; and this mode, so far as regards the power of sale, has been found to answer well. It has saved many estates from the costs of a Chancery suit, and has given rise to very few disputes or questions: it is, indeed, remarkable how seldom the power of sale in a mortgage has either directly or indirectly engaged the attention of the Courts. But the vesting of the fee in the lender is a clumsy procedure, and often occasions great inconvenience and expense.

In a Court of Law, the lender, though he may know nothing of the property, is deemed the absolute owner, but still the real state of the case has compelled the admission that payment of rent to the mortgagor is a good payment until notice of the mortgage be given to the tenant. But a mortgagor is, as it were, a stranger to his own property; if he grants a lease and then mortgages, he cannot distrain for the rent nor otherwise enforce payment of it ; for though a tenant cannot deny his landlord's title, he may show that it has ceased.

In Chancery the real situation and intention of the parties is considered, and the mortgagee is regarded only as the possessor of the title deeds, with a power to make the estate his own, if the money remains unpaid.

Now this state of things is a reproach to the law, and we are confident it is one which need not exist ; for the doctrine of uses, the steam power of our system, supplies an easy remedy. This doctrine, with beautiful precision, enables us to give to a mortgagee exactly what is required for his safety, and at the same time the mortgagor may have the present use of the property. We propose, in short, to give to the mortgagee and to his executors within twenty-one years after his death a power to appoint the premises with a proviso for cesser of such power on payment of the money. This power will of course give to the mortgagee complete and absolute control over the property if he should require it, but in the mean time the mortgagor will remain the owner as he ought. In Jeremy Bentham's scheme for a general registry he would, we believe, on his plan of the country, have had mortgagees represented by blots,—and appropriately enough, for a mortgage in fee cannot be removed without trouble ; but the limitation which we have ventured to propose might be better likened to a net which incloses and secures, but may easily be removed.

We will now consider more minutely the advantages which would result from this mode of limitation.

The mortgagor, so long as he paid the interest and until the principal money was required, would remain in possession of all his rights as owner of the land ; he would be within rules, but still he would have life and powers of acting of which he is wholly deprived by a conveyance in fee simple.

When he paid off the mortgage debt, no reconveyance would be required ; the power of the mortgagee might be made to cease by a simple receipt. This would be very important in practice, and it would save much expense. In case of the death of the mortgagee there would be no inquiry as to his heir at law or devisee of mortgaged estates ; the parties to receive the money, his personal representatives, would be competent to release.

The personal representatives of a mortgagee alone would be competent as well to transfer as release a mortgage; and thus the numerous and perplexing questions which arise, whether mortgaged estates do or do not pass by a devise, would be at an end.

The mortgagee might easily invest himself with the legal estate if he wished, but that would be seldom necessary; for he might sell the estate and appoint it at once to the purchaser.

Of course, if the mortgagor made a lease or other estate after the mortgage, it would be divested by an execution of the power vested in the mortgagee; and the grantee might be evicted by the mortgagee, like a tenant who comes in after a mortgage in fee.

But we incline to think that it would be better in most cases to give the mortgagor, by the mortgage deed, a qualified power to lease; for if without such power he makes a lease after the mortgage, and the mortgagee subsequently wishes to enter into possession of the premises, and the tenant refuses to attorn to him, he, the mortgagee, cannot enforce payment of the rent or otherwise proceed against the tenant, except by bringing ejectment. When the mortgagor occupies any part of the premises, we recommend that there should be an agreement to hold the same as tenant at a rent not less than the full annual value of the premises. In some cases where the mortgagor is in possession, a power to distrain is of the first importance, and that can only be effectually had against assignees under a bankruptcy by the mortgagor being actual tenant to the mortgagee at a fixed rent. It is certainly doubtful whether a mere power to distrain given by a mortgagor can be exercised against his assignees[1].

The numerous questions which have within a few years been discussed in our courts relative to tenants and mortgagees show the importance of placing their respective rights on a clear footing; and we think it only just that a tenancy from

[1] See 4 Mees. & Wels. 699, 702.

year to year should be exempt from the power of a mortgagee, so at least that he may be required to give a regular
notice to quit.

It may be objected, that, unless the mortgagee has some
estate vested in him by the mortgage deed, he may lose rents
due and unpaid when he exercises his power and enters into
possession, and this is true ; but it would only be of importance when the security was a deficient one, and it may without infringing much on the symmetry of our plan be obviated
by limiting to the mortgagee a term of years, subject to the
same proviso for cesser on the power. Or the object may be
equally well attained by a declaration, that an appointment
shall have relation back to the date of the mortgage deed, so
as to pass all rents due and unpaid when notice is given to
the tenants not to pay to the mortgagor.

We will now give the draft of such a form of mortgage
deed as we think would effectuate the improvements we have
suggested :—

This Indenture made the 14th day of August in the year
1839, between John Gray of the borough and county of New-
castle-upon-Tyne, gentleman, of the 1st part, and Tobias Scott
and Luke Kipley, both of the same place, gentlemen, of the
2nd or other part. *Whereas* the said Tobias Scott and Luke
Kipley have, at the request of the said John Gray, agreed to
lend him the sum of £2000, upon having the repayment of
the same with interest secured in manner hereinafter expressed. *And whereas* by indentures of lease and release bearing date respectively the 14th and 15th days of September
1832, the release being made between Thomas Low therein described of the 1st part, the said John Gray of the 2nd part, and
Stephen Twist therein described of the 3rd part, the messuages
and closes or parcels of ground and hereditaments hereinafter
described and expressed to be hereby appointed and assured,
were conveyed : *To the use* of such person or persons, for
such estate or estates, interest or interests, and to and for
such intents and purposes, as he the said John Gray by any
deed or deeds should from time to time, or at any time appoint. And in default of and until such appointment : *To the
use* of the said John Gray and his assigns during his natural

life, without impeachment of waste. And after the determination of that estate by any means in his lifetime : *To the use* of the said Stephen Twist and his heirs during the natural life of the said John Gray. In trust nevertheless for him and his heirs aforesaid. And after the determination of the estate so limited in use to the said Stephen Twist and his heirs as aforesaid : *To the use* of the said John Gray, his heirs and assigns for ever. *Now this indenture witnesseth*, that in pursuance of the said agreement, and in consideration of the sum of £2000 of lawful British money to the said John Gray paid by the said Tobias Scott and Luke Kipley on the execution of these presents, the receipt of which sum the said John Gray doth hereby acknowledge, and of and from the same doth hereby acquit and release the said Tobias Scott and Luke Kipley, their heirs, executors, administrators, and assigns ; the said John Gray doth hereby for himself, his heirs, executors, and administrators, covenant with the said Tobias Scott and Luke Kipley, their executors, administrators, and assigns, that he the said John Gray, his heirs, executors, administrators or assigns, or some or one of them, shall and will well and truly pay, or cause to be paid, unto the said Tobias Scott and Luke Kipley, their executors, administrators, or assigns, the sum of £2000 sterling, on the 14th day of February now next ensuing, together with interest for the same, in the meantime, after the rate of £5 for every £100 by the year, without any deduction whatsoever. *And this indenture further witnesseth*, that in further pursuance of the said agreement, and for further securing the said principal and interest monies expressed and intended to be hereby secured, the said John Gray, by virtue of his said received power, and of every other power enabling him in this behalf, doth by this deed appoint to the uses hereinafter expressed, and doth also hereby grant and release unto the said Tobias Scott and Luke Kipley, their heirs and assigns, all that messuage or dwelling house situate in the township of Bolton in the county of Durham, with the offices, garden and hereditaments thereunto belonging. And also all those closes or parcels of ground situate in the same township, containing together by estimation 100 acres or thereabouts. Boundaries, &c. Together, &c. And all deeds, &c. *To have and to hold* the said messuage, closes or parcels of ground, hereditaments, and all and singular other the premises hereby granted and released, or intended so to be, unto the said Tobias Scott and Luke Kipley and their heirs : *To the uses* following, that is to say : To such uses and upon and for such trusts, intents, and purposes, as they the said Tobias Scott and Luke Kipley or the survivor of them, or the executors or administrators of such survivor, within 21 years after his death, shall from time to time, or at any time, by any deed or deeds appoint. And in default of and until such appointment : *To the uses* expressed and declared of and concerning the same hereditaments and premises in and by the said hereinbefore recited indenture of release of the 15th day of September 1832 : *Provided always* and it is hereby declared, that as to such of the said hereditaments and premises as are now in the occupation of the said John Gray he shall hold and occupy the same as tenant thereof, from year to year, to the said Tobias Scott and Luke Kipley, their heirs and assigns, at and under the yearly rent of £200, payable by two equal portions, on the 14th day of August and the 14th day of February in every year. And it is hereby declared, that if and when the said rent of £200 shall be received by the said Tobias Scott and Luke Kipley, their executors, administrators or assigns, or any of them, the same shall be applied first in or towards payment of the interest due in respect of the said principal sum of £2000, and of all costs and expenses which a mortgagee is entitled to have and retain, and then towards payment of the said principal sum. *Provided also* and it is hereby further declared, that it shall be lawful for the said John Gray to demise the said hereditaments and premises, or any of them, from year to year, or for any term of years not exceeding three years in possession, so only that the best rent be reserved, without fine or premium. *Provided also* and it is hereby declared, that every appointment made by virtue of the powers aforesaid shall have relation back to the day of the date of these presents, so as to carry and pass as well all rents and profits due and unpaid when notice shall be given to any tenant, or occupier of the said mortgaged premises, not to pay the same to the said John Gray, his heirs or assigns, as all rents thereafter to accrue due, so that the said Tobias Scott and Luke Kipley, their executors, administrators, and assigns, may have all usual remedies for the recovery of such rents and profits. *Provided also,* and it is hereby expressly agreed and declared, that upon the payment by the said John Gray, his heirs, executors, administrators or assigns, or any of them, of the principal and interest monies expressed and intended to be hereby secured, which shall be acknowledged by a memorandum or receipt indorsed on these presents, or by some other writing to be respectively signed by the said persons parties hereto of the second part, or the survivor of them, or the executors or administrators of such survivor, the powers hereinbefore given to the persons parties hereto of the second part, and the survivor of them, and the executors or administrators of such survivor, shall cease and determine, but without prejudice to any estate which shall have been previously created by virtue of such powers, or any of them. And it is hereby declared, that in case the said lastly-mentioned powers and every of them shall cease before the said principal and interest monies expressed to be hereby secured shall be fully paid, the same monies shall remain and be a charge on the said hereditaments and premises until the payment thereof. And it is hereby also declared, that in case default shall be made in payment of the said principal and interest monies expressed to be hereby secured, pursuant to the covenant for payment thereof hereinbefore contained, it shall be lawful for the said persons parties hereto of the second part, their executors, administrators or assigns, or any of them, to institute and prosecute a suit to foreclose the equity of redemption of the said mortgaged premises, and to have and exercise any remedy or right which a mortgagee can have or exercise in ordinary cases. And it is hereby expressly declared, that the said proviso for cesser shall not remain in force, or have any effect either at law or in equity, with respect to such of the said hereditaments and premises explained to be hereby granted and released, as shall be sold under the power for that purpose hereinafter contained. *And* it is hereby agreed and declared, that the said Tobias Scott and Luke Kipley shall stand possessed of, and be deemed entitled to, the principal and interest monies expressed to be hereby secured, and the securities for the same, as joint tenants, as well at equity as in law, so that if they or either of them shall happen to die whilst the said principal and interest monies, or any part thereof, shall continue upon the security intended to be hereby made, the survivor of them, or the executors, administrators, or assigns of such survivor, shall have full power as well to give a receipt for the same as to release the mortgaged premises therefrom, as absolutely and effectually as the said Tobias Scott and Luke Kipley could or might have done. *And* the said John Gray doth hereby for himself, his heirs, executors, and administrators, further covenant with the said Tobias Scott and Luke Kipley, their executors, administrators, and assigns, in manner' following, that is to say, [Here may follow covenants to insure, and that mortgagees may sell, with agreement as to application of sale monies, and then usual covenants for the title.]

W. C. W.

ART. IV.—FORFEITURE BY BREACH OF COVENANT.

It is designed to show in the present article, 1st, for what, and to whom a power of entry may be lawfully reserved ; 2dly, by what words, and how such clauses are construed ; 3dly, what amounts to a breach, and how it may be waived ; 4thly, who may enter for a forfeiture ; 5thly and lastly, as to the relief which courts of law and equity administer in aid of the lessee.

1. As to the nature of a condition for the breach of which the landlord may re-enter, the maxim is " *cujus est dare ejus .est disponere,*" and the general rule is clear, that the landlord, having the *jus disponendi* and parting only with a limited interest, may annex to his grant whatever conditions he pleases, provided they be not illegal or unreasonable ; just as, before the statute of *Quia emptores*, the feoffor might have enfeoffed upon condition that the feoffee should not alien, because he had a possibility of *reverter ;* and as, at the present day, the sovereign may grant upon such a condition because of the tenure to himself.[1]

Hence a stipulation that the lessee shall not alien without the licence of the lessor, is a condition which has always been

---

[1] Knight's case, 5 Co. 56 ; Co. Litt. 223 b.

valid and reasonable, as the latter confides in the personal integrity and responsibility of his lessee, and even equity will not in general relieve against a breach.   There appears to be no case in which a question has arisen as to the validity of this restriction with reference to the length of the term ; but Buller, J. intimated in Roe v. Galliers, 2 T. R. 133, that in very long leases it would be bad as tending to a perpetuity.

It was doubted for some time whether the policy of the law would admit of a condition that the lease should be void in case of the bankruptcy or insolvency of the lessee.   The bankrupt, it was contended, by means of being in possession, was enabled not only to obtain a collusive credit, and defraud his creditors, but also to impoverish his estate by expending large sums of money by way of improvements, while the creditors could obtain no benefit therefrom.   This was one of the facts found in the case in which the point was decided.   But the Court of King's Bench unanimously held that there was nothing unreasonable in the lessor making such a stipulation to prevent his estate from getting into the hands of strangers, and the decision has been invariably followed both at law and in equity.[1]   The proviso was coupled in the case in question with a stipulation not to assign without consent, but the junction of such a stipulation appears to be immaterial.   After this decision it was not difficult to maintain the legality on general principles of a condition that the lease should be void if extended or taken in execution ; and accordingly it has been holden that such a stipulation is good even against a seizure under an extent at the suit of the crown.[2]

These appear to be the only conditions worthy of notice as calculated, without the aid of authority, to raise a doubt. Provisoes giving a right of re-entry upon non-payment of rent, non-repair, underletting, appropriating to certain trades, &c. are common, and have never been disputed.   Nor is there anything illegal in requiring the lessee of a public-house to buy all his beer of the lessor, or even, it would seem of a third person, under pain of forfeiture ; but the law annexes

[1] Roe v. Galliers, 2 T. R. 133.
[2] Rex v. Topping, M'L. & Y. 544.

this additional qualification, viz. that the article supplied be good and saleable.[1]

Stipulations which require the lessee to do an act either *malum in se*, or *malum prohibitum*, are clearly void, as well as those which make his estate contingent upon his forbearing to do an act which the law requires to be done for the public welfare.

The doctrine of conditions however, it must be observed, does not rest upon privity of tenure ; though it is only where there is a privity of this nature that a general restriction upon alienation is good. Where a person parts with his whole estate, he cannot bind the vendee not to alien. " If a man be possessed of a lease for lives, or of a horse, or of any other chattel, real or personal, and give or sell his whole interest or property therein upon condition that the vendee or donee shall not alien the same, the condition is void, because his whole interest and property is out of him, so as he hath no possibility of a *reverter ;* and it is against trade and traffic, and bargaining and contracting, between man and man."[2]

But short of this prohibition, which is imposed to prevent perpetuities, the parties to a contract may model it how they please. " If A. be seised of Black Acre in fee, and B. infeoffeth him of White Acre upon condition that A. shall not alien Black Acre, the condition is good, for the condition is annexed to other land, and ousteth not the feoffee of his power to alien the land whereof the feoffment is made, and so no repugnancy to the estate passed by the feoffment."[3]

Another example of a restriction imposed by a party who had no reversion is given in the next section of Littleton. " But if the condition be such that the feoffee shall not alien to such a one, naming his name, or to any of his heirs, or of the issues of such a one, &c. or the like, which condition does not take away all power of alienation from the feoffor, &c. then such condition is good."[4]

In a recent case a lessee for years made a conveyance operating as an assignment of his whole interest in the land, and inserted therein a covenant on the part of the assignee

---

[1] See Holcombe v. Hewson, 2 Camp. 391 ; Jones v. Edney, 3 Camp. 285 ; Thornton v. Sherratt, 8 Taunt. 529.

[2] Co. Litt. 223 a.   [3] Id. 223 b.   [4] Sec. 361.

not to open a public-house on the demised premises without licence, and a clause of re-entry on breach of the covenant, and it was holden that though he had no reversion he was entitled to maintain ejectment.[1]   There was the additional fact, as it would seem from the report, that the lessee reserved a rent payable to himself, but this was not mentioned as an ingredient upon which the judgment was based, nor does it seem within the reason of the law that the mere reservation of a rent where there is no reversion could either sanction a general restriction as to alienation, or that the absence of it would disable an assignee from annexing such other condition to his assignment.

It is an ancient and inflexible principle of law, that a power of re-entry can only be reserved to the grantor; that is, to the person from whom the *legal* estate moves, and to his immediate representative, either personal or real, according to the nature of the estate.[2]   Hence where a mortgagor and mortgagee join in a lease, and the proviso for re-entry is made with the former, neither can take advantage of it; not the mortgagor because he is a stranger to the grant, nor the latter because it is not given to him.[3]   It is here assumed that the title of the mortgagor is set out in the lease, for otherwise if he appear as the or one of the demising parties, the instrument will be good by estoppel.[4]   If the power of re-entry be given to both the lessor and a stranger, it would seem that, though bad for the latter, the former alone may maintain ejectment.[5]   But a condition may well be reserved to the lessor upon doing or omitting to do an act to a stranger; as if a lease be made upon condition " to pay the rent to J. S;" and though there follow the words " and that otherwise J. S. shall enter;" yet the lessor may enter, for the condition is created by the first words.[6]

2. There are various words and phrases which of themselves make an estate conditional, without an express power of entry.   Three of these are enumerated by Litt. ss. 328,

[1] Doe v. Bateman, 2 B. & C. 168.
[2] Co. Litt. 214 a.
[3] Doe v. Adams, 2 C. & J. 232; Doe v. Laurence, 4 Taunt. 23.
[4] Doe v. Goldsmith, 2 C. & J. 674.
[5] Co. Litt. 213 b, n.; Doe v. White, 4 Bing. 276.
[6] See Co. Litt. 213 b, n. (1).

329. The first is " on condition," as if A. lease to B. upon condition that B. pay to A. yearly a certain rent. Where a memorandum of agreement expressed that A. let to B. in consideration of the rents and conditions thereinafter mentioned, and contained the words, " it is further stipulated and conditioned that B. shall not assign, transfer, &c." the court held the latter words to constitute a condition, though the instrument was not under seal. It was observed, that no precise form of words was necessary to raise a condition. It was sufficient if it appeared that the words were intended to have the effect of creating it.[1] Another form mentioned by Littleton is, " provided always" that the said lessee do pay to the said lessor such a rent. These words often serve to limit or qualify a former clause, and then they do not make a condition; as if a lease be made without impeachment of waste, " *provided* that he shall not do voluntary waste;" or a grant of a rent-charge, " *provided* that the grantor shall not charge his person."[2] So if it be covenanted by the indenture that the lessee shall make the reparations, provided always that the lessor shall find timber, or that he shall scour the ditches, or the like, provided always that he shall carry the dung to such a field.[3]

Lord Coke lays it down, that to ascertain when these words make an estate conditional three things are to be observed:
—1st, that the proviso do not depend upon another sentence nor participate thereof, but stand originally of itself; 2nd, that they be the words of the bargainor, feoffor, lessor, &c.; and 3d, that the proviso be compulsory to enforce the bargainee, &c. to do an act. If these concur it is immaterial in what place in a deed the proviso comes, for having the force of a condition it shall have reference to the estate and be annexed to it. Nor is the force of the words lessened by reason of their being joined with others which are the words of the lessee, as " *provided always,* and it is covenanted and agreed between the said parties, that the lessee shall not alien."[4] This was holden to constitute both a condition and a covenant; and

[1] Doe v. Watt, 8 B. & C. 308; Co. Litt. 204 a.
[2] Lord Cromwell's case, 2 Co. 72.
[3] Id.
[4] Simpson v. Titterell, Cro. Eliz. 242.

it was said to be a general rule that where a proviso is that the lessee shall perform or not perform a thing and no penalty to it, this is a condition, otherwise it is void ; but if a penalty is annexed, it is otherwise. So in a grant of the lieutenantship of a forest, the words " provided always, and the said A. B. doth covenant and agree that he shall not cut down any wood growing upon any part of the premises," were holden to be the words of both parties and to have the same effect.[1]

One decision appears to go still farther : the words were, " it is covenanted and agreed between the parties, that H. doth let the lands for five years, *provided always* that W. shall pay to H., during the term, 120*l*. per annum ;" and this was holden to be not only a good reservation of rent but a condition also.[2]

A third form given by Littleton is the " *ita quod ;*" *so that* the said B. do pay or cause to be paid such a rent. This seems equivalent in most respects to the proviso, and to be a word either of condition or qualification according as it originates, or is annexed to, another sentence.

The effect of words which of themselves import a condition is thus shown in the case of Doctor and Student, cited Co. Litt. 213 b, n. (1). Feoffment *upon condition* that he shall pay to J. S. 20*l. and that otherwise J. S. shall re-enter.* Here, though J. S. cannot re-enter, the feoffor can, for the condition was created by the first words ; and though he intends the advantage of this to J. S., it does not signify.

In the grant of an annuity the word " for" amounts to a condition, as showing the cause or consideration of the grant. Thus, if an annuity be granted " for" one acre of land, if the acre be evicted by an elder title, the annuity ceases.[3] But not so with a grant or conveyance of land. If a man makes a feoffment in fee "to do," or "with the intent," or " to the end or purpose" that the feoffee shall do such an act, none of these words make the estate conditional, for in judgment of law they are not words of condition.[4] Yet such precise words are not required to avoid a lease for years as to avoid a freehold. Therefore a clause " and the said lessee shall continually dwell

---

[1] Earl Pembroke v. Barkley, Cro. Eliz. 384.
[2] Harrington v. Wise, Cro. Eliz. 486.
[3] Co. Litt. 204 b.
[4] Id. 204 a.

upon the capital messuage of the said manor upon pain of forfeiture of the said term," amounts to a condition.

There are other words commonly used to introduce a condition, but which do not, like those before given, make the estate conditional of themselves. Such as " if it shall happen," " in case that," &c. and these require an express clause of re-entry ;[1] therefore if A. grant land to B. to have and to hold to him and his heirs, " and if" or " but if it happen that the said B. do not pay 10*l.* at Easter," without more words, this is not a good condition ; but if these words be added, " it shall be lawful for A. to re-enter," it will be a good condition.[2] By a memorandum of agreement for letting land for twenty-one years, it was stipulated in the following terms : " and it is also further agreed and clearly understood, that *in case* the said [lessor], or his heirs, executors, and assigns, should want any part of the said land to build or otherwise, or cause to be built, then the said [lessee], or his heirs, executors, or assigns, shall and will give up that part or parts of the said land as shall be requested by the said [lessor,] by his making an abatement in proportion to the rent charged, and also to pay for so much of the fence, at a fair valuation, as he shall have occasion from time to time to take away, by his giving or leaving six months notice of what he intends to do."—"And it is also further agreed that after the [lessor], or his heirs, &c. *have taken* so much of the said land not leaving one acre, or as much as will satisfy [the lessee], then [the lessee] shall be at full liberty to relinquish the remaining part of the land." The Court of Common Pleas held that for want of a clause of re-entry the stipulation had the effect of a covenant only, and not a condition.[3]

There is a material difference between words of condition and words which determine the estate by way of limitation. At common law an assignee might take advantage of the latter, while he could not of the former ; at the present day the important distinction is, 1st, that the one absolutely puts an end to the estate, while a breach of the other may be waived or relieved against ; and 2d, that in the one case the

[1] Litt. s. 330, 331.
[2] Cruise, Dig. 4, p. 426.
[3] Doe v. Phillips, 2 Bing. 13.

z 2

emblements belong to the tenant and in the other to the land-lord. The words "until," or "so long as," "during," "whilst," &c. are apt words of limitation; as if a lease be made to A. until B. comes from Rome, or so long as A. shall continue unmarried; or for 100 years if the lessee shall so long live, or during coverture, &c., as soon as the event happens, the lease absolutely expires.

The most usual course, and one which is recommended by Littleton, is to insert an express clause of re-entry, and we shall presently have occasion to observe that there is no dif-ference at the present day between a condition or proviso which makes the lease upon a given event absolutely *void,* and a proviso for re-entry generally. The framing of such a clause requires however some attention, for although the rule of construction differs from that which is applied to con-ditions, particularly where the proviso embodies also a cove-nant, (which is usually the case,) and thus becomes the lan-guage of both parties, yet nothing will be *intended* in favour of a forfeiture. A rational and common sense meaning will be put upon ambiguous words,[1] and the courts will look to the whole instrument to collect the intention of the parties in the use of them, but they will not extend the proviso to any thing beyond the reach of the words used. In a lease in the usual form, after a covenant by the defendant that he would pay the rent, &c. and would not assign the premises, or any part thereof without leave of the lessor, followed the words, " provided always that if the said rent shall be in arrear for twenty-one days, &c. or if all or any of the covenants or agreements *hereinafter* contained on the part of the lessee to be done and performed according to the true intent and meaning of these presents, shall happen to be broken in any respect, that then it shall be lawful for the lessor to re-enter," &c. There were no covenants on the part of the defendant after this proviso, but only a covenant on the part of the les-sor that the lessee paying the said rent and performing all and every the covenants *hereinbefore* contained on his part to be performed, &c. should quietly enjoy. The action was brought for an alleged forfeiture by assigning without leave, and it was contended that the court might so marshal the

---

[1] Doe v. Elsam, M. & M. 191; Doe v. Sherwin, 3 Camp. 135.

words, viz. by making the proviso in this instance change place with the covenants, that the one may be consistent with the other, and the whole have effect, or construe the words in the latter covenant, " that the lessee *paying* and *performing*," &c. to be in effect a covenant by him to perform the preceding covenants, and then those covenants would be drawn down to the subsequent part of the lease, as if they had been repeated after the proviso. Lord Ellenborough, C. J., inclined to construe the two covenants together, since both respected the period of enjoyment, and the words " hereinafter" in the one, and " hereinbefore" in the other, evidently related to the same stipulations; but without professing to be free from considerable doubts, his lordship thought the safest course was to give to the instrument a sense according to its letter. Bayley, J., suggested that the draft might have contained other stipulations after the proviso which were struck out before engrossment, and, on the ground that the court could not clearly see what the intention was, concurred with the other judges in giving judgment for the defendant.[1] The general rule was here acknowledged, that the intention if manifest shall prevail ; and that the courts will transpose the stipulations if the sense and meaning of the parties require it. On the other hand, where the proviso was, that if " the lessee, his executors, or administrators, or either of them," should become bankrupt, the lessor should re-enter, it was ruled to be broken by the bankruptcy of the executor in his private capacity, though the term would not have passed to the assignee; Park, B., observing, " that where the words are so clear we cannot go into the question as to the intention of the parties. They must be bound by their own express stipulation however absurd we may think it." The court refused a new trial.[2]

But the more important consideration is the structure of the proviso itself, so that it may embrace all the covenants negative and affirmative. In Doe v. Stevens, 3 B. & Ad. 299, the lease contained covenants by the lessee, 1st, to pay the rent ; 2dly, to lay out 150*l.* in repairing and improving the premises; 3dly, well and sufficiently to repair, support, sustain, maintain, amend, and keep the premises ; 4thly, to insure the buildings during the time against fire; 5thly, not to permit any reed

---

[1] Doe v. Godwin, 4 M. & S. 265.
[2] Doe v. Davies, 6 C. & P. 614.

stack to be made, or any considerable quantity of pitch to be kept or laid in or upon any part of the premises without carefully housing the same; 6thly, to permit and suffer the lessor to view the premises; and 7thly, not to assign without leave of the lessor. There was a proviso for re-entry "if the rent should be in arrear for fourteen days, or the lessee should assign without leave of the lessor, or *do or cause to be done any act, matter, or thing whatsoever* contrary to or in breach of any one or more of the covenants thereinbefore contained." Then followed a covenant by the lessor "that the lessee, his executors, &c. paying the rent and *performing all and every* the covenants and provisoes according to the true intent and meaning of the lease, should quietly enjoy the premises." The breach alleged was the neglect to repair, and the Court of King's Bench, after taking time to consider, held that this was not covered by the proviso for re-entry. "The words," said Lord Tenterden, C.J., "*do or cause to be done,* import an act, and there is nothing in the other parts of the instrument from which we can clearly collect that it was the intention of the parties that it should apply to an omission to do an act. We are therefore of opinion that the mere omission to repair cannot be considered as *doing or causing to be done* an act, within the meaning of the proviso."

The case of Doe v. Marchetti, 1 B. & Ad. 715, is precisely the converse of this. The covenants were "that the said S. her executors, &c. should not suffer any sort of buildings to be erected in the curtilage or garden behind, but use the same as a garden and curtilage only; nor suffer any window shutters or other projections to be in the back or front walls thereof, nor permit any of the walls or buildings to be raised or otherwise altered from the plan thereof in any respect, without the previous written consent of the said Sir L. V. Palk, or of his heirs or their steward." To which the following proviso was added, "and if the said G. H. his executors, &c. shall by the space of thirty days next after notice for that purpose *make default* in performance of any or either of the clauses or agreements herein contained, it shall be lawful for the said Sir L. V. Palk, or his heirs, into the said premises to re-enter, and the same to have again and enjoy as if these presents had not been made." The defendant, tenant of the lessee, made a variation from the plan referred to, by erecting a portico on the demised premises before the front wall without licence, upon which, and more than thirty days before the commencement of the action, Sir L. V. Palk gave notice to the lessee and the defendant to remove immediately all encroachments and projections, stating that, unless the premises were restored to their proper state, he should proceed to recover possession. The portico was not removed, and an ejectment was brought for the forfeiture. The Court held that though the expression " make default" had been applied to negative covenants as well as to affirmative ones, yet, taking the whole clause of re-entry together, it must be taken to be confined to those covenants which are to be *performed* by the lessee. " Here the forfeiture is to be incurred," observed Littledale, J., " not merely if default be made or the act done which is covenanted against, but if there be a default of performance after thirty days' notice. The case of forfeiture therefore must be one in which a notice can have been given, and in which the lessee may have an opportunity of performing some covenant of the lease in consequence of such notice ; as, for instance, a covenant to keep in repair, which, though in some degree negative, is also of an affirmative nature."

It is difficult to imagine a really negative covenant which can be covered by such a proviso, and notwithstanding the intimation from the bench, we are not aware of any case in point. A covenant, affirmative in its nature, may be put in a negative shape, as, for instance, instead of " that the lessee shall repair," it may be said " that he shall not suffer the premises to grow into decay." So a negative covenant may be superinduced by an affirmative ; as in the above case, a stipulation might have been added that " the lessee should remove all erections which a surveyor should certify to be in violation of the covenant," and then the proviso would have reached it. It is probable that the judges had in view some such case as this, for the reasoning above quoted shows that the proviso would be equally inapplicable to the covenant, if there had been no stipulation as to notice.

The right of re-entry should be reserved not only to the lessor " and his assigns," but also to his heirs or executors, according to the nature of the estate, for it has been holden that, if a man makes a lease for years upon condition that

if the rent be in arrear it shall be lawful for the lessor
" and his assigns" to re-enter, the condition is not commensurate with the lease, for want of the word " heirs," but
determines with the life of the lessor, and that consequently
after his death the right of entry is gone.[1]   The same construction has been applied to a covenant with the lessor " and
his assigns" for payment of rent, which therefore determines
by the lessor's death.[2]   But the words " during the term"
would probably be sufficient in both cases.

The annexation of a penalty to the breach of a particular
covenant does not prevent by construction the operation of
a general proviso for re-entry, though there are covenants to
which the proviso can apply; but it may give the lessee an
alternative.   Thus where the lease contained, in addition to
the usual covenants, a covenant to use, consume and spend
upon the premises all the hay, dung, &c. under a penalty of
5l. for every ton carried off; and also a clause of re-entry,
which enumerated every covenant in the lease except that to
consume the hay, &c. on the premises, and then provided that
for the breach of any of the covenants in the lease the lessor
might re-enter; the court held the fair meaning of the covenant
and proviso to be, that, if the hay, &c. be removed without
payment of that sum, the right of re-entry shall accrue.

In further illustration of what has been said relative to the
principles of construction, we quote the case of Doe d. Lady
Wilson v. Abel, 2 M. & S. 541.   The demise was of a field,
which the defendant had occupied as tenant from year to year,
and the defendant covenanted " that if the lessor or person
entitled to the freehold or inheritance should be desirous at
any time during the term to take all or any part of the land
demised for building thereon and for yards and gardens to
such buildings, it should be lawful for the lessor or her assigns,
or person entitled as aforesaid, to enter and come into and upon
all or any part or parts of the said land to make such buildings
as she or they should think proper, and generally to do all
such acts as should be requisite and necessary in any such
case, without any interruption by the defendant, his executors,
&c.: provided always that the lessor, or person entitled as
aforesaid, should give or leave notice in writing of such inten-

[1] Co. Litt. 215 b, n.   [2] Co. Litt. 47, a.

tion to the defendant, his executors, &c. six calendar months, at the least, previous to the time of entering upon the said land or any part thereof for the purposes aforesaid, or any of them, and provided also that the lessor should in every such case allow or pay to the defendant, his executors, &c., for each and every acre of the said land so taken, the yearly rent of 8*l.* 8*s.* and so in proportion for any greater or less quantity than an acre." There was also a proviso that the lease should be void and the lessor be at liberty to re-enter in case of non-payment of the rent, or if the defendant should make default in performance of any of the covenants. The lessor conveyed away part of the land, and two years afterwards gave notice of her intention to take all the residue for building and other purposes expressed in the proviso ; that she should enter for such purpose at a day six months after the notice, and that from thenceforth the defendant's rent would cease. At the expiration of the notice the lessor's steward went to the field and demanded possession generally, but was not accompanied by any surveyor, builder, or building materials, nor had either been engaged or bespoke. The defendant refused to surrender, contending that the covenant did not entitle the lessor to repossess himself of the land, but merely to enter for the qualified purpose of building, and to take it as it should be required for that purpose. But the court, looking at the manifest intention of the parties as it was to be collected from the whole clause, and particularly to the stipulation for abatement of rent, held that the proviso gave a general right to retake the land for the purpose of building, and not merely a right to enter and take it foot by foot as the building advanced.

3. As to what amounts to a breach. It may seem superfluous to observe, that a covenant not to "assign" is not broken, at least at law, by underletting or granting an under lease, for whatever period, so long as any reversion remains in the lessee.[1] This is a restriction which, though recognized and sanctioned both in courts of Law and Equity, is nevertheless one which is not favoured ; it is not deemed included amongst "the usual covenants," and the breach must, at law, be as it were literally proved. So the depositing the

---

[1] Crusoe v. Bugby, 3 Wils. 234.

lease by way of security for a debt is not a breach of a covenant " not to assign or part with" the lessee's interest therein.[1] A covenant that the lessee shall not assign does not bind the assignee,[2] so that if the lessor waives the first, he cannot prevent any subsequent assignment; nor would the executor of the lessee in such a case be restrained from assigning over.[3] Where the lessee, who was under a covenant that he, his executors or administrators would not underlet or assign, became bankrupt, and his assignees sold the lease, which eventually came back by assignment to the bankrupt again, and he contrary to the covenant underlet, it was holden that, as the covenant did not extend to prevent an assignee from underletting, and as the bankrupt was discharged from his covenants as lessee by reason of his assignees having accepted the lease, the right of re-entry was at an end.[4] Where, however, the proviso names the executors and administrators of the lessee, the personal representative cannot assign, though the estate be encumbered with debts. Hence it was said by Ashurst, J., in Doe v. Harrison, 2 T. R. 425, that such a term for the purpose of assignment could not be considered as legal assets. Nor could it be so deemed for the purpose of charging the executor, though it is assets for the purpose of execution, for the point which was once a subject of great doubt is now considered as settled, that the sale of such a term by the sheriff under a *fi. fa.* is not a breach of the condition any more than the devolution of it on the personal representative.[5] The principle is that the proviso does not extend to an assignment by operation of law, and therefore it is not broken by the bankruptcy or insolvency of the lessee.[6] Still further it had been decided that a stipulation prohibiting the " lessee, his executors, administrators *and assigns*" from parting with the term, extends only to an assignee by the act of the party, and therefore that the *assignee of the estate* may sell without committing a breach.[7] But the prohibition attaches upon

---

[1] Doe v. Bevan, 3 M. & S. 353.
[2] Philpot v. Howe, Amb. 480 ; Paul v. Nurse, 8 B. & C. 486.
[3] Cox v. Brown, 1 Ch. 170.
[4] Doe v. Smith, 5 Taunt. 795.
[5] Doe v. Carter, 8 T. R. 57.
[6] Goring v. Warner, 1 Eq. Ca. Ab. 100 ; Crusoe v. Bugby, *ante.*
[7] Doe v. Bevan, 3 M. & S. 353.

his assignee. In consequence of these decisions, the practice of stipulating expressly for the events of bankruptcy, insolvency, or seizure in execution, has become common.

If, however, the lessee wilfully does any act contributing in any degree to the assignment, that will be a breach. Thus if he gives a warrant of attorney, or suffers judgment by default, for the purpose of enabling the plaintiff to take the term in execution, the condition is broken.[1] A specific bequest of the term does not, it seems, amount to a breach.[2]

An assignment void in point of law does not constitute a breach of the condition. In Doe d. Lloyd v. Powell, 5 B. & C. 308, the lessee being under a covenant not to "grant, assign over, pass away, or depart" the premises demised, under pain of forfeiture, executed in January an assignment of all his property, real and personal, to trustees, for the benefit of his creditors. The trustees acted upon the assignment till the April following, when a docket was struck against the lessee founded on the assignment as an act of bankruptcy; and the term with the other effects was taken by the assignees. It was held that, the deed being void *ab initio*, there was not in contemplation of law an assignment by the bankrupt.

The principle of this decision is inconsistent with that of Doe v. Shewin, 3 Camp. 134. There, the lessee, being bound to insure and keep insured the premises, had neglected to pay the annual premium within the fifteen days limited by the policy. But the company afterwards accepted the premium, and gave a receipt in the usual form, whereby the instrument was restored to validity. But Lord Ellenborough, C. J., ruled, that, as there was an interval (about sixteen days), during which the landlord was exposed to the risk of fire, the covenant was broken, and the landlord entitled to recover at law—whatever relief there might be for the tenant in equity. It appears that the Court of Exchequer afterwards granted an injunction on payment of the costs of the action, but these were not paid, and the defendant became bankrupt. The application was then renewed on behalf of the assignees, but refused.[3] In subsequent cases, the court has refused

---

[1] Doe v. Carter, 8 T. R. 300. [2] Fox v. Swann, Sty. 483.
[3] Doe v. Shewin, 3 Camp. 134.

to grant an injunction against an ejectment for the breach of a covenant to insure against fire.[1]

It need scarcely be observed that, if the lessee does assign in violation of the covenant, the assigment is good to charge the assignee ; also, that if he assigns over in the same way, he ceases to be liable as assignee, though chargeable on the covenant not to assign.[2]

The term " bankruptcy " has a technical meaning, and denotes the event of the party becoming actually subject by adjudication to the bankrupt law, but the word "insolvency" has a wider signification, and though coupled with the word " Bankruptcy," means not only being brought up, or petitioning the Insolvent Debtors' Court, but a general inability to pay his debts. This is the ordinary meaning of the word, and the sense in which it will be taken unless the context shows that it was intended to have the more limited meaning. Hence, though an adjudication by the Insolvent Debtors' Court will be conclusive evidence of a breach, it is not the only evidence.

" I take insolvency to mean," said Le Blanc, J., in Bayly v. Schofield, 1 M. & S. 338, " as it respects a trader, that he is not in a situation to make his payments as usual, and it does not follow that he is not insolvent because he may ultimately have a surplus upon the winding up of his affairs." Bayley, J., observed in the same case, " Insolvency means that a trader is not able to keep his general days of payment, and that he is not to be considered as solvent because possibly his affairs may come round." A difficulty, however, in meeting a particular debt or demand is not evidence of insolvency, particularly for the purpose of working a forfeiture. It must be of a more general and extensive description ; a general composition or what is said to resemble a composition, the paying every creditor a little as it comes to hand.[3]

In Doe v. Rees, 4 B. N. C., 384, the defendant had obtained his discharge under the Insolvent Debtors' Act in January 1836 ; the lessor was a creditor to a considerable amount. He received rent which became due in respect of

[1] Reynolds v. Pitt, 19 Ves. 134 ; White v. Warner, 2 Mer. 459.
[2] Paul v. Nurse, 8 B. & C. 486.
[3] See Cutten v. Sanger, 2 Y. & J. 469.

the premises at Christmas 1837, and laid the demise in January 1838. The only proof of " insolvency" was the discharge, and the fact that the debt remained unpaid. But the former had been waived, and as to the latter, Tindal, C. J., said, " It is contended that the non-payment of a debt due to the lessor of the plaintiff constitutes a continuing insolvency. If so, any one debt due from a tenant to a landlord would constitute the tenant an insolvent. I think that such is not the meaning of the condition. Insolvency means a general inability to pay debts."

The onus of proof lies of course on the lessor, and though in the *construction* of the language of a proviso for re-entry, the courts incline neither to the one side nor the other, they hold the party seeking to enforce it strictly to the *proof* of that which he alleges as a breach. The rule is to presume nothing by way of evidence in favour of forfeiture. If the covenant be an affirmative one, the plaintiff must give negative evidence. Upon a covenant to insure, evidence that the defendant has refused invariably to show the policy, and the non-production of it at the trial after notice, is not even *primâ facie* evidence of a breach for this purpose, though it might be sufficient in an action of covenant.[1] Hence the propriety of adding a stipulation that the defendant shall show the policy or receipts when demanded, or that the non-production thereof shall be deemed sufficient evidence of a breach.

There is a peculiarity affecting the remedy by entry for non-payment of rent which should never be lost sight of in framing the proviso or the covenant. By the Common Law, unless the rent be made payable elsewhere, the lessee is not bound to go off the land to pay it ; and the lessor, in order to work a forfeiture, must demand the precise sum in person, or by an attorney lawfully constituted by warrant, at the front door of the house, or if there be no dwelling-house, on the most notorious and principal part of the premises, on the day when it becomes due, and about the time of sun-set; not before that period, nor so long after that there is not sufficient light to count the money.[2] The demand must be

---

[1] Doe v. Whitehead, 2 Jur. 493, Q. B.

[2] Maund's Case, 7 Co. 112 a ; Saund. 287, n. 16.

made though there be no one present to represent the lessee. If the condition be for payment within a given time after the rent day, then the demand must be made a convenient time before the last day.[1]

The inconveniences to which landlords were subjected by reason of the rule requiring these niceties have been partially removed by the statute 4 Geo. II., c. 28, s. 2, which enacts, "that in all cases between landlord and tenant as often as it shall happen that one half-year's rent shall be in arrear and the landlord or lessor to whom the same is due hath right by law to re-enter for the non-payment thereof, such landlord or lessor shall and may, without any formal demand or re-entry, serve a declaration in ejectment for the recovery of the demised premises, or in case the same cannot be legally served or no tenant be in actual possession of the premises, then to affix the same upon the door of any demised messuage, or in case such ejectment shall not be for the recovery of any messuage, then upon some notorious place of the lands, tenements, or hereditaments comprised in such declaration in ejectment, and such affixing shall be deemed legal service thereof, which service or affixing such declaration in ejectment shall stand in the place and stead of a demand and re-entry, and in case of judgment against the casual ejector or non-suit for not confessing lease, entry and ouster, it shall be made appear to the court where the said suit is depending, by affidavit, or be proved upon the trial in case the defendant appears, that half a year's rent was due before the said declaration was served, and that no sufficient distress was to be found on the demised premises countervailing the arrears then due, and that the lessor or lessors in ejectment had power to re-enter, then and in every such case, the lessor or lessors in ejectment shall recover judgment and execution in the same manner as if the rent in arrear had been legally demanded, and a re-entry made," &c. To sustain an ejectment under this statute it must be proved, not only that half a year's rent was due and that the lessor for the default had power by the terms of the lease to re-enter, but also that no sufficient distress could be found or got at upon any part of the premises, the whole having been carefully searched.[2] Unless these circumstances

---

[1] Maund's case, 7 Co. 112 a; Saund. 287, n. 16.
[2] See Doe v. Wandlass, 7 T. R. 117.

concur, the lessor is thrown back to the ceremonials before noticed, so that the relief given by the act is at best only partial and imperfect. The statute, however, dispenses with a demand in cases to which it applies, notwithstanding the proviso contains the words " being lawfully demanded." [1]

It is therefore highly expedient to provide that no demand of rent shall be necessary. This stipulation was always holden valid, and it should never be omitted.

In no other case is a demand of performance necessary in order to sustain an ejectment, unless required by the terms of the lease.

The proviso only operates during the term ; hence, if the lessee holds over so as to become tenant from year to year, though he may be subject to the terms of the lease, he is not liable to forfeiture in other respects. [2]

If with knowledge that the covenant has been broken, the lessor distrains, or does any other act amounting to a recognition of an existing tenancy, he waives the forfeiture and cannot afterwards take advantage of it.

It must first be observed that there is no difference as to this point, at the present day, between a proviso for re-entry, and a stipulation that the lease shall be void. It has long been settled, that an actual entry is unnecessary in order to determine an estate of this kind ; [3] and it is equally well established that the word " void" means only " voidable," [4] and as on the one hand none but the lessor has the option of avoiding the instrument, [5] so on the other, any act of recognition will establish it again. To an action in a bond against a surety for payment of the rent, the defendant pleaded a proviso in the lease, that if the rent should be unpaid by the space of forty days, the demise &c. should be utterly void to all intents and purposes ; that at a period before the arrears sued for became due, the rent had been unpaid by the space of

---

[1] Doe v. Alexander, 2 M & S. 525.   [2] See Johns v. Whittey, 3 Wils. 140.
[3] See per Curiam in Doe v. Masters, 2 B. & C. 492.
[4] Doe v. Banks, 4 B. & A. 401 ; Daken v. Cope, 2 Russ. 170.
[5] Doe v. Birch, 1 M. & W. 402 ; Rede v. Farr, 6 M. & S. 121 ; Roberts v. Davey, 4 B. & Ad. 664.

forty days, whereby the indenture became void.   On demurrer judgment was given for the plaintiff, on the ground that the proviso did not vacate the lease, except as against the lessee, the principle of law being that a party shall not take advantage of his own wrong.[1]

The question of waiver is one of fact for the jury, but there are some acts which of themselves are deemed conclusive and upon which a jury will be directed to find for the defendant.   Such is the levying a distress for the rent subsequently to the breach relied on, and with knowledge thereof.[2]   A demand of such rent also (unless qualified) followed up by payment, appears to be evidence of the same nature; but the acceptance of rent without demand is equivocal.[3]   A landlord is not to refuse a payment made without action, for he is equally entitled to the rent whether he insist on the forfeiture or not;[4] though if it be accepted without any mention of the breach, there might be fair ground to presume a waiver.   Of course the acceptance of rent which became due *after* the breach is conclusive;[5] but there can be no question of waiver unless the breach is complete at the time of the act done.   Thus where the proviso was on non-payment within twenty-one days, and the landlord distrained *before* but continued in possession *after* that time, there being no sufficient distress, it was ruled that he had not waived his right to re-enter.[6]

It is not uncommon to find a covenant to repair generally, and a covenant to repair within a given time after notice, with a general proviso for re-entry.   These are treated as independent covenants, upon either of which the lessor may re-enter,[7] and differ from a covenant to repair and at all events within three months after notice, which is one qualified stipulation.[8]   In these cases, if the lessor gives notice to repair according to the terms of the latter, he impliedly waives the benefit of the former covenant;[9] but a general

[1] Rede v. Farr, 6 M. & S. 121.
[2] Pennant's Case, 3 Co. 64, *sed qu.* since 8 Ann. c. 14.
[3] Id. Doe v. Nash, 1 M. & W. 402.   [4] Id.
[5] See Amsby v. Woodward, 6 B., C. 519.   [6] Doe v. Johnson, 1 Stark. 411.
[7] See Wood v. Day, 7 Taunt. 646.   [8] Horsfall v. Testar, 7 Taunt. 385.
[9] Doe v. Menx. 4 B. & C. 606.

notice requiring the party to repair, not mentioning any time and not purporting to follow the special covenant, has not this effect, it being no more than a demand of performance.[6]   In Doe v. Lewis, 5 Ad. & Ell. 277, after a general covenant to repair, there followed a stipulation that the lessor and his assigns should be at liberty to enter at all seasonable times to view the state of the premises, and upon every such view to give or leave notice in writing for the lessee of all defects, &c. ; and in case he should neglect or refuse to repair the said defects within two calendar months afterwards, it should be lawful for the lessor, &c., with workmen and labourers, to enter and do such repairs as he or they should think necessary ; and that the lessee should repay the money expended with his next half year's rent, or in default the lessor should have power to distrain for the same as rent. Then followed a proviso, that if the rent or any such increase should be behind for fifteen days, or if the lessee should not in all things well and truly perform all the covenants, the lessor should be at liberty to re-enter.   The premises being out of repair, the lessor gave a notice requiring certain things to be done, and stating that in case of neglect the premises would be put in order, and the lessee be charged with the costs.   The repairs were not done by either party, and at the expiration of the notice the action was brought.   It was holden that by giving such notice the lessor had waived his right of re-entry, and that his only remedy was to do the repairs himself, and distrain according to the warning given in case the charges were not paid.

An agreement to enlarge the time for repairing does not operate as a waiver of the right, but at the expiration of the time the lessor may maintain ejectment without a fresh notice.   On this ground proceeded the judgment in Doe v. Brendley, 4 B. & Ad. 84.   The lease contained a covenant to repair, and a proviso for re-entry in case of non-repair within three months after notice.   A notice was given, but before its expiration the plaintiff commenced an ejectment.   At the trial a juror was withdrawn by consent, the plaintiff finding that he could not maintain the action ; and by an order of court, the defendant was to put the premises in repair by a

[1] Roe v. Paine, 2 Camp. 520.

given day, being six months from the time when the notice
was given.   Having failed to do so, another action was
brought, and held maintainable without a new notice.

The receipt of rent before the expiration of the notice does
not of course amount to a waiver, since the forfeiture is not
complete until that time.   So where the covenant is so
framed as that the continuance of the act or omission amounts
to a new breach, the doctrine of waiver is inapplicable.
Where the covenant was not to alter, convert, or *use* the
rooms then used as bed-rooms for any other purpose than
bed or sitting rooms for the occupation of the lessee himself or his family; and the lessee had let part of them to
a lodger, but the lessor had received rent after he knew of
such occupation; it was holden that though a conversion or
alteration would be a breach complete at once, the using
constituted a new breach every day, of which the landlord
might take advantage.[1]   So of a covenant "to insure and
keep insured" the premises, and lodge the policy with the
lessor, the court held the true construction to be, not that
the lessee should effect one policy and keep that on foot, in
which case the breach would have been waived, but that he
should always keep the premises insured by some policy or
another, and that there was a continuing breach for any portion of time that they remained uninsured.[2]   Where a lease of a
colliery provided that if the works should stop or cease at any
time for two years, the lease should be void; it was holden
that the landlord might make it void at the end of any two
years during which there had been a continued cesser to
work, even on the day after he had received the rent.[3]   In
Doe v. Bliss. 4 Taunt. 735, the tenant, in violation of his covenant, had underlet part of the premises, year after year,
with the knowledge of the landlord, who nevertheless received rent after it; and the Court of Common Pleas held
that he had not lost his right of re-entry.   It would seem,
however, from the report, that the action was brought on a
new underletting.

[1] Doe v. Woodbridge, 9 B. & C. 376.
[2] Doe v. Peck, 1 B. & Ad. 428.
[3] Doe v. Bancks, 4 B. & A. 401.   This decision was doubted of by Lord
Eldon in Dakin v. Cope, 2 Russ. 170.

Again, to constitute a waiver it is essential that the lessor, when he does the act, should have knowledge of the forfeiture. Hence, where after a forfeiture incurred by underletting, the lessor accepted rent, and it was evident from his having, when applied to, refused permission to underlet, that he was not aware of the fact, it was held that he had not by acceptance of the rent waived his right of re-entry.[1] So where the son of the lessor, acting as his agent, during his father's illness, had, after notice of a breach, demanded rent, but it was not shown that the lessor himself was cognizant of what had been done, the court held there was no evidence of a waiver. "The son," observed Parke, B., "had probably an authority to receive the rent, but not to grant a new lease by waiving the forfeiture of the former one."[2]

Acquiescence before breach, which may with greater propriety be denominated a "dispensation" than a "waiver," equally prevents the lessor from insisting on the forfeiture. In one case, where the condition was that the lessee should not permit any person to inhabit the premises who would use certain trades, the lessor lived next door and witnessed the conversion of the premises to their obnoxious uses by the assignee of the lease for upwards of six years, and then brought an ejectment for the forfeiture, yet he was held entitled to recover. It did not appear that he had received any rent since, and the court held that mere knowledge and acquiescence did not amount to a waiver ; that there must be some act affirming the tenancy; but Mansfield, C. J., suggested that if it had appeared that a great deal of money had been laid out by the defendant in improving and repairing the premises, that would have been a strong circumstance from which a jury might imply a consent to the alteration.[3] There can scarcely be a doubt, that, had the question been left to the jury, as it certainly would be at the present day, they would have come to a different conclusion. In a recent case the lessor agreed with the person in possession to grant a new lease to take effect at the expiration of the old one, and it was held that he could not afterwards insist on the forfeiture occasioned by the lessee

[1] Doe v. Harrison, 2 T. R. 425. See Pennant's Case, 3 Co. 64.
[2] Doe v. Birch, 1 M. & W. 402.
[4] Doe v. Allen, 3 Taunt. 78.

having assigned or underlet without a licence in writing.[1] Where the lessee being under a covenant to insure in the name of himself and the lessor, let the lease and counterpart remain with the lessor, an attorney, as a security for money lent, and after having from him an abstract in which it was stated merely that the tenant was to " insure and keep insured the premises," &c. effected the policy in his own name only, Abbott, C. J., put it to the jury, whether, after seeing the abstract, the defendant did not as a reasonably prudent man, think he was doing all that was necessary, for if so, although there was no express dispensation, the lessor would not be entitled to recover; and the jury found for the defendant.[2] Where after a breach by not completing the houses in proper time, the lessor advised the defendant to " take to " the premises, and it appeared that at the time he had an annuity secured on them, Abbott, C. J., said, " that if he had had no interest in them before, the lessor could not after such advice, have insisted on the forfeiture, but under the circumstances it was no more than advising him to make the best of his security, and there was no waiver."[3]

A licence to assign amounts to a perpetual dispensation of a covenant not to assign without licence. This was settled in Dumper's Case, 4 Co. 119, and has ever since been considered law, though it has never received the approbation of the profession.[4] The condition was, that the lessee *or his assigns* should not alien the premises to any person or persons, without the special licence of the lessor. Afterwards the lessor licenced the lessee to alien or demise the land or any part of it to any person or persons whomsoever. The lessee assigned, the assignee devised to his son and executor who died intestate, and his administrator assigned to the defendant. The court resolved that the alienation by licence had determined the condition, so that no subsequent alienation could break the proviso or give cause of entry to the lessors, for that they could not dispense with an alienation at one time, and the same estate remain subject to the proviso after. Upon the same principle, if a lease be made to three upon condition

[1] Doe v. Curwood, 1 H. & W. 140.	[2] Doe v. Rowe, 2 C. & P. 247.
[3] Doe v. Eykins, 1 C. & P. 154; R. & M. 29.
[4] See Doe v. Bliss, 4 Taunt. 735.

that they or any one of them shall not alien without the assent of the lessor, and afterwards the lessor gives a licence to ône, the other two may assign without it.[1] So if he licenses the alienation of a part, the lessee may alien the whole, for a condition cannot be apportioned by act of the parties, and as the lessor cannot enter into the part aliened by licence, he cannot enter at all.[2]

There is less inconvenience arising out of the doctrine of this case than might have been anticipated, because its authority is admitted only where there is an actual, express dispensation or licence given according to the requisitions of the lease. Thus, if the lessor by some act of acquiescence amounting to a waiver loses or gives up his right to insist on the forfeiture, this does not bind him as to future alienations.[3] And where the lessee was prohibited from letting or assigning without a licence *in writing*, it was holden that a parol licence to let part, though sufficient to prevent the lessor from setting up that letting as a breach, did not prevent his re-entry for letting the residue.[4]

The person who recovers for a condition broken, is in of his first estate. The recovery defeats all rights and incidents annexed to the estate of the lessee and all his mesne incumbrances.[5] The lessor is entitled to the emblements, and it is not necessary for this purpose that the breach should be entirely the act of the party himself, for where the forfeiture is incurred immediately by act of law, as by bankruptcy or seizure in execution, yet this is but the consequence of some act or default of the tenant with which in law he is chargeable.[6]

We have before observed that at Common Law a right of entry could not be reserved to any but the lessor and his heirs or executors, according to the nature of his estate. The same principle required that it should not be granted over, and therefore, if the reversion were assigned, the condition was gone, for the grantee could not take advantage of the condition, nor could the grantor, as he had nothing left in the estate. Another maxim of law is that every condition must defeat the entire estate, and that a condition cannot be so framed as to make one and the same estate in any lands cease

---

[1] Leeds v. Crompton, Cro. El. 816, cited ib. [2] Ib.
[3] Doe v. Bliss, 4 Taunt. 735. [4] Roe v. Harrison, 2 T. R. 425.
[5] 1 Rol. Ab. 474. [6] Davis v. Eyton, 7 Bing. 154.

as to one person and remain as to another, or cease for one time and revive afterwards.[1]   But if a man make a feoffment in fee of Blackacre and Whiteacre upon condition, &c., and for breach thereof that he shall enter into Blackacre, this is good.[2]   Again, a condition cannot be apportioned by act of the parties so as to become void as to one part of the land, and remain good as to the other.   Thus if the lessor of three acres grants away the reversion of one, neither he nor the assignee can enter for the condition broken, for he that enters for a condition broken, must have been in of his old estate, and that he could not be when he had granted away a part.[3]   But a condition might always have been apportioned by act of law.   As if a man seised of two acres, the one in fee, and the other in borough-English, has issue two sons, and leases both acres for life or years, rendering rent with condition, the lessor dies, in this case by this descent, which is an act in law, the reversion, rent, and condition are divided. Also it may be apportioned by act and wrong of the lessee, as if he makes a feoffment of part and the lessor enters for the forfeiture, there the condition remains for the residue, for none shall take advantage of his own wrong.[4]

Such being the common law, it was enacted by the statute 32 Hen. VIII. c. 34, s. 1, " that as well all and every person and persons and bodies politic, their heirs, successors and assigns which have or shall have any gift or grant of our said sovereign lord, of any lordships, manors, lands, tenements, rents, parsonages, tithes, portions, or any other hereditaments, or of any reversion or reversions of the same, &c.,—as also all other persons being grantees or assignees to or by any other person or persons than the king's highness, and the heirs, executors, successors and assigns of every of them, shall and may have and enjoy like advantages, against the lessees, their executors, administrators and assigns, by entry for non-payment of rent or for doing of waste or other forfeiture; and also shall and may have and enjoy all and every such like and the same advantage, benefit, and remedies by action only for not performing other conditions, covenants and agreements contained and expressed in the indentures of their said leases,

---

[1] Mildmay's Case, 6 Co. 40 a.   [2] Co. Litt. 202 b.
[3] See Dumper's Case, 4 Co. 120 ; Knight's Case, 5 Co. 55.
[4] Dumper's Case, sup.

demises or grants, against all and every the said lessees, their executors, &c. as the said lessors or grantors themselves or their heirs should or might have had, &c."

Notwithstanding, the words of the act appear to put the assignee precisely in the assignor's place, the phrase " other forfeiture" is taken to refer to forfeitures of the same nature as those mentioned, viz. such as are incident to or for the benefit of the reversion, as for keeping the houses in repair, scouring of ditches, preserving of woods, or the like, and not for the payment of any sum in gross delivery of corn, wood, &c.[1] Covenants or stipulations running with the land, of which alone the assignee can therefore take advantage, are defined in modern language to be such only as concern the nature, value, or mode of occupation of the thing demised. Hence it has been doubted whether the assignee of the reversion can take advantage of a. condition of re-entry, if the lessee shall assign without licence.[2] It must be observed that though the assignee of the lessee may not be liable on the covenant by reason of its not running with the land, he is so far bound to perform it that the lessor himself or his heirs may enter for the breach of it the same as he might have entered on the lessee himself. In this respect covenants and conditions widely differ. Hence, where the breach was that the defendant who had taken the lease by assignment had omitted to insure, the court forbore to enter into the question, whether he might have been sued on the covenant, holding that by not doing so he had at all events, as against the lessor, committed a forfeiture.[3]

The alterations made by this statute are chiefly these. That assuming the condition to be one which affects the reversion, or, in ordinary language, runs with the land, an assignee of the whole estate of the lessor may bring ejectment for the forfeiture. So if he have not the whole estate, provided he have some reversion in the whole of the demised premises, he may equally avail himself of the condition. As if lessee for life be, and the reversion is granted for life. So if lessee for years be, and the reversion is granted for years, the grantee for years shall take benefit of the condition in respect of the word " executors" in the act.[4] But where only

---

[1] Co. Litt. 215 a.
[2] Lucas v. How. T. Ray, 250.
[3] Doe v. Peck, 1 B. & Ad. 428.
[4] Co. Litt. 215 a.

a reversion in part of the demised premises is granted, as in the instance just mentioned, the case remains as at common law, and neither the assignee nor the lessor can enter for a breach. The condition is wholly gone, but the covenants are divisible, and each may sue thereon in respect of his particular reversion.[1]

It is important also to observe that the statute does not vest in the grantee a right of action or of entry for a breach committed before the execution of the grant or assignment. A right of entry, so far as it is a chose in action, is not assignable. Therefore, if after a breach committed, the lessor conveys away the reversion, neither can maintain ejectment for the forfeiture.[2]

An assignee is a person who has the estate to which the condition is annexed, whether he comes to it by conveyance in pais, or by act and operation of law. If tenant for life or in tail with power to lease, make a demise with proviso for re-entry, the remainder-man has the benefit of it. But if lessee for years underlet, and then assign his reversion, and the assignee purchase the reversion in fee and take a conveyance to himself, he can no longer avail himself of the covenants of the sub-lessee, the reversion to which they were annexed being extinguished.[3] So a person who comes in by title paramount is not an assignee, as the lord by escheat.[4] A surviving wife cannot avail herself of the conditions in an under-lease of her land made by the husband.[5] If an executor demise and die intestate, the administrator de bonis non is a stranger to the covenants in the lease.[6]

5. As to relief against forfeitures. It is the standing rule of Courts of Equity, that a forfeiture shall not bind where the thing may be done afterwards, or where a full compensation may be made. Hence, when the tenant failed in performance of a covenant to lay out a given sum by a given time in repairs, and the landlord had commenced an ejectment, the court interfered by injunction upon the terms of the lessee paying all costs at law and in equity, and expending not only the stipulated amount, but so much in addition as would put the premises in the state in which they would have been

---

[1] Kitchen v. Buckley, 1 Lev. 109.
[2] See Fenn v. Smart, 12 Ea. 444.
[3] See Webb v. Russell, 3 T. & R. 393.
[4] Co. Litt. 215 b.
[5] Co. Litt. 46 b.
[6] Bailey v. Drew, 2 Lev. 100.

had the covenant been duly performed; for the principle is full compensation, and the increase of the price of labour and materials must not be thrown on the landlord.[1] Where therefore, from the nature of the covenant, a full compensation cannot be made, or where the court cannot estimate its amount, there can be no relief. On this ground, where the breach is general non-repair, assigning or underletting, or mismanaging the estate, the court will not in general interfere.[2] An injunction has been repeatedly refused where the action proceeded on the breach of a covenant to insure against fire.[3]

This jurisdiction is participated in one instance by courts of law; where, before the statute 4 Geo. II. c. 28, if an ejectment were pending for a forfeiture by non-payment of rent, the defendant might have procured a stay of proceedings by paying the amount due and all costs into court. And now by that statute it is enacted " that if the tenant or tenants, his, her or their assignee or assignees, do or shall at any time before the trial in such ejectment pay or tender to the lessor or landlord, his executors or administrators, or his, her or their attorney in that cause, or pay into court where the same cause is depending, all the rent and arrears, together with the costs, then and in such case all further proceedings in the said ejectment shall cease and be discontinued." This enactment is not confined to such ejectments as are provided for by the second section, viz. where there is no sufficient distress on the premises, but extends to all actions founded on non-payment of rent; and a mortgagee of the lease is entitled to the benefit of it, though he has not become a party to the action.[4] After trial, a court of law will not now interfere, the statute being construed to legalize the practice which before obtained only to a certain extent, viz., upon the application of the tenant *before* trial.[5] But where the tenant has not appeared and judgment has gone against the casual ejector, the proceedings have been stayed even

---

[1] Saunders v. Pope, 12 Ves. 282.

[2] Wadman v. Calcraft, 10 Ves. 67.

[3] Reynolds v. Pitt, 19 Ves. 134; White v. Warner, 2 Mer. 459; see Doe v. Shewin, 3 Camp. 135, n.

[4] Doe v. Roe, 3 Taunt. 402.

[5] Roe v. Davis, 7 Ea. 363; Doe v. Masters, 2 B. & C. 490.

after execution, and the premises ordered to be given up.[1] The application is in form to stay proceedings upon payment of the rent and costs, and it may be made to a judge at chambers.[2]

When the action is for other breaches besides that of non-payment of rent, the courts, upon the equity of the statute, will allow the tenant to pay into court the rent and costs, and prohibit the lessor from availing himself of such breach upon the trial.[3]

The foregoing enactment does not in any way interfere with the jurisdiction of courts of equity; but by the second section, "in case the lessee or lessees, his, her or their assignee or assignees, or other person or persons claiming or deriving under the said leases, shall permit and suffer judgment to be had and recovered on such ejectment, and execution to be executed thereon without paying the rent and arrears, together with full costs, and without filing any bill or bills for relief in equity within six calendar months after such execution executed, then and in such case the said lessee or lessees, his, her or their assignee or assignees, and all other persons claiming and deriving under the said lease, shall be barred and foreclosed from all relief or remedy in law or equity other than by writ of error for reversal of such judgment in case the same shall be erroneous, and the said landlord or lessor shall from thenceforth hold the said demised premises discharged from such lease."

There is a proviso "that nothing therein contained shall extend to bar the right of any mortgagee or mortgagees of such lease or any part thereof who shall not be in possession, so as such mortgagee or mortgagees shall and do within six calendar months after such judgment obtained and execution executed, pay all rent in arrear and all costs and damages sustained by such lessor, person or persons entitled to the remainder or reversion as aforesaid, and perform all the covenants and agreements which on the part and behalf of the first lessee or lessees are and ought to be performed."

L.

---

[1] Doe v. Roe, sup.
[2] Ca. Pr. C. P. 6.   [3] B. N. P. 97.

ART. V.—THE LAW OF JUDGMENTS.

THE law respecting judgments has been so materially altered by the late Act 1 & 2 Vict. c. 110, ss. 11 and 13, that some remarks on the subject cannot but prove interesting.

It is well known that, at the common law, a judgment creditor could not, except in special cases, attach the land of his debtor. This was altered by the legislature by 13 Edw. I. s. 1, c. 18 ; which enacts that it should be in the election of such a creditor to have a writ of *fieri facias*, or that the sheriff should deliver to him all the chattels of the debtor (saving only his oxen and beasts of his plough,) and " the one-half of his land." The latter words appear to be ambiguous, and a question was raised, whether they extended to the land which the debtor had at the time of the judgment being recovered, or that which he had when execution was sued, and it was determined that half of the land which the debtor had at the time of the judgment being given, and at any time afterwards, was liable.' So that as Cruise writes, a judgment binds all the lands whereof the debtor was seised at the time when the judgment was entered, or which he afterwards acquires ; and no subsequent act of his, not even an alienation for a valuable consideration to a purchaser without notice of the judgment, will avoid it.[2] But it is remarkable, that, though it was held that the sheriff might, under the words we are now considering, extend leasehold lands,[3] it was also held that such lands were not bound till execution was sued.[4] Of course trusts, or equitable estates, or interests, were not liable ; nor were copyhold lands.

The most remarkable question upon this ancient statute occurred very recently:—Lands were limited to such uses as A. should appoint, and in default of appointment to A., his heirs and assigns. A judgment is then duly entered up against A. Subsequently, A. appoints the lands to B. for a term of 500 years. The judgment creditor then sues execution, and the question was, whether the lands vested in B.

---

[1] 2 Inst. 395 ; 10 Vin. Abr. 562 (t).   [2] 2 Cruise Dig. 58.   [3] 2 Inst. 395.
[4] Fleetwood's case, 8 Rep. 171 ; 10 Vin. 567, pl. 11.

could be taken. The case appears to have been chiefly argued and decided with reference to this rule, that a party taking under a power, takes from the date of the appointment, just as if the limitation to him had been inserted in the deed creating the power instead of the power; and, consequently, that B.'s estate was prior to A.'s and could not be liable to judgments against A. This decision is certainly of high authority, for it has not only the sanction of the court in which it was first made, but has since been acted upon by the court of Chancery.[1] But it must be observed, that at the time the judgment was entered up against A., the lands were *his;* he had a fee simple, though defeasible by virtue of the power. Do the words of the statute, "his lands," fairly include such an estate? And we believe it is acknowledged that they do; and if A. had conveyed without reference to his power, his alienee would have had no defence against the judgment. It might then have been strongly urged, and it appears that in Chancery the point was made, but the foundation of the judgment creditor's right, the statute of Edward, was not alluded to, A.'s estate in the lands was charged or affected by an act of parliament, can A., by his own act, defeat a charge or right so created and given? A bankrupt was never allowed to defeat the estate which the legislature enabled the commissioners to convey.[2] The only answer given to this was, " the plaintiff is merely a judgment creditor, without any lien by contract *or other title* than what her judgment gives her." It is submitted that if the statute of Edward had been remembered, this could not have been said.

We come now to the 29 Car. II. c. 3, s. 10, by which it was enacted, that it should be lawful for every officer to whom any writ should be directed, at the suit of any person upon any judgment, to deliver execution of all such lands and hereditaments as any other person should be in any manner or wise seised or posessed in trust for him, against whom execution was sued, like as the officer might have done if the said party against whom execution should be sued, had been seised of such lands or hereditaments of such estate as they

[1] Doe v. Jones, 10 Barn. & Cr. 459; Skeeles v. Shearly, 3 Myl. & Cr. 112.

[2] Doe d. Coleman v. Britain, 2 Barn. & Ald. 93.

should be seised of in trust for him, at the time of the said execution sued.

Upon this enactment it has been determined that the debtor must have the sole equitable interest, not one depending upon the payment of debts or the like.[1] It has also been held that an equity of redemption is not within the words of the act.[2]

It does not appear to have been decided, but the general impression we apprehend is, that if a debtor had only the trust of a term, that is, the equitable interest in a term of years, the land could not be extended under this clause. Lord Thurlow's observation was, execution shall be delivered of lands just as if the debtor had been seised, if there be but a term it is impossible he can be seised.[3] It will be observed that the clause is not carefully worded ; in the former part it is seised or possessed, but in the latter only seised. But this is narrow ground to take, and perhaps if the question were now considered, the clause would be thought applicable to leaseholds as well as freehold lands.—(See Doe d. Phillips v. Evans, 1 Crom. & Mee. 450.) If a debtor's interest in a term is simple and precise, though it be but an equity, there cannot be any greater difficulty in practice in extending the lands than if the estate of the debtor were an equitable freehold or fee simple. Lord Ellenborough's decision in Scott v. Scholey[4] was right, on the ground that the debtor had not the sole right in the term.

It will be observed that the above enactment only extends to lands in which the debtor has an equitable interest at the time execution is sued ; but Chancery holds that if a party who purchases an equitable interest, though he gets also a conveyance of the legal estate, has notice of a judgment, he is bound by it.[5]

Here we may notice the protection which a satisfied term used to afford to purchasers, for if it was assigned in trust for the purchaser before execution was sued, a judgment creditor of the vendor could not have the land during the term. But Chancery holds a judgment to be a lien upon any equitable in-

---

[1] Doe v. Greenhill, 4 Barn. & Ald. 684.   [2] Lyster v. Dolland, 1 Ves. jun. 431.
[3] 1 Ves. jun. 435.   [4] 8 East, 467.   [5] Tunstall v. Trappes, 3 Sim. 286.

terest whatever the debtor may have, and that if the purchaser had notice, he is bound by it, and therefore a term was no protection if notice could be proved.—(See Tunstall v. Trappes, 3 Sim. 286.)　　It should be observed, that where the estate or interest of a debtor is legal, a judgment is no lien in equity : [1] hence a legal term might be purchased, though there was notice of a judgment, if no execution was sued out.　　In the case of a satisfied term, the trust of which was simply for the owner of the estate, it may be doubted whether a purchaser might not have been free from the judgment though he had notice, for it might have been argued, and may still be contended, in a case not within the new law, that a judgment is not a lien in equity where it is a lien at law; and that the judgment was a lien by the 10th section of the statute of frauds, upon the lands in the term, though the interest of the debtor was but equitable, and consequently there was no place for an equitable lien.　　In stating this, we are aware of the doubt expressed by Sir Edward Sugden, whether, with respect to lands extendible by force of the 10th section of the statute of frauds, Chancery does not give the judgment creditor an equitable lien *ultra* his remedy under the statute.　　Mr. Coote is in error in stating in his book on Mortgages, that this question was determined in Tunstall v. Trappes, just cited ; it does not appear to have been mentioned, and the facts, as stated, did not allow of its being discussed.　　In that case the judgment debtor had a mere equity of redemption, subject to several charges, and the fee was vested in a trustee to discharge the incumbrances. Cranmer, who had notice of the judgment, had the fee conveyed to him, and he, after paying the several charges, lent a further sum to the judgment debtor, Shadwell, V. C. decided that Cranmer was entitled to priority over the judgment debt, as to such of the charges paid off by him, as were created prior to the time when he had notice of the judgment, but as to the residue of the sum lent by Cranmer, the judgment creditor had priority.　　A similar decision was made by the same judge, in the same cause, in favor of a judgment creditor who had neglected to register his judgment.

After this short sketch of the law as it lately was, we pro-

---

[1] See Forth v. Duke of Norfolk, 4 Madd. 503.

ceed to consider the late very important enactments respecting judgments.

The recital or preamble is, " Whereas the existing law is defective in not providing adequate means for enabling judgment creditors to obtain satisfaction from the property of their debtors, and it is expedient to give judgment creditors more effectual remedies against the real and personal estate of their debtors than they possess under the existing law." This is followed by several enactments relating to judgments, two of which we must set out fully.

Sect. 11. " That it shall be lawful for the sheriff, or other officer to whom any writ of elegit, or any precept in pursuance thereof, shall be directed, at the suit of any person, upon any judgment which, at the time appointed for the commencement of this act, shall have been recovered, or shall be thereafter recovered in any action in any of her majesty's superior courts at Westminster, to make and deliver execution unto the party in that behalf suing, of all such lands, tenements, rectories, tithes, rents, and hereditaments, including lands and hereditaments of copyhold or customary tenure, as the person against whom execution is so sued, or any person in trust for him, shall have been seised or possessed of at the time of entering up the said judgment, or at any time afterwards, or over which such person shall, at the time of entering up such judgment, or at any time afterwards, have any disposing power which he might, without the assent of any other person, exercise for his own benefit, in like manner as the sheriff or other officer may now make and deliver execution of one moiety of the lands and tenements of any person against whom a writ of elegit is sued out."

Sect. 13. " And be it enacted, That a judgment already entered up, or to be hereafter entered up against any person in any of her Majesty's superior courts at Westminster, shall operate as a charge upon all lands, tenements, rectories, advowsons, tithes, rents, and hereditaments, (including lands and hereditaments of copyhold or customary tenure) of or to which such person shall, at the time of entering up such judgment, or at any time afterwards, be seised, possessed, or entitled for any estate or interest whatever, at law or in equity, whether in possession, reversion, remainder, or expectancy, or over which such person shall, at the time of entering up such judgment, or at any time afterwards, have any disposing power which he might, without the assent of any other person, exercise for his own benefit, and shall be binding as against the person against whom the judgment shall be so entered up, and against all persons claiming under him, after such judgment, and shall also be binding as against the issue of his body, and all other persons whom he might, without the assent of any other person, cut off and debar from any remainder, reversion, or other interest in or out of any of the said lands, tenements, rectories, advowsons, tithes, rents, and hereditaments ; and that every judgment creditor shall have such and the same remedies in a court of equity, against the hereditaments so charged by virtue of this act, or any part thereof, as he would be entitled to in case the person against whom such judgment shall have been so entered up, had power to charge the same hereditaments, and had, by writing under his hand, agreed to charge the same with the amount of such judgment debt, and interest thereon : Provided that no judgment creditor shall be entitled to proceed in equity, to obtain the benefit of such charge, until after the expiration of one year from the time of entering up such judgment, or in cases of judgments already entered up, or to be entered up before the time appointed for the commencement of this act, until after the expiration of one year from the time appointed for the commencement of this act, nor shall such charge operate to give the judgment creditor any preference in case of the bankruptcy of the person against whom judgment shall have been entered up, unless such judgment shall have been entered up one year at least, before the bankruptcy : Provided also, that as regards purchasers, mortgagees, or creditors, who shall have become such before the time appointed for the commencement of this act, such judgment shall not affect lands, tenements or hereditaments, otherwise than as the same would have been affected by such judgment if this act had not passed : Provided also, that nothing herein contained shall be deemed or taken to alter or affect any doctrine of courts of equity, whereby protection is given to purchasers for valuable consideration, without notice."

The 11th section applies only to judgments " recovered" in an action. It has been suggested that lands may be freed from being *extended* under an elegit, through the operation of a joint power. Thus, if lands are limited to such uses as A. and B. shall jointly appoint, with remainder to A. the real owner in fee, it is contended, that a person purchasing and having an appointment made to him under the joint power, would be free from any judgment *recovered* against A. To this it may be objected : 1. That a party cannot defeat a charge imposed upon his estate by act of parliament ; and that the act gives the judgment creditor a lien upon the estate of A. in default of appointment, whether it be legal or equitable, and that this lien A. cannot discharge by concurring in the exercise of the joint power. 2. Supposing the lien upon the estate of A., in default of appointment, to depend upon the existence of that estate, and to fail when it is determined, that estate gives A. a "disposing power," which he might, without the assent of any other person, exercise for his own benefit, and, therefore, the land is subject to the lien, though it be transferred to a purchaser under the power.

It seems to have been thought that the proviso, with which the 13th section concludes, extends to even the lien or charge created by the 11th section, but that we think is clearly a mistake. The position of the proviso and the nature of it are both against the conclusion. The doctrine of courts of equity respecting protection to purchasers without notice has never been applied to legal liens. Suppose under the old law a cestui que trust and his trustee had conveyed an estate to a purchaser, who paid his money without notice of any judgment, but, in fact, unknown to him, execution had been sued out previously to the conveyance being signed, would the purchaser have held free from the debt?—We apprehend clearly not. The 11th section gives a legal right, and this, according to the doctrine in question, cannot be defeated by a legal estate or right subsequently acquired. The proviso in question has a proper subject to which it may be applied, and in connexion with which we find it, why then extend it to restrict a right to which it has properly no application? If this proviso is applicable to cases within the the 12th section, a creditor would in some cases have a less effectual remedy than he had before; he might be defeated by a conveyance to a purchaser without notice.

The 11th section seems to apply to leaseholds, whether the debtor have the legal or only an equitable estate therein, and if so, the same are now liable from the time of the judgment being entered up. This is a most important point. If under the statute of Edward, which had only the word "*lands*," leaseholds might be extended, it is impossible to deny that the words of the 11th section are sufficient to comprise them; besides the strong argument arising from the Act being for creditors, we have the words "tenements," and seised or *pos-*

sessed." If this be so, the protection which a satisfied term used in certain cases to afford against judgments is gone nay, such a term might prove injurious to a purchaser. Suppose by means of some device the fee could be vested in a purchaser free from the legal lien of the judgments of the vendor, if there happened to be a term in trust for the vendor, that would be liable to the judgments and would enable the creditor to extend the lands in the hands of the purchaser. Assuming that leaseholds were held not to be within the words of the 11th section, it might be said, that the trust of the term gave the party an absolute disposing power over the lands therein comprised.

The 13th section enacts that every judgment, however entered up, shall operate as a charge upon all lands in which the debtor has any estate or interest whatsoever, or over which he has a sole disposing power; it does not say equitable charge; but the creditor shall have the same remedy in a court of equity as if the debtor had charged his estate or interest by writing; but this remedy is made subject to the doctrine of courts of equity, whereby protection is given to purchasers without notice.

Assuming that through the operation of a joint power, or other device, the legal lien given to a judgment creditor by the 11th section may be defeated, whether the purchaser has notice or not, the question arises whether the charge created by the 13th section is likewise defeated. It is contended that it is; on the ground that the charge attached only on defeasible estate, and that the second member of the 13th section only shows how the charge may be worked out, and does not alter its nature. If this be so, and there is some occasion for the construction, the 13th section is almost, if not altogether, a dead letter, for the court of Chancery has long been used to do all that this section could do if qualified, as suggested. But, we think, Chancery will not deal so ungraciously with this enactment as to decide that there is no life in it; and, indeed, though the words are not so well pointed as they might be, considerable astuteness is required to show that they have only the effect attributed to them. The object of the framer of the clause, probably, was to preclude the argument (1) that a judgment is only a general charge and not a specific lien and (2) that it is not equivalent to a charge by the agreement of the party, and seeing that the act is remedial and in favour of common honesty, a court will not search with eagle's eyes to defeat it. In consequence of the difficulties which oppose any endeavour to discover equitable interests and liens, the sympathy of a court of equity has always been with a purchaser without notice, but the feeling will not, it is apprehended, be with a purchaser who purchases with notice, or who neglects, or studiously avoids searching the register provided by this act, and so wilfully shuts his eyes against the dangers he might easily escape without any difficulty, and at a trifling expense.

Consider how the point would have been before the statute of uses and of frauds. The use under the joint power is a springing use, which cannot arise without the consent of the party having the ultimate use; would not a purchaser of the springing use have been held liable to a judgment against the sole owner of the beneficial interest in such use, of which he, the purchaser, had notice? Suppose, before the act we are now considering, an equity of redemption had been limited to such uses, and upon and for such trusts and purposes, as the mortgagor and a trustee should by any deed executed by them in the presence of four witnesses appoint, and in default of appointment, to the use of the mortgagor in fee; could a purchaser of the equity have been advised to rely upon an appointment as a protection against judgments, of which he had notice? If Chancery would have so protected a charge created by its own authority, it would not be unwilling to enforce a lien consigned to its care by act of parliament. We should say, then, that a purchaser indulges a hope as vain as it is dishonest, who expects, by any contrivance, to escape a judgment of which he has notice; for the judgment creditor does not now rest merely on his judgment, as the Chancellor objected, perhaps hastily, in Skeeles v. Shearley, but on the protection given by the 13th section of the Act before us. The technical rule, that a limitation under a power should be considered as if inserted in the instrument creating the power, is not of such overwhelming authority and excellence, as to reconcile us to its sway when it issues in what may be deemed a fraud, and requires the submission of the first principles of equity.[1] And as we have abundant authority to say that we may look to the previous acts of a party exercising a power, it would not, perhaps, be stretching the jurisdiction of Chancery beyond its accustomed limits, if we desired that it could not be shown that the party claiming under a power had a guilty conscience.

But we have still a further argument why the charge imposed by the 13th section should not be allowed to be defeated by the operation of the proposed joint power, or any other similar shift. The charge in question is not distinguished by the act by the appellation of equitable charge, and may, perhaps, be likened to an agreement for a lease, or an interesse termini, which, though cognizable in a court of law, is best worked out in Chancery.

Suppose this case were before a court of law. A., on a purchase has the land limited to such uses as he and B. shall appoint, or to such uses as B., with the consent of A., shall appoint, with remainder to A. in fee. A. agrees to grant a lease to commence at a future day, and then before the day he and B. appoint to C. by way of mortgage and without notice of the lease. The day arrives and the lessee enters. Afterwards, during the lease, C. would enter, and treats the lessee as a trespasser. Is it not plain that a court of law would protect the lessee, and tell C. that before he acquired his title, virtue had gone out of A., and that to the extent of the lease the land was bound ? And it is also plain that equity could not interfere in such a case ; it might be hard upon C.; but would it not have been a greater hardship upon the lessee ? Now the only difference between this case and a case which might arise between a judgment creditor and a mortgagee is this, that in the former the lease arose directly and simply from the act of A.; in the latter the charge, though occasioned by the act of A., is only imposed upon the land by act of parliament. But is there any good ground why the lease should work a suspension of the power, but the charge not ? A. cannot be ignorant either of the lease or of the charge ; but a mortgagee may be honestly ignorant of the former, but cannot of the latter, without wilful and

[1] See 3 Mee. & Welsby, 572, 653.

culpable negligence. The act provides that no judgment shall have the benefit of its provisions until registered according to the 19th section.

The question will probably come before a court of law, and it will then be decided whether a charge imposed on an estate by act of parliament can be defeated by any act of the party subsequent to the charge ; and if it should be held that such a charge cannot be so defeated, we apprehend it will be immaterial in a court of law whether the purchaser had notice or not ; and unless the creditor seeks to enforce his charge in Chancery, that court cannot, we think, interfere on behalf of the purchaser.

It might, too, be held, that the purchaser was a person claiming under the donee of the power, and therefore subject to the charge by the very words of the act.

It will perhaps be said, that the proviso with which the 13th section concludes shews that a merely equitable charge was intended, but we doubt whether the words will bear that construction. They are very general ; and import no more than that Chancery may help a purchaser or mortgagee without notice, if it can consistently with its peculiar doctrines. It should be enquired what is the doctrine of courts of equity respecting protection from judgments ? This doctrine, it is clear, does not affect judgments which are a lien upon or may be enforced against an estate by virtue of an act of parliament, so that it may be strongly urged, this proviso is an empty sound ; it is too vague and indefinite to control the express charge created by clear words ; for if that had been intended, it would have been easy for the legislature to have said, the charge we give to a judgment creditor shall not affect a mortgagee or other purchaser without notice, but instead of that, it contents itself with a mere saving of any doctrine courts of equity hold respecting protection to purchasers without notice, a doctrine, which, perhaps, it would puzzle the whole of the Chancery bar to define and expound. For instance, Sir Edward Sugden states it as a question too difficult for him to determine, whether a judgment affecting an equitable estate or interest, within the operation of the 10th section of the statute of frauds, is or is not subject to the equitable doctrine of notice.

If the proviso authorises and compels a court of equity to say, that the charge cannot be enforced against a purchaser, against whom notice cannot be proved, the only effect of the enactment is, that a judgment is now an equitable charge, where the debtor has the legal estate, for it has long been a charge upon every modification and degree of equitable interest, and not merely upon a moiety of the proceeds,[1] for the whole, it appears, are liable.

It should be observed that the present doctrine of Chancery respecting judgments has no reference to the legal estate, it depends simply upon the fact of notice. Hence, supposing under the old law a judgment was entered up against the owner of an equity of redemption, and the same was subsequently sold to a purchaser without notice of the judgment, we apprehend the purchaser would hold free from the judgment, though the legal estate remained outstanding. But supposing the same facts under the new law, with the addition that the judgment creditor, before the sale of the equity, gave notice of his judgment to the party having the legal estate, would the purchaser be free from the judgment? We think not; for the judgment creditor might say, my charge upon the equity is the same now as if it had been made by an agreement in writing. But a judgment considered as a charge by an agreement in writing should be subject in Chancery to the equitable doctrine of getting in the legal estate without notice of any charge; and this, perhaps, is the real object of the proviso before us.

In cases where the legal estate is already in a mortgagee or otherwise out of the owner, a judgment creditor, whether he gave notice of his charge to the party having the legal estate or not, may be entitled to rank among the equities, however they may be created, according to the date. If so, a second mortgagee, or a mortgagee who has only an equitable estate, will have now little advantage over a judgment creditor, except that he may have power to sell the pledge, without going into Chancery.

Upon the whole we think no device will exempt a purchaser from the charge created by the 11th section, and that he must

---

[1] Tunstall v. Trappes, 3 Sim. 300.

also be subject to that created by the 13th, unless he gets the legal estate without notice.

We apprehend it will be held that a mortagee's interest in the mortgaged premises is not subject to the charge of the 13th section, though the words are sufficient to comprise it.

But we must now conclude. We have thought it may be useful to bring before our readers these various views ; for the subject will doubtless engage the earnest attention of the practitioner, and sooner or later must be fully discussed in our courts. In the meanwhile our advice to purchasers and mortgagees is, search the register and rely not upon any device to sponge off or squeeze out the debts of the person under whom you claim.

Since writing the above, Sir Edward Sugden's new act " for the Better Protection of Purchasers against Judgments, Crown Debts, Lis pendens, and Fiats in Bankruptcy" just passed, (4 June, 1839,) has been put into our hands. This enactment coming from the hand of a master should, we think, have contained the whole law respecting judgments, and have settled the doubts which have from time to time arisen. But instead of doing so it has confounded the subject to such an extent, that we doubt not litigation will flourish within the precinct. Our readers are aware that the 4 & 5 W. & M. c. 20 required that all judgments should be docketed, and that section 3 enacted, that no judgment not docketed should affect purchasers or mortgagees. The act of 1839 enacts, that no judgments shall hereafter be docketed under the act of W. & M., but it does not repeal the act. But the substance of the act of W. & M. being taken away, can the 3d section have any operation ? In other words, suppose a judgment now recovered is not registered pursuant to the act of 1838, will it affect lands in the hands of a purchaser? It may be said, *lex neminem cogit ad impossibilia,* and that docketing of judgments being prohibited the penalty for not docketing is gone. This is a very serious question, for if a purchaser can be affected by a judgment not registered, he is in as bad a case as before the year 1692.

The most important provision of the act of 1839, so far as regards our present purpose, is section 5, which enacts, that as against purchasers and mortgagees without notice of any such judgment, (quære, *any* judgment, or a judgment registered pursuant to the act of 1838,) it shall not bind or affect any lands or any interest therein further or otherwise, or more extensively in any respect, although registered, than a judgment would have bound such purchaser or mortgagee before the act of 1838, where it had been duly docketed. It appears, then, that the act of 1838 is to have no operation either at law or in equity, unless the purchaser or mortgagee has notice ; but the section before us seems to say, that without notice a judgment, at least if registered, shall have the same operation as a docketed judgment ; but this very important provision is only an implication. The enactment is, without notice, no judgment shall bind further or otherwise, although registered, than a judgment would have bound before the act of 1838, if docketed. But the act does not say, in express terms, as it should, that a registered judgment without notice shall have the same effect as a docketed judgment before the act of 1838 ; and we do not observe that the registering of a judgment is made equivalent to the docketing under the stat. of W. & M. Assuming that the inference is allowed, and that a registered judgment without notice shall have the same effect as a docketed judgment, the result of the section before us is, that without notice the old law will decide the question, with notice the new law must be referred to, and this it must be admitted is very unsatisfactory.

Sect. 4 enacts, that after a judgment shall have been entered five years it must be re-entered, otherwise the same shall be void ; but we apprehend that though a judgment is not re-entered it will not be void against a purchaser who has notice of it ; and if so, so far as regards the act of 1838, which depends upon notice, the 4th section is a nullity.

Most of the sections in the new act before us are expressly extended to purchasers or mortgagees, but the 12th section, which gives protection against secret acts of bankruptcy, mentions only purchasers. Is this intended ? And does the wording of the previous sections exclude mortgagees from the benefit of the section ?

Section 13 of the new act is a copy of section 86 of the Bankrupt Act, 6 Geo. 4, c. 16. What is intended by the repetition ?

W. C. W.

ART. VI.—ADVENTURES OF AN ATTORNEY.

Adventures of an Attorney in Search of Practice. London. 1839.

This book consists of a selection of cases in which an attorney was or might have been employed, interspersed with reflections on the line of conduct most likely to promote success in the profession, and pieces of advice to young practitioners as to the proper mode of demeaning themselves towards clients of all sorts. The title, therefore—evidently suggested by " Adventures in search of a Horse"—strikes us to be ill-chosen ; for, coupled with the name of the hero, Mr. Sharpe, it led us, and probably has led many others, to anticipate neither more nor less than an exposure of the tricks of the knavish members of the body, which is not the main object, nor even one of the main objects, of the publication.

As the plan was probably borrowed from Mr. Warren's " Passages from the Diary of a late Physician," the author might as well have gone a step further and borrowed the title too. " Passages in the Life of an Attorney" would convey a fair general notion of the contents. This work, however, is obviously the bonâ fide production of a practitioner,—the result of his own actual experience or that of his acquaintance and cotemporaries, so that direct practical conclusions may confidently be drawn from it ; and we gladly avail ourselves of the opportunity to comment on a few topics of professional interest which come home to the feelings or pockets of all.

The commencement runs thus, aptly enough pourtraying the unreasoning and unreasonable eagerness of a beginner :

" There is something vastly agreeable in the first day of a professional life : clerkship, servitude, and drudgery are all at an end ; one no longer asks the hour, with sore consciousness of being too late for office, or dire misgivings of having been inquired for ; and racking one's wits in vain for some new excuse, not yet exhausted, of " gone to the Temple," " examining an abstract," or " serving a notice !" I was in such a desperate hurry to begin, though I had not a client nor the dream of one, and was filled with lofty ambition to do the thing well, and start with all the magnificence of a house, I had not patience to wait till I could find one, but engaged a first floor over a shop, bought a desk and half-a-dozen chairs second-hand, incarcerated the first stray lad I could catch, in a dark cell eight feet by six, tied up old precedents with new tape, and then painted my name gorgeously on the door posts' with all the dignity of " Mr. Sharpe, Solicitor," at full length.

" Such was my self-complacency at the independence of my novel position, that I believe I rung my hand-bell for my clerk half a score of times in the course of an hour, merely for the pleasure of having it answered; though there was charity in the act, for without this stimulus to attention he would inevitably have gone to sleep for lack of better employment. * * * *

" How long this interesting state of indolent expectation might have continued, had I waited for clients to come to me, I cannot say; but after a week or two I began to find it as *ennuyant* as it was profitless, and resolved, as nobody seemed willing to find me out, to try my luck in finding out them. It was very clear that my extraordinary merits were still unknown, and an attorney, though he ought certainly to " blush unseen," if he blushes at all, cannot by any means afford to waste his sweetness on the desert air. Hence I changed my plan; left word with my clerk that if any body called I was ' gone to the Temple,' and sallied forth on a Paul Pry expedition among all my friends and acquaintances : but I verily believe that the demon of ill-luck, if there is such a deity in heathen mythology, presided over my first essays. Not a soul had called on me for three weeks, except two or three idle lads to see ' how I got on,' when, while engaged on one of my marauding expeditions, a certain noble lord of very large property, hitherto unprovided with a solicitor, and to whom I had been favourably mentioned by a common relative, drove up to my door, and called to instruct me to file an information against the trustees of an important charity. ' Gone to the Temple' was as unintelligible to his noble ears as if my clerk had reported me ' gone to the devil;' perhaps, in his opinion the expressions were synonymous, as in truth, I have often considered them myself: however this may be, I never saw any more of his lordship, or heard another syllable of his instructions, (except that another solicitor had filed the information,) though on three successive mornings I left my card at his mansion in Grosvenor Square; at no cost of time, for I had nothing else to do, but at an immense expense of coach-hire, omnibuses not then being in fashion. It is all for the best : I have since seen and heard much of his lordship; he is a worthy man, but his notions, however becoming his high rank, would never have agreed with my temper at that early time of day; and had we quarrelled, I should have lost clients in his connexion that I have still retained, and value far more highly.

" This was a bad beginning, *but I made the best of it,* as has been my rule through life."

He clearly made nothing of it, as the moral could hardly have been drawn till long afterwards. It is not in early youth, or when smarting under a first disappointment, that a man becomes an optimist.

A few days afterwards he is solaced by a call from a gentleman who wishes to bring an action, though clearly without a leg to stand upon. He is told as much; the opinion is confirmed by that of a junior counsel; but the litigant, still unconvinced, goes to another attorney, brings the action, and succeeds—

" I met him a few days after the trial, and our conversation was rather amusing.

" ' Well, Wright, you have gained the day !'

" ' Yes, to be sure : but little thanks to you.'

" ' I admit it ; for I still think you were all wrong.'

" ' Ay; but wiser folks thought me all right.'

" ' Scarlett never thought so, whatever the jury might.'

" ' But Scarlett did think so, and said so.'

" ' Oh yes ! he told the jury so of course, and they were fools enough to believe him ; but did he tell *you* so, at your consultation?'

" ' He said nothing at the consultation ! he never once asked me to sit down ; but he cocked his eye at the attorney, nodded to the other counsel, poked the fire, and I saw at once it was all right. I paid two guineas or more for that cock of the eye ; but it don't matter for that, so long as that rascal can't rob me and laugh at me to boot ; and he would have done both had I followed your advice.'

" ' Well, don't cry till you are out of the wood; he'll move for a new trial, and will get it, take my word for it ; and then Scarlett himself will tell you who is right.'

" My friend made a wry face at this prediction, and had his opponent then chanced to meet with him, and taken him between wind and water, he would gladly have drawn stakes; but as my ill-luck would have it, I was again out, for a new trial was *not* moved for, my friend recovered damages and costs, and has ever since voted me a fool, and himself the very cleverest biped in creation ; yet the case was as clear as the daylight. I earned, by this matter, 2*l.* 14*s.* 6*d.*, and lost my client and my legal repute into the bargain."

This is one of the adventures which we should wish to make known as extensively as possible. The result of an action depends, and always must depend, on a variety of circumstances unconnected with the merits ; a lawyer can apply the law to the facts as stated in his instructions or his brief, but it is impossible to foresee how they will turn up in Court, what figure the witnesses will cut in the witness box, or by what sort of jury the question will be tried. This is the real cause of the glorious uncertainty of the law ; yet not only is the whole set down to the account of the profession as a body, but each individual member is made answerable for the result in each individual case. No professional man is ever permitted to exclaim :

> " 'Tis not in mortals to command success,
> But we'll do more, Sempronius, we'll deserve it."

His next client is a sort of Baron de Bode, a gentleman who had been urging a claim to a large amount on the government during the better portion of his life. Mr. Sharpe's old master had hitherto managed the business, but the affair was awfully complicated, the papers were in a foreign language which no one left in the office was acquainted with, and the prospect of an auspicious termination was slight ; so the client was not only permitted, but recommended, to transfer himself ; and Mr. Sharpe's whole energies were thenceforth directed to the case. He succeeds to the full extent of the demand, receives full credit for his exertions, with forty-one pounds five shillings and six-pence,—the precise amount of his bill, and is never employed again. He accounts for this strange instance of ingratitude by supposing that he had offended his client's delicacy by advising him not to supersede a bankruptcy of some thirty years standing, which the old gentleman, after paying off every creditor he could hear of, had resolved on doing for the express purpose of reviving every description of liability.

All the rest of our hero's early clients treat him in the same manner ; he lost them, he assures us, as fast as he got them, without any fault of his own, *except* that he often ruffled their self-love. At the outset, also, he was culpably neglectful of a precaution, which, if a man wishes to make a good impression, it may be as well to take before going to join an ordinary party, much less before undertaking the conduct of affairs : he neglected to inform himself of the connexions and previous history of the persons with whom or for whom he was to act. For example, he is introduced to a Lady Carysfort, who, with her two sisters, Mrs. Walsingham and Miss St. Clair, was entitled to the accumulations of a large property. She asks : " will this affect my rights under my aunt Carisbrook's will ?"

" I began to feel alarm ; I had never heard of such a will, nor of such a person, and the plain course was to say so.

" I never heard of the will of Mrs. Carisbrook !

" ' The Countess of Carisbrook,' laying a slight emphasis on the word ' Countess,' ' bequeathed to me 500*l.* per annum, so long as my father lived.' "—p. 36.

He next calls on Mrs. Walsingham, and informs her that it would be necessary for him to see her husband on the subject :

" ' I cannot imagine, Sir, what Mr. Walsingham can have to do in the matter ! it is *my* money, not Mr. Walsingham's !'

" ' I believe Madam, it is not comprised in your settlement, and of course, therefore, his concurrence is necessary.'

" ' It is *not* of course, Mr. Gregory Sharpe, nor shall I ask Mr. Walsingham's concurrence in any step that I think proper to take.'

" ' I beg pardon for persisting in a point which seems irksome to you, but you must be aware that in contemplation of law, you and Mr. Walsingham have a common interest and are identified.'

" ' Identified, Sir ! identified with Mr. Walsingham ! a common interest with Mr. Walsingham !' raising her voice at every period, till at last it almost amounted to a scream.

" ' Well, Madam, perhaps you will oblige me by at least speaking to him on the subject.'

" ' *I* speak to Mr. Walsingham ! speak to *him* on the subject ! or on any subject whatever ! ! ! Indeed, Sir, you must excuse me ;' rising at the same time to ring the bell."—pp. 36, 37.

He is bowed out, and returns to Lady Carysfort, who asks him another question :

" ' I cannot answer that question precisely without seeing the settlement. Sir William may take an interest in it, or your children.'

" ' My children, Mr. Sharpe ! my children!'

" The exclamation was uttered with a shriek ; the poor lady immediately became hysterical ; Miss St. Clair sobbed audibly ; and Sir

William strided across the room, evidently embarrassed. The very lap-dog on the rug displayed his fangs, and growled out his indignation. Here was another pretty mess that I had made of it! I began to think the whole family crazy; and commissions of lunacy crossed my vision; how could I apologise, unconscious as I was of offence.

"'Mr. Sharpe!' said Sir William sternly, and suddenly paused.

"'Really, Mr. Sharpe,' sobbed out Miss St. Clair, and was again silent.

"'Oh! Mr. Sharpe, if'—and poor Lady Carysfort was mute from utter exhaustion.'"—pp. 38, 39.

The mystery is soon explained. Mr. and Mrs. Walsingham had been separated by deed for the last fifteen years: whilst Sir William and Lady Carysfort's union was one which " would have subjected more plebeian folks to certain pains and penalties."

There is truth and good sense in the following:

" If I may judge from my own experience, there is no greater fallacy than to conclude that the friends gained at school or college are sufficient to launch you in the sea of life. I had such ephemeral acquaintance by the hundred; but they rarely stick by one for any practical good : the majority of them are themselves embarked in the same great adventure of professional speculation, and consequently have themselves to look to first, and little leisure and less inclination to assist others who may perchance hereafter prove their rivals. Moreover, the frankness of youth discloses its defects as well as its merits, and it is rare indeed that boys carry their favourable recollections of a schoolfellow to the age of maturity. *It is among those with whom business, in its proper sense, brings us first acquainted, that we must seek to establish a connection;* and if that connection is to be permanent, their tastes, their tempers, and their habits, must be as much the subject of our study, as the redress of their injuries, or the protection of their rights. Such is the self-importance of mankind, that it is thought no common favour by a senior to allow a young man even one opportunity of rendering himself acceptable in his profession. Clients are not very ready to intrust themselves to juvenile advice; and if by the entreaty or influence of friends, or by any other accident they are induced to do so, not only do they expect most deferential gratitude, but they scan with an illiberal and almost inquisitorial eye, every word and gesture that in men of longer standing would be overlooked."—pp. 42, 43.

No man is a prophet in his own country : it is difficult to

persuade people to trust their lives or property to a youngster whom they may have caught pelting their ducks or stealing their apples, whatever legal or medical ability he possesses; but it is by no means equally clear that boys rarely carry their favourable recollections of a schoolfellow to maturity ; i. e. when the recollections *are* favourable.   But no one, man or boy, can have above one or two friends in the strict acceptation of the term, and even they may have relations or connections with prior claims to such interest as they can exert.   When therefore the candidate feels himself growing impatient and angry at neglect, we recommend him to calm his fluttered feelings and soothe his self-complacency by reflecting, that there is no reason why tried men should be set aside for untried ones, and that he himself would think it very hard if, when he had established a connection, his clients should abandon him from caprice or be lured away from him by solicitation.

The next adventure introduces us to a different class of characters :

"A man constantly on the look-out, can hardly fail of finding something to do.   Though my success in Boyle's affair got me very little money, it acquired me some credit for capability.   A public inquiry of great national importance was in progress : an insulated matter connected with it required professional investigation, and many solicitors of ten times my experience having declined the duty, not only because it was unpopular in itself, but attended, as was supposed, with some little personal risk, I was invited to undertake it. I was so very green at this time, that I was unconscious of the favourable position in which I stood, and the advantage it gave me in fixing my own terms, for time pressed : I was to embark within four-and-twenty hours of receiving my instructions, and, as I have noticed, nearly a dozen attornies having already refused the office, the government was so driven into a corner, that I might have named what compensation I pleased, it would have been promptly given. The same *insouciance* about the position of my employers, misled me here.   I was summoned to the Foreign Office.   At the end of a long apartment, busily occupied in papers from which he seemed unwilling to take his eye, sat a young man scarcely older than myself, and dressed in the extreme of fashion, with whiskers and moustaches of no common dimensions ; they were at that period much less common than at present ; his heels were decorated with gilt spurs of extraordinary length; his trousers braided *en militaire*, and in fact his whole costume partook of the style of military undress. It was *not* Lord Lyndhurst, then Sir John Copley, though the very next day I recollect meeting this learned Solicitor-General, in consultation with his yet more learned colleague, in precisely the same equipment."—pp. 54, 55.

The dandy secretary is disposed to treat him with *hauteur*, but Mr. Sharpe contrives to establish his own claims to respect by means which strike as not particularly well adapted to the end, and the interview proceeds:

" ' Well, Sir, this is a delicate affair; you will I am sure act with prudence and caution; in case of unforeseen difficulty, you will address yourself to Sir Charles ————. How soon can you start?'

" ' In an hour if you wish it.'

" ' Very well; you will receive your further instructions from the Attorney-General, and you will write to us by every post. Good morning, Mr. Sharpe:' and I was bowed out accordingly. Extraordinary to say, I was afterwards informed, by good authority too, that I had ' made a favourable impression on Lord Cl————.'

" The Attorney-General was carefully minute in the delivery of his instructions. Sir John Copley lounged into the room for five minutes, examined me with his glass as though I had been a kangaroo, adjusted his black stock before the mirror, played about his spurs with a spruce jockey-whip elegantly mounted with gold, and then lounged out again with the grace and foppery of a French dancing-master! but I suppose this was in keeping with the saloons of Carlton House.

" I proceeded on my journey, and succeeded in my mission; it would have been difficult to fail under the guidance of one so clear and so acute as Gifford; I was absent for five weeks, I was only five nights in bed, and received for my services exactly one hundred pounds!!! Had I known my men better, I might have had five times as much."—p. 57—59.

We presume this adventure to be based upon Mr. Powell's Milan expedition, which he executed with equal credit and, (we trust,) more profit to himself; but when (if ever) he gives his own version of the affair, we doubt whether any mention of gilt spurs or jockey-whip will be found in it, or whether he will state that Gifford's instructions were clearer than Lord Lyndhurst's in that or any other transaction in which opportunities for comparison were afforded. The whole description, in short, is a gross caricature.

The next sketch is in much better keeping :—

" Mr. Bedworth was an *oratorical* tradesman of strong politics, and had made himself conspicuous by his ill-judged and ostentatious violence on many occasions. He became obnoxious to the public press, and was libelled and abused as virulently as the fondest lover of notoriety could desire : he applied to me for counsel.

" ' I am a very ill-used man, Mr. Sharpe.'

" ' I think you are, Sir, but I thought you were the last man to complain of hard usage in the good cause.'

" ' That is very true, and I don't complain ; but these detestable papers must be put down. It is a foul shame that this licentious ribaldry—this tyrannical despotism of the press, should be tolerated : to a man of less iron nerve than myself, such unmerited calumny would be fatal ; to a man more open to suspicion than myself, it would be ruin.' I was not then aware that Mr. Bedworth had been twice a bankrupt, three times insolvent, and, in a word, ' on the town,' for the last five years."—pp. 60, 61.

*   *   *   *

" ' Very well, Mr. Bedworth ; the first then is the affidavit. see you are called a ' gaol-bird,' a ' rogue of enterprize,' and a ' gazetted thief ;' your name is not specified certainly, but you have no doubt, I presume, that you are the party intended ?'

" ' None at all, none whatever : ' the principal speaker ' at this celebrated meeting, could be nobody but me, Sir. I was undoubtedly the principal speaker there. I moved the first resolution ; I seconded the third ; I spoke on the fourth ; I opposed the amendment ; and finally, I returned thanks to the chair. Indeed, I may say that nobody of any consequence took any part in the affair, but myself.'

" ' Then it is unquestionable, Mr. Bedworth, that you are the ' gaol-bird ?' '

" ' I am, Sir.'

" ' And the ' rogue of enterprize ?' '

" ' I am, Sir.'

" ' And a ' gazetted thief ?' '

" ' I am, Sir. I am the ' gaol-bird,' the ' rogue of enterprize,' and the ' gazetted thief :' all in one—*Tria juncta in uno,* Sir.'

" ' Well then, we must deny it all on oath.'

" ' That is easily done.'

" ' I will prepare the affidavit to-night, if you will favour me with a short narrative of the last few years of your trading life.'

" ' What has that to do with it ?' (*in obvious alarm*).

" ' We must go into court with clean hands, you know ; and not only deny the charge, but all colour and foundation for it.' "—pp. 64, 65.

*   *   *   *

" To cut short a long story, though not wanting in instruction, the bill [be elects to indict] was preferred six times, before it was returned a true bill ; the press caught scent of the proceedings, and revenged themselves by new libels that piqued my wrong-headed client into renewed exertion ; and finally his costs swelled up to three hundred and sixty pounds.   He then libelled *me* for having deceived him : paid me with a bill at twelve months, which was dishonoured ; and at the end of some three years, and not before, my costs were paid, and my public-spirited client for ever lost to me, not less, however, to my satisfaction than to his."—p. 67.

We believe it was Madame de Sevignè who remarked of the religious ladies of her day, that they gave themselves to God when man would have nothing to do with them.   On the same principle, or absence of principle, tradesmen seldom or ever devote themselves to the affairs of the public till they have proved themselves utterly incapable of managing their own.   Examine into the composition of the new Town Councils, or review the lives of the leading city orators for the last fifty years, and it will be found that Mr. Bedworth is a fair sample of a numerous class that would soon grow into an intolerable nuisance, if they were not occasionally lashed back into their original obscurity by the press ; and one of the worst evils inflicted by the present ministry on the community, is the encouragement they have afforded to this class. Can any one doubt, that, had Mr. Bedworth been one of the worthies of Birmingham, he would have been nominated by Lord John Russell or the Lord Chancellor to the magistracy ?

" One axiom on the question of costs is so obviously true, that we cannot avoid surprise at our clients so often losing sight of it.   If they wish only to pay their attorney like a shoe-black, they will soon have only shoe-blacks for their attornies.   No man can limit himself as to the extent of costs, without cramping his exertions to a degree that may prove highly injurious to his client's interest.   The casualties and accidents of litigation are so frequent, and sometimes so expensive, that they occasion more expenditure than even the whole of the proceedings that go on in the accustomed course ; and if the cause of action is not of sufficient importance to warrant costs out of the ordinary routine, if necessary, it is wiser and more honest to advise the client to submit to his loss."

This axiom is illustrated by an instance in which it became necessary to dispatch a witness in a chaise and four a journey of a hundred miles, to procure a document which Mr. (now Baron) Gurney had declared indispensable at the consultation the evening before the trial. But its justice is almost self-evident, and any man of sense will see, on a moment's reflection, that he has positively no alternative between tying down his solicitor to a fixed sum (in which case any unforeseen emergency may prove fatal), and giving him *carte blanche.* That bills of any sort, much less bills for law proceedings, will ever be paid without a murmur, is what we are not visionary enough to expect ; but there are one or two considerations regarding them which professional men should take every opportunity of pressing on the attention of their friends.

A law-suit must always involve some disputed question or questions, to be decided by a given tribunal, on written or oral testimony or both. Unless the point be a very clear one, the result will depend in a great measure on the selection and classification of the evidence. Competent persons must consequently be employed to select and classify it ; the documents must be procured, and the witnesses be ready when required. Now take an average bill of costs for bringing or defending an action, and it will be found that all the more startling items are reducible to the elements indicated above—for attending witnesses, examining them, conveying them to and keeping them at the assizes (often more than one half of the gross amount), searching records, preparing briefs, and fees to counsel. It will appear, also, that the rate at which the attorney is allowed to charge for his labour, is lower than any other class of men, of the same station in society, would insist upon. How, then, we would ask, is the proposed reduction to be effected ? Causes cannot be tried without witnesses ; witnesses will not attend at their own expense ; nor will persons capable of applying law to facts, be ever got to examine witnesses or take the other requisite steps, without an adequate remuneration. As for pleadings, they are already curtailed as much as they well can be, and certainly do not average more than five pounds a case; whilst the probable demand for counsel may be estimated from the known eagerness of clients to select the best, without reference to cost. It follows inevitably, in our opinion, that the promises held out by law reformers of the radical class, are all based on delusion, and that far the greater part of the declamation levelled against attorneys, is unjust as well as impolitic. The only sure mode of preventing abuse is to elevate legal practitioners as a class, and no body of men were ever yet exposed to calumny for any length of time, without having their character deteriorated or their progress retarded by it; if only because the self-respect of the existing members is unduly lowered, and recruits of the better order are thereby prevented from joining them.

There is one remark on the subject of costs which we regret to find in such a work :

" I lament to add that I never heard of counsel relinquishing fees for a successful pauper ; though I have known many in which the attorney of that pauper has been left to pay such fees out of his own pocket."—p. 85.

No one who knows anything of the constitution of the bar can doubt that many of its members would readily work for nothing if they might, or even pay handsomely for an opportunity of distinguishing themselves; but the introduction of such a practice would be fatal to their respectability, and the etiquette of the profession is consequently opposed to it. Moreover, there is really no analogy between the cases. The counsel knows nothing of the parties but what may be collected from the brief; the fee bears a very small proportion to the sum total of the costs, and an occupied man would find it more advantageous to give back his fees in doubtful cases at once, than to enter into the additional communication or correspondence required for ascertaining the precise circumstances of the alleged object of charity.

At the same time, Mr. Sharpe has been singularly unlucky if he never heard of instances of liberality on the part of counsel whose standing was sufficiently high to secure them from the suspicion of undue motives. We have not the slightest doubt of the truth of his statement (pp. 85—87) to the effect that attornies often make considerable sacrifices both of time and money for the unfortunate. Why should he endeavour to throw suspicion, by invidious comparisons, on barristers, who, according to every reasonable presumption, would naturally act in the same manner if they could? If he will take the trouble to ascertain the names of two or three gentlemen who are said to be in the habit of taking low fees (or none) from the attorneys on whom they principally depend for business, we do not think he will be anxious for the rest of the bar to imitate them.

There is another allusion of the same sort which we believe to be totally unfounded :

" I can suggest no better rule for an attorney to follow in cases of this kind, than honestly to inform himself, by the opinion of an honest counsel, by which I mean a man who will give you credit, *which few of them will do,* for consulting your client's interest in disregard of your own, what is the proper course to pursue, and to take that course, utterly regardless of any reproach which the client may subsequently make."—p. 137.

If a counsel, after stating the legal bearings of the case, is asked in consultation what is the proper course to take, he will of course advise that which is most for the client's interest. To suppose otherwise, is to suppose that both attorney and counsel are rogues. No suspicion the counsel might happen to entertain of the attorney's motives, would modify his own opinion; yet surely the bar might be allowed credit for penetration enough to distinguish between honesty and knavery, and charity enough to give honesty its due.

Startling as bills of costs are admitted to be, a case is narrated to show that there are occasions when even an expensive law-suit may be the means of saving money. Thus, an action is brought against a commercial firm for repudiating a contract made in their name by a person falsely assuming to act by their authority. They are startled at the probable expense, and settle the demand, thereby rendering themselves liable to a host of other claimants. The instance is well intended, and it is to be hoped the over-prudent will profit by it.

In the following passage, again, the same feeling prevails, though the author's candour prevents him from withholding a

qualification which completely obviates the inference originally intended to be drawn:

" I have sometimes witnessed a great deal of overbearing insolence
from barristers of every standing; but never except from men naturally coarse, and like some solicitors that I have described, mere
adventurers, though often successful ones, in their profession. So far
however, as my own experience has gone, these men are exceptions
to the general rule. I recollect one occasion about eighteen years
ago, when a learned barrister was defending a prisoner whom I was
prosecuting, his eloquence was at a loss for a better argument, and
therefore in addressing the jury, he charged me with having falsely
instructed counsel ! his client was convicted, and thus the jury showed
their sense of the value of the charge. I was then so young that I
knew not how slight was the insult conveyed by such professional attacks; but being my opponent's equal in all the adventitious circumstances of education and social position, and somewhat his superior
in birth and connexion, I resented the supposed affront by giving him
my card. I cannot describe my amazement, when instead of receiving the hint in silence, he tossed it from him with an air of affected
indifference, saying, ' I throw it back with contempt;' but taking
especial care at the same time to fix the attention of the judge on
this daring violation of forensic privilege, so as to avoid the bare
possibility of unpleasant consequences. The obliging interposition
of Mr. Law, the present recorder, healed my wounded feelings; or I
might have been betrayed by anger into a very disagreeable position.
These attacks however are, as I have observed, rarely made on solicitors of acknowledged character; nor, in truth, could I quote another such instance towards myself in nearly twenty-five years'
acquaintance with the courts; it is because it is almost unique, that
I think it worth mentioning."—p. 217—219.

Things are come to a fine pass, indeed, if a barrister is not
to deny the truth of his opponent's instructions without being
forced to fight the gentleman who furnished them; and we
would just hint to Mr. Sharpe, that he who really wishes to
demand satisfaction for an insult, never adopts a line of conduct calculated to attract attention or lead to a fracas. He
should have waited till the court broke up, and then requested
explanation through a friend. But we have given in a preceding article (ante, p. 263) a sufficient answer to this charge,
and it is so decidedly against a barrister's interest to offend
an attorney, that, even without Mr. Sharpe's concluding ad-

mission, it might be taken for granted that such instances as that above-mentioned are exceedingly rare.

"The usual style of insolence," he continues, " is of a very different description : it is a supercilious hauteur that implies total disregard of the attorney, the client, the cause, and the fee. On the latter point, I incline to think that the disregard is entirely assumed, but in all other particulars, it is too natural to be insincere."

We should be glad to know how he reconciles this opinion with the one hazarded at p. 223 :

" Barristers have at least as much, if not more, sensibility, about the failure of clients, than ourselves, however they may affect a lofty disregard of the emoluments of their profession. I have often been amused at the indirect appeals, and sometimes the downright mendicity, of cousins, connexions, and friends, for a stray brief, or a casual motion, on behalf of a 'relation at the bar, if my engagements to other gentlemen allowed me !' "

The first sentence of this paragraph alleges that they do care for something besides the fee ; the second corroborates our statement as to their direct interest in adopting a different line of behaviour from that which Mr. Sharpe, despite of his exceptions and qualifications, is evidently most anxious to fix upon them. Indeed, in discussing this class of subjects, he is singularly illogical and inconsistent, from a reason which the next extract may suggest:

" We are excusable in resenting any imputation against our conduct as gentlemen, let it proceed from whom it may, or any sneering recognition of our station. But we are not entitled to assume a professional equality with the bar, merely because it draws its immediate support from us.¹ There is, it is true, an exclusive temper in its conventional etiquette, that in these liberal times is perfectly ridiculous. *I have known a brother refuse to dine with a brother in an assize town*, the one being counsel, the other attorney, because it was held contra bonos mores at the bar mess. Springing as this does from the jealous feeling that barristers entertain of each other, lest undue means should be exerted in familiar intercourse to obtain briefs, it is not less confessedly disgraceful to themselves as a body, than it

---

¹ Just as merchants or wholesale dealers draw their immediate support from shopkeepers. What has this to do with their social position ?

is offensive to those whom it insults : this exclusiveness reflects no discredit on our class, though much, avowedly, on their own. Against offences of this kind we cannot protect ourselves ; but against any offered to us individually, we easily may, by always observing that self-respect which commands respect, invito animo, from others. I have mentioned the only instance that has ever occurred to myself, in which I could fairly quote language applied to me by counsel, of which I feel justified in complaining ; and I attribute my exemption from an annoyance to which I have daily seen others exposed, principally to the care which I have always anxiously taken never to lay myself open to reproach for conduct unworthy of an honourable member of my profession ; but in some degree also to a demeanour implying at once perfect equality of station, and yet respectful deference to superior knowledge and professional rank. We should recollect that as the military officer is nobody except on the parade, or in the ball-room, so the lawyer loses all distinction out of Westminster Hall, and when we meet in the world, we meet on equal terms : this is perfectly consistent with the discipline of the ranks."—pp. 224, 5.

Two of the characters in "Pelham" are made to discuss the question whether illegitimacy presents an insuperable bar to a man's being perfectly a gentleman. They decide that it does not, *provided the individual has self-respect and strength of mind sufficient to subdue any consciousness of inferiority,* which would be fatal to that ease and independence of demeanor which are absolutely essential to the character. Just so, if an attorney feels no consciousness of inferiority—and most assuredly there is no earthly reason why an attorney, well educated and well connected, should feel any consciousness of the sort—he will find himself, during periods of social intercourse, on a perfect footing of equality with the bar. In fact, we could name many members of what is called the inferior branch of the profession, who, from literary reputation or political influence, would be received with much more consideration in general society than an undistinguished member of the bar. But the worst of it is, a great deal of paltry jealousy, originating in this very consciousness, prevails ; and it is perfectly clear to our minds, that Mr. Sharpe has hitherto tried in vain to convince himself of the actual existence of that perfect equality he is contending for. If so, why is he eternally harping on the point ? or why so angry at the very limited, description of exclusiveness which is still thought necessary to sustain, not the rank or the dignity, but the bare independence and respectability of the bar?

In a hasty review of the personal demeanour of some of the leading counsel, Mr. Serjeant Talfourd is described as not merely courteous but cordial; yet (in a passage quoted in a former number, but which cannot be quoted too frequently) Mr. Serjeant Talfourd thus vindicates the etiquette which has proved so offensive to his cordial and (in this instance) well-judging admirer:

" From this extraordinary position arises the necessity of the strictest etiquette in form, and the nicest honour in conduct, which strangers are apt to ridicule, but which alone can prevent the bar from being prostrated at the feet of an inferior class. But for that barrier of rule and personal behaviour, solicitors would be enabled to assume the language and manner of dictators; and no barrister could retain at once prosperity and self-respect, except the few whose reputations for peculiar skill are so well established, as to render it indispensable to obtain their services. It is no small proof of the spirit and intelligence of the profession as a body, that these qualities are able to preserve them in a station of visible superiority to those on whom they virtually depend. They frequent the places of business; they follow the judges from town to town, and appear ready to undertake any side of any cause; they sit to be looked at, and chosen day after day, and year after year; and yet, by force of professional honour and gentlemanly accomplishments, and by these alone, they continue to be respected by the men who are to decide their destiny."

At the same time the rules are by no means so unsociable as Mr. Sharpe supposes; and we rather think that the gentleman who refused to dine with his brother, did so because he preferred a circuit party to a family one. It is perfectly well known that a majority of the bar are taken from the class from which the higher order of attornies are supplied; it is ridiculous to suppose that the common ties of relationship are to be severed, or the ordinary rules of social intercourse to be neglected, for the sake of what would then become a ridiculous system of etiquette. All that is required is, that a man shall not get business by unworthy means—

amongst which *huggery* certainly stands pre-eminent—but each individual case is now decided by the principle, and the bare fact of dining with an attorney would prove nothing if the inference were rebutted by relationship or even by the character of the diner-out.

The rule as to travelling is so generally misunderstood, that we gladly avail ourselves of this occasion to justify it. A barrister may join or leave the circuit per coach, but he must travel from one circuit town to another in a private conveyance of some sort. To suppose that this rule was instituted with a view to dignity, is preposterous; for a postchaise, a gig, or a saddle-horse, is certainly not more dignified than a coach. It is simply a rule of delicacy, it being deemed improper for counsel to be mixed up with parties and witnesses. It is also maintained from considerations of convenience; since, the coach accommodation being necessarily limited, it was thought as well to leave it for the clerks, and enforce a system of mutual accommodation. This rule, however, is now constantly infringed with impunity.

We are the less surprised at Mr. Sharpe's erroneous opinions on these matters from finding, that, with all his shrewdness of observation, he is superficially acquainted with society, and makes strange blunders regarding its constitution and its rules. Thus, he represents a young married woman, residing in Bryanstone Square, as setting out on a ride with a young man early in the forenoon, staying out all day, and returning late in the evening, just time to prevent her husband and friends from starting in pursuit of her—all without exciting the slightest suspicion, and apparently without the slightest consciousness of impropriety.

In another place he thus speculates on fashion:—

" He had scarcely left Cambridge, when he became introduced to one of those minor circles which dub themselves fashionable, because they have acquired the ease and style of high-bred folly, however far removed by birth from the patrician class; *in truth, in these modern days of liberality, there are but two fashionable classes of society, however those classes may be subdivided: the men of academic education form the one; the educated by hook or by crook, form the other;* now and then they interlace with each other, but still the line of demarcation is broadly marked; the superior class branch out in manifold directions, and according to taste or circumstances, associate themselves with a political, a scientific, a professional, or a literary *coterie;* the half-educated aspire to the same elevation, and occasionally attain it; the large herd of intermediate talent, who have no intellectual pretension to rank in any particular study, are hangers-on in the set they happen to fancy, and make up for learned deficiency, by boldly asserting the exclusiveness of their peculiar circle; *men, like these, form the bulk of the fashionable world;* whether that world rolls along in the coroneted carriage through the streets and squares of aristocracy, or crowds the scientific hall, or lounges in the library chair of the club-room, or with more humility of aspiration, retails the gossip of the House over the good things of a civic table, *or speculates in Russell Square on the prospects of the leader on the circuit,* such is the material of which it is composed."—pp. 301, 302.

If we are to understand this literally, every educated man must be a man of fashion, for every educated man must belong to one of these two classes; and yet if the large herd of intermediate (?) talent form the bulk of the fashionable world, there must surely be more classes than two. But every one knows that fashion is necessarily of an exclusive character, and that society never was and never can be divided as this gentleman pretends. Most of the higher class are now educated at a University; but nine out of ten of those educated at a University have no pretension to mix with the higher class; which, generally speaking, can only be reached in one of three ways—birth, wealth, or celebrity.

Let us see whether our author has been more successful in his attempt to divide and classify his own branch of the profession, which he prefaces by some remarks on their relative position in society. Forty or fifty years ago, he tells us, an attorney's title to be ranked even among the middle classes was very equivocal; " Mr. Latitat was the rogue of every farce—the knave of every novel,"—and the nature of legal business adapted it to the character of the practitioner. "The bulk of professional practice was to be found in petty personal disputes or delinquencies—in small controversy between small people." Within the last century, however, our commercial system has grown up; whilst the immense increase of public companies and parliamentary business have largely contributed to swell the stream of professional profit, and at the same time to purify its source, by giving a legitimate and acknowledged value to the solicitor's services. " This gradual elevation of our duties has naturally led to the introduction among us of many young men from that rank of life, who, less than half a century ago, would have spurned the calling as derogatory to their birth; and attornies in the higher walks of the profession have, in many instances, established for themselves an acknowledged title to rank with the first circles.''

Such is his solution of the change, and it is by no means destitute of ingenuity, but we are not quite satisfied with it, because it refers to causes which affect only the profession of the law, in defiance or forgetfulness of the undoubted fact, that many other callings have been simultaneously advancing towards respectability. About the time that a Mr. Latitat was the rogue of every farce, Parson Adams was drinking ale in Lady Booby's kitchen without any consciousness of degradation, literary men drew their chief subsistence from begging dedications, and half-pay officers were only too happy to play the part of led-captain to a squire. Within the last half century, the educated classes have gradually succeeded in emancipating themselves from the undue preponderance of rank and wealth ; a feeling of self-respect has been communicated to all ; and it seems to us more logical to attribute the elevation of solicitors to the general diffusion of property and education, than to any change peculiar to themselves. The fact, however, is undeniable, and it matters comparatively little on what principle it is accounted for. But here's the rub :

" Though by this accession of better born, and therefore generally better educated men, we have improved our social position, and can now enumerate hundreds among us, who are not less gentlemen by birth, by feeling, and by manners, than we are by act of parliament, there still remains too much of that low business which was once the staple of our trade, not to attract many low people into the profession ; the rather because if once admitted there, the best prizes are as open to them as to others, if by happy accident they can insinuate themselves into the first or second class of competition : indeed to be an attorney is itself a great step in life, a sort of gentility of station, in the estimate of the lower ranks of shopkeepers and mechanics ;

nor does it require any great outlay of money to give a son a title to the name, provided no lavish expenditure has been made in his previous education. Let it not be supposed that I feel contempt for this laudable and even humble ambition ; far from it, for I profess principles too liberal, as well in politics as I trust in Christian faith, to deride it ; but I still think myself at liberty to protest against the absurdity, as well as the silly pretension of placing a boy of sixteen in an attorney's office, without any preparatory education beyond the Latin grammar, and too often less than that, simply to qualify him to be a gentleman, whilst his brothers are tinkers and tailors, and his father a Bow-street runner or sheriff's officer."—pp. 195, 196.

The expedients, he says, by which these worthies contrive to eke out a livelihood are various. Some consort with insolvents ; some with expectant heirs, blacklegs, and money-lenders ; others buy up bad debts and make themselves useful to roguish tradesmen, who stand in need of a sharp practitioner to evade a contract or stave off a liability ; but all contribute their quota towards the contumely that is showered upon the body. Nice associates, by the way, for the bar! and illiberal indeed must be the advocate who ever ventures on an exposure of such practices !

According to Mr. Sharpe, there are three maxims to be invariably observed in dealing with gentry of the kind : never enter into a *without prejudice* negociation with them ; never admit them to an interview, or, if forced into personal communication, call up the whole of your establishment as witnesses :

" I am not enjoining caution that I do not practise. Some years ago an attorney called on me—a man whose word I would not have credited had he pledged it with a halter round his neck. The door from my own office into my clerk's was wide ajar, and he saw me at my desk as he stealthily entered ; however he had the decency to ask,

"' Is Mr. Sharpe at home ?'

"' No ;' replied the clerk.

"' No ! why I see him in his office.'

"' He is not at home, Sir.

"' Well I must speak to his ghost then,' he rejoined, approaching my room ; there was no time to be lost ; I rose from my seat, rushed into the clerk's office, nearly overturning the intruder in my haste, and angrily exclaimed to my clerk, ' What do you mean by this, you

young rascal? did I not tell you when Mr. Tricker called to deny me?
I tell you I am *not* at home, Sir; I am attending the Common Pleas!'
and slamming the door in his face, and audibly turning the key, I
left him aghast at finding for once his own impudence outdone! He
left the place as soon as he recovered from his amazement, and I
never was troubled by him again. It is not always so easy to release
yourself, and if you are condemned to be closeted and rudeness is out
of place, *the simple course is to ring forthwith for your common law
clerk, and desire him to search for a letter of the 30th February last, in
the largest bundle of papers in the room!* You have no other chance of
safety with a professed affidavit-monger."—pp. 206, 207.

The seventeenth and eighteenth chapters contain some sa-
gacious observations upon witnesses. Of all witnesses in an
honest cause, an intelligent child is the best. Of all witnesses
in any cause, a woman is the worst, unless she happens to be
very pretty and engaging, for then she will answer the purpose, whatever it be, most successfully. "The counsel
examining in chief ogles her with one eye, and the jury with
the other, while a marked suavity of demeanour seduces the
fair *debutante* into perfect ease; the gallantry of the bench,
let his lordship be as old as Methuselah, bestows somewhat
more than a transient glance, and wanders into a conversational familiarity on every doubtful or hesitating answer."
He illustrates this proposition by describing the effect produced by a witness called to discredit a witness of his own:

"To discredit her testimony, a young lady of only two-and-
twenty, the daughter of the defendant, was called. She was uncom-
monly pretty, I might even say beautiful, and the elegance of her
manners and dress rendered her irresistible. Wilde, who was my
counsel, was horror-struck with the apparition: he leaned over the
desk to me, after attentively eyeing the jury, ' Sharpe, we are done!'
and 'done' we were most assuredly, though her evidence, strictly
weighed, was not worth a straw, for the jury gave us but five pounds,
and we thought ourselves fortunate in getting even that, under such
untoward circumstances."—pp. 252, 253.

There may be some foundation for this calumny on the sex,
which has been confirmed by poetical authority:

> "The pretty creatures fib with such a grace,
> There's nothing so becoming to the face."

It is also a remarkable fact, that some of the most ingenious and pertinaciously maintained impostures on record have been carried on by women.—Elizabeth Canning, for example, or the Somersetshire girl, Bowditch—but we doubt whether Serjeant Wilde would have given himself up for lost at the first appearance of a pretty woman in the box.

A child's evidence is of course unanswerable, and one of the most famous crim-con cases of modern times was brought to light by a child.

We have only room for one quotation more; but we cannot well make up our minds to omit a curious hoax played off upon the principal newspapers, towards which Mr. Sharpe entertains no friendly feelings:

" I recollect once being at a dinner party of young men, none of them contemptible in point of ability, and some of them far otherwise. By way of evening amusement, we selected each our daily paper, and affecting the tone of familiar acquaintance, addressed letters to the editors in such terms as we considered most likely to irritate, that we might have the pleasure of judging by their ' answers to correspondents' how far we succeeded in penetrating their anonymous hides. At our next meeting we brought their various replies; they were entertaining, inasmuch as if their wit was somewhat scanty, they at least furnished each of us with a sobriquet for the evening, that afforded no little pleasantry among ourselves. All dealt very much in alliteration, and most affected the laconic. I cannot recollect the whole of them, but they were very similar, and the Times was especially nettled, though I cannot now recall the cause of offence. ' Old Nick is a ninny! we know him better than he thinks we do; we wish he would send his balderdash to papers that have more room for it.' ' Bounce is a booby,' was the retort of another; if I remember right, it was the Chronicle. ' A fool who writes a clerk-like hand may be assured that we were not hoaxed sufficiently to reach the second page of his letter;' was John Bull's somewhat Irish disclaimer of being duped. A fourth answered in obvious wrath, ' Fairplay looks as foolish as when he was dragged out of the horsepond! he forgets that we were by; we could tell him all about it if necessary!' It gave us some gratification to see, that, even in their mysterious hiding places, these self-important worthies did not feel quite comfortable when attacked with daggers, as pointed if not as poisonous as their own; for there was not one letter that remained unnoticed, nor one answer that did not show the eager wish to throw back the mortification that had been inflicted."

He proceeds to enumerate some instances in which an unjust and injurious tyranny has been exercised by the press, and calls loudly for an alteration of the law on that account; but he forgets to mention another alteration still more needed —he forgets the ruinous expense to which newspaper proprietors are exposed in the shape of costs, even where they are confessedly conferring a great benefit on the public by the exposure of villainy, quackery or fraud. Mr. O'Connel has managed to delay the reform of this crying grievance during three or four years by bringing in, or pretending to bring in, a Bill on the subject, but it is to be hoped that another session will not be allowed to pass away without a remedy.

In conclusion, we cordially recommend this book as a clever, amusing and instructive one, both to professional and general readers, but we should be glad to find all illnatured allusions to the bar omitted in future editions, because we are convinced that any bickering or ill-will between the two branches of the profession must infallibly deduct from the respectability and influence of each. The public, on such occasions of difference, have an awkward habit of believing both parties.

H.

ART. VII.—SCOTCH PROCEEDINGS IN LUNACY.—CASE OF YOOLOW.

Report of the Proceedings under a Brieve of Idiotcy, Peter Duncan against David Yoolow, tried at Coupar-Angus, 28—30 Jan. 1837. With an Appendix of Documents and an Introduction. By Ludovic Colquhoun, Esq., Advocate. Edinburgh. 1837.

THIS Report seems not only well adapted to serve as a precedent for future proceedings of the kind,—the object the editor had more particularly in view,—but also to throw light on the Scotch law regarding persons of unsound mind, and put medical men and others on their guard against an undue readiness to form presumptions of mental incapacity. The speeches of the counsel also contain numerous passages well worthy to be cited as specimens of forensic reasoning and eloquence. We can hardly err, therefore, in devoting a few pages to the case.

The law of Scotland, as explained by Mr. Colquhoun in a well-written introduction, divides persons labouring under mental disabilities into two classes: 1. Those who are in such a state as to make it necessary to take both person and property under the protection of the law; 2. Those where the party possesses sense enough for his personal guidance, but is unfit to be trusted with the management of his property.

The process for determining whether an individual belongs to the first class is termed Cognition and Inquest: a writ or brieve is issued, and a jury or inquest, summoned by the sheriff, decides, much in the same manner as in England.

The legal remedy prescribed for the second class is that of Interdiction,—" a legal restraint laid upon those who either through their profuseness, or the extreme facility of their tempers, are too easily induced to make hurtful conveyances, by which they are disabled from signing any deed to their prejudice, without the consent of curators, who are called Interdictors.[1]" This species of restraint may be imposed by the sentence of a superior court on the application of the heir or next of kin, or without such application where the court discover signs of mental weakness in the party to a suit; or the individual may impose an interdiction, equivalent to a judicial sentence, on himself, by executing a bond whereby he engages to do no act affecting his property without the consent of certain curators whom he selects. This is by no means an unwise or unnecessary provision, for patients subject to periodical accessions of the malady are generally quite conscious of its approach; and persons versed in medical jurisprudence will have no difficulty in recalling the case of a gentleman of fortune who came regularly to put himself under the care of a keeper a day or two before his power of self-control was lost. If the agnate or nearest of kin refuses to

---

[1] Ersk. Inst. B. 1, T. 7, s. 53.

interfere, or there be no agnate, the better opinion is, that the Court has no power to interfere—a defect which Mr. Colquhoun proposes to supply by enabling the Lord Advocate to set the fitting process in action.

The case before us is one of cognition and inquest; the question being, whether David Yoolow was or was not in a state of imbecility rendering him unfit for the ordinary concerns of life. The trial took place at Coupar-Angus in January, 1837, before Mr. Sheriff L'Amy and a jury of fifteen; Mr. Patrick Robertson and Mr. Alexander M'Neill appearing as counsel for the pursuer, and Mr. Duncan M'Neill and Mr. Charles Neaves for the defender. Never was case better contested, and seldom has our attention been called to one in which such ample scope was afforded to forensic fact and metaphysical subtlety, the admitted facts being of a kind on which no positive conclusion could be based.

After a little preliminary altercation as to the order in which counsel should be heard—which the sheriff terminated by deciding that the old Scotch system should be followed in preference to that recently imported from England for civil causes in the Court of Session—the case for the claimant was opened by Mr. A. M'Neill:

" You will have an opportunity of seeing this person, and forming your own estimate of his capacity. He will either be produced to you, or you must visit him at his residence. My statement is, that he is a complete imbecile—not absolutely bereft of reason—but totally unable to manage his own affairs. He is now fifty-two years of age, and has all his life been treated as a child. In early youth he met with an accident, which brought on paralysis and fever—the effect of which on his constitution, bodily and mental, was to arrest all advancement; and he has remained in a state which cannot strictly be called second childhood, as he has never been enabled to emerge from first childhood. He has been constantly attended as a child."

Being compelled to admit that Yoolow was well versed in the Bible, the advocate endeavours to obviate the inference by stating that considerable scriptural knowledge was often found in combination with idiotcy. For example, Bossuet once offered to give an idiot an apple, if he would tell him where God was. The answer of the idiot was : " I will give you two, if you will tell me where he is not." Again, the following lines are attributed to an idiot :

> " Could we with ink the ocean fill——
> Were the whole earth of parchment made,——
> Were every single stick a quill,
> And every man a scribe by trade,——
> To write the love of God above,
> Would drain the ocean dry,
> Nor could the scroll contain the whole,
> Though stretched from sky to sky."

It is very possible that the writer of these lines, as well as Bossuet's acquaintance, were deemed incapable of managing their affairs : we have heard one of the greatest poets of the age termed an inspired idiot, and we ourselves have some clever acquaintance, who, if they knew their own interest, would apply for an interdict without delay ; but we do not believe that the repartee or the verses could have emanated from a mind affected at the time to imbecility.

The case being thus opened, a visit to the alleged idiot was proposed, and resisted on the ground that he was quite capable of attending the inquest according to the established practice. The sheriff ruled that, after hearing the defender's opening statement, the jury should proceed to a personal examination of Yoolow at his residence. Accordingly, Mr. Neaves, the junior counsel for the defenders, made a brief statement with the view of putting the jury on their guard :

" It is my duty to warn you, that in now seeing and conversing with David Yoolow, it will be necessary for you to summon up all that conscientious caution and impartiality which your oaths have bound you to observe in a question so seriously affecting the interests of a fellow-being. Yoolow must be presented to you under great and singular disadvantages; and allowances of no ordinary kind must be made, before a true estimate of his condition can be formed. You will be struck on beholding him with defects and peculiarities, which it is impossible for any one to contemplate without uneasiness and pain. A cripple and a paralytic from his boyhood, you will find his limbs decrepit and deformed, his arms and hands misshapen and contorted so as to be useless for the needful purposes of life, and his eyes, countenance, and whole frame agitated by fearful and convulsive motions, that seem incompatible with regular volition or intelligence. His articulation, also, has been much affected by his disease, and adds another difficulty to the task which you have to perform—another obstacle to your arriving at the truth. I do not fear that such men as you, bent simply on discharging your duty, will allow any fastidious feelings to operate with you ; but I do fear, that you may be led to associate and confound together, things that are essentially different— bodily infirmity and mental incapacity. It is not the external husk that you are to regard. It is the mind within that you are to search for, and measure if you can reach it. And I have no hesitation in telling you, that within that unpromising and forbidden frame of body, there does reside a mind and soul possessed of all the faculties and powers which belong to a rational, an intellectual, and a moral creature."

The inquest then adjourned to Yoolow's residence, where he underwent a trying examination, which lasted about an hour.

Yoolow was asked if he was aware that there was a proceeding going on at Coupar-Angus for the purpose of trying his case? He answered, " Yes—and I hope you will soon bring it to an end." He was asked, if he knew that the object of the trial was to ascertain the state of his mind? He answered, " My mind is strong enough, though my body and bones are weak."

In answer to other questions put to him, he stated that he had been at school at Kettins, till he was about nine years of age, and that he had learned to read, but had not been taught arithmetic. He mentioned the name of the schoolmaster of the parish, and also that of the minister, Mr. Symmers. He stated the dates, and the length of time since the death of his father and sister respectively. He said that his sister, Miss Yoolow, had been kind to him. He stated that his father had left him 600*l.* which was in the bank ; that he formerly got 20*l.* of interest, but last year only 12*l.* The sheriff having remarked that this was two per cent. interest; he said it was. The sheriff then put down seven shillings successively, which Yoolow reckoned up ; whereupon a half-crown and a sixpence were put down, and he readily added to the seven shillings the half-crown and the sixpence, and said that the whole was ten shillings. Being shown a guinea note of the National Bank, he said that it was a guinea note, and that the value of it was a pound and a shilling. At first sight, he said it was a note of the Commercial Bank, but almost immediately corrected himself, and said it was of the National Bank. He was asked as to the extent of his farms, which he stated correctly, and said that one of them was held from Mr. Murray, and another from ' the Laird of Pitcur.' He stated the amount of rent payable to each landlord, and that part was payable in money and part in grain, and specified the quantities of grain. Being asked what would happen if he did not pay the laird (landlord) the rent of the farm? he answered, that he would be turned out. Being asked, if he were the landlord, what would he do with the farm? he answered, ' I would let it, I suppose.' Being asked whether he read the newspapers, he answered that he did—the Weekly Journal. He was asked what it was that he read in the newspaper? He answered, that it was the price of grain. Being asked, what is the price of wheat? he answered, thirty-eight shillings a quarter. Being asked how much is in a quarter of wheat? he answered, eight bushels. To the question whether he read his Bible? he replied, that he did. Being asked if he understood what he read? he answered, ' I think I do.' He was asked, whether the soul perished with the body? He answered that it did not. Being asked what became of it? he answered, ' If you are good, it goes into happiness; if not, into misery.' He was asked how many ploughs he had labouring, and how many horses? which he answered correctly. Being asked who were his sister's trustees? he named them all. Being asked what he would do with his money at his death? he answered, ' I cannot take it with me.'. He was asked if he were dying would he not think it right to leave some part of his money to his relations? he answered, ' part of it.' He was asked, if a deed were offered him to sign, giving away his property, would he sign it? He said, ' I should like to know what was in it.' Being asked, how his money was applied? he answered, ' In providing raiment to me, and the like.' He was asked the distance from Mill of Peattie to Coupar-Angus? which he answered correctly. He was asked the distance to Dundee? and answered, that he did not know. He was asked if there was any town further off than Dundee? He answered, ' Yes—Edinburgh, but I never was there; and Glasgow, and Greenock, and Paisley.'

As the party were leaving the room, Yoolow called back Mr. M'Neill, and said : " You are my counsel, and I hope you will do what you can for me—I hope I'll not be plagued with these people coming back again."

The witnesses on both sides were next examined ; namely, fifteen for the prisoner, and eleven for the defender. Amongst them were several of the most celebrated professors of medical jurisprudence and (if they will forgive the term) mad-doctors of Scotland, but we cannot say that their depositions are much calculated to strengthen the reliance we have been wont to place in testimony of the sort. They constantly confound mere ignorance or credulity with incapacity ; and lay down maxims admirably adapted to promote the interest of their own calling, but not at all calculated to attract or command the acquiescence of other classes of the community. We will give a few specimens, beginning with Dr. Christison, who enjoys a very high reputation in this department of knowledge.

Dr. Robert Christison : " I asked him then what interest he got for his money in the bank ? He answered, ' Twenty pounds.' I then asked him, ' Whether that was for the year or half-year ?' and he answered, ' Oh ! for the year.' ' And what money have you in the bank ?' He answered, ' £1200.' Then Mr. Symmons asked, ' How much that was the hundred !' He said he could not tell ; and added, that he was ' no good hand at arithmetic.' I asked him if ever he read the newspapers ? He answered, with seeming pleasure, ' Oh, yes.' I asked, ' Are you a great politician ?' He answered, ' I never meddle with politics.' I asked him if he ' knew who was prime minister just now ?' He thought a little, and then answered, ' No : but I can tell you fine who is king—its King William ;' and this was said with seeming pleasure, which appeared childish. I said, ' Although you do not meddle with politics, there are some branches of them which, as a farmer, you should know about ; for instance, *what is your opinion of the Corn Bill ?*' He answered, ' I ken naething about that.' I asked, ' What is it intended for ?' He answered, ' To sell the corn, I fancy.' "

We have heard a gentleman relate that having occasion to consult Bearcroft, he placed before him a very simple arithmetical calculation, but was told to set it down in words at length, the learned counsel being utterly unable to comprehend figures. What is still more conclusive, it will presently be seen that one of the medical witnesses could not answer the very question put by Dr. Christison to Yoolow.

The other questions are still more preposterous, and before repeating this sort of testimony we recommend Dr. Christison to be at the pains of ascertaining the precise degree of political information prevalent amongst the inferior order of agriculturists. Only the year before last a west country farmer being asked why he voted against the old member, replied, " I've tried un six years and corn dont rise, so now I'se gie a turn to tother;" and an old lady at Exeter, was heard exclaiming a fortnight after Sir William Follett's return—"Here's a pretty member—bread *ris* already."

Dr. *William Malcolm* : " I got him on the subject of the Bible ; and, at my desire, he read part of it, and seemed to know the meaning of what he read. But this did not shake my opinion as to his being a man of unsound mind, as it is not uncommon for lunatics, and other persons of unsound mind, to be acquainted with the Bible. There are several persons of this description in a state of hopeless *insanity*, and insane upon every point but the Bible ; but I hold an *idiot* to be a person who is totally void of understanding. I asked him if he had heard of the Reform Bill, *and that farmers of his extent of land were entitled to a vote?* But this seemed to be all a blank to him. Yoolow's appearance, also, is very much that of an imbecile person. I understood that when Yoolow was about eight or nine years of age he had a fever, which ended in decrepitude and paralysis, which weakened his mind. He appeared very much excited when I saw him. There was a profuse perspiration on his forehead, and his hands and feet were constantly moving about ; and I was afraid of his falling from his chair. *There was no cause at all for this excitement.* At this interview I was perfectly satisfied that Yoolow was a man of unsound mind."

On cross-examination the same witness states : " I thought that he was in possession of the farm as tenant, when I said he was entitled to vote under the Reform Bill.—If you had been aware that the farm was held by trustees, would you have considered Yoolow as éntitled to vote?—I am not a lawyer, and am not able to answer that question. In the Perth Asylum, there are two or three lunatics who have great knowledge of the Scriptures. One of these is insane on every other point; and if you ask him a question on any subject, he answers by quoting a passage from the Bible, mentioning chapter and verse."

What has this to do with a capacity for reasoning on scriptural subjects? Yet not one of these medical gentlemen, who have made mental maladies the study of their lives, ever dreams of distinguishing between understanding and memory.

" Mr. *George Anderson*, Surgeon: What questions did you put? I put the questions to him, how many shillings were in five shillings, and how many shillings were in ten shillings; but he had difficulty in answering how many shillings were in ten shillings, though he said that ten shillings was half a pound. How did you put the question to him as to how many shillings were in ten shillings, or in five shillings? What words did you use? I used the words, ' How many shillings are in ten shillings?' and ' How many shillings are in five shillings?' And he did not know how many? He did not. Then he knew that ten shillings was half a pound, but he did not know that ten shillings was ten shillings; was it so? Yes. You may take time to answer the question I am going to put:—If £1200 is laid out at interest, and yields £20 of interest yearly, how much is that per cent. by the year? I am not able to calculate that without pen and ink, not being conversant with such matters. If you had the use of pen and ink, could you calculate it?—there are pen and ink, take them. I cannot say that I could calculate it with the use of pen and ink. Did you put any questions to David Yoolow to ascertain his notions of right and wrong? I did not. Did you ask him if he had any knowledge of, or belief in a future state? I did not.

Re-examined by Mr. *Robertson*, and desired to explain his answers relative to the ten shillings :—I must have meant to say, that Yoolow did not understand that ten shillings made half a pound, but that he did know how many shillings were in ten shillings.

Cross-examination resumed by Mr. *D. M'Neil:*—" You said that you also asked him how many shillings were in *five* shillings, and that he did not know—what explanation do you give as to that ? I must have fallen into a mistake, when I said that I asked how many shillings were in five shillings. What, then, was the question you asked David Yoolow relative to the five shillings, and what was his answer? I am embarrassed, and cannot tell."

We shall give but two extracts from the depositions for the defence.

The Reverend *James Flowerdew:* " I found he possessed a very considerable acquaintance with the Scriptures. I shaped my questions to him, so that I might discover whether he knew the Scriptures mechanically merely, or whether he was intelligent upon the subject. I paid less attention to his quotation of texts than to his application of them. I examined him both on the Mosaic and Christian dispensations; and I put questions to him in regard to the doctrines of the Gospel, with the view to ascertain whether he understood them; and I found that he not only thoroughly understood them, but gave reasons in support of his belief, not from texts merely, but other reasons which satisfied me he had reflected and reasoned on the subject. * * * * I asked him whether any miracles were performed under the Jewish dispensation. He said there were. I then asked him if there was any difference between the miracles under the Jewish dispensation and those under the Gospel. He said there was. I asked what that difference was. He answered, that the first were miracles of judgment, and the others were miracles of mercy and compassion. There was another question I asked him, the answer to which struck me very much, and satisfied me that he was capable of something like a process of reasoning. I asked him if the apostles wrought miracles. He said they did. I then asked him if they used any name in working their miracles; and he said they did:— that they used the name of Jesus, saying, ' in the name of Christ or Jesus,' when they wrought their miracles. I then asked him if Christ used any name when he was going to

work miracles, and he said ' No.'   I then asked him what he
would infer from the different mode in which Christ wrought
miracles from the apostles — and he replied without the
slightest hesitation, ' a divine person.' "

Dr. *John Argyle Robertson:* " He understood money
matters very well.   I asked him the meaning of a receipt?
He answered, it was a discharge for sums paid.   I asked
him what was the use of a receipt?   He said it was to prevent a second demand being made for payment.   I asked
him what would be the effect if I destroyed a bank-note?
He said you would be a loser.   I asked him what effect it
would have upon the bank?   He said the bank would be
gainers.   I asked him what was the meaning of being a
cautioner?   He said it was being a guarantee for another's
debt.   I asked him if the principal could not pay what would
happen?   He said, if the cautioner could not pay he would
be put in jail."

Mr. Robertson fought his losing case with all the tact,
eloquence, and readiness that would have been expected from
him—

" The first point to which I direct your attention is, the general
history of Yoolow's life, as admitted on all hands.

" If it were true, as some of the opposite witnesses have not hesitated to say, that Yoolow was a man of *strong* mind,—if that mind
had not been at all affected by his bodily state of decrepitude, I ask
you, how you can account for the limited nature of his occupations?
It might be right to give a due portion of time to the Scriptures, but
why should he never have done any thing else ?—or why did he only
change from these to a Book of Hymns, or the Pilgrim's Progress,
the visions of which, it appears, disturbed this vigorous intellect?
The confinement of the mind to this one book, to the exclusion of
every other subject, is a strong indication of imbecility.   I do not
say that he was bound to know the merits of political questions, but
he might at least have known that his own landlord was member for
the county in which he lived.   Most people, surely, so situated,
would have known that fact.   If possessed of any understanding, he
must have heard of the Reform Bill, which it is proved he had not.
But supposing him indifferent to politics, why, if a strong-minded
man, or a man of sound mind, did he not betake himself, in some
degree, to other subjects than religion?   Why did he confine himself
to that single topic, to which it is notorious that persons of unsound

mind so often recur, and of which such striking examples were mentioned to you as existing in the Perth asylum?"

With all due deference to Mr. Robertson, there is nothing at all strange or uncommon in the circumstance. The majority of bedridden persons in Yoolow's rank of life read nothing but the Scriptures; and if the doctrine were extended a little further, it would embrace all who profess what are called Evangelical opinions, who are wont to condemn every kind of reading, not of a strictly devotional character, as profane.

" Then, it seems, he dislikes the visions of the Pilgrim's Progress,—they disturb his mind. Is that a proof of soundness? He can't eat fruit,—because by eating fruit our first parents fell! He asks people ' are ye canny?' What nonsense is this!—Does he believe in witchcraft?—Then comes his string of interrogatories—' Are you a doctor? The hills, are they as far as the end of the world? Manna doctors rise when it is snawing? I haena to rise when it's snawing.—I am better off than doctors.' There is a strong-minded man! Then he submits to be asked how many two and two make; and, instead of being angry, he says—*four*. But of late it would appear that his power of calculation has become wonderful. How this recent attainment has been acquired, I know not: but he can now answer questions which puzzle every body, except my learned friend opposite, whose knowledge of figures is notorious. But will they succeed in making him a man of sense? What if my learned friend and I were to carry on such conversations, as seem to have been Yoolow's delight; ' Duncan, are ye canny?—Peter, we haena to rise when it's snawing.—Na, Duncan, we are better off than doctors.' Would this be the language of sense, or of imbecility?"

Yoolow is not the only person who has felt his mind disturbed by the visions of the Pilgrim's Progress, nor the only person who has held silly conversations with his servants. But the main fallacy in this paragraph consists in the artful change of the terms of the question; as if the defender were called upon to prove the strength, instead of disproving the imbecility, of his intellect.

" I pass over his ignorance of the prime minister. I acknowledge it is often difficult to answer who is prime minister. Whether it be Lord Melbourne, or the Duke o' ——, or any other O', may be at times a puzzling inquiry to wiser men than Yoolow. But then it seems Yoolow knew who was king—and he announces his knowledge in a way incontestably proving his silliness. On the subject of the corn laws, of which he ought to have known something, all that Dr. Christison could extract from him, was a conjecture that they were to sell the corn.

*   *   *   *

"In the middle of a conversation on other matters, Yoolow cannot refrain from expressing how much he is delighted with David Ballairdie's buttons.

"Gentlemen—contemplate for a moment this picture. Here is a man of fifty-four years of age, who, like the veriest child, is 'pleased with a rattle, tickled with a straw,'—and gazes with infantine ecstacy at a brass button ! The fact speaks volumes ; and I may observe, that the beauty of these buttons is the only subject of conversation that Yoolow is proved ever to have originated. I beg pardon—I must correct myself. I understand it is not *David,* but *Saunders* Ballairdie, who is the gentleman with the buttons—these buttons which are more interesting to Yoolow than the deed of settlement of his sister. Look, gentlemen, at this unhappy creature's estimate of different objects. He does not know that his landlord is member for the county. He does not hear of the Reform Bill —though I should have thought that the noise of Coupar-Angus would have reached his ears at the first election. To all these things he is indifferent—he cares not what passes in the state—he sees no occasion for reform so long as Ballairdie's buttons glitter in the sun."

These are the most striking passages of this clever but unsatisfactory address, which is completely demolished, argument after argument, by Mr. M'Neill—

"Gentlemen (said Mr. M'Neill), when I remember the great attention with which you listened to the evidence, and that each of you had an opportunity of seeing and conversing with the defender ; when I think of the time that has already been occupied in this trial, and the many inconveniences and discomforts to which you have unavoidably been exposed in the course of it, and how very little, if at all, the result of it now depends upon me—it is with considerable reluctance that I trespass on your patience, or add another moment to the many hours of fatigue you have already undergone. But if there is any ground at all for the perseverance and the confidence with which the cause has been pressed on the part of the pursuer, I cannot but feel that it may be fraught with fearful consequences to my unfortunate client. If the sad dispensation which, in early life, deprived him of bodily power, was attended with the farther deprivation of all mental faculties, then indeed would he be a fit object, not only for your greatest pity and commiseration, but for the protecting interference of the law, were it not that other circumstances, to which I shall have occasion to allude, render such interference in his case unnecessary. If he does truly labour under that double deprivation of bodily power, and of mental faculties, your verdict, whatever it may be, can bring neither gladness nor sorrow to him. But if, as I firmly believe to be the case, there does dwell within that feeble and shattered tabernacle a reflecting mind, now watching with anxious solicitude the fate of this inquiry—a mind conscious of the disadvantages to which it is exposed, and yet sensitively alive to all the sympathies of our nature —by circumstances accustomed, if not compelled, to rely on its own resources for employment, and in solitude driven to feed upon itself, unrelieved by those calls to active exertion which in other cases help to break gloom and banish despair—if that is truly the condition of my client, I can picture no consequences more fearful, no fate more appalling, than that such a man should, through any mistake on your part, or through any failure of duty on mine, be subjected to the endless and countless mortification of unmerited degradation, of unjust control and subjection to minds perhaps weaker in power and in virtue than his own, and of sad and hopeless excision from the mass of rational beings. You will, therefore, I am sure, pardon the anxiety which prompts me still to solicit your attention to the grounds on which I confidently ask your verdict in his favour."

He then quotes a number of authorities to prove that mere deficiency of mental power is not sufficient to disqualify a man for the management of his affairs—that hesitation of speech, nervous affections, uncouth gestures, or absence of mind, have often induced a mistaken supposition of insanity; and that above all it is a most imperative duty to distinguish between the actual acquisition of knowledge and the capacity.

"The most knowing savage from the Sandwich Islands, or the shrewdest serf from Russia, would be found totally ignorant of many things which we know to be familiar to persons of limited knowledge among ourselves. We even see in our own country men of the strongest natural parts, who, from their avocations, their dispositions, or the position in which their lot has been cast, have not extended the sphere of their knowledge half so far as some who are infinitely inferior to them in natural sagacity and mental power."

An amusing instance of mingled ignorance and credulity in men of the highest intellectual eminence is related in one of Mrs. Shelley's delightful volumes of biography:

Racine and Boileau having been named joint historiographers to the king (Louis XIV), it was intimated to them that they were to accompany him in his campaigns. "The poets seem to have been singularly ignorant of everything appertaining to a journey, and to have shown the most amusing credulity. Racine was told that he must take care to have his horse shod by a bargain of forfeit. ' Do you imagine,' said his adviser, M. de Cavoie, ' that an army always finds blacksmiths ready on their march? Before you leave Paris a bargain is made with a smith, who warrants, on penalty of a forfeit, that your horse's shoes shall remain on for six months.' ' I never heard of that before,' said Racine; ' Boileau did not tell me; but I do not wonder; he never thinks of anything.' He hastened to his friend to reproach him for this neglect; Boileau confessed his ignorance; and they hurried out to seek the blacksmith most in use for this sort of bargain. The king was duly informed of their perplexity, and by his raillery in the evening, undeceived them."[1]

The whole of the remarks on the medical evidence are good, but we have only room for a part of the commentary on Dr. Christison's :—

" Dr. Christison, after separately exhausting the three departments of agriculture, arithmetic, and politics, proceeded to put questions to the supposed idiot on the more complex subject of political economy. This part I shall read to you in the doctor's own words : ' I said, although you do not meddle with politics, there are some branches of them, which, as a farmer'—David Yoolow, however, never was a farmer, he is only going to become a farmer now, but Dr. Christison erroneously supposes him to have been a farmer—' which, as a farmer you should know about; for instance, what is your opinion of the corn bill ?' There is a question for you ! There is a question to be put to an idiot ! There is a question to be put to an uneducated countryman, who had no experience in corn, or in trade of any kind ! Pray Mr. David Yoolow, what is your opinion of the corn bill ? That is a branch of politics which you ought to understand ! Really, gentleman, there is in this something so ludicrous, that unless we had heard of it from Dr. Christison himself, I could scarcely have credited it. I am sure if my learned friend opposite had told me that Dr. Christison had put such a question to a supposed idiot, after having tried

[1] Lives of the Eminent Literary Men of France, vol. i. p. 280.

him in the several departments of agriculture, arithmetic, and politics, I should have thought that my learned friend was giving vent to his known humour, and would have given him credit for another excellent joke. The vague terms, too, in which the question was expressed might have puzzled even Mr. Western to answer it. Pray, sir, what is your opinion of the corn bill?—without deigning to say in what respect. Pray, sir, what is your opinion of things in general? would be almost as specific and intelligible a question. David Yoolow, when thus assailed on the subject of the corn bill, which I dare say had never before cost him a thought, honestly answered, ' I ken nathing about that.' But that answer did not deter the doctor from pressing the subject. ' I asked him (says he) what is it intended for ?' That certainly was somewhat more specific; and what was the answer? ' He answered, to sell the corn, I fancy !' A better answer Cobbett himself could not have given, and none of my learned friends or of the learned doctors examined in this cause, have attempted to impugn it."

He thus ingeniously, though perhaps somewhat too sophistically, disposes of the argument founded on Yoolow's peculiarities of temper and caprices :

" Gentleman, I am almost ashamed to stoop to notice the points to which that evidence was directed. I shall merely touch on what appear to be the most important of them. In the first place, then, it is said that he was peevish and fretful, to a degree that was childish, and sometimes, when crossed in trifling matters, took the pet and went to bed. It is not wonderful that an invalid and recluse should be peevish and fretful. It has been remarked, and I believe with truth, that persons constitutionally feeble and decrepit, are generally subject to irritability of temper ; and that even the possession of the most splendid talents, the most exalted genius, and the soundest notions of philosophy, may not secure them against that infirmity ;—a memorable instance of which is said to have occurred in the case of one of the greatest poets and truest painters of the human character, that Britain ever produced. Then it is said that Yoolow had foolish prejudices—that he would not eat fruit, because the eating of fruit caused the fall of man. This may appear to you or to me a foolish prejudice, but both you and I know, that prejudices and aversions of that kind are not confined to idiots,—that they extend even to whole tribes and nations. Jews are said to have a prejudice or aversion to the flesh of swine. The numerous disciples of Mahomed have also prejudices and aversions, in eating and drinking. There are many millions of inhabitants of Hindostan, who, from prejudices or scruples, will not partake of the flesh of animals that are daily eaten by Europeans; and, even in our own country, I have known pious Christians who had conscientious scruples against eating the blood of animals that had been shot or strangled. Another of Yoolow's prejudices brought forward as indicating idiocy, is said to have been his aversion to profane swearing, and his horror of certain persons who indulged in that most sinful and unmeaning practice. To those who are not used to take the name of the Lord in vain, or to hear others do so, without an unpleasant feeling, though they may not be so extremely sensitive, or exhibit their feelings so very strongly as Yoolow, this does appear a most extraordinary fact to be adduced as a proof of idiocy, before a jury of this country. Yoolow may perhaps carry his notions into extremes, and exhibit his religious feelings and scruples in a way that is neither usual nor necessary. But is that a proof of idiocy? When a distinguished character of the last age, on revisiting one of the scenes of early life, was struck with the recollection of an act of disobedience to parental authority which he had there committed, and evinced his contrition for the juvenile and comparatively trivial transgression, by exposing his uncovered head to the inclemency of the elements,—was he bereft of reason? Did the frame of mind which prompted that extreme exhibition of filial reverence and piety, unfit him for the management of his own affairs, and make him worthy of being cognosced as fatuus and an idiot? He, whose intellectual superiority was acknowledged even in the jealous republic of letters, —who, in mental conflict with the great authors and learned men of his time, was admitted to wield a giant's power,—maintaining and advancing the literary reputation of his native land,—chastening the philosophy, and elevating the morals of the Christian world. Tell me not, then, that Yoolow's horror of profane swearing, and his aversion to the society of those who indulge in that vice, is a proof of idiocy."

We presume that the irritable valetudinarian alluded to in the first paragraph is Pope, and the distinguished penitent of the last age, Johnson. We have no distinct recollection of the anecdote; but numerous traits of superstitious weakness, far more open to perversion, might be culled without difficulty from the annals of his life.

"Finally it is said that David Yoolow's amusements, which are admitted to have been harmless, were exceedingly foolish and unintellectual.—Particularly the freak of Grosing, which was so humorously commented upon by my learned friend. Gentlemen, how many of the amusements of all of us are unintellectual, and how many of them, when gravely examined at a distance from the feelings and excitement and levity that prompted to the indulgence in them, appear foolish and ridiculous! Have we not heard of ministers of state and even crowned heads, playing at blind-man's-buff? Do we not daily see men and women, of all ranks, leaping and bouncing on the floor till they are about to fall down with fatigue, and call it dancing? We see the first people in the country galloping across fields and leaping over ditches and hedges, to the fracture of their limbs and the imminent hazard of their necks, all in order that they may, with the assistance of two or three score of dogs, kill a poor frightened wretch of a fox, or get hold of his unsavoury tail, which, after it is got, is worth nothing. We see grave gentlemen, patiently standing for hours up to the middle in water, trying to catch a fish, while they might for sixpence buy more fish than they can catch in a season, and avoid forming part of that exhibition which a great lexicographer is said to have described as a rod and a line, with a worm at one end and a fool at the other. What strange performances and exhibitions have we not seen resulting from the innocent pastime of playing at forfeits! What were the feasts of the Queens of May, and of the Abbots of Unreason? What were, and are, the carnivals and masquerades of past and present times? In short there are seasons when the mind escapes, and ought to escape, from the trammels of thought and reason and recruit itself by unreserved indulgence in innocent folly,—the more absolutely foolish and unintellectual, the more perfect the relaxation. But, if all the strange freaks of our most capricious humours and unrestrained indulgence were to be chronicled for years, and suddenly arrayed against us with the graphic powers of my learned friend, I doubt whether there are many of us who would on the day of trial, appear to be further removed from idiocy than David Yoolow,—or whether the counterfeit dialogue which, in the exuberance of his fancy, my learned friend supposed as taking place between himself and me, would be one whit more absurd than some of the originals."

The sheriff summed up the evidence with clearness and impartiality, and the jury unanimously returned a verdict for the defender without retiring from the box.

[The latest contribution to this branch of learning is *A Treatise on the Medical Jurisprudence of Insanity. By T. Ray, M.D.* Edinburgh, 1859—which we shall probably take an early opportunity of reviewing.]

DIGEST OF CASES.

COMMON LAW.

[Comprising 9 Adolphus & Ellis, Part 1 ; 1 Perry & Davison, Part 4 ; 6 Nevile & Manning, Part 5 : 6 Scott, Part 5 ; 4 Meeson & Welsby, Part 5, and 5 Meeson & Welsby, Part 1 ; 8 Adolphus & Ellis, Parts 1 and 2, also recently published, contain no case which has not been before abstracted.]

AFFIDAVIT.

1. (*Addition of deponent.*) An affidavit by " A. B. of, &c., the plaintiff (or defendant) in this cause," is sufficient without any further addition.

An affidavit commencing thus :—" R. J., late of the city of W., victualler, but now of, &c.," without any further addition, held sufficient.—*Angel v. Ihler*, 5 M. & W. 163.

2. (*Entitling.*) The defendant, whose real name was Humphrey D. R., was described in the writ of summons and distringas thereon as Henry R. On an application to set aside the distringas, he entitled his affidavit as in the cause " B. v. Humphrey D. R., sued as Henry R. :" Held incorrect, there being no such cause until appearance.—*Borthwick v. Ravenscroft*, 5 M. & W. 31.

ALIEN ARTIFICER.

If an alien artificer takes possession of a dwelling-house under an agreement in writing, which provides for the granting of a future lease, the instrument being illegal under 32 Hen. 8, c. 16, the lessor may enter at any time and eject the tenant, although the instrument do not amount to a lease.—*Lapierre v. M'Intosh*, 1 P. & D. 629.

AMENDMENT.

(*Under 3 & 4 Will. 4, c. 42.*) A declaration in assumpsit stated, that in consideration that the plaintiff would employ the defendant to build on a certain plot of ground, a *room, booth, or building*, and to fit it up *according to certain plans* agreed upon, for the sum of 20*l.*, the defendant promised to erect the same by the 28th June, 1838. The defendant pleaded non assumpsit, and that the agreement was rescinded. The contract proved was, that the defendant should place upon a plot of ground, hired for the purpose by the plaintiff, certain *seats and tables*, to be completed *four or five days before* the 28th June, 1838 (the day of the coronation), for 25*l.*; and it did not appear that there were any plans agreed upon. The judge at the trial having directed the declaration to be amended in conformity with the contract proved, the Court refused a new trial.— *Ward* v. *Pearson*, 5 M. & W. 16.

ARBITRATION.

1. (*Enlargement of time.*) An arbitrator who had power to enlarge the time for making his award by indorsement on the order of reference, made the following indorsement :—" I direct that a rule of this Court shall be applied for by counsel's hand, to enlarge the time of making my award." No such rule was applied for ; but the parties subsequently attended meetings before the arbitrator, and made no objection to the regularity of the enlargement : Held, first, that the indorsement was itself a sufficient enlargement of the time : but secondly, that if it were not, the irregularity had been waived.— *Hallett* v. *Hallett*, 5 M. & W. 25.

2. (*Award, when sufficiently final—Proof of allegation of award made.*) Where an action of assumpsit, the declaration in which contained a count upon a promissory note for 22*l*. 11*s*. 9*d*., and a count upon an account stated for 30*l*. was referred to arbitration, and the arbitrator found that the plaintiff had good cause of action for, and was and is legally entitled to have, claim, and recover of and from the defendant the sum of 22*l*. 11*s*. 9*d*., being the amount of the promissory note mentioned in the pleadings in the said cause : Held that the award was bad, inasmuch as it did not dispose of the issue upon the account stated. (2 C. & M. 722.)

In an action upon the award, the declaration stated that the original action was referred by a rule of Court to A. B., who duly made his award of and concerning the premises so referred to him, and did thereby find, &c. The defendant pleaded that the said A. B. did not duly make and publish his award of and concerning the premises referred, in manner and form, &c. : Held, that the production of the award and the rule of Court was sufficient primâ facie evidence to support the issue on the part of the plaintiff, until the validity of the award was impeached by evidence dehors on the part of the defendant. (11 East, 193.)— *Gisborne* v. *Hart*, 5 M. & W. 50.

ARREST.

1. (*Setting aside, time for.*) An application to set aside an arrest made on a judge's order, under the 1 & 2 Vict. c. 110, s. 3, must be made promptly ; and as it seems, within the time for putting in bail.

In order to excuse the delay, on the ground of a previous application at chambers, the rule must be drawn up on reading the summons, or it must be shown by affidavit.—*Sugars* v. *Concanen*, 5 M. & W. 30.

2. (*Discharge from illegal arrest.*) S., a sheriff's officer, arrested the defendant, not then having any warrant, and took him to a lock-up-house. At that time there was a warrant in the sheriff's office, directed to another officer, to arrest the defendant at the suit of the plaintiff. S. went to the sheriff's office, and representing that he had an opportunity of arresting the defendant, got his own name inserted in that warrant. It appeared that this was in accordance with the practice of the office, and it was sworn that the sheriff was ignorant that the defendant had at that time been already arrested. S. took the warrant, and arrested the defendant at the suit of the plaintiff: Held, that the defendant was not entitled to be discharged. (2 W. Bla. 823 ; 9 Bing. 566. See Pearson v. Yewens, 5 Bing. N. C. 489.)—*Robinson* v. *Yewens*, 5 M. & W. 149.

BANKRUPTCY. See PLEADING, 7.

BILLS AND NOTES.

1. (*Presentment of foreign bill payable after sight.*) A bill of exchange was drawn in duplicate on the 12th of August at Carbonear in Newfoundland, payable ninety days after sight, on S. & Co. in England, for the freight of a voyage from Liverpool to Carbonear. The bill was not presented for acceptance to S. & Co. until the 16th of November. Carbonear is twenty miles from St. John's, wit h daily communication between those places ; and from St. John's there is a post-office packet three times a week to England, the average voyage being about eighteen days : Held, that the jury had properly found that the bill was not presented for acceptance within a reasonable time, no circumstances being proved in explanation of the delay.—*Straker* v. *Graham,* 4 M. & W. 704.

2. (*Consideration.*) To a declaration in debt on a promissory note for 24*l.*, dated 3d January, 1837, made by the defendant, payable twelve months after date to the plaintiff, the defendant pleaded that one J. W., before and at his death, was indebted to the plaintiff in 24*l.* for goods sold, which sum was due to the plaintiff at the time of the making of the promissory note in the declaration mentioned : that the plaintiff, after the death of J. W., applied to the defendant for payment ; whereupon, in compliance with his request, the defendant, after the death of J. W., for and in respect of the debt so remaining due to the plaintiff as aforesaid, and for no other consideration whatever, made and delivered the note to the plaintiff, and that J. W. died intestate, and that at the time of the making and delivery of the note, no administration had been granted of his effects, nor was there any executor or executors of his estate, nor any person liable for the debt so remaining due to the plaintiff as aforesaid ; and the defendant averred *that there never was any consideration for the said note except as aforesaid :* Held, that the plea was a good answer to the declaration. (1 C. & J. 231. See Serle v. Waterworth, 4 M. & W. 9.)—*Nelson* v. *Serle,* 4 M. & W. 795.

3. (*Notice of dishonour, evidence of from subsequent admission—Pleading.*) On an issue joined in an action by indorsee against maker of a promissory note, on the fact of presentment, a promise made by the defendant to pay the bill, after it became due, is primâ facie evidence to prove the issue.—*Croxon* v. *Worthen,* 5 M. & W. 5.

4. (*Defence of—Total failure of consideration.*) To an action by the indorsee against the drawer of a bill of exchange, the defendant pleaded that the bill was given in payment of the price of seventeen pockets of hops sold by the plaintiff to the defendant, as hops of a certain grower, and answering certain samples, to be delivered by the plaintiff to the defendant within a reasonable time : that although a reasonable time had elapsed, the plaintiff had not delivered to the defendant any hops answering the samples, *or any hops whatsoever ;* and that there was no consideration for the bill except as aforesaid. Replication, de injuriâ. It appeared that the plaintiff had delivered to the defendant seventeen pockets of hops, but inferior to the samples : Held, that the general allegation in the plea that the plaintiff had not delivered *any hops whatever,* was immaterial, and might be rejected : and that without it the plea showed a total failure of consideration, and was an answer to the action. Held, also, that if the plaintiff relied on the defendant's *acceptance* of the inferior hops, he ought to have replied it.—*Wells* v. *Hopkins,* 5 M. & W. 7.

BILL OF LADING. See PRINCIPAL AND FACTOR.

BOROUGH RATE.

(Appeal against, by whom.) The power of appeal against a borough-rate under 5 & 6 Will. 4, c. 76, is confined to the grounds of appeal against a county rate, under 55 Geo. 3, c. 51, s. 14, and therefore an individual cannot appeal for any personal grievance, or on the ground of the rate being retrospective.—*Reg.* v. *Recorder of Bath*, 1 P. & D. 622.

CHURCH-LEASE. See LEASE, 1.

CHURCH-RATE.

An action for distraining goods for arrears of a church-rate may, under the 53 Geo. 3, c. 127, s. 12, be brought within three months after the *sale* of the goods. *Collins* v. *Rose*, 5 M. & W. 194.

CONSPIRACY.

(Indictment for, when too general.) An indictment charged in the first count, that the defendants unlawfully conspired to defraud divers persons, who should bargain with them for the sale of merchandize, of great quantities of such merchandize, without paying for the same, with intent to obtain to themselves money and other profit. The second count charged that two of the defendants, being in partnership in trade, and being indebted to divers persons, unlawfully conspired to defraud the said creditors of payment of their debts, and that they and the other defendant, in pursuance of the said conspiracy, falsely and wickedly made a fraudulent deed of bargain and sale of the stock in trade of the partnership for fraudulent consideration, with intent thereby to obtain to themselves money and other emoluments, to the great damage of the said creditors.

Held, 1. That the first count was not bad for omitting to state the names of the persons intended to be defrauded, as it could not be known who might fall into the snare; but that the count was bad for not showing by what means they were to be defrauded.

2. That the second count was bad for not alleging facts to show in what manner the deed of sale was fraudulent. (2 Stra. 999; 1 East, 583; 2 B. & Ald. 204.)—*Peck* v. *The Queen*, 1 P. & D. 508.

CONTRACT.

(Cannot be repudiated in part, on ground of fraud.) A. engaged to convey away certain rubbish for B. at a specified sum, under a fraudulent representation by B. as to the quantity of the rubbish which was to be so conveyed : Held, that in an action for the value of the work actually done, A. could recover only according to the terms of the special contract ; although when he discovered the fraud, he might have repudiated the contract, and sued B. for deceit. (3 Camp. 351 ; 9 B. & C. 59; 1 Ad. & E. 40.)—*Selway* v. *Fogg*, 5 M & W. 83.

COPYHOLD.

(Right of copyholder to remove stones fallen on the land.) Where large masses of stone had fallen from time to time from some cliffs above upon the field of a copyhold, and had become thereby partially imbedded in the soil, there being no evidence to show when any particular portion of them had fallen : Held, that they were the property of the lord, and that the copyholder could not remove them for his own profit.—*Dearden* v. *Evans*, 5 M. & W. 11.

COSTS.

1. *(When to be taxed on reduced scale.)* Where a cause is referred at Nisi Prius, care should be taken to give the arbitrator the same power of certifying that it was a fit cause to be tried before a judge as the judge at Nisi Prius would have had ; since otherwise, if he award to the plaintiff a sum under 20*l.*, the Master

will not be warranted in taxing the costs, either as between party and party, or as between attorney and client, except according to the reduced scale given in the "Directions to Taxing Officers," H. T. 4 Will. 4.—*Wallen* v. *Smith,* 5 M. & W. 159.

2. (*Same.*) Where the defendant, just before the assizes, in order to save the expenses of the trial, agreed to withdraw his pleas, and that the plaintiff should be at liberty to sign judgment for 11*l.* 12*s.*, and that on payment of that sum, with costs to be taxed, the proceedings should be stayed: Held that the costs must be taxed on the reduced scale applicable to a verdict under 20*l.*—*Cooke* v. *Hunt,* 5 M. & W. 161.

3. (*Under conditional rule.*) Where a rule was made absolute for changing the venue from Middlesex to the country, on payment of the costs of the application, " and of all costs reasonably and bonâ fide incurred and rendered useless by the rule;" and after taxation of the costs, the defendant's attornies gave notice to the plaintiff's attornies that they abandoned the rule: Held, (Maule, B. dissentiente) that the rule was conditional only, and that the defendant was not bound to abide by it, although the plaintiff had in the meantime incurred the costs of his witnesses, who were on their way to town before the rule was made absolute. (11 East, 319; 2 D. P. C. 182; 5 T. R. 257.)—*Pugh* v. *Kerr,* 5 M. & W. 164.

And see COURT OF REQUESTS ACTS; PAUPER.

COURT OF REQUESTS ACTS.

(*When to be pleaded.*) Where a Court of Requests Act provided that if any person should commence any action in any of the superior Courts against any person residing within the jurisdiction of the Court of Requests, for any debt &c., which *upon the trial* should be found not to amount to 40*s.*, *no judgment should be entered on the verdict,* and if it were entered, should be void, and the defendant should have costs : Held, that a defendant could not take advantage of the act by suggestion on the roll, but was bound to plead it in bar of the action.—*Jackman* v. *Cother,* 5 M. & W. 147.

DEVISE.

1. (*To trustees.*) Devise of freehold premises to trustees, to *set and let* the premises, and out of the rents and profits thereof to pay a debt, and in the next place to pay certain legacies, as soon as the rents and profits would permit, and after the debt and legacies were paid off, to R. B. in fee :—Held, that the trustees took only a chattel interest, for that the power of leasing was expressly confined to the purpose of paying off the debt and legacies.—*Ackland* v. *Lutley,* 1 P. & D. 636.

2. (*Vesting of estates—When devise void for remoteness.*) Devise of real and personal estate to trustees, to permit testator's daughter for her life to take the rents, &c., and from and after her decease the premises were given to such of her children as she then had or might have; if a son or sons, at his or their ages of twenty-three, and if a daughter or daughters, at her or their ages of twenty-one years, in fee, as tenants in common; and in case of the death of any child or children under the respective ages, the share to go to the survivors; in case his daughter should have only one child, if a son, that should live to the age of twenty-three, and if a daughter, that should live to the age of twenty-one, the whole to such child; until his grand-children should attain such ages as aforesaid, the rents to be applied for their maintenance by the trustees; in case such grand-children should all die under age, devise over :—Held, that they took

vested interests, and that therefore the devise was not void for remoteness : (1 M. & Sel. 577.)—*Doe* d. *Dolley* v. *Ward,* 1 P. & D. 568.

HABEAS CORPUS.

1. A judge at chambers has power at common law to issue in vacation a writ of habeas corpus, returnable before himself immediately.

A return to a writ of habeas corpus primâ facie imports verity, and until it is impeached need not be supported by affidavits or otherwise.

Quære, by what mode of procedure the return may be impeached and its truth inquired into.

Semble, that it may be controverted by affidavits.

Quære, whether it can be traversed in pleading, or merely confessed and avoided.

The Court may, in its discretion, allow the return to be amended after it has been filed.—*Reg.* v. *Batcheldor,* 1 P. & D. 516.

2. The Court cannot grant a habeas corpus to bring up a defendant for the purpose of charging him in execution, who is in custody under military arrest.—*Jones* v. *Danvers,* 5 M. & W. 234.

HARBOUR ACT.

By a local act trustees were authorized to take lands for the improvement of a harbour, and in case of a disagreement with the land-owner as to the price to be paid him, or of his refusal to treat, to direct a sheriff to summon a jury, by whom the price was to be assessed. If the jury gave a greater sum than offered by the trustees, or the same sum, they were to pay all the costs ; if a less sum, the costs to be paid equally by both parties ; and in the former event, to be recovered by a distress warrant from a magistrate : Held, that it it belonged to the trustees to have the inquisition of the jury properly drawn up, and that therefore they could not object to the sum awarded by it, or have it brought up by certiorari to quash it, on the ground that it did not state the disagreement or the refusal to treat, so as to show that the jury had jurisdiction, and that it did not state the proportion of the sum assessed to the sum offered, so as to ascertain which party was to pay the costs. *Semble,* that a statement in the inquisition that each party appeared by counsel, was sufficient to show their disagreement as to price, and that it was not necessary for the inquisition to find the proportion of the sum awarded to the sum offered.—*Reg.* v. *Trustees of Swansea Harbour,* 1 P. & D. 512.

HIGHWAY ACT.

Where a parish was divided into eight tithings, each of which, before the new Highway Act (5 & 6 Will. 4, c. 50), maintained its own highways separately, and after the passing of that act each of the tithings elected one or more persons as surveyors, who formed a board for the parish, but rated the tithings separately as before the act : Held, that the parish at large had no power to form a board under sect. 18, and that the rate made by them was bad.—*Reg.* v. *Bush,* 1 P. & D. 586.

HUNGERFORD MARKET ACT.

(*Compensation under.*) By the 11 Geo. 4, c. lxx. the Hungerford Market Company are empowered to make compulsory purchases of land for the use of the market ; and by section 19 all tenants for years, from year to year, or at will, occupiers of any part of the estate called the Hungerford House, &c., or therewith contracted to be purchased by the Company, who shall or may sustain or be put unto any loss, damage, or injury, in respect of any interest whatsoever, for good-will, *improvements*, tenants' fixtures, or otherwise, which they now enjoy, by reason of the passing of the act, shall receive compensation from the Company. While the Company were treating for the purchase of certain premises under the act, a person entered into an agreement to rent them for one year, and that if, with the owner's consent, he should hold beyond the year, he should quit, or be at liberty to quit, at any quarter day, on receiving or giving three months' notice ; that he would not underlet or give up possession to any one, make any alteration without a written consent of his landlord, would keep all the glass entire, and so leave the same, together with all articles mentioned in a schedule, and all *improvements* or additions which he should make during his occupation, for the benefit of his landlord. The tenant occupied, with the consent of his landlord, for several years, while the above negociations were proceeding. He afterwards received due notice to quit, and the purchase by the company was completed : Held, that he was not entitled to compensation from the Company in respect of improvements made by him during his occupation. (2 B. & Ad. 341, 348 ; 4 B. & Ad. 327, 592, 596.)— *Reg. v. Hungerford Market Company, exp. Palmer,* 1 P. & D. 492.

HUSBAND AND WIFE.

(*Action by husband, when wife to be joined in.*) Lands were demised to A. and B. his wife for twenty-one years. A. afterwards granted a lease of them to C. for nine years : Held in an action brought by A. alone, for an injury to his reversionary interest, that the allegation that the reversion belonged to him was well supported, and that the wife need not be joined in the action ; but that even if she ought, the objection should have been taken by plea in abatement.— *Wallis v. Harrison,* 5 M. & W. 142.

And see INSOLVENT, 1.

INDICTMENT. See CONSPIRACY.

INFANT.

Assumpsit to recover the amount of a tailor's bill, for clothes supplied to the defendant's testator in his lifetime. Plea, infancy of the testator. Replication, necessaries ; on which issue was joined. On the trial it appeared that the testator was a minor at the time when the goods were supplied, but it was proved that he had an allowance of 500*l.* a year, besides his pay as a captain in the army. The learned judge at the trial was of opinion that if the minor had a sufficient income allowed him to supply him with necessaries suitable to his condition for ready money, he could not contract even for necessaries upon credit : Held, that this was a misdirection.— *Burghart v. Hull,* 4 M. & W. 727.

INSOLVENT.

1 (*Discharge of feme sole, how to be pleaded.*) In an action against husband and wife, for a debt contracted by her before coverture, they may plead her discharge while a feme sole under the Insolvent Debtors' Act.— *Storr v. Lee,* 1 P. & D. 633.

2. (*Proof of contingent debt.*) Where A. purchased of B. his business of an attorney, the purchase-money to be paid by two instalments, and the conveyance contained a proviso giving A. the power within a limited time either of completing the purchase, or giving B. notice of his abandonment of the contract, in

which case B. was to repay 50*l.* of the purchase-money : Held, that B.'s discharge under the Insolvent Debtors' Act, before the expiration of the time limited for giving such notice, was no answer to an action to recover back the 50*l.* after such notice given ; for that it was not a contingency capable of valuation at the time of the insolvency.—*Brown* v. *Fleetwood,* 5 M. & W. 19.

And see LIMITATIONS, STATUTE OF, 2.

JOINT STOCK COMPANY. See PARTNERS, 1.

JURY.

(*Affidavit of admission of misconduct by juror, admissibility of.*) On a motion for a new trial, the Court will not receive an affidavit by the attorney of an admission made to him by one of the jurymen, that the verdict was decided by lot.—*Straker* v. *Graham,* 4 M. & W. 721.

LANDLORD AND TENANT.

1. (*Action for use and occupation.*) The lessee of a term underlet the demised premises, and his undertenant held over for a portion of a year after the expiration of the term, against the will of the lessee, so that he could not give up possession to his lessor. During such holding over the lessee distrained upon the undertenant for rent previously due : Held, that the lessee was liable, in use and occupation, for the period of the under-tenant's holding over, but not for a whole year's rent.—*Ibbs* v. *Richardson,* 1 P. & D. 618.

2. (*Estate of party in possession under contract of purchase.*) Where a party was let into possession of land under an agreement of purchase, he paying interest after the rate of 5 per cent. per annum upon the purchase-money until the completion of the purchase, which was to be in three months ; and the purchase not being then completed, he continued in possession on the same terms : Held, that this was only a tenancy at will, which might be determined without notice to quit.—*Doe* d. *Tomes* v. *Chamberlaine,* 5 M. & W. 14.

LEASE.

1. (*Church lease by perpetual curate.*) A perpetual curate, whose curacy has been augmented by a grant of lands under the Queen Anne's Bounty Acts, cannot make a lease for three lives without the consent of the ordinary. (4 T. R. 665.) —*Doe* d. *Richardson* v. *Thomas,* 1 P. & D. 578.

2. (*Duration of—Surrender.*) Where a lease is to commence *from* the 25th of March then next, for twenty-one years, fully to be complete and ended, the term does not end until the last moment of the 25th March in the last year.

A lessee who had paid his rent occasionally to a trustee, and occasionally to a cestui que trust, gave up possession on the last day of his term, but before his term was over, to the person who had been trustee, and not to the party then having the legal title : Held, that as the act was equivocal, it did not amount either to a surrender or to a forfeiture of the term.—*Ackland* v. *Lutley,* 1 P. & D. 636.

3. (*Lease or agreement—Lease, when it vests in parish.*) By a written instrument, stamped with a lease stamp, and dated the 25th of February, 1782, E. S., being seised in fee of a house and premises, agreed to demise and let them to a committee for the parish of H., and the committee agreed to accept and take them, for the purpose of converting them into a poorhouse for the use of the parish of H. ; to hold to the said committee, in trust as aforesaid, from the 25th day of March then next coming for the term of ninety-nine years, at the clear yearly rent of 27*l.,* payable half-yearly : and the committee agreed to pay the rent, and

to keep the premises in good and sufficient repair during the term. It was also agreed that a lease and counterpart of the premises should be prepared and executed on or before the first of January then next, with covenants and agreements pursuant to that contract, and such other general clauses as are usually contained in leases; and there was a proviso, that in case the committee or their successors should think it a more eligible plan to purchase the premises in fee at the price of 420*l.*, that then he the lessor should convey them accordingly. No lease was ever executed, but the premises from the date of the instrument were used as a poor-house for the parish of H., and the churchwardens and overseers for the time being of that parish paid the rent to E. S. and his representatives. In an action of assumpsit against the parish officers for the time being of the parish of H., for non-repair of the premises : Held, first, that the agreement operated as a demise for the term of ninety-nine years, and not as a mere agreement for a lease ; secondly, that the lease vested in the overseers of the poor by force of the stat. 59 Geo. 3, c. 12, s. 17, and that the defendants were liable. (5 T. R. 165, n.; 15 East, 244; 3 Taunt. 64; 10 B. & C. 885 ; 4 Ad. & Ell. 274, 478.)— *Alderman* v. *Neate*, 4 M. & W. 704.

4. (*Lease or agreement.*) By an instrument dated December 13th, 1834, A., in consideration of the rents, covenants, and agreements thereinafter mentioned, agreed to grant a lease to B., his executors, &c. of certain premises, to hold the same for the term of two years and three-quarters, wanting seven days, from the 25th day of December instant, yielding and paying a certain rent, payable quarterly, the first payment to be made on the 25th of March then next ; which said indenture should contain covenants on the part of B. to pay the rent, &c., and all such other covenants as were contained in a lease therein referred to ; and B. agreed that he would, if and when requested so to do by A., accept such lease ; and that *until such lease should have been granted as aforesaid, it should be lawful for A., his executors, &c., to distrain for all or any part of the rent which might become due from B., for or in respect of the premises thereby agreed to be demised, at any time after the execution of that agreement:* Held, that the instrument operated as an agreement only, and not as an actual demise ; and consequently, that an agreement stamp was sufficient for it.—*Bicknell* v. *Hood*, 5 M. & W. 104.

LEGACY DUTY.

A testator, by his will, after giving certain legacies, gave, devised, and bequeathed unto his executors, their heirs, executors, and administrators, all the rest and residue of his estate, real and personal, upon trust, at such times as they might think fit, to *sell, convey, or otherwise convert into money* the same, or any part thereof ; and the testator directed that all the residue of his estate should be invested as it should be realized, and should be divided amongst all his children, in such shares and proportions that his son then born should take four shares, any other son or sons which he might have should take three shares each, and his daughters should take two shares each ; but if his son then born should die before twenty-one, and without leaving issue, the testator directed that his next son should take four shares, or, if he should have no other son, then that his eldest daughter should take three shares ; and he directed that in the event of any of his children dying under twenty-one, and without issue, his or her legacy or share should be considered as having lapsed ; and that in case any of his daughters should marry under twenty-one, his trustees should settle her fortune upon such trusts &c. as were specified in the will of his the testator's father with respect to certain bequests of *personal property* to the sisters of the said testator therein contained ; and the testator directed that his trustees should have full power, in making such sales as in the said will were *directed*, to resort to either public or private sale, and to buy in and re-sell, and to defer any sale so long as they might think fit, *and of causing any part or parts of his the said testator's real or personal estate to be valued instead of being sold, and of allotting such parts to any or either of his the said testator's children at the amount of the valuation,* as a part of his or her proportion of his residuary estate, *but to be considered as personal estate,* and subject to the trusts in the said will declared respecting such proportions of residuary estate.

The testator, at the time of his death, had one son and four daughters. The trustees, after the testator's death, sold a large part of the real and personal estate, amounting to 180,000l., and caused the remaining part of the residue, which consisted of real estate, to be valued, and the same was valued at 90,000l., which was the son's share of the residue ; and the sums of 45,000l. each, amounting to 180,000l., were the shares of the daughters. The trustees allotted the estate which had been so valued at 90,000l., to the testator's son, at the amount of the valuation, and retained the sum of 180,000l., the proceeds of the part which had been sold, for the benefit of the four daughters :—

Held, that legacy duty was payable upon the amount of the part which was actually sold, but not upon the part which the trustees had allotted to the testator's son, under the discretionary power contained in the will.—*Attorney-General v. Mangles*, 5 M. & W. 120.

LIBEL. See PRIVILEGES OF PARLIAMENT.

LIMITATIONS, STATUTE OF.

1. (*When it begins to run on contract of indemnity.*) A right to sue upon a contract of indemnity against the costs of an action is first vested when the party to whom the indemnity is given pays the bill of costs, and not when it is delivered to him, and the Statute of Limitations therefore does not begin to run against his right of action until after such payment. (Overruling Bullock v. Lloyd, 2 C. & P. 119.)—*Collinge* v. *Heywood*, 1 P. & D. 502.

2. (*When it operates on insolvent's debt.*) The Insolvent Act, 52 Geo. 3, c. 165, s. 54, by which a right is reserved to creditors to obtain payment out of the future effects of the insolvent, does not prevent the operation of the Statute of Limitations.—*Browning* v. *Paris*, 5 M. & W. 117.

MASTER AND SERVANT.

A. agreed to enter into the service of B., and wrote to him a letter as follows :—
" I hereby agree to enter your service as weekly manager, commencing next Monday ; and the amount of payment I am to receive I leave entirely to you." A. served B. in that capacity for six weeks :—Held, (Parke, B. dissentiente) that the contract implied that A. was to be paid something at all events for the services performed ; and that the jury in an action on a quantum meruit, might ascertain what B., acting bonâ fide, would or ought to have awarded. (1 M. & Sel. 290.)—*Bryant* v. *Flight*, 5 M. & W. 114.

MINE.

(*Construction of reservation of mines in grant.*) A., being seised in fee of certain lands, granted the land to P., his heirs and assigns, reserving to himself, his heirs and assigns, " all and all manner of coals, seams and veins of coal, iron ore, and all other mines, minerals, and metals which then were, or at any time, and from time to time thereafter, should be discovered in or upon the said premises, &c., with free liberty of ingress, egress, and regress, to come in and upon the premises, to dig, delve, search for, and get, &c. the said mines and every part thereof, and, to sell and dispose of, take, and convey away the same, at their free will and pleasure; and also to sink shafts, &c., for the raising up works, carrying away and disposing of the same or any part thereof, making a fair compensation to P. for the damage to be done to the surface of the premises, and the pasture and crops growing thereon."—Held, that, under this reservation, A. was not entitled to take all the mines, but only so much as he could get leaving a *reasonable* support to the surface.—*Harris v. Ryding,* 5 M. & W. 60.

And see WATERCOURSE.

ORDER OF REMOVAL.

A parish, obtaining an order for the removal of a pauper, must send with it, under s. 79, of 5 & 6 Will. 4, c. 76, the whole of the examinations taken before the justices, and not that part of them only on which the order was founded.—*Reg. v. Inhabitants of Outwell,* 1 P. & D. 610.

OVERSEER. See LEASE, 3.

PARTNERS.

1. (*Liability of subscriber to joint stock company.*) A project having been formed for the establishment of a company for the manufactory of sugar from beet-root, a prospectus was issued, stating the proposed capital to consist of 10,000 shares of 25*l.* each. The directors began their works, and entered into contracts respecting them, and manufactured and sold some sugar; but only a small portion of the proposed capital was raised, and only 1400 out of the 10,000 shares were taken :—Held, that a subscriber, who had taken shares and paid a deposit on them, was not liable upon such contracts of the directors, without proof that he knew and assented to their proceeding on the smaller capital, or expressly authorized the making of the contract. (7 B. & Cr. 409; 9 B. & Cr. 632; 10 B. & Cr. 128.)—*Pitchford v. Davies,* 5 M. & W. 2.

2. (*Actions between partners.*) Where A. and B. had been partners in certain transactions for the purchase and sale of wool, having also had other dealings together, and they settled a general account, in which was an item to B.'s debit " to loss on wool," and which showed a balance of 15*l.* against him : and B. signed the account and admitted the balance due :—Held, that A. might afterwards maintain an action to recover the amount of the item for the loss on the wool. Held, also, that it was no answer to such action, that, after the account was settled, the plaintiff had assented to a proposal of the defendant, that he should take out the balance in butcher's meat.— *Wray v. Milestone,* 5 M. & W. 21.

PAUPER.

(*Order to sue in formâ pauperis after commencement of suit, irregular.*) An order for the admission of a plaintiff to sue in formâ pauperis, made after the commencement of the suit, is irregular, and the plaintiff will, in such case, be dispaupered, or compelled to find security for costs. (4 M. & W. 610.)—*Lovewell v. Curtis,* 5 M. & W. 158.

PAYMENT INTO COURT. See PLEADING, 6.

PLEADING.

1. (*Plea of nil habuit in tenementis, what amounts to.*) To an avowry of a distress for rent the plaintiff pleaded that, before defendant had any interest in the premises, they were mortgaged in fee ; that the mortgagor remained in possession, and demised to the defendant ; that the defendant, the mortgage money being still due, demised to the plaintiff; that afterwards, the mortgage money being still due, and interest thereon, and 14*l.*, avowed for by the defendant, being also in arrear, the mortgagee gave notice to the plaintiff to pay the 14*l.* to him instead of to the defendant, and threatened, in case of non-payment, to put the law in force, and was then about to put the law in force, wherefore the plaintiff necessarily paid that sum to the mortgagee, and so the said sum was not in arrear; concluding with a verification : Held, on special demurrer, that the plea was good, being a plea of payment, and not of nil habuit in tenementis, and that it was not bad for setting out the circumstances of the payment, or for concluding with a verification. (4 T. R. 511 ; 6 Taunt. 524.)—*Johnson* v. *Jones*, 1 P. & D. 651.

2. (*Evidence under non assumpsit—Alteration of contract.*) In assumpsit on an express contract, which, on production at the trial, contains an interlineation in a material part, if the plaintiff prove that the instrument was originally executed without the interlineation, and in the form declared upon, the defendant cannot, on non assumpsit, contend that it has been avoided by the subsequent alteration. (3 D. P. C. 630.)—*Hemming* v. *Trenery*, 1 P. & D. 661.

3. (*Frivolous demurrer.*) Where a demurrer, though not absolutely frivolous, is evidently for the mere purpose of delay, the Court will permit it to be taken out of its turn.—*Dawson* v. *Parry*, 6 Scott, 890.

4. (*Nolle prosequi.*) Where a nolle prosequi is entered on a plea which goes to the whole cause of action, the defendant is entitled to judgment on the whole record. (3 T. R. 571 ; 2 Burr. 753.)—*Peters* v. *Croft*, 6 Scott, 897.

5. (*Replication of license to plea of user of way.*) To a declaration in trespass qu. cl. freg., the defendant pleaded that he and the former occupiers of a house and land had for twenty years used and enjoyed as of right a certain way on foot and with horses, &c., from and out of a common highway, towards, into, through, and over the plaintiff's close to the defendant's house and lands, and back, at all times of the year at their free will and pleasure. The replication averred that the defendant, &c. used and enjoyed the right of way mentioned in the plea, but that they did so under the plaintiff's leave and license. At the trial, it appeared that the defendant and the former occupiers of his house and land had an admitted right of way from thence over the locus in quo to the highway, and across the highway to a close called Reddings, and that for the last twenty years they had had a license from the plaintiff to use, whenever they pleased, a way from the defendant's house and lands over the locus in quo to the highway and back, when they had not any intention of going to Reddings : Held, that the replication was not supported by this evidence, and that the plaintiff was bound to show a license co-extensive with the right claimed in the plea, and admitted by the replication.—*Colchester* v. *Roberts*, 4 M. & W. 769.

6. (*Effect of plea of payment into Court as an admission.*) To counts in indebitatus assumpsit, for rent and for fixtures, &c. the defendant pleaded as to all, except 12*l.*, non assumpsit ; and as to that sum, payment into Court of that amount: Held, that the plea of payment into court only admitted that something

was due on a contract for fixtures; and the plaintiff having proved merely that the value of the fixtures exceeded 12*l.*, without proving any contract entered into by the defendant to take those fixtures, that he was not entitled to recover.

A plea of payment of money into court under the general indebitatus counts, only admits a liability upon some one or more contracts to the extent of the sum paid in. (The Court held the ruling of Tindal C. J. in Walker v. Rawson, 1 M. & Rob. 250, and the dicta of Littledale J. and Parke J., in Meager v. Smith, 4 B. & Adol. 673, not to be law.)—*Kingham v. Robins,* 5 M. & W. 94.

7, (*Effect of plea of " not possessed," in trover by assignees of bankrupt.*) In an action of trover, the plea, that the plaintiff was not possessed, puts in issue the right of the plaintiff to the possession of the goods, as against the defendant, at the time of the conversion.

Therefore, in an action of trover against assignees of a bankrupt, such a plea lets in evidence that the goods, at the time of the bankruptcy, were within the order and disposition of the bankrupt as reputed owner, (according to the 6 Geo. 4, c. 16, s. 72), and that the defendants thereupon, as assignees, sold the goods. (4 Bing. N. C. 54, 290.)—*Isaac v. Belcher,* 5 M. & W. 139.

8. (*Several counts.*) The first count of a declaration in case set forth certain deeds whereby the plaintiffs were entitled to a factory, with the steam engine and boiler, and complained that the defendants had disannexed and removed the boiler from the premises, and converted and disposed of it to their own use, to the injury of the plaintiff's reversion. The second count was in trover for the same boiler. Quære, whether the allowance of these two counts was in violation of the rule of H. T. 4 Will. 4?—*Weeton v. Woodcock,* 5 M. & W. 143.

And see Bills and Notes, 3; Insolvent, 1; Set-off; Trover.

POOR RATE.

1. (*Saleable underwood, what is.*) Saleable underwood under the 43 Eliz. c. 2, means such shoots from old stools as are capable of reproduction, and of being treated by the wood-owner so as to yield a succession of profits, and the circumstances to determine this question are matters of fact for the sessions.

Therefore, where a plantation of oaks was cut down last in 1786, and shoots grew up from their stools, which were occasionally weeded, and at the end of fifty years the wood-owner cut some every year, which he sold for colliery purposes and fire-wood, and the sessions decided that they were not saleable underwood; the Court held that they would not disturb their decision, although Coleridge, J., doubted whether the decision was not wrong upon the facts.—*Reg.* v. *Inhabitants of Narberth North,* 1 P. & D. 590.

2. (*Rateability of Bridge—Beneficial occupation.*) A local act of parliament recited that it would be of great utility to the public to build a bridge, and empowered a company to raise a capital sum amongst themselves by shares, and to borrow a further sum, by mortgage or annuity, for the building thereof, and authorised tolls to be taken, and enacted that the tolls should be applied first in discharging the expenses of the act, and paying the mortgagees their interest, and that the surplus should be divided among the proprietors, not exceeding 7½ per cent. on their shares. The excess arising from the tolls beyond the dividend was to be applied in paying off the capital advanced by the proprietors; afterwards to pay off the mortgage debt, afterwards to form a fund for the repairs of the bridge, and then the tolls to cease altogether.

The company raised the sums authorised under the act, and also incurred a further debt in completing the bridge. The tolls, which amounted to 1500*l.* a year, were applied in discharging this further debt and the interest of the money raised. This debt had not been wholly discharged, and no dividend to the proprietors had ever been made :—Held that the Company had a beneficial interest in the tolls till their capital was paid off, and that they were therefore rateable to the poor's rate as occupiers of the bridge.—*Reg.* v. *Blackfriars' Bridge (Manchester) Company,* 1 P. & D. 603.

POWER.

(Execution of by will.) A power was to be executed by will, signed, sealed, *and published,* in the presence of and *attested* by witnesses. The will commenced, " I L. H. S. &c. do publish and declare this to be my last will," and concluded, " I declare this to be my last will. In witness whereof I have to this my last will set my hand and seal," L. H. S. (L. s.) " Witness, A. B. and C."—Held, by Vaughan J., Parke B., Alderson, B. and Coltman, J.—(dissent. Tindal C. J., Bosanquet J., and Gurney B.)—that the publication of the will was not attested so as to satisfy the terms of the power. (Reversing the judgment of the Court of Queen's Bench, 6 N. & M. 259.) *Doe* d. *Spilsbury* v. *Burdett,* 1 P. & D. 670.

PRACTICE.

(Discharging jury.) Where the defendant in trespass justifies the alleged acts of trespass in several pleas, each answering the whole of the trespasses, the judge cannot receive a verdict on some of the issues, and discharge the jury as to the remainder, without consent of the parties.—*Tinkler* v. *Rowland,* 6 N. & M. 848.

PRESCRIPTION ACT. See WATERCOURSE.

PRINCIPAL AND FACTOR.

(When property in goods vests in factor.) T., a corn merchant at Longford, who had been in the habit of consigning cargoes of corn to the plaintiffs, as his factors for sale at Liverpool, and obtaining from them acceptances on the faith of such consignments, on the 31st of January obtained from the masters of two canal boats (No. 604 and No. 54), receipts signed by them for full cargoes of oats therein stated to be shipped on board the boats, deliverable to the agent of T. in Dublin, in care for and to be shipped to the plaintiffs at Liverpool. At that time boat 604 was loaded, but no oats were then actually shipped on board boat 54. On the 2nd February, T. inclosed these receipts to the plaintiffs, and drew a bill on them against the value of the cargoes, which the plaintiffs accepted on the 7th, and paid when due. On the 6th of February, W., an agent of the defendant, who was T.'s factor for sale in London, arrived at Longford and pressed T. for security for previous advances. T. on that day gave W. an order on T.'s agent in Dublin, to deliver to W. the cargoes of boats 604 and 54 on their arrival there. Boat 604 had then sailed from Longford, but boat 54 was only partially loaded. The loading was completed on the 9th, and T. then transmitted to W. in Dublin a receipt signed by the master of the boat, (in the same form as those sent to the plaintiffs), making the cargo deliverable to W. W. received this on the 10th. On their arrival in Dublin W. took possession of both cargoes for the defendant. Held, that the property in the cargo of boat 604 vested in the plaintiffs, on their acceptance of the bill, and that they were entitled to maintain trover for it; but that they could not maintain trover for the cargo of boat 54,

since none of it was on board, or otherwise specifically appropriated to the plaintiffs, when the receipt for that boat was given by the master, (1 Bos. & P. 563 ; 5 M. & Sel. 350 ; 2 Bing. 20 ; 37 R. 119, 783 ; 3 Price, 547 ; 3 M. & W. 15.) *Quære,* whether a document, similar in form to a bill of lading, but given by the master of a boat navigating an inland canal, has the effect of such an instrument in transferring the property in the goods.—*Bryans* v. *Nix,* 4 M. & W. 775.

PRISONER.   See HABEAS CORPUS.

PRIVILEGES OF PARLIAMENT.

(*Privileges of the House of Commons in cases of libel.*) It is no defence in law to an action for publishing a libel, that the defamatory matter is part of a document which was, by order of the House of Commons, laid before the House, and thereupon became part of the proceedings of the House, and which was afterwards, by order of the House, printed and published by the defendant ; and that the House of Commons heretofore resolved, declared, and adjudged, "that the power o publishing such of its reports, votes, and proceedings, as it shall deem necessary or conducive to the public interest, is an essential incident to the constitutional functions of parliament, more especially to the Commons House of Parliament, as the representative portion of it."   And on demurrer to a plea suggesting such a defence, a court of law is competent to determine whether or not the House of Commons has such privilege as will support the plea.—*Stockdale* v. *Hansard,* 9 Ad. & Ell. 1.

RELEASE.

(*Cannot be avoided by parol.*) To a declaration against a defendant as maker of a promissory note, he pleaded that the note was a joint and several note by himself and A., and that A. had been released. Replication, that A. had been so released at the defendant's request, and that the defendant, in consideration of such release at his request, ratified the promise in the declaration, and promised that he would remain liable on the note, as if there had been no such release : Held, that the replication, setting up a parol contract to avoid the release, was bad.—*Brooks* v. *Stuart,* 1 P. & D. 615.

SAVINGS' BANKS ACT.

Where by rule of a savings' bank no claim for any sum of money could be made more than seven years from the death of a depositor, the Court discharged a rule nisi for a mandamus to the trustees of such a bank, to appoint an arbitrator, under 9 Geo. 4, c. 92. s. 45, to decide a dispute as to money, the alleged depositor of which had been dead more than seven years. (2 N. & P. 278.)—*Reg.* v. *Trustees of Northwich Savings' Bank,* P. & D. 477.

SCIRE FACIAS.

Quære, whether a scire facias will lie upon an interlocutory judgment. (12 Mod 500.)—The Court refused to entertain the question or motion.—*Benn* v. *Greatwood,* 6 Scott, 891.

SET-OFF.

(*Plea of, when to be taken distributively.*) When a defendant, under a plea of set-off to the whole declaration, proves a sum of money owing to him from the plaintiff, less than the amount of the claim which the plaintiff has established, the defendant is not entitled to have a verdict entered for him on that issue for the amount which he has so proved, but the issue must be found for the plaintiff ;

unless where the defendant, by all his pleas taken together, covers the whole cause of action. (2 C., M. & R. 547 ; 7 Ad. & E. 595.)—*Tuck* v. *Tuck*, 5 M. & W. 109.

SETTLEMENT.

1. (*By payment of rates.*) On the 5th October, 1835, the pauper took a house at 16*l.* a year, payable quarterly, and the tenancy was determinable by a quarter's notice, given at any period. At the end of the first quarter, 10*s.* a quarter was taken off the rent. He resided in the house until the 26th September, 1836, when he removed to another parish. He left some trifling property behind him in the house, and kept the key of it until the 5th October, 1836, when he completed payment of the year's rent. He was rated to all the rates made during his tenancy, and paid them all except the last rate, made on the 29th September, and confirmed and allowed on the 4th October, and published on the 9th : Held, that there was a hiring and occupation for a year under 6 Geo. 4, c. 57, and that he gained a settlement by payment of rates ; the 4 and 5 Will. 4, c. 76, s. 66, which enacts that after the passing of the act no settlement shall be gained by *occupying a tenement* unless the occupier shall have paid rates in respect of such tenement for one year, not applying to settlements by payment of rates. (1 N. & P. 453; 10 B. & C. 520.)—*Reg.* v. *Inhabitants of St. Mary Kallendar*, 1 P. & D. 497.

2. (*By renting a tenement.*) In 1813 the pauper's children were engaged to work at a mill for three years. T., the owner of the mill, rented three cottages in the parish of B., distant one-eighth of a mile from the mill, for the convenience of the families employed there. The pauper occupied one of the cottages, and agreed to pay 2*s.* a week for the cottage, which was to be deducted out of the children's wages. The children worked for the three years, and some of them for a longer period. The pauper occupied the cottage till 1829, when he quitted on being required to do so, without any regular notice to quit. The pauper was never in the service of the mill-owner. On these facts the sessions decided that the pauper had gained a settlement in B. by occupying a tenement under the 13 & 14 Car. 2, c. 12, subject to a case.—Held, that it was a question of fact for the sessions, whether the occupation of the cottage was ancillary to the services of the children ; and that on the facts stated the pauper had gained a settlement. —*Reg.* v. *Inhabitants of Bishopton*, 1 P. & D. 598.

STOPPAGE IN TRANSITU.

The vendor by a delivery order directed the defendants, who were wharfingers, to deliver to the vendee " 1028 bushels of oats, bin 40, to be weighed over, and the expense of weighing to be charged to the vendor." The vendee afterwards gave an order to the same effect on a sale to the plaintiffs. There were no other oats in the bin, and they were transferred to the plaintiffs in the defendants' books, but never weighed over. The vendor, on the failure of the first vendee, claimed a right of stoppage in transitu :—Held, (without reference to any estoppel against the defendants, the wharfingers,) that the property had passed as between buyer and seller, so as to defeat the vendor's right of stoppage. (2 Campb. 243 ; 1 N. R. 69.)—*Swanwick* v. *Sotheron*, 1 P. & D. 648.

TRANSPORTATION FROM CANADA.

1. The gaoler of Liverpool, in return to a habeas corpus, stated that, by an act of the legislature of Upper Canada, upon the petition of any person charged with high treason, preferred before arraignment to the Lieutenant-Governor of the province,

and praying to be pardoned, such governor was empowered to pardon him on such terms as might appear proper, and that in case any person should be pardoned on condition of transportation for life or for years, and should return to the province contrary to such condition, he should suffer death. The return then stated that the prisoner was indicted for high treason, and, before arraignment, presented a petition, confessing his guilt and praying for pardon; that he received a pardon on condition that he should be transported to Van Diemen's Land for fourteen years, to commence from his arrival there; to which condition he assented; that there being no direct means of transporting him from Upper Canada, it was necessary to take him to Quebec, in Lower Canada, whereto he was taken by the authority of the Lieutenant-Governor of Upper Canada, and by virtue of a warrant of the Lieutenant-Governor of Lower Canada was delivered to the custody of the sheriff of Quebec, until he could be transported; that there being no means of transporting the prisoner directly from Lower Canada to Van Diemen's Land, it was necessary to take him to England, and thereupon by letters patent, sealed with the seal of the province of Lower Canada, and directed to A. B., captain of a vessel, A. B. was commanded to receive the prisoner, and take him to Liverpool, the same being a place which seemed fit to her Majesty, and which was the most convenient in that behalf; that A. B. conveyed the prisoner to Liverpool; and there not being the means of conveying him immediately to Van Diemen's Land, it became necessary that he should be delivered by A. B. into the custody of the gaoler of Liverpool (the party making the return) for safe custody, whilst the means for transmitting the prisoner to Van Diemen's Land were preparing with all dispatch.

Held, that the return was not bad for any of the following objections:—

That the prisoner was not a convict, and therefore could not be transported.

That there was no judgment of transportation.

That the colonial legislature could not authorise transportation *intra fines* of another territory.

That the condition of the pardon being transportation for fourteen years, to commence from the prisoner's arrival at Van Diemen's Land, was bad for uncertainty.

That the transportation had miscarried for want of a continued authority from the Governor of Upper Canada throughout the intermediate places between that province and Liverpool.

That the various documents referred to, and especially the letters patent, under which the prisoner was detained by the party making the return, were not set out.

Quære, if the objections had been good, whether the Court would have discharged the prisoner, if it sufficiently appeared that he was charged with treason.

The name of the prisoner, with the names of several other prisoners, occurred in the recital of the letters-patent set out in the return, but his name was accidentally omitted in the mandatory part of the letters. The return stated that his name occurred in the mandatory part also. The Court ordered the return to be amended so as to agree with the letters-patent, as it was improper that any false statement should appear on the records of the Court; but held that the letters were not material to justify the prisoner's detention.

The Court also refused to attach the party making the return, for such false statement, as it did not appear to have been made wilfully.—*Reg.* v. *Batchelder,* 1 P. & D. 516.

On the same case being brought before the Court of Exchequer, the Court refused to discharge the prisoner, on the ground that, even if the condition of the pardon was not lawful, or the prisoner was not an assenting party to it, he was still liable to be sued for the treason in England, and therefore any subject might detain him in custody until he was dealt with according to law,—*Canadian Prisoners' Case*, 5 M. & W. 32.

TROVER.

(*Pleadings—Conversion.*) To trover for two reclaimed deer, the defendant pleaded, 1, except as to one, actionem non, because he was not guilty ; and 2, as to that one, that he took it damage feasant in his own close, as a distress, which was the conversion complained of : Held, on special demurrer to the latter plea, that it need not have commenced with actionem non. (2 M. & W. 72) : Held, also, (Littledale, J. dubitante), that the plea confessed and avoided a conversion ; that it was not necessary for the defendant to add that he had impounded the deer, or in what manner he had disposed of it, and that if there was any irregularity in disposing of the distress, it should have been new assigned,—*Weeding* v. *Aldritch*, 1 P. & D. 657.

And see PLEADING, 7; VENDOR AND PURCHASER, 2.

USE AND OCCUPATION. See LANDLORD AND TENANT, 1.

USURY.

A. agreed with B. to lend him 200*l.* at the rate of 1*s.* in the pound per month (60*l.* per cent. per annum), to be secured as follows : viz. whenever any portion of the money should be advanced, the borrower was to give a promissory note, payable one month after date, to be renewed as often as it should fall due ; and for each renewal, 1*s.* in the pound was to be paid by way of discount : Held, that the promissory notes so given were within the protection of 3 & 4 Will. 4, c. 98, s. 7, and 7 Will. 4 & 1 Vict. c. 80. (6 Ad. & Ell. 932 ; 5 Bing. N. C. 332.) —*Holt* v. *Miers,* 5 M. & W. 168.

VENDOR AND PURCHASER.

1. (*Right of purchaser to rescind contract on ground of misrepresentation as to title.*) In an action for money had and received to recover back the deposit money paid by the plaintiff on the purchase of an estate, a special case stated, that by the will of the defendant's father, the estate in question was devised to him after the death of his mother, and to his issue in tail, subject to a payment of 2*l.* a year to his sister M. C., with remainder to the testator's own right heirs. In the year 1817, and during the lifetime of his mother, the defendant by lease and release assigned the estate for his own life to his sister M. C. and R. W., upon trust to receive the rents and apply them to keep the tenements in repair, to pay to M. C. her annuity of 2*l.*, and to pay the residue to the defendant. After the mother's death, M. C. (R. W. being dead,) received one quarter's rent, since which the rents had been received by the defendant. In February, 1836, the defendant advertised the estate for sale, and on the 25th of that month the plaintiff purchased it upon a contract stated in the conditions of sale. Amongst other conditions were the following :—" That the premises are to be sold subject to a yearly rent of 2*l.*, payable during the life of M. C., the sister of the defendant ; and which said M. C. having given notice that in consequence of a certain alleged indenture, bearing date August 19, 1817, whereby she alleges the defendant conveyed all his estate and interest in the premises unto R. W. (now

deceased), and the said M. C. for the term of his the said defendant's life, upon certain trusts in the alleged indenture contained, and that no conveyance of the premises could be made without the concurrence of her the said M. C., and who thereby declared she should refuse to execute any such conveyance, the said defendant declared *that the said alleged indenture is a fabrication, and has made a solemn affidavit that he never executed any such indenture, and that such indenture, as far as concerns any supposed signature or mark of him the defendant, is a forgery ;* and the opinion of Sir J. C., his Majesty's Attorney-General, and Mr. K. have been taken as to the necessity of the said M. C.'s concurring in the sale, and were in favour of the defendant's being able, by virtue of the recent act for abolishing fines and recoveries, to make a good title to the premises without the sanction and concurrence of the said M. C.; and the vendor is also prepared to prove that on the trial of an action of replevin of S. v. the said M. C., the presiding judge expressed himself favourably to the right of the defendant to convey without the concurrence of the said M. C.; *the purchaser therefore shall not make any objection on account of the said alleged indenture,* nor be entitled to call for any sanction, concurrence, &c. &c., by or from the said M. C.; but if the purchaser shall think fit, in order to indemnify him or her against all actions, suits, and other proceedings, claims and demands by the said M. C., a portion of the purchase-money (not exceeding 200*l.*) *may remain as a charge by way of mortgage on the premises,* at interest after the rate of 4½ per cent., and that such charge, at the option of the purchaser, shall remain on such security *during the life of the said M. C., and for a period not exceeding twelve months after her decease.*" The plaintiff paid the deposit now sought to be recovered. The jury at the trial found a verdict for the plaintiff for the amount of the deposit, and that the deed of the 19th August, 1817, was the deed of the defendant : Held, 1st, that whether the representation of the deed being a forgery were a warranty upon which the plaintiff might maintain an action or not, the plaintiff had no right to rescind the contract because it turned out to have been untrue. Secondly, that by the stipulation " that the purchaser should not make any objection on account of the alleged indenture," *every species of objection* to the title on the part of the purchaser arising out of the alleged deed was interdicted, and he was precluded from insisting either upon the existence of the deed, or upon its legal effect and operation, as a defect in the title which he had agreed to take.— *Corrall* v. *Cattell,* 4 M. & W. 734.

2. (*Of goods—Specific appropriation by purchaser—Trover—Conversion.*) B. a builder contracted with A. and others, trustees of a new hotel about to be erected by a company of proprietors, to build the hotel, except as to the ironmonger's, plumber's, and glazier's work, for a specified sum, and covenanted to complete certain portions of the work within certain specified periods, being paid by instalments at corresponding dates : and that if he should neglect to complete any portion within the time limited, he should forfeit and pay the sum of 250*l.* as liquidated damages. The agreement then contained a clause empowering the trustees, in case (inter alia) B. should become bankrupt, to take possession of the *work already done* by him, and to put an end to the agreement, which should be altogether null and void ; and that the trustees in such case should pay B. or his assignees only so much money as the architect of the company should adjudge to be the value of *the work actually done and fixed* by B., as compared with the whole work to be done. The course of business during the progress of the work was for the clerk of the works to inspect every article which came in under the

contract, and none were received except on his approval. After the works had proceeded some time, B. became bankrupt. Before his bankruptcy certain wooden sash-frames had been delivered by him on the premises of the company, approved by the clerk of the works, and returned to B. for the purpose of having iron pulleys belonging to the trustees affixed to them; and at the time of the bankruptcy, these frames, with the pulleys attached to them, were at B.'s shop. He afterwards, but before the issuing of the fiat, re-delivered them to the trustees; and the sash-frames being afterwards demanded of them by B.'s assignees, they gave an unqualified refusal to deliver them up.

Held, 1st, that the property in the wooden sash-frames had not passed to the trustees at the time of the bankruptcy.

2dly, That they were not entitled to retain them under the agreement, as being *work already done,* they not having been *fixed* to the hotel; but that even if they were within that clause of the agreement, it could not bind the assignees, inasmuch as their right accrued on the bankruptcy, whereas the option of the trustees was not to be exercised until after the bankruptcy.

3dly, That the refusal of the trustees not having been limited to the *pulleys,* the demand and refusal were sufficient evidence of a conversion by them of the wooden sash-frames, so as to entitle B.'s assignees to recover them in trover.— *Tripp* v. *Armitage,* 4 M. & W. 687.

WAGER.

(*When void as against public policy.*) A wager as to the conviction or acquittal of a prisoner on trial on a criminal charge, is illegal, as being against public policy. *Evans* v. *Jones,* 5 M. & W. 77.

WARRANT OF ATTORNEY.

The Court allowed judgment to be entered up on a warrant of attorney above and under ten years old, on an affidavit that the defendant had been seen and conversed with by the deponent twenty-seven days before the motion was made (4 D. P. C. 44; 5 D. P. C. 221.)—*Powell* v. *Howard,* 6 Scott, 826.

WATERCOURSE.

(*Right to artificial watercourse in mining district—Operation of 2 & 3 Will. 4, c.* 71.) Before the year 1570 a company of adventurers had begun to construct a sough or level, now called the Cromford Sough, for the purpose of draining a portion of the mineral field in the wapentake of Wirksworth in Derbyshire; being remunerated, by agreement with the proprietors of the mines, by a portion of the lead ore raised within the district benefited thereby (technically called the *title* of the sough.) The water from this sough flowed into a brook called Bonsall Brook, and their united waters turned an ancient corn-mill. In 1738 they leased this easement, of continuing and maintaining the sough, to certain parties for 999 years. In 1771, A. obtained a lease for 84 years from the owner of the land through which the sough was made, of the brook, of the stream of water issuing from the sough into it, and of the piece of land on which the corn-mill stood, with the right of erecting mills thereon; and accordingly, in 1772, erected extensive cotton-mills thereon, partly on the site of the ancient corn-mill, and they were worked by the same junction of the two streams. This lease contained a proviso, that if during the term, the stream issuing from Cromford Sough should, by the bringing up of any other sough, or by unavoidable accident, be taken away or lessened, so that there should not come to the mills sufficient water for working them, and the lessor should not be able otherwise to supply it, it should be lawful for A. to take down the mills, and remove them to another piece of ground therein described, of which a lease should be granted for the rest of the term. In 1789, A. purchased from the lessor the absolute interest in the land leased, and in that through which so much of the sough was made as lay within the manor of Cromford. In the meantime another company had in 1771 commenced the construction of another sough on a lower level, called the Meer Brook Sough, (commencing within the manor of Wirksworth), for the purpose of draining a larger portion of the mineral field, under a similar license from the same mine-owners who had before used the Cromford Sough. In 1836, Meer Brook Sough having been so far extended into Cromford as to drain the Cromford Sough, the water supplying A.'s mills was thereby diverted : Held, that under the circumstances A. had not acquired, by his user of the water issuing from Cromford Sough, such a right to it as to entitle him to maintain an action against the proprietors of the Meer Brook Sough ; this being an artificial watercourse made for a particular and temporary purpose, and its water having been originally taken by him with notice that he might be discontinued, and the circumstances not being such as to afford any presumption of a grant by the owners of the mines ; and that he did not acquire such right by force of the stat. 2 & 3 Will. 4, c. 71, s. 2.—*Arkwright* v. *Gell*, 5 M. & W. 203.

WAY. See PLEADING, 5.

WORK AND LABOUR.

(*Assumpsit for, when right of action in, is complete.*) Where A. contracts to do work on materials supplied to him by B., (as where he contracts to survey a parish, and to set down the results of such survey in a map, upon paper furnished to him by B.), his right to sue for work and labour is complete as soon as he has finished the work, and has given B. a reasonable opportunity of ascertaining its correctness ; and if (there being no contract for a specific price) he demand more for the work than a reasonable price, and refuse to deliver it except upon payment of such larger price, that does not preclude him from suing for and recovering a reasonable price.—*Hughes* v. *Lenny*, 5 M. & W. 183.

WRIT OF TRIAL.

(*What cases triable under.*) In an action of indebitatus assumpsit for wages, the damages claimed in each count were 100*l.* The particulars claimed 7*l.* 19*s.* for wages, &c., " and also such further sum, by way of damages, as the jury might think proper to give for the wrongful dismissal of the plaintiff without notice." The amount indorsed on the writ was 12*l.* 19*s.* It appeared that the plaintiff had been engaged at a salary of 60*l.* per annum, and dismissed without any notice ; and he had a verdict for 15*l.* 19*s.*: Held that the case was not triable before the sheriff under the 3 & 4 Will. 4, c. 42, s. 17.—*Jacquot* v. *Boura*, 5 M. & W. 155.

EQUITY.

ACCOUNT.

(*Debt and damages.*) A Court of Equity will not take an account of debts one way and of damages the other, nor in any case where the subject as to which the account on one side is required would not be a matter of set off at law, though it does not follow that where there would be a set off at law, there would necessarily be an account in equity.

Accordingly where the plaintiff in the course of various dealings had given various bills of exchange in payment of goods supplied, and alleged by his bill that a large parcel of the goods furnished were by the fraud of the defendant very deficient in quantity and quality, the Court refused him to grant either an account or an injunction. *Glennie* v. *Imri*, Y. & C. 436.

ADMINISTRATION OF ASSETS.

1. (*Appointment of agent.*) Where book debts were very numerous, the executors of a tradesman were held justified in appointing an agent to collect them, but the amount of per centage to be allowed him was not determined by the Court. —*Hopkinson* v. *Roe*, Bea. 181.

2. (*Carrying on trade.*) Where a testator directed a specific portion of his property to be employed in carrying on his trade, creditors whose debts had arisen in the course of the subsequent trading, were allowed to claim only against such specified portion of the assets.—*Cutbush* v. *Cutbush*, Bea. 184.

3. (*Costs of satisfied legatee.*) Plaintiff in an administration suit held not liable to pay the costs of legatees who had been paid and disclaimed.—*West* v. *Cole*, Y. & C. 582.

4. (*Transfer of stock—Costs.*) The costs of transferring stock from the name of the testator into the names of the executors were disallowed.—*Hopkinson* v. *Roll*, Bea. 181.

AGREEMENT.

(*Consideration—Husband and wife.*) An agreement by a wife to waive the further prosecution of an indictment against her husband for an assault, in consideration of a separate maintenance, though made with the sanction of the Court in which the prosecution was pending, is illegal in respect of the consideration, and is further open to the objection of being made between husband and wife. —*Garth* v. *Earnshaw*, Y. & C. 484.

ALIEN.

(*Money, the produce of land.*) Where lands were devised to English subjects as trustees upon trust to sell, and after payment of mortgages to invest the residue upon certain trusts for the benefit of certain parties, some of whom were aliens : held, upon objection taken by a purchaser under a decree for sale, that the trusts for the aliens (which at the time of the question being raised were still contingent) were good, Fourdrin v. Gowey, 3 M. & K. 383, being overruled by the present case.—*Du Honomelin* v. *Sheldon*, Bea. 79.

ALTERATION OF RECORD. See EVIDENCE, 2.

AMENDMENT. See PRACTICE, 4.

APPEAL.

1. (*Costs on reversal of decree—Construction.*) Held that the order of the House of Lords reversing the decree in *Small v. Atwood*, and dismissing the bill with costs, see 3 Y. &. C. p. 105, applied only to the costs of the suit up to and including the decree in the Court below.—*Small v. Atwood*, Y. & C. 501.

2. (*Costs of staying execution.*) The costs of an application to stay the execution of an order which was afterwards reversed on appeal, were made costs in the cause, contrary to the usual practice, which is for the party applying for such an indulgence to pay such costs.—*Richardson v. Bank of England*, Bea. 153.

CASES OVERRULED.

1. *Foden v. Finney*, 4 Russ. 428. See HUSBAND AND WIFE.
2. *Fourdrin v. Gowey*, 3 M. & K. 385. See ALIEN
3. *Swinford v. Horne*, 5 Madd. 379. See PRACTICE (*in the Exchequer*), 8.
4. *Wetherell v. Weighill*, 3 Y. & C. 244. See TITHE COMPOSITION ACT.

CHOSE IN ACTION.

(*Remedies of assignee in equity.*) The Court will not in ordinary cases assist the assignee of a bond in recovering what is due on such bond, but will leave him to bring his action at law in the name of the obligee.—*Keys v. Williams*, Y. & C. 462.

CONSTRUCTION.

(*Covenant to settle.*) By a marriage settlement certain sums, to which A. the wife was then absolutely entitled in possession, were settled to her separate use for life, remainder to her husband for life, remainder after the death of the survivor upon trust for the children, and in default of children, then as A. should appoint, and in default of appointment, upon trust for her next of kin as if she were sole. And the husband covenanted that in case A., or he in her right should at any time thereafter during the coverture succeed to the possession of or acquire any property, he would settle the same to the separate use of A. for life, and after her death upon the like trusts for the children as were declared as to the settled monies, and in default of children, upon trust as A. should appoint, and in default of apointment for her next of kin as if she were sole. At the time of the marriage a sum of money stood settled as to one moiety in trust for A. for life, for her separate use, and as to the other in trust for her mother for life, with remainder to A. for life, and as to the whole in trust for the children of A., and in default of such children, then as to one moiety in trust as A. should appoint, and in default of appointment for her executors, administrators, or assigns: A. survived her mother, and died in the lifetime of her husband, without children: Held, that the covenant in the settlement attached to the said last-mentioned moiety, and that upon the death of A. it belonged to her next of kin, but the question was not raised till after the husband's death.—*Grofftey v. Humpage*, Bea. 46.

CONSTRUCTION OF STATUTES.

1. (1 *Will.* 4, c. 60.—*Executor of trustee.*) Where the executor of the survivor of three trustees declined to prove his will, held that the case was within the above statute.—*Exp. Hagger*, Bea. 98.

2. (*Same statute, s.* 10.—*Transfer of stock.*) The request in writing mentioned in this act, as to the transfer of stock, means a private request by the party requiring the transfer, and service of an order of Court directing such transfer is not sufficient.—*Madge v. Riley,* Y. & C. 425.

3. (1 *Will.* 4, *c.* 60 ; 4 & 5 *Will.* 4, *c.* 23; *or* 1 & 2 *Vict. c.* 69.—*Mortgagee.*) Where a mortgagee in trust was resident out of the jurisdiction, the Court refused to make an order under either of the above statutes. (Exp. Whitton, 1 Keen 280, is no longer law since the last mentioned statute. Explanation of that case.)—*Green v. Holden,* Bea. 207.

4. (1 & 2 *Vict. c.* 117.—*Government Securities.*) The term "Government Securities" in the Public Monies Custody Act, where it is used in the alternative with 3 per cent consols, held not to include Exchequer bills.—*Exp. Chaplin* Y. & C. 397.

And see Execution of Decrees.

CONTEMPT.

(11 *Geo.* 4 & 1 *Will.* 4, *c.* 36, *s.* 15, *rule* 5.) Where a defendant who was in custody for contempt had been brought up and turned over to the Fleet, but it afterwards appeared that he had not been so brought up till two days after the period fixed by the above statute, he was ordered to be discharged with costs to be paid by plaintiff, though defendant had made no objection at the time of the first order.—*Greening v. Greening,* Bea. 121.

And see Practice (*in the Exchequer*), 10.

COSTS.

(*Defect of parties.*) Where an objection for want of parties was taken at the hearing and allowed, although such objection was not raised by the answer the plaintiff was made to pay the costs of the day.—*Bailey v. Dennett,* Y. & C. 459.

And see Administration of Assets, 3, 4 ; Appeal, 1, 2 ; Equitable Mortgage ; Evidence, 1.

DEBTOR AND CREDITOR.

(*Collateral securities—Remedies in Equity.*) Where a creditor upon a bond (of which he was assignee) had also an equitable mortgage, and upon bill filed against his debtor had obtained on order for sale and for payment of his debt out of the proceeds of such sale, but such proceeds were not sufficient to pay him in full, the Court refused to order the balance to be paid him, but left him to his remedy at law upon the bond.—*Keys v. Williams,* Y. & C. 462 ; (see S. C. 3 Y. & C. 55.)

ELECTION. See Injunction, 2.

EQUITABLE MORTGAGE.

(*Costs.*) Upon a bill filed to enforce an equitable mortgage by deposit without memorandum, costs will be given to the plaintiff as against the personal representatives of the mortgagor.—*Connell v. Hardie,* Y. & C. 584.

EVIDENCE.

1. (*Costs.*) Where a plaintiff enters into evidence of facts sufficiently admitted by the answer, the defendant will be entitled to the costs occasioned thereby, though the plaintiff succeeds in the suit. *Booth v. Booth,* Bea. 125.

2. (*Effect of adding parties.*) Where a bill originally brought by the husband alone for a legacy given to his wife, had in consequence of an objection at the hearing been amended by the addition of the wife as party, held, on the authority of Milligan v. Mitchell, 1 Myl. & C. 443, that the evidence previously taken could not be used.—*Bailey v. Dennett*, Y. & C. 459.

3. (*Interested witness.*) Where part of the parol evidence admitted as to the ademption of portions was to the effect that a testator intended to provide for both daughters equally, the evidence of one of the daughters against the ademption of the other portion was held inadmissible.—*Davys v. Boucher*, Y. & C. 397.

4. (*Notes on brief.*) The notes made by a barrister on his brief on the trial of an action at common law, were admitted in a Court of Equity as evidence of what had been stated by a witness at the trial—*Cattell v. Corrall*, Y. & C. 413.

5. (*Re-examination.*) A witness who had been examined generally in the cause as to the fact of occupancy and perception of titheable matters, ordered to be re-examined before the Master as to the particulars and quantity of the titheable matters.—*Maton v. Huyter*, Y. & C. 457.

And see PRACTICE (*in the Exchequer*), 5, 6, 8.

EXECUTION OF DECREES.

(*Order for costs.*) Court of Equity will carry into effect their orders and decrees for costs, by attaching the stock of the party under the provisions of the 1 & 2 Vict. c. 110, s. 18; and notice of the intended application to the Court to make the order for the charge absolute, is a sufficient application for payment. —*Blake v. White*, Y. & C. 434.

EXECUTOR.

(*Surviving partner—Payment into Court.*) A. upon his retiring from his partnership with B. and C. left his capital in the trade, taking from B. and C. a warrant of attorney for 12,500*l.*; he afterwards mortgaged policies of assurance on his own life to the amount of 7000*l.* as a collateral security for a debt by the firm. He then made his will, whereby he appointed B. and C. his executors, and authorised them upon giving security to employ the 7000*l.* or any part of it in the trade. B. and C. did so employ it without giving security, alleging by their answers that the 12,500*l.* was far more than sufficient to cover what the firm owed to the estate of A., which they said was only 989*l.*, exclusive of the monies received on the policies. On motion made on bill and answer (the bill having been filed by one of the residuary legatees), the defendants B. and C. were ordered to pay into Court the 7000*l.* as well as the 989*l.* *Costeker v. Horror*, Y. & C. 530.

And see PRACTICE (*in the Exchequer*), 10.

FOREIGN PRINCE.

(*Jurisdiction.*) Where a foreign prince brings an action in any of our Common Law Courts, he becomes subject in respect of such action to the jurisdiction of our Courts of Equity as usually exercised in reference to proceedings at common law, and a bill of discovery will lie against such prince in aid of a defence to the action.—*Rothschild v. Queen of Portugal*, Y. & C. 594.

HUSBAND AND WIFE.

1. (*Separation—Charge on wife's allowance—Parties.*) A. by deed made on the separation of himself and wife, covenanted with a trustee on her behalf to pay

either to her or to the trustee for her an annuity during the separation, and by the same deed assigned leaseholds to the trustees to secure such annuity. The wife afterwards borrowed money of B. upon the security of her annuity, which the Court reluctantly admitted she might do, and B. filed a bill against A. and her to obtain the benefit of the charge, but without making the trustee a party, upon which A. filed his bill against the trustee and his wife and B., stating that the trustee threatened to distrain for arrears of the annuity, and praying to be at liberty to pay the arrears into Court, and to be indemnified against the costs of B.'s suit : Held, that such a bill could not be maintained either as a bill of interpleader, B.'s suit being defective for want of parties, or as a bill *quia timet* for the same reason, and because the apprehension of costs is not a ground for such a bill.—*Palmer v. Fraser*, Y. & C. 491.

2. (*Wife's legacy.*) The Court refused to entertain a bill by a husband for a legacy given to his wife, without her being made a party, although the legacy was only 50*l.*, Foden v. Finney, 4 Russ. 428, being overruled.—*Bailey v. Dennett*, Y. & C. 459.

And see AGREEMENT.

INJUNCTION.

1. (*Co-defendant—Collusion.*) An injunction to restrain proceedings at law was granted against one defendant at the instance of a co-defendant, where the latter was a trustee for the plaintiffs, some of whom were infants, and where the attorney in the action also acted as solicitor for the plaintiffs and for the defendant, against whom the injunction was awarded.—*Edgecombe v. Carpenter,* Bea. 171.

2. (*Equitable question—Practice.*) Where the defendant by his answer admitting the plaintiff's title as heir at law, set up an equitable claim, which, if the cause had been brought to a hearing, would have put the plaintiff to his election, the Court refused on motion an injunction to restrain the setting up of outstanding terms, and would not allow the plaintiff to elect in the then state of the cause.— *Ringer v. Blake*, Y. & C. 591.

3. (*Heir at law.*) Where an heir at law who had for some years acquiesced in a will, and who had concurred in the institution of the suit for establishing such will, afterwards brought actions at law impeaching it; an injunction was granted against him while it was referred to the Master to inquire what course it was proper for the trustee under the will to take.—*Edgecumbe v. Carpenter*, Bea. 171.

4. (*Landlord and tenant.*) A yearly tenant with the option of purchasing, having filed his bill for a specific performance against the landlord, the latter after notice to quit brought an action of ejectment against him, whereupon the tenant applied for an injunction to restrain the action, which the Court only granted upon the terms of the tenant continuing to pay the rent without prejudice.— *Pyke v. Northwood*, Bea. 152.

And see PRACTICE, 2.

INTERPLEADER. See HUSBAND AND WIFE, 1.

ISSUE. See MODUS.

JURISDICTION. See FOREIGN PRINCE; SERVICE OF PROCESS.

LEASE.

(*Liability of equitable assignee.*) The equitable assignee of a lease by contract with a prior assignee, to which the original lessee was not a party, and which stipulated that the purchaser under it should not be entitled to call for a legal assignment, having been in possession under such contract : Held liable to indemnify the lessee, after the expiration of the term, for breach of covenant committed whilst he the equitable assignee was in possession. (But see Moores v. Choat, 8 Sim. 508.)—*Close v. Wilberforce*, Bea. 112.

MAINTENANCE.

(*Destitution of parents.*) An increased allowance for maintenance was made out of the property of infants, for the purpose of supporting their parents, who were in a state of destitution.—*Allen v. Coster*, Bea. 203.

MANOR.

(*Conveyance of, in shares—Mode of enjoyment.*)—Under a deed of 1658 a manor with its rights, members, and appurtenances, saving and reserving certain specified lands, was, by a deed of 1682, conveyed to trustees upon trust to permit the persons named in the schedule to such deed, their heirs and assigns, being tenants of the several tenements also mentioned in the schedule, to enjoy a rateable share of the rents and profits of the manor, in proportion to the rents they had paid. Upon a bill filed by a tenant of the manor, who proved that his estate was part of one of the tenements specified in the schedule, claiming to be entitled to the benefit of the trust deed, and to a right of sporting over the manor : Held, 1st, that he could not maintain his claim merely as tenant of the manor, by reason of certain parts thereof having been excepted from the original deed. 2ndly, that a share in the manor, &c. was not so far annexed to the tenements specified in the schedule, as to dispense with the necessity of his showing a distinct title to the share he claimed. 3rd, that a permission to sport was not a proper mode of conferring on those entitled the benefits of the deed, but that the sporting should be let and the rent divided.—*Hutchinson v. Morritt*, Y. & C. 565.

MODUS.

(*Ancient pasture—Pleading—Issue—Value of money.*) The description of " ancient pasture" held to be confined to such land as was then and had continued to be from time immemorial in a state of pasture, and where a modus was pleaded as to *ancient pasture*, it was held that evidence was not admissible to show a modus as to particular lands in the parish alleged to be known by the description of *ancient pasture* ; to which, when in pasture, it was contended that the modus attached ; and an issue was refused in the same case as to whether the modus was not good, in the sense in which the plea was construed by the Court, as to part of the lands, which were the subject of the suit, the evidence in support of the modus so understood appearing to be very slight ; and the Court took an occasion to state the principles upon which an issue is granted or refused.

See also in the same case the observations of the Court as to the alterations in the value of money.—*Cooper v. Byron*, Y. & C. 467.

OUTLAW.

(*Right of, to redress.*) Although an outlaw cannot come into Court to establish a demand, yet he may apply to the Court to set aside an attachment which has been irregularly issued against him.—*Hawkins v. Hall*, Bea. 78.

PARTIES.

1. (*Aliquot share of fund.*) Where a legacy of a sum of money was given to two in equal shares : Held, that either might file a bill for his share. (See Hutchinson v. Townsend, 2 Keen, 675.)—*Hughson* v. *Cookson*, Y. & C. 578.

2. (*Executor de son tort.*) A person who, as the supposed husband of an executrix, had, with her consent, possessed himself of part of the testator's assets, held not to be a necessary party to a bill against the executrix for administration of the estate.—*M'Kenna* v. *Everitt*, Bea. 134.

3. (*Husband and wife.*) The real husband of a woman, who had many years been separated from her, during which time she had married again, held a necessary party to a bill against her for the administration of the estate of her second supposed husband, whose executrix she was.—*S. C.*

4. (*Husband and wife.*) A husband and wife being joined as co-plaintiffs in a suit relating to the separate property of the wife, it was ordered, upon objection taken by the defendant, that the bill should be amended by making the husband a defendant, and adding a next friend, but it was agreed that the drawing up the order should await the decision of the Chancellor in Tullett v. Armstrong. —*England* v. *Downs*, Bea. 96.

5. (*Supplemental suit.*) One of several co-plaintiffs mortgaged his interest, and became insolvent pending the suit ; a supplemental bill was filed by the other plaintiffs against the mortgagee and provisional assignees alone : Held, that the defendants in the original suit, who were accounting parties, ought to have been made parties to the supplemental suit.—*Feary* v. *Stephenson*, Bea. 42.

6. (*Tenants in common.*) On demurrer to a bill by one of two tenants in common, for recovery of the possession of his share, which also prayed for a delivery up of title deeds : Held, that the other tenant in common was a necessary party.— *Brookes* v. *Burt*, Bea. 106.

7. (*Trustee of term.*) On demurrer to an ejectment bill, alleging that plaintiff had abandoned his action of ejectment at law by reason of the defendant's threatening and intending to set up an outstanding term : Held, that the trustee of such term was not a necessary party.—*Brookes* v. *Burt*, Bea. 106.

PETITION.

(*Right of Way—Fences—Mansion-house.*) Held, 1st, that commissioners of partition might annex to one allotment a new right of way over another allotment, the right of way being occasional and for the purpose of repairs. 2ndly, that they might direct new fences to be made to divide the allotments at the expense of the different parties entitled. 3rd, that the mansion-house was properly awarded to the heir at law, though the rest of his allotment was at a distance. —*Lister* v. *Lister*, Y. & C. 540.

PAYMENT INTO COURT.—See EXECUTOR.

PLEA.

1. (*Amended bill.*) Where a plea of want of parties had been submitted to, and the parties pointed out had been added, a further plea for want of parties to the amended bill will not be allowed, unless the necessity for adding such parties arises from the amendments.—*Rawlins* v. *Dalton*, Y. & C. 447.

2. (*Discovery of documents.*) To a bill for an account of tithes, which charged that the defendant had documents in his possession from which the plaintiff's

title and the truth of the matters stated in the bill would appear, the defendant put in a plea denying the perception of any titheable matters, but not denying the possession of documents : Held, that for want of such denial the plea was bad, though the charge in the bill was general, and did not suggest in what manner the production of the documents would falsify the plea.—*Clayton* v. *Earl of Winchelsea*, Y. & C. 426.

3. (*Negative pregnant.*) *Semble*, that a plea of no titheable matters, if it enumerates specially all such matters, should not deny the perception of them in the plural number only, but in the singular also.—*S. C.*

4. (*Of matters inquired after by bill.*) A defendant cannot avail himself in the shape of a plea of matter of which discovery is sought by the bill, and upon this ground a plea of a prior incumbrance to a bill by the owner of a charge seeking for a discovery of prior incumbrances, was held bad.—*Rawlins* v. *Dalton*, Y. & C. 447.

5. (*Prior incumbrancer—Form of.*) The plea of a prior incumbrancer should aver not only that the charge subsisted at the time of the filing of the bill, but that it was at that time in the hands of such incumbrancer.—*Rawlins* v. *Dalton*, Y. & C. 447.

PORTIONS.

(*Ademption—Principles as to.*)—The doctrine of ademption of portions, given by will, by subsequent advancement, does not apply to those cases where the original portion consists of an interest in real estate, and in all cases of ademption it is requisite that both portions should be similar in kind, definite in amount, and certain in enjoyment.—*Davys* v. *Boucher*, Y. & C. 397.

And see EVIDENCE, 3.

PRACTICE.

1. (*Evidence—Supplementary affidavits.*) Where witnesses had been examined *vivâ voce* in the Master's office, under the 69th order 1838, affidavits made by them afterwards to supply defects in their evidence were held inadmissible.—*Hopkinson* v. *Roe*, Bea. 181.

2. (*Injunction.*) An order *nisi* to dissolve the common injunction obtained after exception to the answer has been filed, is irregular, though a general impression to the contrary had prevailed.—*Howes* v. *Howes*, Bea. 197.

3. (*Investment.*) The Court refused to order the investment of money, which it ordered to be paid into Court, where the notice of motion upon which the order was made did not state that an application would be made at the same time for its investment, and one of the parties did not appear.—*Robinson* v. *Wood*, Bea. 206.

4. (*Notice of motion—Amendment.*) A plaintiff on the same day on which he gave notice of a motion for an injunction and receiver, but after service of the notice, amended his bill under a previous order : Held, that the notice of motion was discharged.—*Gouthwaite* v. *Rippon*, Bea. 54.

5. (*Parties abroad—Process.*) Where a necessary party is out of the jurisdiction, it is not sufficient to state that he is so, but the bill must go on to pray process against him.—*Brookes* v. *Burt*, Bea. 106.

See also as to same point *Munoz* v. *De Tastet*, before Sir J. Leach, V. C., reported in note to *S. C.*

6. (*Sale under decree.*) A Master's report approving of a contract for sale cannot be confirmed on a petition of course, with consent of the clerks in Court of all parties; but a special petition stating all the facts is requisite.—*Bailey* v. *Todd*, Bea. 95.

7. (*Transfer of stock into Court—Fees.*) One guinea only is allowed to the broker of the Accountant-General for the transfer of stock into Court, and where executors had upon such a transfer employed their private broker, the additional amount paid by them to him was disallowed.—*Hopkinson* v. *Roe*, Bea. 181.

PRACTICE.—(*In the Exchequer.*)

1. (*General rule as to.*) Where the practice in the Exchequer is not settled, the Court will follow the practice in Chancery; and in such a case, an order which had been obtained contrary to the settled practice in Chancery was discharged with costs.—*Jones* v. *Thomas*, Y. & C. 455.

2. (*Amendment.*) Where a plaintiff had, upon a motion to dismiss his bill, obtained special leave to amend, and had afterwards taken exceptions to the further answer of the defendant, which the latter submitted to: It was held that the plaintiff could not obtain, as of course, an order to re-amend, and for the defendant to answer the amendments and exceptions at the same time.—*Dixon* v. *Snowball*, Y. & C. 445.

3. (*Amendment—Parties.*) Where an official assignee was omitted as defendant, leave was given at the hearing to amend, by adding him as such.—*Wood* v. *Wood*, Y. & C. 581.

4. (*Amendment—Supplemental bill.*) *Quære* whether under an order to amend by adding parties, a plaintiff may file a supplemental bill. (See Greenwood v. Atkinson, 5 Sim. 419.)—*S. C.*

5. (*Commission to take answer.*) Under a commission to take the answer of two defendants, the answer of one only may be taken.—*Hall* v. *Connell*, Y. & C. 528.

6. (*Enlarging publication—False allegation.*) The statement made to the Court, in order to obtain an order to enlarge publication, that the party applying for it has material witnesses to examine, is not a mere matter of form, and where such a statement was false, the order was discharged.—*Brunt* v. *Wardle*, Y. & C. 503.

7. (*Notice—Mistake.*) Where there was a commission to take an answer, provided notice was given to J. S., the solicitor of the plaintiff, who was also one of the commissioners, and the other commissioners gave him notice of their intention to execute a commission *to examine witnesses:* Held, that such notice was sufficient, as J. S. could not have been deceived by it.—*S. C.*

8. (*Re-examination of witness.*) The order for re-examination before the Master of witnesses in the cause can only be made upon special application, even though they are to be examined upon new matters. (Swinford v. Horne, 5 Madd. 379, said to be overruled.)—*Jones* v. *Thomas*, Y. & C. 455. (See *S. C.* 3 Y. & C. 227.)

9. (*Revivor.*) Where the decree in the original suit directed the payment of a sum by the party on whose death the suit had become incomplete, a new decree for payment must be made in the revived suit against his representatives.—*Harries* v. *Johnson*, Y. & C. 583.

10. (*Supplemental bill.*) Where one of two executors, being in contempt for want

of answer to the original bill, had been discharged under *Sugden's* Act : Held, that a supplemental bill might be properly filed against him, and that, he being again in contempt, the bill was properly taken *pro confesso* against him.— *Hughson v. Cookson,* Y. & C. 578.

And see CONTEMPT ; INJUNCTION, 2 ; SERVICE OF PROCESS, 1 ; SHORT CAUSE ; SOLICITOR AND CLIENT, 1.

PRODUCTION OF DOCUMENTS.

1. (*On motion by defendant.*)   Where, in a suit for an account and an injunction, founded on an allegation of error and fraud in the accounts rendered by defendant, the plaintiff, by his bill, stated that a report had been made by an accountant, which, he said, the defendant ought to inspect and explain ; it was ordered, on motion by the defendant before answers, that he should have one month's time to answer from the time of notice being given him that the said report had been left with the plaintiff's clerk in court for inspection ; but an order for the defendant to inspect other documents relating to the accounts not denied to be in possession of the plaintiff, was refused.— *Shepherd v. Morris,* Bea. 175.

2. (*Privileged communication.*)   In a suit to impeach the validity of a charge upon a living, on the ground that it had been taken in trust for the bishop of the diocese, upon whom the act of parliament under which the charge was made imposed a trust in regard to it, such suit being brought against the son of the bishop, to whom the charge had been transferred by his father : Held, that a correspondence between the bishop, who was then deceased, and his solicitor, and a case submitted on his behalf to counsel, as to the validity of the charge, some years before the institution of the present suit, and also a correspondence in contemplation of the present suit between the defendant and the solicitor of the late bishop, who was not the solicitor of the defendant, were not privileged.

Distinction between the knowledge of the solicitor and the knowledge of the client.—*Greenlaw v. King,* Bea. 137.

QUIA TIMET.   See HUSBAND AND WIFE, 1.

RECEIVER.

(*Poundage.*) After a receiver had been appointed in an administration suit, money belonging to the estate was, with the consent of the parties owing it, who were insurance companies, ordered to be paid directly into Court, without passing through the hands of the receiver, and to the exclusion of his right to poundage. *Haigh v. Grattan,* Bea. 201.

RULE IN SHELLEY'S CASE.

Real and personal estate was devised to a feme covert for life, for her independent use and benefit, with remainder to her husband for life, with remainder to the heirs of her body in tail, with remainders over ; and then followed a declaration in the will that all the aforesaid limitations were intended to be in strict settlement : Held, in accordance with the certificate of the Court of C. P., 4 Bing. N. C. 1, that, subject to her husband's life estate, the wife took an estate tail in the realty and an absolute interest in the personalty.—*Douglas v. Congreve,* Bea. 59.

SEPARATE USE.

1. (*Future coverture—Anticipation clause.*)   A devise and bequest in trust for an

unmarried woman, to her separate use, and so that she should not be able to aliene : Held, effectual upon any subsequent marriage, both as to the separate use and the restraint upon anticipation.

A proviso in restraint of alienation, though in general terms, following a gift to the separate use of an unmarried woman, was construed as intending to be confined to the period of any subsequent coverture, and was held to operate to that extent. *Tullett* v. *Armstrong*, Bea. 1. (An appeal against the decision is pending.)

2. *(Same point.)* *Scarborough* v. *Borman*, Bea. 34.

3. *(Same point.)* *Clark* v. *Jaques*, Bea. 36.

4. *(Settlement by wife.)* By settlement made on the first marriage of a woman, property to which she was entitled in reversion was settled in trust for her to her separate use, exclusive of her then intended husband, or any other husband. Her first husband died, and she married again : Held, that the trust for her separate use still attached.—*Dixon* v. *Dixon*, Bea. 40.

And see PARTIES, 4.

SALE UNDER DECREE.

(Delay of purchaser.) Where the purchaser under a decree had been guilty of delay, a re-sale was ordered, unless he paid the money into Court by a given day, and in the event of a re-sale, it was also ordered that he should make good the loss, if any, and pay the costs on all proceedings.—*Gray* v. *Gray*, Bea. 199. See Smith's Chanc. Pract. 205.

SERVICE OF PROCESS.

1. *(Jurisdiction.)* Service of subpœna for payment of costs on a party out of the jurisdiction, held to be irregular : distinction between this case and that of Davidson v. Marchioness of Hastings, 2 K. 509.— *Hawkins* v. *Hall*, Bea. 73.

2. *(Original irregularity.)* A party who has attached and arrested a party under a service of process which is afterwards held to be irregular, cannot serve him with process whilst the detention so induced still continues. *Quære*, whether a party, discharged from custody on the ground of irregularity, is bound to avail himself of his discharge, to quit the prison and return home without delay? — *Hawkins* v. *Hall*, Bea. 73.

SHORT CAUSE.

(Foreclosure suit.) It is contrary to the practice to advance a foreclosure suit to be heard as a short cause, unless with the consent of the defendant. See Rashleigh v. Dayman, 2 Mad. 947.—*Lewin* v. *Moline*, Bea. 99.

SOLICITOR AND CLIENT.

1. *(Taxation of costs.)* Where the common order for taxation had been obtained under circumstances which rendered a special application proper, upon an application by the solicitor to discharge such order, the Court refused to enter into the consideration of circumstances, which might have been sufficient, had a special application been made, to support an order for taxation, the old rule, which was different, having been altered.—*Gregg* v. *Taylor*, Bea. 183.

2. *(Taxation of costs—Client abroad.)* Where a client, residing abroad, applies for the taxation of his solicitor's bill, he must give security for the costs of the proceedings.— *Re Pasmore*, Bea. 94.

And see PRODUCTION OF DOCUMENTS, 2.

SPECIFIC PERFORMANCE.

1. (*Compensation—Increase in value since contract.*) Where, after a protracted suit, specific performance was decreed, the conveyance to be dated at the time when a good title was first shewn, an increase in the value of the estate, which had arisen from the dropping in of lives between that time and the time previous to it, when the vendor had been ready to convey, was considered a subject of compensation, but the principle upon which the increase in value should be computed, which the Court observed to be a question of difficulty, was not settled at the hearing.—*Townsend v. Champernowne,* Y. & C. 505.

2. (*Costs—Time of title shewn—Date of conveyance.*) Where, by the Master's report, which was confirmed, it appeared that the plaintiff had a good title at the commencement of the suit, but that he did not shew a good title till about two years before the Master's report: Held, that though a specific performance was decreed, the defendant was entitled to the general costs of the suit; but that he should pay the costs of discussing certain additional points referred to the Master, as to which he failed, and that, as to the costs in the Master's office generally, each party should pay his own, the defendant having taken many insufficient objections. The date of the conveyance was ordered to be on the day on which a good title was reported to be shewn.—*S. C.*

3. (*Fraud—Absence of professional adviser.*) The circumstances that the vendor had not the assistance of a professional adviser, and that the contract was made while he was drinking with the purchaser's solicitor, the evidence not going to shew that he was intoxicated, were not held sufficient ground for refusing specific performance, there having been no design on the purchaser's part to keep the vendor from employing a solicitor, and the price being fair.—*Lightfoot v. Heron,* Y. & C. 586.

4. (*Misstatement—Waiver.*) In the conditions of sale it was stated and stipulated that a certain deed, affecting the title of the vendor, was a forgery, and that the vendor had made an affidavit to that effect, and that the purchaser should not take any objection to the title by reason of such deed. Afterwards the purchaser refused to complete, and brought an action (in the Exchequer) for the deposit, and obtained a verdict, the jury declaring the deed to be genuine, subject to the opinion of the whole Court as to whether the contract was thereby rescinded. The whole Court, sitting at common law, held that it was not; and upon a bill filed by the vendor for a specific performance, Alderson, B. held that he was bound by that opinion, and decreed a performance.—*Cattell v. Corrall,* Y. & C. 413.

STATUTE OF LIMITATIONS.

(*Trust for payment of debts.*) A trust for payment of debts will not prevent the operation of the statute in a will of personal estate. Lord Brougham's judgment in Jones v. Scott, 1 R. & M. 255, having been reversed by the House of Lords.—*Evans v. Tweedy,* Bea. 55.

TITHE COMPOSITION ACT.

(*Jurisdiction of commissioners.*) The commissioners under this act (6 & 7 Will. 4, c. 71,) have power to put an end to tithe suits only so far as they interfere with the making of the award under the act; and upon this ground a motion to stay proceedings in such a suit, though supported by an affidavit of the assistant commissioner, stating that he would be unable to make his award until the matters in difference were determined, was refused. (But see We-therell v. Weighill, 3 Y. & C. 244.)—*Girdlestone v. Stanley,* Y. & C. 481.

TRUSTEE.

(*Liability of—Probate.*) One of two trustees and executors having joined in probate of a will, held to have become thereby liable for loss to the testator's estate occasioned by its having been retained in trade with his knowledge by the other executor, who was also a partner of the deceased ; but the widow of the testator, who was tenant for life of a moiety, and who had assented to the retainer, was declared liable to indemnify the trustee to the extent of the interest she was entitled to.—*Booth v. Booth,* Bea. 125.

And see CONSTRUCTION OF STATUTES, 1, 2, 3.

WILL.

1. (*Construction—Books.*) The manuscript note-book of Dr. Willis, made during his attendance on George III. held to pass by his will under the general description of all his books in a particular residence where such note-book was found.—*Willis v. Curtois,* Bea. 189.

2. (*Construction—General clause—Survivor.*) Where there were different bequests to different classes of children, followed by a general clause that the shares of all such legatees as died under twenty-three should go over to the survivor and survivors, such clause was construed distributively as to each class, and the word "survivor" was taken in its usual sense.—*Cromeck v. Lumb,* Y. & C. 565.

3. (*Construction—Husband and Wife.*) Where there was a bequest of 300l. to A. and his wife for their own use and benefit, followed by a direction that if A. should be indebted to the testator at the time of his death, the debt should be deducted from the legacy, and A. died in the lifetime of the testator, owing to him 250l. which remained unpaid at the testator's death: Held, that the wife was entitled to the whole of the 300l.—*Davies v. Elmes,* Bea. 131.

4. (*Construction—Issue.*) Lands were devised to A., the testator's widow, for life, with remainder to trustees upon trusts "to pay and divide the rents unto and among all the brothers and sisters of the testator who should be living at the time of A.'s death, and to their issue male and female after the respective deceases of his said brothers and sisters for ever to be equally divided between them :" Held, that the words issue male and female were words of limitation, and that the children of a sister who died in the lifetime of A. took no interest.—*Tate v. Clarke,* Bea. 100.

5. (*Construction—Locality of subject—Personal ornaments.*) A testator having three places of residence at A., B. and C., after having devised to his nephew his messuages at A., next bequeathed to him his house at B. which was leasehold, and the will then proceeded, "and I also give to my said nephew all my carriages, horses, implements, and my live and dead stock and chattels in and about the said house and premises, and also my household goods and furniture, pictures, plate, linen, china, liquors of all sorts and brewing vessels, and likewise my watches and *personal ornaments*:" Held, that the household goods in each of the three residences passed by this request.

Quære whether a bust passed under the above words, and what is the meaning of "personal ornament."—*Willis v. Curtois,* Bea. 189.

6. (*Construction—Misdescription.*) Testator gave an annuity to trustees during the life of A. and her five daughters in trust for A. during her life, and after her

death for her said daughters and the survivors and survivor; and while more than one should be living to be divided between them in equal shares. At the time of the will and at the testator's death A. had five sons and one daughter : Held that the annuity went after A.'s death to such one daughter. (Harrison v. Harrison, 1 R. & M. 72.)—*Lord Selsey v. Lord Lake*, Bea. 146.

7. (*Construction—Principal or Interest.*) Testator gave a sum of 15,645*l.* secured to him as a charge upon an estate, upon trust after making certain payments thereout to accumulate the interest thereof for twenty years, and at the expiration thereof the trustees to stand possessed of *the interest of the said sum*, upon trust to make certain payments; and he also directed that the trusts of the sum of 15,642*l.* should be dealt with as the trusts of a certain other term, and that subject thereto *the said sum and the interest and accumulation* should be in trust for a certain class of children; and there was a direction that the capital should sink into the estate upon which it was charged : Held, that the accumulated interest only of the said sum after payment of the sums charged on it was given to the children specified.—*Scott v. Earl of Scarborough*, Bea. 154.

8. (*Construction—Remoteness.*) A bequest of a residue to a class of children, some of them unborn at the death of the testator, followed by a clause that the shares should not be payable till the children attained twenty-three; and by another general clause that all legacies in the will should be vested in each of the legatees at twenty-three; and also that the shares and legacies of such as died under that age should go over to the survivor : Held void for remoteness. —*Cronsck v. Lumb*, Y. & C. 565.

9. (*Construction—Vesting.*) A bequest of a fund to trustees upon trust to set apart sufficient to raise an annuity to be applied for the maintenance of certain children, then living, till the youngest attained twenty-three, and then the principal to be divided among such children, would of itself give an immediate vested interest to such children; see Rop. Leg. p. 500; but by the effect of a subsequent general clause giving over the shares of such as died under twenty-three; it was held that the vesting was postponed till that age.—*S. C.*

10. (*Construction—Vesting—Period of distribution.*) A testator gave the accumulation of the rents and profits of real and personal estate at the expiration of twenty years after his decease to such of his grandchildren, *then* (at the time of his making his will) born or thereafter to be born during the lifetime of their respective parents, as should attain twenty-one or marry with consent, and whether born or unborn when any other of them should attain the age aforesaid. At the expiration of the twenty years there were several grandchildren who had attained twenty-one, but two of the testator's children were still living : Held that the shares of the grandchildren who had attained twenty-one were vested, subject to open and let in the claim of any other grandchildren who might attain the same age, and in the meanwhile the interest only of the vested shares was to be paid.—*Scott v. Earl of Scarborough*, Bea. 154.

BANKRUPTCY.

[Containing 1 Montagu and Chitty, Part 1 ; and 3 Deacon, Part 3 ;—omitting cases noticed in former digests.]

ACT OF BANKRUPTCY.

(*Acquiescence of creditor.*) The bankrupts had for some time been carrying on business, under a deed of arrangement for the benefit of the petitioning creditor, when an affidavit of debt is made by him, and notice given to them under the 1 & 2 Vict. c. 110, s. 8, preceded by an intimation from his solicitor that it would be a mere matter of form. After this, a release having been refused to them according to the terms of the original deed of arrangement, they file a bill against the creditor to obtain it, but the suit is compromised, and another agreement is executed, providing for a final release and settlement. Two days after the execution of this agreement the term of the notice expires, and after this, some dispute arising as to the due performance of the agreement, the creditor issues a fiat, grounded upon the above notice and affidavit of debt : Held, on petition by bankrupts to annul, that no act of bankruptcy had been committed by reason of the assent of the creditor, and the fiat was annulled with costs.—*Exp. and re Brown*, Mont. & Ch. 177.

> N.B. The ground taken by the judge, Sir J. Cross, was different from that taken by either party in the argument, the petition relying chiefly on the release.

ADVERTISEMENT.

(*When stayed.*) The Court will not, on petition by bankrupt to annul, grant an order to stay the advertisement, unless probable cause is shown for supposing that the petition will be granted.—*Exp. and re Rhodes*, Dea. 697.

AFFIDAVIT OF DEBT.

(*Second affidavit.*) Where a creditor, who had filed an affidavit under 1 & 2 Vict. c. 110, for a debt of 100*l.* upon which security was given, filed another affidavit, alleging a debt of 3612*l.*, there being no other debt than that on which the first affidavit was filed, the Court refused to order the second affidavit to be taken off the file.—*Exp. and re Rose*, Mont. & Ch. 142.

AGENT.

(*Common agent—Appropriation—Special case.*) Where a debtor and a creditor have employed the same agent, a remittance by the debtor to such agent, for the purpose of being paid over to the creditor, must be so applied by the agent or his assignee, even though the estate of the agent has a claim against the remitting party ; and upon this principle, where a Belgian house had, through the agency of the bankrupts, consigned to a house in China goods, for which the latter house remitted bills to the bankrupts, who were also their agents, which they directed to be appropriated, as well as the balance of a previous remittance, in payment of the Belgian house, to whom they also sent at the same time, through the bankrupts, a letter announcing the appropriation, the date of such letter and of the last remittance from China being subsequent to the date of the fiat : It was held by the Lord Chancellor, upon a special case, affirming the judgment of the Court of Review, that the bills, as also the balances on the previous account, must be handed over to the Belgian house.— *Re Douglas*, Mont. & Ch. 1.

ANNULLING.

(*Concert.*) A fiat, taken out by bankrupt's father, apparently with the view of defeating a judgment creditor, annulled on petition of the latter, there being no estate to administer.— *Exp. Gaitskells re King*, Mont. & Ch. 160.

APPEAL.

(*Form of—Special case.*) Appeals from the Court of Review can only be brought before the Chancellor in the form of a special case, unless he should otherwise direct, and he will not give such direction except under special circumstances.

The settlement of the special case rests entirely in the discretion of the Court below, and no appeal will lie as to the mode in which it is settled.— *Exp. Stubbs re Hall*, Dea. 549.

And see PETITION OF REHEARING.

ASSIGNEES. See PRACTICE, 2, 15 ; PRINCIPAL AND SURETY.

BANKRUPT.

(*Description of.*) A. and B. traded under firm of A. and B. Being indebted to C., it was agreed that they should carry on business as his agents, and that the firm should be called " The Grove Mills Company." *Quære*, whether a fiat issued against them under the latter name, upon a debt contracted by them as the firm A. and B., is valid.— *Exp. and re Brown*, Mont. & Ch. 177.

BANKRUPT TRUSTEE.

(*Dividends.*) Bankrupt trustee not allowed to receive dividends on the trust fund, though the sum was only 200*l*. and parties consented.— *Exp. Strettell re Raikes*, Mont. & Ch. 165.

And see PRACTICE, 12, 13.

CERTIFICATE.

(*Staying—Laches of creditor.*) The Court refused to stay a certificate till the determination of an action, brought by the petitioner against a third party, against whom he had a claim assigned to him by the bankrupt as a security ; there appearing to be no sufficient reason why he should not have proved before. — *Exp. Pheasant re Sherwood*, Dea. 625.

And see PRACTICE, 17.

COMMITMENT.

(*Irregularity.*) Various objections to a commitment, founded on clerical errors and verbal mistakes, were overruled.— *Exp. Green re Elgie*, Dea. 700.

COMPOSITION.

1. (*Defective agreement.*) The Court refused to enforce an agreement, entered into between the bankrupt and his surety and the assignees, to annul the fiat on full payment of all debts, although it appeared there was enough to make

such payment on the debts then proved, because the condition of the composition clause, 6 Geo. 4, c. 16, s. 133, had not been complied with, and because other creditors might yet prove.—*Exp. and re Nainby*, Dea. 587.

2. (*Special agreement.*) Where a bankrupt, at the date of his bankruptcy, was entitled (as the Court held) to a vested interest as tenant for life in reversion of an estate, subject to a condition of residing in the mansion house, and after having obtained his certificate became entitled in possession, and then entered into an agreement with his assignee, whereby he undertook to reside in the mansion, in order to keep alive his estate, a certain portion of the rents being reserved to him, the rest to be paid to the asssignee, which agreement was never affirmed by the creditors ; the Court, on petition of the bankrupt to restrain the assignee from receiving the rents according to the agreement, and on cross-petition from the assignee, affirmed the agreement, to the extent of declaring it binding so long as the bankrupt continued in possession ; and they intimated an opinon that the condition of forfeiture had determined by the bankruptcy.—*Exp. and re Goldney*, Mont. & Ch. 75.

COSTS.

(*Competing fiats.*) On a petition to supersede the first fiat, on the ground of delay in opening, it appearing that the petitioner was aware that something had been done towards opening the fiat, and that he had endeavoured to prevent the prosecution of it ; his petition was dismissed, and no costs were given him.— *Re Wood*, Mont. & Ch. 69.

And see PRACTICE, 15, 20.

DIRECTION OF FIAT.

In the following cases the Court refused to alter the direction of the fiat or to depart from the rule in the first instance :—

1. In a case where no particular ground for the application is stated in the report.—*Exp. Brett*, Mont. & Ch. 70.

2. Where it was alleged that the act of bankruptcy was a fraudulent conveyance, and that the fraud would be more easily discoverable in London.— *Exp. Meeking re Bray*, Id. 71.

3. Where the bankrupt resided in Cornwall, but the majority of creditors in number and value, and the witnesses to the act of bankruptcy, resided in London.—*Re Hugo*, Id. 74.

4. Where eighteen creditors resided in London, and three only at the place of the bankrupt's residence.—*Re Hellyer*, Ibid.

5. Where all the creditors but one resided in London.—*Anon.* Id. 142. See also *Anon.* and *Re Allen*, Id. 146.

6. Where there were no creditors at the place of the bankrupt's residence.— *Re Binks*, Id. 143.

7. Where creditors to the amount of 10,000*l.* out of 14,000*l.* desired the removal.—*Re Smith Wright*, Id. 144.

8. Where the petitioning creditor and the witnesses to the act of bankruptcy resided in London, and the alleged object was to invalidate a preference. —*Re Mansfield*, Id. 145.

9. In a case where the bankrupt had, for a period of three years, ending within two years of his bankruptcy, resided and traded at a place other

than his then place of residence, and was largely indebted there, and since he left it had five times changed his abode.—*Re Hewitt*, Dea. 586.

The Court altered the direction of the fiat in the following cases :—

10. Where the bankrupt carried on trade in two places and resided at one, but there was another place nearly central between the two first-mentioned places, and nearer than either to the majority of creditors.—*Re Warner*, Mont. & Ch. 72.

11. Where the petitioning creditor, the witnesses to the act of bankruptcy, and the major part in value of the creditors, resided in London.—*Anon.* Id. 142.

12. Where two of the commissioners were creditors, and two resided at a distance, and the fifth generally declined to attend, and only four, out of creditors, to the amount in all of 60,000*l.*, resided in the neighbourhood of the bankrupt's residence.—*Re Geach*, Id. 145.

EQUITABLE MORTGAGE.

1. (*Costs of assignees.*) If a petition for sale of an equitable mortgage is rendered necessary, through a misconception by the assignees of their rights, they cannot claim costs, except out of the general estate of the bankrupt.—*Exp. Bate re Gough*, Mont. & Ch. 58.

2. (*Substitution by parol—Costs.*) Where the leases of several houses were deposited by bankrupt, together with a written memorandum, to secure a debt, and the creditor afterwards gave up some of them to the bankrupt, and took other leases in their stead as a substituted security, but without any written memorandum : Held, upon petition for the sale of the whole, that the creditor was entitled to costs as to the whole.—*Exp. Cobham re Halls*, Dea. 609.

EVIDENCE.

(*Proceedings in Chancery.*) On a petition to prove against the separate estate of one of three bankrupts, upon a bond given by them in conjunction with a surety, evidence de bene esse was admitted of proceedings in Chancery, in a suit by the obligee of the bond against the estate of the surety.—*Exp. Walker re Fidgeon*, Dea. 672.

FIAT.

(*Abatement by death.*) *Semble*, that a joint *fiat* becomes altogether of none effect in this Court by death of one bankrupt ; but *quære*, whether the Lord Chancellor may not give effect to it against the survivor?

In such a case, where a fresh creditor had petitioned for a new *fiat*, a preference was given to the original creditor, who petitioned on amended papers; and no costs were given to the second creditor.—*Exp. Norris re Norris*, Mont. & Ch. 159.

And see DIRECTION OF FIAT; PRACTICE, 6.

FORFEITURE.

(*Effect of bankruptcy on condition.*) *Semble*, that a condition of forfeiture in the event of grantee ceasing to reside in a particular mansion house, is determined by his bankruptcy.—*Exp. and re Goldney*, Mont. & Ch. 75.

JURISDICTION.

1. (*Chancellor.*) The Lord Chancellor intimated an opinion that he had not original jurisdiction even as to annulling the fiat, where the matter had come

before the Court of Review, on a petition to reverse the adjudication, and he qualified the observations of Lord Brougham in Exp. Keys, 1 Mont. & A. 226, and 3 Dea. & Ch. 263.—*Exp. Stubbs re Hall*, Dea. 549.

2. (*Contempt.*) The Court of Review has jurisdiction to enforce by its process any orders of the Lord Chancellor in bankruptcy. (1 & 2 Will. 4, c. 56, s. 8); accordingly where, before the institution of the Court, the Lord Chancellor had dismissed a petition with costs, and the petitioner, after the usual processes against him from this Court, had been ultimately committed for contempt: Held, that such commitment was regular.—*Exp. Green re Elgie*, Dea. 700.

3. (*Officers of the Court.*) An application by a registrar, who had resigned, for an order on the accountant to pay him the arrears of his salary, was refused by the Court, on the ground of want of jurisdiction. The registrar had become insolvent, but his assignee had declined to receive payment of the arrears.— *Exp. and re Bousfield*, Mont. & Ch. 41.

OFFICIAL ASSIGNEE.

(*Right of, to commission.*) It was held by *Sir G. Rose* that the official assignee was not entitled to commission on any sum of money realized under the fiat, whether belonging to the bankrupt or not; but in this case the money on which commission was charged was the proceeds of the sale of a mortgaged estate, the whole of which was paid over to the mortgagee, and *Sir J. Cross* laid stress upon that circumstance.—*Exp. Whisson*, Dea. 646.

PETITION OF REHEARING.

(*Lapse of time—Special circumstances.*) Where the agent of a party abroad had presented a petition of appeal against a decision of the commissioners rejecting a proof, and failed in such petition, a petition of rehearing, presented six months afterwards by the principal himself, who did not come to England till after the hearing of the previous petition, and who alleged that had he then been in the country he could have produced other evidence than that relied on by his agent, was entertained by the Court, and such further evidence was gone into.— *Exp. Jackson re Warwick*, Dea. 651. (See *S. C.* reported as Exp. Whitmore, 3 Dea. 365, and 3 M. & A. 627,—L. M. No. 44.)

PETITIONING CREDITOR.

1. (*Laches—Second Fiat.*) Petitioning creditor allowed, at his own costs, to issue a second fiat, the time for opening the fiat having gone by, through his inadvertence, without prejudice to any other docket.—*Exp. Partridge re Knibb*, Mont. & Ch. 165.

2. (*Costs.*) A creditor issued a fiat, which he forbore to prosecute, in order to enable the bankrupt to settle by arbitration some disputed accounts between himself and partners. The award was not made till more than a year after the issuing of the fiat, when the creditor applied for leave to issue another, which was refused to him both by the Court of Review and the Lord Chancellor.— *Exp. Foljambe re Hewitt*, Dea. 628.

And see FIAT.

PRACTICE.

1. (*Affidavit.*) Where no proceeding is pending, an affidavit cannot be filed before the petition which it is to support; but it is otherwise where there is a matter depending in Court.—*Exp. Green*, Dea. 700.

2. (*Assignees—Service.*) An order to prove cannot be made in the absence of the assignees, without personal service of the petition upon them. Service on the solicitor to the fiat will not do.—*Exp. Baker re Scott*, Mont. & Ch. 156.

3. (*Bankrupt.*) In *Exp. Goodman re Nainby*, (see Proof, 1,) the bankrupt applied to be heard by counsel, but was refused.—Mont. & C. 151; Dea. 631.

4. (*Before adjudication.*) Quære, whether, before adjudication, the bankrupt can petition to supersede on a legal objection?—*Exp. and re Brown*, Mont. & Ch. 177. See next case.

5. (*Same.*) A petition by alleged bankrupt to attend adjudication by counsel, for the purpose of opposing it, was refused; but petition was retained, with stay of advertisement of bankruptcy found, and the petitioner to apply instantly for a *supersedeas.*—*Exp. and re Foulkes*, Mont. & Ch. 68.

6. (*Competing fiats.*) An application under a separate fiat, for an appropriation of funds, will not be ordered to stand over by reason of the pending of a petition to supersede such fiat in favour of a subsequent joint fiat; the Court observing that the success of such petition would not affect the order.—*Re Haddon*, Mont. & Ch. 42.

7. (*Costs.*) Where parties out of Court agree upon the terms of an order, save as to the costs, the Court will not decide upon that point without opening the whole order.—*Exp. Bate, re Gough*, Mont. & Ch. 58.

8. (*Inspection of documents.*) Where an affidavit, in answer to a petition, referred to certain exhibits, which did not appear to be mutual accounts, or documents between the parties, an application of the petitioner to have copies of them before the hearing was refused.—*Exp. and re Parr*, Dea. 607.

9. (*Opening fiat.*) Non-attendance of witness to prove bankruptcy held to be no ground for enlarging time of opening fiat.—*Re Hillsdon*, Mont. & Ch. 74.

10. (*Petitioning creditor's bond.*) Fresh bond allowed to be filed, on petition to amend error in previous one.—*Re Dulcken*, Mont. & Ch. 73.

11. (*Proof.*) Bankrupt's wife allowed to prove for herself and children.—*Exp. Thring*, Mont. & Ch. 75.

12. (*Proof—Bankrupt Trustee.*) The Court refused to allow a petitioner to prove against a bankrupt trustee, on the ground that he had managed the accounts for the bankrupt, and was therefore better able to depose to the debt.—*Exp. Collingdon, re Anderson*, Mont. & Ch. 156.

13. (*Same.*) Where bankrupt trustee had not surrendered, one of the *cestui que trusts* was allowed to prove for herself and the rest.—*Exp. and re Forrester*, Mont. & Ch. 143.

14. (*Proof—Separate estate.*) The Court refused to hear counsel on behalf of the separate creditors, where they had not been served with the petition.—*Exp. Walker, re Fidgeon*, Dea. 672.

15. (*Removal of assignee.*) Assignee who had been elected in his absence, and without consent, removed at his own costs.—*Exp. Hammond, re West*, Mont. & Ch. 74.

16. (*State of facts.*) State of facts cannot be amended while before the registrar, but his report must be first made.—*Re Turner*, Mont. & Ch. 73.

17. (*Staying Certificate—Attestation.*) A petition to stay a certificate ought to state that the certificate was signed, but the omission of such a statement was considered immaterial, where the certificate was lying in the office when the petition was presented.

An attestation to such a petition in the following form, " Witness, A. B., solicitor to the petitioner," (A. B. being the solicitor presenting the petition,) was held sufficient.—*Exp. Stocken, re Stocken*, Mont. & Ch. 232 ; Dea. 610.

18. (*Superseding—Onus probandi.*) On petition to supersede, the usual course is, after the petition has been opened, to call upon the respondent to support the fiat, but where there is no question as to the strictly legal requisites, but an objection, such as that of acquiescence by creditor is relied on, *semble*, that the petitioner should begin.—*Exp. and re Brown*, Mont. & Ch. 177.

19. (*Superseding—Parties.*) Where one of two bankrupts, under a joint commission, is dead, his representative must join with the survivor in a petition to supersede, and a consent in writing to the petition is not sufficient,—*Re Steel*, Mont. & Ch. 73.

20. (*Supplemental petition — Costs.*) *Quære*, whether a supplemental petition, containing facts, or a fuller statement of facts, which might have been introduced and fully stated in the original petition is regular ? Such a petition having been filed but not used at the hearing, the petitioner succeeding on the original petition, no order was made as to costs of supplemental petition.—*Exp. and re Brown*, Mont. & Ch. 177.

21. (*Taxation of Costs—Service.*) A petition by one assignee to tax a bill must be served on the other assignees.—*Exp. Fosbrooke, re Fisher*, Mont. & Ch. 176.

And see DIRECTION OF FIAT.

PRINCIPAL AND SURETY.

(*Interested assignee.*) Where the principal and surety had concurred in an equitable mortgage to the creditor of an estate, in which each of them had an interest, and both principal and surety afterwards became bankrupt, and the creditor was appointed assignee of the surety, and presented a petition for sale of the estate, such an order was refused, till a *quasi* assignee should be appointed to protect the interest of the surety and his creditors in the matter.—*Exp. Haines, re Barnett*, Mont. & Ch. 32.

2. (*Proof by surety.*) Where a party accepted bills for the accommodation of the bankrupt, which the latter redeposited with his bankers as a security for the floating balance due to them from him, and the bankers proved for the whole of such balance, and the acceptor of the bills then paid such bills in full :— Held, that he was not entitled to receive back from the bankers the dividends received by them in respect of the amount due on the bills, but was only entitled to stand in their place as to future dividends on that sum. (Exp. Brunskill, 4 Dea. & Ch. 442.)—*Exp. Holmes, re Garner*, Dea. 662.

PROOF.

1. (*Extinguishment of Debt by proceedings at law.*)—A creditor having taken the bankrupt in execution, died before the date of the *fiat*. Some time afterwards the bankrupt was discharged from custody by a judge's order, the action having abated, and the executor of the creditor not having revived the judgment, or attended the warrant: Held, that the right to prove the debt was not gone —*Exp. Goodman, re Nainby*, Mont. & Ch. 151.

2. (*On joint security against separate estate.*) Where the three bankrupts joined with a surety in a bond, which was deposited with the bankers of the firm, for the purpose, as it was held against the bankrupts, of securing the floating balance due from them to the bank, though in a suit instituted in chancery by the

bankers against the estate of the surety, it was decided, that as far as he was concerned the bond was intended to be security only for the balance due at the time of its execution (See Walker v. Wardman, 11 Bligh, N. S.; L. M. No. 41.) It was held, that proof might be made for the whole amount of the bond against the separate estate of one of the bankrupts.—*Exp. Walker, re Fidgeon,* Dea. 672.

3. (*Security—Payment into Court.*) A creditor took a mortgage with power of sale from one of three partners, who afterwards died, devising the estate to the two surviving partners. They become insolvent, and assign their property to two trustees, who with the sanction of the creditor enter into an agreement for sale of the mortgaged estate, the purchaser to pay off the mortgage debt by instalments. A *fiat* afterwards issues against the surviving partners: Held, that the creditor might prove under it for the whole of the mortgage debt, but it was ordered that the dividends on such proof should be paid into Court, subject to further order.—*Exp. Smyth, re Steel,* Dea. 59.

4. (*Usury—Renewable bills.*) Where the bankrupt had borrowed 1600*l.* upon a bill for three months, renewable at his option for three other months, till the expiration of eighteen months; the original proposal having been for a loan for that time, and the bankrupt agreed verbally to pay interest at the rate of 10½ per cent per annum, upon each of such bills: Held, upon proof tendered on one of such bills, that it was bad for usury, the whole transaction being a manifest evasion of the 3 & 4 Will. 4, c. 98, s. 7. And *quære*, whether one three months bill at such a rate of interest, as between drawer and acceptor, is within the protection of the statute?—*Exp. Terrewest, re Poynter,* Mont. & Ch. 146; Dea. 590.

[An appeal against this decision is now pending before the Chancellor.]

And see PRINCIPAL AND SURETY, 2.

TAXATION OF COSTS.

(*Deceased Solicitor.*) The representatives of a deceased solicitor are not liable to the costs of taxation of a bill of such solicitor, though more than one-sixth of the amount be taken off. Nor where the assignees were liable to such representatives to pay the costs of an action brought against them for some of the costs, were they allowed to set off against such liability their costs of the first-mentioned taxation.—*Exp. Hammond, re Jackson,* Mont. & Ch. 136.

USURY. See PROOF, 4.

APPEAL ON REPORTED CASE.

The decision in Exp. Whitmore, 3 M. & A. 627; 3 Dea. 365; L. M. No. 44, was confirmed on a re-hearing, although further evidence was adduced that the account of the dealings, in respect of which the petitioners claimed a right of proof against the separate estate, was kept separate, both in the books of the bankrupt and in those of the petitioners.—*Exp. Jackson, re Whitmore,* Dea. 651.

ECCLESIASTICAL COURTS.

[Containing cases in 1 Curt. Part. 3.]

ADMINISTRATION.

1. (*Parties—Next of kin.*) The party who would be entitled to administration under the statute, must be cited before the Court will grant administration to a third party.—*In the Goods of Barker,* 592. (Prerog.)

2. (*Parties—Assignment.*) Where all interest under a will is assigned to trustees by a sole executor and legatee, administration will only be granted to his assignees after he has been cited.—*Mayhew v. Newstead,* 593. (Prerog.)

ADMINISTRATION BOND.

1. (*Discharge of sureties.*) Where A. and B., who had appointed C. their attorney to take out administration for their use and benefit, never called upon him for an inventory and account, and had given him three years to pay the balance which was due to them under the administration; C. having become insolvent, the Court refused to deliver up the administration bond to A. and B. for the purpose of being put in suit against C.'s sureties.—*Murray v. M'Inerheney,* 576. (Prerog.)

2. (*Inventory.*) The Court refused to deliver out the administration bond, for the purpose of being put in suit at law, for non-delivery of an inventory within the time assigned by the bond, no previous proceedings having been instituted against the administratrix in this Court, and an inventory having been given in previous to the application.—*Crowley v. Chipp,* 456. (Prerog.)

ALIMONY.

(*How forfeited.*) Where a wife who had been decreed alimony in a suit instituted by her against husband, had gone abroad for the purpose of evading compliance with a writ of *habeas corpus* issued against her by the King's Bench commanding her to produce her children, the Court held that this was no defence to a monition against her husband to compel payment of alimony.—*Greenhill v. Greenhill,* 462. (Consist.)

And see INSOLVENT.

BRAWLING.

On articles against a clergyman for brawling and disrespectful conduct to his superior (the case being only in part proved), he was monished and condemned in 75*l. nomine expensarum.*—*Office of the Judge* v. *Morley,* 470. (Arches.)

CHURCH-RATE.

1. (*Adjournment*—*Place and time of polling.*) Where the notice of a meeting in vestry, for the purpose of granting a church-rate, stated that the meeting would be immediately adjourned to the Town Hall, and the chairman accordingly did so adjourn it: Held, that the adjournment did not affect the validity of the rate, and that the Town Hall was not an improper place for taking the poll.

Held, also, that eleven hours was a sufficient time for taking the poll, 785 being the greatest number proved to have voted on any previous occasion.— *Baker* v. *Wood,* 507. (Arches.)

2. (*District*—*Mother Church.*) Under 58 Geo. 3, c. 45, s. 71, the inhabitants of the district are liable to be rated during twenty years, not only for the repairs of the mother Church, but for the expenses of worship in it.—*Chesterton* v. *Farlar,* 345. (Consist.)

3. (*Inequality*—*Omission.*) A rate was held not to be bad for irregularity because it omitted the occupants of houses under 20*l.* annual value, of which the land-lords were rateable to the poor under the local acts 17 Geo. 3 and 7 Geo. 4, and because it also omitted other parties alleged to be in a state of destitution.— *S. C.* (Privy Council.)

4. (*Power of churchwardens*—*Postponement of rate.*) Where the parishioners refuse to make a rate for necessary repairs, the churchwardens may make one of their own authority, and the postponement of a rate for a year was held tantamount to a rejection. Decided expressly on the authority of Gandeon v. Selby, unreported case before Sir W. Wynne.—*Veley* v. *Burder,* 372. (Consist.) (N. B. this is the Braintree case.)

5. (*Same point.*) Report of the judgment of Sir W. Wynne in the case of Gandeon v. Selby, extracted verbatim from the notes of the late Sir Christopher Robinson, 394.

6. (*Retrospective.*) Although the church rate be not on the face of it retrospective, the party libelled may allege that it is so; and in this case a rate admitted to have been made in a considerable part for the purpose of paying a debt incurred by the churchwardens of the previous year, was held bad.—*Chesterton* v. *Farlar,* 345. (Consist., Arches and Privy Council.)

CHURCHWARDEN.

1. (*Neglect of duty.*) In order to sustain *criminal* proceedings against church-wardens for not repairing or keeping in proper order the parish church, and for neglecting and disobeying the lawful orders and directions of the Archdeacon, proof must be given that the churchwardens have personally neglected their duty, or have wilfully disobeyed the orders of the Archdeacon.—*Office of the Judge* v. *Palmer,* 7. (Consist. and Arches.)

2. (*Quaker.*) A Quaker having been elected to the office of churchwarden, the Court (of the Archdeacon of London) declined compelling him to undertake the office. —*Adey* v. *Theobald,* 447.

And see CHURCH RATE, 4, 5.

COSTS.

(*Husband and wife.*) The husband is liable to the costs of the wife unless she has a separate income sufficient for her support and for the payment of costs.—*Belcher* v. *Belcher,* 444. (Arches.)

And see PAUPER.

DIOCESE OF LINCOLN. See JURISDICTION, 2.

EVIDENCE.

(*Credibility of Witness.*) An exceptive allegation to impeach the credibility of a witness by contradicting his evidence in the cause, is only admissible as to such parts of his testimony as have a material bearing on the issue.—*Trevanion* v. *Trevanion,* 406. (Consist.) *S. C.* on appeal in Arches, 486. N. B. An appeal from this decision is now pending before the Privy Council.

INSOLVENT.

1. (*Alimony.*) The Court refused on a suit for divorce at the instance of the husband to allow alimony *pendente lite* to the wife of an insolvent, though his father had considerable property and had supported the son, but proceedings were stayed till some small maintenance should be afforded to the wife.—*Bruere* v. *Bruere,* 566. (Consist.)

2. (*Fund in Court.*) The balance of a sequestration account remaining in the registry, ordered to be paid to the assignee under the Insolvent Act of a deceased incumbent, though no personal representative before the Court.—*Little Hallingbury, Essex,* 656.

JURISDICTION.

1. (*Brawling.*) The Ecclesiastical Court has jurisdiction in offences of brawling, independently of the statute 5 & 6 Edw. 6, c. 4.—*Office of the Judge* v. *Morley,* 470. (Arches.)

2. Letters of request from the commissary of Buckingham go to the Court of Arches and not to the chancellor of Lincoln.—*S. C.*

PAUPER.

(*Who may sue as—Costs.*) A party who by his business or profession is capable of obtaining a livelihood, even though he may have been discharged under the Insolvent Act, is not entitled to proceed in *formâ pauperis,* but in such a case the Court refused to tax the costs of his wife against him, declining at the same time to appoint a day for the hearing at his prayer.—*Walker* v. *Walker,* 560. (Consist.)

PLEADING.

In criminal suits the articles should state the whole transaction, in order that the defendant may give an affirmative issue.—*Taylor* v. *Morley,* 470. (Arches.)

PRESUMPTION OF DEATH.

1. A person who had embarked in 1835, on his way from Manilla to London, in a vessel which had never since been heard of, nor any one on board, was presumed to be dead.—*In the Goods of Hutton,* 595. (Prerog.)

2. (*Priority of death.*) A husband, his wife and child, having perished together by shipwreck, administration granted to the husband's effects as of a widower.—*In the Goods of Murray*, 596. (Prerog.)

PROCESS.

(*Citation—Residence.*) Before the Court will pronounce a party in contempt, for the purpose of proceeding in the cause, his residence must be shown to have been within the jurisdiction of the Court at or before the time of the issuing of the citation.—*Carden v. Carden*, 558. (Consist.)

WILL.

1. (*Execution of power.*) The Court refused to grant administration with the will annexed of a will executed in pursuance of a power in a settlement, neither the settlement nor a copy of it being produced.—*In the Goods of Monday*, 590. (Prerog.)

2. (*Improper influence.*) Where the testatrix was an old bedridden woman, eighty years of age, living in a state of great destitution, but entitled to considerable property, for the recovery of which a suit was pending, and the party propounding the will, under which he took a considerable benefit, was her solicitor in such suit, and the will was drawn by a friend of his, who, before he went to the testatrix, was informed by the propounding party what would be the probable instructions of the testatrix, and actually made in his house a rough draft of the supposed will, from which he put leading questions to the testatrix as to what her intentions were, though there was no other evidence of undue influence or incapacity, the will was rejected at the instance of a sole legatee under a will ten years old.—*Sankey v. Lilley*, 397.

3. (*Insanity.*) Where the Court was satisfied of the insanity of a testator, as well by proofs apparent on the face of the will as by affidavit, administration was granted as of a dead intestate, but the will was directed to be deposited in the registry.—*In the Goods of Bourget*, 591. (Prerog.)

4. (*Same.*) Although the testator had been found under an inquisition of lunacy to to be of unsound mind, and to have been so from a time anterior to the date of the will, there being no appearance of folly on the face of the will, the Court refused, on motion founded on affidavit, to grant administration as of an intestate. —*In the Goods of Watts*, 594. (Prerog.)

5. (*Proof of handwriting.*) Where no persons could be found who could make the usual *affidavit* as to the handwriting of the deceased, a will and codicils were, with the consent of all parties, admitted to probate upon comparison of the signatures with other known signatures of the deceased.—*In the Goods of Carey*, 592. (Prerog.)

6. (*Revocation by letter.*) Where the testatrix, while labouring under mortal disease, but in full possession of her faculties, directed letters to be written to her executor, with whom she had deposited the will, directing him to destroy it, which he, from some scruple, did not do, causing the will to be forwarded to the testatrix, who died before its arrival in ignorance whether it was destroyed or not, but with the continuing intention of revoking it : Held, that this was a revocation.—*Walcott v. Ochterlony*, 580. (Prerog.)

7. (*Revocation—Parol evidence.*) Parol evidence held admissible to rebut the presumption of revocation arising from marriage and birth of children, and some of such evidence being expressions of the testator impugning the chastity of his wife: Held, that it was no objection to its admissibility that it tended to bastardise the issue, the evidence not being adduced for that purpose.—*Fox v. Marston,* 494. (Prerog.)

8. (*Simultaneous papers.*) Where three papers, severally marked Nos. 1, 2, and 3, all executed by the testator under the same circumstances and at the same time, were propounded, the Court, although it rejected the two first, as incomplete and doubtful, admitted the last, which was in these words : No. 3, " This is a codicil to my last will. I give my servant George one hundred pounds."—*Reynolds v. Thrupp,* 568. (Prerog.)

HOUSE OF LORDS.

———

[Containing cases in 1 Maclean & Robertson, Part 1.]

———

ACCOUNT. See ARRESTMENTS; INTEREST.

APPEAL. See PRACTICE, 1, 2, 3, 4.

ARRESTMENTS.

1. (*Priority of security—Account—Assignation.*)   A. held an assignation of certain outstanding claims of the granter of the assignation as a security for certain specified debts, and in relief of certain specific obligations.   Another party, also creditor of the granter, raised an action against him, and on the dependence thereof used arrestments in the hands of A., and of the trustee of the debtor in the assigned debt, and of the factor for the trust: Held, (affirming the judgment of the Court of Session,) that A., in accounting with the arrester, was entitled to take credit in the first place for the amount of debts and obligations specified in the assignation, and all expenses relating thereto; 2ndly, for all sums paid to or for the behoof of, and for all furnishings to the granter, the common debtor prior to the arrestments; and, thirdly, for all sums paid to or for the behoof of the common debtor after the arrestments, but in virtue of obligations contracted prior thereto.

    Held, on the merits, that A. was properly allowed his costs, and that the interlocutor was right in not giving costs to the other parties, appellants and respondents.—*Clyne's Trustees, v. Dunnet*, 28.

And see TRUST.

ASSIGNATION. See ARRESTMENTS; COMPETITION.

AUGMENTATION. See WARRANDICE.

CITY OF LONDON.

(*Quo Warranto—Special customs—Stat. 11 Geo. 1, c. 18, sec. 11—Jurisdiction.*) On quo warranto for exercising the office of alderman of London, the defendant pleaded two customs, viz. 1st, a custom that "the Court of Mayor and Aldermen of the city of London, from time immemorial, have had the cognizance and determination of the election and return of every person elected into any place or office at any wardmote court, whenever the merits of such elections were brought into question, and of examining and determining whether any person returned to them as an alderman of any ward of the city, is, according to the discretion and sound consciences of the mayor and aldermen, a fit and proper person, and duly qualified in that behalf. And secondly, a custom " that whenever it should happen that the inhabitants of any ward should three times return to the Court of Mayor and Aldermen the same person to be an alderman of any such ward, who should upon such several returns, according to the former custom, be adjudged and determined not to be a fit and proper person to support the dignity and discharge the duties of an alderman, the Court may nominate, elect, and admit a fit and proper person, being a freeman of the said city, out of the body of the whole citizens, to be an alderman of such ward so made destitute of an alderman: Held, confirming the judgment in the Exchequer Chamber, that the customs were reasonable and legal customs, and not repealed by or inconsistent with the statute of the 11 Geo. 1, c. 18, sec. 11, or the bye law of the 13 of Anne, which relate only to elections at wardmotes: Held, also, that the Court of Mayor and Aldermen have exclusive cognizance of the fitness of the person elected, and that the issues as to that point were immaterial, and that the judge below properly refused to receive evidence thereon, and rightly discharged the jury, without the consent of the parties, from giving any verdict thereon.—*The King* v. *Johnson*, 1.

COMPETITION.

(*Priority of payment—Presumption—Assignation.*) A party lending money over an estate in fee simple, stipulated to receive as collateral security, in addition to a heritable bond and disposition in security, in his favour, assignation of certain securities of a prior date: in a question between a party holding an incumbrance intervening between the assigned incumbrances and the bond and disposition in security: Held, (there being no evidence to the contrary,) that the presumption was that the prior incumbrancers were paid with the money of the assignee, and that (affirming the judgment of the Court of Session) the assignation conferred a preference over the intermediate incumbrancer.—*Mackenzie* v. *Orr*, 117.

COSTS.

1. (*Appeal for.*) The House of Lords will not entertain an appeal for costs, and parties will not be allowed to escape from the rule, where, appealing for costs in substance, they mix up their appeal with some other matter of merits. Per Lord Chancellor.—*Clyne's Trustees* v. *Dunnet*, 28.

2. (*Pauper—Bond of caution.*) No objection to a warrant for interim execution that a printed copy of the petition has not been laid before each of the judges; nor is it an objection to such warrant for payment of costs, that the party obtaining the warrant has sued in formà pauperis, and that his own agent alone signed the bond of caution.—*S. C.*

3. (*Default of appearance—Pauper.*) No appearance having been made for the respondent, who sued in formà pauperis until the case was called on for hearing, when his printed case was presented at the bar of the House of Lords, he was by the indulgence of the House, allowed to be heard, but was refused his costs, though he would otherwise have been fully entitled to them on the merits.—*S. C.*

CUSTOM   See City of London.

DEATH-BED DEED.

(*Liege poustie, heir.*) A party, in the event of his pre-deceasing his parents, made a conveyance to them, and the survivor, whom failing, to any persons he might name; whom failing, to any person they might name. His parents predeceased him, leaving a trust conveyance of their whole property in favour of trustees named. He thereafter executed a deed on death-bed, conveying his whole estate to trustees named, declaring the purposes, and revoking all deeds inconsistent therewith: Held, (affirming the judgment of the Court of Session,) that the first deed, neither singly nor taken in connection with the second deed, was effectual to disinherit the heir, the event on which it was to take effect not having happened : Held, that the first deed was inconsistent with the death-bed deed, and revoked by it : Held, also, that the death-bed deed could not be coupled with the first, or with the first and second deeds, so as to exclude the challenge of it by the heir, and was void as against him.—*Clyne's Trustees v. Clyne*, 73.

ENTAIL.   See WARRANDICE.

EVIDENCE.

1. (*Oath of common debtor.*) A party holding an assignation of certain claims, as a security, subject to the arrestment of another party in respect of money due to such party from the assignor is entitled, as against such party, to prove by the oath of the common debtor, items of account between himself and the common debtor not otherwise established.—*S. C.*

2. (*Immaterial issues.*) Held that evidence on immaterial issues is properly rejected, and that the jury may be discharged without consent of parties from giving evidence thereon.—*The King v. Johnson*, 1.

FRAUD.

(*Breach of trust.*) A party executed a settlement in favour of certain trustees, who accepted and chose an agent to act for them.   The agent, in conjunction with one of the trustees, the husband of the cestui que trust, who was also heir at law of the trustee, procured the said cestui que trust to make up a title to part of the trust estate, passing over the trust, and thereupon to execute a disposition in his favour, on the ground that it was in security of advances for the trust.   The agent thereupon took infeftment and executed a conveyance in favour of third parties : Held, (affirming the decision of the Court of Session) that the agent was bound in the first instance without awaiting the result of an accounting to restore the estate in integrum against the real security created by the disposition and infeftment.—*Frazer v. Stevens's Trustees*, 171.

INTEREST.

(*Security—Account.*) A. having a heritable bond over an estate in respect of money lent, and having by assignation certain prior securities on the same estate, the arrears of interest due on which securities were from omissions not assigned till a subsequent period, when they were separately conveyed to the same party ; and the interest on the loan having been paid prior to the assignation of the securities : Held, (affirming the judgment of the Court of Session) that A. was not bound to apply the interest paid on the loan before the assignment of the arrears due on the prior incumbrances in reduction of the interest due on such last mentioned incumbrances in diminution of his prior security, but was entitled to refer it to the account for which he had the least available security.— *Mackenzie v. Orr*, 117.

PATRONAGE.

(*Church—Jurisdiction.*) A. was validly and effectually presented to a church and parish in Scotland by the patron, but was rejected by the presbytery of the bounds, on the sole ground that a majority of the male heads of families communicants in the said parish had dissented, without any reason assigned, from his admission as minister : Held, that the presbytery acted illegally and contrary to the provisions of the statutes, and particularly 10 Anne, c. 12, in rejecting the presentee, and that the objection to the jurisdiction of the Court of Session ought to be repelled.—*The Presbytery of Auchterader v. The Earl of Kinnoul*, 223.

PAUPER. See Costs, 2.

PLEADING.

(*Matters in issue.*) A court of appeal will not readily listen to an objection that certain documents relied upon to prove certain facts are inadmissible on the ground of such documents not being in issue, where such objection was not made below and no injustice appears to have been done. Per L. C.—*Sir C. Halkett v. Nisbet's Trustees and others,* 53.

PRACTICE.

1. (*Preliminary pleas—Right of appeal.*) In a reduction, the defender pleaded certain pleas which he designated preliminary. A record was ordered to be made up on these pleas, on which the defender reclaimed, when the Court (on the ground that the defences pleaded as preliminary were the only defences pleadable in causa on which it might be necessary to make up a record) adhered. The record was then prepared, and the defender repeated his former pleas, but without again designating them as preliminary. The ordinary "repelled the dilatory defences" reserving a question arising out of these pleas to be discussed with the defences on the merits. On reclaiming, the Court adhered : Held, that an appeal against the judgment was competent without leave of the Court.— *Clyne's Trustees v. Clyne,* 72.

2. (*Interim execution.*) The directing interim execution is in the discretion of the Court of Session, and no appeal against an interim order can stay the process.— S. C.

3. (*Jury trial.*) In an action in which the main question in dispute was whether a party had intromitted with his father's effects, the Lord Ordinary found, 1st. That further investigation was necessary; and, 2nd. That no sufficient cause was assigned for departing from the general rule for ascertaining disputed questions of fact, and therefore remitted the cause to the jury roll. On reclaiming, the Court refused the desire of the note as incompetent; Quoad ultra, of consent recalled the interlocutor of the Lord Ordinary, hoc statu, in so far as it contained findings in the cause, and remitted to proceed as shall be just. An application was then made to re-transmit the cause to the Ordinary Roll of the Court of Session, which was refused. On reclaiming, the interlocutor refusing was re-called, and the Court remitted to the Lord Ordinary to re-transmit the cause to his Lordship's Court of Session Roll, and to order a proof by commission. The House of Lords reversed the judgment, but on the ground that the Lord Ordinary was right in directing a trial by jury as the question was one which it is fit and proper so to try.

    Semble, an interlocutor of a Lord Ordinary directing trial by jury, cannot properly be the subject of a reclaiming note to the Inner House, or of an appeal to the House of Lords.—*Montgomerie v. Boswell,* 136.

4. (*Appeal.*) Whether when appealing against a judgment of the Court of Session it is competent to include in the appeal interlocutors of the Lord Ordinary in the cause which have not been previously made the subject of a reclaiming note, *quære?—Clyne's Trustees v. Dunnet,* 29.

PRESUMPTION. See Competition.

QUO WARRANTO. See City of London.

STATUTES.

10 Anne, c. 12. See Patronage.

11 Geo. 1, c. 18, s. 7. See City of London.

TEINDS. See Warrandice.

TRUST.

1. (*Breach of—Notice of—Discharge of diligences of inhibition and arrestment.*) A trustee without the concurrence of his co-trustee joined with one of the cestui que trust in disposing of part of the subject of the trust to the agent for the trust, in security for certain advances made by the agent, but not for the purposes or within the scope of the trust: Held, that it was incompetent for the trustees, without special power in that behalf, and wholly incompetent for one of them acting alone, so to pledge the trust estate ; and that no third party cognizant of the terms of the trust could be held to have made the advances on the faith of the trust estate ; and that diligences of inhibition and arrestment obtained in respect of such disposition were properly recalled and discharged without caution or consignation.—*Stuart v. Carnegie*, 192.

And see Fraud.

WARRANDICE.

(*Entail—Augmentation of teinds—Liability of heir.*) Sir John Wedderburn of Gosford, having sold the lordship of Innerwick, with the parsonage and vicarage tiends thereof, warranted the teinds from future augmentations ; Sir Peter, the son of Sir John, made up titles to him by service as heir of line, and with his wife executed mutual taillies of their respective estates, but without the statutory fetters against alienation and debts ; under these taillies Charles Wedderburn, his second son, became heir of provision in Gosford, and grantee under a general disposition with express burden of debts ; and Pitfirrane, the property of the wife, was settled on the eldest son : on the death of Charles, Sir John, his son, made up his title by general service to him, as nearest heir male of line, of taillie and provision, and succeeded to the estate of Gosford and the other property comprised in the general disposition, and sold part of the estates ; at a subsequent period he became infeft of the lands of Pitfirrane and surrendered Gosford to his younger brother Henry, who took on himself the obligations to which Sir John was subject, on the bankruptcy of of Henry, a sum of money was claimed and allowed to Sir John in respect of these obligations. The appellant was served heir of line taillie and provision to Sir John, his father : Held, affirming the judgment of the Court of Session, that the appellant was liable to the obligation of the warrandice entered into by his ancestor.—*Sir Charles Halkett v. Nisbett's Trustees*, 53.

LIST OF CASES.

———

COMMON LAW.

EQUITY.

BANKRUPTCY.

ECCLESIASTICAL.

HOUSE OF LORDS.

ABSTRACT OF THE PUBLIC GENERAL STATUTES.

(2 & 3 Victoria—*continued.*)

Cap. 23.—An Act to consolidate and amend the Laws for collecting and securing the Duties of Excise on Paper, made in the United Kingdom.

[19th July, 1839.]

Cap. 24.—An Act to repeal the Duties and Drawbacks of Excise on Bricks, and to grant other Duties aud Drawbacks in lieu thereof, and to consolidate and amend the Laws for collecting and paying the said Duties and Drawbacks.

[19th July, 1839.]

Cap. 25.—An Act to remove Doubts as to the charging certain of the Duties of Excise on Glass. [19th July, 1839.]

Cap. 26.—An Act to provide for the Enactment of certain Laws in the Island of Jamaica. [19th July, 1839.]

Cap. 27.—An Act for regulating the Proceedings in the Borough Courts of England and Wales. [19th July, 1839.]

S. 1. Empowers the judges of courts of record named in schedules A. and B. to the 5 & 6 Will. 4, c. 76, to make, alter, and revoke rules for appointing the times, proceedings, process, appearances, practice, and pleading, and the fees of the attorneys : no such rules, or order revoking or altering them, to be of any force until allowed and confirmed by three of the Judges.

S. 2. Courts to be held four times at least in the year, and with no greater interval than four calendar months.

S. 3. After 1st September, 1839, all personal actions in the Borough Courts to be commenced by writ of summons.

S. 4. Act may be amended or repealed this session.

Cap. 28.—An Act for more equally Assessing and Levying Watch Rates in certain Boroughs. [19th July, 1839.]

S. 1. The council of every borough named in either of the schedules to the 5 & 6 Will. 4, c. 76, may levy a watch rate on the occupiers of all lands, &c. within the borough, which shall be watched by day and night, and which shall by order of the council be declared to be the watch rate ; such rates to be made upon an estimate of the *net annual value* of the land, i. e. of the rent at which they might in their actual state be expected to let from year to year, the average costs of repairs, insurances, and tithe commutation rent-charge, being paid by the tenant : no rate to exceed in a year 6d. per pound on the net annual value, except in the boroughs in which at the passing of the 5 & 6 Will. 4, the sum thereby authorized to be levied exceeded the watch rate which might have been then raised, by 6d. in the pound : Provided, that the act shall not extend to either of the Universities, nor to affect the liability of the borough fund to make good any deficiency of the watch rate towards the expenses of the police, nor to make more liable lands entitled to exemption or deduction by any local act.

S. 2. For these purposes the council are to have all the powers given them respectively as to the borough rate and watch rate, by the 5 & 6 Will. 4, c. 76, or any subsequent act.

S. 3. Act may be amended or repealed this session.

Cap. 29.—An Act for the better Protection of Parties dealing with persons liable to the Bankrupt Laws. [19th July, 1839.]

S. 1. All contracts, dealings and transactions by and with any bankrupt really and bonâ fide made and entered into before the date of the fiat, and all executions and attachments against his lands or goods bonâ fide executed and levied before the date of the fiat, to be deemed valid, notwithstanding any prior act of bankruptcy, provided the persons dealing with the bankrupt or on whose account the execution or attachment issued, had not at the time notice of any prior act of bankruptcy: nothing herein contained to give validity to any payment by way of fraudulent preference, or any execution founded on a judgment on a warrant of attorney or cognovit given by way of fraudulent preference.

S. 2. Act may be repealed or altered this session.

Cap. 30.—An Act for Apportioning the Spiritual Services of Parishes in which two or more Spiritual persons have Cure of Souls generally throughout the Parish. [19th July, 1839.]

Cap. 31.—An Act to continue until the first day of June One thousand eight hundred and forty-one, and to the end of the then Session of Parliament, the Local Turnpike Acts in England and Wales, which expire with this or the ensuing Session of Parliament. [29th July, 1839.]

Cap. 32.—An Act to continue until the end of the Session of Parliament next after the Thirty-first day of May One thousand eight hundred and forty-one, certain allowances of the Duty of Excise on Soap used in Manufactures.
[29th July, 1839.]

Cap. 33.—An Act to indemnify such Persons in the United Kingdom as have omitted to qualify themselves for Offices and Employments, and for Extending the Time limited for those purposes respectively until the Twenty-fifth day of March One thousand eight hundred and forty; and for the Relief of Clerks to Attornies and Solicitors in certain cases. [29th July, 1839.]

Cap. 34.—An Act to confirm certain Rules and Orders of the Supreme Courts of Judicature at Fort William and Madras, and to empower the same Courts, and the Supreme Court of Judicature of Bombay, to make Rules and Orders concerning Pleading. [29th July, 1839.]

Cap. 35.—An Act to continue for One Year Compositions for Assessed Taxes, and to alter the period for the Expiration of Game Certificates, and for granting Licenses to deal in Game. [29th July, 1839.]

Cap. 36.—An Act to regulate the Duties to be performed by the Judges in the Supreme Courts of Scotland, and to increase the Salaries of certain of the said Judges. [29th July, 1839.]

Cap. 37.—An Act to amend and extend until the First of January One thousand eight hundred and forty-two, the Provisions of an Act of the First Year of Her present Majesty for exempting certain Bills of Exchange and Promissory Notes from the Operation of the Laws relating to Usury. [29th July, 1839.]

Cap. 38.—An Act to amend the Jurisdiction for the Trial of Election Petitions.
[17th August, 1839.]

S. 1. The 9 Geo. 4, c. 22, and so much of the 42 Geo. 3, c. 108, as requires the parties on Irish election petitions to interchange lists, to be suspended until the end of the second session of the first parliament which may be called after the dissolution of the present: this enactment not to revive Acts repealed by the 9 Geo. 4, c. 22.

S. 2. Defines what shall be considered an election petition. No such petition to be received unless subscribed by some person claiming the right to vote at the election, or to have been returned, or alleging himself to have been a candidate.

S. 3. Recognizance to be entered into by petitioners, according to the form in Schedule A. annexed to the Act.

S. 4. Prescribes form of affidavit of sufficiency and description of sureties.

S. 5. The speaker to appoint an examiner of recognizances, to hold his office during the pleasure of the speaker.

S. 6. Speaker to appoint a deputy during illness, temporary disability, or unavoidable absence of examiner.

S. 7. Recognizances to be perfected before the examiner, or one justice, and in the latter case to be certified by the justice and delivered to the examiner.

S. 8. Gives an option of paying the amount of the recognizance into the Bank of England, on the joint account of the party and the examiner, instead of finding sureties.

S. 9. Declaration of trust to be made of monies so paid in.

S. 10. Provision for change of trustees.

S. 11. No election petition to be received unless indorsed by a certificate of the examiner that the recognizance, &c. have been perfected.

S. 12. Names of sureties to be entered in a book to be kept in the office of the examiner.

S. 13. Sitting member, or electors defending the return, may object to the insufficiency of the sureties: ground of objection to be stated in writing, and delivered to examiner of recognizances within ten days after the presenting of the petition, if the surety objected to reside in England; or within fourteen days if in Scotland or Ireland.

S. 14. Notice of objections to be put up in the examiner's office, and objections to be heard by him not less than three or more than five days after their receipt; petitioners to have copies.

S. 15. Examiner empowered to inquire into sufficiency of sureties on the grounds stated in the notice only, and to receive evidence on oath or affidavit, and to award costs.

S. 16. In case of death of a surety (stated as a ground of objection), the sum for which he was bound may be paid into the Bank.

S. 17. Examiner to report to the speaker whether the sureties are unobjection-able or not, and to make out a list of the petition, on which he shall report that they are unobjectionable.

S. 18. Petitioners may withdraw petitions on giving written notice to the speaker, and to the sitting member or his agent: in such case to be liable to costs incurred by the sitting member.

S. 19. If the speaker be informed, by a certificate subscribed by two members, of the death of a member petitioned against, or returned upon a double return, whose election or return is complained of, or that he has been summoned to the House of Peers, or if his seat be resolved by the House to be vacant, or if he declare that it is not his intention to defend his return, notice shall immediately be sent by the speaker to the returning officer, who shall cause a copy to be affixed on the county or town hall, or nearest parish church, and it shall also be inserted in one of the two next London Gazettes.

S. 20. Within fourteen days after the presentment of a petition, or within thirty days after notice in the Gazette that the seat is vacant, or that the sitting member will not defend his return, electors may petition to be admitted parties to defend the return, &c. and shall be admitted with or in the room of the sitting member.

S. 21. Members who have given notice of their intention not to defend, not to be admitted parties against the petition.

S. 22. At the beginning of every session, on the day after the last day allowed for questioning the returns, the speaker shall by warrant appoint six members (not being petitioned against or petitioners) to be a committee, to be called the General Committee of Elections: such appointment to take effect unless disapproved of by the house within three days.

S. 23. If the house disapprove the appointment, the speaker to make a new appointment within three days, and so toties quoties.

S. 24. The disapproval may be general, or special as to any particular members.

S. 25. The speaker may appoint anew members not specially disapproved of.

S. 26. The appointment of each member to continue until the end of the session, or until he ceases to be a member, or resign his appointment, or the committee report that he is disabled by illness, or until the committee be dissolved.

S. 27. Cases of vacancy in the general committee to be made known to the house by the speaker, and proceedings to be suspended until the vacancy be supplied.

S. 28. Committee to be dissolved in case of continued absence of more than two members, or if by reason of irreconcileable disagreement of opinion it cannot discharge its duties, or on resolution of the house.

S. 29. Appointments to supply vacancies, and re-appointments of the general committee, to be made by the speaker, in like manner as before.

S. 30. All election petitions to be referred to the general committee for the purpose of their choosing select committees to try them: speaker to communicate to the house and to the general committee reports of the examiner as to the sureties, and notices of the death or vacancy of the seat of members, &c.; and where petitions are withdrawn, or the examiner reports against the sureties, the order for referring the petition to the general committee shall be discharged; and the committee shall not proceed on any petition referred to by notice in the Gazette, according to s. 19, until thirty days after its insertion, unless the petition of parties admitted to defend the return be referred to them in the mean time: and where the proceedings are so suspended, the petition to be struck out of the list, and re-inserted at the bottom of it.

S. 31. Speaker to appoint time and place of first meeting of the general committee; but no member to act on it until sworn at the table.

S. 32. No business to be transacted unless four members are present, and no appointment of a select committee by the general committee to be of force unless four members then present agree in it.

S. 33. Committee to make regulations for conduct of their proceedings.

S. 34. Committee clerk to attend general committee, and make minutes of their proceedings, to be laid before the house.

S. 35. If at the dissolution or suspension of proceedings of the committee there be business before them appointed for a certain day, the speaker may adjourn it.

S. 36. Alphabetical list of the members of the house to be made at the commencement of the session.

S. 37. Members above sixty years old to be excused from serving upon election committees, on claiming in their place or in writing.

S. 38. Members having leave of absence, or offering such excuse as the house shall resolve to be sufficient, to be excused from serving during leave of absence or pleasure of the house: and every member who has served on one election committee, and claiming to be excused, not to serve again during the session.

S. 39. Members whose returns have not been brought in within due time, petitioners, and members petitioned against, disqualified from serving during the continuance of such ground of disqualification; and members appointed to serve on a committee disqualified from serving again for seven days after its final report.

S. 40. A corrected list, distinguishing the excused and disqualified members, to be printed and distributed with the votes.

S. 41. The list may receive further corrections for seven days after.

S. 42. The lists so finally corrected to be referred to the general committee, who shall select six, eight, ten, or twelve persons qualified to serve as chairmen of committees, and who, if willing to serve, shall be formed into a " chairmen's panel," not to serve otherwise than as chairmen: members to continue on it till the end of the session, or until discharged by leave of the house.

S. 43. The remainder of the lists to be divided into five panels of equal number, the order of which to be decided by lot, and to be the panels whence all members shall be chosen to serve on committees.

S. 44. Power to the general committee to correct the panels from time to time.

S. 45. General committee to supply vacancies in the chairmen's panel, and increase its numbers if thought necessary.

S. 46. Power to chairmen's panel from time to time to make regulations for the distribution of the duties of chairmen.

S. 47. The general committee to determine how many committees shall be chosen in each week, and to give three weeks' notice of the day of choosing any election committee.

S. 48. Such notice to be given to the petitioners, the sitting members, to parties who have petitioned to be admitted to defend, and in certain cases to the returning officers.

S. 49. Provision for the case of parties afterwards admitted to defend the return.

S. 50. Lists of voters, intended to be objected to, to be delivered in to the clerk of the general committee ten days before the day appointed for choosing the committee.

S. 51. General committee to choose from the panel in order of service six members not disqualified or excused, for the trial of any petition; each panel to serve for a week.

S. 52. In case of disagreement in choosing a committee, the general committee to adjourn it to the following day, and so on: and all committees to be chosen for petitions according to their order on the list.

S. 53. When the committee is chosen, the parties to be called in, and the names read over to them.

S. 54. The general committee to proceed in order with all the petitions appointed for that day.

S. 55. The parties to be called in again within half an hour after they have withdrawn, when they may object to disqualified or excused members: and if the general committee allow the disqualification, a new committee to be chosen.

S. 56. Notice to be given to every member chosen.

S. 57. If any member chosen shall prove by the next day that he is disqualified or excused, a new committee to be chosen.

S. 58. When the six members are finally chosen, the members on the chairmen's panel to notify to the general committee the name of the member appointed by them as chairman of the select committee.

S. 59. The select committee to be reported by the general committee to the house.

S. 60. Members of select committee to be sworn.—(9 Geo. 4, c. 22, s. 30.)

S. 61. Members of the select committee not present within an hour after the meeting of the house to be taken into custody by the serjeant at arms, &c.

S. 62. If any such member is not present within three hours after the meeting of the house, the swearing of the committee to be adjourned.

S. 63. If on the day to which it is so adjourned all the members of the committee do not attend and be sworn within an hour after the meeting of the house, the committee to be discharged.

S. 64. Petitions and lists to be referred to the committee, and the time and place of meeting to be appointed by the house.—(9 Geo. 4, c. 22, s. 30.)

S. 65. Provision for election of new chairmen if necessary.—(See 9 Geo. 4, c. 22, s. 37.)

S. 66. Committees not to adjourn for more than twenty-four hours, without leave of the house, &c.—(9 Geo. 4, c. 22, s. 42.)

S. 67. Committee-man not to absent himself; committee not to sit until all the members be met; and on failure of meeting within one hour, to adjourn.—(9 Geo. 4, c. 22, s. 43.)

S. 68. Absentees to be directed to attend the house.—(9 Geo. 4, c. 22, s. 44.)

S. 69. If any committee be reduced to less than six by the non-attendance of its members, it shall be dissolved, except in particular cases provided for.

S. 70. Committees to be attended by a short-hand writer.—(9 Geo. 4, c. 22, s. 38.)

S. 71. Committee empowered to send for and examine persons, papers and records: and witnesses misbehaving may be reported to the house, and committed to the custody of the serjeant at arms.—(9 Geo. 4, c. 22, s. 39.)

S. 72. Giving false evidence before a committee declared perjury.—(9 Geo. 4, c. 22, ss. 49, 62.)

S. 73. Evidence to be confined to objections particularized in the lists delivered to the general committee, and to the specified heads.—(9 Geo. 4, c. 22, s.15.)

S. 74. Select committee shall try the merits of the petition, and their determination to be final, and to be reported to the house.—(See 9 Geo. 4, c. 22, s. 40.)

S. 75. Committee may report their determination on other matters to the house.—(9 Geo. 4, c. 22, s. 41.)

S. 76. While the committee is deliberating, the room to be cleared, &c.—(9 Geo. 4, c. 22, s. 47.)

S. 77. Questions to be decided by a majority of voices; chairman to have a casting vote.—(9 Geo. 4, c. 22, s. 47.)

S. 78. The names of members voting for or against any resolution of a committee to be reported to the house with the final report, and no member to be allowed to refrain from voting on a division.

S. 79. Committees not to be dissolved by the prorogation of parliament, &c.—(9 Geo. 4, c. 22, s. 56.)

S. 80. Costs when to be incurred by petitioners, &c.—(9 Geo. 4, c. 22, s. 57.)

S. 81. Costs when incurred by parties opposing petitioners.—(9 Geo. 4, c. 22, s. 58.)

S. 82. Costs when incurred where no party appears to oppose a petition.—(9 Geo. 4, c. 22, s. 59.)

S. 83. Costs upon frivolous objections to voters.—(9 Geo. 4, c. 22, s. 15.)

S. 84. Costs upon unfounded allegations against parties or their agents.

S. 85. Mode of ascertainment and taxation of costs.

S. 86. Costs occasioned by delay in appointing the select committee, to be taxed off.

S. 87. Persons appointed to tax costs empowered to take affidavits.

S. 88. Provision for recovery of costs on speaker's certificate.

S. 89. Persons paying costs may recover their proportionate shares from other parties liable.—(9 Geo. 4, c. 22, s. 64.)

S. 90. Recognizances when to be estreated for non-payment of costs, &c.

S. 91. Power to sue returning officer for neglecting to return any person duly elected.—(9 Geo. 4, c. 22, s. 66.)

S. 92. Act to commence from the end of this session, and to continue to the end of the second session of the next parliament.

S. 93. Provision for pending petitions.

S. 94. Act may be amended or repealed this session.

Cap. 39.—An Act to amend an Act passed in the last Session of Parliament, for abolishing Arrest on Mesne Process in Civil Actions except in certain Cases, for extending the Remedies of Creditors against the Property of Debtors, and for amending the Laws for the Relief of Insolvent Debtors in England.

[17th August, 1839.]

S. 1. The provision in the 1 & 2 Vict. c. 110, s. 115, limiting the payment for insertion of advertisements of the Insolvent Debtors' Court in newspapers to 3s. each, repealed; such advertisements hereafter to be inserted for a reasonable compensation.

S. 2. Insolvent Debtors' Court empowered to appoint commissioners to receive recognizances of bail at a greater distance than ten miles from London.

S. 3. Parties empowered to enter into recognizances before such commissioners.

S. 4. Commissioners of the Insolvent Court to make rules and orders for regulating the amount and the taking of recognizances.

S. 5. Commissioners of the Court on circuit empowered to take such recognizances.

S. 6. As soon as the sureties have justified, and the recognizances are filed, the Court shall order the discharge of the insolvent.

S. 7. Act to commence 1st Oct. 1839, (except as to s. 1).

Cap. 40.—An Act for Procuring Returns relative to the Highways and Turnpike Roads in England and Wales.   [17th August, 1839.]

S. 1. Justices of the peace within their respective jurisdictions to appoint a time and place for the surveyors of the highways to deliver to them returns to the matters stated in schedule A. annexed to the Act; and to give notice to them to make such returns, and to the constables, requiring their attendance at such meetings.

S. 2. Justices to receive returns, and examine the surveyors as to the truth of them, and sign and attest the same.

S. 3. Constables to receive from the clerks of the peace copies of the schedule A., and deliver them to the surveyors; and to attend the meetings, and receive and transmit the returns, with a list of the parishes &c., and of the surveyors to whom delivered, to the clerks of the peace and town clerks at the Epiphany quarter sessions.

S. 4. Surveyors of the highways also to attend the meetings, and deliver the accounts therein particularly required, under a penalty not exceeding £10 nor less than £5.

S. 5. Clerks of trustees to transmit to the Secretary of State returns according to the form in schedule B., under the same penalty in default.

S. 6. Penalty on officers making false returns.

S. 7. Recovery and application of penalties.

S. 8. Justices before whom returns are made by surveyors to administer to them the declaration therein set forth.

S. 9. Making false declaration a misdemeanor.

S. 10. Copies of this Act, and of schedule A., to be transmitted by the Queen's printer to the clerks of the peace, who are to distribute them among the acting justices, and deliver copies to town clerks for distribution : and clerks of the peace and town clerks to receive and transmit returns to the Secretary of State, to be laid before Parliament.

CAP. 41.—An Act for Regulating the Sequestration of the Estates of Bankrupts in Scotland. [17th August, 1839.]

CAP. 42.—An Act to improve Prisons and Prison Discipline in Scotland.
[17th August, 1839.]

CAP. 43.—An Act to suspend until the end of the next Session of Parliament the making of Lists and Ballot and Enrolments for the Militia of the United Kingdom. [17th August, 1839.]

CAP. 44.—An Act to prevent until the end of the next Session of Parliament Ships clearing out from a British North American Port loading any part of their Cargo of Timber upon Deck. [17th August, 1839.]

CAP. 45.—An Act to amend an Act of the Fifth and Sixth Years of his late Majesty King William the Fourth relating to Highways. [17th August, 1839.]

S. 1. Proprietors or directors of railroads to maintain gates across each end, whenever a railroad crosses or shall hereafter cross any turnpike road, highway, or statute labour road, and to employ persons to open and shut them so as to prevent danger or damage : penalty 5l. for each day's neglect, with costs.

S. 2. Penalties and costs to be recovered and applied as directed by the 5 & 6 Will. 4, c. 50.

S. 3. Act to commence 30th September, 1839.

CAP. 46.—An Act to authorise the Trustees of Turnpike Roads to reduce the Scale of Tolls payable for Overweight. [17th August, 1839.]

CAP. 47.—An Act for further improving the Police in and near the Metropolis.
[17th August, 1839.]

S. 1. So much of the 29 Geo. 2, c. 25, as requires the appointment of constables at courts leet, repealed.

S. 2. Parts of parishes within fifteen miles from Charing Cross may be added to the metropolitan police district by order in council.

S. 3. Places so added to be within the 3 & 4 Will. 4, c. 89.

S. 4. Repeal of the 6 & 7 Will. 4, c. 50, except as to appointment of commissioners of police justices for Berkshire and Buckinghamshire, under 10 Geo. 4, c. 44.

S. 5. Metropolitan police constables to have all the powers of constables in those counties, and on the river Thames, &c.

S. 6. Provision for sum required to defray charges of Thames police, horse patrol, &c.

S. 7. Constables may be sworn in to act for the royal palaces, and within ten miles thereof.

S. 8. Additional constables may be appointed in case of need, at the charge of persons making application for them.

S. 9. In addition to the returns already required, a statement of the number of persons belonging to the police force shall annually be laid before parliament.

S. 10. Horses and police vans in the service of the police exempted from turnpike toll : penalty of 5*l.* for fraudulently claiming the exemption.

S. 11. Police constables to be in attendance at the police and criminal courts within the police district, to execute summonses and warrants.

S. 12. All summonses and warrants in criminal proceedings to be executed by police constables.

S. 13. Constable to deliver any warrant directed to him to his superintendent, &c. who shall by indorsement appoint constables to execute it.

S. 14. Penalty of 10*l.* on constables for neglect of duty.

S. 15. No constable to resign without leave in writing from his superintendent, or a month's notice of his intention, on pain of forfeiture of all arrears of pay, and a penalty of 5*l.*

S. 16. Constables dismissed or ceasing to hold the office, to deliver up all clothing, accoutrements, &c. to the superintendent, under penalty of a month's imprisonment and hard labour.

S. 17. Penalty of 10*l.* for unlawful possession of accoutrements, &c., and for assuming the dress of police constables for any unlawful purpose.

S. 18. Penalty of 5*l.* for assaults on any of the police in the execution of their duty.

S. 19. Employment in the police not to prevent the party from receiving half-pay.

S. 20. Salary of commissioners of police to be 1200*l.* a year.

S. 21. Commissioners, surgeon, receiver, and clerks in the office to be within the 4 & 5 Will. 4, c. 24.

S. 22. Superannuation fund to be provided for constables.

S. 23. Rates of allowance from the fund.

S. 24. Repeals the 2 Geo. 3, c. 28.

S. 25. Boats employed in the sale of liquors, slops, &c. between London Bridge and Limehouse Hole, to be subject to the provisions of the 7 & 8 Geo. 4, c. lxxv.

S. 26. Persons receiving ship stores from seamen, &c. to be guilty of a misdemeanor.

S. 27. Persons cutting or damaging ropes, cables, &c. of any ship lying in the Thames, to be guilty of a misdemeanor.

S. 28. Persons wilfully letting fall articles unlawfully obtained from any vessel, into the Thames, or conveying them away, may be taken into custody, and shall be guilty of a misdemeanor.

S. 29. Persons framing a false bill of parcels for the purpose of escaping detection, and preventing the seizure of any thing by the police, to be guilty of a misdemeanor.

S. 30. Persons found on any canal, dock, wharf, boat, &c. in possession of any instrument, &c. for unlawfully obtaining or secreting wine, to be guilty of a misdemeanor.

S. 31. Persons piercing casks, &c., opening packages, &c., on board any ship, or on any wharf, &c. to be guilty of a misdemeanor.

S. 32. Persons breaking or injuring packages with intent to spill or drop the contents, to be guilty of a misdemeanor.

S. 33. Superintendents or inspectors of police may board vessels to observe the conduct of parties employed in lading or unlading, to preserve the peace, and to prevent or detect offences.

S. 34. Superintendents, inspectors, or serjeants, having just cause to suspect that a felony has been or is about to be committed on board a vessel, may enter it and take up suspected persons.

S. 35. Power to superintendents and inspectors to seize unlawful quantities of gunpowder on board ships.

S. 36. Penalty on officers of vessels lying between Westminster Bridge and Blackwall for having on board guns loaded with ball, or firing guns in the night.

S. 37. Penalty for heating combustible matters on board of vessels.

S. 38. Penalty on keeping open fairs between eleven p. m. and six a. m.

S. 39. Fairs within the metropolitan police district may be inquired into by the commissioners of police; and if they be declared unlawful, after notice, the booths, &c. to be removed, and persons fixing them, &c. taken into custody.

S. 40. On the owner or occupier of the ground entering into recognizances, the question as to the right of title to any fair may be tried in the Court of Queen's Bench.

S. 41. Freemen of the vintner's company to be subject to all provisions of acts for the regulation of licensed victuallers.

S. 42. Houses for the sale of wine, spirits, beer, or other distilled or fermented liquors, not to be opened on Sundays, Christmas Day, or Good Friday, before one p. m., except for refreshment to travellers.

S. 43. Penalty on publicans supplying liquors to persons apparently under the age of sixteen.

S. 44. The regulations of the 9 Geo. 4, c. 61, respecting public-houses, extended to other houses and places of public resort.

S. 45. Penalty on keepers of cook-shops, &c. making internal communications with adjoining public-houses, &c.

S. 46. Power to the commissioners of police to direct the superintendents to enter unlicensed theatres, and take away persons found there : penalty on persons opening or letting places for such purposes, or performing, &c. therein.

S. 47. Penalty on the keeping or using places for fighting or baiting animals.

S. 48. Power to commissioners to authorise superintendents to enter houses which are stated by two householders, on oath, to be commonly reported and believed by them to be kept as gaming-houses, to enter such houses and take into custody persons found there. Penalty of 100*l.* or six months' imprisonment on the parties keeping such house. Penalty of 5*l.* on persons found there.

S. 49. Proof of gaming for money, &c. not to be deemed necessary in support of informations for gaming.

S. 50. Penalty of 5*l.* on pawnbrokers receiving pledges from children apparently under the age of sixteen years.

S. 51. Power to commissioners of police to regulate the route and conduct of persons driving stage carriages, cattle, &c. during the hours of divine service.

S. 52. Provision for regulations for preventing obstructions in the streets during public processions or rejoicings.

S. 53. Proprietors of stage carriages not to be liable for penalties by reason of their drivers deviating from the prescribed route.

S. 54. Penalty of 40s. on certain specified nuisances committed in any public thoroughfare within the police district.

S. 55. Penalty of 5l. on firing cannon within 300 yards of dwelling-houses.

S. 56. The using of dogs to draw carts, &c. prohibited after 1st January, 1840, under a penalty of 40s. for the first, and 5l. for subsequent offences.

S. 57. Street musicians to depart when required to do so, under a penalty of 40s.

S. 58. Persons found drunk in any public thoroughfare, and guilty of riotous or indecent behaviour, and persons guilty of violent or indecent behaviour in any police station-house, to be subject to a penalty of 40s., or imprisonment for seven days.

S. 59. Penalty of 5s. on persons using carriages without the owner's or driver's consent : children apparently under the age of twelve so doing, to be detained and delivered to the parents or guardians.

S. 60. Penalty of 40s. on certain specified nuisances in any street or public place within the police district.

S. 61. Power to constables to destroy dogs reasonably suspected to be mad : penalty of £5 on the owners permitting them to go at large, after information or belief of their being mad.

S. 62. Compensation for hurt or damage in the commission of any offence under the Act, not exceeding £10.

S. 63. Constables may apprehend, without warrant, any persons committing offences within their view, and where name and residence cannot be ascertained.

S. 64. Constables may apprehend, without warrant, idle and disorderly persons disturbing the peace, or whom they have just cause to suspect of having committed or being about to commit any felony, misdemeanor, or breach of the peace, or persons loitering about at night, &c.

S. 65. Power to constables to apprehend, without warrant, persons charged with aggravated assault, so recently committed that a warrant could not have been obtained.

S. 66. Power to police constables (and persons aggrieved) to apprehend and detain persons found committing any misdemeanor ; and to the former to stop and search any vessel or carriage reasonably suspected to contain stolen goods.

S. 67. Power to constables to stop and detain, till inquiry made, carriages removing furniture in the night, to evade rent.

S. 68. The horses, carriages, &c. of offenders may be detained as a security for penalties and expenses.

S. 69. Persons apprehended without warrant to be taken to the station house, till brought before a magistrate, or giving bail.

S. 70. Power to police constables to take recognizance at station houses on petty charges.

S. 71. Power to the constables, in case of felony or grave misdemeanor, to bind over persons making charges, when the police courts are shut.

S. 72. Condition of the recognizances.

S. 73. Penalty of £5, or a month's imprisonment, on all misdemeanors and offences under the Act, for which no special penalty is before appointed.

S. 74. Nothing herein to repeal local Acts containing penalties.

S. 75. Meaning of the word " magistrate."

S. 76. Convictions to be made by one police magistrate, or two county justices, in districts where no police court is established.

S. 77. Provisions for commitment on non-payment of penalties.

S. 78. Interpretation clause.

S. 79. This Act to be construed as one Act with 10 Geo. 4, c. 44.

S. 80. Act may be amended or repealed this session.

CAP. 48.—An Act to amend Two Acts of the Third and Fourth and Fourth and Fifth Years of his late Majesty King William the Fourth, for Consolidating and Amending the Laws relative to Jurors and Juries in Ireland.
[17th August, 1839.]

CAP. 49.—An Act to make better Provision for the Assignment of Ecclesiastical Districts to Churches or Chapels augmented by the Governors of the Bounty of Queen Anne ; and for other purposes. [17th August, 1839.]

CAP. 50.—An Act to extend and amend the Provisions of the Acts for the Extension and Promotion of Public Works in Ireland ; and for the Recovery of Public Monies advanced for the Use of Counties, Parishes, and other Districts in Ireland, on the Faith of Grand Jury Presentments and Parochial Assessments.
[17th August, 1839.]

CAP. 51.—An Act to Regulate the Payment and Assignment in certain cases of Pensions granted for Service in her Majesty's Army, Navy, Royal Marines, and Ordnance. [17th August, 1839.]

CAP. 52.—An Act for the further Regulation of the Duties on Postage until the Fifth day of October, 1840. [17th August, 1839.]

S. 1. Empowers the lords of the treasury, by warrant, to alter, fix, reduce, or remit all or any of the rates of postage on letters, and to subject them to rates of postage according to the weight ; and a scale of weight to be named in the warrant, without reference to distance ; and to fix and limit the weight of letters to be sent by post ; and from time to time to alter and repeal such reduced rates, and establish others, and to appoint at what time the rates shall be paid, viz. whether on posting or receipt of the letter, or at either of those times at the option of the sender. Warrants to be inserted in the Gazette ten days before coming into operation, and to be laid before parliament within fourteen days.

S. 2. The rates of postage to be fixed by such warrant, to be charged by and paid to the postmaster general.

S. 3. Empowers the treasury by warrant to suspend any parliamentary or official privilege of franking, whether under 1 Vict. c. 35, or any other act; and to make regulations for the future exercise of official franking.

S. 4. Treasury empowered to suspend and make new regulations in respect of the twopenny and penny posts.

S. 5. Treasury empowered to direct that letters on stamped paper, or inclosed in stamped covers, or having a stamp affixed, (the stamp being of the value expressed in the warrant,) shall, if within the limitation of weight to be fixed under this act, pass free of postage.

S. 6. Treasury may direct commissioners of stamps to provide dies, &c. for denoting the rates of duties.

S. 7. Commissioners of stamps to keep a separate account of the stamp duties under this act, and to pay them over according to treasury warrant.

S. 8. Rates on stamped covers to be deemed stamp duties, and subject to the stamp acts.

S. 9. Letters to be posted, conveyed, and delivered, as the postmaster general, with consent of the treasury, shall direct.

S. 10. Masters of all outward bound vessels required to take bags of letters.

S. 11. Treasury may reduce or alter gratuities to masters of vessels carrying bags of letters.

S. 12. The word " letter" in this act to include newspapers and all articles transmitted by the post, but not so as to deprive newspapers of privilege of passing post-free. Interpretation clause of 1 Vict. c. 36, adopted into this act.

S. 13. Three of the lords of the treasury to be a quorum.

S. 14. Act to cease on 5th October, 1840, except as to duties then payable, and proceedings for recovery of duties and penalties.

S. 15. Act may be amended or repealed this session.

CAP. 53.—An Act to amend an Act of the last Session of Parliament for making temporary Provision for the Government of Lower Canada.

[17th August, 1839.]

CAP. 54.—An Act to amend the Law relating to the Custody of Infants.

[17th August, 1839.]

S. 1. The Lord Chancellor and Master of the Rolls in England and Ireland, on petition of the mother of any infant in the sole custody of the father or guardian, may make order for access of the petitioner to the infant, at such times and under such regulations as he deems convenient and just; and if the infant be within the age of seven years, that it shall be delivered to the custody of the petitioner until attaining that age.

S. 2. On all complaints under this act, affidavits sworn before a master in Chancery to be received, and parties deposing falsely therein to be guilty of perjury.

S. 3. Orders made under the act shall be enforced by process of contempt.

S. 4. No order to be made in favour of any mother against whom adultery shall be established by judgment in crim. con., or sentence of an ecclesiastical court.

S. 5. Act may be amended or repealed this session.

CAP. 55.—An Act to suspend, until the First Day of August One thousand eight hundred and forty, certain Cathedral and other Ecclesiastical Preferments, and the operation of the new Arrangement of Dioceses upon the existing Ecclesiastical Courts.

[17th August, 1839.]

CAP. 56.—An Act for the better ordering of Prisons. [17th August, 1839.]

S. 1. Extends the powers of the 4 Geo. 4, c. 64, and 5 Geo. 4, c. 85, to all gaols, &c., except as to classification of prisoners; subject to 5 & 6 Will. 4, c. 38, and 6 & 7 Will. 4, c. 105, and this act.

S. 2. So much of the 4 Geo. 4, c. 64, as provides that no classification of prisoners shall be made contrary thereto, repealed: and the persons authorized by law to make rules for the government of prisons, shall be empowered to make rules for a different classification or for the separation of prisoners; the secretary of state to certify the fitness of rules before they are enforced.

S. 3. Any prisoner may be separately confined during the whole or any part of the imprisonment.

S. 4. *Separate* confinement not to be deemed *solitary* confinement within any act prohibiting the latter for more than a limited time. Regulations as to the cells for and nature of separate confinement.

S. 5. Prisoners to be divided into at least five classses: 1. debtors; 2. prisoners committed for trial; 3. prisoners convicted, and sentenced to hard labour; 4. prisoners convicted, and not sentenced to hard labour; 5. prisoners not included in the foregoing classes: and separate rules to be made for every class of prisoners.

S. 6. General rules set forth, which are to be observed in every prison, in addition to the others in force in the prison.

S. 7. Keepers may appoint deputy keepers, with approval of visiting justices.

S. 8. Repeal of so much of 4 Geo. 4, c. 64, as requires keepers to account to convicts for the net profits of their labour; no officer to have a profit from prisoners' work; allowance by visiting justices to prisoners against whom no bill is found, or acquitted on their trial, to be such as appear to them reasonable, and not to be given to the prisoners till their discharge.

S. 9. Return required by 5 Geo. 4, c. 85, to be made in the form of schedule A. to that act, and the returns of the Millbank penitentiary no longer to be made.

S. 10. Return required by 4 Geo. 4, c. 64 (schedule B.), to be made in the form of the schedule to this act.

S. 11. Insufficient prisons may or reported as such under the 4 Geo. 4, c. 64.

S. 12. Plans of new or enlarged prisons to be sent and approved by secretary of state. Limitation on his power of disapproval.

S. 13. If three calendar months elapse after receipt of the plan, without notification from the secretary of state of his disapproval, the plan may be put in execution without his certificate of approval.

S. 14. Provisions for prisons for which there shall be no clerk of the peace or chief magistrate to perform the duties required by the 6 Will. 4, c. 38.

S. 15. Chaplains to be appointed in every borough gaol and house of correction.

S. 16. Chaplains of certain prisons to hold no other benefice: power in certain prisons to appoint assistant chaplains.

S. 17. Offenders, against whom a sentence of death is recorded, may be kept to hard labour.

S. 18. The 7 Will. 4 and 1 Vict. c. 13 (Millbank Penitentiary Act) extended to persons under sentences of transportation not mentioned in that act.

S. 19. Provision as to convicts removed from the penitentiary as incorrigible.

S. 20. One pentagon in the penitentiary to be set apart for confinement of soldiers or marines under the mutiny acts.

S. 21. Superintendent of that pentagon, appointed by superintending committee or visitor, to be the sole superintendent therein; but nothing herein contained to prevent the soldiers and marines from being taken to the chapel or infirmary.

S. 22. Persons attemping to introduce forbidden articles into prisons may be apprehended, and on conviction before a justice, fined not exceeding 5l. or not less than 40s., to be paid towards the expenses of the prison; and in default to be committed to gaol for not more than a month.

S. 23. Interpretation clause.

S. 24. Keepers appointed by the style of governors to have all the powers and duties of the gaoler or keeper.

S. 25. Act to commence 1st Jan. 1840.

S. 26. Act may be amended or repealed this session.

CAP. 57.—An Act to continue, until six months after the commencement of the next Session of Parliament, an Act of the last Session of Parliament, for authorizing her Majesty to carry into immediate execution by Orders in Council any Treaties for the Suppression of the Slave Trade. [17th August, 1839.]

CAP. 58.—An Act to make further Provision for the Administration of Justice, and for improving the Practice and Proceedings in the Courts of the Stannaries of Cornwall; and for the Prevention of Frauds by Workmen employed in Mines within the County of Cornwall. [17th August, 1839.]

CAP. 59.—An Act for taking away the Exemption, except in certain Cases, of Officers of the Militia to serve as Sheriff. [17th August, 1839.]

CAP. 60.—An Act to explain and amend an Act passed in the First Year of his late Majesty King William the Fourth, intituled " An Act for consolidating and amending the Laws for facilitating the Payment of Debts out of Real Estate." [17th August, 1839.]

S. 1. The provisions of 11 Geo. 4 and 1 Will. 4, c. 47, extended to authorize courts of equity to direct mortgages as well as sales to be made of the estates of infant heirs and devisees, and of lands devised in settlement, and to authorize such sales and mortgages in cases where the tenant for life, &c. or first executory devisee, is an infant.

S. 2. The surplus of money arising from any sale or mortgage under the recited act or this act, to descend in the same manner as the estates sold or mortgaged would have done.

CAP. 61.—An Act for the Improvement of the Navigation of the River Shannon. [17th August, 1839.]

CAP. 62.—An Act to explain and amend the Acts for the Commutation of Tithes in England and Wales. [17th August, 1839.]

CAP. 63.—An Act to remove Doubts as to the Charging the Duty of Excise on Hard Soap, until the Eleventh day of October One thousand eight hundred and forty. [24th August, 1839.]

CAP. 64.—An Act to defray the Charge of the Pay, Clothing, and contingent and other Expenses of the Disembodied Militia in Great Britain and Ireland; and to grant Allowances in certain Cases to Subaltern Officers, Adjutants, Paymasters, Quarter-Masters, Surgeons, Assistant-Surgeons, Surgeons' Mates, and Serjeant-Majors of the Militia, until the First day of July One thousand eight hundred and forty. [24th August, 1839.]

CAP. 65.—An Act to amend the Mode of Assessing the Rogue Money in Scotland, and to extend the Purposes of such Assessment. [24th August, 1839.]

CAP. 66.—An Act to reduce certain of the Duties now payable on Stage Carriages. [24th August, 1839.]

CAP. 67.—An Act to amend an Act of the Fifth and Sixth Years of the Reign of King William the Fourth, intituled An Act to amend the Law touching Letters Patent for Inventions. [24th August, 1839.]

S. 1. Repeals so much of the 5 & 6 W. 4, c. 83, s. 4, as provides that no extension of the term of a patent shall be granted, if the application be not prosecuted with effect before the expiration of the term originally granted.

S. 2. The term of a patent right may be extended, where the application for such extension has not been prosecuted with effect before the expiration of the term from any other causes than the neglect or default of the petitioner; provided that the petition be presented six calendar months before the expiration of the term, and sufficient reason be shown for the default.

S. 3. Act may be amended or repealed this session.

CAP. 68.—An Act to continue, until the Thirty-first day of August One thousand eight hundred and forty, an Act of the First and Second years of her present Majesty, relating to legal proceedings by certain Joint Stock Banking Companies against their own Members, and by such Members against the Companies. [24th August, 1839.]

The statute 1 & 2 Vict. c. 96, continued to 31st August, 1840.

CAP. 69.—An Act to authorize the Purchase or Building of Lodgings for the Judges of Assize on their Circuits. [24th August, 1839.]

S. 1. The powers given to the justices in sessions by the 7 G. 4, c. 63, to contract for the improving or building of lodgings for the judges of assize, extended by enabling them to purchase houses, or land for erecting thereon houses, as lodgings for the judges.

S. 2. Houses, &c. so purchased to be conveyed in trust in the same way as in the recited act is directed as to land.

S. 3. Act may be amended or repealed this session.

CAP. 70.—An Act to amend the Act of the Ninth year of King George the Fourth, to provide for the Administration of Justice in New South Wales and Van Diemen's Land, and for the more effectual Government thereof, and for other Purposes relating thereto; and to continue the same until the Thirty-first day of December One thousand eight hundred and forty, and thenceforward to the end of the then next Session of Parliament. [24th August, 1839.]

CAP. 71.—An Act for regulating the Police Courts in the Metropolis. [24th August, 1839.]

S. 1. The present police Courts and police magistrates continued.

S. 2. The queen in council may alter the number and situation of the Courts; the number of magistrates limited to 27.

S. 3. Vacancies to be supplied by the crown from barristers of four years' standing.

S. 4. Magistrates, clerks, &c. exempted from serving on juries.

S. 5. Provides for appointment of clerks, ushers, doorkeepers, and messengers.

S. 6. No magistrate or officer of the courts to vote at or interfere in elections for Middlesex, Surrey, London, Westminster, Tower Hamlets, Finsbury, Marylebone, Southwark, Lambeth, or Greenwich, under a penalty of £100.

S. 7. Receiver of metropolitan police to be receiver under this act.

S. 8. Provisions of 10 G. 4, c. 44, as to powers and duties of receiver, extended to him when acting under this act.

S. 9. Provides for salaries of magistrates, receiver, clerk, and officers.

S. 10. In case of the establishment of a civil Court for recovery of small debts, the queen may appoint the metropolitan magistrates to take the duties thereof.

S. 11. The crown may direct an issue from the consolidated fund towards the expenses of this act.

S. 12. Magistrates to attend from 10 to 5 o'clock, and at other times in cases of urgent necessity, &c.

S. 13. Acts directed to be done by a justice of the police office, or by a neighbouring justice, may be done by any of the police magistrates.

S. 14. One of the magistrates may do any act directed to be done by more than one justice, except at petty sessions.

S. 15. Magistrates to meet quarterly for reporting to the Secretary of State.

S. 16. Secretary of State may make rules for conducting the business of the court.

S. 17. Process in respect of matters arising within the metropolitan police district need not be indorsed, in order to be executed out of the district by the constable to whom directed.

S. 18. Summons for persons residing within metropolitan police district to appear at any place without the limits specified in this act, void.

S. 19. Magistrates may proceed by summons, and if the party summoned does not appear thereto, may issue warrant.

S. 20. Summons may be served by delivery of a copy to the party; or to his wife, servant, &c. and explaining it to them.

S. 21. Warrant for the apprehension of any person may be issued without summons, good grounds for doing so being stated on oath.

S. 22. Powers to magistrates for enforcing the attendance of witnesses.

S. 23. Persons giving false evidence liable to the penalties of perjury.

S. 24. Persons suspected of having or conveying stolen goods, and not accounting for them, guilty of a misdemeanor, and liable to a penalty of £5.

S. 25. In case of information given that there is reasonable cause for suspecting that any goods have been unlawfully obtained and are concealed, magistrates may issue warrant to enter houses (by force if necessary) and search for and take them, and take into custody persons suspected to be privy to their concealment.

S. 26. Persons from whom stolen goods are received to be brought before and examined by the magistrates, and on conviction subject to a penalty of £5, or imprisonment for 3 months.

S. 27. Power to order the delivery of goods stolen or fraudulently obtained, and in possession of brokers and other dealers in second hand-property.

S. 28. Property unlawfully pawned, &c. may be ordered to be restored to the owner, although produced without the issue of any search warrant.

S. 29. Power to order the delivery of possession of goods charged to have been stolen or fraudulently obtained, and in the possession of a constable: not to bar the right of any person to sue the party to whom delivered within six months.

S. 30. Unclaimed stolen goods delivered to the receiver may be sold after 12 months for the benefit of the police superannuation fund.

S. 31. Power to award costs on hearing of charges.

S. 32. Power to award amends for frivolous informations.

S. 33. Penalty of £10 on common informers compounding informations.

S. 34. Power to the magistrates to diminish the informer's share of a penalty.

S. 35. Power to mitigate penalties in all cases, except under revenue acts.

S. 36. Power to remand or enlarge prisoners on recognizances.

S. 37. Disputes about wages for labour done on the river, &c. (except by Trinity ballastmen) to be settled by the magistrates, provided the amount in question do not exceed £5.

S. 38. Power to direct compensation for wilful damage by tenants.

S. 39. Power to the magistrates to deal summarily in cases of oppressive distresses on weekly or monthly tenants, or yearly tenants under £15 rent.

S. 40. Power to order the delivery of goods unlawfully detained, and under £15 value, to the owner : Proviso as to action for recovering possession of them at law within six months.

S. 41. If the guardians of the poor, or overseers of a union or parish, and medical officer, shall certify any house to be in a filthy and unwholesome condition, the magistrate may order it to be cleansed, and the expenses to be recovered by distress.

S. 42. No other justice to take fees within the police district : penalty £100.

S. 43. Table of fees to be hung up in the police courts.

S. 44. Mode of proceedings in informations in the police courts.

S. 45. Mode of recovery of penalties and forfeitures.

S. 46. Accounts to be kept of fees and forfeitures received, and delivered quarterly to the receiver, and the amount paid to him.

S. 47. Certain penalties and forfeitures to be paid to the receiver : but not to extend to penalties under the revenue acts.

S. 48. Forms of information and conviction to be according to schedule (B).

S. 49. No proceeding before any of the police magistrates to be quashed for want of form, or removed by certiorari.

S. 50. Appeal to the quarter session against summary orders and convictions, where the penalty is above £3, or imprisonment for more than a month.

S. 51. Distress by warrant of the police magistrates not to be unlawful for want of form.

S. 52. Plaintiff not to recover for any wrongful proceeding under this act after tender of amends : in case of refusal of amends, defendant may pay money into court.

S. 53. Limitation of actions for acts done under the act.

S. 54. Act to commence the day next after its passing, and 3 & 4 W. 4, c. 19, and 7 W. 4 & 1 Vict. c. 37, then to cease, except as to offences already committed and penalties incurred.

S. 55. This act, and 10 G. 4, c. 44, and 2 & 3 Vict. c. 47, to be construed together as one act.

S. 56. Penalties in proceedings under revenue acts to be recovered and paid as if this act had not been passed ; and this act not to give an appeal from any convictions under such acts.

S. 57. Act may be amended or repealed this session.

Cap. 72.—An Act for enabling Justices of Assize and Nisi Prius, Oyer and Terminer, and Gaol Delivery, to hold Courts for Counties at large in adjoining Counties of Cities and Towns, and conversely. [24th August, 1839.]

S. 1. Justices of assize, &c. empowered to hold courts for any county at large, and also for any county of a city, county of a town, borough, or other jurisdiction locally situated within or adjacent to the county at large, in any court-house whether in or belonging to the county at large, or in or belonging to the other jurisdiction, and to adjourn from the one to the other : and all evidence given and things done at such court shall be deemed and alleged to have been given and done within the county, &c., within which the court would have been held but for this act : but not to authorize the holding of any court more than three miles out of the jurisdiction for which it is holden.

S. 2. Act may be amended or repealed this session. [24th August, 1839.]

Cap. 73.—An Act for the Suppression of the Slave Trade. [24th August, 1839.]

Cap. 74.—An Act to extend and render more effectual for five years, an Act passed in the Fourth Year of His late Majesty George the Fourth, to amend an Act passed in the Fiftieth Year of His Majesty George the Third, for Preventing the Administering and Taking Unlawful Oaths in Ireland.

[24th August, 1839.]

CAP. 75.—An Act for the Better Regulation of the Constabulary Force in Ireland.

[24th August, 1839.]

CAP. 76.—An Act to restrain the Alienation of Corporate Property in certain Towns in Ireland, until the First day of September One thousand eight hundred and forty.

[24th August, 1839.]

CAP. 77.—An Act for the Better Prevention and Punishment of Assaults in Ireland for Five Years.

[24th August, 1839.]

CAP. 78.—An Act to make further Provisions relating to the Police in the District of Dublin Metropolis.

[24th August, 1839.]

CAP. 79.—An Act for the better prevention of the Sale of Spirits by unlicensed Persons in Ireland.

[24th August, 1839.]

CAP. 80.—An Act to empower the Commissioners of Her Majesty's Woods, Forests, Land Revenues, Works, and Buildings to raise a Sum of Money for making additional Thoroughfares in the Metropolis.

[24th August, 1839.]

CAP. 81.—An Act to authorize for One Year, and from thence to the end of the then next Session of Parliament, the Application of a Portion of the Highway Rates to Turnpike Roads in certain cases.

[24th August, 1839.]

S. 1. Justices to inquire at special sessions for highways into the revenues and condition of the repair of turnpike roads, and, if necessary, to apportion a part of the highway rate to the trustees of any turnpike road.

S. 2. If the surveyor refuse to pay over such portion of the rate, the same to be levied on his goods.

S. 3. Power of appeal to the quarter sessions.

S. 4. Act to extend only to England.

S. 5. Act may be amended or repealed this session.

S. 6. Act to continue for a year, and from thence to the end of the then next session of parliament.

CAP. 82.—An Act for the better Administration of Justice in detached parts of Counties.

[26th August, 1839.]

S. 1. Any justice of the peace may act in all things relating to any detached part of any other county surrounded in whole or in part by the county for which he acts: and all acts of justices, and constables, &c. in obedience to them, shall be as good, and all offenders may be committed, tried, &c. in like manner as if such detached part were to all intents part of the county for which the justices act.

S. 2. Expenses of prosecution of offenders to be repaid by the county to which such detached part belongs.

S. 3. " County" to include parts of a county having a separate commission of the peace.

S. 4. Act may be amended or repealed this session.

CAP. 83.—An Act to continue the Poor Law Commission until the Fourteenth day of August One thousand eight hundred and forty, and thenceforth until the end of the then next Session of Parliament.

[26th August, 1839.]

The poor law commissioners, assistant commissioners, secretaries, and other officers empowered to hold office and exercise its powers until the 14th August, 1840, and thenceforth until, &c., subject to removal, &c. by the crown.

CAP. 84.—An Act to amend the Laws relating to the Assessment and Collection of Rates for the Relief of the Poor. [26th August, 1839.]

S. 1. In case the contribution of the officers of any parish of monies required by the board of guardians of the parish or union, for the performance of their duties, be in arrear, the officers may be summoned before two justices to show cause why the contribution has not been paid, and the justices may issue a warrant for levying the arrears, and costs, from such officers, in the same manner as a poor rate.

S. 2. Orders heretofore made by the poor law commissioners for the appointment of collectors of poor-rates, &c. declared valid.

S. 3. This Act not to affect the right of vestries to give directions for the custody of documents under the 58 Geo. 3, c. 69.

S. 4. The 4 & 5 Will. 4, c. 76, and this Act to be construed as one Act.

S. 5. Act may be amended or repealed this session.

CAP. 85.—An Act to enable Justices of the Peace in Petty Sessions to make Orders for the support of Bastard Children. [26th August, 1839.]

S. 1. The powers of the justices in quarter sessions to make orders on putative fathers of bastard children, under the 4 & 5 Will. 4, c. 76, s. 72, transferred to justices in special or petty sessions : but notice to the putative father need only be given 7, instead of 14, days before the sessions.

S. 2. Powers to justices to enforce attendance of witnesses.

S. 3. Parties charged may enter into recognizances for trial of the charge at the quarter sessions and payment of costs, and in such case the justices shall not proceed with the charge, but all further proceedings shall be had before the quarter sessions.

S. 4. Interpretation clause.

S. 5. Act may be amended or repealed this session.

CAP. 86.—An Act to amend an Act passed in the Session holden in the Sixth Year of His late Majesty King William the Fourth, for amending the Laws relating to Bankrupts in Ireland. [26th August, 1839.]

CAP. 87.—An Act for improving the Police in Manchester for Two Years, and from thence until the End of the then next Session of Parliament.

[26th August, 1839.]

CAP. 88.—An Act for improving the Police of Birmingham for Two Years, and from thence until the End of the then next Session of Parliament.

[26th August, 1839.]

CAP. 89.—An Act to apply a Sum out of the Consolidated Fund, and the Surplus of Ways and Means, to the Service of the Year One thousand eight hundred and thirty-nine, and to appropriate the Supplies granted in this Session of Parliament. [27th August, 1839.]

CAP. 90.—An Act for raising the Sum of Twelve millions twenty-six thousand and fifty pounds by Exchequer Bills, for the Service of the Year One thousand eight hundred and thirty-nine. [27th August, 1839.]

CAP. 91.—An Act to continue until the First day of January One thousand eight hundred and forty-one an Act of the last Session of Parliament, relating to the Bank of Ireland. [27th August, 1839.]

CAP. 92.—An Act to explain and amend an Act of the First and Second Years of Her present Majesty, so far as relates to Fines and Penalties levied under the Revenue Laws in Ireland. [27th August, 1839.]

CAP. 93.—An Act for the Establishment of County and District Constables by the Authority of Justices of the Peace. [27th August, 1839.]

S. 1. Where it shall appear to the justices in quarter sessions of any county, that the ordinary peace officers are not sufficient, it shall be lawful for them to set forth the same by a report under the hands of a majority of the justices present, and to declare how many constables are in their opinion needed, and the rates of payment expedient to be paid, and such report shall be sent to the secretary of state : Provided, that the number of constables shall not be more than one for every 1000 inhabitants, according to the last census.

S. 2. Quarter sessions may from time to time, with consent of the secretary of state, increase or diminish the number of constables.

S. 3. Rules for the government, pay, clothing, &c. of the constables to be made by the secretary of state and laid before parliament.

S. 4. One chief constable of the county to be appointed by the sessions with the approval of the secretary of state, or two for a county divided for the purpose of returning members to parliament : and the same chief constable may by agreement be appointed for several counties or parts of counties.

S. 5. Notice of proceedings under this Act to be given with the notice of holding the sessions, on the requisition of five justices for the county.

S. 6. The chief constables, subject to the approval of two justices in petty sessions, to appoint the other constables, and a superintendent in each division, and at his pleasure to dismiss them, and to have the general government of all the constables, subject to orders from the justices in quarter sessions, and to the rules established for the government of the force.

S. 7. Chief constable empowered to appoint a deputy in case of his illness or necessary absence ; to act also in case of vacancy of the office of chief constable, but not for more than three calendar months.

S. 8. Constables to be sworn in before a justice, and to have the powers and duties in the county and any adjoining county, of constables at common law or under any statute ; and the provisions of the 1 & 2 Will. 4, c. 41, extended to them.

S. 9. Constables disqualified during their office, or for six calendar months afterwards, from voting at or interfering in elections of members for the county for which they are appointed, or any adjoining county, or any city or borough within them ; under a penalty of 20*l.*

S. 10. Constables appointed under this Act not to employ themselves in any other office, and to be exempt from serving on juries and in the militia.

S. 11. Act not to prevent constables from receiving half-pay.

S. 12. Penalty of 10*l.* on constables for neglect of duty.

S. 13. No constable to resign without leave in writing from the chief constable or superintendent, or a month's notice of his intention, on pain of forfeiture of all arrears of pay, and a penalty of 5*l.*

S. 14. Constables dismissed or ceasing to hold the office to deliver up all clothing, accoutrements, &c. to the chief constable or superintendent, under penalty of imprisonment for a month.

S. 15. Penalty of 10*l.* on unlawful possession of accoutrements, &c. and on assuming the dress of constables for any unlawful purpose.

S. 16. Penalty of 5*l.* on publicans harbouring constables during the hours of duty.

S. 17. Chief constables to attend at quarter sessions and make reports concerning the police, and obey orders and warrants of the justices; and superintendents in like manner to attend at petty sessions.

S. 18. Allowances to be made to the chief constable for extraordinary expenses in the exercise of the duties of the constables; to be examined and audited in quarter sessions.

S. 19. Justices may, with the approval of the secretary of state, appoint constables for one or more divisions of the county only, with the like powers: but with one police establishment only.

S. 20. Expenses of putting the act in force to be defrayed out of the county rate.

S. 21. Where the act is adopted for one or more divisions of a county only, the quarter sessions may increase the county rates on those divisions accordingly.

S. 22. Provisions of the 55 Geo. 3, c. 51, to apply to the increased rates hereby authorized.

S. 23. County treasurer to keep separate accounts of the rates levied under this Act.

S. 24. Nothing in the Act contained to enable justices to appoint constables within boroughs incorporated under 5 & 6 Will. 4, c. 76.

S. 25. On the appointment of constables under this Act, the powers of constables within the county (except high constables and special constables) to cease and determine; except as to the collection of arrears of rates: but not to prevent or invalidate the appointment of parochial constables.

S. 26. The power to appoint and pay constables under acts for watching any town, &c. where the population is more than 10,000, to continue for two years.

S. 27. All detached parts of counties, hundreds, &c. liberties, and parishes (except the boroughs before mentioned) to be considered for the purposes of this Act as part of the county, hundred, &c. by which it is surrounded, or with which it has the longest common boundary.

S. 28. Interpretation clause.

S. 29. Act may be amended or repealed this session.

Cap. 94.—An Act to exempt the Parliamentary Grant to the Heirs of John Duke of Marlborough from the Payment of the Duty of One shilling and sixpence in the pound. [27th August, 1839.]

Cap. 95.—An Act for improving the Police in Bolton for Two Years, and from thence until the End of the then next Session of Parliament.
[27th August, 1839.]

Cap. 96.—An Act to authorize Her Majesty, until Six Months after the Commencement of the next Session of Parliament, to carry into effect a Convention between Her Majesty and the King of the French relative to the Fishing on the Coasts of the British Islands and of France. [27th August, 1839.]

Cap. 97.—An Act for funding Exchequer Bills. [27th August, 1839.]

EVENTS OF THE QUARTER.

ALTHOUGH the results of the last Session remain to be stated in the present Number, our trimestrial summary will be short, the Bill for the Improvement of the Metropolitan Police Courts being the only important step yet taken by the government (for the two or three other Law-bills did not originate with them) towards redeeming the pledge given in the Queen's name, that law reform should receive their earliest and best attention. The mere passing of this Bill, too, proves nothing; for it rather confers the power of making improvements than makes them, and we doubt whether a Home Secretary, like Lord Normanby, will be found capable of carrying out its principle. He has begun badly : for example, a power of raising the salary of the magistrates to 1200*l.* was conferred for the express purpose of raising the standard of qualification ; and the first act of the Home Office is to stipulate with the newly-appointed magistrates that (with the exception of the chief) they should rest satisfied with 1000*l.*—the object being, we understand, to silence the narrow-minded cavils of some radical stickler for economy. In fact, things are come to such a pass, that the wilful contravention of the plain intentions of the legislature is now deemed a title to public confidence in a ministry—

"In the Municipal Bill," says a zealous defender, "the House of Commons enacted, that the town councils should by election appoint magistrates in corporate towns : the Lords substituted a power of nomination by the Crown. What does the Minister having the executive power do ? Why, request that the town-councils would hold a similar election to that which they would have held if the House of Commons provision had become law ; and invariably, or nearly so, he appoints the persons so elected.—(See Mr. Gisborne's Pamphlet.) Here, then, it is the executive power that secures to corporate towns the advantage of popular magistrates."[1]

The advantage in question has been rendered rather problematical by what recently took place in Birmingham, and we incline to think that, had Lord John Russell been consulted, he would have begged the writer to choose some other topic of commendation. But we quote the passage to illustrate the folly of trusting anything to his or his colleagues' discretion, and shew the depth to which political morality must have sunk, when the organ of a party can venture to employ such arguments. "True, the government are unable to carry any one measure of consequence; true, scheme after scheme is defeated through their incapacity, and principle after principle surrendered by

[1] *The Edinburgh Review,* No. 141, p. 267, *note.*—At p. 275 we find enumerated amongst Whig performances "the consolidation into one volume of the Commercial Laws of the Empire." We should be glad to know where this volume is to be procured.

their fears. But they have no silly scruples about the distribution of their patronage, no weak reluctance to trusting demagogues with power. Neither the administration of justice, nor the security of property, nor the preservation of the peace, is held too sacred to be sacrificed at the shrine of popularity; and so long as they retain the loaves and fishes, their friends are certain of the fragments."

The only plausible apology for the reduced salary is, that the government have notwithstanding secured the services of such men as Mr. Long and Mr. Jardine.

Of the Bills that failed during the last session, the most remarkable were the Admiralty Court Bill, the Copyhold Enfranchisement Bill, the Copyright Bill, and the Registration of Electors' Bill. As their failure was principally attributable to the press of business or defect in form, they will all doubtless be reproduced without delay. We trust that the Attorney General will at length be induced to put the last, the Registration Bill, into a shape less calculated to attract opposition, since every year brings fresh evidence of the indecent haste and extreme carelessness with which the Reform Bill was prepared. Do what they will, it is quite impossible for the revising barristers to reduce its inconsistent and clumsily expressed provisions to uniformity; yet though a short declaratory act, an appeal court, and an improved machinery for giving the required notices, would set every thing to rights, the government officials will do nothing because they cannot clog the measure with one essentially distinct. Can it be seriously contended that a change of the tribunal is inextricably involved in an alteration of the law?

No equity reform measure failed, because none was introduced. The law reformers in both houses contented themselves with talking about it. Yet it is quite impossible for the present state of things to last: the judges are admitted on all hands to be hopelessly unequal to their work, and four years is the shortest period within which a case of difficulty can arrive at a conclusive hearing. We regret to say that the arrears in the Queen's Bench, also, have increased to such an extent as to leave the judges of that court very little chance of subduing them without assistance. Another case like Stockdale and Hansard, and they are undone.

We have heard nothing more about the closing of the Common Pleas. It seems that the Chief Justice wisely shrinks from the responsibility of declaring the warrant illegal, and prefers abiding by the decision of the legislature; but will parliament re-establish an injurious monopoly merely to save the judges the painful necessity of enforcing the attendance of the bar?

It is said that Lord Melbourne, who hates exertion of any sort, is wont to receive the tidings of a bishop's death with an exclamation by no means respectful to the Right Reverend bench, and, under existing circumstances, he might well be betrayed into similar marks of impatience by the unlooked-for death of a judge. When a prime minister is free to take fitness as the test, he is seldom much embarrassed in his choice; but when he has to decide with reference to party services and the comparative security of seats, he may be pardoned for procrastinating. To the best of our information, he has not yet decided who is to succeed Mr. Justice Vaughan. The candidates most confidently named are Mr. Erle, Mr. Serjeant Talfourd, Mr. Wightman, and the Solicitor General. There has also been a rumour to the effect, that Sir William Follett would have the refusal; and if Sir William Follett could be persuaded to accept an appointment so much below his well-founded pretensions, it is not improbable that the offer would be made, for the ministry would thus get rid of a formidable opponent and gain credit for a good action at a blow.

We shall endeavour to collect a few biographical particulars regarding Mr. Justice

Vaughan for our next number; and there is another member of the profession, recently deceased, to whom we should have made a point of paying a similar tribute of respect had we not been anticipated by a writer in *The Legal Observer.* We allude to the late Mr. Edgar Taylor, whose literary and legal attainments were of a very high order.

The examination of articled clerks applying to be admitted will take place as usual during the last ten days of next term. The examiners are Messrs. Austen, Harrison, Metcalf, and Ranken, with one of the Masters of the Common Law Courts.

Lord Abinger's charge to the Grand Jury of Leicestershire has been reprinted in a cheap form in compliance with a suggestion from the *Times,* and has already gone through several editions. It is a production of great eloquence and ability, and precisely such as ought to emanate from a judge; for, without alluding to party politics, it calmly calls attention to the dangers which menace our institutions, and summons the well-affected to the defence of them. It is no fault of the speaker if such passages as the following lead to awkward inferences:

"Gentlemen, entertaining these opinions, I cannot do better on this occasion than borrow from her Majesty's proclamation, which has just been read to you, the precept which she has thereby commanded me, as one of her judges, to inculcate, which is, that I should exhort you to follow that example which her Majesty informs you she has determined to set to her people, *of discountenancing all vice, immorality, and impiety, and generally all those persons who, by their conduct and character, are disturbers of the public peace;* and, on the other hand, to give countenance and encouragement to those only who show by their conduct a disposition to fulfil the duties of religion, and support the authority of the law. Indeed I will venture to say, that if every gentleman would strictly adhere in his own sphere, and within the circle of his own influence, to the injunctions contained in this, her Majesty's proclamation, the necessity of providing gaols and new systems of prison discipline would be greatly diminished."

As was cleverly said in one of Coleman's farces, "Let every man's reform, like his charity, begin at home, and society, like Thames water, will purify itself."

Oct. 26, 1839.

Notices to Correspondents.—We have sent an answer to the address given by B. T. The bill in equity alleged to have been filed by one highwayman against another, about which "SENEX" inquires, is stated at length in the first volume of "Westminster Hall."

LIST OF NEW PUBLICATIONS.

A Digest of the Law of Evidence on the Trial of Actions at Nisi Prius. By Henry Roscoe, Esq. of the Inner Temple, Barrister at Law. Fifth Edition, with considerable Additions. By C. Crompton and E. Smirke, Esqrs., Barristers at Law. In 12mo. price 1*l*. 2*s*. boards.

[We have not had time to examine this Edition, but the high character of the Editors is a sufficient guarantee for its accuracy.]

The Law relating to the Public Funds; and the Equitable and Legal Remedies with respect to Funded Property; including the Practice by Distringas, and under the Statute 1 & 2 Vict. c. 110, with references to the Cases on the Foreign Funds and Public Companies, and an Appendix of Forms. By James John Wilkinson, Esq., of Gray's Inn. In 12mo. price 12*s*. boards.

A Selection of Precedents, from Modern Manuscript Collections and Drafts of actual Practice; forming a System of Conveyancing, with Dissertations and practical Notes. By Thomas Jarman, Esq. of the Middle Temple, Barrister at Law. The Third Edition. By George Sweet, Esq. of the Inner Temple, Barrister at Law. Vol. 5, in royal 8vo. price 1*l*. 5*s*. boards.

Commentaries on Equity Jurisprudence, as administered in England and America. By Joseph Story, LL.D., Dane Professor of Law in Harvard University. Second Edition, Revised, Corrected and Enlarged. In Two Volumes, royal 8vo. price 1*l*. 14*s*. boards.

[Reviewed ante, p. 61.]

A Treatise on the Law of Easements. By C. J. Gale, Esq. and T. D. Whatby, Esq. Barristers at Law. In 8vo. price 16*s*. boards.

Dr. Robinson's Magistrate's Pocket Book; or an Epitome of the Duties and Practice of a Justice of the Peace out of Sessions, alphabetically arranged. Third Edition, with considerable Alterations and Additions; an extensive Collection of Forms of Commitments and Convictions; and a copious Index. By J. F. Archbold, Esq. Barrister at Law, price 1*l*. 6*s*. boards.

The Law of Bills of Exchange, Promissory Notes, Checks, &c. By Cuthbert W. Johnson, Esq. of Gray's Inn, Barrister at Law. Second Edition, in 12mo. price 7*s*. boards.

Commentaries on the Law of Agency, as a Branch of Commercial and Maritime Jurisprudence, with occasional Illustrations from the Civil and Foreign Law. By Joseph Story, LL.D., Dane Professor of Law in Harvard University. In royal 8vo. price 14*s*. boards.

[To be reviewed in a future number.]

Martin's Practice of Conveyancing Precedents, with practical Notes. By C. Davidson, Esq. of the Middle Temple, Barrister at Law. Vol. 3, Part 2, in royal 8vo. price 15*s.* boards.

A Copious and Practical Treatise on the Game Laws, including all the Statutes connected therewith, in which every Section is analysed and Practical Information annexed thereto, and the Law and Practice of Appeals against Charges by Surveyors of Taxes, together with all the Cases and Decisions of the Judges thereon down to the present time, and numerous Practical Forms : to which are prefixed a Chapter on the Property in Animals Feræ Naturæ, and a Chapter on the Forest Laws. By John Bell, A.M. of Lincoln's Inn, Barrister at Law. In 12mo. price 7*s.* 6*d.* boards.

The Magistrate's Pocket Companion, containing a Practical Exposition of the Duties of a Justice of the Peace out of Quarter Sessions, alphabetically arranged. By William Eagle, of the Middle Temple, Esq. Barrister at Law. In 12mo. price 15*s.* boards.

A Practical Treatise on the Qualifications and Registration of Parliamentary Electors in England and Wales; with an Appendix of Statutes, including the Act to amend the Jurisdiction for the Trial of Election Petitions, 2 & 3 Vict. c. 38, with Notes. By G. P. Elliott, Esq. of the Middle Temple, Barrister at Law. In 12mo. price 10*s.* 6*d.* boards.

[To be reviewed in a future number.]

INDEX TO VOL. XXII.

London; Printed by C. Roworth and Sons, Bell Yard, Temple Bar.